YOGI BERRA

Eternal Yankee

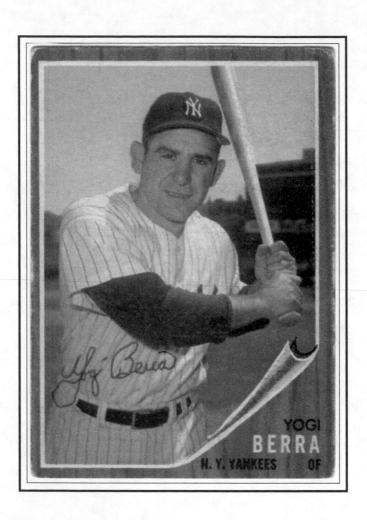

YOGI BERRA

Eternal Yankee

Allen Barra

W. W. NORTON & COMPANY

New York • London

Copyright © 2009 by Allen Barra

All rights reserved
Printed in the United States of America
First Edition

For information about permission to reproduce selections from this book,
write to Permissions, W. W. Norton & Company, Inc.,
500 Fifth Avenue, New York, NY 10110

For information about special discounts for bulk purchases, please contact
W. W. Norton Special Sales at specialsales@wwnorton.com or 800-233-4830

Manufacturing by RR Donnelley, Harrisonburg
Book design by JAMdesign
Production manager: Julia Druskin

Library of Congress Cataloging-in-Publication Data

Barra, Allen.
Yogi Berra : eternal Yankee / Allen Barra. — 1st ed.
p. cm.
Includes bibliographical references and index.
ISBN 978-0-393-06233-5 (hardcover)
1. Berra, Yogi, 1925– 2. Baseball players—United States—Biography.
3. Baseball coaches—United States—Biography. 4. New York Yankees
(Baseball team) I. Title.
GV865.B46B37 2009
796.357'092—dc22
[B]

2008045799

W. W. Norton & Company, Inc.
500 Fifth Avenue, New York, N.Y. 10110
www.wwnorton.com

W. W. Norton & Company Ltd.
Castle House, 75/76 Wells Street, London W1T 3QT

1 2 3 4 5 6 7 8 9 0

Yogi Berra: Eternal Yankee is lovingly dedicated to

my late father, Alfred Barra, who never got tired of being called "Yogi,"

the late Willie Morris, who must have asked me a dozen times, "Which book are you going to do first, Bear Bryant or Yogi Berra?"

the late Leonard Koppett, who helped plant the seed for this book several years ago and never quit asking, "Did you start the damn book yet?"

my wife, Jonelle Bonds, the Common House of Time spheric modula.

and most of all,

to Yogi, for making this book necessary.

Contents

Chronology

1920s–1930s

May 12, 1925   Lawrence Peter Berra is born in "the Hill" section of St. Louis, Missouri, to Pietro and Paulina Berra, from Malvaglio, Italy.

1938?   The likely year in which Larry Berra and his friends went to the movies and saw a travelogue featuring an Indian fakir. One of his friends thought Larry looked like the yoga expert, or "yogi."

1939?   Larry drops out of school after the eighth grade to find work. Later, at the urging of his brothers and a local priest, his parents agree to let him pursue baseball.

1940s

1941   Yogi and his boyhood friend, Joe Garagiola, try out for the Cardinals at Sportsman's Park in St. Louis. General Manager Branch Rickey offers Joe a contract and a $500 signing bonus. To Yogi, Rickey reluctantly offers just $250. Yogi turns him down.

Nov. 11, 1942   Yankees GM George Weiss offers Berra a contract on the recommendation of a St. Louis businessman, Leo Browne.

1943   Yogi's professional debut for the Norfolk Tars in the Class B Piedmont League for about $74 a month—about a dollar a day after rent. Meets Phil Rizzuto at a game with the Norfolk Air Station Tigers.

1944–1945   After receiving his draft papers, Yogi joins the Navy at the suggestion of an officer who promises him some playing time before being shipped out.

Midshipman Berra volunteers for top secret duty in a tiny LCSS rocket boat that serves at Normandy; later sees action on the southern coast of France.

The Giants Mel Ott offers $50,000 for Yogi's contract; Yankees president Larry MacPhail shrewdly declines.

1946   As a Newark Bear in the International League, Yogi competes against future stars such as Jackie Robinson. Roommate Bobby Brown will later become president of the American League.

Sept. 22, 1946 Major league debut, at Yankee Stadium, batting against Philadelphia's Jesse Flores. Hits a home run in his first game.

Winter 1947   Larry MacPhail takes the team on an exhibition tour of Puerto Rico, Venezuela, Cuba, and Panama. Manager Bucky Harris lauds Berra to the press, who are introduced to Yogiisms.

July 1947   Yogi Berra Day at Sportsman's Park in St. Louis. Tells the hometown crowd, "I want to thank everyone for making this day necessary."

Sept. 30, 1947 Berra and Frank "Spec" Shea become first rookie pitcher-catcher battery to start in the World Series (against the Brooklyn Dodgers). Yankees win, but Dodgers base runners give him fits.

Oct. 2, 1947   Hits the first pinch-hit home run in World Series history.

Oct. 4, 1947   Almost catches the first no-hitter in World Series history: Bill Bevens gives up a double to Cookie Lavagetto with two out in the ninth and loses.

Oct. 6, 1947   Yankees beat Dodgers four games to three, earning Yogi the first of ten World Series rings. Back in St. Louis, he shows Pietro and Paulina his Series check for the astonishing sum of $5,830.

1948   Meets the beautiful Carmen Short, a waitress at Biggie's Steakhouse in St. Louis. She becomes "the third girl" he has ever dated.

Oct. 1948   Manager Bucky Harris is fired, and Casey Stengel is hired, beginning the most fruitful manager-player relationship in the game's history. Casey will come to refer to Yogi as "*Mister* Berra, my *assistant* manager."

Jan. 26, 1949 Yogi and Carmen are married in St. Louis at St. Ambrose Catholic Church, where his parents were wed.

Spring 1949 Hall of Fame catcher Bill Dickey works with Yogi to sharpen his catching skills. Dickey, says Yogi, "learned me all of his experience."

Oct. 9, 1949 Despite a bad thumb, Yogi catches four games as the Yankees whip the Dodgers four games to one in the World Series, earning Yogi his second ring. Berra explains wearing protective gloves during workouts: "The only reason I need these gloves is 'cause of my hands."

Dec. 8, 1949 First son, Larry, is born.

1950s

1950   Yogi has one of the most sensational seasons by a catcher ever, batting .322 and driving in 124 runs with 28 home runs, but the MVP award goes to his friend Phil Rizzuto.

March 8, 1950 Off-season contract standoff with George Weiss ends after a public plea to Weiss from Stengel. Yogi gets a $5,000 boost.

July 1, 1950 A brash twenty-one-year-old left-hander from New York, Edward Ford, makes his Yankee debut. He wins nine of ten decisions before giving up the next two years to military service. When he returns in 1953, Ford and Berra become the greatest big-game battery of all time.

Oct. 7, 1950 Yankees become World Champions for the second straight season, beating the Philadelphia Phillies in four games.

July 12, 1951   Yogi catches his first no-hitter as Allie Reynolds blanks
                  Cleveland, 1-0.

Aug. 1951   Yogi's first *Sport* magazine cover.

Sept. 23, 1951   Second son, Tim, arrives.

Sept. 28, 1951   Catches the second no-hitter of his career as Reynolds
                  blanks the Boston Red Sox, 8-0. With two outs in the
                  ninth, Yogi drops a windblown pop by Ted Williams, giv-
                  ing baseball's greatest hitter a second shot. Williams pops
                  it up again, and Yogi puts it away.

Nov. 8, 1951   Berra edges pitchers Ned Garver and Allie Reynolds for
                  his first MVP. The Dodgers' Roy Campanella, Berra's
                  greatest rival for best catcher in the game, wins the
                  National League award.

Oct. 10, 1951   Yankees defeat the Giants four games to two, taking their
                  third consecutive World Series.

Sept. 1952   Becomes first catcher to hit 30 home runs in a season.

Oct. 7, 1952   Yankees defeat Dodgers for fourth consecutive World
                  Series. Yogi bats just .214 in the seven games but hits two
                  home runs.

Oct. 5, 1953   Winning 99 games during the regular season, Yanks beat
                  a sensational Brooklyn Dodgers team that had won 105
                  games. Yankees are first team to win five consecutive
                  World Series.

Oct. 1954   The Yankees have their best season under Stengel, win-
                  ning 103 games, but finish second to the Indians' 111.

Nov. 1954   Yogi, .307 with 22 home runs and 125 RBIs, wins his sec-
                  ond AL MVP.

Sept. 30, 1955   Jackie Robinson steals home in Game One of the World
                  Series off Whitey Ford. Yogi becomes, literally, hopping
                  mad. The "Safe or Out" argument goes on to this day.

Oct. 7, 1955   Yogi hits .417, but the Yankees finally lose the World
                  Series to the Dodgers.

Oct. 15, 1955   The Japanese discover Yogi. During the Yankees' good-
                  will tour of Japan, Yogi is handed a Japanese newspaper

with an article about him. "I can't read it," he says. "It's in Japanese."

Dec. 4, 1955   Yogi, who hit 27 home runs with 108 RBIs, wins his third MVP. Campanella, with 32 home runs and 107 RBIs, wins his third NL MVP.

Feb. 7, 1956   Berra is named vice president of the Yoo-Hoo Chocolate Soft Drink Company. A woman asks him if "Yoo-Hoo" is hyphenated. "No, ma'am," he explains, "it isn't even carbonated."

Sept. 5, 1956   With his 236th home run, Yogi ties Gabby Hartnett's all-time record for catchers.

Oct. 8, 1956   Yogi leaps into Don Larsen's arms after the first perfect game in World Series history.

Oct. 10, 1956   Yogi ties Lou Gehrig's record by leading the Yankees in RBIs for the seventh straight season, an achievement even Babe Ruth and Joe DiMaggio failed to accomplish.

—Yankees avenge the previous year's Series loss to Brooklyn by beating the Dodgers four games to three. Berra drives in ten runs, two with titanic home run shots off Don Newcombe, the NL's MVP.

Dec. 13, 1956   Third son, Dale, is born.

May 16, 1957   "The Copa Incident." Berra, Ford, Bauer, Kucks, Mantle, and wives join Billy Martin to celebrate his birthday at the Copacabana. Insults aimed at Sammy Davis Jr. spark a brawl, and a delicatessen owner winds up with a broken nose and jaw. Hank Bauer is accused, Billy Martin is blamed, and everyone is fined. An angry Berra is docked $1,000 by Yankee co-owner Dan Topping, though Yogi insisted, "No one did nothin' to nobody."

June 10, 1958   The Rizzuto-Berra bowling emporium opens in Clifton, New Jersey. The *Daily News*'s Dick Young reports that Yogi and Phil have each invested more than $50,000 of their own money. The alley features a trophy case of Yogi-Scooter memorabilia. "I'm bowling 300 but hitting .221," says Yogi.

Aug. 15, 1958	The *Sporting News*, "The Bible of Baseball," prints a rumor that the Yankees will trade Yogi to the Cardinals for Stan Musial. Yogi calls the rumor "a compliment."
May 5, 1959	Paulina Berra passes away with Yogi at her bedside.
May 10, 1959	Berra makes an error against the Washington Senators, snapping his all-time record of 148 consecutive games without a miscue.
July 1959	Yogi, Carmen, and the boys move into a handsome English Tudor–style house in Montclair, New Jersey, with a two-acre yard.
Aug. 3, 1959	Yogi is voted Player of the Game when his two-run homer off Don Drysdale at Memorial Coliseum in Los Angeles wins the second All-Star game of 1959.
Aug. 9, 1959	Yogi hits his 300th home run. His friend Elston Howard wins the game with a home run.
Sept. 19, 1959	Yogi Berra Day at Yankee Stadium. This time he gets the speech right.
Dec. 1959	Yogi and Carmen travel to Italy as goodwill ambassadors for an organization that distributes baseball equipment to Italian children. They attend the opera at La Scala in Milan. Yogi enjoys it, "even the music."

1960s

Oct. 1960	Berra plays in a record eleventh World Series, this time against the Pittsburgh Pirates. In the seventh game, he nearly wins it for the Yankees with a dramatic three-run homer in the sixth that gives New York the lead, but the Bucs win on Bill Mazeroski's famous home run. Yogi drives in eight runs in his last World Series as a regular.
Oct. 18, 1960	Casey Stengel fired as manager after twelve seasons and seven World Series championships. Following the press conference, he promises reporters that he will never again make the mistake of being seventy. Ralph Houk takes over the job.

Oct. 24, 1963   Eighteen days after they lose the World Series to the Los Angeles Dodgers, the Yankees name Yogi their new manager. The move surprises many younger writers who don't recall that Yogi had been Casey's assistant manager.

Aug. 20, 1964   "The Harmonica Incident." After losing a series to the Chicago White Six, the slumping Yankees are treated to a harmonica recital on the team bus by infielder Phil Linz. Egged on by Mantle and Ford, Linz continues to play after Berra tells him to stop. Yogi loses his temper, slaps the harmonica away, and the next day the much-ado-about-nothing is all over the country's sports pages.

Perhaps sparked by the incident, the Yankees turn the season around and roar back to win the pennant.

Oct. 15, 1964   The Yankees lose the World Series to the Cardinals, despite outscoring them 55-27 over seven games. Most baseball observers applaud the rookie manager's handling of the team and marvel that he came within one game of winning the World Series despite an injury to Whitey Ford.

Oct. 16, 1964   A day after losing the Series, the Yankees fire Berra as manager. Fans are shocked by the callousness of the Yankee regime. Cardinals manager Johnny Keane is hired as the replacement.

Nov. 17, 1964   Less than a month after the Yankees fired him, his old acquaintances George Weiss and Casey Stengel bring Yogi to the New York Mets as a coach.

May 11, 1965   Just before his fortieth birthday, Yogi retires as an active player. He knows it was time to go: "It's hard for me to see the ball."

Oct. 16, 1969   Berra's Luck lives on. The Miracle Mets, who finished in ninth place in 1968, win the World Series, beating a powerful Baltimore Orioles team in just five games.

1970s

Jan. 21, 1971   In a staggering display of stupidity, Hall of Fame voters leave Berra, probably the greatest catcher the game has ever seen, 28 votes short of Cooperstown.

Jan. 19, 1972   Given a year to nurse their guilty consciences, baseball
                   writers vote Yogi, along with Sandy Koufax and Early
                   Wynn, into the Hall. When asked how he pitched to
                   Berra the few times he faced him, mostly in exhibitions,
                   Koufax says with a laugh, "Carefully."

April 2, 1972   Mets manager and Yogi's good friend Gil Hodges dies of
                   heart attack. Four days later, Berra signs a two-year con-
                   tract to manage the Mets.

July 22, 1972   Yankees—finally—retire Yogi's number. 8, six months
                   after he is elected to the Baseball Hall of Fame and nine
                   years after his last at-bat as a Yankee. The Mets are in San
                   Francisco, so Larry Jr. accepts for his father.

Aug. 7, 1972   Yogi is inducted into the Hall of Fame.

Oct. 10, 1973   The Mets clinch the NL pennant, defeating the Cin-
                   cinnati Reds in the playoffs. Yogi has now managed two
                   teams to pennants, one in each league, the first man since
                   Joe McCarthy to do so.

Oct. 21, 1973   The Mets lose a thrilling seven-game World Series to the
                   Oakland A's.

Aug. 6, 1975   The Mets fire Berra, though the team's record of 58–53
                   isn't bad.

Dec. 5, 1975   With the enthusiastic recommendation of his old team-
                   mate Billy Martin, who had replaced Bill Virdon as man-
                   ager one-third into the season, Yogi is hired as Yankees
                   coach.

1980s

Dec. 16, 1983   Yogi is named manager of Yankees, replacing Billy
                   Martin.

April 28, 1985   Berra is fired by Yankees management—over the
                   phone—after just sixteen games. Yogi vows to have
                   nothing to do with the Yankees as long as George
                   Steinbrenner is the owner.

1986   Berra's New Jersey neighbor, John McMullen, owner of
                   the Houston Astros, offers him a job as coach with the

Astros. In his first year, Berra's Luck strikes again, and Houston wins the NL West, but loses an exciting playoff series to the New York Mets.

1989   Yogi retires from baseball.

1990s and beyond

Dec. 1998   The Yogi Berra Museum and Learning Center opens its doors on the campus of Montclair State University in New Jersey.

Jan. 7, 1999   Yogi and George Steinbrenner reconcile their differences and meet to shake hands at Yogi's museum.

May 12, 2005   Yogi celebrates his eightieth birthday to national acclaim. He and Carmen have been married fifty-five years and have ten grandchildren.

Feb. 23, 2007   Yogi and Don Larsen watch a replay of the perfect game from the 1956 World Series along with a packed house at the museum. It's the first time that either man has seen the game since they played in it fifty-one years earlier.

July 22, 2007   Yogi is elected to the Shrine of the Eternals by the Baseball Reliquary, an organization dedicated to "fostering an appreciation of the historical development of baseball and its interaction with American culture." Previous inductees include Bill Veeck Jr., Jim Bouton, Satchel Paige, and Marvin Miller. Yogi's longtime backup catcher, Charlie Silvera, accepts the award for him.

Aug. 13, 2007   Death of Phil Rizzuto.

YOGI BERRA

Eternal Yankee

Introduction

Inventing Yogi Berra

He was the guy who made the Yankees
seem almost human.

—MICKEY MANTLE

SOMETIME IN THE summer of 1941, two of the great legends of baseball narrowly missed making a connection that would have radically
altered baseball. Some historians place the date in 1942, but the two men
with reason to remember it best, Yogi Berra and Joe Garagiola, say, and I
have taken their word, it was 1941.

Lawrence Peter Berra, a then somewhat stocky, ungainly looking
sixteen-year-old Italian-American kid from the "Dago Hill" area of St.
Louis, had attracted the attention of the best organization in the National
League for a tryout in Sportsman's Park. Jack Maguire, a scout for the St.
Louis Cardinals, told his boss, general manager Branch Rickey, that Berra
had a powerful left-handed swing, a great arm, and heaps of potential.
Rickey wasn't sure; he was more interested in another kid from the Hill,
Joseph Henry Garagiola, a year younger than Berra. Garagiola was thought
by Rickey to be faster, smoother, and more polished. Dee Walsh, another
Cardinals scout, talked Rickey into signing Garagiola with a $500 bonus,
but Rickey was skeptical about offering anything at all to Berra.

Rickey had been getting reports on both boys all summer, not just from
his scouts but also from two of his outfielders, Enos Slaughter and Terry
Moore, who occasionally showed up to give pointers at the WPA baseball
school at Sherman's Park. Rickey's initial offer to young Berra was a
contract—but no bonus. To a boy that age, a professional baseball contract,
even without a bonus, was nothing to be scorned. But Lawrence, displaying
the kind of stubborn integrity that would, in just a few years, stymie the

most powerful organization in sports, balked. "In the first place," he would tell sportswriter Ed Fitzgerald nearly two decades later, "I knew it was going to be tough enough to convince Mom and Pop that they ought to let me go away. But if Joey was getting $500 for it and I wasn't getting anything, they would be sure to think it was a waste of time for me."[1]

Hedging, Rickey offered $250. Branch Rickey was the most influential executive in baseball—by the end of the decade, it was estimated that nearly 37 percent of all big league players had been developed in one of his farm systems—and Larry's brash reply took him aback: "No, I want the same as Joey's getting."[2] Rickey did not mention to Berra how much a month he would be earning under the contract, and Berra never asked. "That didn't matter to me. I would have taken anything. All I was interested in was that if Garagiola was getting $500, I wanted $500, too."[3] Yogi would later take pains to emphasize that he wasn't jealous of his pal, but he was convinced, from years of sandlot and street games, that he was as good a ballplayer as Joe. Garagiola disagreed. "Yogi wasn't better than me," recalls Joe. "He was much better. There were a lot of good ballplayers on the Hill at that time, and 'Lawdy'—as his friends called him, echoing his mother, who couldn't pronounce 'Larry'—was the best. You know how kids choose up sides with a bat, one hand on top of the other until you reach the end of the handle? When the last hand got to the top, the first thing said was 'We want Lawdy.' "

Jack Maguire argued with his boss, but Rickey was intractable: Berra would never be more than a Triple-A player. He was too clumsy and too slow, Rickey said, to be a genuine big league prospect. Maguire never understood Rickey's decision. Berra's coaches, and certainly his opponents, did not find him either slow or clumsy, though he often *appeared* to be both. Branch Rickey was, simply, the greatest judge of talent the baseball world had ever seen and, perhaps, with the possible exception of a man whose path would cross Yogi's, the greatest front office man in the game. In his time, Rickey pegged Jackie Robinson, Roberto Clemente, and dozens of other great players as future stars; he had been a catcher himself and was capable of evaluating all body types. He understood that baseball was a game that benefited from all manner of physical tools. Yet, Rickey, against the advice of his own scout, would not put out the additional $250 to sign Larry Berra. It was the most colossally shortsighted blunder ever made by a baseball executive, surpassing even Boston Red Sox owner Harry Frazee's dealing Babe Ruth to the Yankees in 1920. Frazee, at least, got the incredible sum of $425,000 in cash and loans.

If, that is, Rickey's decision was a blunder. In later years, a counterstory would circulate that Rickey was actually being shrewd: he knew he wouldn't be with the Cardinals much longer, he was preparing to leave the St. Louis club for the Brooklyn Dodgers, and his real intention was to "hide" Berra and sign him for Brooklyn. Joe Garagiola points out that just a couple of months after the tryout, after Rickey had moved to the Dodgers, he contacted Berra to offer him a contract. "Rickey tried to sign Yogi after he went to work for the Dodgers," says Joe. "Why would he have kept a file on him if he hadn't intended to sign him for Brooklyn?"

In 1961, when his autobiography was published, Yogi flat-out denied that Rickey had tried to "hide" him. "I've never believed that . . . From everything I've heard about him, he's too big a man to do anything like that."[4] In recent years, probably from hearing the opposite version so much, Yogi .... he .... the .... on the .... In a 1999 interview with Bob Costas, he said that he believed Rickey had intended all along to keep him for the Dodgers. It's easy to see why: this explanation offers a simple, logical reason for a decision that seems otherwise inexplicable.*

The problem is, there isn't any evidence to support this interpretation. Rickey himself never mentioned it. In his 1965 book, *The American Diamond: A Documentary of the Game of Baseball*, Rickey devoted a brief entry to "Yogi and Campy"—Berra and Roy Campanella, the great Dodgers catcher whose extraordinary career parallels Yogi's. "In the last decade," wrote Rickey, "the two dominant catchers in baseball were Roy Campanella of Brooklyn and L.P. Yogi Berra of the New York Yankees. By 1955 they were at the top of their game, and each had earned the Most Valuable Player award in his respective league for the third time. Both men were clutch hitters with extra-base power, both were powerfully built but deceptively fast, both were very smart behind the plate . . . both Campy and Yogi had splendid throwing arms . . . They have hit over 550 home runs between them, surpassing all catchers in history in this department . . . Baseball may never see two such talented men for a long time."[5]

There isn't a word about Rickey's having passed up a chance to sign Yogi in St. Louis in 1941, or, in fact, of Rickey's having contacted Yogi later when

---

*Though Yogi himself might have offered the simplest and best explanation for Rickey's puzzling decision in his 1961 book: "I think it's just that it was getting harder to get players as the war went along, and he remembered me and figured it would be worth a few hundred dollars to see if I could help him. Anyway, it didn't make any difference." (Berra and Fitzgerald, *Yogi*, p. 64)

Rickey was with the Dodgers and Berra had signed with the Yankees. Such an omission was unusual for Rickey, who was an encyclopedia of facts and memories. Murray Polner, Rickey's best biographer, doesn't recall a mention of Berra in any of Rickey's papers. "I tend to disbelieve the story of Rickey's trying to 'hide' Yogi for the Dodgers," says Polner. "Rickey was a notorious tight wad, but painfully honest. He wouldn't have set up a prospect for the Dodgers while working for the Cardinals. He wouldn't have paid Garagiola $500 of Cardinal money if he didn't think Joe was major league caliber."

And if Rickey was still doing his job for the Cardinals, he would have signed Yogi Berra for them if he thought Yogi was a genuine prospect. The only plausible explanation for Rickey's later failure to mention his contact with Yogi would seem to be his ego: he simply did not want to admit that he missed signing one of the greatest players in the game's history.

There is another possibility as to what happened with Rickey and Berra, but it rests on tenuous evidence. In a 1949 profile of Yogi in *Collier's* magazine, a writer named Gordon Manning stated that in the September after the tryout, Rickey phoned Berra "and said he would contact him in a few days"—presumably when his contract with the Cardinals was up—"but Yogi, confused by the Great Man's double-talk, signed with the Yanks after scout Johnny Schulte had duplicated Joe's bonus on a tip from Leo Browne."[6] Where would Manning have gotten this information? Surely not from Rickey. Either Berra mentioned it to him during their interview or Manning misunderstood something Yogi did say. If it's true, then it would seem Rickey did try to "hide" Yogi from the Cardinals, but I have seen no mention of a September call from Rickey anywhere.

Many years later the phrase "Berra's Luck" would make its way into articles about Yogi. Looking back on his career, it was amazing how many times something seemingly bad would turn out not merely well but better than Yogi or anyone could have anticipated. Rickey's failure to sign Yogi is the first known example of Berra's Luck. After the tryout in Sportsman's Park, Larry was hurt and humiliated. He went home empty-handed, while his pal, a lad younger than he was, went home to his parents not only with a contract but with $500, more in one lump sum than his family would otherwise have come across in decades.

If fate, like an angel in the films of Frank Capra—an Italian immigrant born about the same time as Yogi's father—had tapped him on the shoulder and said, "Don't let it bother you, you will go on to the winningest career in the history of American sports, your words will be quoted by movie stars and presidents, and you will be rich enough to take care of your parents and your whole family," Larry Berra could not possibly have believed him.

———

ONE OF THE most popular staples of adventure comic books is parallel universes, where "What if?" stories show us what might have happened if, for instance, Batman's parents had lived or if Superman's Krypton had not exploded. The life of Yogi Berra, who enjoyed those comic books nearly as much as he enjoyed baseball, would have made for a fascinating series of "What if?" stories. If Branch Rickey had stayed in St. Louis or if he had just offered Yogi the $500, what might Berra's career have been like? And how might the world as we know it be different? Given Berra's natural talent and capacity for hard work, he would have been a Hall of Famer had he spent all or most of his career with the Cardinals—though, oddly enough, his career at catcher, his natural position, would have been slowed by the earlier maturity of Joe Garagiola. Rickey's judgment was correct at least as to where the two youngsters stood in 1941; Joey was more developed as a backstop and would catch more games in his first two seasons as a Cardinal than Berra would in his first three seasons with the Yankees. Also, in New York Berra had the great Bill Dickey to bring him along, and Yogi's progress would almost certainly have been even slower without the help of the fabled catcher. Still, there was no holding back a player of Berra's talent. He would hit more home runs in his first four seasons than Garagiola would hit in his entire career.

After 1946, Garagiola's rookie year, the Cardinals would not win another pennant until 1964, when they would face a Yankee team in the World Series managed by . . . Yogi Berra. Between 1947 and 1963, though, the Cardinals finished second five times and third four times. It's likely that Berra would have made the difference in at least a couple of those pennant races. If the Cardinals had boasted Berra during that span, they might well have challenged the Dodgers for National League supremacy. Yogi, a St. Louis boy, would have been, along with Stan Musial, one of the two most popular players in the history of America's greatest baseball town. St. Louis fans relished nicknames—they gave one to an entire team, the 1934 "Gashouse Gang" Cardinals, as well as nearly everyone on it: "Dizzy" and "Daffy" Dean, "Pepper" Martin, Yogi's first great baseball idol "Ducky" Medwick, and Yogi's early instructor "Country" Slaughter. In the 1940s, their greatest player would be Stan "The Man" Musial. "Yogi" would have been an instant favorite. Playing against the Dodgers in the National League, though, would have pitted Berra against the other great catcher of his time, Roy Campanella, so, had he been a Cardinal, Yogi wouldn't have been an automatic selection to start the All-Star game every year as he was for the Yankees. It also isn't certain that he would have won three Most Valuable Player awards. However, it seems safe to say that Berra, had he played for the Cardinals those seventeen seasons, would have been one of his league's best players, an obvious Hall of Famer, and that St. Louis would have won a couple more pennants. A statue of Yogi would probably be standing next to Stan the Man's outside Busch Stadium.

The more intriguing "What if?" is: "What if Branch Rickey had signed Yogi for the Brooklyn Dodgers?" The possibility is so monumentally disruptive to the existing order that to even contemplate it leaves one dizzy; it's like one of those science fiction stories where the protagonist changes something in the past then returns to the present to find everything altered. The Brooklyn Dodgers were the only other team of that era with the potential to challenge the Yankees for baseball supremacy. To many Americans, the Dodgers were America's team; even in the Deep South (where their games were broadcast on the Armed Forces Network) they were often seen as small town underdogs whom millions rooted for against the cold, corporate, big-city Yankees. The Dodgers of the late 1940s and 1950s, the Dodgers of Jackie Robinson, Roy Campanella, Duke Snider, Pee Wee Reese, and Gil Hodges, produced as many household names as the Yankees of the same period. Yogi would have been a spectacular fit— what the rest of the country called malapropisms would have been regarded in Brooklyn as heightened awareness.

From the first year Berra played more than 80 games, 1947, through 1963, his last year as a player with baseball's most dominant team, the Yankees won 1,649 games during the regular season and lost 989, a won-lost percentage of .625. The Dodgers, over the same span, were the second best in baseball, 1,560–1,080 for .591, a difference of .034. Take away Yogi—who never finished lower than fourth in the MVP voting from 1950 to 1956—from the Yankees and replace him with anyone besides Campanella. It's more than reasonable to assume that the Yankees would have won an average of three fewer games per season and that the Dodgers with Yogi would have averaged at least three more wins. If Yogi had been a Dodger then (and if my three-wins-per-season average is correct), the Brooklyn/Los Angeles Dodgers of 1947–1963 would have been baseball's most dominant team, with a record of 1,600 to 1,610 wins, while the Yankees (again holding to Yogi's value of three wins per season) would have won fewer than 1,600.

What about the World Series? The Yankees won fourteen pennants over those seventeen seasons, and the Dodgers won eight. Take Yogi out of pinstripes and put him in Dodger blue, and I would wager that at the least the difference would be split. Yogi's presence could have been enormous in Brooklyn's heartbreaking pennant races of 1950, when they lost to the Philadelphia Phillies Whiz Kids, and in 1951, when they lost to the New York Giants on Bobby Thomson's last swing of the season. Those were just two of the five Dodgers' second-place finishes over those seventeen seasons. As a Dodger, Yogi could easily have turned World Series history on its head. Between 1947 and 1963, the Yankees and Dodgers faced each other in seven World Series, with the Yankees winning five. The Yankees' edge in victories in those series is surprisingly small just 20 wins to the Dodgers' 18. Though four of those Dodger victories came in 1963, a season in which Yogi played just 64 games, so perhaps 1963 should be left out of the equation. That leaves the Yankees with 23 World Series victories over the Dodgers between 1947 and 1956. How many of those games could Yogi have turned around? Well, if he had turned around as many for the Dodgers against the Yankees as he actually did for the Yankees against the Dodgers, the Dodgers, not the Yankees, would have been baseball's dominant team over those seventeen seasons.*

And here's a really scary thought: given Yogi's amazing track record handling young pitchers, what might he have done with Sanford Koufax, who made his debut with the Brooklyn Dodgers at the age of nineteen? In 1961, Koufax finally lived up to his incredible potential, with 18 wins and 269

---

*Perhaps the most intriguing question about the Yogi-as-a-Dodger scenario is: Who would have been the Dodgers' catcher—Yogi or Campy? There are some who would regard the question of which of the two great catchers to start as a problem. I think having Yogi Berra and Roy Campanella on the same team and wondering where to play them is a problem all managers would like to face. For one thing, both Berra and Campanella were capable of playing other positions—Campy played all his major league games at catcher, but in the Negro Leagues he was a capable first baseman, third baseman, and outfielder—and in addition to having both their bats in the lineup on most days, the Dodgers could have had the option of using one to relieve the other in, say, second games of doubleheaders. Imagine having Yogi Berra or Roy Campanella as your *backup* catcher! Campanella lost quite a few games to injury, and in those situations they could have pulled Berra out of, say, left field and put him behind the plate.

If they played together, Berra would have been the starting catcher because he reached the major leagues sooner than Campanella. It's true that Yogi's skills behind the plate were honed considerably by Bill Dickey, but if Yogi had been on the Dodgers, Branch Rickey would certainly have seen to it that Berra had first-rate coaching.

strikeouts, breaking Christy Mathewson's fifty-eight-year-old National League record of 267. Prior to that, in six seasons, Koufax had been just 36–40 in 103 starts. Is it unreasonable to assume that Sandy would have fulfilled that potential a little sooner with Yogi catching? In 1958 Roy Campanella suffered a horrendous auto accident that paralyzed him and ended his career. (In any event, by 1957 he was thirty-six and winding down, appearing in just 103 games and hitting only .242.) What if Yogi had had a shot at working with Koufax when he was twenty-two or twenty-three?*

In either scenario, on any team, Yogi's greatness would have emerged. He would have become an American folk hero and icon no matter what team he played for, but if he had not been a Yankee, I would not have written this book. He would have wound up living in St. Louis or, God forbid, Hollywood, and I would not be living less than ten miles from the Yogi Berra Museum and Learning Center and would not have the privilege of regarding Yogi as a neighbor. And if Yogi had not been a Yankee, would he truly be the national hero he is today, particularly to non-Yankee fans all over the country? It seems paradoxical, but Yogi Berra is known and loved by millions who hate the team he played for, the team that regularly beat *their* teams. Of what other former athlete could something similar be said? As Mickey Mantle said, "He was the guy who made the Yankees seem almost human."[7]

I don't really remember if I was a Yankee fan in my youth—ours was a Willie Mays household that revolved around the daily checking of box scores to compare Mays's productivity with Mickey Mantle's. Like millions of people around the country, I never felt I had to root for the Yankees to love Yogi, and like everyone else, whatever my feelings about the Yankees—I distinctly remember rooting against them when they played Mays and the Giants in the 1962 World Series—I always loved Yogi. But, I asked myself as my daughter and I wandered through Yogi's museum, do we really appreciate Yogi Berra?

Everyone *loves* Yogi—or as the title of a play based on his life which he was too shy to attend says, *Nobody Don't Like Yogi.* But do we really take him—I know this sounds strange, but hear me out—*seriously* enough?

---

*To my knowledge, the only writer to have considered the possibility of Yogi as a Brooklyn Dodger was Gordon Manning. in *Collier's*: "What a daffy Dodger Yogi would have made!" Manning wrote that Berra didn't care for the idea: " 'Brooklyn,' he says with obvious distaste. 'What a place. Anytime we play at Ebbets Field in a spring exhibition or somethin' I always gotta leave the house two hours early. I know I'm going to take the wrong subway, so I gotta allow time for gettin' lost.' "

Everybody acknowledges that Yogi was a truly great player, but has he ever really been given his due? When it came time to vote for the All-Century team in 1999, Yogi finished second to Johnny Bench, 704,208 votes to 1,010,403. I don't want to sound as if I'm knocking Johnny Bench, another of my favorite players, but Yogi Berra was unequivocally the greatest catcher in the history of baseball, as good a hitter as Bench and an even better defensive catcher, and as every Yankee fan knows, the biggest winner in baseball history in terms of pennants and World Series rings. He was the cornerstone of the most dominant baseball team of the twentieth century, the only team to win five consecutive World Series, the 1949–1953 Yankees. It's entirely possible that Johnny Bench, given the chance to play with the same teammates as Yogi, would have collected just as many rings—maybe. But Yogi *did* win them. Yogi was the glue that held the Yankees together between the fading of Joe DiMaggio and the rise of Mickey Mantle.

I don't want to spend too much time on the Bench versus Berra argument now—you'll find a detailed comparison of their careers in Appendix A—but for now suffice it to say that Yogi is, by all objective measurements I can find, the greatest player at baseball's most demanding position. There are, after all, only sixteen catchers in the Hall of Fame, and with good reason, considering the wear and tear catching takes on the human body and the skills one must possess to be just a competent catcher in the first place. Catchers' equipment is commonly referred to as "the tools of ignorance," and the man who coined the phrase should be horsewhipped: no other position demands such intelligence, instinct, and leadership skills, and at no other position are great players so underappreciated. (As Joe Garagiola told me, "Catchers are the fire hydrants at the Westminster dog show.")

Moreover, Yogi was an extraordinary player in other ways, a smart base runner and, though no one would mistake him for DiMaggio in the outfield, competent enough to have played 74 games in the outfield as the Yankees broke him in to the catcher spot and then, in his mid-thirties, to become the team's semiregular left fielder, thus getting his successor Elston Howard into the lineup and continuing to contribute to his team when his own primary skills were fading.* As a manager, he won two pennants, one in both leagues, taking both teams to the final game of the

---

*Carlton Fisk played 31 games in the outfield for the Chicago White Sox at age thirty-nine—he had made eight previous outfield appearances in his career before that—but not many other catchers have been able to make the move so late in their career.

World Series. As a coach with the New York Mets and Houston Astros, he was involved in two of the most thrilling postseason series ever, the 1969 World Series and the 1986 National League Championship Series.

You can find all of that in the record book. Modern baseball analysts hotly debate the existence of such things as clutch hitting and other "intangibles," with most denying them. But this reality was not doubted in Yogi Berra's day. Branch Rickey, no mystic when it came to the analysis of baseball, called Yogi one of the greatest clutch hitters he had ever seen. Mantle said it best, recalling a tight situation in the World Series, "There was no one I would rather see batting in that situation than Yogi, unless it was me."[8] No one has yet succeeded in offering a satisfactory explanation as to what clutch hitting is, but nearly everyone Yogi played with or against insists that whatever definition you want to use, it applies to Yogi Berra. In the final analysis, the question of whether or not clutch hitting is real may not be as important as the fact that so many players *believe* that it is real. Just as there are no atheists in foxholes, there are no agnostics in dugouts in the late innings of close games. Yogi's teammates wanted to be on his side in tough, tight situations, and the guys on the other team didn't want to face him when they felt the game was on the line.

This leads to the question of intangibles. *Webster's New World College Dictionary* says intangibles "cannot be easily defined, formulated or grasped." Nothing drives analysts nuttier than fans who rate players by their supposed "intangibles," which Bill James once called "a fan's word for talents that don't exist." Twenty-five years of writing about sports has left me uncertain as to whether or not I believe intangibles actually exist; I rather feel like the Irish peasant woman who, when asked by the writer Sean O'Faolain if she believed in the fairies, replied indignantly, "I do not." But, she cautioned, "They're there." Intangibles may be in the eye of the beholder, but it's also possible that some things we lump under the heading of intangibles might simply be things we have not yet found a way to quantify—or which do exist but can't be quantified. What they call "being good in the clubhouse" (meaning a player who fosters good vibes and inspires confidence), the capacity for capitalizing on opponents' strengths and weaknesses, the faculty for passing on experience to younger players (as Yogi did to future Hall of Fame second baseman Craig Biggio, whom he steered away from the catching position while with Houston), and the handling of pitchers come under the heading of intangibles. Not for nothing did Casey

Stengel, the most successful big league manager ever, refer to Yogi as, "*Mister* Berra, my assistant manager."

Deny the existence of clutch hitting and the value of intangibles, and you are in conflict with those who saw Yogi Berra play. Define clutch hitting and intangibles any way you like; whatever definition you put on them, the men who played with and against Yogi Berra thought he possessed them. As a player, manager, and coach, Yogi played on more winning teams and was involved in more legendary games and more famous plays than any player in the history of the game. In fact, far, *far* more than anyone else. He is so much ahead of whoever is in second that I cannot at the moment imagine who that might be. He helped put World Series rings on the hands of pitchers whose names are now forgotten by all except the most rabid Yankee fans, pitchers such as Frank "Spec" Shea, Joe Ostrowski, Tom Ferrick, and a score of others. And if you don't believe they Lawson should be included in their number, you can ask him.

His life and career are a virtual cutaway view of the game of baseball in the twentieth century.

———

AND YET, THE question persists. Do we take Yogi Berra seriously enough? And the answer, I think, is no. Joe Garagiola gives a surprising reply to the question "What's the first word that springs to mind when you think of Yogi?" "Underrated," says the man who has known him since childhood. And Garagiola is right, as is ESPN's Jayson Stark in his book, *The Stark Truth: The Most Overrated and Underrated Players in Baseball History.* Stark regards Berra as not merely the most underrated catcher of all time but the most underrated player. And Stark is correct in pointing out that Yogi occupies a peculiar niche: unlike other underrated players, Berra has not been forgotten: there has simply been a wrong turn taken somewhere in regards to what he should be remembered for.

That Garagiola should call Yogi underrated is, of course, ironic, since it was Joe who helped create the mindset that caused him to be underrated. Through decades of telling Yogi stories, many real and some apocryphal, to audiences of millions during Joe's days at NBC, he undermined the perception of Berra as a great player and competitor and replaced it with the image of an amiable clown who was lucky enough to have been around when the Almighty handed out roster spots on winning teams. I don't imply that that was Joe's intention, but the stories, repeated endlessly on television and paraphrased in newspapers and magazines and then in subways, in offices, and in bars, created a pseudo-Yogi that took on a life of its own, a caricature of the real man.° This wasn't all Joe's doing by any means; Yogi Bear, the cartoon creation with whom the original Yogi was none too pleased, made his debut three years before Garagiola began telling Berra stories on NBC's national baseball broadcasts. (And who'd have guessed back in the early 1960s when Yogi Bear was the most famous cartoon character on TV that forty-five years later the first Yogi would once again be more familiar to audiences than the animated bear he inspired?)

It must be admitted, too, that Yogi himself has done his share to perpetuate the pseudo-Yogi. The Aflac commercial, currently among the most popular on television, is a case in point. If you haven't seen it, which means you've been in solitary confinement on the moon for the last couple of years, it presents Yogi in a barbershop (presumably one near his home in Montclair) dispensing pseudo-Yogiisms such as "If you get hurt and miss work, it won't hurt to miss work" and "They give you cash, which is just as good as money." The commercial is funny, but the lines don't sound like Yogi.

On the day I write this, June 4, 2006, in a column headed "As Yogi Berra Never Said," the syndicated columnist James J. Kilpatrick writes, "In 1953, the New York Yankees won their fifth World Series in a row. Their popular catcher, Yogi Berra, took it in stride. 'It's déjà vu all over again,' he said. The trouble is, he never said it. It's also probable that he never said of a particular restaurant, 'It's so crowded nobody goes there any more.' And if Berra was the first to remark, 'The future ain't what it used to be' the evidence is hard to come by."

Actually, Yogi did say (or at least reliable witnesses swear he did say) "It's déjà vu all over again." But nobody remembers it being after the 1953 Series: they remember he said it after Mickey Mantle and Roger Maris hit back-to-back home runs in 1961. Yogi most certainly did say, in regard to dining at a particular restaurant, probably Toots Shor's, "Nobody goes there any more, it's too crowded." However, he never said he was the first

---

°Berra himself has always been a bit ambivalent about Garagiola's version of Yogi. "It was good for him to say all he has said about me over the years," he recalled for Tom Horton in his 1989 memoir, *Yogi: It Ain't Over,* "and it had been good for me, too. At least it was not bad. That's the way I would like to say it. It wasn't bad . . . We were childhood friends and still are and will always be. Joe is not the only one who used me as a stooge, if that is a good word (I am not sure it is, but I'm going to use it anyway). He was the most well known. A writer friend suggested I use 'foil' in place of 'stooge.' It didn't work for me." (p. 59)

to say it, and to my knowledge no one, least of all Yogi, has ever claimed that he said "The future ain't what it used to be."

If Yogiisms have become a light industry, then the debunking of Yogiisms practically qualifies as one. Kilpatrick is far from the first to set up a straw Yogiism just to knock it down.

Generally speaking, there is a significant difference between the genuine Yogiisms and the pseudo-Yogiisms, and it is this: the things Yogi said that he actually said usually make sense in fewer words than most anyone else would use. "When you come to the fork in the road, take it" refers to the quickest way to get to his house (it's the same distance whether you keep to the right or left). That "You can't think and hit at the same time" will be confirmed for you by any great hitter. Yogi never said that being able to think wouldn't help you to hit—quite the contrary. As he phrased it in a Q&A session at the 1998 Montclair Booktober Fest, "You do your thinking before you got up to bat. We used to spend a lot of time before the games talking about certain pitchers, what they threw, and what was the best way to hit them in certain situations. We did a lot of talking and a lot of thinking about hitting. We just didn't stand there thinking when we were up to bat." Another man with a great eye, French photographer Henri Cartier-Bresson, said as much about his profession: "Thinking should be done beforehand and afterwards—never while actually taking a photograph." No one laughed at him.

"Why buy good luggage? You only use it when you travel" just seems like plain good sense to me. "It ain't over till it's over" was supposed to have been coined by Yogi during the Mets' 1973 pennant race, and he turned out to be right: it *wasn't* over until it was over. (Yogi, for his part, thought that Rocky Bridges might have said it first; in any event, he insisted he always tried to say "It *isn't* over until it's over.")

"Ninety percent of this game is half mental"? Who knows better what the percentage is? And, as anyone can tell you who has ever tried (including Bear Bryant, who was no one's idea of an amiable clown but who was always quoting his favorite Yogiism), you *can* observe a lot just by watching. And so on. True Yogi fans, of course, make a distinction between real Yogiisms—distilled bits of wisdom which, like good country songs and old John Wayne movies, get to the truth in a hurry—and the famous malapropisms, such as when he told the fans at Yogi Berra Day in St. Louis, "I want to thank everyone for making this day necessary." And who can say for certain that the St. Louis fans *didn't* make the day necessary?

The commercials are merely Yogi's most recent jujitsu on the media, who long ago created a semifictional persona described by Yogi himself as "a kind of comic-strip character, like Li'l Abner or Joe Palooka."[9] They've been doing it to Yogi for nearly sixty years now, and for nearly sixty years Yogi, instead of doing what almost anyone else would have done, nursing resentment and allowing bitterness to fester, has had the last laugh by turning the psuedo-Yogi into a cash cow. No one, of course, has more of a right to benefit from any image of Yogi than Yogi himself. But though it has helped make him the most famous living former athlete, one of the most quoted Americans of the last two centuries, and, in the words of the *New York Daily News'* Bill Madden, "the most recognizable figure in America,"[10] it may have cost him something as well. Namely the full measure of respect that should be accorded a man of Yogi's accomplishments. An exhibit at Yogi's museum traces the evolution of an American legend in such pop cultural artifacts—let's call them Yogiana—as baseball cards, comic strips, milk cartons, soft drink bottles, and figurines, as well as books, including his 1961 autobiography, *Yogi*; his 1966 instruction manual, *Yogi Berra's Baseball Guidebook*; reflections on his ten championship series, *Ten Rings*, co-written with Dave Kaplan; and published in 2008, *You Can Observe a Lot by Watching: What I've Learned About Teamwork from the Yankees and Life* (also co-written with Kaplan).

What there *isn't* in that glass case is a copy of a comprehensive biography of Yogi,° which, if you think about it, is absolutely amazing and a fact that has slipped under the radar of Yogi's enormous fandom. Surely he is the greatest ballplayer never to have had a serious biography—a gap in baseball history that I hope to fill with this book. In fact, for all of his fame and the endless stories affirming or debunking Yogiisms, there has been little written about Yogi and his enormous role as the most valuable player of the greatest of all baseball dynasties. He is excluded (by his own wishes) from most oral histories of the Yankees in that period, and thus his role has been kept to a minimum in most narratives of the Yankees from World War II on. He is, of course, prominent in most of his teammates' memoirs, including those of Whitey Ford, Phil Rizzuto, and Mickey Mantle, as well as those of his manager and mentor, Casey Stengel, and, of course, Joe Garagiola.

Partly this is because Yogi, contrary to his public image, is a painfully shy and deeply private man who is extremely uncomfortable in formal inter-

---

°At the time I wrote this, I had not yet seen Carlos DeVito's 2008 biography, *Yogi: The Life and Times of an American Original*.

views. But those who encounter him in informal situations can attest that he is surprisingly quick and engaging. At the Montclair Book Center in 1998, he was autographing copies of *The Yogi Book: "I Really Didn't Say Everything I Said!*, when I showed him a copy of his autobiography, *Yogi*, which he had signed for me thirty-seven years earlier. "Do you remember signing this for me at the Menlo Park shopping center in 1961?" I asked. "Yeah," he replied with a grin. "How 'ya been doin'?"

Baseball historian Dom Forker, working on a history of the 1955–1964 Yankees, received this reply from Carmen Berra some seventeen years ago: "If you know Yogi, as I'm certain you do, you know he hates to give interviews. He doesn't like to talk about himself. Do you want to hear about our six grandkids?" (This was in 1990; it's eleven grandkids now.) "That told me as much about Yogi as any interview," says Forker. "He just wanted to talk about his grandchildren. Charlie Keller, his teammate for years with the Yankees, told me 'Yogi isn't much with about himself, you're going to need all the help you can get.' Charlie was right."

How shy is Yogi Berra? In 1998, after the team from Tom's River, New Jersey, won the Little League World Series, they paid a visit to the Yogi Berra Museum in Montclair. Berra, in the middle of a congratulatory address to the boys, began to tear up. Yogi's reticence to play the public figure has often caught sportswriters nurtured on the pseudo-Yogi by surprise, leading them to the conclusion that Yogi was some sort of media creation. Jack Mann, later a columnist for the *Detroit Free Press*, came to New York in the mid-1950s and met Berra while writing for the *New York Herald Tribune*. He was told he would be wowed with Yogi quotes, but he never got anything in the locker room worth using. By 1967, when he chronicled the fall of the Yankee empire for a book, he concluded that "Yogi Berra wasn't really a character. . . . He wasn't even especially interesting. If there had not been a Yogi Berra, it would have been necessary for those attempting to write cute copy about the Yankees to invent him, and they did."[11] Mann was on the verge of an insight, but he was so focused on debunking the popular notion that he missed the real point: the Yogi Berra that everyone read about in the papers every day and heard about on television *was* an invention. The real Yogi was no cliché, and he was nobody's invention but his own.

PART ONE

Chapter One

King of the Hill
(1925–1942)

His name is Yogi something or other.
Ain't that a hell of a name?

—I LH HII/\IHIIH,

Commander VFW Stockham Post

TUCKED INTO THE southwestern corner of St. Louis, "the Hill," named for its proximity to the highest point in the city, is a neighborhood, an enclave, and a state of mind. Located just south of the River des Peres and Interstate 44, and bounded by Kingshighway Boulevard on the east, Hampton Avenue on the west, Columbia and Southwest Avenues on the south, and Northrup and Manchester Avenues on the north, the Hill remains today almost as exclusively Italian-American as it was a century ago. In fact, Larry Berra, growing up there in the late 1920s and early 1930s, recalled but a single non-Italian family, German Catholics, in his neighborhood. Joe Garagiola remembered a diminutive Jewish dry goods merchant named Gianin who spoke Italian fluently, "And I don't just mean Italian. I mean all the *dialects*. He could talk to Neapolitans, Sicilians, Lombards. He could communicate with some of them better than they could among themselves." Garagiola's own mother never looked at the downtown St. Louis store ads, as Gianin had everything that she needed.

As late as the 1960s, this neighborhood was still widely referred to as "Dago Hill." "You'd travel around the country," says Garagiola, the Hill's second-most famous émigré, "in California, in Boston, in Texas, and Florida, and somebody would say to you, 'Oh, the Hill! You're from Dago

Hill.' " The Hill's historian, Gary Mormino, author of *Immigrants on the Hill*, says, "You started to see the term 'Dago' phased out in the ethnically-conscious sixties. A lot of locals tell you now that they find it offensive, but the truth is for a long time they got a kick out of using the term." Larry, as a young man, was always happy to use the term. In 1949, during a radio show hosted by sportscaster Bill Slater, he happily informed thousands that he hailed from "Dago Hill." "Four network vice-presidents nearly dropped dead when that uncomplimentary national reference went out over the air," said Slater. "But that didn't faze Yogi."[1]

The ancestors of many current residents began arriving toward the end of the nineteenth century; that so many Italians are still there is due to the fact that homes are rarely listed on the open market and are usually sold by word of mouth to relatives and friends. "The most pleasantly fragrant neighborhood in St. Louis," as it was dubbed by one Midwestern magazine because of the redolent aroma of Italian cooking, the Hill may host the finest assortment of Italian restaurants and bakeries to be found in the country. To hear some residents talk, the only Italian restaurants as good as those to be found on the Hill are those that *used* to be on the Hill. Longtime residents still debate the merits of bygone restaurants the way baseball fans do old ballplayers. Marian Ossana, current Hill resident and mother of Diana Ossana, Academy Award winner for the screenplay for *Brokeback Mountain*, recalls one restaurant: "Sala's was on Daggett, and we had to park under or nearly under the viaduct to go there. I remember that we sometimes got a 'Sala's Special,' which was luscious ham and roast beef on double-decker toasted Italian bread. They did a huge carryout trade with a big carryout counter just as you entered the restaurant. My husband and others in the family loved their T-bone steaks."*

The first Italian immigrants to settle on the Hill at the end of the nine-teenth century were attracted by jobs at the nearby St. Louis Smelting and Refining Company; the facility produced clay products, an industry that would provide many decades of work for members of the Berra and Garagiola families. By the late 1890s, worshippers at the Hill's first Roman Catholic church, St. Aloysius, were noticing that nearly half the congrega-tion spoke Italian. The neighborhood's most famous landmark, St. Ambrose Catholic Church, an impressive Lombard Romanesque brick and terra-cotta structure on the corner of Marconi and Wilson, was dedi-

---

*In Ossana's 1994 novel *Pretty Boy Floyd*, co-written with Larry McMurtry, someone remarks, "I'll dress up and we can go to Sala's on Dago Hill. It's a real nice place."

cated in 1926, modeled after San Ambrosia in Milan. Visitors to Church Plaza are greeted by a seven-foot-tall bronze statue, *The Italian Immigrants*, by St. Louis–born sculptor Rudolph Torrini, which depicts a couple who look as if they could have gotten off the same boat as the young Vito Corleone.

Pietro Berra and Giovanni Garagiola didn't arrive in America on the same boat. Pietro—or Pete, as he would be known to some of his Americanized friends—probably came over in 1909; Joe Garagiola recalls his father saying that he arrived in 1911. They had known each other back in the old country in Malvaglio, a small town in the north of Italy near Milan. That made them "Hill Guineas," slang used by southerners to denote those born in the mountainous north. Yogi didn't find the "guinea" reference offensive: "It's all right with me because everybody knows that's where the best Italian cooks come from." Pietro knew a girl in Malvaglio by the name of Paulina. They decided that they would eventually be married and move to America, and like many thousands of his countrymen before and after him, Pietro went ahead to the New World to earn the money to pay for their future. From California to Colorado and back to Missouri, he took work as a farmhand, a construction worker, and a bricklayer, wherever there was work he could do with his hands. Many years later, Yogi would recall, he and his father would go to the St. Louis Arena to see a boxing match or hockey game, and his father would remind him that he had helped build it. Pietro eventually found work at the Laclede-Christy Clay Products kiln, alongside his own boyhood friend, Giovanni Garagiola, and sent for Paulina.

The difficulties that most Italian laborers endured on first arriving in this country were illustrated by a public notice printed in a newspaper in 1895 to recruit laborers for the Croton Reservoir near New York City: common labor, white, would be paid $1.30 to $1.50 a day, while common labor, colored, would receive $1.25 to $1.40. At the bottom of the scale was "common labor, Italian," for $1.15 to $1.25. Things would not improve until America's industrial base, fueled by World War I, expanded.

The essentials of Pietro Berra's story were repeated millions of times between the 1890s and 1920s; only the names of the specific towns and the occupations differed. Generally derided by WASPs as Wops—one hypothesis is that the term was an acronym of "without papers," as many Italians were classified at Ellis Island—they were taken in by an America with a voracious appetite for cheap unskilled labor. Their lot was described by Richard Gambino:

The Italians went to work, saved their meager wages, and brought over their relatives. In 1910, the Bureau of Labor estimated that 95% saved twenty-eight to thirty dollars per month. At a time when they made less than forty dollars per month, this represented an incredible sacrifice! Their reputation for hard work, self-maintenance, and frugality made them attractive to the hard-boiled employers of the time. Thus, they were recruited for work all over the United States . . . These Italian families literally settled "on the other side of the tracks" from the beginning. Italians labored in lumber camps in Michigan and built projects like the Ashokan Dam in New York State. They became workers in shipyards—the now defunct Brooklyn Navy yard was a large employer of Italian-Americans in my boyhood. They built canals and roads everywhere. They became iron ore miners in Michigan, Wisconsin, and Minnesota, phosphate miners in the South, and stone miners in the quarries of New England. In Florida, they manned the cigar factories of Tampa, and in the Midwest, they worked the stockyards of Chicago and Kansas City, and the brickyards near "Dago Hill" in St. Louis. On both coasts, they became fishermen, the predecessors of the Italians found today in San Francisco's Fisherman's Wharf . . .[3]

It would be the children of these Italian immigrants who settled in Brooklyn and the Hill and Fisherman's Wharf who would form the nucleus of the greatest dynasty in baseball history. From 1936 to 1953, the Yankees, led by a handful of players who grew up in Italian-American communities on the east and west coasts and in the heartland would win thirteen pennants and twelve World Series in eighteen seasons.

There are contradictory stories about when and where Pietro and Paulina were married. In his 1961 book, Yogi says the marriage took place in the first St. Ambrose, exactly when he didn't know, though he thought family tradition placed the year as 1911. Twenty-eight years later, in his memoirs, he thought his parents might have been married in Italy after Pietro had worked for some time in America. More certain is that they bought a house on Elizabeth Avenue in the Hill, number 5447. Within a few years, Giovanni Garagiola had raised enough money to send for his girl back in the old country, and they moved directly across the street, 5446. The "Hill Guineas" from Malvaglio were now full-fledged American *cittadinoes* (citizens) working at the same plant and living on the same block.

Larry's parents were one of a great many Berras on the Hill, none of whom, as far as Pietro knew, were relations. In 1961, recalling facts for his autobiography, Yogi would remember a Berra's real estate company, a furniture store,* a chiropractor, and "a big-shot politician who was a Democratic committeeman."⁴ Garagiola remembers the man as "Midge," the 24th Ward alderman, who both his and Yogi's father would go to for help on neighborhood concerns. Over the years on trips back to the neighborhood, Midge Berra would tell Joey to "say hello to my cousin Yogi." "Once Yogi became a Yankee," Joe quipped, "he picked up all kinds of relatives." But Midge Berra, in the eyes of his constituents on the Hill, had earned the honor of being considered Yogi's cousin. "Men like FDR and Harry Truman were idols to my father," Garagiola would write nearly half a century after leaving the Hill, "but Midge Berra was a reality."⁵

Pietro and Paulina would have five children; the oldest, Michael, was born in Malvaglio on a trip back to the old country in 1917. Lawrence Peter—Lorenzo Pietro, actually—their youngest boy, was born May 12, 1925. "My mother never called him Lawrence," says Yogi's sister Josephine, "and tried to call him Larry. It came out 'Lawdie.' "⁶ So, then, did the rest of the family, and then his schoolmates and pals. "Lawdie" would stick until superseded in his early teens by "Yogi."

The Hill was a tough neighborhood, and the residents were proud of that. On a visit back home in 1946, a neighbor told Garagiola, "Gioi"— Italian for Joey—"you the firsta boy what comes from the Hill with a name witha ends a,e,i,o getta name in the paper and no killa somebody."⁷ Though most Italian-Americans knew little about the so-called Mafia besides what they read in the papers, they nonetheless enjoyed the mystique the secret society accorded them. In fact the Hill, like most other Italian-American communities, enjoyed a crime rate lower than that of most other foreign-born groups.†

There were several reasons for the strong sense of order on the Hill. One was the concept of *La Famiglia*, of which the father was the unchallenged head but the mother was the center. Each played a distinct role in keeping the children in line. The mother declared the rules, the father enforced them. "No matter who it was who was mad at me," Berra told Ed Fitzgerald, "Mom or Pop or both of them, it was always Pop who hit me. Mom would never do it, she would just tell him and he would take care of it."⁸ Nothing else illustrates the differences in attitudes toward child rear-

---

*Marian Ossana still has furniture "which I've been dragging about all of these years from Berra's Furniture Co. on the Hill, and it's held up well."

†This was true at the beginning of the twentieth century, as detailed in a book entitled *The Italian in America* by E. Lord, J. Trevor, and S. Barrows published in 1905, and proved to be equally true nearly sixty years later in a study by James W. Vanderzanden, *American Minority Relations*. (Information from Gambino, *Blood of My Blood*.)

ing over the last seventy-odd years than Yogi's calm acceptance of his father's easy use of the hands in maintaining discipline. Several times in his memoirs and in interviews he would mention that his father hit him when he was a boy; he'd always mention it casually, in passing, and with no trace of anger or resentment. "If it was something that Mom thought she could explain to us, and fix up that way, she would try it. Not Pop, though, he never talked; he was all action. All the other fathers were the same way. There wasn't any juvenile delinquents on the Hill."[9]

Outside authority such as police were rarely needed, largely because mothers and fathers, backed by the unquestionable force of the Catholic church, held the hormonally charged young men in check. "No trouble was so big," Garagiola would recall in his autobiography, "that Father Palumbo couldn't straighten it out. You were taught early that Saturday is take-a-bath-day, get-to-Church-for-Confession, and help-Mama-fill-out-the-weekly-envelope-to-drop-in-the-basket-at-Mass-on-Sunday-day."[10]

Another reason for the relatively low crime rate was, as Yogi would recall many years later, "There really wasn't much of anything to steal."[11] And even if there had been, there were no cars for them to make their getaways in. "I think it's the cars more than anything else that get the kids in trouble today. Anyway, we never had that problem. Even our parents didn't have cars."[12] There was some petty thievery which usually involved cookies or other small items from the neighborhood bakery. The boys would pool their change until one of them could purchase a dime's worth of day-old buns while the others swiped whatever was easily available and concealable. More often, it was fruit from the huge market on 39th Street, which, because of its size and the swarms of customers roaming the aisles, was virtually impossible for management to police. The loot was typically pieces of small fruit such as apples, swiped while the boy in the group who was the best talker—often Joey, Yogi would insist—kept the clerks busy. On the rare occasions when someone got caught, the store manager, after conferring with the boy's parents, had himself a free delivery boy or floor sweeper. "We never did anything bad enough to get into trouble with the cops," said Yogi.[13]

When Larry and his schoolmates turned twelve, they got their first chance to play organized baseball in a YMCA league. They called themselves the Stags, after the soccer team, and they were the only team in the circuit that didn't have real uniforms. Their "uniform" was a white tee shirt, and they were at once proud and resentful of the fact. No merchant in the Hill area would come up with the money to sponsor the team, not because they didn't have it, but because of their disdain for baseball.

Occasionally, when the boys felt daring, they would actually steal a watermelon, then bring it back to the Stags' "clubhouse," an empty garage where they would meet to play cards and store their equipment and which cost them $12 a month to rent. Larry, Tony, and Mike Berra sold papers—the *Globe-Democrat* and the *Post-Dispatch*—after school, but that money, always, went home to Mom. Since the ten cents a month in dues did not cover the rent for the clubhouse, the Stags were forced into a crash course in street capitalism. They bought dime boxes of cigarettes and sold the twenty smokes for a penny apiece; they'd accumulate enough cash to buy boxes of candy for three cents each and sell them for a nickel. Larry never got high grades in arithmetic, but he had a head for business. The most creative fund-raising activity involved a renewable resource; almost every family on the Hill depended on a vegetable garden, and vegetable gardens depended on a fresh supply of fertilizer. In the 1930s, most home deliveries were still made by horse-drawn wagons, and sometimes the arrival of a wagon would inspire the boys to spring into action. When a horse did the inevitable, one or more of the boys would scoop it up and take it to the nearest customer, who might give them a nickel or even a dime if the horse had been generous. One old man by the name of Franck didn't want to part with his coins and would dash out to retrieve the horses' droppings himself; Larry or one of his friends would get in his way just long enough for their teammates to grab it first.

Larry found one more way to make a couple of dollars that was a little tougher but more lucrative than selling horse manure. Frank Mariani, a boxing trainer and former light- and welterweight fighter, put on amateur boxing shows at a club on the Hill. He taught Larry the ropes and featured him in several of his fight cards, paying him anywhere from five to ten dollars a bout, depending on the house. The money was sensational, and the boys were usually packed in good protective headgear, so there was little chance of injury. Berra was short for a thirteen year old, but exceptionally quick and strong. He won eight of nine fights before the club folded, mostly against tough Irish kids who had grown up in neighborhoods adjacent to the Italians on the Hill. His one loss, a decision, was later avenged. His parents, assuming that he had no aspirations for a career in the ring, had no objection to his boxing, and the money was a windfall.

———

THE HILL WAS the quintessential Italian-American community, but it was far from typical. It differed from many in at least one major respect: it wasn't a slum. As Gary Mormino puts it, "The Hill isn't a collection of tenement buildings. It's a neighborhood with houses, yards, and lots of room for kids to play in. In some ways it had and has more in common with suburban neighborhoods in towns all across America than with, say, the Italian sections of the Bronx or Brooklyn or South Philadelphia"—the latter being where my father grew up. The Hill today has changed in many ways since Larry and Joey grew up there, but it's still their old neighborhood, still with houses painted, as Yogi once put it, "within an inch of their lives,"[14] with lawns like putting greens. Carmen Berra once cracked that first-time visitors to the Hill were disappointed that they didn't see a salami "hanging out of every window." But the neighborhood remains unmistakably Italian. In fact, Italian flags hang to the right of U.S. flags on houses, and fire hydrants are painted in the Italian tricolor, while many doors have stained-glass windows and perhaps every fourth front yard displays a statue of the Virgin Mary or St. Francis of Assisi. St. Ambrose stills stands like a bastion of the traditions and values of the people in its congregation. Trucks from Fazio's, the magnificent bakery (now bakery and specialty foods), are still seen making the rounds, and Joe Fassi's Sausage and Sandwich Shop, on the corner of Dugan and Sublette at the end of the Berras' block, is still a hugely popular family restaurant. It was an ice cream parlor in 1926, the year after Yogi was born, and later, after Prohibition, a bar was added. As boys, Yogi and Joey would come home from school and then run down to Fassi's to fetch a bucket of cold beer to greet papas Berra and Garagiola when they arrived back home from the clay works. Yogi and Joe didn't walk to Fassi's for the beer, they ran. "Rushing the beer can," Yogi recalled, "wasn't something we did if we happened to think of it. We had better think of it, or else."[15]

Today, customers can view Fassi's Wall of Fame adorned with photos of Berra, Garagiola, and the legendary broadcaster Jack Buck, who moved into the neighborhood in 1954.

The Hill has always been a paradise for boys who love sports, particularly games from the old country like soccer° and bocce.† In America the

---

°Seven of the seventeen players on the 1950 U.S. World Cup team were from St. Louis, and four of the starters grew up on the Hill. Their 1–0 victory over heavily favored England in a preliminary round is still regarded as one of the biggest upsets in World Cup history. Their story was told in *The Game of Their Lives* by Geoffrey Douglas, which was made into a critically acclaimed docudrama in 2005.

†St. Louis remains one of the bocce hotbeds of the country, as reflected in the handsome Italia America Bocce Club built in 1975 on Marconi Avenue, home of the 2006 United States Bocce National Championships. In the 1999 video biography, *Yogi Berra: Déjà vu All Over Again*, hosted by Bob Costas, Yogi and his boyhood pals met at the club to reminisce.

love of these sports and others has blossomed; it was amazing the number of different games that could be played in one weekend or even on a single day when Pietro and Paulina's family was growing up. On a typical Saturday, when chores and errands were done, it wasn't unusual for Hill kids to play some street hockey, get in a couple hours of baseball, and then head for the local YMCA. Lou Barioli, one of Yogi's schoolmates, recalls, "On Saturday night we walked all the way to the Y on Grand Avenue to swim and play some basketball. We'd be home by ten. We looked forward to that all week."[16] In retrospect, the Hill was a community ideally designed to produce athletes. In addition to Berra and Garagiola and the members of the 1950 American World Cup soccer team, there was Ben Pucci, who became a star football player at Washington University and went on to play pro ball with the Buffalo Bills and Cleveland Browns in the All-American Football Conference, Jimmy Hayes, who became a standout fullback at the University of Illinois; Freddy Hotmann, who was a catcher for the Yankees after World War I; and Jim Goodwin, who played for a year for the White Sox.

They even found time to invent some games of their own, one of which, called "bumby," was demonstrated by Yogi and his friends for Bob Costas during a 1999 documentary. The "bottom man" squats on all fours, while the next two "players" lean forward, hands on the shoulders of the man in front of him; the final player—Costas, in this case—jumps on the back of the last man, as if mounting a horse, and the first three move together like a snake and try to shake him off. The conditioning bumby must have demanded of its players is apparent in the video, as the then seventy-four-year-old Yogi had no trouble supporting the weight of three grown men.

It was an idyllic existence for a boy, its pleasures untinged by the misery caused by the Depression in the outside world. The parents, many of whom had been born in the old country, mostly kept their jobs through the 1930s, and the ones who couldn't hang on had a staunch safety net in their family and friends. Jacob Riis, the activist journalist and social reformer, found the percentage of paupers among Italian-Americans to be the lowest of any ethnic group.° Their children, who had never known any other kind of life, were scarcely aware of the existence of soup kitchens, Dust

---

°The Irish, Riis noted in his classic *How the Other Half Lives*, had the highest percentage of paupers among their population, 15 percent, with so-called "native" Americans, meaning American-born Protestants, only a little behind at 12 percent, while the rate among Germans was 8 percent. Italians, he was surprised to find, had a percentage of pauperism of less than 2 percent.

Bowl victims, and welfare. "We grew our own vegetables," Mickey Garagiola, Joe's brother, told Bob Costas. "We kept chicken coops." They also hunted rabbits for food and for "points" to earn admission to football games. "We used to work our 'points' to get in to see St. Louis University play football at Walsh Stadium."[17] One of their chief duties was ridding the playing field of varmints. Larry's primary weapon was the stone: the arm that would one day gun down American League base stealers was honed gunning down rodents on a gridiron. Their work done, Larry and his friends would stride into the stadium and, much to the surprise of the appalled ticket holders, stuff their dead rabbits under their seats while they watched the games. A rabbit's value didn't end there, as Mickey Garagiola explained: "You'd soak a rabbit in wine for a couple of days and it was as good as filet mignon."[18]

On Sunday morning, it was understood that every family member who could walk would be at Mass. The only exemption was for those who were too sick to get out of bed, and as Yogi would later recall, "If you were going to say you were sick, you'd better make sure you were, cause if you weren't at Mass in the morning, you sure weren't going to be playing ball in the afternoon."[19] Paulina, like most of her neighbors, often got up before dawn, went to five o'clock Mass, and had a table full of bread, doughnuts, milk, and coffee ready when the family arose for breakfast. Sunday dinner in Italian families was the big meal of the week, and while Pietro and the children were in church, she'd begin preparation of the Sunday meal, which generally began with an antipasti plate of ham, salami, and bologna with slices of bread, followed by risotto, small chunks of meat or fish, and salad spiced with escarole and chicory. From there, the meal evolved into what Yogi would call "serious eating," usually two main courses—chicken and either beef or lamb. On special occasions there would be the glory of most Italian-American households on the Hill: ravioli. Sunday dinner, like all family meals, was governed by strict but simple rules: no one reached for anything until Papa Berra had helped himself, and no one left the table before he did.

That was how the Berras ate on Sundays and on special occasions, but on weekdays, even during the Depression, the Berra household wasn't exactly a soup kitchen. A standard dish might be liver, veal, pork chops, or *carne e patata* (meat and potatoes) with a side dish of spaghetti and, of course, the big salad bowl in the center of the table. And always there was bread, lots and lots of bread. And if Larry didn't appreciate how hard his father worked to put it on the table, he did one night in the middle of supper when he picked off a couple of chunks of bread and left the rest lying on the table. Out of nowhere his father's hand flew out and slapped him on the side of the head so hard he was almost knocked out of the chair. Larry was stunned; what had he done to earn that? "What do you think I buy bread for?" his father said. "To eat, not to waste."[20]

Later, when he was with the Yankees and the team would play in St. Louis, Yogi would bring teammates over for Sunday dinner. For Phil Rizzuto, it was like a homecoming; for non-Italians such as Whitey Ford, Bill Skowron, and Gil McDougald, it was heaven. In 1954 the Browns moved to Baltimore and became the Orioles, ending the Yankees' trips to St. Louis. "You know," Whitey Ford would later crack, "we didn't win the pennant in 1954, even though we had one of our best teams. And after the season when we were fishing around for a reason why we didn't win some of us would say it was because we didn't get to eat at the Berras' house."

Always, there was sports, filling up every free moment in a boy's schedule and often many more besides. "We didn't go home for lunch," says Joe Garagiola, "we'd save time by bringing lunch with us." This was a problem for some on Fridays; Catholics at that time were not permitted to eat meat, so the usual ingredients of an Italian sandwich were *proibito*. Yogi's solution was to bring a loaf of Italian bread filled with bananas and hot mustard. Some of the guys, remembers Joe, "couldn't take it. I remember once we lost our shortstop, who got sick watching Yogi eat that sandwich."

Like many a second-generation Italian-American boy, Larry could see no practical application in the things that were being taught in school. The reason for this is difficult for nearly anyone not born in that time or place to understand, particularly when considering the pride that Italian-Americans took in achieving social status in the New World. The reason was perhaps best expressed by Richard Gambino, who was chairman of a program for Italian-American studies at Queens College in New York during the 1960s, the only such program in the United States at the time: "The Italian immigrant was poorly equipped for the American economy, except for his powerful motivation to work for his family . . . In short, the pride that comes from seeing and feeling one's efforts and skills mingled with some result. The Italian-American seeks to do something the result of which he can demonstrate to his family. Herein lies another important component of his pride. 'With these hands I built *that* wall.' '*This* is my restaurant,' etc."[21]

The value of abstract learning intended to improve one's life outside the community was not readily apparent to many of the immigrants' children and certainly not to young Lawdie, whose grade-school years would inspire many a bogus Yogi story. The most popular has his teacher saying "Larry, don't you *know* anything?" with Berra replying, "Ma'am, I don't even *suspect* anything." (Did the teacher write that one down to pass it on for posterity?) On the other hand, Yogi's school years may also have inspired a legitimate one, if we trust Berra family lore. Apparently someone asked young Larry, when he was around the age of twelve, "How do you like school?" "Closed," he replied.

Pietro blamed his youngest son's indifference to schooling on sports. He may have been right. "He felt that I spent too much time playing," Yogi remembered. "It was football and soccer in the fall and winter, and baseball in the spring and summer. I loved every sport there was."[22] But Pietro, like most fathers on the Hill, held a special contempt for baseball, which he did not understand and which had no connection with his own youth. Even the local storekeepers who were willing to sponsor boys' soccer teams and provide uniforms regarded baseball as "a bum's game." The Southwest Drugstore bought tee shirts for the Stags soccer team, but the baseball team wore old overalls and plain tee shirts. Lou Baroli, who grew up with Yogi and Joe, recalls that when they played kids from better-off neighborhoods who had uniforms, "it was more or less an incentive to play harder, to beat them."[23] There weren't enough mitts to go around; kids in the field often borrowed gloves from their opponents at bat. Larry did not own a mitt until he played American Legion ball. "It goes without saying," he said in *Yogi*, "that we never had spikes when we were kids. How could we ask our fathers to buy us shoes you couldn't wear to church?"[24]

To paraphrase the Duke of Wellington, pennants were won on the sandlots of the Hill. Those who were later caught by surprise when Yogi Berra became a successful big league manager didn't know of his reputation in the rabid and competitive sports culture of the Hill. "Yogi made our neighborhood games possible," according to Joe Garagiola. "He was the great organizer. He engineered the whole project of turning an abandoned clay mine, which was really the neighborhood dump, into our baseball field. Yogi was the project foreman, and had us hauling in rusty wrecked cars along the foul lines to be our dugouts."[25] By the time the kids would show up to play, Larry would have everything ready and organized. The lack of equipment forced him to be ingenious; bunches of magazines strapped around legs would pass for shin guards. On one occasion, he "borrowed" and ended up ruining one of Pietro's brushes to paint a gridiron. American footballs were tougher to improvise; Yogi solved the problem by organizing a squad of Hill boys outside the football practices for the St. Louis University team. When an errant kick sailed over the fence, the first man to grab it would wing it to Larry, who had the best throwing arm and would relay it to the next man down the line, usually Joey, and so on. "Those poor equipment managers," says Garagiola, "didn't have a prayer."

His prowess in every sport made him a schoolyard legend. According to one story, which sounds as if it could have been lifted from a biography of Bear Bryant, Larry and some Hill boys were playing soccer in Tower Grove Park while the Southwest High School football team was scrimmaging on a nearby field. One of the high schoolers shanked a punt; Larry, wearing an old pair of sneakers handed down from one of his brothers, scooped it up and boomed it back. The Southwest coach, Lou Kittlaus, stopped the scrimmage on the spot and came over to try and talk Larry into coming to his school and playing on the team. Berra declined; he liked football but wasn't sure it was his sport. In another story that sounds less plausible, the manager of another team tried to distract Berra by telling him he couldn't hit a ball to the outfield wall. Yogi supposedly smiled and stepped out of the batter's box and said, "For ten bucks?" Their bluff having been called—that some of Yogi's friends remember the coach's name indicates that the story has at least a kernel of truth—the opposing team was humiliated when Berra parked the next pitch over the wall. It's doubtful that *any* Hill boy, particularly one said to be as taciturn as Berra, would have made a bet for the ridiculous sum of ten dollars. But *something* happened, and to the boys who were there, the story loomed larger than Babe Ruth calling his shot in the 1932 World Series.

———

A MISS BELTRAMI—her first name is lost to history—lived on Elizabeth Avenue in the Hill, the Garagiola side of the street, and she sponsored Larry's group for the Cardinals Knothole Gang, an idea promoted by Branch Rickey to help build a future fan base by getting kids into the ballpark. Every Saturday an adult affiliated with the organization would take a group of kids for free to Sportsman's Park. For Larry, his first Cardinals game wasn't so much a dream come true as a dream beyond anything he previously knew of. His brother had taken him to some games of the St. Louis Flyers in the American Hockey League; he would sleep in the afternoon so he could stay up late enough to go to the Flyers games, which were all played at night. But the Cardinals were bigger than life. That they had to sit in the upper-left-field seats so far from the action only made things seem bigger and more important. "I used to worship the ballplayers," Yogi would later say, meaning the Cardinals of the Gashouse Gang era—Frankie Frisch, Spud Davis, Leo Durocher, Dizzy and Daffy Dean, Frank Orsatti (one of the growing number of Italian-American players in professional baseball in the mid-1930s), and, most of all, the slugging outfielder, Joe "Ducky" Medwick, who, like Larry, was short, quick, and powerful. In the mid-1930s, Medwick was one of the best players in the National League; he would win the triple crown in 1937 and finish with a lifetime batting average of .324. He was probably the first professional athlete Larry had met face to face; he was certainly the first one to know Larry well enough to call him by his first name. Neither could have guessed that in about ten years' time, Berra's nickname would be as famous as Medwick's and that Ducky would be Yogi's instructor on the New York Yankees or, most amazing of all, that they'd be voted into the Hall of Fame within four years of each other—Medwick in 1968 and Berra in 1972.

Some Hill boys would scramble to the local news agency after school to try and make a little money selling papers. Larry's favorite corner was Southwest and Kingshighway, where he frequently caught Ducky coming and going. "Joe Medwick was my idol and my favorite player, too," Berra would recall. "He gave me a nickel every time he bought a paper, and the paper was three cents, and he said 'Keep the change,' " It never occurred to Larry to ask for his hero's autograph. "Had I known his autograph would be worth money, I would have asked for his name on something."[26] On the other hand, as Berra pointed out later, he never asked President Reagan for his autograph, either.

When Berra told his friends about his famous customer, they listened with open mouths. The next day, they all gathered on his corner to watch him sell a paper to Ducky Medwick. More than that, Medwick recognized him and called him Lawdie. After that, recalled Joe Garagiola, "you could have charged admission to stand at Yogi's corner."[27]

The Stags' biggest rivals were the Edmonds, a team in the Recreation Intermediate League, whose uniforms were provided by their sponsor, a well-known restaurant. The Stags knocked themselves out trying to beat their economically advantaged rivals, but wound up finishing a close second in league standings. The next year, the league rules specified that each team had to have a sponsor; the unadopted Stags drifted apart, though they had made such an impression on the Edmonds that several of the best players, including Larry and Joey, were asked to join. This amounted to a whole new skill level for both boys and prepared them for the important jump they were to make in the next couple of years.

———

"THROUGH THE MASTERY which the Yogi attains over his thought and his body," wrote the nineteenth-century German religious philosopher Karl Kellner, "he grows into a 'character.' "[28] As it is with yogis, so it was with Yogi.

There are a score of stories regarding the origin of the most famous—or second-most famous, if you want to give the nod to Babe Ruth—nickname in American sports, but as Yogi once told me, "Most of them aren't true." Sometime in the 1980s, after Yogi was firmly established as an American institution, it became common to read that Whitey Ford had hung the nickname on him. Joe Garagiola insists that it was given to Yogi by Bobby Hofman, a St. Louis boy (though not a Hill product) whom Yogi met in American Legion ball and who would play seven years for the New York Giants. Phil Rizzuto muddled the issue somewhat by saying in interviews that Yogi himself had offered conflicting stories as to his nickname. Yogi's stories may have been confusing, but they were never conflicting; his explanations were always the same on the major points.

First, he didn't get the moniker in the big leagues but back in American Legion ball. Second, it was given to him by Jack Maguire Jr., son of the Cardinals scout. When he was thirteen or fourteen, Lawdie and his friends, among them Hofman and Maguire, went to the movies, and before the feature saw a short travelogue about India. One scene that made an impression on them involved a man identified both as a Hindu fakir and a yogi—though a yogi is defined as a person who practices yoga, whereas a fakir can also be either a Hindu or Muslim itinerant beggar. Clearly it was the first definition that applied to the man in the movie. According to Yogi's autobiography, when they walked out of the movie house, Jack said, "You know, you look just like a yogi. I'm going to call you Yogi."[35]

But recalling the moment for Bob Costas nearly forty years later, Berra added a new wrinkle: "We didn't have any dugouts in American Legion ball, or any benches. When I sat on the ground with my legs crossed, Jack said I looked like a yogi." Why, exactly? If there weren't any benches, all the boys had to sit on the ground. There was something about Lawdie that set him apart, a quality of calmness and concentration that was instantly associated with the Indian in the travelogue, as evidenced by the fact that the tag stuck even with those who hadn't seen the travelogue. "I never saw a nickname catch on faster than Yogi," says Garagiola. Almost immediately, his friends, family, everyone referred to him as "Yogi." Even Paulina exchanged "Lawdie" for "Yogi." It was almost as if he went to sleep one day as Larry and woke up the next as Yogi.

It was probably no accident that Larry became Yogi in St. Louis in the 1930s. No American city then or now was so mad for baseball, and at no period in baseball history did more players acquire lifelong nicknames. As Bud Abbott reminded Lou Costello in their immortal "Who's On First?" routine, "They give these players peculiar names these days."*

Though the nickname took with his friends and family, it was a bit longer before Yogi officially won out over Larry in the outside world. In 1951, by which time Berra had collected four World Series rings, a Most Valuable Player award, and had made the cover of *Sport* and several other national magazines, the Yankees' rookie pregame announcer, Bob Sheppard, found that fans were asking, "Who's this Larry Berra? Is he related to Yogi?" Sheppard sought out Yogi in the clubhouse and told him he thought he should announce him as Yogi from now on since that was how the fans seemed to know him. "Sure," Berra replied. "What the heck, call me Yogi. Everybody else does."

Not everybody, or at least not everybody all the time. "There's none of that 'Yogi' stuff at home," Carmen Berra once said to an audience at the Yogi museum. "At home, he's Larry." Joe Garagiola, though, insists, "Carmen once got an anniversary card signed 'Yogi Berra.' " According to Joe, Carmen asked her husband if he signed his last name so she wouldn't think it came from another Yogi.

———

"I HAD NEVER been able to see any sense in my going to school," he said in *Yogi*. "The harder the arithmetic problems got, the less I could see that knowing this stuff was ever going to do me any good."[30] He played hooky as often as he dared and worked on his parents to let him quit; he got through the eighth grade, he would say, only because some good-natured teachers at the Wade School figured out a way to graduate him.

———

*Abbott and Costello first performed "Who's On First?" on the Kate Smith radio show in 1938, perhaps a year before Larry became Yogi, inspired in large part by the heavily nicknamed Cardinals Yogi grew up rooting for (Dizzy and Daffy Dean are both mentioned in the sketch). In 1945, they performed it on screen for the film *The Naughty Nineties*; unable to acquire the St. Louis Cardinals' logo, Abbott was identified as a coach for the fictitious St. Louis Wolves.

Following his narrow escape, the priest and the Wade School principal met with Larry and his parents in their house one night to discuss his future. The conversation wasn't heated, because all parties were agreed on the essential point: Larry would be better off working than in a classroom. It probably wasn't a tough decision to make; many kids who grew up during the Depression were forced to quit school and find work to carry their weight in the family. All of Larry's brothers had jobs on the Hill—Tony in a bakery, Mike at the local shoe factory, and John waiting tables at Ruggeri's, one of the best restaurants on the Hill.

The question wasn't so much should Larry work, but where. His first job was in a coal yard where coal dust was pressed into blocks (nearly all Hill houses were heated by coal-burning stoves). Yogi hated the work, which was wrapping the coal blocks for delivery, not because it was difficult but because it was dirty. If the weather was good, he would leave the coal yard about three and meet his friends on the baseball field. The owners of the coal yard soon determined they could get along without him; it would not be the last job on the Hill he would lose to afternoon baseball. None of them paid much, but the weekly earnings of $25 or so was nothing to scorn during the Depression. Paulina would give Yogi back perhaps $2; he didn't need much more, largely because he was too shy to go out with neighborhood girls. "I was a case," he would say, "I was so bashful. All I was interested in was playing ball."[31] He got in more trouble because of baseball, he insisted, than the other guys did because of girls.

Pietro soon lost patience, and another council was held at the Berra household with older brothers Tony, Mike, and John in attendance, as well as Father Coester from St. Ambrose and Joe Causino from the local YMCA. The Father explained again to Larry that there was nothing wrong with the game of baseball, but that its role in his life had now become detrimental. It was redirecting his time and attention away from the far more important pursuit of making a living. The boy turned to Joe Causino for support: "You always told us that the thing a man is most interested in is what he ought to spend his life at. I remember you said if you like something so much, you eat and sleep and think it, then that's what you ought to do."[32] Okay then, Causino replied. What is it you want badly enough to work at it, what's it going to be? Surrounded by his father, brothers, parish priest and baseball coach, virtually all the male figures of authority in his life, Larry began his first major step toward creating his own life. "Baseball," he told them. "Baseball is what I want."[33]

His father must have been more dumbfounded than angry. He failed to

understand his son's passion for this strange game, and he couldn't begin
to comprehend how anyone could think of it as work. Understanding the
reluctance of Pietro Berra to let his son pursue a career as a professional
athlete is almost impossible for someone raised in a later time and culture.
Richard Gambino summed up the mentality in *Blood of My Blood*:

> In addition to their recreational values, games . . . also permitted enjoy-
> ment of the competitive spirit among men. Yet the competition was kept
> within bounds, avoiding the excess that has become so much a part of
> modern life not only in games and sports but in business, professional
> and social life. Ours is a society in which the competitive spirit runs
> amuck. Despite his notorious 'ferocity,' the typical Italian-American man
> is aghast at the fierce, frenzied, serious competitiveness displayed in
> what he regards as trivial areas of life . . . The traditional Italian-
> American's first response when exposed to this kind of behavior is that it
> is *pazzia* [madness] . . . [I]t is madness to become emotionally controlled
> by a sport, a game or a career, as are so many Americans. To invest one's
> ego and emotions in the kitty of such activities is to lose the perspective
> of sane manliness. Manhood is too important to be staked on games.[34]

How could baseball possibly be regarded as a business? The attitude
was expressed perfectly by Mama Garagiola a few years later when she saw
her first game at Sportsman's Park: "Why do people pay to see men play?"[35]

Why indeed? Everyone on the Hill agreed that the best baseball player
in the family, maybe in the entire Hill, was Larry's older brother, Tony, who
had already acquired the nickname Lefty. Tony never had a chance to try
his skills above the semipro level; he would not go against his father's
wishes. But Tony went to bat for his younger brother, and Pietro shrugged
and gave in. In retrospect, it's easy for any parent to see why Papa Berra
had serious doubts about his son's pursuit of a baseball career. What is not
so easy to understand is why he finally gave his approval. Though it has
always seemed like a paradox to outsiders—and indeed, often appears that
way to Italians themselves—the father's authority was absolute, yet boys,
as they came of age, were expected to develop the independence of spirit
to disobey. They would, after all, soon be out in the world on their own and
raise families of their own. There was a point at which the father recognized that the son's will had become too strong to overrule. This was
Larry's moment to assert himself.

So Lawdie would get his chance so long as he continued to work while he played ball. If it was obvious after a reasonable time that he wasn't going to make it, he would give up baseball and look for a "real" job. "It seemed," said Yogi on reflection, "like a fair deal to me."[36]

───

"SO," YOGI WOULD sum it up years later, "I had a happy childhood." It was not quite over yet. In fact, Yogi would never lose that sense of play he knew as a young boy; baseball, in any form, at any level, would always be fun for him. On the other hand, practically from the time he decided that baseball was what he wanted to do, he took it seriously. He would never be able to make a clear division between play and work: "I took my job home with me from the ball game," he would say nearly half a century later, "what I mean is that I took my job everywhere."[37] His on-the-job training began at the American Legion Stockham Post.

Probably none of the TTill boys knew who Gunnery Sergeant Fred W. Stockham was or that he had given his life for his country in the Marine Corps in 1918. Stockham, an orphan, had served as a recruiting officer in St. Louis before World War I; he saved the lives of several men in his outfit during a gas attack on the front lines in France, including a St. Louis man, Barret Mattingly, who championed Stockham for the Congressional Medal of Honor and was instrumental in having St. Louis VFW Post 4 renamed in his honor. Nearly forty years after Stockham's death, Yogi Berra would find himself living less than three miles from Stockham's unmarked grave in Montclair, New Jersey.

In retrospect, it looks like a straight shot from the Stockham Post to the New York Yankees. For Yogi, it seemed like more of a winding trail. The experience Berra gained against such a high level of competition would prove invaluable; in two consecutive years, Stockham Post went to the semifinals of the National American Legion Tournament, losing one year to a team from Burwyn, Illinois, and the next year to a squad from California, the Sunsets, who fielded a star player named Gene Mauch. Twenty-two years later, Mauch would be manager of the Philadelphia Phillies and Berra of the Yankees, and they would narrowly miss facing each other in the World Series.

Yogi played second, third, outfield, and caught. He hit with eye-popping authority, but it didn't always seem that way to spectators. He would pull pitches on the outside corner to right field and sometimes hit pitches off the fists to center; he was as likely to hit a fastball at eye level over an outfielder's head as he was to strike out on the same pitch. Leo Browne, the

Post commander, wrote a letter to Bob Burnes of the *St. Louis Globe-Democrat* which summed up the seventeen-year-old Berra: "He does everything wrong, but it comes out right. We tried him at every position except pitcher and he can play all of them. He's got short legs, but he runs good . . . He swings at everything in sight. His form is all wrong and the coaches can't make him wait at the plate, but he's the best hitter I've ever seen." (One is reminded of Fred Astaire's famous screen test that listed his deficiencies but added, "Can dance a little.") Browne included one more thing in his letter. "His name is Yogi something or other. Ain't that a hell of a name?"[38]

Burnes came out to see Berra play. Unfortunately, Yogi was at third base that day and wasn't sharp. This should have been irrelevant, as no one ever thought third base was Berra's natural position. The problem was, what *was* Berra's natural position? He didn't have the lithe look of an infielder, and though he ran well, he didn't *look* as if he could cover enough ground to play the outfield. Most assumed that he could make it as a catcher. He had the arm and seemed to have the toughness required for the game's most exacting position, but he lacked polish and authority behind the plate. But he could hit, so he'd play somewhere.

Yogi and Joey worked out regularly at Sportsman's Park, part of the crowd who comprised "the donkey brigade."* The two Elizabeth Avenuers got slightly better treatment than the others when Yogi would smuggle a bottle of Pietro's homemade "Dago Red" to the Cardinals clubhouse man, Butch Yatkeman, who would let them wear team uniforms and work out on the field.

———

THE CARDINALS' REFUSAL to sign Yogi would become the stuff of legend, but what's often forgotten is that the city's other team, the lowly Browns, passed on him as well. At the urging of Jack Maguire, Browns scout Lou McQuillen took a good look at Berra and told his bosses he thought Yogi had the makings of a great ballplayer. They offered him a contract to start out with one of their farm clubs, but no signing bonus. Their reasoning seems to have been similar to the Cardinals': Berra didn't *look* like a ballplayer, or at least a typical one. It was simply too hard for

---

*The origin of the term seems to be forgotten, but Garagiola recalls that it was generally used by the groundskeepers at Sportsman's Park for the kids who were most persistent in their efforts to get into the ballpark. "We'd wear down their resistance. We'd wait so long that they'd finally just wave us in."

most observers to get past Yogi's appearance and his often unorthodox style of play. He rounded the bases quickly but looked so damned awkward hitting the ground when sliding; he could throw well from the outfield or from the catcher's position to second base, but he seemed to fall over doing it; and, *damn*, he could give a baseball a ride, but some of the pitches he swung at!

Yogi was stung. It seemed as if three years of what he regarded as hard work was all in vain. "Ever since I had been a little kid, I had been used to having the other guys laugh at me because of my looks and poke fun at me because I was so clumsy, but I had always been as good a ballplayer as any of them and better than most of them, so I never minded. Now, for the first time, I didn't even have that. Nobody wanted me as a ballplayer."[39]

The summer of 1942 was the worst of Yogi's life. Joey was off to Springfield, Missouri, to begin his career as a professional ballplayer. Yogi was just a semi-amateur, picking up a few bucks here and there playing semi-pro. His brother Mike got him a job at Johansen's Shoe Company as a tack puller on ladies' shoes. It wasn't a bad job, as he remembered it, but all he could think of was that he wasn't a baseball player. In October, the Yankees lost to the Cardinals in the World Series, their first World Series defeat since 1926. The day after the final game, there was a knock on the door of 5447 Elizabeth Avenue, from as unexpected a visitor as would ever make an appearance in Yogi Berra's life. A man they had never met, John Schulte, shook hands with Pietro and Larry and told them that he was the bullpen coach for the New York Yankees. He had been authorized by the team to offer Larry a contract that paid $90 a month for Larry to play with a Yankees' farm club in Norfolk, Virginia, in the Piedmont League. Oh, yes, there was the matter of the bonus—the Yankees were offering him $500. Stunned and dizzy with joy, the Berras shook hands and agreed. All of a sudden, Yogi Berra had a chance to be what he always wanted to be, a big league ballplayer. Of course, he stayed on at the shoe factory until it was time to report to the training camp at Excelsior Springs, Missouri; Mama Berra still needed the money. But Lawdie's allowance was raised to $3 a week.

The phrase Yogi's Luck or Berra's Luck was decades away from being coined, but here on Elizabeth Avenue it had just been born. It may not have been luck after all. The man who had passed on a chance to sign Yogi, Branch Rickey, was fond of saying, "Luck is the residue of design." The design that had brought Schulte to the Berras' front door hinged around a man by the name of George Weiss. In the fall of 1942, Yogi Berra had never heard his name and did not know that, with the possible exception of Rickey, Weiss was considered the shrewdest executive in baseball. Nor could Yogi know that for nearly the next three decades, with two franchises, their names would be inextricably entwined. Weiss would beat Berra into the Hall of Fame by one year.

Shortly before Yogi left for the training camp, a telegram arrived. It was from the office of the general manager of the Brooklyn Dodgers of the National League. Branch Rickey wanted Larry Berra to travel to Bear Mountain, New York, the site of the Dodgers training camp and sign a contract. There would be a bonus. Yogi never found out how much, but since Rickey remembered Berra, it may be presumed that he remembered that he would sign for no less than $500. But Larry Berra, through luck or the residue of design, was now the property of the New York Yankees.

Chapter Two

Larry Berra,
They Call Him Yogi . . .
(1943–1946)

What you have to remember about Yogi is that all he ever wanted was to be a baseball player.

—JERRY COLEMAN

GEORGE MARTIN WEISS was known by some of the beat writers who covered the Yankees as "Lonesome George" because, as one of them put it, "He always seemed to be." He was, depending on whom you talked to, humorless, cheap, cold hearted, honest, racist, ruthless, and fair. The late Leonard Koppett summed him up this way: "He never lost a poker game because of a warm impulse." Many of his players respected him, and more than a few despised him. To a man, they all agreed he had a heart of brass. Jerry Lumpe, who played with the Yankees from 1956 through 1959, says, "Weiss cared nothing about the players as people. We were meat, and our only reason for existing was for what we could do for George Weiss and the franchise." Hank Bauer, a standout hitter and outfielder for Yankee championship teams of the 1950s, called the Yankees front office men in that period "cold-hearted bastards. You can quote me. I loved my team, my teammates, and the city, but, boy, getting what you deserved from those S.O.B.s was a fight. No matter what you did, every contract talk was a struggle, and the one you struggled with was George Weiss." Bob Turley, the first Yankees pitcher to win the Cy Young award (in 1958), recalls, "When you talked salary with George Weiss . . . , it was like pulling teeth.

Except that *they* were pulling *your* teeth. Most of the negotiations were done by phone, and they didn't take any collect calls."

Weiss was a Yale man, and while living in New Haven had honed his skills as a promoter of baseball. A semipro team he purchased for peanuts outdrew New Haven's Eastern League team, partly because Weiss was willing to give the locals what they wanted: baseball on Sunday and big-name talent. In those days, you could pay top stars to barnstorm in minor league games on Sundays. Weiss offered Ty Cobb cash to ride a train down from Boston when the Tigers were playing the Red Sox; Cobb came to New Haven, played with one eye counting the gate, and demanded more money for the next game. Weiss gave him the then eye-opening sum of $800 a game. It was worth it. Cobb not only sold tickets, he helped Weiss bury the Eastern League competition. In 1919, the Eastern League own-ers, acknowledging that they were overmatched, decided to quit trying to beat Weiss and let him join them. Owning an Eastern League franchise was Weiss's legitimate entry to professional baseball.

In 1932, he parlayed that into a position with Colonel Jacob Ruppert's New York Yankees as director of the farm system. His genius for organiza-tion rivaled Branch Rickey's; at its peak, the Yankees network included more than twenty first-rate minor league franchises and, in twenty-nine seasons, helped produce the stars for nineteen pennants. And though Weiss was ultraconservative, he routinely took chances that other men in his position did not take. In 1934, his scouts told him that a promising minor leaguer from the Pacific Coast League was a poor bet to recover from an injury and make it to the Yankees; Weiss took a chance on Joe DiMaggio anyway. And in 1942, he rolled the dice on seventeen-year-old Yogi Berra on the advice of a man he had known as an umpire back in the Eastern League.

Leo Browne was a rich man, a dealer in oil and fuel. He was also a base-ball fan, the type of man who enjoyed helping out young prospects. A friend of Johnny Schulte, a native of St. Louis who lived there when the Yankees' season was over, Browne, after conferring with Schulte, wrote the letter about Yogi to Bob Burnes of the *Globe-Democrat* trying to stir up interest in Yogi. He finally thought to contact Weiss, whose eye for talent and business acumen had impressed Browne back in Connecticut. There aren't too many baseball men who solicit player evaluations from former umpires, but Weiss respected Browne's judgment, and his attention was grabbed by something in Browne's letter: "All this kid wants is $500 to sign. Whatever you want to give him a month, he'll take it." Yogi was underage, so Pietro signed the contract for him. The Berras waited, but no one said anything about the bonus. In fact, months later at Norfolk, hungry and in need of cash, Yogi would ask the team's GM, Jim Dawson, what had happened to it. He was told that the five hundred was contingent on his making the Yankees and that he wouldn't get it until the year was out.

Yogi had just learned his first lesson in dealing with the game's shrewdest bargainer: read the fine print. He didn't complain, he determined to work harder. "I can truthfully say," he would conclude eighteen years later, "that it was when they gave that business about it [the bonus] not coming to me until I had stuck with the ball club for a year that I made up my mind I was going to see to it that I got everything that was coming to me from then on, and I think I have."[1] And he did. The Yale man with the reputation as the toughest negotiator in the game would, before the decade was out, meet his match in the high school dropout from the Hill. George Weiss would discover, as Branch Rickey had before him, that Yogi Berra had a clear sense of his own value, whether he could articulate it or not.

───

YOGI REPORTED TO Excelsior Springs, Missouri, spring home of the Kansas City Blues of the American Association. Manager Johnny Neun put him in a few intrasquad games, but when the exhibition season began Berra was assigned to a lower level team for seasoning, the Norfolk Tars of the Class B Piedmont League. The brief excursion to Excelsior Springs had been a lark; now Larry Berra was, for the first time in his life, plunged into the world outside the Hill. He was not yet eighteen.

Norfolk was not only his introduction to professional baseball but also to the Second World War. Berra scarcely gave a single thought to the trouble in Europe before leaving St. Louis. So it appears to have been with many Italian-Americans, such as my father, who once told me, "I never really thought about the War until I heard from my draft board. I just assumed that it would be a matter of time, probably a short one, before I would be in the Army or Navy, and my family did, too. I never heard anyone voice the slightest reservation about going to war against the 'old country.' " So strong were the boundaries of family, neighborhood, and culture that the enormity and complexity of world events made no impression until one became directly involved. Though some federal government officials feared that elements of the Italian-American community might have allegiances to the Fascist regime in Italy, they proved to be completely loyal to the United States. In Richard Gambino's words,

It is one of the most remarkable facts of American history that a people whose recent roots are in a land where no governmental authority was respected overwhelmingly supports the authority of America with their labor, sacrifice, and blood.[2]

No one knows how many Italian-Americans were in the U.S. armed forces during World War II because the War Department did not classify personnel by ethnic background. Michael Musmanno, author of *The Story of the Italians in America*, estimated the figure at considerably more than a million. In 1961, New York Governor Nelson Rockefeller, in a speech to Italian-American war veterans, stated, "The services mustered over one million, five hundred thousand of Italian descent."[*] If true, this would come to more than 10 percent of the armed forces from 1941 through the end of the war.

Norfolk, Virginia, the headquarters for the Fifth Naval District and thus for the Atlantic Fleet of the U.S. Navy, was preparing for war, and it soon became obvious to Berra that his life would revolve around circumstances far too large for him to control. In the spring of 1943, Norfolk and its neighboring city, Newport News, were boomtowns, jammed with Navy personnel and defense workers far in excess of the town's facilities. Whatever Southern charm Norfolk may have possessed was trampled in the mad rush of perhaps 750,000 people in a town with a native population of fewer than 190,000. Everywhere there were long lines—waiting for streetcars and taxis, and in restaurants and grocery and department stores. Alcohol flowed; liquor was not sold for individual drinks in Virginia, but "setups" were available everywhere. This being a much cheaper and quicker way to achieve inebriation, alcohol-fueled rowdiness was rampant, overwhelming the local police, both civil and military. In Italian families, drunkenness was *proibito*, and Yogi had never witnessed such public displays. Too shy to approach girls and hundreds of miles from friends and family, Yogi often found himself shut off from his principal form of entertainment—movies—due to the long lines, and for entertainment was forced to fall back on the solitary diversion of comic books.

His biggest problem wasn't the competition on the baseball field. The Piedmont League was Class B, and he quickly saw that many of the young

---

[*]George Creel, head of public relations for the U.S. Department of War during World War I said, "The Italians in the United States are about four percent of the whole population, but the list of casualties shows a full ten percent of Italian names."

players had no more experience than he had, and the ones who did were either major league retreads or career minor leaguers who didn't have his talent. His problem was in fueling that talent. His salary was $90 a month, and no adjustment was made for the wildly inflationary prices the war had brought to Norfolk. The players were paid twice a month, and after taxes were withheld, the $45 had shrunk to about $37, or, in Yogi's estimation, about half of what he could have made shining shoes at the bus terminal. He found a roommate to share the rent, Bill Sukey, a pitcher for the Tars, but after rent was paid, he still had to cover part of his uniform costs, tip the clubhouse man, and eat—and, if he could somehow find the change, see an occasional movie and maybe buy a pack of cigarettes. "I never got too hooked on cigarettes," he later said, "'cause I couldn't afford them. Maybe starvation kept me from getting cancer."[3]

There was just about a dollar a day left over for eating and anything else. As the dollar scarcely covered the eating, there wasn't much of anything else. For the first time in his life, he was forced to borrow money, or at least to try to, as most players on the Tars were in pretty much the same situation he was. One player he remembered fondly was Jack Phillips, a first baseman, who always seemed to have change to spare. The two would become teammates on the Yankees. Yogi was worse off than the others in one way: he was Italian. Even during the heart of the Depression, meals at the Berra household, as in most Italian-American homes, were small feasts. Now, searching his pockets for money to buy sandwiches, he could understand his father's angry response to bits of bread he had wasted at the family table. He and Bill Sukey usually ate cheaply at luncheonettes or "dog wagons." Years later, when he described the hard times at Norfolk to his sons Larry, Tim, and Dale, the boys would pretend to play violins, and their father would laugh.

In the summer of 1943, though, hunger was no laughing matter. More than twenty years before Marvin Miller started the players union, Yogi led a strike, of which he was the rank and file. Hunger made him shrewd. Shortly before a Tars game, he noticed that both of his team's other catchers were hurting—you certainly *can* observe a lot by watching—and realized he had the team's manager, Shaky Kain, over a barrel. He told his skipper that he was too weak to play, and Kain dug into his own pocket and sent his only catcher to the nearest concession stand, where Yogi imitated Babe Ruth attacking a pile of hamburgers. He got two hits that night. Emboldened, he decided to try the hunger act again. He approached Kain about getting a raise in salary; Kain went to Dawson, who in turn had to get permission from the Yankees front office, a man named Ed Barrow, the Yankees' business manager for twenty-seven years. Yogi learned two things from his request: first, the team will not offer if you don't ask, and, second, even to get just a $5 per month raise from the New York Yankees was no small matter.°

Actually, Larry learned three important things at Norfolk. According to Irv Goodman, who profiled Berra for *Sport* magazine in 1958, Norfolk's opposition, and sometimes even their hometown fans, began getting on the young Larry about his looks. "The slurs," Goodman wrote, "offended, and Yogi gritted his teeth and slammed his bat, and his manager, Shaky Kain, had to take him off into a corner for a talk. 'Look,' Kain said, 'This is gonna happen. More to you than to others. And in language worse than you've been hearing. You gotta learn not to get mad. They're the characters who pay your salary. Let 'em holler all they want. Figure they're entitled. If you ever show them, or show anyone, that they're getting to you with the needle, you're dead. Ignore. That's what you gotta do. Ignore.' Yogi says it was a hell of a speech, and he followed Shaky Kain's advice to the letter. He ignored it."[4]

Relief came from home. Somehow, Paulina understood from the tone of her son's letters that he wasn't eating properly. Yogi wasn't ever quite sure how she knew, but, he surmised, "Moms aren't supposed to know all they know, but they do."[5] Unbeknownst to her husband, Mama Berra would slip her youngest boy a few dollars in the mail. She would also caution him, in Italian, not to let his father know that he was hungry, or he might make him come home.

Then local relief arrived. Yogi had become a favorite with the Norfolk fans as well as those in surrounding Piedmont League towns, including Roanoke, Lynchburg, Portsmouth, and Richmond. Life was good; there wasn't much money, but he was playing ball, away from home for the first time in his life, and finding out that the rest of the country wasn't so bad. He enjoyed the travel and the little ballparks, and the fans responded in kind. In those days, it was common for fans to bring goodies to their favorite players, and Yogi was singled out by a woman—she must have been Italian—who came to the Tars games every Sunday. Every week she

---

°One player who earned some interesting concessions from the franchise was a pitcher named Allen Gettel. Gettel, who pitched for the Yankees in 1945–1946 and bounced around the major leagues until 1955, only pitched in Norfolk's home games. A farmer, he stayed home to tend his crops when the Tars were on the road, a service that was deemed beneficial to the war effort. It also kept Gettel out of military service.

brought him a hero sandwich stuffed with salami and provolone, which Yogi did not share with his teammates. The hero was for Yogi what spinach was to Popeye; against Roanoke (whose manager was the Hall of Famer and former Washington Senators outfielder Heinie Manush), he exploded with 12 hits and 23 RBIs in two games. The $500 bonus no longer seemed so far away. Not all the league's pitchers, of course, were as bad as the ones on Roanoke. In fact, hits didn't come easy in the Piedmont. "That was a dead ball league," he would recall. "I don't know what it was. Only one guy in the whole league, I think, hit .300.° Jack Phillips, on our team, led the league in homers with eight, and I hit seven. Then in the playoffs, they gave us live balls and I hit four home runs."[6]

His hitting made it possible to ignore his 16 errors at catcher, a high mark for the league (though his fielding percentage was around the league average; his error total was high because he caught so many games) He was green but willing, in his first game, a night contest, a batter hit a pop foul, and Berra wasted no time telling his teammates "I got it! I got it!" The ball dropped about ten feet away from him. Learning to read the arc of a pop fly in night lights was just one of the many skills he would acquire. But after a rough start he caught on, hitting .253 in 111 games. Another year at that rate and a call-up from the parent club might be in sight. Yogi was looking forward to an explosive 1944, and he got one.

While he waited, he played with such unbridled enthusiasm that he left some of his teammates open-mouthed. "You should have seen me in Norfolk," he would tell *Life* magazine five years later. "One time I was so anxious to start catchin' that I went behind the plate without my mask on."[7]

The image of Yogi as a guy who came to play was vivid with everyone who saw him play in his youth. "What you have to remember about Yogi," Jerry Coleman would remember, "is that all he ever wanted was to be a baseball player."

———

LATER, YOGI WOULD say he never knew who "they" were. A lot of American boys in small towns knew the people staffing their draft boards by heart. For Yogi's part, "I knew they were the draft board and all that, but I didn't know any of them."[8] He recalled having spoken to someone connected with the military who told him to come and see him at the end of the season; that was as much as he understood. He knew he'd be in the

———

° Actually, the two top hitters in the league hit .333.

service soon, but he had no idea when or where. When he got his first notice from the St. Louis draft board, he requested that his papers be sent on to Norfolk. While the papers were en route, the Tars played a fund-raising exhibition with the team at the Norfolk Air Station. There were some names on the opposing team Yogi was familiar with, including Fred Hutchinson (who had already played 30 major league games with the Tigers and who would manage the Cincinnati Reds against Yogi and the Yankees in the 1961 World Series); Hugh Casey (who had won 46 games in the previous four seasons with the Dodgers); Sam Chapman (already a four-year veteran with the Philadelphia A's); Eddie Robinson (who had played a few games with the Indians in 1942 and would be Yogi's teammate for three seasons in the 1950s); a talented twenty-six-year-old Red Sox out-fielder who, according to a chant by Boston fans, was "better than his brother Joe," Dominic DiMaggio; and, best of all, a diminutive infielder from Brooklyn named Phil Rizzuto. Yogi and Rizzuto hit it off immedi-ately. "I liked him right away," says Yogi. "I wasn't very tall, and he was the first big league ballplayer I saw that I could eat soup off his head."[9] Rosters and media guides would shuttle Yogi back and forth from 5'7" to 5'8" for his whole career; Rizzuto was generally listed at 5'5", but was awarded an inch by the PR department when he made it to the Bronx.

———

YOGI TALKED TO the warrant officer at the Norfolk naval training sta-tion, Gary Bodie, who told him that most of the big leaguers in uniform were getting ready to be shipped out. Yogi told him he would be drafted soon, and Bodie suggested that he join the Navy, and Bodie could try to get him on his team to play some ball before being shipped out. When the sea-son ended, Berra took his physical in Richmond and was asked what branch of the service he wanted; he picked the Navy. Something occurred to him: How much time would they give him before he was government property? He hadn't been home for a while, and there might be time to dash home for a Sunday dinner. It turned out the Army would have allowed him about three more weeks than the Navy, but it was too late. The clerks were too lazy to tear up the paperwork and start over, and due to a snafu his papers were processed without regard to Bodie's request. Yogi was in the Navy. As he did throughout his life, he rolled with the punch: "I did not know it at the time, but this was a big thing in my life. The three extra weeks in St. Louis were not as important as I thought they were."[10] He was beginning to enjoy the outside world.

After passing his physical, he left for the naval base at Bainbridge, Maryland, and six weeks of boot camp. His routine was interrupted by an emergency at home; his mother was facing surgery. The Navy and the Red Cross sent him back and let him stay until Paulina was strong enough to go home. Assured by her doctors that she was doing fine, Yogi got back on the train and headed for Little Creek, Virginia, not far from Norfolk, where he would train for amphibious service. He discovered that in the Navy, as in the Army, the philosophy was to hurry up and wait. In the evenings there was little to do but read comic books and watch movies at the base—at least he didn't have to stand in line to see them. But things were about to get interesting. One night, as Yogi and his mates watched Clark Gable and Spencer Tracy in *Boomtown*, the film was stopped and the lights went on. Enlisted men were ordered back to barracks. Officers lined the men up and asked for volunteers for duty aboard rocket boats. Yogi didn't know what rocket boats were—scarcely any of his pals seemed to know, either—but someone called them rocket ships, and that got his attention. He hadn't been in the service long enough to learn that you weren't supposed to volunteer for anything, so he found himself on a fast track for the adventure of a lifetime.

The rocket boats turned out to be small landing craft, LCSSs (Landing Craft Support Small), whose purpose was to spray rockets on the beach before troop landings. There were duller things to train for. Some of the men got the hint that they might be participating in a major troop landing, perhaps the invasion of Hitler's Fortress Europe that the papers were always writing about. "I didn't think about it being dangerous," said Yogi, "I was sick of hanging around all day. I wanted to be doing something."[11] The volunteers were sent to a training base just south of Baltimore to meet their rocket boats. They weren't impressed. These were not the kind of boats that looked as if they could sustain ocean voyages. The LCSS was new, a thirty-six-foot-long craft made of wood and steel that had been tested by the Allied navies during the recent invasion of Sicily. Though the Navy liked to call them ships, the men who served on them referred to the craft derisively as "big bathtubs." Yogi quickly perceived that his boat "really wasn't much of anything except a platform to carry out a whole lot of live firecrackers."[12] The strategy was for a transport ship to approach the shallow water of a beachhead and release its cargo of eight LCSSs, which would then move closer to sweep the beach of enemy guns. In addition to the rockets, the LCSS was armed with antiaircraft weapons, twin .50 caliber machine guns mounted in a ball turret like those used on bombing aircraft. Each boat was to be manned by just an officer and six sailors.

If Yogi and the other volunteers thought they were in for a lark, they soon understood that the Navy regarded this as serious business: their mail was censored, and they weren't allowed to leave base. They were told not to mention the boats or their training in their letters. Yogi wasn't indignant over the censorship: "It made me feel important."[13] He and his mates began five weeks of intensive practice in the techniques of loading the rockets, firing, and hitting their targets. They began to talk amongst themselves; it looked like they might be getting ready for something big.

After a couple of weeks, his unit was sent to Lido Beach, Long Island, then shipped to Bayonne, New Jersey, with Yogi about five pounds heavier as a result of his assignment as a soda jerk during the interim. The unit boarded an LST (Landing Ship Tank) for Boston, a journey that made Yogi nostalgic for the Army he missed getting into. It was here that Seaman Second Class Lawrence Berra experienced seasickness for the first time. The heat, noise, and cramped quarters reminded him of the stories Pietro had told of his first trip to America from Italy, and Yogi later confessed, "Whenever Pop starts telling me what it was like coming over from the old country in steerage, I tell him it must have been like the first class compared with what we had."[14] While embarking from Boston, the unit joined a convoy off the coast of Nova Scotia near Halifax. His system now accustomed to the pitch of the ocean, Berra began to enjoy the trip, though "I would have liked it better if they had let us sleep more, but in the Navy, they hate to have those loudspeakers idle. I can still hear them, 'Now hear this: Clean sweep down fore and aft. Sweep all trash over the fantail.' "[15] Yogi was able to trump his dad's stories of ocean sailing in at least one way—when Pietro came to America, he didn't have to worry about a torpedo or mine caving in the side of the ship. But the convoy arrived in Glasgow, Scotland, without incident. Finally stationed in Plymouth, England, the unit sweated out the wait before D-Day, receiving almost daily reports of German submarine attacks in the area. Berra was on at least one patrol outside the harbor, but saw no action. Early in June, Yogi and the crew boarded the U.S.S. *Bayfield*, a Coast Guard transport that carried the six LCSS boats within firing range of Omaha Beach. Theirs was to be the smallest craft to take part in the biggest invasion in world history.

Just before dawn on the morning of June 6, 1944, their rocket boat was lifted on the davits and lowered over the side and, in Yogi's words, "expendable as hell, we headed in for Omaha Beach."[16] The classic description of the Allied armada at that moment was written by Cornelius Ryan in *The Longest Day*:

> Never had there been a dawn like this. In the murky, gray light, in majestic, fearful grandeur, the great Allied fleet lay off Normandy's five invasion beaches. The sea teemed with ships . . . Outlined against the sky were the big battle wagons, the menacing cruisers, the whippet-like destroyers. Behind them were the squat command ships, sprouting their forests of antennae. And behind them came the convoys of troop-filled transports and landing ships . . . Circling the lead transports, waiting for the signal to head for the beaches, were swarms of bobbing landing craft, jam-packed with the men who would land in the first waves.

Ryan's account of the invasion, particularly at Normandy, is comprehensive, but if he were going over the details, there were boats in front of those landing craft too small to have been noticed by history,° and Yogi Berra was in one of them.

As Yogi would remember the moment, "It was scary but [it was] really something to see. I was only eighteen, and I didn't think anything could kill me. I didn't know enough to be scared. I had my head up over the side of the boat all the time, looking around like it was the Fourth of July in Forest Park and after the fireworks we were gong to go over and get some hot dogs and cokes."[17] It's a good thing that Berra and his shipmates didn't think too hard about the situation they were in, because of all the craft participating in the Normandy invasion, the LCSSs were the most vulnerable. The sailors were shielded by only a couple of inches of steel, which afforded them little protection, as an enemy cannon or mortar shell could easily have dropped right on its open deck. If enemy fire ignited one of the rockets, the entire craft and its crew would be obliterated.

When Berra looked over the edge to see the show, his lieutenant yelled at him, "You better put that goddam head down if you want to keep it!"[18] Yogi took his advice. He didn't get along with the craft's officer, an Ensign Holmes, "not on D-Day and not before and not after."[19] But on the morning of the invasion, they were a smoothly functioning team. The strategy was to watch the lead boat fire a test rocket; if it reached the beach, then the others would move up to the same range and fire. If the first rocket

---

°Ryan's classic history of D-Day mentions four different kinds of landing craft, but makes no mention of the tiny LCSSs.

failed, they would all move in closer and wait to see what happened to the next test rocket. Amidst the smoke and noise and choppy waters, it wasn't easy for the sailors to get a good bearing on how close they were. But the first rocket lit up the beach, and to their relief, according to Berra, "we were closer than the hitter is to the left-field screen at Fenway Park." All the boats let loose with their payloads, "and it was like nothing I had ever heard or seen in my life."[20] "I couldn't see all the bloodshed that they showed in the movie 'Private Ryan,' but I did see a lot of guys drown."[21]

The little LCSSs had done their part, and by the afternoon everyone could relax a bit. Their orders were to stay close to the shore till at least June 9 in order to provide cover fire if the Germans launched a counterattack, but none came. On June 8, the storm everyone had feared on June 6 finally came, and the little crafts were battered. To prevent them being swamped, they were tied up to a line of Liberty ships that had been sunk close to the shore to form a breakwater. It looked as if things would be okay. Then, suddenly, three fighter planes appeared overhead. The LCSSs had orders to shoot at any plane that came below cloud level, so Yogi and the other gunners opened fire, hitting one of the planes. The pilot made it out of his burning plane, and when his parachute hit the water, he swam toward Yogi's boat. Berra yelled to his mates to keep the pilot covered while he helped him out of the water. He expected to hear German; instead, he got an earful of American curse words—they had shot down an American fighter. The sailors were apologetic, but unashamed. Their aim was good even if they couldn't see the plane's markings.

The storm got worse, snapping the cable that secured the LCSS to the Liberty ship. Berra's boat soon flipped over, and the tiny crew was faced with the absurd situation of having survived D-Day only to risk drowning after the shooting had stopped. But clinging to the hull of one of the Liberty ships, they all hung on till rescued. Berra and the rest of the crew spent the next two weeks back on the *Bayfield*, relaying messages between Omaha and Utah beaches and helping new arrivals through the minefields. The work was nerve wracking, particularly when the Luftwaffe found a couple of functioning aircraft and sent them to harass the anchored ships. Finally, after thirteen days, the exhausted sailors were given some rest. Apparently the order was not passed on to the Germans. As soon as the men hit the sack, the general quarters alarm sounded. A German bomb fell near the *Bayfield*'s aft, but caused no serious damage. "I wouldn't have cared if it did," said Yogi. "I was too tired to be scared."[22]

Thirty-five years later, Berra would recall that General Eisenhower had been on the *Bayfield*. "I never saw him then, but he saw me play in some World Series, and I met him. I never talked about D-Day. It didn't seem right, but now I wish I had."*

———

AFTER A REST at Portsmouth, Yogi's squadron, about forty men, jumped on an LCI (Landing Craft, Infantry) for the port of Bizerte in Tunisia, then a bustling North African coastal town of some 60,000. Living in tents close to the beach and with nothing much to do but shuffle around piles of depth charges for destroyers, Berra found little to remember about Bizerte besides the novelty song "Dirty Gertie from Bizerte" ("Like a lot of other tourist attractions," Yogi said, "I never saw her").[23] He had so many immunization shots that he "felt like a pin cushion."[24] A promotion to Seaman First Class upped his pay to $84 a month—that was $84 without taxes, uniform costs, or living expenses, and with movies for free. He was sending money home to Paulina and, the boredom notwithstanding, feeling better about life. Things were about to get livelier.

The Allied invasion of southern France in 1944 was deemed by many analysts as a bad bet, but Eisenhower's instinct that the Germans were spread too thin and the southern coast of France was lightly defended turned out to be correct. But the fighting was bloody enough for those who were there. Yogi would later recall the August 15 assault on Marseilles, part of an operation designated Dragoon, as being scarier than Omaha Beach, probably because no one knew what to expect at Normandy, whereas at Marseilles they knew exactly what was coming. On Yellow Beach, their designated target area, there was an enormous hotel that had been damaged by shellfire but which the Germans had fortified with mortars and machine-gun nests. The LCSSs moved in within a couple hundred yards of the shoreline and began raking the hotel. In the wave directly behind them were Royal Navy ships firing at targets beyond the hotel. In the midst of the barrage, someone on Yogi's boat screamed for the crew to hit the deck; Berra, who was cradling a rocket, tried to duck under the gun mount and dropped his load; it did not go off or you wouldn't be reading this book. "Nothing else happened," Yogi recalled for the *New*

———

*A number of sailors thought that Eisenhower was aboard their ships on D-Day. The radios on each ship relayed a radio message from the general that sounded so clear that it seemed as if he was speaking through each craft's PA system. According to Cornelius Ryan, Eisenhower was at the 101st Airborne Division's headquarters at Newbery watching the first Allied planes prepare to take off.

York Daily News' Joe Trimble, "and when the boat seemed to get back on an even keel, me and the rest of the guys poked our heads out from under cover to see what was up. We found out then that a British shell had hit a yard from us because they had shortened their range too much. Lucky it was a dud."[25]

The barrage continued. Yogi was nicked by a bullet from one of the German machine guns, earning him a Purple Heart. Shortly afterward, a rocket blew the nest away. Berra, manning the twin .50s, began, along with the other gunners, to cut down the Germans as they fled the hotel. When American troops landed to secure the area, they were met by an enthusiastic swarm of townspeople—"Old people, kids, even some dogs"—waving flowers, offering bottles of wine, and singing *La Marseillaise*. "It was a wacky war," Yogi thought. "A half hour after we were getting shot at by the Germans, the French were welcoming us."[26]

———

AS THE INVADING Allied armies moved inland toward Germany, there were whispers that a great many Navy personnel, now unneeded in the European theater, would be shipped to the Pacific. None of Yogi's crew was enthusiastic about the possibility, but after two invasions, they earned a break. The next postcard Paulina Berra received from her youngest son was postmarked Naples, Italy.

The unit was lodged in an inn overlooking the Bay of Naples, about as nice a place to spend a month during World War II as could be found. He even found time for a quick trip to the Isle of Capri. "It was like being a tourist," he remembered, "except that you didn't need any money. Any American sailor or GI could make friends in a minute as long as he had a good supply of chocolate and cigarettes, and I made sure I did."[27] The only snag, as Yogi soon discovered, was, to paraphrase George Bernard Shaw on the Americans and British, Italian-Americans and Italians "were two peoples separated by a common language." The dialect Yogi had been raised with, heavily tinged by Pietro's Hill-Guineaisms and American slang was, much to the chagrin of Berra's buddies, nearly impenetrable to Neapolitans. He could communicate with basic words, but a great deal of subtext was lost in the exchange.

Ready for adventure, he bumped into a friend from the Hill named Bob Cocoterra. Cocoterra, who had enlisted in the Army, was driving his jeep from Naples to Milan; Yogi had brief thoughts of going up with him and then heading for the town of Malvaglio to see where his parents had been raised, but the Allies hadn't quite pushed that far north. He would settle for Rome. His CO, when asked what the plans were for the unit, shrugged; they might leave tomorrow, they might be here for another month, who knew? Yogi took a chance. "What could they do, shoot me? Me, with a Distinguished Unit Citation, two battle stars, and an ETO [European Theatre of Operations] ribbon, not to mention a Good Conduct Medal. I was practically a hero."[28] (Yogi neglected to mention the Purple Heart.) Seaman First Class Lawrence Berra, tourist, stayed at a first-class hotel, saw the catacombs and the Coliseum, and, knowing how much it would thrill his mother, went to the Vatican and saw Pope Pius XII greet an enthusiastic throng from his balcony. After four days, he hitched a ride back to Naples, the first of Pietro and Paulina's offspring to see the old country.

The term now over, clear to Berra, the squadron was next shipped to Oran in northern Algeria, a seaport of nearly half a million, most of them Muslim. On Christmas Day, 1944, Yogi, a few of his mates, and a few score French Catholics attended midnight Mass. On New Year's Eve they boarded a troop transport, popped some bottles of champagne, and headed back to the United States. At Norfolk, he was given a physical and a series of routine psychological tests designed to identify the effects of stress in combat. Then, with a month's leave, he boarded a train for St. Louis and the Hill. Two days after leaving Norfolk, he was showing his medals to his teary-eyed mother. He never showed her his Purple Heart because he didn't have it. Assuming that it would upset Paulina to find out what it was for, he never applied for the medal.

Berra seldom spoke of his war experiences, and many of the sportswriters who covered him in the 1950s never knew he had been at Normandy. In 1984, while coaching for the Houston Astros, he talked a little about it to Jim Palmer and Tim McCarver, the broadcasting tandem for the Astros-Dodgers game in Los Angeles. A writer from the *Los Angeles Times* overheard the conversation. "Yogi," he wrote the next day, "survived D-Day and George Steinbrenner, and all in 40 years."

———

SEAMAN FIRST CLASS Berra's next posting was in New London, Connecticut. To anyone in the Navy, this meant submarines; New London had been the site of the first U.S. Navy submarine base way back in 1915. (Today, it is home to 8,500 sailors and sixteen nuclear-powered attack submarines.) Back in Norfolk, a doctor asked him, "Were you scared over there?" "No," he replied, perhaps thinking of submarine duty. "Not at the time. But I am now."[29] "I volunteered for the rocket boats," he said years later when sorting through his feelings, "although I don't regret the time spent, not one day. But . . . I didn't want to go under water . . . I didn't even want to go *on* water again, and thinking back on that so-called troop ship makes me, well, not shudder, but shake my head."[30]

As it turned out, the job the personnel officer had in mind was with Welfare and Recreation, and his assignment was taking care of the base's movie theater. Also, somebody had looked at his record and found out he had done some amateur boxing in St. Louis. He spent his time taking tickets, managing equipment for the football team, and helping to build the base's baseball field. It was better than riding around in a floating bathtub waiting for a shell to drop in your lap, but it was frustrating. He couldn't understand why he had not been assigned to the baseball team; it still hadn't gotten through to him that in the military the squeaky wheel gets the grease.

Over the winter of 1944–1945, he began to pester Commander Robert H. Barnes about seeing the manager of the baseball team; sometime in late winter, Barnes gave in. In theory, it was to Yogi's advantage that the team's skipper, Jim Gleeson, was a major league ballplayer (though it might be more correct to say Gleeson had *been* a major league outfielder, as he quit in 1942, his fifth and final season, after batting just .200 in nine games with Cincinnati). He might have been expected to recognize professional talent—and Berra was professional and had talent—but Yogi in his sailor suit didn't look much like any ballplayer Gleeson had ever seen. "What do you do?" Gleeson asked skeptically. Berra answered, adding that he belonged to the Yankees and had spent a season at Norfolk before the Navy. Gleeson replied that he looked more like a wrestler or a fighter. Yes, said Yogi, he had done some amateur boxing back in St. Louis, but he really was a ballplayer. Gleeson remained skeptical. Maybe it was the suit; maybe it was Yogi in the suit. "In my opinion," Berra said in his autobiography, "those sailor suits don't add anything to anybody's appearance. But I think I looked worse in mine than most guys did. Because of my weight, which was around 195 then, like it still is [in 1961] I've always looked smaller than I really am. Between those tight blue pants with all the buttons and that ridiculous white sailor hat, I must have been a sight."[31]

It wouldn't be the last time that the sight of Yogi in a sailor suit would cause someone to doubt that he was a ballplayer. Gleeson and his coach, Ray Volpe, a minor league pitcher in the Yankees chain, drilled Berra with a barrage of baseball questions to see if he was for real. "I wish I had a picture of the interview or a soundtrack of the conversation!" Gleeson told Joe Trimble in 1954, "Yogi seemed implausible . . . He insisted he belonged to the Yankees, and I thought he was laying it on. We decided to test him with a quiz, asking about the managers and the other teams in the Piedmont League and facts about the cities. He answered correctly."[32] The soon-to-be twenty-year-old minor league veteran seemed to know more about professional baseball than they did. They told him to report in April for the first practice of the Raiders.

The first time Yogi got to bat, he erased all doubts that he could play, stroking the first few pitches, in Gleeson's words, "far, high and wide." Gleeson knew "We had a diamond in the rough, and I mean rough. He had no polish as a ballplayer except when he was at bat. His manner of speech, and his appearance, seemed to be the biggest subject of mockery in those days. But almost from the time he made his first appearance, the fans seemed to recognize his colorful manner."[33] He certainly was colorful in the outfield, where he turned routine fly balls into adventures, but whether he looked good or not, he made the plays—or most of them, at any rate—and he hit a ton, though in such an unorthodox manner as to astonish both his teammates and the opposition. In a game at New London he reached for a pitch high and away and tomahawked it into left field for a double. The catcher was Gus Niarhos, who would later be Yogi's teammate on the Yankees. Gus turned to the umpire and exploded: the pitch Berra had hit was one he called as a pitch-out! The ump waved him away; Niarhos, the ump said, should have told Yogi.

The competition was first rate, service teams and semipro clubs stocked with veterans and prospects such as himself, and when he was off duty, he had the chance to pick up an odd fifty bucks or so playing semipro ball himself. On one fortuitous day, he picked up $100 at the expense of a cocky semipro team that wanted to wager on the game's outcome. It was the equivalent of a month's wages for a first class seaman, and the biggest payday he had yet had in baseball.

He got to travel to Boston with the New London Raiders and play in an exhibition game against the Braves at Braves Field, the first time he had set foot on the field of a major league ballpark since he had performed for Branch Rickey back in St. Louis. The Yogi Berra legend may be said to have begun just a few days later. On June 25, 1945, the New York Giants stopped at New London on their way back from a series with the Braves in Boston. Gleeson and his old friend Mel Ott, the Giants manager and part-time outfielder, were watching batting practice. Gleeson told Ott to take a good look at his odd-looking phenom. There was perhaps no prominent major leaguer better suited to appreciate Berra's unorthodox talents. Ott, scarcely taller than Yogi at 5'9", was a six-time National League home run champion known for his peculiar "foot-in-the-bucket" stance in which he cocked his right leg and brought it down as he stepped forward to meet the ball. "I came away from New London," Ott told Joe Trimble in 1954, "with only one thing in mind. I wanted to get that little catcher"—at this point, Yogi was spending more time behind the plate than in the outfield—"He seemed to be so right, even though he was doing everything wrong. Why, he made two hits on wild pitches!" (The hits came in an exhibition game against the Giants when Yogi faced perhaps his toughest major league pitcher up to that time, the Giants' Ace Adams. Adams had led the National League in appearances from 1942 through 1944 and led the league in saves in 1944 and 1945.)

On the train ride back to New York, Ott made his decision. "I figured Berra would develop into a catcher worth $100,000 in a few years. That fluid swing of his reminded me of Johnny Mize"—Mize, the Cardinals' big first baseman, had led the NL in home runs and slugging in both 1939 and 1940 and would eventually be elected to the Hall of Fame. "I talked things over with Stoneham [Giants owner, Horace], and then went to MacPhail [Yankees general manager, Larry]. The next day I made an offer of $50,000 for the little catcher."[34] The "little catcher," whom Branch Rickey could have had for a $500 bonus, was now worth $50,000—actually more, as it turned out. As Ott would later tell sportswriter Tom Meany, "I figured some day he would develop into a $500,000 catcher."[35] MacPhail did not recognize Berra's name when Ott came to see him about buying Yogi's contract and apparently did not think to ask George Weiss, who did know. MacPhail stalled, apparently indicating to the Giants that he was willing to make the deal while he conferred with the team's chief scout, Paul Krichell. "I wanted to get a look at this kid who sold Ott a bill of goods on the strength of one ball game—and a $50,000 bill of goods at that."[36] Krichell, who had been with the Yankees since 1913, had a brief mental file on Berra and gave it to his boss. MacPhail figured that if Berra was worth $50,000 to Ott, he was worth at least a look to the Yankees. He contacted Yogi at New London.

On his next leave Yogi hopped on a train and walked into the Yankees' Fifth Avenue office dressed in the same unfortunate Navy blues that he wore when he interviewed with Jimmy Gleeson. MacPhail's jaw dropped—was it too late, he wondered, to get that $50,000 from the Giants? Nine years later, he recalled his reaction. Berra, he told Meany, walked into his office and said, "You want to see me, Mister?" MacPhail thought, "This guy can't be a ballplayer. He looks like the bottom man of an unemployed acrobatic team"—which, minus the unemployed, was what Yogi had been when playing "bumby" on the Hill when he was a kid.[37] But Berra did make an impression on MacPhail. "His last remark that afternoon convinced me that I was dealing with a professional ballplayer. We shook hands, and Berra said, 'Who do I see about my expenses for this trip?' "[38] Yogi wasn't trying to be a tough guy: "I just figured the Yankees had more money than I did."[39] Later, Yogi would recall that MacPhail was very nice to him. Stories would circulate about funny things MacPhail thought when he first laid eyes on his new prospect, but, said Yogi, "He didn't make any wisecracks to me."[40]

After his initial surprise, MacPhail quickly figured that there had to be more to Berra than what met the eye. He figured that if Mel Ott was willing to pay $50,000, then Berra was at least worth keeping around long enough to try him out at Newark, the Yankees' Triple-A franchise in the International League. MacPhail invited Yogi to stick around and see a Yankees game; he went to the stadium with John Schulte, the bullpen coach who had signed him. It was his first glimpse of the shrine of baseball—or at least that's the way it looked to Yogi with Monument Park at the end of the cavernous center field.*

Schulte took Yogi into the Yankees clubhouse, where Pete Sheehy, the clubhouse man, walked in and saw Schulte standing next to a strange fellow in a sailor suit. Who the hell is that? he asked Schulte. Yogi later admitted, "I never had much luck impressing the clubhouse boys."[41]

━━━━━

DURING THE FALL of 1945, the war over, Yogi, despite being worth $50,000 to another team, worked as a clubhouse boy for the Navy Raiders while waiting to be mustered out. During the football season, he washed the players' uniforms, shined their shoes, and packed equipment for when the team was on the road. The Raiders, like many service teams, had an excellent football squad, drawing from a wide talent pool of collegiate and

---

*During the Q&A session of the 2006 Watch the World Series with Yogi event, Berra said he didn't recall seeing Babe Ruth's plaque on his first visit to Yankee Stadium. In fact, he didn't; Ruth's wasn't added until 1948. In 1946, the only people honored were Miller Huggins, Jacob Ruppert, and Lou Gehrig.

pro players. Yogi liked the work and enjoyed being part of the team. The Raiders' biggest road game was played at Yankee Stadium against a black team from the Tuskegee Institute in Alabama. During the trip to New York, he met Pete Sheehy's assistant, "Little Pete" Previte. While stuffing towels in the players' lockers, Yogi told Previte that he was property of the New York Yankees, that he would be playing for Newark the next year, and that he'd be using one of the lockers himself in about two years. Little Pete looked at this funny-looking kid with the ridiculous nickname standing there with an armful of towels and thought he was nuts. Two years later, Little Pete was bringing Yogi clean towels along with boxes of baseballs to be signed for the fans. In time, requests for Berra's signature on a ball became overwhelming, and Previte had to learn to imitate Yogi's signature. "He can sign my name so good," Yogi would say, "the bank would take it on a check."[42]

On May 6, 1946, six days before his twenty-first birthday, Seaman First Class Lawrence Berra was honorably discharged from the U.S. Navy. He celebrated back on the Hill, expecting to hear from the Yankees any day about an assignment to Kansas City. The telegram from MacPhail's office arrived, but it wasn't for assignment to Kansas City; Yogi was told to report to the Bears clubhouse in Newark, New Jersey. He would be just a half step from the greatest organization in baseball and the fulfillment of a dream. But it was a half step many promising young players before had tried and failed to make. In the words of future teammate and American League president Dr. Bobby Brown, "It's only about twelve miles from Newark to Yankee Stadium. But it's the longest twelve miles in America." No one thought to notify the Newark team that Berra was due to arrive. He caught up to the Bears in Rochester at the same time that Walter Dubiel, a twenty-seven-year-old veteran of two seasons with the Yankees (1944–1945), during which he had posted a 23–22 record, got there. When the players came back to their hotel after beating the Red Wings, they found Dubiel, whom they were expecting, and Berra, whom they were not. Yogi, wrote a magazine journalist a few years later, "looked like a young fellow whom Dubiel might have hired to carry his luggage."[43]

———

THE POSTWAR NEWARK that Yogi saw was much more vital than the rust belt victim it would become. It was a city of neighborhoods of various ethnic enclaves—more like Brooklyn than Manhattan, many thought. Before it dispersed into suburban New Jersey, the Jewish community in the 1940s and 1950s, described by Philip Roth in *The Great American Novel* and *The Plot Against America*, was pious, hard working, and baseball mad—as were the Italian-American sections where Yogi could generally be found having dinner after games, in family restaurants not much different from those he had known in the Hill. He wasn't homesick, but he chafed at not being played right away. He wasn't going to get any experience sitting on the bench.

The current incarnation of the Newark Bears plays in the independent Atlantic League and is best known for providing holding patterns for major league veterans, often ex-Yankees, such as Jim Leyritz and Ruben Sierra, who are looking to make it back to the majors for a few more games. (They also got some national publicity when forty-four-year-old Rickey Henderson, just for the love of the game, DH'ed in 2003 and part of the 2004 season.) In 1946, the Bears were the launching pad for the Yankees' best young prospects. Berra caught up with the team in Rochester, New York, full of hope and enthusiasm, and immediately began letting the Bears know what he'd already made clear to Larry MacPhail—that whatever others thought of him, he had a clear sense of his own worth. The Bears manager was George "Twinkletoes" Selkirk, an outfielder for the Yankees from the glory years of 1934 through 1942 and the first outfield replacement, in fact, for Babe Ruth. Selkirk was still playing some outfield while he skippered Newark. He told the clubhouse boy to issue Berra a uniform. Yogi, who had not taken an at-bat at this level of professional ball, found the cap too small and was miffed to discover there was no number on the back of his shirt. He wasn't placated by the clubhouse boy's trick of splitting the seam in the back of the cap to make it "one size fits all." And this was not the right way to start out. He rolled the uniform into a ball and brought it back. I'm not trying out, he told them, I'm *playing* for this team.

Not right away, he wasn't. Selkirk had two catching prospects, Mike Garbark, who had caught some games with the Yankees during the war years, and Charlie Fallon, who were both much more experienced behind the plate than Berra, and Selkirk considered them both much more reliable than this clumsy-looking kid. The Yankees front office, though, had long-term concerns that outweighed Selkirk's desire to win at Newark. Bill Dickey, the backbone of the Yankees from 1929 until 1943, was, at age thirty-nine, coming to the end of a great career, limping through the 1946 season, in which he would bat just 134 times. Most of the playing time that year went to Aaron Robinson, who showed some power with 16 home runs in just 330 at-bats, but who had passed his thirty-first birthday in the middle of the season. MacPhail guessed that 1946 represented the peak of Robinson's ability, and his judgment would prove to be correct. (Robinson would catch fewer than 400 games during the remainder of his major league career with four teams.) The Yankees would soon need a replacement, and MacPhail wanted one who could hit; Dickey, in addition to being a great defensive catcher, had hit over .300 eleven times during his career and had driven in more than 80 runs seven times.

No catching prospect in the organization looked as if he could match those numbers except the unpolished Berra. So the word came down from the front office: start polishing him. Yogi quickly showed that all he needed was playing time. In 77 games, against pitching not a great deal tougher than what he would face in the majors, Berra hit an eye-catching .314 with 15 home runs and 59 RBIs, numbers that projected to around 30 home runs and 120 RBIs over a full season. Yogi's stats were all the more impressive considering that he was shuttled back and forth from the outfield (where he played 20 games) to catcher. Also, he had played through a fractured thumb and a bad ankle sprain. In the field, things were rougher. In a game against Rochester, he nailed a runner trying to steal second base—literally, hitting him smack on the left shoulder. What made the game legendary for Berra was a later throw to second base that hit the umpire. Bobby Brown, his roommate with the Bears, recalls the two throws as "amazing. I'd never seen either one of those things happen in a game, and here both of them happened just a couple of innings apart."

He was noticed, indeed. The second time the Bears played Montreal, the Royals' manager, Clay Hopper, caught on that Berra was a dead pull hitter and shifted his fielders to the right side of the diamond the way Cleveland manager Lou Boudreau positioned his men when Ted Williams was at bat. Hopper gave Berra a demonstration of the kind of smarts he'd be facing at the top level: Yogi went hitless the first time against the shift. In turn, Berra showed the opposition that he could think, too. By repositioning his feet in the batter's box a few inches and slowing down his swing, he was able to dump singles into left field that turned into doubles. He went five for seven in one stretch before Hopper, in frustration, ordered his defense to stop shifting. Yogi caught the attention of a general manager as well. Bucky Harris, who would be managing him less than a year later in the Bronx, was Buffalo's GM in 1946. "If I had a gun," Harris later told Joe Trimble, "I'd have shot the little pest a hundred times. Every game we played against Newark, he murdered us."[44]

The Bears didn't murder many opponents, though, and finished fourth, twenty games out of first place. But then, no one won much of anything in the International League except for Montreal, led by the league's batting champion, the sensational Jackie Robinson who, it was rumored, was being groomed to become the first black player in the major leagues. Berra knew that Robinson was a natural. "Anyone could see that he had the speed and the moves and a great batting eye. There wasn't any question in my mind that he was good enough to play [in the big leagues]. Some of us were just wondering *when* he was going to get a chance."[45]

Extra playoff games were an economic necessity for the minor leagues in the 1940s, and so the Bears season did not end until September 18, having been extended by the strange system which gave a fourth-place finisher like Newark a shot in the postseason. The final game is remembered today not for Robinson's performance but for Berra's—in fact, it featured perhaps the worst performance of Yogi's entire professional career. As the years rolled on and Yogi's collection of World Series rings grew, his admirers noted with awe how even-tempered he always seemed to stay in tight situations. As with all admirable traits, Yogi's calm and even cheerful demeanor under pressure reflected the strength of his character, but it was a strength that he had to cultivate. A crowd of 20,000, enormous for a minor league game, saw the Bears take a 4–3 lead into the ninth inning. Herb Karpel, who earlier in the year had lasted just 1⅔ innings with the Yankees in his only major league stint, was in for starter Duane Pillette. Karpel got Robinson and Lou Riggs and, pitching to Les Burge, was a strike away from ending the game. Karpel, on a 2–2 count, threw what looked like a perfect strike, and the Bears began to celebrate, but umpire Artie Gore saw it differently and called it a ball. On the next pitch, a frustrated Karpel gave up a home run to Burge to tie the game. The Bears on the bench got all over Gore but, as Yogi recalled, "It didn't do any good. It never does."[46]

Gore tossed Selkirk and several of his players. The exasperated Bears changed pitchers again. They gave up two more hits; on the second, a Bears outfielder fired the ball home in what looked to Yogi to be sufficient time to nab the runner. Gore again disagreed. Berra exploded and charged Gore, ramming into him. The entire infield ran in to restrain Yogi, who later admitted that if his teammates hadn't been there, he'd have struck the umpire. It's a good thing he didn't, because things turned out badly enough for him as it was. The league's president, Frank Shaughnessy, after interviewing Gore and Selkirk, fined Berra the staggering sum of $500. Obviously, few first-year minor league ballplayers were capable of paying such a fine—Yogi's roommate, Bobby Brown, who had signed for a

$30,000 bonus, must have been the only Bear who could. Weiss and MacPhail weren't terribly distressed; feistiness wasn't the worst thing a young ballplayer could be guilty of, and the Yankees covered the fine. But it was sobering for Yogi, knowing how close he had come to taking a swing at Gore and possibly getting himself thrown out of baseball before he had even had a chance to make the major leagues. As he had done and would continue to do throughout his career, he chalked up the incident as a lesson learned and resolved to not ever make the same mistake again. He would have many a beef with an umpire before his career was over, but he would be fined only one more time in his nineteen-year career, and that for relative pocket change. (The Bears lost the series to the Royals, four games to two.)

Listening to the radio on the train ride from Montreal, someone yelled "Shush!" when a sports item was announced. The Yankees, stumbling to a third-place finish in the American League, seventeen games behind the rival Red Sox, had decided to finish the year by giving a little seasoning to their best minor league prospects: Brown, Berra, pitcher Vic Raschi, and outfielder Frank Coleman were being called up to the parent team for the final week.

Unlike the other rookies, Yogi had been to Yankee Stadium, but that didn't diminish his feeling of awe at walking into the Yankee clubhouse again—this time, he was a Yankee. Years later, he would recall the moment for Bob Costas: "Imagine, me, a kid from the Hill in St. Louis, coming into the Yankee clubhouse with all those guys I'd been hearing about. It was the biggest thrill of my life." He remembered Joe DiMaggio's first words to him: "How ya' doin', kid?"[47] DiMaggio did not remember saying that to him. "Contrary to what I have seen written," he told writer Tom Horton in 1989, "I did not see him in the clubhouse . . . For some reason, I didn't meet Yogi that way." Yogi thought DiMaggio had greeted him warmly because they were both Italian; DiMaggio had no recollection of that, either. He did recall that "Larry Berra, and that's what we called him then, looked like a fire hydrant walking up to the plate. I really don't know what I thought . . . he looked like a showoff but he didn't have anything to show off . . . When I say showoff, I don't mean he swaggered like some of these guys do now . . . When I say showoff I mean he was swinging three bats. Most of us used two. He had all three going, and then he flipped two of them away and you had to watch."[48]

The new recruits arrived in time for a sparsely attended, late-season, Sunday afternoon doubleheader. Berra studied the contours of the ballpark, noting that the right-field porch was just 296 feet from home plate. He was ready to play. After, that is, some practical considerations. "When do we eat?" he asked Pete Sheehy. Fortified, he donned pinstripes for the first time. "I tried not to get too jazzed up. It was probably a token look-see, nothing to get too excited about. Nothing doing. My blood was tingling. How could any twenty-one-year-old kid not be excited about playing for the *New York Yankees*?"[49] Yogi got a break that day. His pitcher was the thirty-nine-year-old Spurgeon Ferdinand "Spud" Chandler, who was enjoying his best major league season. He went into the game against Connie Mack's Philadelphia A's with a record of 19–8 and an ERA of slightly over two runs per game. Yogi remembers that his greeting for Yogi was almost the same as DiMaggio's: "Hello, kid." Spud's advice to Berra was to just relax and call the pitches. If Spud didn't like the call, he'd shake it off until he got what thing he liked.

In the second inning, Yogi strolled up to the plate at Yankee Stadium for the first time, wearing the number 47 on his broad back, not the immortal number 8 Yankee fans would later come to know. The pitcher was Jesse Flores, and the A's catcher, Buddy Rosar, a former Yankee, welcomed him with "This ain't Newark!" Rosar had heard about Berra, as had most of the fans in attendance, who were there at this point in the season just to catch a preview of what might be in store for their team in 1947. "I hear there's a big league team in Philadelphia," Yogi replied amiably. As if to belie his reputation as a hitter who swung at everything, Yogi took his first big league pitch, a fastball in the corner, for a called strike. Flores then greeted Yogi with his first major league curveball. The pitch was outside. For the first time, Yankee fans and players saw Lawrence Berra extend his powerful wrists and whip the bat into a baseball. There was a resounding crack, and the ball soared deep into the right field seats, well beyond the 296-foot mark. The Yankees went on to win, 4–3. Joe DiMaggio had a vivid recollection of the home run: "I will never forget this, he hit a pitch, a ball so far out of the strike zone I would never swing the bat* . . . Not only was it a ball, I really don't think I could have hit it. I mean hit it, not out of the park like he did, I mean that I couldn't have put my bat on the ball."[50] Someone else remembered the moment as well. In the center-field bleachers, a seventeen-year-old pitcher named Ed Ford, who had just signed with the Yankees, watched the ball fly into the right-field seats and wondered if some day this squat fellow would hit home runs like that on his behalf.

---

*Meaning if DiMaggio had been a left-handed hitter.

So Yogi Berra hit a home run in his first major league at-bat . . . or so the legend goes, or at least as reflected in Gene Schoor's 1976 *The Story of Yogi Berra*, written for young adults. Actually, Yogi did hit a home run in his first major league game, but not in his first major league at-bat. Over the years, as Yogi stories were told and retold, the reality became simplified for easier recall, even by Yogi. Forty-three years later, in the biographical video *Déjà vu All Over Again*, Bob Costas asked Berra, "Did hitting a home run your first major league at-bat make you think it was going to be easy?" "No!" Yogi replied emphatically.[51]

By that time, Yogi must have forgotten that it didn't actually happen his first time up, but the second time he came to bat (which is logical, as it was in the fourth inning). The next day, September 23, in the *New York Daily News*, Jim McCulley gave this report:

> Stoically situated and going no place else this wandering season, the Yanks tried out a couple of recruits from Newark against the Athletics in the first game of a Stadium-doubleheader yesterday, and both rookies performed with acumen to hand Spud Chandler his 20th victory, 4–3 . . .
>
> About 20,000 fans were present to watch shortstop Bobby Brown and catcher Larry (Yogi) Berra break into the major leagues in Yankee livery.
>
> Berra, a 21-year-old ex-sailor who resembles Charlie Keller in stature and at bat, collected two hits in four trips. The second time up, in the fourth, he hit a home run with Keller on base which served up the victory for Chandler . . .
>
> Berra's rap smashed into the lower bleachers in right and was hit off Flores.[52]

As Berra circled the bases during his home run trot, Mel Allen, the Voice of the New York Yankees, announced in his sonorous Alabama drawl, "That's Larry Berra, they call him Yogi!" And then his signature, "How 'bout that!"

———

AFTER THE GAME, Paul Krichell introduced Berra to another Yankees prospect who had signed with the team that day. "Larry," said Krichell, "I want you to meet Eddie Ford. Eddie, this is Larry Berra."[53] It was the first and last time that the most famous batterymates in baseball history would know each other as "Larry" and "Eddie."

IN HIS SECOND game, Yogi hit his second major league home run. On his way home, while waiting for a train to Boston at the 125th Street station, he noticed that Joe DiMaggio was eyeing him quizzically— DiMaggio, the first great Italian-American national celebrity, the greatest player in the game. Finally, Joe smiled and Yogi grinned back at him. "So what?" he told the Yankee Clipper. "I can hit homers, too."[54]

On the next Tuesday, with four games left in the season, Yogi played his first game in Fenway Park. Over the next few decades he would experience more memorable baseball moments in Fenway than any park besides Yankee Stadium. The experience did not stir him. "When I first saw it," he said in 2005 at the Yogi Berra Museum, "there wasn't any Green Monster, The wall wasn't even green—it was covered with ads." The Green Monster wasn't green until the following season, which was also when lights were installed. (The Red Sox were the third-to-last major league team to play home night games.)

In the first inning, Ted Williams, by consensus the greatest hitter in the game, walked to the plate, where a squat, smiling catcher looked up at him and said, "How ya' doin'?" Williams couldn't believe his near-perfect eyes. "It was in 1946, and I was at home plate waiting for another pitcher to come in . . . Well, I looked at him—hadn't heard of him before. The shin guards were four inches too tall for him, and the chest protector is way down, too long for him. And all I could think of was 'Who are they trying to fool with this guy?' "[55] Like Humphrey Bogart and Claude Rains in one of Yogi's favorite movies, *Casablanca*, it was the start of a beautiful friendship.

Within a couple of weeks, the folks on the Hill would be celebrating the World Series debut of one of their favorite sons, a local boy who, in four years, had gone from Stockham Post American Legion ball to the biggest sporting event in America. The local boy was not Larry Berra, but Joe Garagiola, whose Cardinals had won the National League pennant. *How 'bout that!*

Chapter Three

A Silly Hitter
(1947)

He will be the most popular player on the Yankees since
Babe Ruth . . . People are going to love this little guy.

—BUCKY HARRIS

YOGI HAD NO way of knowing it, but his legend had already begun. His roommate, Bobby Brown, delighted in telling teammates and reporters that Yogi was an avid reader of comic books. Brown, who was using baseball to pay his tuition to medical school, carried his medical books with him on road trips. Late one night, tired from the traveling and studying *Boyd's Pathology of Internal Medicine*, he told Berra to turn off the light. In a minute, Yogi told him, he wasn't finished with his comic. A moment later, he said, "Gee, that was a good one. How'd yours come out?" The story has been repeated so many times over the years that it almost seems as if it has to be apocryphal. But more than forty years later, Brown still insists that it's true, and, moreover, "I didn't tell it to make fun of Yogi. I just thought it was a good story. I thought from the start that Yogi was bright and fun to be around. And let me say something else: I read his book later, and it was a lot better than mine."

Like Molière's bourgeois gentleman who had been speaking prose his whole life and didn't know it, Yogi Berra, it seems, had been making unintentional Yogiisms without knowing it. Now there were people out there ready to record them for posterity, and soon the world would know them.

THE 1947 NEW York Yankees were a team poised precariously between the two greatest dynasties professional baseball has ever seen. From 1936 through 1943, the Yankees won seven American League pennants and six World Series. In fact, from 1936 to 1939, they won the World Series every year. None of the pennant races were close; to even call them races at all is misleading. Over those four seasons, the Yankees, even besting their Murderers' Row teammates of the previous decade, won the American League by 19½ games, 13 games, 9½ games, and 27 games, respectively. In the Series, they won 16 of 19 games from the National League, including 11 in a row—from the last three games of 1937 against the New York Giants through the four games in 1939 against the Cincinnati Reds.

New York's talent during those years proved overwhelming. In all four seasons, the Yankees led the American League in runs scored and fewest runs allowed, which pretty much says it all. They had the game's best all-around player in Joe DiMaggio and the league's—many said the game's— best catcher in Bill Dickey, and from 1936 to 1939 they had Lou Gehrig, still adding to his record of consecutive games played. The pitching staff was rock solid, featuring the outstanding righty-lefty tandem of Red Ruffing and Lefty Gomez—a combined 146–69, for a winning percentage of .679 over those four years. In 1940 the Yankees slipped to third place, but rebounded to take it all in 1941. The 1942 team actually won two more games than the 1941 edition, but somehow contrived to lose four out of five games in the World Series to the St. Louis Cardinals, it was an aberration, everyone believed, that would be corrected after the war when all the great talent returned. But when the talent returned in 1946, the Yankees finished a shocking third, wearing out three managers in the process. In retrospect, 1946 seems like a minor dip on a near unbroken record of success that would continue for many more years, but at the time, their 1946 record sent some serious warning signals throughout the Yankees system.

———

YOGI STARTED HIS off-season watching Joe Garagiola play baseball. The Cardinals had finished in a dead heat with the Brooklyn Dodgers and played a best-of-three playoff for the National League pennant, which the Cardinals won in two. Yogi and his brothers saw the seventh and final game of the World Series against the Red Sox at Sportsman's Park. In the eighth inning, the Berras and thousands of others gasped as Ted Williams slashed a foul ball that split a finger on Joey's throwing hand. He was replaced by Del Rice. Yogi picked a good game to see; this was the one where Enos Slaughter won the Series for the Cardinals with his electrifying dash from first to home on Harry Walker's line drive single to left center. Slaughter saw that Boston shortstop Johnny Pesky held on to the relay throw too long and ran right through third base coach Mike Gonzales's stop signal.* Yogi wasn't just enjoying himself, he also learned something—the way Slaughter took advantage of what seemed like a minor gaffe turned out to be the winning play in the Series. "It was a good lesson in winning baseball."[1]

Garagiola hadn't hit much that season, a dismal .237 with three home runs in seventy games, exactly as many as Yogi had hit in seven games with the Yankees. In the World Series, though, Joe out-hit the two best hitters in the game with a .314 average compared to .259 for Ted Williams and .222 for Joe's teammate, Stan Musial. All through the Series, said Yogi, "everybody on Elizabeth Avenue was drinking more Dago Red than usual."[2]

The prides of Elizabeth Avenue soon found work for the off-season in the hardware section of the Sears, Roebuck and Co. store in downtown St. Louis, something unimaginable for young stars today. Yogi had to admit, "We didn't take it very seriously. It was just a way to make a few dollars so we wouldn't have to dip into the bank account for spending money."[3] Yogi, says Joe, "wasn't much of an expert on hardware. One guy came up to our counter and asked for a specific kind of screw. Yogi went blank. He pointed to the various jars with all the screws and said, 'I can't tell one from another. I think you'd better pick them out yourself.' I burst out laughing, but I don't guess the customer found it funny."

————

LARRY MACPHAIL HAD worked for the Cincinnati Reds and Brooklyn Dodgers before joining the Yankees. A heavy drinker and workaholic, he was the poor man in a high-powered triumvirate—the others were Dan Topping and Del Webb—that purchased the Yankees from the heirs of beer magnate Colonel Jacob Ruppert in 1945. Abrasive often to the point of rudeness, MacPhail never hesitated to push new ideas that he thought might create new revenue streams. At the end of the 1933 season, the Cincinnati Reds were in receivership, having sold less than 2,900 tickets a game. MacPhail was hired as general manager to jolt the Reds' dwindling financial base back to life, and proceeded to do so with startling swiftness, bringing night baseball to the major leagues and putting the Reds games

*Or perhaps, as Glenn Stout and Richard A. Johnson contend in *Red Sox Century*, Pesky "did not pause or freeze with the ball," he "simply made an average play in a situation that was already lost." Two different films of the play, insist Stout and Johnson, show no clear hesitation on Pesky's part.

on radio. (Several owners were still suspicious of radio in the early 1930s, suspecting that it would hurt ticket sales by giving the games away for free—the same argument many of them would make two decades later about television.) He had fits of near craziness but often righted himself in time to make even his worst moments work to his advantage. While with the St. Louis Cardinals minor league team in Columbus, just before moving to Cincinnati, he phoned a furniture store about the delay of a delivery to his office; refusing the secretary's explanation, he went into a rage, insulted her, and hung up. The woman was taking no guff. She phoned him back and told him precisely where to get off. Instead of prolonging the shouting match, MacPhail took a cab to the store, calmed her down—though it is not recorded that he apologized—and hired her as his personal secretary. She would work for him at Cincinnati and later at Brooklyn.

Dan Topping owned a company that manufactured tin plating. His grandfather had been president of Republic Steel. He was well known in New York sporting circles and was majority owner of two professional football teams—though in the 1940s even two pro football teams didn't begin to approach the prestige of being part owner of one big major league baseball team.

Del Webb's outside interests were equally intriguing. As a building contractor whose chief investments were in and around Phoenix, Arizona, he made a fortune developing a series of shopping centers that catered to the new suburban lifestyle, and motor hotels to accommodate a rapidly mobile population. (He was also farsighted enough to build subdivisions, replete with golf courses, near his shopping centers.) Webb also had some of the shadiest business connections of any man in major league baseball, acting as the contractor for Benjamin "Bugsy" Siegel's Flamingo Hotel on the strip in the burgeoning town of Las Vegas.*

Webb and Topping had the money, MacPhail was the baseball man. They purchased the Yankees—and nearly as important, its minor league affiliates—in 1945 from the Ruppert family for $2.8 million, roughly half of what Alex Rodriguez makes in a month today. The two businessmen allowed MacPhail to buy nearly 10 percent of the Yankees, loaning him

---

*Webb did an excellent job of keeping his relationship with Siegel out of the press. The two were closer than Webb's Yankees partners knew. A few years ago, while visiting the border town of Bisbee, Arizona, I struck up a conversation with the proprietor of the legendary Copper Queen Hotel, who showed me an old guest book which contained the signatures of both Del Webb and Bugsy Siegel, who had checked in the same day in 1945, less than three hours apart.

more than $900,000 to enable him to make the purchase. He was named president of the team. For the next two seasons, MacPhail managed his and their interests very well, so much so that after two years he was able to sell back his stock to his partners for a sizable profit. While MacPhail was in the Yankees front office, things were lively. Pressured to show a profit so he could pay back his partners, MacPhail wasted little time in doing for the Yankees what he had done for the Cincinnati Reds. In 1946, he ordered the installation of the most sophisticated and expensive lighting system in the major leagues, a move that helped the Yankees set a new franchise attendance record of over two million. (The average per-game attendance of 29,400 nearly doubled the previous Yankee Stadium high of 15,300.)

The end of World War II allowed a wide field for MacPhail's genius. Using connections in the War and State departments to take advantage of relaxed restrictions on travel, he took the team on a swing through the Caribbean and Latin America, including a series of exhibition games in San Juan, Puerto Rico; Caracas, Venezuela; Havana, Cuba; and Panama. He saved money by bunking the players at Army bases. Some of the older players grumbled about the toll the tour took on them, darkly hinting to selected beat writers that it might have been the reason for the team's mid-season sag. DiMaggio was among the loudest complainers. MacPhail wanted him in Puerto Rico even though Joe's foot was still in a cast from his heel operation. Though DiMaggio said little publicly, there was no shortage of pals in the sportswriting crew for Joe to air his gripes to. MacPhail ignored DiMaggio's discontent—the Yankees' Latin tour had practically been a license to print money, and in 1947 the trip would be longer and cover even more territory.

Yogi, though, was no tired veteran, and was anxious to play anywhere: "To me it was fun. It was baseball."[4] For a twenty-one-year-old kid who had scarcely left his neighborhood in St. Louis until three years earlier, Yogi had now seen much of the eastern seaboard and some of France, Italy, and North Africa; he would now be on a whirlwind tour through the hotbeds of Latin baseball. He was having a ball. Nothing fazed him, not even in Caracas when a Venezuelan policeman, reacting to political unrest, grabbed Yogi on the way into the ballpark and began frisking him for a gun. Yogi assumed the man was a fan who was glad to see him and hugged the bewildered officer right back.

Bucky Harris, the Yankees' fourth manager in two years, was having a ball, too. Joe McCarthy (who had managed the team since 1931 and won a team record 1,460 games) had stepped down rather than take the heat when the team floundered early in 1946. Or at least that's the way it was reported; in fact, the Yankees were 22–13 at that point and not playing all that poorly. But McCarthy did not get along with the Yankees' new owners and sensed a growing discipline problem, exacerbated by a clash with Joe Page, whom he threatened to send down to Newark if he didn't shape up. "You want to send me to Newark, send me to Newark," Page answered. McCarthy quit shortly afterward. The Yankees cited his recurring gallbladder problems, but it couldn't have hurt that much, as less than two years later he was back in baseball, managing the Red Sox. (The persistent rumors, though they never saw print, were that McCarthy was battling the bottle.)

McCarthy's resignation was a shock to the team and the fans. His seven World Series titles were the most of any manager up to that time and has been equalled only by Casey Stengel. Bill Dickey, McCarthy's replacement, found that he was temperamentally unsuited for the position, and no one was particularly excited about the prospect of Johnny Neun, who was at the helm for just fourteen games.

Bucky Harris had not managed since 1943, when his Phillies won just 38 of 90 games and finished a dismal seventh of eight teams in the National League. From 1935 to 1942 he had been at Washington, where the Senators finished above .500 only once, 1936, when they won 87 and lost just 71. MacPhail hired him after the 1946 season with the understanding that he would be managing the team the following season. Bucky was happy to be a Yankee, and so was his new outfielder-catcher. But despite the number of proven players on the roster, Harris knew he didn't inherit a guaranteed champion. Among the veterans there were several serious concerns. Tommy Henrich, nicknamed "Old Reliable" because of his reputation for clutch hitting, was thirty-seven and had hit only .251 with 19 home runs in 1946. The pitching looked promising, but Red Ruffing, long-time ace of the staff, was now gone, and Spud Chandler, who had gone 20–8 the previous campaign, was thirty-nine and didn't look to match that record again. (He would finish 9–5 in 1947.) Randall Pennington "Randy" Gumpert had been a huge surprise in 1946, starting in 12 games, relieving in 21 others, and posting an 11–3 record with a dazzling 2.30 ERA. But Gumpert hadn't pitched at all in the majors from 1938 until 1946, and he seemed an unlikely candidate to repeat. (He would appear in just 24 games in 1947 and finish the year with an ERA of 5.46.)

One of Harris's biggest concerns was his shortstop, Phil Rizzuto, a terrific fielder and base runner. But he had hit .257 with two home runs the year before, and at age thirty he didn't figure to be getting better. Indeed, in 1947 Phil Rizzuto looked like a man whose opportunity for greatness had passed him by. Born in Brooklyn in 1917, Rizzuto, at 5'6" and around 160, was one of the smallest players in the major leagues. In his rookie year, 1941, he hit .307, stole 14 bases, led the American League in double plays, and had the best range of any shortstop in the circuit. He was just as good in 1942, with a .284 average, 22 stolen bases, more double plays, and an even better range. When he returned from the military in 1946, he had to feel his way back into the lineup. He liked Bucky Harris. "You could trust him and he had an ego, but he was not full of himself," Rizzuto wrote in his 1994 account of his glory years with the Yankees, *The October Twelve*.[5] The remark was probably intended as a shot at Casey, who had passed him over at a tryout for the Brooklyn Dodgers. Nearly sixty years later, Casey's snub still hurt: "It's not that I was rejected—rejection is part of living—it was that I was made to feel like a fool for showing up." As it turned out, "Scooter," as he came to be called for his ability to glide into the hole to his right or left and scoop up ground balls, was lucky. Like his soon-to-be best friend on the Yankees, Yogi Berra, if Phil had gone to the Dodgers, he would have had to compete for his position with another future Hall of Famer—in Rizzuto's case, Pee Wee Reese. In any event, Rizzuto was a Joe McCarthy man, "the best manager I ever saw,"[6] and he never hesitated to let anyone know it.

When Rizzuto was finally, with Yogi's support, inducted into the Hall of Fame in 1994, some writers objected that his career statistics weren't impressive enough to merit Cooperstown. Perhaps not, but it should be noted that Rizzuto gave up three of his best years of his career to the U.S. Navy. Ted Williams, among others, recognized the value of the diminutive Yankee shortstop: "A lot of people said that Rizzuto was too small, but, damn, those two guys [Rizzuto and Berra] knew how to beat you. Makes me sick to think about it."[7]

The 1947 Yankees had strengths, of course, such as slugging outfielder Charlie "King Kong" (named for his enormous biceps) Keller, who had hit 19 home runs in 1946, but no one thought that Keller could carry the team. The biggest star on the team was also the biggest question mark. In 1947 Joe DiMaggio wasn't merely the most famous ballplayer in America, he was already anointed as a legend for his 56-game hitting streak in 1941 and for being the keystone of the only team to have won four straight World Series. But DiMaggio had had his weakest season in 1946, hitting just .290 (35 points below what would be his career average) with only 25 home runs. He had had an operation to remove a bone spur in his left heel over the winter, and it had not healed properly; the decision to have a second operation meant that he would miss the season opener, and no one knew how much more. Simply put, the Yankees were a dynasty teetering on the brink. On the bright side, there was a powerful right-hander named Allie Reynolds, who, although inconsistent, had shown flashes of brilliance at Cleveland, and a smart-looking right-hander, Vic Raschi, who, at twenty-eight, was a bit old to be looking at his first full major league season, but looked ready to win when he took the mound. And, there was Lawrence Peter Berra.

But where was Berra to play? In 1947, the Yankees had other viable catchers. In fact, Aaron Robinson was more than capable. One of the few bright spots on the 1946 team, he hit .297 with an on-base average of .388, and hit thirteen home runs in just 100 games. The trouble was that in the spring of 1947, Robinson was close to his thirty-second birthday, and the Yankees couldn't see much of a future for him. Sherm Lollar had just been acquired from the Cleveland Indians and would prove to be a fine big league catcher, a seven-time All-Star, and a three-time Gold Glove winner. But Lollar had nothing like the pop in his bat that Yogi had. Either of those two might do, but the Yankees did not look for players who could do—they looked for players who could do *more*.

When Yogi arrived in St. Petersburg at Miller Huggins Field—named for the diminutive Yankee manager who won three World Series between 1918 and 1929—he was as surprised as other rookies at his first sight of the facility. The Yankees were first class in their traveling arrangements and hotels, but most of the players had seen better clubhouses in the minor leagues. Compared to Yankee Stadium, with its spacious lockers, carpeting, training room, and players lounge, the clubhouse at Huggins Field looked like something in a down-and-out high school. The lockers didn't even have hooks for clothes, just nails, and there was scarcely enough room for the more than four dozen players crowding into it. Perhaps the point was to create a Spartan atmosphere; if so, many rookies missed the subtlety of the point. Whitey Ford didn't hedge: "The clubhouses in Norfolk and Binghamton were better. This clubhouse was a piece of shit."[8]

Those who were there in the spring of 1947 say the consensus was that Yogi would probably play the outfield while learning to catch. Phil Rizzuto remembered the coaches saying things like "We'll stick him in the outfield—if he can play it." In any event, this is pretty much what the Yankees did, but there were two problems with this plan. The first was that Berra wasn't going to learn how to catch while playing in the outfield; second, Berra wasn't much of an outfielder. In truth, his problem in the outfield was the same as his problem behind the plate: inexperience. At that point he had played fewer than 190 minor league games and just a handful of major league games. "He wasn't slow," recalled Mel Allen, "I mean, he wasn't fast, but he had better than average speed. He could run as well as most of the Yankee outfielders in spring training. He hesitated too much when a ball was hit—he didn't get a good break on it. But he could hang on to just about anything he could reach, and he had a good arm." The numbers agree with Allen's observation: in 74 games in the outfield in 1947 and 1948, Berra made just three errors and his .980 fielding percentage was a shade above the league average. But he got to fewer balls than other American League corner fielders.

Bucky Harris's plan was to move Henrich from right field to center until DiMaggio had recovered from his operation, alternating Berra in right with right-handed hitting Johnny Lindell, a converted pitcher and an off-season cop in California. Harris hedged his bets by finding Yogi a veteran instructor: Joe "Ducky" Medwick, the man he had sold papers to back in St. Louis little more than a decade before, was on hand to school Berra in the use of an outfielder's finger mitt and in the art of breaking properly toward line drives that were sliced away from him. Berra was thrilled to see his hero again. "He said he didn't remember me," Berra said in answer to a questioner at his annual Watch the World Series with Yogi event, "but he was glad to see me again, anyway." So was Bucky Harris, who could now get down to the job of molding Berra into the superstar he thought he could be. And Frank J. O'Shea was happy to see Yogi, too.

"Spec" Shea—he dropped the O' while playing in the bigs and got his nickname from the freckles, or "speckles," with which he was covered— was an amiable Irishman from Connecticut who was as happy as Yogi to be getting his shot with the Yankees. For a couple of years, they were nearly inseparable, both as roommates and off the field. Later, he would drive over to New Jersey with Yogi to pick out the Berras' first house. Shea liked the house and advised Yogi to buy it; Yogi, at first, wasn't so sure. "It's a big house," he told his teammates. "All it's got in it is rooms."[9] During games, Shea had an aggressive wise guy persona that kept Yogi loose. Shea's favorite target was the Yankees' greatest enemy, Ted Williams. Once, with Shea needling him from the dugout, Williams stepped out of the batter's box to ask, "Who's that popping off over there? Is that Shea?" "Yeah, that's him," replied Yogi. "Tell him to get out on the mound," Williams growled.[10]

Shea was fond of saying that he brought Yogi luck. Once, at the St. Petersburg dog track, they were down on their luck and went bust. Grantland Rice, then regarded as the dean of American sportswriters, recognized Yogi, took pity on him, and gave him a quiniela ticket, one in which the bettor picks any two dogs to finish first and second or second and first. Their picks won, and Yogi and Spec went back to the hotel feeling rich, splitting $114. In turn, Shea admitted that Berra brought him some luck, too: "Yogi reminds me of World Series."[11]

Bucky Harris was happy for the distraction that Yogi's presence brought to a troubled training camp. Instead of focusing on age and injuries, the baseball press quickly zeroed in on Larry Berra—his prodigious home runs, his nickname, his demeanor, his bon mots, and not necessarily in that order. In what seemed like no time at all, Berra became the most written about in sports since another rural, visual stylist, Jay Hanna "Dizzy" Dean. Harris played up Yogi to the press.

"Don't think he's a dope," Bucky told writers at a press conference. "Try to remember that he hasn't had much schooling and is at a disadvantage in conversation. Just don't sell him short when he's up there at the plate. He's going to kill a few people with that bat, and they won't think he's funny at all. I'll make a prediction about Yogi. I say within a few years he will be the most popular player on the Yankees since Babe Ruth. I know that Henrich and Rizzuto and DiMaggio have a lot of fans who admire them. They are great ball players. But I mean more than that. People are going to love this little guy because he's such a character. They're going to feel sorry for him when he makes a mistake and go wild when he does the right thing to win a ball game. He's funny to look at and sometimes he makes ridiculous plays. But he's got personality and color. That's crowd appeal, and it makes people pay their way into the ball park."[12] Harris's remarks were picked up by newspapers not just in the Northeast but all over the country; even before the 1947 season began, fans were wondering who this character named Yogi really was.

As Harris predicted, Berra's good nature and popularity helped protect him when he goofed—and there were plenty of goofs in those first couple of seasons. The down side was that practically before he took his first at-bat in the 1947 season, Yogi Berra had become a caricature. The caricature was more real to the public than the man, and caricatures don't have feelings.

Even among the many who liked and admired Yogi, the attitude was often grossly condescending. Harris, for instance, wasn't shy about referring to his star prospect as "The Ape." "Did you see The Ape hit that ball today?" he beamed after a practice in Puerto Rico. With DiMaggio out, the writer wanted to know, might Berra be the Yankees new cleanup hitter? "Do you think The Ape could do it?" Harris responded.[13] Harris set the tone for the press, and before long the press was gleefully reprinting every story and joke about Berra's looks: that he was the only catcher in the league who got better looking when he put on the catcher's mask, that he was the captain of the "All-America Ugly Team" (this by way of Boston Red Sox pitcher Mike Ryba, who, in Yogi's words, "would never win any beauty contest himself"),[14] and that opponents were tossing bananas at him. Teammates, too, joined in. Yankees outfielder Charlie Keller had a picture taken with Yogi. Keller said he was going to send it to his wife—any time she thought her husband wasn't so good looking, Keller said, she should take a look at Yogi.

Even the umpires got into the act. The first time Berra came to bat with Bill Summers behind the plate, he was greeted with, "Welcome to the club." "What club?" asked Berra. "The all-ugly club," replied Summers. Berra told Summers that he must be the president, "and we both had a laugh."[15] Laughing off the taunts and crude jokes was Yogi's way of dealing with them; among the smarter people who covered the Yankees, it won him some friends. "Yogi is one of nature's noblemen," sports columnist Arthur Daley wrote in *The New York Times*, "An honest heart beats beneath that rough exterior. No ballplayer is ridden as cruelly or unmercifully as he. But he accepts it all with a *homely grin* [emphasis added]. He hasn't the quick wit to retort in kind, so he laughs it all off."[16] Daley was wrong about the wit; when rubbed the wrong way, Yogi was fully capable of a sharp retort. When someone crossed the line with a joke about his looks, Yogi got off one of his all-time best lines: "I never saw anyone hit the ball with their face."

Scribes were learning that they could not, at least not publicly, make fun of the black ballplayers, but for an Italian kid from Dago Hill, it was open season. More than half a century later, Larry Doby, the first black player in the American League and later Yogi's friend and neighbor in Montclair, New Jersey, reflected on the abuse Yogi took. "The stuff people said about him was really nasty. They always seemed to think it was funny, which made it even nastier, I guess, because that made it all right to say it, and I have to be honest with you, I repeated a few of those jokes myself. And it never once occurred to me in those early years that I was hurting Yogi's feelings. The black guys around the league, there weren't many of us, but when we would get together and talk, we knew we were all going through something *together*. That made the abuse a little easier to take. Now that I'm older, I wonder who helped Yogi take all that abuse."[17]

Who did help Yogi? There was, at least, some camaraderie on the Yankees, particularly among the Italian-Americans who formed the core of baseball's all-time greatest dynasty. The 1947 Yankees roster featured future Hall of Famers DiMaggio and Rizzuto, as well as Rizzuto's backup, veteran Frank Crosetti, playing out the last two years of his career (batting only once that year) and preparing for a twenty-year stint as the Yankees' third-base coach, and, as the season progressed, pitcher Vic Raschi and utility infielder Johnny Lucadello. All of them had experienced to some degree the casual bigotry aimed at Italian-Americans, shrugged it off, and come back as champions. Casey Stengel thought the Italians to be "the second best at hitters" among the team's various ethnic groups.*

For the most part, though, it was Yogi against the world—or rather, Yogi disarming the world by laughing along with everyone else, no matter how cutting the jokes. Did the quips and taunts get to him? Hank Bauer, who joined the Yankees late in the 1948 season, felt that it was an insult to Berra to assume he wasn't affected by all the jokes and stories. "Do you think he was stupid?" said Bauer. "Of course he heard what everyone was saying. Of course people hurt his feelings. He fought back the smartest way he knew how, by going along with the jokes, rolling with the punches." Yogi may have rolled with the punches, but that didn't mean he forgot them. That some of the remarks stung is evidenced by his still remembering many of them years later. When he co-wrote his autobiography with Ed Fitzgerald in 1961, Yogi devoted several pages to recounting the nastiest quips. And thirty-eight years after that book, in a volume of memoirs written with Tom Horton, he asked rhetorically, "How come when I was really being hurt in the press, nobody asked me if it did?" The jibes did hurt, he admitted. "But I think it made me work that much harder."[18]

The remark that really stung Berra's pride, though, was made by Rudd Rennie of the *New York Herald Tribune*. "You're not really thinking of

---

*The first, at least when Casey was writing his memoirs in 1960, were "the colored players." Casey, who had experienced every wave of ethnic immigration into the game that was to be seen in the twentieth century, wrote, "Now when I broke into baseball and years ago, we used to have Irish and German and Polish players. And then the greatest players came from the South. Then they came from Texas, and then they came from Chicago . . . The Germans are passing out, the race has gotten mixed up so much, and it's the same with the Irish. They don't talk and act like the ones did that had just come from Ireland." (Stengel and Paxton, *Casey at the Bat*, pp. 104, 114)

keeping him, are you?" Rennie asked MacPhail. "He doesn't even look like a Yankee." When he heard about the remark, Yogi appeared to shrug it off: if he was good enough to be playing for the New York Yankees, he couldn't be a bad ballplayer.

What wasn't readily apparent to those seeing Berra for the first time was that he *was* a good ballplayer. Yes, he could play the outfield and catch, but in 1947 he wasn't playing either with much grace or distinction. The redeeming part of Yogi's game was supposed to be his hitting, but those who watched him in the batting cage and at exhibition games often found themselves unable to believe their eyes. The trademark of Yankee hitters was discipline, but it seemed as if Berra would swing at anything. He regularly got good wood on pitches that were or appeared to be above eye level, and even pulled pitches that were wide of the strike zone. Steve O'Neill, the Detroit Tigers manager, summed it up for reporters in front of the batting cage. "That fellow," said O'Neill, shaking his head, "is a silly hitter."[19] Leo Durocher, one of Yogi's heroes when he was a member of the St. Louis Cardinals' Gashouse Gang and not a stranger to comical antics and retorts himself, saw Berra firsthand in a couple of exhibition games in the spring of 1948. His reaction was similar to O'Neill's. "He can hit," said Leo in a remark that was widely quoted, "what he can reach. But big league curve balls will kill him."* That was considered the ultimate insult for a young player: he can't hit a curve ball.

O'Neill, Durocher, and other critics were missing the point. As Hank Bauer put it, "All those people talking about Yogi's strike zone should have paid less attention to where the ball was thrown and more attention to where it landed." Bobby Brown was quoted as saying, "Yogi has the biggest strike zone in the U.S. It goes from his ankles to his nose, from his breastbone to as far as he can reach."[20] (Only a doctor would use a word like "breastbone" when evaluating a baseball player's skills.) But, says Brown, "I never meant 'strike zone' in the sense that the umpire would call a strike in all that area. What I meant was that Yogi was able to swing effectively at any ball thrown in that zone." Brown is right. Berra's short powerful legs were a solid anchor, and his long arms enabled him to reach pitches which most batters couldn't get to; his wrists were so strong he could whiplash pitches that were low or outside, pitches that would be, at best, fouled balls

*To his credit, when Durocher realized he was wrong, he didn't hedge about admitting it. "I'll be darned. I don't know how he does it, but he does it. How do you pitch to a guy like that?" he told a *Life* magazine writer in the July 11, 1949, issue.

for most hitters. In addition, Yogi had phenomenal hand-eye coordination. Berra was one of the hardest of his or any other era to strike out. Though he was called a free swinger for all of his major league career, he never struck out more than 38 times in a season. For his career, he would strike out just 414 times. Phil Rizzuto, a classic slap hitter, was judged by many to be the most difficult hitter to fan in the late 1940s and early 1950s. Rizzuto struck out just 398 times, 16 fewer than Yogi, in 1,661 games; Berra played in 2,120 games. Rizzuto had only 38 home runs in his major league career; Yogi finished with 358. Consider Berra's batting eye from another perspective: in his first five seasons, Mickey Mantle struck out 479 times, 65 more than Yogi in his entire career.

There was one other very important point about Berra's unique batting style, and if sportswriters and opposing managers and players didn't know it, opposing pitchers soon would: there was no "book" on how to pitch to this guy, no way in a tight spot to waste a pitch by throwing it a little high or a little low or a few inches to the outside. The only safe pitch to throw him when ahead on the count was one in the dirt in front of the plate or over the catcher's head, neither of which a pitcher could do with runners on base.

In 1947, though, even the Yankee coaches hadn't caught on to the effectiveness of Berra's unorthodox batting style. Third base coach Charlie Dressen played straight man to one of Yogi's most famous punch lines. Trying to school Yogi in working the count, Dressen would tell him over and over, "Don't let them sucker you into swinging at the bad ones. Make them get that good one over the plate. You've got to think when you're up there. Think!"[21] To which, after taking three called strikes, Berra is supposed to have replied, "You can't hit and think at the same time"; or, "How do you expect me to hit and think at the same time?" Yogi does admit to saying some variant of the above, but as he told me in 2005, "All I meant was that you can't stand up at the plate trying to think while the ball is comin' at you. There isn't time. You do your thinkin' *before* the ball gets there."

Part of Yogi's mystique would always be that he just walked up to the plate, saw the ball, and swung. As Casey Stengel was fond of saying, "Berra knows how to pitch to everybody in this league except himself."

———

As ROGER KAHN wrote in *The Era*,

1947 . . . seemed to be a comfortable time. We loved our radios in 1947. Any typical Tuesday night, we heard on the large boxy Imperial Model

Cape Hart Radio Phonograph (with Flip-o-Matic record changer) the *Bob Hope Show*, with Jerry Colonna and Vera Vague, and, as a special guest star, dancer-actor-singer Van Johnson. A little later came the *Milton Berle Show* and after that the *Red Skelton Show*, in which Red played the famous country bumpkin, Clem Cididdlehopper. . . .

. . . The mood was materialistic, like the mood of our own present, but at the Stork Club or El Morocco late in the 1940s, women did not look like women of today. Hair was lacquered. Cuts were severe . . . With all the corseting and girdling women's bottoms seemed unitary, so to speak, like the rearmost segment of a honeybee."[22]

Lawrence Peter Berra was not quite so materialistic as some. He couldn't afford to be. His salary for the 1947 season was $5,000—not bad at all by the standards of other rookies, but not quite enough to make him give up that job in the hardware store. Unlike Joe DiMaggio, he shared a room with another rookie, Spec Shea, at the Edison Hotel on 47th Street just off Broadway; they split the $9.00 a day cost and saved a little more sometimes by riding back from Yankee Stadium with Mel Allen.*

New York, Yogi quickly observed, was far from dull: "All those restaurants, supper clubs, newsstands, music, movies, shows, Automats, you name it."[23] On Berra's salary, though, there wasn't much left over for entertainment after he paid for necessities and sent money home to Paulina. Since Yogi wasn't much of a drinker, his favorite evening entertainment was going to the movies. Some writers suggested derisively that he was The Three Stooges' biggest fan; in fact, as mainstream films went, Berra's tastes were somewhat elevated. Like George Bernard Shaw and T. S. Eliot, he loved the Marx Brothers, and his favorite actress was Greer Garson.†

Jimmy Cannon, perhaps the most influential sportswriter of the time, also lived at the Edison and often bumped into Yogi around Times Square. One day he saw Berra in the lobby and asked him what he had been doing with himself. Nothing much, replied Yogi. What's there for a guy in this town to do? Or some variant. What he meant, of course, was how much of

---

*According to Allen's best biographer, Stephen Borelli, in *How About That! The Life of Mel Allen,* his car was "a metallic-gray Buick convertible that had red-rimmed wheels and red seats. The engine purred so softly that the young players barely knew the car was running as it made its way through Harlem and Central Park. 'We wished we could get a ride all the time,' said Yogi." (p. 96)

†In a 2002 YES Network interview with Michael Kay, Berra was quick to identify his favorite movie: *Mrs. Miniver,* the story of an English middle-class family's experiences in the first months of World War II, which starred, of course, Greer Garson.

the town can you enjoy when you're living in New York on $5,000 a year and sending some of it home? Cannon chose to take Berra literally, wrote it up in his *New York Post* column, and a new Yogiism was born.

———

IT WAS A wonderful thing, Yogi would recall fourteen years later, being twenty-two years old and playing ball for the New York Yankees. "I wasn't making an awful lot of money, but I wasn't worrying about that yet . . . It was a kick just walking into that clubhouse and taking my uniform with the number eight on the back off the hook and putting it on."[24]

The Yankees' 1947 home opener was against the Philadelphia A's. New York's opening day lineup didn't look all that imposing. Thirty-nine-year-old Spud Chandler was the starting pitcher, and thirty-two-year-old Aaron Robinson was the catcher. George McQuinn, age thirty-nine, had been given his unconditional release by the A's in December and was the best the Yankees could come up with at first base. Light-hitting Billy Johnson started at third, Charlie Keller in left was a proven commodity (though he would play only 45 games that year due to a back injury). With DiMaggio out, the rest of the outfield—Johnny Lindell in center and Lawrence Berra in right—didn't have fans or sportswriters thinking pennant.

The second baseman was the undistinguished George "Snuffy" Stirnweiss, who had batted just .251 with no home runs in 1946. The Yankees had had a popular, power-hitting second baseman in Joe Gordon, but MacPhail had dealt him to the Cleveland Indians for a pitcher, Allie Reynolds, who had won only 11 of 26 decisions with Cleveland in 1946. The trade was not popular with most Yankee fans, nor with some New York sportswriters. Red Smith, the most respected if not the most influential columnist of his time, wrote that MacPhail was closer to being a circus promoter than a baseball executive, to which MacPhail replied, within earshot of other writers, "Watching 'The Big Indian' "—Reynolds was part Creek and became affectionately known to his Yankee teammates as "The Big Chief" or "Chief"—"is a helluva lot more fun than watching some f——g seal with an oboe."[*25] In truth, MacPhail was part circus promoter and part

———

*When he wrote that line, Smith didn't know that the hard-throwing Reynolds came to the Yankees largely on the recommendation of Joe DiMaggio and Tommy Henrich, both of whom hated hitting against him. MacPhail apparently wanted the Indians' Red Embree, whose ERA in 1946, 3.47, was actually better than Reynolds's 3.89. MacPhail decided to trust the judgment of DiMaggio and Henrich.

baseball executive, though this wasn't obvious on opening day, as the Yankees lost 6–1. Berra went 0-for-4.

Yogi had a much better time when the Yanks went back to Washington to make up the rained-out opener. President Harry Truman threw out the first ball. Though Berra had played a handful of games the previous year, he was technically a rookie in 1947, and the fans were waiting for him. He gave them something to see, with four straight hits to left, right, through the middle, and down to the right-field corner. In the clubhouse after the game, he was so excited he was shaking. A writer asked him if it was because of his sensational opening day performance. No, Yogi told them, it was because he had played in front of the President of the United States. On April 30, he finally got a chance to play in front of the whole family when the Yankees played the Browns in St. Louis; he got box seats for his mother and father, Josie, Tony, Mike, and John. The Yankees picked this night to give just about their worst performance of the season, losing 15–5. Larry, playing right field, was hitless in four at-bats. "But Mom made ravioli for me after the game anyway."[26]

As the season went on, Yogi's inexperience became more apparent. Behind the plate, he often looked bad trying to block pitches in the dirt, and his powerful arm was erratic. "The guy *fields* with his bat," said *New York Daily News'* Dick Young.[27] But even at bat, Berra's game still had holes. He needed more practice hitting left-handed pitchers, and Harris began to sit him down when a lefty was starting. Once, after popping up with runners on base, he ambled out to right field in a visible funk. DiMaggio whispered some advice to him: "Always run out to your position, kid. It doesn't look good when you walk. The other team may have gotten you down, but don't let 'em know it."[28]

It wasn't the only time that a remark from DiMaggio had a profound effect on Yogi. Pitcher Ed Lopat recalled a doubleheader with the Washington Senators in 1948 where the Yankees won the first game and settled to a 3–3 tie in the second when the game was called on account of darkness. Berra had begged out of the second game, and his replacement, Charlie Silvera, failed to drive in a run in four at-bats with men on base. Yogi was swapping jokes with the other players when DiMaggio, exhausted from the grueling twin bill, peeled off his sweat-soaked shirt and said to Berra, "What the hell's wrong with you? You're 23 years old and you can't catch a double header? My ass." Lopat added it was the only time he ever heard DiMaggio say anything like that in the clubhouse.[29] All young players need something to spur them on, and DiMaggio's words must have done that for Yogi; 1948 would be the first of 12 seasons in which Yogi would catch at least 100 games.*

Privately, Harris asked his players to take it easy on Yogi.† Privately, too, Bucky asked the beat writers to go easy on his most promising rookie as he matured. "He can be a great ballplayer," Harris told reporters. "He won't be if his spirit is broken by criticism. Remember he's very young and has a lot to learn. In a few years, he'll be the biggest player in the game—the closest thing to Babe Ruth. But only if you fellows help the public to understand and love him instead of making him look like a simp."[30] Such paternalism was necessary. Before one game, Johnny Lindell got into a heated discussion with a journalist in front of the outfielders' locker room. What point of baseball strategy the debate was about is lost to time, and though the discussion was friendly, it was loud enough for nearby players to hear. After a couple of minutes, Yogi surprised both his teammate and the writer by jumping into the argument, repeating some of Lindell's points in an imitation of Lindell's Colorado twang. Billy Johnson was of the opinion that Yogi meant well and was merely backing up his teammate, but whatever happened, the writer was angered and accused Berra of acting like a bush leaguer. Embarrassed, Yogi walked off silently. Lindell told Harris about the incident, who politely invited the writer into his office, heard him out, and explained that Yogi was just trying to be one of the boys and he should cut him some slack. The writer supposedly went out of his way to be friendly when he encountered Yogi again.

The return of DiMaggio to the lineup eased the pressure on Berra, but created a new problem. With Tommy Henrich, Joe DiMaggio, Johnny Lindell, and Charlie Keller available to play the outfield, and Aaron Robinson doing a solid job behind the plate, there was no position for Berra. When he did crack the lineup, he sometimes appeared to be in a fog. A few days after DiMaggio's return, Berra started in right field with Joe in center. A not particularly hard fly ball was hit between them, and Yogi, closing in fast, heard his teammate call out. Assuming this meant for him to make the play—DiMaggio was still running gingerly—Berra went

*If, indeed, DiMaggio actually said that to Berra in 1948, or it was after a doubleheader against the Washington Senators. The Yankees played no doubleheaders that season where they won the first game and played to a 3–3 tie in the second. Billy Johnson recalled DiMaggio saying something to Yogi about catching doubleheaders, but couldn't remember which team the Yanks had played.

†No one talked about this at the time, but Joe Page mentioned it to W. C. Heinz more than thirty years later for his book *Once They Heard the Cheers*.

full speed for the ball and smacked right into DiMaggio. It wasn't clear who, if anyone, was at fault, and despite DiMaggio's protest that no one was hurt and that it was his fault for not properly working out the signals, the writers predictably unloaded on the St. Louis greenhorn. "I called for the ball, all right," Joe told reporters after the game, "but Yogi was too anxious to help me. He knows all about that bad heel of mine and figured he was doing something to save me."[31] "They made it sound," recalls Phil Rizzuto, "like it was a play from out of the old Daffiness boys of the Brooklyn Dodgers. You know, like Babe Herman, who was always dropping balls and running into people. And of course, it was Yogi who was made to look daffy."

Sometimes even when Yogi did something right, he was made fun of. On June 15 at Yankee Stadium, the Yankees swept a doubleheader from the Browns. Berra caught the second game. In the seventh inning with the score tied, the Browns had Jeff Heath on third base with one out when Johnny Berardino laid down a squeeze bunt off Vic Raschi. The ball hit the ground directly in front of the plate. Yogi sprang up so quickly that he fielded the ball before Berardino was able to make it out of the batter's box. Yogi spun around and tagged him out. He then had the presence of mind to turn and look for Heath, who was streaking in from third base, and got him by about a foot. For good measure, he then reached up and tagged the home plate umpire, Cal Hubbard. The play made Yogi just the twentieth major league catcher since 1900 to make an unassisted double play, something so difficult that Mickey Cochrane, who was widely considered one of the two best catchers of the first half of the century (the other being, of course, Bill Dickey), never did it.° The Yankees won, 2–1.

In the locker room, a grinning Berra told the press, "I just got the ball and tagged everyone I could see." "Including the ump?" they wanted to know. "Yeah," replied a happy Yogi. "Including the umps!" Rizzuto, dressing at the next locker, turned to Tommy Henrich and said, "Watch how they twist *that* one."[32]

That was nothing compared to how "they" twisted a line from Yogi's speech on Yogi Berra Appreciation Day at Sportsman's Park in St. Louis.†

°On August 17, 1962, against the Kansas City Athletics, Berra became the first catcher to do it twice. Interestingly, both plays, fifteen years apart, came when Yogi was a substitute catcher.

†Curiously, the exact date of Yogi's most famous speech has been forgotten. In his 1961 autobiography and in his 1986 memoirs, all he remembered was that it was a night game. In no story or book written about Yogi over the years is the exact date mentioned.

The neighbors back on the Hill had been delirious the previous fall when Joe Garagiola and the Cardinals won the World Series. Now another hometown boy had made good with the most famous baseball team of all. Yogi was presented with "a pile of stuff," including a new Nash sedan. Pietro, Paulina, and the rest of the Berras, the Garagiolas, and other neighbors were there, as well as several former members of the Stags baseball club. There was only one problem: Yogi had to stand in front of the crowd and deliver the first speech of his life. He asked Bobby Brown for help; the doctor's advice was to keep it short and sweet. He wrote it out on a piece of paper for Yogi: "I'm a lucky guy, and I'm happy to be with the Yankees. I want to thank everyone for making this night possible." Berra, who wasn't scared at Normandy, was terrified in front of the hometown crowd. Instead of reading his speech as Brown had written, Yogi got tongue tied and said, "I want to thank everyone for making this night necessary." Future historians covering the event wrote it up as if Berra did not know the difference between the words "possible" and "necessary" and turned Yogi's two-sentence thank you into the most famous baseball oration since Lou Gehrig told Yankee fans that he considered himself the luckiest man on the face of the earth. "No wonder," Yogi reflected fourteen years later, "I got the reputation of being a character."[33]

It probably didn't help that his fielding had become an almost daily source for sportswriters' jibes. The nastiest was from New York Post columnist Milton Gross, who wrote, "As a catcher, Yogi not only was a hindrance to the defense . . . but also to the pitchers, who had little confidence in him. There was also the suspicion held by some of the Yankees better thinkers that Yogi, living in constant dread and fear of base-stealing forays against him, signaled for fast balls to get the drop on runners when the situation clearly called for curve balls."[34] Gross may have had a point about the pitchers lacking confidence in Yogi, but as much could have been said about almost any young catcher. The truth was that Berra was not always calling for fastballs, and when he did call for breaking balls, his pitchers didn't always trust him. In a game against Boston, Joe Page shook off Yogi, thinking he could get a fast ball past Ted Williams. Williams sent the ball

---

The New York Times archives doesn't mention the 1947 Yogi Berra Day at all, probably because the function was sponsored by the St. Louis Browns and not the Yankees. Dave Kaplan, director of the Yogi Berra Museum and Learning Center, believes it happened in July; if so, and it was as Yogi remembered a night game, then it was probably the second game of a July 12 doubleheader with the Browns. A cursory examination of the available archives in St. Louis papers of the time has failed to confirm the date.

soaring into the right-field seats. Bucky Harris let the entire dugout know that Yogi had called for a curve ball over the inside part of the plate. At the end of the inning, Harris winked at Page; in the future, he told him, he should have a little more faith in his catcher's judgment.

―――

ON MAY 13 at home the Yankees beat the Browns 9–1. Berra selected a low-and-away fast ball and cracked it over the right-field fence for a grand slammer. As he trotted past second on the way to third, Charlie Dressen, hands on his hips, shook his head and said, "Bad pitch. It was a bad pitch." "Looked good to me," Yogi said with a grin as he headed for home.

―――

DiMAGGIO AND MACPHAIL had been on a collision course since Joe was pressured into making the San Juan appearance after his heel surgery. MacPhail had arranged for a newsreel crew to film and interview DiMaggio, Charlie Keller, and Aaron Robinson. The crew was late getting to Yankee Stadium, and by the time they arrived, the three were getting ready to take batting practice. Like the good Yankees they were supposed to be, the trio was all business and refused to postpone their batting turns to accommodate the cameramen. MacPhail was furious and fined Keller and Robinson $50 apiece, but DiMaggio, presumably because he was DiMaggio, was fined $100. For good measure, he also fined Don Johnson and Johnny Lindell for daring to suggest that players shouldn't be asked to take time off from work, without pay, for publicity functions.

In addition to being a tyrant, MacPhail was also a bully. When Phil Rizzuto and George Stirnweiss met with a representative of the fledging rebel Mexican League, MacPhail summoned them to his office and told them they were not to meet with the man again. Rizzuto, laboring under the misapprehension that he lived in a free society, told MacPhail that they just wanted to hear what the man had to say. MacPhail told them in no uncertain terms that if they were seen talking to a Mexican League official again, they would be suspended. This being three decades before Marvin Miller became the first executive director of the players union, Rizzuto and Stirnweiss had no alternative but to comply. "Whoosh," said Rizzuto years later when recalling MacPhail for Roger Kahn. What does that mean, Kahn asked. "Nothing," replied Rizzuto, "just thinking about MacPhail makes me go 'Whoosh.' "[35]

The mood in the clubhouse was turning black. Some spoke of open rebellion, but DiMaggio, the team's unofficial leader, called for peace. Privately, though, he nursed his grudge against MacPhail. A few days after the fine, before a game with the Red Sox, MacPhail scheduled a home run derby between New York's and Boston's right- and left-handed hitters with $100 prizes. Ted Williams, who like all left-handed hitters loved the short 296-foot fence in Yankee Stadium's right field, topped the lefties. None of the right-handers were able to get a ball over the fence in the spacious left field. DiMaggio, though, hit one when it counted during the game. In the locker room, one of MacPhail's assistants brought Joe a check, telling him that the Yankee GM thought he was entitled to the right-handed prize money. DiMaggio told him to give the check to the Cancer Fund.

Despite MacPhail's bullying tactics—or perhaps because they succeeded in unifying the team—the Yankees began playing with deadly precision. In June they reeled off 19 consecutive wins, and by the third week in July it was obvious that there wasn't going to be a pennant race. What was amazing about the streak was that the Yankees did it without most of their best players. Allie Reynolds missed two weeks, and Spec Shea missed starts with a sore arm. Yogi had a terrible throat infection and was out for nearly three weeks. Spud Chandler had bone chips in his elbow that ended his career. DiMaggio played in pain. But there was always someone ready to step in when a regular went down. "There never was a mentally tougher team than the 1947 Yankees," said Bobby Brown.

On September 26, before the last weekend in the season, Mel Allen asked Larry MacPhail to come to home plate before a game with Washington. A stunned MacPhail was presented with a silver tea service with the inscription

> To Larry MacPhail,
> greatest executive in baseball,
> whose zealous efforts were a major factor
> in our 19 game streak and the winning
> of the American League pennant.
> *From his Yankees, 1947.*

The players, who had chipped in for the gift, stood stone-faced while MacPhail wept. MacPhail had no friends on the team, but no one doubted that he had earned the tribute—and they all knew that the money they had kicked in would be more than made up for by their World Series checks.

THE YANKS WOUND up winning 97 games and finishing 12 in front of
the Detroit Tigers. MacPhail's gamble on Allie Reynolds hit the jackpot:
Reynolds went 19-8 and paced the staff. Yogi's unheralded roommate,
Spec Shea, went 14–5, and Joe Page was sensational in the bullpen, winning 14 games, saving 17 more, with an ERA of 2.48. The pitching made
up for the relative—relative for a Yankees team, that is—lack of power.
DiMaggio was the only hitter with more than 20 home runs, and no one
had as many as 100 RBIs. But there was talent up and down the lineup,
and sometimes on the bench. Yogi made a substantial contribution, filling
in at both catcher and in the outfield and, sometimes, pinch-hitting. In 83
games, he had 11 home runs and 15 doubles, hit .280, and drove in 54
runs. This was exactly the kind of production Larry MacPhail had hoped
for. Simple arithmetic indicated that given a full season he would drive in
at least 100. Though he felt it was his natural position, Yogi still hadn't settled down as a catcher. He wasn't shy about seeking advice from veterans
on how to handle base stealers. The Red Sox's Birdie Tebbetts—like Berra,
a catcher who would eventually become a manager—advised him not to
waste time worrying about them because most base stealers steal on the
pitcher. This was a bit of wisdom that most major league managers were
surprisingly slow to understand. (It wasn't until the early 1970s that most
of the big windups that enabled runners to get a jump on the pitcher had
been coached out of the game.) Just keep throwing the ball the best you
can, Tebbetts told him, you learn to throw by throwing.

Their opponent in the 1947 World Series was the Brooklyn Dodgers. As
the poor relations in New York's baseball family—the Dodgers had never
won a World Series and had lost to the Yankees in five games in 1941—
they needed no special incentive to want to beat the Yankees. Nonetheless,
during spring training Larry MacPhail had poured a barrel of gasoline on
the fire. MacPhail had lured Charlie Dressen away from the Dodgers to
coach third base, which irritated Branch Rickey and Dodgers manager
Leo Durocher. Leo also claimed that MacPhail had offered him the
Yankees managing job in 1946, but that he had turned MacPhail down.
Rickey and Durocher then raised a ruckus by accusing MacPhail of having
invited two known gamblers—Connie Emmerman, owner of the Cotton
Club, and Max "Memphis" Engleberg—to his box during a Yankees-
Dodgers exhibition in Havana back in March. MacPhail blew up and filed
libel charges against Durocher. The upshot was that the Yankees and

Dressen were punished by Commissioner Albert Benjamin "Happy" Chandler, who suspended Dressen for thirty days for violating his verbal agreement with the Dodgers. The Dodgers, though, got slammed far worse when Durocher was suspended for the entire 1947 season for "conduct detrimental to baseball" and "association with known gamblers."

All this, of course, paled in the wake of the real story of the 1947 World Series—Jackie Robinson was about to become the first black player in the history of the fall classic. Years later, Berra would insist that the significance of that event made little impression on him. "I always thought, what the heck, sure, there's gonna be black guys and lots of 'em pretty soon. If they can play ball, why not let them play?"[36]

Yogi had no negative feelings about blacks in baseball. He had had little contact with them up to that time. Partly this was due to growing up on the Hill. Italians and blacks in other major cities were often crowded into ghettoes side by side, resulting in friction and violence. The Hill, in contrast, was a neighborhood, insular and relatively self-sustaining. Its residents had little contact with black neighborhoods and thus saw no reason to feel threatened by a different culture.

Privately, though, Berra did have trepidations about playing against Robinson. Not about his color, but about his speed—his and that of other teammates such as Pee Wee Reese and Pete Reiser. Robinson, the National League's Rookie of the Year, had won the stolen base crown with 29—a high total in an era when most runners hugged the bases and waited for batters to hit home runs. Bucky Harris wanted Yogi's bat in the lineup, and when it was announced he would start at catcher, reporters, hungry for any tidbit that might develop into a story, asked him how he was going to contain the Dodgers' speedsters. Berra half-heartedly reminded them that he had held his own when playing against Robinson in the minors, where Jackie had never stolen on him. He tried to sound confident, but DiMaggio later told him he could see his knees shaking all the way from center field.

It was a measure of how unlikely the Yankees' pennant victory had been that their pitcher and catcher in the first game of the World Series, the first ever to be televised, were both rookies. No other team had ever started a rookie battery in the Series. Shea, who probably spent his best years in the military, was just two days short of his twenty-seventh birthday, and his success in the 1947 season was probably the biggest of many Yankee improbables that year. In the clubhouse the day before the first game, Berra and Shea were autographing baseballs when a writer asked Spec how he felt. It was just another ball game, Shea replied—you just had to get twenty-seven outs. Berra was a bit more apprehensive: "Yeah, but them shadows come awful early here this time of year." "He was worrying about those hits," thought Joe Page, "with the ball coming out of the sunlight and then into the shadow of those three decks." According to Page, one of the writers shot back, "C'mon, Yogi, stop worrying about it. You don't figure to get a hit anyway." After the writer walked away, Berra said, as if to himself, "Them writers think I'm kiddin', but they don't have to get up there and hit. They don't have to do nothin'." W. C. Heinz, who overheard Yogi, was impressed: "It's a truth I have never forgotten, anytime I've interviewed an athlete, or anytime I've had to lay a critique on one."[37]

Much has been made of Berra's ineptitude in stopping the Dodger base runners in the 1947 World Series, but what films remain show that the blame, or most of it, should be placed on Yankee pitchers, who let Robinson and Reese get big jumps off first.* It should also be pointed out that the Dodgers' base running in the first two games was largely irrelevant: the Yankees won the first game 5–3 and the second 10–3 behind Allie Reynolds. The Dodgers *had* stolen five bases off Yogi, causing Connie Mack, who had just completed his fiftieth season as a manager, to tell reporters that it was "the worst World Series catching I ever saw."[38] If Connie had been in a more generous mood, he might have noted that a rookie with just 57 games of major league catching experience had just

---

*In Birdie Tebbetts's 2002 memoir, *Birdie: Confessions of a Baseball Nomad*, he recalls bumping into Berra in the lobby of the Edison Hotel right after the first game of the Series:

> It was Yogi's rookie year. This was, of course, his first World Series. In the first game, Jackie Robinson got on base and took a big leadoff, teasing and taunting the pitcher. On the first pitch, he took off for second. Yogi's throw was in the dirt, and very late, and after that every time a Dodger got on base he made Yogi's life miserable. The press was merciless and called Yogi a clown.
>
> Sixty years later, I remember the conversation I had with Yogi. I remember it because it was the first time we talked. I only knew him as a Yankee and I was playing for somebody else. I found out that Yogi was a real down-to-earth, nice man. Always has been. Very real. Something in baseball that we sometimes lose sight of is the fact that there are great players out there who are real.

As they passed in the hotel lobby, Berra turned and said to Tebbetts, "Hey, I want to talk to you. You saw what happened out there today. These guys are driving me crazy."

> "Hell, yes, I saw it, and it wasn't your fault, Yogi. Your pitchers aren't holding the runners on."
>
> . . . And that was the first conversation I ever had with Yogi. The fact that he stopped me and brought it up made me feel pretty good. Later on, when he became manager of the Yankees, he wrote me a letter about something or other. I kept it—a nice letter that sounds like the way he talks. (p. 5)

called the first two games of a World Series and was on the winning side in both.

Nonetheless, Berra had doubts about his ability. After the first game, he sat in his dressing stall with his head down, looking as if the Yankees had lost. W. C. Heinz, who recognized potential when he saw it, walked over and said, "Yogi, forget it. You guys won, and you'll have a better day tomorrow." Berra shook his head. "I guess I ain't very smart," he said. Heinz took offense that a mere rookie would question his judgment on a ballplayer, even if the ballplayer was the person he was talking to. "Yogi, let me tell you something," he said. "I was the one who asked you last year when the Cardinals were in the Series and you were home in St. Louis. I asked you if you went to the games, and you said, 'No, I don't like to watch games.' I said, 'Why not?' You said, 'It makes me nervous, just to watch.' It makes you nervous to watch because you're always playing the game, I don't know. I think that you're not smart enough, because you have a fine baseball brain. Yogi said, 'I don't know, I don't know if you're right.' "[39]

Harris gave in to Berra's critic and put Sherm Lollar behind the plate for Game Three with veteran Bobo Newsom starting. The Dodgers shelled Newsom and his relief for nine runs. Sparked by a DiMaggio home run, the Yanks pulled within two runs in the seventh, and Harris sent Berra in to pinch-hit against Ralph Branca. Branca challenged Berra, and Yogi hit it over the right-field fence and onto Bedford Avenue. It was his first World Series home run and the first pinch-hit homer in Series history. But the Dodgers manager, Burt Shotten, called in reliever Hugh Casey, and the Dodgers won 9–8.

It was the fourth game, though, which proved to be Berra's first memorable World Series contest. The Yankees' starter, Bill Bevens, would become one of the strangest footnotes in baseball's record book. Bevens was thirty in 1947 and would turn thirty-one just eighteen days after his only World Series. He had pitched only four seasons in the majors, two of them during the roster-depleted war years, compiling a mediocre record of 40–36. In 1947 he was just 7–13; that he would be picked to start the fourth game of the World Series illustrates how shallow the Yankees talent pool was. In Game Four, though, Bevens was very nearly unhittable. The Yankees scored solo runs in the first and fourth innings and the Dodgers got one back in the fifth, in large part because Berra, on a Pee

*But, of course, Yogi later admitted he went to one of the World Series games to root for Joe Garagiola.

Wee Reese steal of second, threw the ball into center field. Reese came around to score. Third baseman Billy Johnson didn't think the throw was all that bad and suspected that the middle infielders, Rizzuto and Stirnweiss, got confused about who was supposed to take it. In any event, the Yanks were leading 2–1 going into the ninth, and Bevens had not given up a hit. A thirty-year-old pitcher with just four more wins in his career than losses found himself just three outs away from the first no-hitter in the World Series.

With two outs, Bevens walked Al Gionfriddo, who got a jump on Bevens and broke for second base. This time Berra made a fine throw, Rizzuto made the tag, and the Yankees thought the game was over. But Gionfriddo got the call. Bucky Harris then did a daring thing: he had Pete Reiser walked intentionally, putting the winning run on first base and bringing to bat Eddie Stanky, who had little power but a genuine propensity for getting on base. But Shotten didn't want a walk, he wanted power. He pulled Stanky and pinch-hit with Cookie Lavagetto, a .261 regular season hitter with three home runs in 69 at-bats. Lavagetto was no slugger, but he had more pop than Stanky. Harris's strategy violated the cardinal rules of baseball, but more than forty years later Berra defended his manager: "Cookie Lavagetto was thirty-five and on his last legs, and the scouting report said you could get him with fastballs. But he hit an outside fastball to right for a double, and Eddie Miksis [running for Reiser, who had a bad leg] slid across with the winning run."[40]

As he walked off the field, Bevens broke down in tears. In the clubhouse, Yogi cried with him. Years later, Roger Kahn determined that Yogi had called for the correct pitch after all: Bevens had fired a high and away fastball past Lavagetto for the first strike, then Yogi put down one finger for a fastball and a hand waggle to indicate up and away. "I didn't want to throw it there," Bevens told Kahn years after the fact. "I don't know if I wanted to throw a fastball, but I definitely didn't want to throw him a fastball up and away." Then why did you throw it? Kahn asked. "Because that's what Berra called for. Yogi was a smart kid, whatever you hear." Why, then, did you call for an outside fastball, Kahn asked Yogi. "Because that's what them scouting reports told me to do," Berra replied.[41]

As it turned out, the game cost Bevens more than a no-hitter. Pitch counts were something that few managers or coaches paid attention to back then; pitchers in the 1940s were expected to finish their own starts no matter how many pitches they threw. Since he was working on a no-hitter, no one seriously thought about taking Bevens out of the game, and by the time he walked Reiser intentionally in the ninth, he had thrown more than 140 pitches. If there had been a lapse in strategy, it wasn't the intentional walk so much as Harris's refusal to bring in Joe Page to pitch the ninth inning—or at least to pitch to Lavagetto. Today, that would have been an automatic. Instead, Bevens was left in, and ruined his arm. He pitched 2⅔ innings in the seventh and final game, gave up two hits, and never pitched in the major leagues again. The Yankees released him the following spring.

Yogi was ripped in the press for his failure to throw out either of the base runners in key situations. No one mentioned that Bevens's allowing the runners to get the jump was the reason they were able to steal. Nearly forgotten, too, was the fact that Bevens had little control over his pitches for much of the game—or, as Yogi would recall, "He was wild, but had great stuff."[42] The intentional walk to Reiser was the tenth he had issued in the game, which was why his pitch count was so high. The result was that Yogi, who deserved to be playing in Game Five, sat on the bench and watched his roommate beat the Dodgers 2–1. Yogi started Game Six and got two hits as the Dodgers caught up with Allie Reynolds and won 8–6.

For the all-important Game Seven, the Yankees found themselves in a state of near crisis. According to Spec Shea's son, Frank Jr., Bucky Harris held a team meeting to determine who would pitch the seventh game. "As my father told the story," says Shea Jr., "no one would volunteer, claiming sore arms or not enough rest. My father volunteered and they all laughed at him. He had started Game One and Game Five. He would be starting Game Seven with very short rest, as the Subway Series was played over seven straight days. After a long debate, it was decided he would pitch. After the meeting, the general manager* promised him a $1,000 bonus for having the guts to start. He started and only lasted into the second inning. He had little stuff because of limited rest. The Yankees ended up winning and became champions. But after all that, my father would say, with a laugh, 'Those blankedty-blanks never paid me the $1,000!' " But with a sensational relief effort from Joe Page, the Yankees won 5–2 and took the Series.

Red Barber, in his 1982 memoirs, would recall it as "the greatest Series ever played."[43] Berra's first World Series was undistinguished, a .158 average in 19 at-bats and the pinch-hit home run. But in the postgame delirium of the locker room at Yankee Stadium, no one cared. He was young, a

*This could have been George Weiss, who was named general manager before the start of the 1947 season, but more likely it was team president Larry MacPhail.

Yankee, and a World Series winner. Yogi put his arm around Bucky Harris and thanked him for having so much faith in him; Harris told Yogi that next season he would be the Yankees regular catcher.

There was a bizarre postscript. MacPhail showed up in the locker room, apparently drunk, and, some thought, flushed from crying. He told a stunned roomful of players and coaches that he was retiring. Later that night at a party at the Biltmore, MacPhail, apparently still drunk, threw a punch at John McDonald, the team's road secretary. No one ever found out why. In any event, MacPhail didn't dampen the enthusiasm of the players. Within a few days, everyone got their World Series checks. Yogi's share was $5,830, which was $830 more than he had been paid for the regular season. He didn't deposit it right away; he took it home to St. Louis to show Pietro and Paulina. It was the biggest check anyone in the Berra family had ever seen or imagined. "I think they realized then," he said years later, "that baseball was not a bum's game."[44]

PART TWO

Chapter Four

A Rather Strange Fellow
of Very Remarkable Abilities
(1948–1949)

You . . . are superlative.

—CASEY STENGEL to Yogi Berra

IN THE WINTER of 1948 Yogi Berra had a car, the one the fans had given him at Yogi Berra Day, a World Series ring, and more money than he had ever dreamed of. He had everything but a girlfriend.

He and Joey dropped by to see the boys down at Riva's candy store and went to the YMCA to play some basketball and swim. They also played some hockey—or played *at* hockey. "We were bums," says Garagiola. "We could skate okay, but we couldn't skate and hit the puck. Yogi would lose his balance when he would pull the stick back to hit it, and we had to pull up every time we got too close to the net for fear of crashing into it." Avid St. Louis Flyers fans, they posed for publicity pictures dressed in Flyers uniforms and took turns stumbling across the ice trying to slap pucks into the net. When the *St. Louis Post-Dispatch* published the photos of the "Catchers on Ice," everyone—Yogi and Joe, the folks in the neighborhood, and St. Louis sports fans—had a good laugh. When the pictures showed up in New York papers, though, Red Patterson, the Yankees PR director, felt otherwise. "He had a conniption fit," recalls Garagiola. "All he could think of was Yogi getting hit in the eye with a puck"—the players wore no face guards back then—"and ordered him to stay off the ice." Yogi was impressed by their concern. "They're like my own family," he told Joe.[1]

Automobiles had given Yogi and Joe a new sense of freedom and greater range for their activities. Joe had a new girlfriend, Audrie Ross, who wasn't Italian and lived on the other side of town. Yogi didn't have a girl-friend yet, and when he did, she wasn't Italian either.

Carmen Short, Yogi said later, was just the third girl he had ever dated. Without having seen the other two, it's hard to believe they could have been better looking. Mel Allen thought Carmen was one of the most beautiful women he had ever seen. "She was a knockout. If they had sent her from Central Casting for a movie on Yogi's life, they would have rejected her as too good-looking." Besides not being Italian, Carmen was many things Yogi was not: not from St. Louis (her family was from Salem, Missouri, about two hours northwest), not a school dropout, and not part of a world that revolved around the New York Yankees. Carmen, a waitress at Biggie's steakhouse,* had helped the restaurant's owner, Julius "Biggie" Garagnani, address envelopes and mail subscription cards for Terry Moore Day the season before. She had met Moore's wife, who occasionally came by the restaurant. Somehow, when Berra was pointed out to her, she thought he was Moore, and when Yogi approached her for a date, she was appalled. It was a bad start to a beautiful relationship.

It got better quickly. Yogi asked Charley Ray, Biggie's partner, to inter-cede on his behalf, and Berra shyly explained to her that he was not mar-ried and that while he did play baseball, the Cardinals were not the only team in the game—*he* played for the World Champion New York Yankees. "I could hardly believe my luck," Yogi would say later, "when it turned out she liked me as much as I liked her." But Yogi had more going for him than luck. "He was honest. And simple," she told *Sports Illustrated* in 1984. "Wasn't a show-off. I was dating a lot of college boys at the time, and I liked him in contrast."[2] She found Yogi "masculine. Very strong. Physically and mentally, or I should say psychologically. I think he's very sexy."[3] As she said with a laugh in an interview for a documentary on Yogi's life, "I went after *him*—really, he didn't have a chance."[4]

Yogi and Carmen double-dated with Joe and Audrie, dining out at their pick of St. Louis's superb restaurants and going to movies and basketball games—Yogi was getting a crash course in the importance of money. The relationship went so well so quickly that Yogi began to have second thoughts. He stood her up once—*once*. "I did it," he told Joe Trimble, "because I was afraid things were getting too serious. I didn't want to get involved with no girls just then . . . I was afraid to call her up and say I

---

*The steakhouse has often been identified as Stan and Biggie's—Stan being St. Louis's biggest sports hero, Stan Musial. But that partnership didn't begin until 1950. Musial later opened his own restaurant.

wasn't coming. I just didn't show up, and it made her look bad with the other people. She got good and sore, which I knew she would. "[5] Carmen let him know in no uncertain terms that it had better not happen again. "I was young myself," she said, "and not too anxious to settle down either. I had other boyfriends and was enjoying myself working at Biggie's." (She was doing quite well, too, making up to $90 a week including tips. Yogi could scarcely believe waitressing could be that lucrative.) "Besides, there was my kid sister Bonnie to think of. She and I were living together in a small apartment, and we were both working for Biggie."[6]

Yogi broke off the relationship with Carmen. In addition to romantic troubles, he was also having medical problems—or at least the Yankees thought he was. George Weiss was convinced that the cause of a terrible throat infection Yogi had suffered from over the summer was his tonsils and insisted that he have them removed. Berra balked, but finally agreed to go through with the surgery—if the Yankees paid for it. Weiss blinked and agreed to foot the bill.

After the holidays, Yogi, while selling sporting goods at Sears, Roebuck and Co., began to think about trying to patch things up with Carmen. Biggie, who loved to have athletes hanging around the restaurant, was upset that Yogi wasn't coming by. Bumping into Berra downtown, he told him that he should drop by the place, Yogi said he'd like to but he thought that Carmen was mad at him. Biggie assured him that if he showed the proper contrition, things could be smoothed over. He did, and in her wisdom Carmen forgave him. This time Yogi had to face it: he was in love. When it came time to leave for spring training, he found it hard to tear himself away from Carmen and get back to baseball.

Yogi began 1948 spring training with a new number. When he came up from Newark in 1946, he had been given number 38 and was switched to 35 for the 1947 season. When Aaron Robinson was traded, Yogi got his number 8, Bill Dickey's old number. It was quite an honor, and quite a number to live up to. Dickey would later help to see that he earned it.

Spring training was exceptionally rough for Yogi. He was injured three times and there were whispers among the press that he might not be quite so durable. In a mid-March exhibition game in Clearwater, he suffered a bad ankle sprain sliding into a triple against the Phillies. Dr. Gainer, the team physician, insisted on X rays; Yogi, oblivious to the possible seriousness of the injury, spent that night and the next ten at the local dog track. On March 26, in Sarasota, he got back in the lineup against Boston and collapsed at home plate when his ankle buckled after a big swing. That took him out of the lineup for two more weeks. On April 12 the Yankees played an exhibition game against the minor league Birmingham Barons at Rickwood Field. Much ballyhooed by the Alabama press, the game was a homecoming for Melvin Israel, a.k.a. Mel Allen, the Yankees announcer, who was born in Birmingham in 1913. In attendance were such luminaries as former Alabama football star Riggs Stephenson, who had starred in the big leagues with the Indians and Cubs from 1921 to 1934 and retired with a .336 batting average. Attending as Allen's guests were two local celebrities, both rabid baseball fans, former Alabama football coach Frank Thomas and his protégé, current Kentucky and future Alabama football coach Paul "Bear" Bryant. (Bryant had been tutored by Allen in the early 1930s when both attended the university.)

The game was a big one for DiMaggio and Henrich, both of whom hit home runs, but a bust for Yogi. George Wilson, a Barons outfielder, hit a foul off Yogi's right hand that sent him to a Birmingham hospital for three stitches between his second and third fingers. Yogi missed opening day, and when he returned to the lineup his play was sluggish. Whether because of inexperience or a sore hand or a combination of both, he was ineffective against left-handed pitchers. The Red Sox had a mediocre left-hander named Earl Johnson, whose one definite talent was his ability to get Berra out with sweeping curve balls. A writer asked Yogi what pitch Johnson had that was so effective. "How do I know?" Yogi replied, "I ain't seen it yet."[7]

———

CARMEN SAVED ALL the letters Yogi wrote to her during the 1948 season. One of them reads

Darling, When I'm around you I'm always in the mood for love . . . I love you so much . . . I'm sure glad that you don't want to go out with any other boys and I don't want to go out with any girls . . . I mean that. I love you— I love you."

From another:

Honey, Remember that song "Saturday Night Is The Loneliest Night of The Week"? And I mean it, darling, it really is lonesome without you . . . I'll be playing in the game today, and I hope I can hit a home run for you . . . Darling, you said I won't have any time to miss you. What do you mean? I do miss you always. I am always thinking about you.[8]

Yogi was still suffering some mild anxiety at this point in his life, though he had confidence that things would work out. He was still unsure about his catching, but felt that as long as he continued to hit, the Yankees would keep him and he'd improve. As for Carmen, he decided to take no more chances. In Washington to play the Senators, he asked Bobby Brown to help him pick out an engagement ring. "I had never exactly asked her," he reasoned, "but I was pretty sure she would take it or else why would she keep going out with me all the time."[9]

When the Yankees were in St. Louis to play the Browns, Carmen went to the games with Tony and Mike. She wanted Yogi back in town again, this time for the July 13 All-Star game at Sportsman's Park, and she hedged her bet by stuffing the All-Star ballot box for her boyfriend. "I campaigned all over town," she later confessed, "and I not only got everybody else to send in ballots, I filled out every one I could get my hands on myself."[10] He made it, in the third spot on the roster behind Buddy Rosar of the A's and Birdie Tebbetts of the Red Sox, but did not play.

The night before the game, Yogi asked Carmen to dinner with the family. Paulina pulled out all the stops. Unsure of what words to use—"I didn't know the first thing about how you were supposed to ask a girl if she should marry you"[11]—Yogi decided to let the ring speak for him. When Carmen turned to talk to his brother Tony, Yogi put the box with the ring on her plate. When she saw it, she was silent, but, said Yogi, "you should have seen the expression on her face."[12] The ring was a perfect fit.

"I got kidded a lot, naturally, but I didn't mind," Yogi said years later. "They could call me homely all they wanted to. I had a beautiful girl and nobody could deny that."[13]

———

EARLY IN 1949, Yogi bumped into Pete Reiser, a St. Louis native who had been traded by the Dodgers to the Boston Braves. Yogi handed him an invitation and asked him if he was coming to the wedding. Reiser smiled and assured him he was. "Good," said Berra, slipping the invitation back into his pocket. "No sense in wasting an invitation."

———

PROFESSIONALLY, THE FALL of 1948 was something of a downer for Yogi. In place of the euphoric feeling after the World Series win the previous year, he went back to St. Louis with the knowledge that the Yankees were only the third-best team in the American League. He knew there would be changes, but he had no idea what they'd be. The season of 1947 had seemed like the start of a fabulous new era for Yogi and the Yankees. Now it did not seem that way. During 1948 DiMaggio was outstanding, hitting .320 and leading the league in home runs, RBIs, and total bases. But Shea went from 14–5 to 9–10, Chandler was gone, Rizzuto hit just .252, first baseman George McQuinn hit only .248 with 11 home runs, Charlie Keller played in only 83 games and hit .267, and Joe Page's ERA swelled to 4.25. The Yankees finished behind Cleveland and Boston. The Indians went on to beat the Boston Braves four games to two in the World Series.

Though Bucky Harris had been Yogi's staunch supporter, he had not quite kept his promise to make him the regular catcher—Berra caught just 71 games, compared to 82 for Gus Niarhos, who hit .266 without a single home run all season. Yogi continued to improve as a hitter: he was .305 with 14 home runs and 24 doubles in just 125 games. He missed by two having his first 100 RBI season, a fact that certainly did not go unnoticed by the fans, press, or front office. But signs of his immaturity as a catcher were undeniable. On June 11, 1948, in a game against the Indians, Yogi unwittingly incited a near riot. Left-hander Tommy Byrne, not known for his control, was having a rough time serving up strikes to Indian hitters. Berra, already known for his nonstop chatter behind the plate, had not yet learned when to muffle it when dealing with umpires. He began to bait Cal Hubbard, a man who did not take kindly to such things. Standing nearly 6'5" and weighing enough to be a pro football lineman—which in fact he had been for both the Green Bay Packers and New York Giants— Hubbard kept his temper for a while, but finally blew up when Yogi turned to him on what he thought was a close pitch and yelled, loud enough for many fans to hear, "You missed it! You missed it and you know it!" That was bad enough, but when Yogi began kicking the dirt around home plate, Hubbard was boiling. But Hubbard kept his temper; Berra did not. After throwing the ball back to Byrne (who was himself mouthing insults to Hubbard) Yogi spun around and said—again, loud enough for many fans to hear—"Just say you missed it and I'll shut up!" Hubbard ripped off his mask and jerked his right thumb upward to indicate Berra was out of the game. Bucky Harris and Charlie Dressen screamed to no avail. The game ground to a halt as Yankee fans threw everything from peanuts to Cracker Jack onto the field. Phil Rizzuto said he had never seen anything like it: "I swear, it was as bad as if we had been playing in Brooklyn."

Even in Brooklyn, though, it was rare for a fan to jump out of the stands and throw a beer can at an umpire, but that's what happened in Yankee Stadium that day. The incident was shocking for a number of reasons, the obvious one being that Yogi had seemed like such an easygoing guy that everyone was startled by his loss of temper. Yet another surprise was that the normally placid Yankee fans had become so enamored with Yogi that they were ready to attack an umpire who they thought was abusing their guy. In any event, American League president Will Harridge leveled a bruising $100 fine on Yogi, and Bucky Harris, afraid that all the league's umpires would have it in for the Yankees unless a sincere apology was forthcoming, told Yogi to make peace before the next game in full view of the fans. Just before the game, Yogi, mask tucked under his arm, walked over to Hubbard, grinned sheepishly and said, "You shouldn't take me serious, Cal. After all, I ain't really *ferocious*."[14] Hubbard laughed and shook hands. Who could stay mad at this guy?

It was the first time Yogi had had a near-calamitous confrontation with an ump since he bumped into Artie Gore in Newark two years earlier. It would never happen again.

Despite his growing popularity, Yogi's future in baseball was up in the air by the end of the season. Two men had believed in him. Now Larry MacPhail—for all his shortcomings, MacPhail always thought highly of Yogi—had lef the organization, and Bucky Harris would soon be gone. George Weiss did not like Bucky. Despite Bucky's record of success, Weiss referred to him derisively as "a four-hour manager" who worked an hour before the game and all during it, but during the rest of his waking hours, Weiss thought, Harris wasn't totally absorbed with baseball.

"Berra's Luck" struck again just before the 1948 season ended. When Bucky was fired, Yogi lost a manager who liked him and supported him with the tough New York press. He could have no way of knowing that the Yankees' new choice for a manager would be the greatest stroke of luck of his career.

―――

THE END OF January 1949 was a tumultuous time for much of the planet. On January 25, just five days after President Harry Truman began his full term in office, forces from the Communist Party of China entered Beijing—or as most Americans knew it then, Peking. On the same day, David Ben-Gurion was elected the first prime minister of Israel. All through the Midwest, a series of horrendous storms over three weeks killed tens of thousands of cattle and sheep.

But it was a good day on January 28 on the Hill when Yogi and Carmen were married at the Second St. Ambrose Church in the same parish his mother and father had been married in. Carmen prepared for the marriage by taking instruction from the St. Ambrose priests and converting to Catholicism. "I didn't have any religion of my own," she told Joe Trimble. "I became a Catholic because it seemed to me that a religion that had such a grip on Yogi must be a good one."[15]

They drove the Nash to New Orleans for their honeymoon. Later, at a sports banquet in Florida, Cardinals announcer Harry Caray, a second-generation Italian-American himself, kidded Yogi on the subject of marrying a girl named Short. "What happened," he wanted to know, "to all the girls"—meaning Italian girls—"on the Hill?" "They had their chance," said Yogi.

———

WHEN YOGI ARRIVED at the Yankees spring training camp in St. Petersburg on February 22, he found his new manager waiting for him.

Like most of the players, Yogi knew very little about Charles Dillon "Casey" Stengel except what he had seen in the papers. Yogi's best friend, Phil Rizzuto, knew Stengel and didn't much care for him. He summed up his feelings in his 1994 book, *The October Twelve*, about the 1949–1953 Yankee champions: "Mr. Stengel was not my cup of tea. If I were marooned on the proverbial South Sea island, Stengel would not be on a list of people I would want to help me build signal fires."[16] The source of Rizzuto's dislike of Stengel may have been his rejection at age sixteen (or seventeen, depending on which version of the story you hear) at a tryout for the Brooklyn Dodgers. According to Rizzuto, Stengel turned him down because he was too small—not an entirely unreasonable judgment on Stengel's part, considering that the 5'6" Rizzuto was usually listed at about 150 pounds during his playing years and probably weighed a good ten to twenty pounds less than that as a teenager. But Stengel, Rizzuto would later insist, really rubbed it in, telling him to "go get a shoeshine box."

The story doesn't sound quite right. Casey *liked* small, scrappy players, and there's no evidence that he ever went out of his way to insult those who weren't quite good enough for his teams. Steven Goldman, author of the brilliant analysis of Casey's evolution as a manager, *Forging Genius*, also doubts the shoeshine box story: "I reviewed Rizzuto's versions of the story, and they don't ring true. *Someone* may have told him to get a shoeshine box, but it was probably an opposing player or a scout or maybe a Dodgers coach. Rizzuto never told the story the same way twice. It was only later, when he had reason to be angry at Stengel—or thought he did, when the Yankees released him in 1956—that the story came to focus on Casey. Rizzuto probably came to believe that Stengel said it, but I doubt he actually did." If Stengel remembered the Dodgers tryout, he never mentioned it, and went out of his way to praise Rizzuto over the years, calling him "the greatest shortstop I ever saw" in his autobiography.[17]

There might have been another reason as well: DiMaggio, at a stage in his career where he would have balked at any new manager, did not like Stengel, and Rizzuto idolized DiMaggio. They were Joe McCarthy men, and the McCarthy clique on the Yankees never quite warmed up to Casey. But Yogi Berra was not a McCarthy man.

All Berra knew was the gossip he heard from the players and what he read in the papers. He might have seen John Drebinger's piece in The New York Times which said Casey had been born in 1890 in Kansas City—K.C. became Casey. Drebinger described Stengel as a "onetime hard hitting outfielder, manager of both major and minor league clubs, sage, wit, raconteur, as glib with the wisecrack as the late Jimmy Walker."[18] Yogi might also have read that at his first Yankees press conference, Stengel pulled a faux pas on a par with anything Yogi had ever said: "I want first of all to thank Mr. *Bob* Topping for this opportunity," thus reminding the world of what *Dan* Topping wanted the world to forget, namely his brother Bob, who had been garnering unwanted headlines for the family because of his much-publicized marital difficulties with actress Arlene Judge. Some thought that the clown image that preceded Stengel meant that he was lovable, or at least likeable. Many did end up liking him, but it wasn't easy. He provided good copy for sportswriters, but he suffered no one he thought to be a fool, even veteran baseball writers who had worked for years in the newspaper capital of America. Once, talking to a dugout full of reporters, he responded to a statement by the highly respected Harold Rosenthal of the *New York Herald Tribune* by saying, in full earshot of everyone, "Yer full of shit and I'll tell ya why." Rosenthal was so offended that he told Roger Kahn he would never speak to Stengel again—which, of course, was impossible as long as he was writing about the Yankees. Still, recalls Kahn, Rosenthal bristled for several years afterward when he heard someone say, "Casey must have been a sweet old guy."[19]

When Yogi had first come to the Yankees, writers were fond of saying that he seemed to be a character out of a Ring Lardner story. Now, he was about to meet a man who *was* a character out of a Ring Lardner story.

IF CASEY STENGEL had not existed, even the great Ring Lardner could not have invented him—though he did reinvent him. Lardner had a genius for incorporating the language of everyday ballplayers into his short stories; some of it was no doubt refined, but Lardner never tried to hide the source of his inspirations. "Just keep talking," he supposedly told Stengel when Casey was an outfielder with the Brooklyn Dodgers, "and I'll get my story."

Precisely how revolutionary Lardner's writing style was is evidenced by an essay written by, of all people, Virginia Woolf. While criticizing writers such as Sinclair Lewis for their self-consciousness as Americans, Woolf, who wouldn't have known a declaration of ball four from the Balfour Declaration, noted that "Mr. Lardner is not merely unaware that we [British] differ; he is unaware that we exist . . . Mr. Lardner does not waste a moment in thinking that he is using American slang or Shakespeare's English—whether he is proud of being American or ashamed of not being Japanese; all his mind is on the story. Hence, incidentally, he writes the best prose that has come our way." Commenting further on Lardner's most famous story, "You Know Me Al," she wrote that it was "a story written often in a language which is not English . . . To what does he owe his success? Besides his unconsciousness . . . With extraordinary ease and aptitude, with the quickest strokes, the surest touch, the sharpest insight he lets Jack Keefe the baseball player cut out his own outline, fill in his own depths, until the figure of the foolish, boastful, innocent athlete lives before us. As he babbles out his mind on paper there rise up friends, sweethearts, the scenery, town, and country—all surround him and make him up in his completeness."[20]

Casey would have objected to the use of the adjectives foolish, boastful, and, probably, innocent if they had been applied to him—most likely, he would also have disputed Woolf's use of interior monologue in *To the Lighthouse*—but otherwise it's clear that Lardner's fictional portraits of ballplayers like Casey were based largely on his intimate knowledge and understanding of their language and character. In Casey Stengel, Lardner struck literary gold. The mind boggles at what Lardner, who died in 1933, would have been able to accomplish had he lived long enough to meet Yogi Berra, the only man in baseball capable of challenging Casey Stengel as a verbal stylist.

However, on Columbus Day, October 12, 1948, when the announcement was made that he had been given a two-year contract to become the Yankees' fifth manager in two years, Stengel's verbal dynamics couldn't cover the fact that his big league record was lackluster. He had managed in the Eastern, American Association and Pacific Coast leagues in Worcester, Toledo, Milwaukee, Kansas City, and Oakland for a dozen years and had nine seasons of major league managerial experience with the Dodgers and Braves, with very little to show for it but a trunkful of terrific stories. His minor league teams had won 1,037 games out of 1,967, for a more than respectable won-lost percentage of .528. He had won two pennants, but the second had come two full decades after the first. More to the point— at least the point of most New York sportswriters—he had never managed a single inning in the American League. He had won something in the National League: in the spring of 1944, the *Sporting News*, the self-proclaimed Bible of Baseball, had taken a poll of more than 150 baseball writers on major league managers. Bill "Deacon" McKechnie of the Cincinnati Reds was regarded as the most studious, Leo Durocher was considered to be the feistiest, and Casey Stengel handily beat out Jimmy Dykes and Charlie Grimm for the title of funniest. It was an honor of sorts, considering that Casey was not even managing in the majors at the time, having been fired by the Boston Braves in 1943.

The younger writers knew the stories about Casey, such as the legendary day in 1919 when he was playing for the Pittsburgh Pirates and won over a heckling Brooklyn Dodger crowd by walking up to the plate and doffing his cap to release a sparrow—or at least that's the way the story came to be told. Even if it wasn't true, it said something about Stengel that so many people thought such a tale and a couple of dozen others would have been told about him.

The journalists' sentiments on hearing he was hired were probably best summed up by one of Casey's early biographers, Joseph Durso: "It was as though the State Department had borrowed Emmett Kelly from Ringling Brothers and introduced him as the government's new Chief of Protocol."[21]

Eastern writers might have been forgiven for not knowing much about Stengel's peripatetic career, but if they'd done their homework they'd have known that the Pacific Coast League was no circus. Many thought its talent level wasn't far below that of the major leagues, and superb managers had come out of it, including Paul Richards, Al Lopez, and Bobby Bragan. But none of the New York writers had the vision and experience of George Weiss, who, by 1948 had been administering minor league systems for the Yankees since 1925 in the Eastern League—where his first manager had been Casey Stengel. Weiss knew what no one else did, namely that Stengel had never had first-rate talent to manage and had usually exceeded expectations. With the right talent, there was no reason why Stengel couldn't win at a major league level. When Weiss told his bosses that he thought Stengel could manage the Yankees he must have known he was betting his job on it.*

Casey Stengel, at fifty-eight, was by far the oldest manager ever hired by the Yankees. Stengel played fourteen seasons in the major leagues, including 177 games over three seasons for the New York Giants, where he became a protégé of the most pugnacious and perhaps the greatest manager of pre–World War II baseball, John McGraw. He had had just two truly memorable days as a player. The first came on October 10, 1923. Casey, after having made few contributions to the Giants' pennant run, hit a line drive to his opposite field, left, off Yankee reliever Joe Bush into the deepest part of Yankee Stadium; he beat the relay home for an inside-the-park home run. Damon Runyon described him thusly: "The warped old legs"—Stengel was just thirty-three but looked much older—"twisted and bent by many a year of baseball campaigning, just barely held out under Casey until he reached the plate . . . Then they collapsed."[22] In Stengel's defense, it should be pointed out that he lost a shoe rounding third and practically stumbled to home plate.

That hit won the game and was all the more memorable because it came during the first radio broadcast of a World Series game, with the histrionic Graham McNamee providing such verbal fireworks that some listeners later said they nearly had heart attacks. (In 1927, when McNamee worked the radio broadcast of the Dempsey-Tunney "Long Count" rematch, many listeners *did* die of heart attacks.)

Two days later, on October 12, Casey hit another home run to beat the Yankees. They were the only two games McGraw's Giants would win against their hated crosstown rivals. Less than a month later, McGraw traded Stengel to the dismal Boston Braves. Casey loved McGraw, but he never forgot the humiliation of that trade. Like Yogi, he covered the hurt with a quip: "It's lucky I didn't hit three home runs in three games, or McGraw would have traded me to the 3-I League." (The 3-I was the

---

*Though Weiss may have hedged his bet. Although it has never been confirmed through other sources, Stengel said in his autobiography, "I had a verbal agreement with them—I don't have it in writing and they don't—that if in one year they didn't like my work too well or I didn't like their methods, I could leave despite my two-year contract." (Stengel and Paxton, *Casey at the Bat*, p. 173)

Illinois-Indian-Iowa league.) In truth, though, he had made so little impression as a player that many years later, when schooling Mickey Mantle on the intricacies of Ebbets Field, Mantle was amazed to learn that his manager had once been a big league player.

The New York writers were not wrong in calling Stengel a clown; where they were wrong was in failing to realize that he was a great deal more than a clown. In fact, the Emmett Kelly comparison was appropriate. Stengel, like Kelly, was a professional entertainer, but also studious and serious about his craft. He was smart and intensely competitive, but always, behind the professionalism was an enormous capacity for having fun. It fueled his love for baseball. Though neither man knew it at the time, this made Casey Stengel the perfect manager for Yogi Berra, and together the two men would, beginning with their first season in 1949, ⁣⁣⁣⁣⁣⁣⁣⁣⁣⁣⁣⁣

———

STENGEL IDOLIZED JOHN McGraw and learned from him, but he was no disciple. Or, stated another way, if McGraw had written a Bible on his era, then Casey, by the time he joined the Yankees, was ready to write the New Testament. The art of platooning, for instance; invented by the Boston Braves' George Stallings before World War I and refined by John McGraw, in 1949 Casey Stengel was ready to perfect it. "I used to play with the dead ball," he said in his autobiography, "and this gives me a different slant than some of the other managers. I saw baseball change with a lively ball, and I watched men manage with a lively ball. I found out you had to have different methods in pitching, you had to have different methods of how to run a game. And you had to execute so as to get the best out of each player, even if it did embarrass him at times. That meant platooning him, which will cause embarrassment every day." What Stengel meant by embarrassment was that no player likes to be told that he hits left-handed pitching much better than right-handed, or vice versa, or that he is, when combined with another player of limited but specific talents, a terrific player but that when on his own, playing full time, he might be no better than mediocre. "I know a lot of players never understood my platoon system," he wrote in summing up his years with the Yankees, "and neither did a lot of other people. They say that now that I'm through running the Yankees, there won't be so much platooning in baseball. Well, I'll say this—I don't think we'd have won the ten pennants in my twelve years without it."[23]

IN A VOTE of more than 200 baseball writers before the season, nearly 100 picked the Boston Red Sox (with former Yankee manager Joe McCarthy) to win the pennant, while just under 40 percent picked the Cleveland Indians. The Yankees got just six first-place votes. The Indians looked like a genuine powerhouse. Rookie Gene Bearden had won 20 games in 1948, as had the remarkable Bob Lemon, who chipped in five home runs as a pinch-hitter. Bob Feller won 19 and Satchel Paige, finally getting a chance to show his stuff in the big leagues at who knew what age, was 6–1 with an ERA of 2.47. Future Hall of Fame shortstop Lou Boudreau hit .355 the season before with 18 home runs, while near–Hall of Fame third baseman Ken Keltner had hit .297 with 31 home runs and 119 RBIs. Former Negro Leagues star Larry Doby proved to be as good as everyone thought, batting .301 with 14 home runs in 121 games. And most galling of all, Joe Gordon, dealt to Cleveland for Allie Reynolds, had responded by hitting 32 home runs and leading the team in RBIs with 124. The Red Sox appeared even more formidable. With twenty-two-year-old Billy Goodman (a .310 hitter in 1948) playing mostly at first base, future Hall of Famer Bobby Doerr (27 home runs and 111 RBIs) at second, the under-rated Vern Stephens (29 home runs, 137 RBIs) at shortstop, and slick-fielding Johnny Pesky at third base, the Red Sox had a sensational infield, and of course in Ted Williams they had the man regarded as the game's best hitter. The pitching was more suspect than the hitting, though in Mel Parnell (15–8 in 1948) the Red Sox looked to have a genuine southpaw ace.

Stengel's plan to rejuvenate the Yankees was nothing less than a radical overhaul of the team's philosophy, beginning, as Berra was quick to note on arriving at Miller Huggins Field in St. Petersburg, with a refresher course in the basics, a plan that no doubt failed to endear Casey to a great star like DiMaggio. He also tried to impose some of the discipline that Weiss thought had been lacking under Harris—or, as some players felt, Casey was the instrument with which Weiss was trying to impose discipline. Specifically applied in St. Petersburg, this meant just one night a week, Thursday, at the local dog track, where some Yankees had practically been paying rent. Stengel quickly found out something about his new team: man-agerial rules were for other players, not Joe DiMaggio, and if DiMaggio vio-lated them, the other Yankees would soon follow suit. One Friday night, DiMaggio showed up at the puppy park, as some of the players called it, "dressed real flashy," as Yogi noted, in white slacks and a bright tropical shirt, according to Joe Trimble.[24] (But how would Yogi have known that if he was not at the track himself?) DiMaggio, like Rizzuto, made no bones about his being a Joe McCarthy man and didn't hesitate to flaunt a Stengel dictum. The Thursday night rule went into the discarded pile.

Casey was careful both at the time and in later years not to knock his predecessors: "Mr. McCarthy was a great manager—he won eight pennants with the Yankees in fifteen years . . . A lot of the talent he developed was still on the Yankees when I got there. But I had to find out how to use this talent to win my way. I had to play my own system."[25] In practical terms, this meant alternating right-handed hitting Billy Johnson with left-handed Bobby Brown at third base, and in the outfield righty hitter Hank Bauer with lefty Gene Woodling; it also meant switching Tommy Henrich, who had a bad knee, between outfield and first base, which put less stress on his legs. Charlie Keller could still hit, but had to be rested because of back trouble. Casey knew that such tactics would anger some of his veterans: "They will be mad at the manager, because the manager didn't play them regular. I didn't like to see it, but it did happen with a number of men." There was a cure for such anger: "They just had to realize that the best way to show the manager up is by working hard and keeping in shape, so you can play well when you get the chance."[26]

The art of platooning included knowing when *not* to platoon. There were a few players Stengel knew enough to leave alone. Joe DiMaggio, for instance: "Well, naturally, you don't platoon a man like DiMaggio."[27] Amazingly, for a man who was fifty-eight years old when the season started and who had managed for nine seasons in the big leagues, DiMaggio was the first Hall of Fame–caliber player Stengel had ever had close to his prime.° DiMaggio instinctively disliked his new manager, which may or may not have had anything to do with his own managerial ambitions. (Most historians are convinced Joe wasn't serious about managing, despite the persistent rumors.) Whatever his reasons, DiMaggio did not take to Casey from the start and was noticeably distant when George Weiss asked him to be present at Stengel's October 12 press conference. Joe showed up, but looked very much as if he wished he were somewhere else.

°Casey actually had an amazing number of Hall of Famers—eight—but they were either there too late, like Hack Wilson, who played 67 games at Brooklyn in 1934, or too early, such as Warren Spahn, who pitched just 4 games for Stengel with the Boston Braves in 1942. Casey was lucky enough to have Ernie Lombardi catch 85 games for him in 1942. Lombardi, age thirty-four, led the NL in batting, .330, but batted just 309 times and drove in only 46 runs.

Someone else Stengel did not want to platoon was another player who didn't like him, Phil Rizzuto. Sometimes, though, Rizzuto listened to Casey. In spring training, Stengel spotted a flaw in Rizzuto's throw stemming, Casey felt, from an arm injury he had suffered in 1948. He suggested that Phil stop trying to throw bullets to first on balls he had fielded deep in the hole to his right; instead, his manager suggested, Phil should try lofting the ball to first base. "And he did whether I wanted him to or not."[28]

The third—and, as it turned out, the most important—player Stengel did not want to platoon was Yogi Berra. Stengel quickly surmised that the 1949 Yankees, even with a physically sound DiMaggio, would not have as much punch as previous Yankee pennant winners. There was, he saw, a partial solution for that: get Berra into the lineup on a regular basis. Casey already had enough good hitting outfielders, and anyway, he already understood a principle that many managers would not clearly comprehend until Earl Weaver began to articulate it in the 1970s. Namely, if you got better than average hitting from the men playing the key defensive positions—catcher, shortstop, second base—then you likely had a jump on the opposition. If a platoon of players at one of those positions could produce something like a .300 batting average and perhaps 20 home runs, it would be a considerable boost to the team; if *one* player could produce those numbers, it was a bonanza.

The prerequisite, of course, was that a catcher or infielder be capable. First basemen and outfielders could get by with mediocre or even inept fielding, if they were above-average hitters. Shortstops were involved in too many plays to excuse poor fielding, and this was much more true of catchers, who were not only on the line for every pitch but were often *calling* for that pitch. Stengel knew that Yogi's hitting could make him into the most valuable catcher in the league. He knew something else that many others did not: namely, that Berra had the tools to become a great catcher as well, which would turn him into the most valuable *player* in the league.

———

OVER THE WINTER, Berra met an accountant who lived near the Hill to seek some advice on his taxes. The accountant asked him how much he was going to make in the upcoming season; Yogi, as reluctant as all players were in that era to openly discuss their salaries, told him it wasn't any of his business—not yet, at least, as he was secretly anticipating a salary struggle with the Yankee front office. Well, okay, the accountant replied, how much do you expect to be paid the next year, 1950? More, Berra answered, than the Yankees expect to pay me.

Berra had been paid $8,500 for the 1948 season, and having assessed his value to the team, thought he deserved something around $15,000 the next year. George Weiss shook his head no; a raise of $1,500 was all he was willing to offer Yogi for hitting .305 and just missing the 100 RBI mark. It was the first but far from the last of the salary struggles Berra and Weiss would have. The Yankees' publicity man, Red Patterson, had developed a rating system for American League ballplayers, dividing a player's runs driven home by his total number of at-bats. To no one's surprise, Berra finished behind Joe DiMaggio and Ted Williams, the league's best hitters; the big surprise was that Joe Gordon, Vern Stephens, and Bobby Doerr were the only other AL players to finish ahead of Yogi. Berra made use of Patterson's chart in his negotiations with an exasperated Weiss.

Berra, Weiss said, should remember that he was lucky to be a Yankee; Yogi told him that he was indeed lucky, but that the Yankees weren't exactly suffering with him. If he didn't get more than $1,500, the twenty-three-year-old told the most powerful GM in baseball, he'd quit and go find work back in St. Louis—though, as he admitted many years later, "I don't think I was serious about that."[29] But Weiss wasn't sure.

Weiss eventually offered a $3,500 raise to $12,000—not what Yogi wanted, but a great deal more than Weiss had planned to pay. Weiss was the toughest salary negotiator in baseball, but the stumpy little catcher from St. Louis who had never graduated from high school was studying his moves: "Even while I was giving in, I was memorizing the things Weiss was telling me about how the Yankees believed in paying a ballplayer all that he was worth as soon as he had proved it. Okay, I figured, maybe I hadn't proven it yet, but when I did, I was going to remind them."[30]

A few years, a couple of World Series rings, and an MVP award later, Weiss invited the Berras to his house in Connecticut, where he had a surprise for Yogi: his first contract with the Yankees—the one for the season he played in Norfolk for $90 a month, back when Weiss was the Yankees' farm director. (The only other first contract Weiss had kept was Joe DiMaggio's.) He was proud, Berra thought, that he got me so cheap. Perhaps it was also a concession on Weiss's part. It was almost as if he was saying to Yogi, Well, those days are gone forever.

———

YOGI KNEW, OF course, that he'd never pry really significant money out of Weiss until he had won a starting catcher's role, and to attain this, he would have to work very hard, very quickly. While Yogi learned, Casey was putting the Yankee pitchers through a course in fundamentals. An early exhibition series with the Brooklyn Dodgers—a team many of the Yankees thought that, if they won the pennant, they'd be facing in the World Series—jolted Stengel. The Brooklyn base runners were running wild pretty much as they had done on Yogi in the 1947 World Series. But Stengel's eye caught something that Bucky Harris and others had not. "Our pitchers," said Casey in his inimitable way, "hadn't been brought up in the American League to have perfection in holding men on the bases, and the new pitchers we had from the minor leagues had poor moves to first base, second base, third base . . . It made Berra look bad as a catcher again, because the pitchers did nothing to protect him."[31] Stengel and his new pitching coach, Jim Turner, schooled their men to eliminate the high leg kick that allowed base runners such big jumps; they also told the pitchers to concentrate more on the hitters and less on the base runners.

"The Dodgers," thought Casey, "had some first-class talent. Pee Wee Reese was a great base runner. As a base stealer, he'd only get caught five times in twenty to thirty attempts. Jackie Robinson was a sensational base runner. He was a thrill-runner. He'd get on base and bluff you, then he'd give it a run and be safe." Stengel admired Dodger sluggers Gil Hodges and Duke Snider, but the Dodgers catcher, Roy Campanella, made an even bigger impression on him: "He looked like he had a fat stomach, but that stomach didn't bother him at all, and he was a splendid low-ball catcher—he could squat behind home plate with his fanny actually touching the ground."[32] It was the first meeting of the two men who would come to define the position of catcher, two men who would clash many times over the next several seasons as friendly warriors.

Yogi Berra and Roy Campanella had an amazing number of things in common, beginning with their Italian-American heritage. "Campy," as he was already widely known in 1949, had had to wait till the previous season to get past the major league's color barrier because his mother was African-American, though his father was a second-generation Sicilian. (Campanella, he noted in his autobiography, *It's Good to Be Alive*, "means little bell in Italian.")[33] He was born in Philadelphia three and a half years before Yogi, and like Berra, to a large family—the Campanellas had six kids, outnumbering the Berras by one. Both came from families that had weathered the Depression by holding together, with the kids working at odd jobs. Little Roy, like Little Lawdie, sold newspapers. Both excelled at numerous sports, including boxing, and both shunned the academic life. "All I thought about mainly," Roy said in his memoirs, in a phrase that could have come out of Yogi's own autobiography, "was getting out after school and playing ball."[34] Both grew to a height of 5'8", though most rosters listed Roy at about five to ten pounds heavier than Yogi's given weight of 194. And, finally, when it came to catching, both men idolized Yogi's new coach—as a boy, Campanella had tacked pictures of hometown Philadelphia A's star Mickey Cochrane to his wall next to those of the other great catcher of his day, the Yankees' Bill Dickey.

———

"LAST NIGHT," *The New York Times* reported shortly after Stengel's hiring, "Casey went into a huddle with George M. Weiss, general manager of the Yankees. It is a fair guess that there will be many such sessions in the next few weeks, for all interested parties realize there is much work to be done before the Yankees can ever hope to reclaim their baseball leadership."[35] No one yet had any idea how much work it would take.

Casey, who was now in the American Leugin, did not select his own coaches, but in his words, "decided to go by the recommendations of Mr. Weiss, with the understanding that if I wasn't satisfied with the work of the men he brought in, they would not stay one full season." This doesn't sound quite right; if the Yankees were to win the pennant, it would have to be taken as an indication that the coaches had done good work, and if they didn't it would almost certainly be taken as an indication that Casey had not, in which case he would be in no position to demand new coaches. At any rate, it's likely that Weiss would not have brought in new men without at least some feedback from the manager he was going out on a limb to hire. Signing Bill Dickey was Weiss's idea, but, Casey said, "That sounded like a very good idea to me."[36] The only Yankee coach retained from Bucky Harris's team was Frank Crosetti, who remained coach of the infielders but also became third base coach. John Schulte, the bullpen coach who had signed Yogi, retired and went back to St. Louis.

Bill Dickey, who was inducted into the Hall of Fame in 1954, was regarded by many as the best catcher the game had ever seen. A quiet man who lived his life outside the limelight, Dickey was, in 1949, the most revered living ex-Yankee. He had been the anchor of the greatest Yankee dynasty up to that time, the team that won four consecutive World Series from 1936 to 1939, driving in more than 100 runs in each of those seasons. All in all, Dickey was on seven World Series winners and batted .313 over seventeen years. In 1949, though, the Yankees didn't want Dickey as a batting coach; they were more interested in his reputation as a great receiver. He had led American League catchers in fielding percentage four times, put-outs six times, and assists three times, but never in passed balls.

Over the winter, the *Sporting News* reported that "Berra is a question mark in so far as his availability as a catcher is concerned. Stengel says that the bridegroom has been returned to the backstop squad quite definitely, that Bill Dickey will take him in hand on March 1 and attempt to achieve the same sort of success he enjoyed with Aaron Robinson. However, the Yogi hasn't got the fingers for accurate throwing"—Berra's fingers were considered stubby for a catcher, and he had been forced to paint his finger-nails so his pitchers could read his signals—"and it is possible that he will go right on pitching curves to second base."[37] Within a very short time, Bill Dickey would have the *Sporting News* and everyone else looking at Yogi without question marks.

———

SPUD CHANDLER, YOGI'S first batterymate in the major leagues, was once asked why he thought Berra was not a good catcher when he first came up. "He was in tough shape," replied Chandler, "for two reasons. One, he was worried about his catching. And, two, he had good reason to worry—he was not a good catcher." Said Chandler, "Yogi was so self con-scious that he did not know how to give the signs. He gave them way out of his leg, way out on his knee. I called time and told him: 'Berra, they are going to pick your teeth (steal the signs) if you don't get the signs down in your crotch. Don't let the signs hang out that way, they will steal us blind.' He tried but when he hid the signs, it was still hard for me to see his stubby fingers, and I crossed him up a couple of times. He would call for a curve ball and I saw the fastball sign, so I hummed him a fastball. The second time I did, he called time and came out. He said in plaintive voice, 'You crossed me up!' I countered, 'The hell I did—I didn't cross you up, you crossed yourself up.' "[38]

Dickey quickly perceived that Berra's biggest problem was a simple lack of experience. Much has been made by Yogi and others of the remarkable job Dickey did in turning him into a great major league catcher, but the truth is that Dickey couldn't have done it if Berra not had possessed the intelligence and innate tools of greatness in the first place.

In the spring of 1949, Berra turned twenty-four. He had had less than one full season's worth of minor league games behind the plate, and so far with the Yankees had caught just 122 games. No one had ever really taught him to catch; what he knew he had picked up on the run. Dickey gave him a crash course in catching fundamentals and mechanics and then drilled him over and over and over. "None of the stuff I'm teaching him is really hard," Dickey told a reporter, "but the only way to learn it is by practicing it over and over again, until some days you get sick and tired of doing it. Like I sometimes did when I was a kid."[39]

Dickey's emphasis on repetition tested Berra's determination, a quality which some had failed to see in Yogi. What Dickey found was that he would tire of giving instructions before his pupil tired of carrying them out. Berra was squatting too far behind the plate; Dickey taught him to catch with his throwing hand behind his glove to protect it. Setting up several inches closer to the plate, Dickey told him, would make it easier to hold on to or block pitches in the dirt. Positioning himself so far back in the batter's box also put him at a disadvantage when trying to throw runners out at second base; against most good runners, Dickey told him, a few inches is going to make the difference. Many had questioned Berra's arm, but Dickey saw that the problem wasn't his arm strength but his balance when he threw. He must position his foot correctly and step forward with his left foot as he was about to throw. That way, he would be throwing with his whole body and not just his arm. The greater velocity would keep the ball down and cut down on those famous high hard ones that sailed into center field.

Yogi was also schooled in the difficult and dangerous job of taking throws from the outfield with runners coming home. No catcher can ever earn respect unless he is ready to take a hit from a runner trying to score. The question is where he can best position himself to take the throw and make the tag. The catcher has a split second to decide whether he will go out and meet the ball or nail the runner as he slides in. The latter is a bang-bang play, meaning catcher takes throw, turns toward runner, and—bang! "The worst part of it," Yogi said in reflection, "is that you're not properly braced for it, and that's when you get bowled over good. The runner has all the advantage and the catcher has to do all the worrying. I know because I have got hit a few times."[40] He could have added that as a base runner he had run into a few catchers himself.

How good a job Dickey did with Berra may be judged by how good a teacher Yogi himself became. In 1966, McGraw-Hill published *Yogi Berra's Baseball Guidebook: Basic Plays and Playing Techniques for Boys*,* which outlined and illustrated the fundamentals for playing each position. The catcher's chapter was particularly instructive:

---

*Yogi could have had no idea that, forty years later, girls, including my daughter, would be studying his book as they prepared for high school softball.

- On fouls and pop-ups: "The catcher yanks the mask off his face and *holds onto it*! He does not get rid of the mask until he has spotted the ball in the air and knows its direction. Only then does he toss it away and go after the ball. If the catcher just threw off the mask before taking a look for the ball, he might throw it in the wrong direction and step on it while chasing the popup."

- On plays at the plate: "Deliberately blocking the plate can be ruled 'interference' by the umpire. The catcher straddles home plate, just the way an infielder straddles his base. He grabs the throw and lets the runner slide into the tag. The catcher doesn't have to worry about the runner trying to go around him; just as the catcher can't block the base line, the runner has to stay inside the markings."[41]

- On working with the pitcher: "Very early in the game the catcher learns a great deal about his batterymate. He finds out what's working best for the pitcher that day, whether he's having trouble controlling his fastball or his curve. He also finds out if the pitcher has lost all of his stuff and can't fool any of the batters. I've caught Whitey Ford when he couldn't control any of his pitches except the fastball . . . The thing to do is to stay with the pitch that's working best, and use the other one sparingly, to cross up the batter."[42]

Most instructive was a lesson Dickey began to drum into Yogi's head almost from the start. The idea was that the catcher was the quarterback of a baseball defense and that his responsibilities went beyond catching a ball. He was the manager's eyes and ears on the field, and more often than not, his decision would be the one that a game hinged on. For instance, a good catcher had to be able to make the correct decision about whether or not the pitcher had to come out of the game, and he could not allow his judgment to be affected by personal relationships. "Now," he wrote in 1966, "Whitey is my good buddy; we've been friends since he came to the Yanks way back in 1950. But I've never hesitated to tell the manager that Whitey should be removed from the game, even though my buddy wants to stay in there and continue pitching. We all know the good of the team comes first . . . If a pitcher gets angry because the catcher recommended his removal, he was never a friend to begin with!"[43]

The now married Yogi Berra who came out of 1949 spring training was a different player than the one who had come out of camp the year before. He was confident, aggressive, and ready to be a star. And he knew who to thank for his newfound maturity: "I always say I owe everything I did in baseball to Bill Dickey. He was a great man."[44] Dickey had helped mold a catcher whose achievements would surpass even his own. "Within two years," Dickey told every reporter who would listen, "Yogi Berra will be the best catcher in the American League."[45] Dickey's judgment on such matters was usually unerring, but in this case it was off. Berra would become the best catcher in the American League within just a few months.

One of Yogi's most famous Yogiisms was also one of his most accurate: Bill Dickey did indeed learn Yogi "all of his experience." But that doesn't mean Yogi didn't get experienced by others. The Cleveland Indians' Jim Hegan was regarded as the best defensive catcher in the league. He shared with his Yankee rival a trick of the trade for avoiding swollen hands: "Falsies," he told the *Daily News'* Bill Madden, "I used to put them in my glove for extra padding. Nice and soft, that foam rubber. Today they make 'em out of plastic, so you can't use 'em in gloves anymore."[46]

―――――

THE ONLY SOUR note of the spring training season came when Yogi totaled his new Pontiac after he had given the Nash to his brother Johnny. On the way to the ballpark he lost control of the car and crashed into a palm tree. "I look up," he would later tell a reporter for *Life* magazine, "and there's two palm trees comin' at me—a big one and a little one. I tried to hit the little one, but I missed."[47] He had been reaching for a bottle of shampoo, he later explained, which must have resulted in one of the strangest police reports of the year, particularly since the report indicated that the Pontiac was only traveling at a speed of 15 miles per hour at point of impact.

―――――

BLESSED FOR THE first time in his professional career with frontline big league talent, Stengel determined to blaze a bold path. A pall fell over the team when it was announced that DiMaggio's heel would keep him out perhaps half of the season. Having already decided that Berra was to be his regular catcher, Stengel now decided to thrust even more greatness upon him: Yogi would replace Joe as the man the Yankee attack was built around. Berra was reluctant to accept the burden of such leadership, particularly as it involved replacing one of his own idols; how could he, a kid from the Hill, possibly replace the great DiMaggio? But it was not so radical an idea as it first seemed. Berra had proven his ability to hit major league pitching from, literally, his first day as a Yankee. Going into the 1949 season, Yogi had a .295 batting average for 784 at-bats and had driven in 156 runs in 215 games. Projected over a 154 game season, Yogi's RBI pace would be about 111. It was obvious to Casey that the surest thing he had to a guaranteed 100 RBI man was Yogi Berra.

Berra's development would be the second-biggest factor in overhauling the Yankees. The biggest would be Weiss's hiring of an undistinguished former major league pitcher as pitching coach. "Milkman Jim" Turner—old timers have offered several explanations for the nickname, ranging from his habit of rising early to his actually having been a milkman—had survived for nine seasons, finishing his career during the war years as a reliever with the Boston Braves, the Cincinnati Reds, and finally, the Yankees. This impressed Casey, who also had a long playing career despite minimal talent. Turner was thirty-three when he finally got his shot at the majors and had two outstanding seasons, his rookie year of 1937 with the Red Sox in which he won 20 games, and his fourth, when he went 14–7 with an ERA of 2.89, helping the Reds to reach the World Series where they beat the Detroit Tigers four games to three. That was pretty much it. In the other seven years of his career he won just 25 games and lost 42. He fought hard for everything he'd ever gotten as a ballplayer and had just one genuine stroke of luck, but it was a big one: he had been noticed by George Weiss and Casey Stengel, for whom he had pitched two seasons in Boston. Stengel had also seen him handle pitchers when Turner was managing for Portland in the Pacific Coast League. Under Bucky Harris, Charlie Dressen had coached the pitchers, and, most thought, indifferently; things would be different with Turner. There had been men known as pitching coaches before Turner—particularly Earle Brucker of the Philadelphia A's—but many regarded Turner as the first pitching coach, the first man to make a career of it.

Stengel and Turner had more to work with than most sportswriters realized. Pitching had actually been the strong point of the 1948 team, which finished second in the league with an ERA of 3.75. The Yankees weren't in a class with the seemingly invincible Cleveland Indians, who gave up better than half a run per game less, but it was a pretty good staff, anchored by three strong starters—Vic Raschi, Ed Lopat, and Allie Reynolds, who among them had won 52 and lost 26. If Turner could hold this nucleus together while adding just one more starter and maybe finding a capable reliever, there was no reason why the Yankees couldn't win it all—no reason, perhaps, except an amazing rash of injuries.

Turner set to work with a thoroughness and professionalism that quickly earned him the devotion of a hungry bunch of players. Raschi, Reynolds, and Lopat had never won anything in the big leagues and were desperate to shine. Turner would work with them and the rest of the staff to form a legendary unit whose linchpin was an unproven twenty-four-year-old catcher. "The Project" was what Turner called it. First of all, Turner wanted his boys near each other. Yogi and Carmen left the Edison Hotel, just five blocks from Times Square, and, in the days when the Bronx's Grand Concourse was still a desirable address, moved to the more spacious Grand Concourse Hotel, just two blocks from Yankee Stadium, where Libby and Ed Lopat were living. Their rooms looked out on the ballpark.° By 1951, Allie, Ed, Vic, and their families would all be living near each other in New Jersey. They all got along with each other, and everyone, of course, got along with Yogi.

————

BERRA SPENT HOURS with his starting pitchers. There was much to talk about. For instance, they all needed to memorize the book on every hitter in the league. Reynolds, Raschi, and Lopat all let Berra know what sequence of pitches they intended to throw against which hitters in which situations. These were smart, tough, determined men, emboldened by Jim Turner's confidence in them, and though they had all worked with Yogi, they were wary of giving him the control of calling their game. Wisely, Berra did not try to assert his authority, partly because he had none and partly because he felt that in time they would come to trust him.

Allie Pierce Reynolds was the toughest of the three. He came to the Yankees with a gigantic chip on his shoulder, largely because of an unfair reputation as a quitter. His nickname was "Chief," owing to the Creek Indian blood on his father's side of the family. Like all ethnic nicknames of the period, it was a term of rough affection of the kind his teammates intended when they referred to DiMaggio as "Big Dago" and Crosetti and Berra as "Little Dago." Sports were Allie's ticket to college; he had been a terrific all-around athlete at Oklahoma A&M (later renamed Oklahoma State University) though he had to battle his father, a preacher for the Church of the Nazarene, for the chance to play football. He was a superb

°Larry spent most of the first fifteen months of his life there. As a toddler, he pushed toys out of the window and onto the roof of the grand ballroom down below; Carmen would give the bellhop a dollar to slip out the window and onto the roof to retrieve them.

athlete in all sports.* He went to college on a track scholarship and could run the 100-yard dash in 9.8, and was a good enough running back that in a later era he might have considered going professional with the National Football League. He didn't think about baseball seriously until he suffered a knee injury in his sophomore year, and didn't think about pitching until A&M's baseball coach, Henry P. Iba, asked him to throw some batting practice after watching him make throws from the outfield. "I tried it because I didn't have anything else to do except piddle around with intramural ball."[48] The idea was a bust; the players got no fielding practice because Reynolds struck every batter out. Coach Iba counseled him to consider baseball—not only would it be easier on his knee but the money was far greater. An offer from the Cleveland Indians—quel irony!—was even better, particularly the signing bonus of $1,000.

The knee injury kept him out of the war. He endured four seasons of frustration in which he was able to win just four more games than he lost. Most Cleveland sportswriters thought his problem was endurance; he was able to complete just 41 of his 100 starts, a disappointing total for 1940s baseball. The insulting tag "The Vanishing Indian" began to appear beside his name in print on days after he was lifted for a reliever. Reynolds had tremendous stuff, but while with Cleveland he walked nearly as many batters as he struck out; by the time he reached the seventh inning or so he had generally expended a full game's worth of energy.

The Cleveland organization did not suit him: "No one took an interest in you . . . Cleveland played hard to finish fifth or sixth every year. There was no intense desire on the Indians. Lou Boudreau was a young manager. He had problems. It was tough to get veterans on the bus at certain times."[49] Casey Stengel and Jim Turner, he quickly found out, had no trouble getting the veterans on the bus on time. In fact, the veterans saw to it that everyone got on the bus on time. The Yankees under Stengel became known as a team that policed itself, and Allie Reynolds would be one of the enforcers. Reynolds came to the Yankees in 1947 when he was thirty-two,†

---

*Once he drove with Tommy Henrich to Berra's house to play some bocce, the traditional Italian game of lawn bowling that Italians felt demanded more skill than horseshoes. Reynolds had never heard of the game before he saw Yogi's bocce court. Henrich asked Allie how he thought he'd do. "Quite well," Reynolds replied, "because I'm good at all sports." And he was. (Halberstam, *Summer of '49*, p. 73)

†There seems to be some confusion over Reynolds's birth date, which was fostered by Reynolds himself. In Dom Forker's book, *The Men of Autumn*, he said, "I retired after the 1954 season. That year I was 13–3. Not too bad for a guy who was 37." (p. 10) Indeed not, and even more impressive for a pitcher who was thirty-nine, which in fact

an age at which most pitchers are looking for a place to wind down their careers. He quickly found that the Yankees were different: "When I was traded to the Yankees, it was like going from a church supper to the Stork Club [the legendary Manhattan nightclub]."[50]

Pretty much the same could be said for Edmund Walter Lopat, a left-hander who was thirty when he came to the Yankees from the White Sox in 1948 after several years of wandering in the minors and spending four seasons at Chicago, where he was 50–49. Born to a Polish immigrant named Lopatynski in New York, his career was saved in 1946 when at the age of twenty-eight, the White Sox fired manager Jimmy Dykes and hired former pitching great Ted Lyons. Lyons got hitters out by regularly changing the speed of his pitches and the angle of their delivery; he tantalized them by throwing stuff that looked easy to hit but which was seldom in a hittable part of the strike zone. Lopat wanted to know everything Lyons could teach him, and he began by showing him how to throw an agonizingly slow curve ball. Turner and Weiss had seen him and thought he had enough to become an even bigger winner with the Yankees' great fielders behind him.

Lopat's "junk"—as disgusted hitters called it—was even more effective when it followed Raschi's or Reynolds's hard stuff. In the words of Allie Reynolds, "Lopat was like a wind up doll that needed WD40 and new cogs. The hitters' mouths used to water while they waited to hit. When they came back, they were foaming at the mouth. Lopat drove hitters nuts."[51]

Raschi did not throw as hard as Reynolds, but he had better control. Like Yogi, Victor John Angelo Raschi, born in Springfield, Massachusetts, was the son of Italian immigrants, and like Yogi, he had put in seasoning time with the Newark Bears. Unlike Yogi, Raschi's passion was to graduate from college, and the Yankees used that to lure him into signing by paying for his education at William & Mary. A stint in the service delayed his development as a pitcher, and a nearly full season with Yankee Hall of Fame pitcher Lefty Gomez kick-started it again. By 1949, with a new batterymate, a pitching coach who believed in him, and a terrific infield, he was ready for greatness.

Jim Turner wanted a five-man rotation but settled for a quartet, the fourth member a fastball-throwing left-handed Irishman named Tommy

---

was Reynolds's age in 1954. The early Yankee guidebooks listed Reynolds's birth year as 1917. Why Allie gave out the wrong information isn't known, but presumably he was self-conscious about being twenty-eight in his rookie season. (ESPN.com's Rob Neyer suggests it was common practice for players to shave a year or two off their age.)

Byrne, a pitcher with a penchant for wildness. (He would be the only Yankees starting pitcher to have more walks that season than strikeouts.) Turner treated Reynolds, Lopat, and Raschi like his own sons; Yogi was in no need of a new father, but he was happy to let Turner treat him as a nephew. To outsiders, Turner's boys were a team within a team, and on game day they were all business and didn't care whether or not they were liked. Indians manager Al Lopez, himself of Mexican-American ancestry, was once driven to call Lopat a "Pollack sonofabitch." Roger Kahn, then a reporter in his early twenties, recalls approaching Reynolds and Raschi before a big series for a quote and being told what he could do to himself. Kahn asked Turner why his pitchers were so hostile. "Baseball," Turner politely explained, "ain't no fuckin' tea party."

———

THAT THE 1949 Yankees would finish ahead of the Red Sox and the Indians was the next to the last thing most writers expected. The last thing was that the Yankees could win without DiMaggio, Henrich, and nearly all of the other regular stars out of the lineup for so much of the season. In addition to DiMaggio missing the first 65 games, Tommy Henrich played in just 115, Johnny Lindell in 78, Charlie Keller in 60, and, most costly of all, Yogi Berra played in only 116. The Yankees should have been doomed. That they weren't was due to three principal factors.

First was the Turner-led pitching staff, which finished second in the league in ERA, first in strikeouts, first in saves, and first in fewest hits allowed. The big three—Reynolds, Raschi, and Lopat—finished a combined 53–28. Tommy Byrne, despite his wildness (he led the league in walks) was 15–7, and best of all, Joe Page, with Turner clamping down on his visits to Toots Shor's saloon, rebounded from his 1948 off-year to the level of his 1947 effectiveness, with 13 wins, 27 saves, and a 2.60 ERA.

The second reason for the Yankees' success was Stengel's amazing smoke-and-mirrors job in juggling the lineup. No Yankee led the league in any hitting category. So frequently were his stars injured that by season's end the top three Yankee hitters—DiMaggio, Henrich, and Berra—had appeared in just 17 games together. At second base, Stengel settled on a twenty-four-year-old former (and future) Marine pilot named Jerry Coleman, who, at a little more than 160 pounds, wasn't much bigger than Rizzuto. Coleman, like his shortstop teammate, had little power, but he could hit a lick and was terrific on the double-play pivot. But outside of Berra, Rizzuto, and Coleman (none of whom played in as many as 130 games), there were no regulars; DiMaggio, of course, played regularly when not hobbled by injuries, but he appeared in only 76 games. Casey alternated the smooth-fielding Billy Johnson and hard-hitting Bobby Brown at third base and used seven different players at first, including Henrich, Johnson, and, toward the end of the season, the great veteran slugger Johnny Mize, whom the Giants had dealt to the Yankees late in the season. In the outfield, right-handed hitting Johnny Lindell and left-handed hitter Cliff Mapes, neither of whom were good enough to start for the Yankees under normal conditions, made solid contributions (including 13 home runs and 23 doubles) in fill-in roles. Hank Bauer, who had hit only .180 in 19 games near the end of 1948, pla-tooned brilliantly with Gene Woodling, the two combining for a .271 bat-ting average and 15 home runs. "It was hard to believe," said August R. Mauch, the legendary trainer whom some called the most valuable Yankee of the season.° "Casey would take a guy out of the lineup, and the substitute would do better than the original. He moved players around, he switched positions, he did everything, and everything seemed to work." By one estimate, Stengel used more than 100 different lineups during the 1949 season.[52]

The third reason why the Yankees were able to stay together was Berra, who led the team in RBIs with 91 and held together a staff of pitchers with a seemingly infinite variety of temperaments, styles, and pitches. In his book on the Big Three, *Reynolds, Raschi and Lopat*, Sol Gittleman relates that at first the pitchers made their own pitch selection: "Each of the three, using a system of signals that they would change frequently, dictated what pitch would be coming. Gradually as the season progressed, Reynolds would say at the beginning of an inning, 'Yogi, you call the pitches for a while.' Eventually, Berra got completely on the same wave lengths as his two powerful right-handers. With Lopat, Berra's reflexes were so quick that he could adjust to anything that the left-hander threw. Over the course of the year, Lopat stopped giving signals, and so did Yogi. Berra proved not only to be a good listener, but what every catcher must be: the subtle psychologist and manipulator of his pitchers."[53]

°Mauch, who was both a doctor of naturopathy and a chiropractor, was one of the pio-neers of sports medicine. In the course of his career, he worked sixteen seasons with the Yankees. He also worked with two NFL championship teams, the 1955 Cleveland Browns and the 1956 New York Giants. Among his celebrity patients were George M. Cohan, Jimmy Durante, Admiral Richard E. Byrd, and George Bernard Shaw, whom he rubbed down at the McAlpine Hotel in 1926.

THE 1949 PENNANT race between the New York Yankees and the Boston Red Sox pitted two of the great natural forces in baseball head-on: Ted Williams's power of concentration and Yogi Berra's gift of gab. Increasingly secure behind the plate, Yogi began to enjoy himself and chatter with opposing players. Cleveland's Larry Doby, later Yogi's neighbor in Montclair, said he was "warned" about what to expect when he came to bat against the Yankees when Berra was catching. "I thought they meant that he was abusive or nasty or something. I wasn't prepared for what I got. He'd say stuff like, if we were playing in Cleveland, 'Where's a good place to go for dinner after the game?' If you try to answer while you're trying to hit, you're thinking and hitting at the same time—which Yogi said you cannot do." Williams was a tougher nut.

Rizzuto believed that Berra's constant chatter distracted Williams: "Ted hated a blabbermouth catcher, which Yogi was. But he could not hate Yogi. 'Have a good dinner last night?' Yogi would ask. 'Didn't eat, wanted to stay quick for today's game.' Or 'The food is all bad here in New York.' Or 'Maybe just shut up you ugly bastard.' 'If you leave a tip, the food gets better,' Yogi would say. Even Allie Reynolds might wish that the two guys at home plate would shut up and that the little one would give him a sign."[54]

Yogi did shut up, briefly, during the 1949 pennant race. In the heat of the summer, Stengel became infuriated when the Yankees lost a game to the Philadelphia A's. Eddie Joost, who had played for Stengel at Boston in 1943 and often bumped heads with his manager, took revenge by stroking several key hits against the Yanks. After one A's victory, Stengel stormed into the dining car and yelled, "That club in Philadelphia is making you look like fools! They are taking the food right out of your mouths. So I'm telling you all now: I don't ever want to see any of you getting chummy with them! You don't even talk to them." Joost, knowing nothing of Stengel's order, strode up to the plate in the next Yankees-A's game and politely tapped Berra on the shin guards with his bat. "Hey, Yogi, what's going on?" he asked cheerfully. "Usually," Joost recalled, "we'd have a little chat before getting down to business. Only this time, Yogi doesn't say a word. I try again. He won't even look up at me. I get on base and then move over to second. Phil Rizzuto was standing behind me. I say, 'Hey, Scooter, what's wrong with Yog?' No response. I ask him again, and under his breath, real nervous, Phil says, 'Don't talk to me. The Old Man says we can never speak to you guys again. He'll fine us if we do. He's mad at you because he says you can't beat Boston or Cleveland, but you always beat the hell out of us.' "[55]

Casey, though, held no grudges and admired opponents who went all out to beat him. In 1952, he phoned Joost to let him know he was picking him for the 1952 American League All-Star team at shortstop, behind Rizzuto. By then, Joost was playing for the woeful Washington Senators and happily chatting away with Yogi before every at-bat.

———

THE YANKEES STARTED hot and maintained their surprising lead over the Red Sox all through the summer—in fact, they were in first place for all but four days of the 1949 season. In May, against the Tigers in Detroit, the Yankees got a scare when a practice throw hit Yogi in the side of the head while he was looking at something in the stands; it was the last time, he later said, that he ever dropped his concentration during practice throws. He was carried off the field on a stretcher and taken to a local hospital, where one local beat writer wag—his identity has been lost to time—cracked: "X Rays of Berra's head revealed nothing." The joke didn't bother Yogi: "Because they first used that one on Dizzy Dean, and he wasn't too bad."[56]

At mid-season, even without DiMaggio in the lineup, the Yankees were soaring. Red Sox fans stuffed the All-Star ballot boxes for their man, Birdie Tebbetts, who outpolled Yogi by more than 200,000 votes, though Berra still made the team. He would finish the year with 15 more home runs and 43 more RBIs than Birdie. On the Fourth of July, in the first game of a twin bill with the Red Sox at Yankee Stadium, the Yankees were leading 5–4 in the ninth inning but the Red Sox loaded the bases on Vic Raschi with only one out. Boston outfielder Al Zarilla slashed a line drive single to left field—or what should have been a single—but it was a low liner and Johnny Pesky, the runner on third, fearing the ball might be caught by Yankees left fielder Cliff Mapes, retreated to within a few feet of the bag. Mapes fielded the ball on one hop and fired home. The throw was accurate but high; Berra reached up to snag it but kept his right foot on the tip of home plate. He made no attempt to tag the sliding Pesky, who would have evaded the tag in any event because the throw had been so high. Yogi then turned to umpire Joe Paparella, who was in the process of making a safe call on Pesky: "I was giving him all the help I could. I kept holding the ball in my glove and yelling 'He's out! He's out! I don't have to tag him! The throw beat him and he's out on a force!' " His quick-wittedness prevented the run from scoring, and the Yankees went on to win. "It meant a lot to me," he later said, "because I was getting pretty tired of the wise guys who kept putting me away by saying things like, 'That Berra may be dumb, but at least he can hit.' I knew the rules of baseball backwards and forwards."[57]

The Yankees stayed hot throughout July. On the fifteenth, they played the second game of a doubleheader against the hapless Browns at Sportsman's Park in St. Louis. The family and most of the rest of the neighborhood from the Hill came out to root Yogi on, but in the first game, as often happened in St. Louis, Yogi failed to live up to expectations. Luckily, the gang stuck around for the second game. Against Browns ace Ned Garver, Yogi sent two blasts not merely over the right field but over the pavilion roof. In three years as a regular, Yogi had never been able to hit a home run in front of his own people. Now, in one game, he had two that soared completely out of the park. "Mom's lasagna tested better than ever that night when I went back home with Tony, Mike, John and Pop."[58]

Despite the plague of injuries, the team held steady, but on August 7, playing at home in another summer doubleheader with the Browns, they courted disaster. The Yankees humiliated St. Louis 20–2 in the first game. Yogi was the chief target for vengeance, having hit a grand slammer in the first game and a three-run homer in the second game. Browns starter Dick Starr had had enough. He threw a fastball—or at any rate, a pitch that was fast enough to break Yogi's left thumb. For good measure, reliever Karl Drews hit Jerry Coleman and Yogi's replacement, Gus Niarhos, and then, just to emphasize the point, Tommy Henrich. The pitch bruised a nerve in Henrich's arm. In twenty-first-century baseball Drews would have received a warning and possibly an expulsion and fine when he hit Berra, but this was 1949, and Drews was left in the game long enough to very nearly cost the Yankees the pennant. Tommy Byrne tried to retaliate for the Yankees but was too wild to hit the evasive Browns batter. He got off with a warning from the umpire Bill Summers.° Browns manager Zach

---

°Hank Bauer thought that Summers may have had his own motivation for letting the Browns throw at the Yankees during the August 7 doubleheader in which Berra and Henrich were hurt. On August 5, Summers had tossed Yogi from the second game of a twin bill for constantly arguing his calls. "I don't mind a little beefing now and then," Summers told reporters after the game, "but this was more than I could take. He kept it up for minutes at a time, batter after batter. I finally told him that one umpire in the game was enough, and that I was the one who was staying." (*New York Daily News*, August 6, 1949) Summers insisted there were no hard feelings from the August 5 game; at least, he said, Yogi didn't use foul language like most American League catchers. And on August 6, Summers sat down next to Yogi on the Yankee bench, and the

Taylor insisted, absurdly, that the hitting of four batters with pitches wasn't deliberate.

"This whole business of beanballs is something I guess they'll never settle," Yogi later reflected. "Nobody ever admits to throwing at a hitter, but everybody knows it's done . . . Everybody talks about brush-back pitches instead of beanballs, but that's strictly a matter of words. When a guy is throwing at you, you don't care what he calls it."[59] In the rough and tumble baseball of the late 1940s, beanballs were just part of a rough game: Berra's reaction was to simply shrug and say he forgot to duck.

If Yogi was philosophical, Casey was furious. "Imagine a couple of clowns like that," he railed to reporters in the postgame clubhouse. "They couldn't make the grade on this club for four years"—both Starr and Drews had been dealt by the Yankees to the Browns in 1948, so they may have had some personal motivation "and they haven't been able to make it with the Browns, either. They've been getting their ears pinned back, so this is the way they try to get even."[60] With Berra's injury, Stengel now seemed on the verge of cracking up. Having no one else on whom to vent his frustration, he turned on his star catcher. When Yogi shuffled around the clubhouse every day before games, Stengel would needle him in front of reporters: "This is a stranger to the ball club. He doesn't do any work around here, but we may be able to find something for him one of these days. I can't let you see him play right now, because he says he has an ache or something."[61]

Stengel needed someone to take this frustration out on, and it certainly wasn't going to be DiMaggio. He pushed, prodded, and needled Berra every day, challenging him to get back into the lineup. Carmen was back in St. Louis, pregnant with their first baby, and Yogi thought he could convalesce faster around his family. But Stengel would have none of it. Yogi wouldn't think of defying his manager and continued to suit up and travel with the team, but otherwise he dug in his heels. Casey rode him, but "I didn't care. I wasn't playing until I wasn't hurting."[62] The experience revealed a practical, hardheaded side of Yogi. He played by the rules Casey put down, but outside those rules he refused to let the ball club intrude. Yogi had a strong sense of himself that would not be diminished by even his manager's criticism. He knew the stories of ballplayers who had tried to

two kidded each other. Yogi told him he was going to switch jobs and become an umpire because he could see better; Summers shot back that Berra couldn't pass the umpires' intelligence test.

return to the lineup too soon after injuries and ruined their careers. Dizzy Dean, for instance, of his hometown Cardinals, who, in the 1937 All-Star game, had taken a line drive off the bat of Earl Averill that broke his big toe. Dean forced himself back into the lineup too soon, changed his pitching motion, and ruined his arm. Yogi understood that it was management's job to win now and let the future take care of itself; it was a player's job to look out for his own future.

Charlie Silvera did a capable backup job while Berra was out. Contrary to what Casey was implying to reporters, Berra didn't need to find something to do—he was busy working with Jim Turner and the pitchers to fill Silvera in on strategy and tactics. Silvera hit .315 in 130 at-bats, 38 points higher than Yogi's average, but the difference between the two catchers was glaring: Silvera didn't hit a single home run all season. Meanwhile, Stengel continued to needle. When Yogi asked to spend some time in St. Louis, Stengel shot back, "Sure, shake with the left hand and let some of them grab that thumb. Maybe you'll shake yourself into shape there. They'll think you're a hero!" [63] Worse, Stengel prodded others into getting onto Yogi's case. Billy Johnson recalled a game against the Senators in early September: "I can't remember exactly, but it was our last western trip— back then, anything that wasn't Eastern Seaboard was considered west. It was just before Labor Day. I was so wound up with the tension of the pennant race and so pressured by Casey that I did something I've regretted ever since. Yogi was sitting alone and I walked up and said, 'You know, Yog, if you don't get back in the lineup soon, it's just possible if we win that there's gonna be a team meeting and someone's gonna stand up and suggest that maybe Berra doesn't deserve a full share of the World Series money because he didn't play enough games when it mattered.' It was a bush league thing to do. All I can say is that I wanted him back in the lineup real bad, we all did." Johnson apparently had not checked the team stats; the guy he accused of not having played enough games when it mattered was leading the team in RBIs.

Yogi would end up leading the team with 91 RBIs; aside from Tommy Henrich, no other Yankee drove in more than 80. Henrich, like Berra, would have had a bunch more, but on August 28 against the White Sox in Chicago he crashed into a wall chasing a fly ball, fracturing two vertebrae and bruising a third. All season long Henrich had been sustaining serious injuries and putting himself back into the lineup—on July 25, he broke a toe but cut a hole in his shoe, put on a black sock so it wouldn't be noticed, and went out to play. But this time the back injury was too much, and it seemed as though his season was over. It was not; he would not only come back again, but would collect four hits in the World Series. After hearing his medical report following the wall crash, though, it seemed to many that not only was Henrich through but the Yankees as well. Red Smith, a writer certainly not given to hyperbole, declared, "Without reservation or equivocation, the Yankees lost the 1949 pennant" when Henrich's body met the fence at Comiskey Park.[64]

Stengel never lost heart, even while kneeling over the prostrate form of Henrich. "Lie down," he told his veteran outfielder. "Don't get up. Take it very easy." Henrich was in pain, but Casey's words were balm. "For the first time that season," Henrich recalls, "I thought, 'He loves me. I really mean something to him.' " No sooner had the thought jumped into Henrich's head than he heard his manager whisper, "Lie down and give me time to get someone warmed and got this clown [the pitcher] out of here."[65]

Berra wouldn't budge. "It hurts, it hurts," he told Stengel one day when he thought he had taken enough. "I didn't ask to get it broke, and I ain't gonna play until it's right."[66] On September 1 against the Browns, Charlie Silvera was struck on the top of his head when a Browns player overswung. Now Stengel was down to just a single catcher, Gus Niarhos, who was not a bad receiver but as a hitter was roughly to Silvera what Silvera was to Berra.

Though not sure he was ready, Yogi returned to the lineup on September 7. The situation was critical, and everyone agreed that half a Yogi was better than none. With inches of tape wrapped around his thumb, he could scarcely grip a bat and swung virtually one-handed. He had to put a sponge inside his mitt to deaden the impact of Reynolds's and Raschi's fastballs. But the crowd of more than 66,000 at the stadium left no doubt about where their sentiments lay. They gave Yogi a thunderous ovation when his name was announced in the lineup and when he came to bat in the first inning. Hank Bauer, a rookie that season, was surprised at the fans' fervor: "We hadn't expected that. I mean, I really liked Yogi, and I really thought he was our most valuable player, but I didn't realize how much our fans loved him. The ovation he got on his return was bigger than DiMaggio's, which was something since this was Yogi's first year as a regular. I think Joe might have been a little jealous." The Yankees split the two games with the Red Sox (the middle game was rained out). Berra went hitless, but by throwing two runners out he left no doubt in anyone's mind that the Yankees' first-string catcher had returned.

DiMaggio had rejoined the team back in June and would hit .346 the rest of the season. But the Red Sox came alive, and on the next-to-last weekend they swept three games from the Yankees, one each on Saturday and Sunday at Boston and the third on Monday at Yankee Stadium, dumping them into second place. Stengel was ready to despair. DiMaggio had come down with a virus, Berra was playing in pain, and the pitching was shaky. On Tuesday, while getting ready for a game with the A's, the phone in Casey's office rang. Since any call might be from George Weiss, Stengel answered. "Is this Casey?" asked a voice with a sharp New York edge. "Yeah," he shot back, "Who's this?" It was a twenty-year-old pitcher named Eddie Ford calling from Binghamton. Stengel's mind raced; Ford was a left-hander, and everyone knew about left-handers. He was skinny and feisty, a tough Irish kid from New York on whom he had gotten a good report from Paul Krichell, one of the army of fine scouts that Weiss had out there combing the country. Binghamton's season was over, Ford told him, and he was ready if the parent club needed him, adding that he had gone 16–5 in the Eastern League's Yankee affiliate. "You may think I'm cocky," he told Casey, "but I can win for you. I've learned everything I can learn in the minor leagues."[67] Stengel thought for a moment then growled that he'd let him know if the Yankees needed him.

Who did this little wise ass think he was that he could pitch for the Yankees in a pennant race?

———

DOWN THE STRETCH, the Yankees had three games at Yankee Stadium with the Philadelphia A's, not a great team that year but one that finished eight games over .500 and was itching to spoil the Yankees' season. As it turned out, some Yankees had more on their minds than the A's or the upcoming season closers with the Red Sox. DiMaggio, for instance, was fretting about his batting average and the humiliation of finishing the season under .300. "He hit a shot to shortstop Eddie Joost," Jerry Coleman recollected, "and Joost jumped way up and caught it. It was a hell of a play. So now I'm out there at second base waiting as DiMaggio comes by, mumbling to himself like he'd always do, as he was going to centerfield. Berra unloads one of those Hail-Mary throws over my head, and it hits DiMaggio right in the head, and Joe goes down. He looks up and sees me looking at him, and he figures I'm the guy who let the ball go through. He picks it up and he one-hops me and hits me on the knee; he knew what he was doing. *You fancy Dan sonofabitch, catch the goddam ball.* He's hobbling around, I'm on the ground holding my knee, Berra's standing at home plate with his hands down, looking innocent. That was the tension of DiMag going for that .300 batting average."[68]

———

MANY THOUGHT THAT Red Sox manager Joe McCarthy had the Yankee's number. It all came down to the last two games of the year, games that will live forever in Yankee lore. Needing both wins for the pennant, the Yankees fell behind 4–0 in the first game and came back for a 5–4 win. The next day they won 5–3 to take the hardest fought pennant race in team history.

As with so many great pennant races in what many would later call the golden era of New York baseball, the World Series against the Brooklyn Dodgers had an anticlimactic feel. DiMaggio, still playing in pain (and underweight from a virus), tired though, with his thumb still sore, did very little at the plate—they had just three hits in 34 at-bats between them for a combined batting average of .088. But scarcely any one of the Yankees hit except Bobby Brown and skinny Jerry Coleman, who, amazingly, had nine of the Yankees' 20 RBIs. Reynolds pitched a shutout, beating Don Newcombe 1–0 in the opener, and Raschi lost a 0–1 heartbreaker to Preacher Roe in the second game. The Yankees won the last three, finally exploding for ten runs in the final game. Raschi hadn't been at his best, lasting into the seventh inning but allowing five runs, but he was good enough to win.

Afterward, Al Abrams of the *Pittsburgh Post-Gazette* came up to Yogi in front of his locker. " 'What did you say to Raschi when you went out to the mound to talk to him in the fifth inning?' he asked. 'I said, You're wild, buddy, you're wild.' 'Wasn't that obvious?' asked the reporter. 'I don't know whether it was obvious or not obvious,' Yogi shot back. 'All I know is that he was wild.' "[69]

For Yogi, there was one big difference between the 1949 World Series and the victory over the Dodgers two years earlier. In the first game, Pee Wee Reese stole second; it was the only Dodgers steal the entire Series. Before the fifth and final game, Shirley Povich wrote in *The Washington Post*, "Casey Stengel restored Yogi Berra to the Yankee line-up today despite the Dodgers' base-stealing threats. 'We can use Yogi's hitting,' said Stengel, 'and they can't steal any bases on him when he's up there with a bat in his hands, can they?' "[70] As it turned out, Yogi's contribution wasn't with the bat in his hands but behind the plate. Yogi gunned down the last three Dodgers attempting to steal, including Jackie Robinson.

In the euphoria of the postgame locker room, all the pressures, irritations, and animosities built up during the season were forgotten. The Yankees had, after all, overcome almost unbelievable handicaps to take everything, and everyone realized that it was Stengel's cunning and tenacity that had made the difference. Some thought—and still do—that the Yankees were incredibly lucky to have won a championship that year. But in truth, the only luck the Yankees had that season was all bad, at least in terms of individual breaks. Collectively, their luck was spectacular, the kind of luck Branch Rickey spoke of when he called luck "the residue of design." It has been suggested that if DiMaggio, Henrich, and Berra had not missed about 150 games between them—to say nothing of the seventy-odd injuries that kept other players out of the lineup—then the 1949 Yankees might have set an all-time record for victories. As it was, 97 wins during the regular season and the four in the World Series were enough.

Topping and Webb held a victory party for the team at the Biltmore Hotel. Old-time vaudevillian William Frawley, who would soon be known as Fred Mertz on *I Love Lucy* (and thirteen years later played a Yankee coach in the Mantle-Maris vehicle *Safe at Home*) sang "Carolina In The Morning," Ray Bolger danced, and Yogi and Carmen's favorite comedian, Bob Hope, told jokes.

It was more than October that lent an autumnal air to the party. Everyone sensed, without it being said, that this was the end of an era, that the Joe McCarthy gang that was the core of the team would soon be gone. Joe DiMaggio was thirty-four and had played barely half a season in 1949; everyone knew that even if he made it through 1950 he would never again be the Joltin' Joe of legend. Tommy Henrich would be forty in 1950 and could no longer play the outfield. Charlie Keller was just thirty-two at the end of the 1949 season, but his herniated disc would force him into an early retirement. In September, Phil Rizzuto had turned thirty-two; who knew if he could ever hit .275 again? Johnny Mize was a golden pickup near the end of the season, but he would be thirty-seven before the next season would be over. Johnny Lindell was thirty-two. Vic Raschi, Ed Lopat, Tommy Byrne, and Joe Page were all over thirty; Allie Reynolds was thirty-five. Spec Shea, who had been so effective in 1947 and 1948, was 1–1 in 1949 and had what looked like permanent arm trouble. As the year came to a close and the afterglow of their pennant and World Series triumph faded, the reality set in: Stengel's Yankees were an aging team without an established superstar to lead them.

A COUPLE OF days after the party, Yogi and Carmen were back on the Hill, moving in with Pietro, Paulina, and sister Josie. Once again, his mother gaped in awe at the numbers on her son's World Series check of $5,665.54, which was nearly half of Lawdy's 1949 salary.° Why indeed did people pay so much money to see men play?

YOGI AND CARMEN settled in to wait for the baby to arrive. Yogi's days were filled with light exercise, bowling, and soccer, but with a child coming, he could not afford not to take an off-season job. Soon, restaurant owner Henry Ruggeri was passing out cards announcing

Your Genial Host Lawrence (Yogi) Berra,
World's Champion Yankee Catcher,
Greets You From Ruggeri's.

Yogi's brother John and Joe Garagiola's brother Mickey were already working there, and Yogi was happy to fill in the hours shaking hands. The only part he objected to was wearing a tuxedo.†

AS FOR YOGI and Casey, there would be plenty of time for Berra to heal from the harsh words Stengel had spoken in moments of stress. After all, he had been lavish enough in his praise during the season. After Yogi's great play to beat the Red Sox on July 4, a Boston beat writer asked Stengel

°The amount was smaller than Yogi's 1947 World Series check because there were fewer tickets sold, the 1949 Series being two games shorter.

†It was Ruggeri's that Yogi was referring to when he supposedly said, "Nobody goes there any more, it's too crowded," though Yogi quote detectives have traced a similar statement to Charlie's in Minneapolis. It is, of course, far from inconceivable that he said it about both and perhaps many other restaurants as well. Legend says that Dorothy Parker said it about Chasson's in Beverly Hills, which well may be true. The words appeared in print for the first time in a February 20, 1943, issue of *The New Yorker* in a story by John McNulty entitled "Some Nights When Nothing Happens Are the Best Nights in This Place"—which in fact pretty much sounds like something that came from Yogi. It's possible that McNulty first heard it from Dorothy Parker. But whoever said it first, it's highly unlikely that Berra, who was eighteen in 1943 and playing baseball in Norfolk, Virginia, would have heard it from either.

That Dorothy Parker and Yogi Berra might have coined precisely the same witticism is a breathtaking notion that will surely send some scholars into frenzied research.

if, with the rash of injuries to Yankee outfielders, he might consider switching Yogi back to the outfield. "I'd switch Berra only in the worst emergency," Stengel said loud enough for the clubhouse to hear and one eye on Yogi, who was sitting at his locker. "The kid's doing great. Why has our pitching staff been so good? Berra, that's why! He handles those pitchers real good. He's throwing all right, and they're not running on them. They better not! The way he's throwing now, Ty Cobb couldn't steal a base on him!"[71]

———

WHATEVER CASEY HAD said in the scorching heat of the 1949 pennant race, his sentiments about Yogi were summed up near midseason, when Yogi had walked into the clubhouse as Casey was entertaining the press. Phil Rizzuto, he said, was having a great year and helping to hold the wounded team together. The praise was not hyperbole: Rizzuto would hit just .275, but he would be the only Yankee to appear in as many as 128 games and have more than 500 at-bats that season. "Phil is the one man," Casey told the reporters, "who was sure to land on the All-Star team." "What about me?" Berra asked in a voice halfway between kidding and hurt. Casey turned to his field manager. "You," he said, loud enough for the press corps to hear, "are superlative."

When talking about his prize catcher to the press, Casey was more reflective. "*Mister* Berra," he said, "is a rather strange fellow of very remarkable abilities."[72]

The Berras of Elizabeth Avenue,
1934. Back: (left to right) John,
Mike, Paulina, and Tony.
Front: Josie, Pietro, and
Larry, age nine.
(Courtesy of the Yogi Berra Museum
and Learning Center)

The Italian Immigrants, by
St. Louis–born sculptor
Rudolph Torrini, stands in
front of St. Ambrose
Church, where Yogi and
Carmen were married.
The statue commemorates
the immigrant families who
settled on the Hill.
(Photograph courtesy of
Rudolph Torrini)

The Hill Gang. Two members of the Stags sandlot baseball team made it to the major leagues—Joe Garagiola (bottom left) and "Lawdy" Berra (middle row, second from right). Everyone followed Paulina Berra's lead and called him "Lawdy"; she could not pronounce "Larry."
(Courtesy of the Yogi Berra Museum and Learning Center)

Yogi the Bear. Berra joins the Newark Bears in April 1946. "It's only about twelve miles from Newark to Yankee Stadium," said his Bears roommate, Bobby Brown, "but it's the longest twelve miles in America."
(Courtesy of the Newark Bears)

Kings of the Hill. Lawdy and Joey at Yankee Stadium in the summer of 1947. Garagiola's defending World Series champion Cardinals were in town to play the Dodgers, and Joe dropped by.
(Courtesy of the New York Yankees)

Yogi Berra Day at Sportsman's Park, 1947. Yogi thanks fans for making this day
necessary.
(Courtesy of the St. Louis Mercantile Library / University of Missouri)

5447 Elizabeth Avenue, the Hill, St. Louis. Pietro, Lawrence, and Paulina
Berra, circa 1947.
(Courtesy of the Sport Media Group)

"I'll make a prediction about Yogi. I say that within a few years he will be the most popular player on the Yankees since Babe Ruth," said Bucky Harris. The men with the most famous nicknames in American sports history shake hands at Sportsman's Park, St. Louis, on Babe Ruth Day, June 20, 1948. Ruth would die of cancer just eight weeks later. (Courtesy of the National Baseball Hall of Fame)

Yogi on ice. Berra, like all the Hill kids, was a multi-sports player. Here he works out with the St. Louis Flyers hockey team in the off-season, 1948. This picture was circulated in papers around the country; when Yankees PR director Red Patterson saw it, he hit the ceiling: "There was a piece of our valuable bric-a-brac down on the ice where he might lose an eye." Yogi's reply to Patterson's wire was typical: "A guy has to stay in shape, doesn't he?"
(Courtesy of the St. Louis Mercantile Library / University of Missouri)

"The best day of my life." Lawrence Berra and Carmen Short are married on January 26, 1949, in St. Louis. Joe Garagiola and his wife, Audrie, are on the left.
(Courtesy of the St. Louis Mercantile Library / University of Missouri)

Maître d' Berra displays menu for Henry Ruggeri, who surely must have known it by heart. (Courtesy of the Yogi Berra Museum and Learning Center)

Yogi and Carmen, 1950.
(Courtesy of the Sport Media Group)

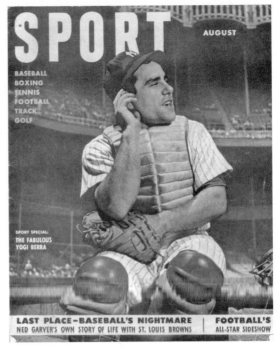

The start of a beautiful relationship. Yogi's first cover on *Sport* magazine, August 1951: "The Fabulous Yogi Berra" by Ed Fitzgerald. The title says it all.
(Courtesy of the Sport Media Group)

When it came time to sign, they were all smiles. Behind the scenes, Yogi waged fierce battles with the toughest of all general managers, George Weiss—and more often than not, Yogi won. Casey Stengel (right) is happy to have his great catcher for the 1951 season. (Courtesy of the Sport Media Group)

"Who are they trying to fool with this guy?" was Ted Williams's reaction when he first saw Yogi behind the plate in 1946. The two enjoyed many memorable conversations at home plate.
(Courtesy of the Sport Media Group)

"He learned me all of his experience," Yogi said of Bill Dickey, the Hall of Fame catcher who was an integral part of the Yankee teams that won four straight World Series from 1936 to 1940. Dickey's instruction helped Yogi to better his mentor's record.
(Courtesy of the Sport Media Group)

The Big Four: (left to right) Berra, Allie Reynolds, Vic Raschi, and Eddie Lopat. They formed the nucleus of the only team in baseball history to win five straight World Series. Only Yogi is in the Hall of Fame.

(Courtesy of Lou Requina)

"Yogiiiiiii!" Carmen Berra, in labor, screamed from her hospital bed in dismay on hearing that her husband had dropped a foul pop off the bat of Ted Williams that would have given Allie Reynolds a record second no-hitter in one season. Over the years, many have called the pop-up an easy play, but Reynolds thought otherwise: "The wind was blowing the ball away from him. I hoped to make a grab for it. I was afraid I spiked Yogi on the hand when I jumped over him." On the next throw, Yogi called for a pitch in the same location; Williams popped it up again to the same spot, and Reynolds had his no-hitter. September 28, 1951, Yankees vs. Red Sox, Yankee Stadium. (Courtesy of the Sport Media Group)

Murderers' row. There were no black players on the Yankee roster in 1951, but the players themselves were ready for change. Here fight fans Yogi Berra, Allie Reynolds, and Joe DiMaggio greet the two greatest boxers of the era, Sugar Ray Robinson (far left) and Joe Louis (far right), in the Yankee clubhouse.
(From the collection of Bert Randolph Sugar; photographer unknown)

Three kings follow a suit. The American League's MVPs for 1950 (Phil Rizzuto), 1951 (Berra), and 1952 (Bobby Shantz, wearing cardboard crown). In those days, even superstars had to supplement their incomes with off-season jobs. Yogi takes the measure, and Phil writes up the order.
(Courtesy of the *New York Daily News*)

"He's still out!" Game One of the World Series, September 28, 1955. To this day, Berra remains as adamant that Jackie Robinson was out as he was when arguing with umpire Bill Summers in the third photo of a sequence taken by *New York Daily News* photographer Frank Hurley. The second photo seems to bear Yogi out, but a closer look at the first photo reveals that Berra moved into the batter's box, preventing the Dodgers Frank Kellert from swinging at the pitch from Whitey Ford. According to the rules, "Each runner, other than the batter, may without liability of being put out, advance one base when, while he is attempting to steal a base, the batter is interfered with by the catcher." There's no denying it: the ball is still on the way in that first photo, and Yogi's position prevents Kellert from swinging. Verdict: Sorry, Yogi, but Jackie was safe.
(Courtesy of the *New York Daily News*)

Yogi and Campy rehash the Dodgers'
victory in the 1955 World Series. "A
close shave," Campanella reflected—
after the two catchers won their
league's MVP awards for the
third time.
(AP Images)

Yogi after dark. Like most of
New York's famous athletes in
the 1950s, Yogi's favorite
postgame hangout was Toots
Shor's saloon on West 51st Street
in Manhattan, also the favorite
haunt of Frank Sinatra, Jackie
Gleason, Ernest Hemingway,
and Joe DiMaggio. Here Berra
offers a Yogism to Shor (left) and
legendary heavyweight champion
Jack Dempsey (right), whose
Broadway restaurant was as
popular a nightspot as Shor's.
(Courtesy of the Toots Shor family)

All tied up. Friendly enemy
Roy Campanella tries to put
the choke on Yogi after the
Yankees came back to tie up
Brooklyn in the fourth game
of the 1956 World Series.
Ralph Branca (center) is
amused. Yogi hit .360 for
the Series with 10 RBIs in
seven games.
(Courtesy of the St. Louis
Mercantile Library / University
of Missouri)

Whitey and Yogi display their new contracts for the 1957 season outside Yankee Stadium. Whitey got $35,000; Yogi, $58,000.
(Courtesy of the *New York Daily News*)

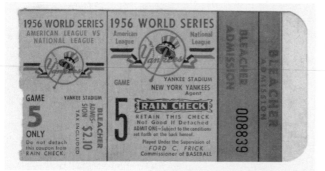

The perfect ticket. Stub from Don Larsen's perfect game in the 1956 World Series.
(Courtesy of Joe Murphy, South Orange, New Jersey)

The usual suspects. Mickey Mantle, Whitey Ford, Yogi, Charlene Bauer, Hank Bauer, and John Kucks (left to right) leave the district attorney's office following the May 16, 1957, Copacabana incident. None of the Yankees appear to have been involved in the brawl, but they all received fines anyway. In Yogi's words, "No one did nothin' to nobody."
(Courtesy of the Sport Media Group)

Yankees from Dixie. Yogi, Whitey, Casey, and Mickey guested in "Hillbilly Whiz," the October 1, 1957, episode of *The Phil Silvers Show* on CBS. Dick Van Dyke played Hank Lumpkin, a hotshot southpaw from Tennessee whom Silver's Sgt. Bilko tries to sell to the Yankees for the astonishing sum of $125,000. Whitey Ford (left) and Yogi are disguised as southern gentlemen; Van Dyke (right) is blocking our view of Phil Silvers. Yogi's closing line: "Arrivederci, ya'll."

Yogi digs in. Berra and Phil Rizzuto break ground for a forty-alley bowling emporium, which opened on June 10, 1958, in Clifton, New Jersey. (Leonard Detrick, *New York Daily News*)

The good-humored man. While other ballplayers squandered their salaries on the high life, Berra invested in numerous ventures such as snack bars. They made money, but some of the profits inevitably were earmarked for treats for local kids. (Courtesy of the Sport Media Group)

"Smarter than the average bear."
Yogi Bear, Hanna-Barbera's jovial,
wisecracking "pic-a-nic"
basket–stealing cartoon bear, pic-
tured here with his lifelong mate,
Cindy, made his debut in 1958 on
The Huckleberry Hound Show and
soon became as popular as his
namesake. Berra didn't seem to
regard the cartoon bear as an
honor, even though the character's
voice and mannerisms weren't
modeled on the original Yogi but
on Art Carney's Ed Norton of *The
Honeymooners*. (Was Carmen
Berra the inspiration for Cindy?)
(Image copyright Hanna-Barbera;
courtesy of Joseph Barbera)

Yankee fans thank Yogi
for making this day
necessary. Clockwise
from bottom left:
Larry, Pietro, Carmen,
and Timmy.
(*Life* magazine, 1959)

Chapter Five

Mister Berra . . . My *Assistant* Manager (1950–1951)

There are so many legends about Yogi that it is very difficult
to separate fact from fiction.

—ERNEST HAVEMANN,
Life magazine

IN 1954—by which time Yogi Berra had accumulated six World Series
rings, one more than Babe Ruth had in his entire career—the esteemed
literary critic Jacques Barzun wrote, "Whoever wants to know the heart
and mind of America had better learn baseball." The heart of baseball in
the 1950s was New York, with three major league baseball teams that won,
between 1947 and 1958, eighteen of the possible twenty-four pennants
and ten of the twelve World Series. At the heart of New York baseball was
the Yankees, and the heart of the Yankees was Yogi Berra.

"In that era of general good will and expanding affluence," wrote David
Halberstam of the 1950s, "few Americans doubted the essential goodness
of their society. After all, it was reflected back at them not only by contemporary books and magazines, but even more powerfully and with even
greater influence in the new family sitcoms on television. These—in con-
junction with their sponsor's commercial goals—sought to shape their audience's aspirations." Reflecting on the mood of America in the years after the
war, Halberstam continued, "They were optimistic about the future. Young
men who had spent three or four years fighting overseas were eager to get
on with their lives; so, too, were the young women who had waited for them
at home."[1] The post–World War II rush to have children would later be
described as the baby boom. (Everything else in the United States seemed

to be booming, so why not the production of children as well?) It was a good time to be young and get on with family and career.

Which is precisely what Lawrence Peter Berra—son of Italian immigrants, child of the Great Depression, World War II veteran, and catcher for the World Champion New York Yankees—was doing as the second half of the American Century began. Yogi's dreams were not those of many young Americans of the next century; he possessed no keen desire for wealth, status, or power. By age twenty-four he had already attained just about everything he could imagine that was good in life. He was playing the game he loved, and his hard work was being rewarded with a good living. On December 8, 1949, Larry Jr., eight pounds, five ounces, was born. Yogi, Carmen, and Larry Jr. were living with Paulina and Pietro in the house Yogi had grown up in. (Yogi's brothers had moved out by now, but sister Josie was still at home.) He had not yet fulfilled his dream of buying Mom and Pop a new house, as Joe DiMaggio had been able to do for his folks when he made the major leagues. But that was coming; for now, there was enough space for six in the eight-room house, and his parents were happy with the new basement Yogi had fixed up.

Weather permitting, he played golf during the day with St. Louis's reigning sports hero, Stan Musial; if he had to wear a tuxedo at night for a couple of hours and greet people at a restaurant, it was a small price to pay. It was uncomfortable, and sometimes the sight of him in it put off potential customers who thought they were approaching an establishment out of their price range. One such couple who seemed to be on a first date was reassured by Yogi, "It's just like a hamburger joint, only with tablecloths and a bigger menu."[2]

There was just one spider on the valentine of Yogi's life, and it arrived in the form of a big, fat envelope with a return address that read "New York Yankees Baseball Club."

———

IN DECEMBER OF 1949, a name was dropped forever from the Berra household—or rather, one Larry was dropped and another added. With the birth of Larry Jr., Carmen began to call her husband by the same name as the world was coming to know him. "From that point on," she would later recall for sportswriter Bill Madden, "there was no confusion about two Larrys in the house."[*]

———

[*]"If it's a girl," Carmen said in the August 13, 1949, issue of *Collier's* magazine, "we're going to call her Becky Ann, and if it's a boy, he'll be Larry, Jr.—*not* Yogi!"

A few months later, early in the 1950 season, equipment manager Pete Sheehy walked into the clubhouse with a box full of autographed baseballs. "Who the hell is Larry Berra?" he asked, holding up a ball to the Yankees catcher. "That's my real name," replied Berra with a shrug. "Well," said Sheehy, "that's not what the fans know you as. That's not what they want. From now on, sign 'Yogi.'" And from then on, he did. One day umpire Bill McGowan asked him to sign a couple of balls; a minute later, he turned to Yogi and hollered, "Who the hell is *Larry* Berra?" That clinched it for Yogi.

———

BY THE START of the 1950 season, Yogi Berra, to his and his family's amazement, had become a household name. In the heat of the 1949 pennant race, three of America's most widely read magazines, *Life*, *Look*, and *Collier's*, had sensed what the fans already knew: there was something unique about Yogi, and sent writers to profile him. *Life's* story appeared first. "Why Pitchers Get Nervous," by Ernest Havemann, featured a provocative tag: "Squat Yogi Berra, the Yankee catcher, has been known to hit wild pitches for home runs. He has also hit palm trees"—a reference to Yogi's misadventure with the bottle of shampoo while driving his new Pontiac—"and a responsive chord in female fans." The piece was a compendium of Yogi stories, both real and imagined, that had collected to date. There was the report of the X ray on his skull after the batting practice beaning and Bobby Brown on Berra's propensity for swinging at odd pitches. Havemann wrote, "Yogi can use his bat like a golfer, blasting the ball out of the sand trap, like a cop reaching toward the far line of cars with a night stick . . . Yogi is designed along the lines of a Percheron rather than a race horse; he stands only 5'-7½" tall but weighs 187 pounds, wears a size 17 collar and 42 coat, and has forearms and calves as thick as wagon tongues. Being knock-kneed as well as barrel-shaped, he gives the impression of being welded together from hips to knees and of running only from the knees down like a fat girl in a tight skirt." And, later: "On the polite and professional Yankees, who are by and large an all-American dream of the lithe, long-limbed, Yogi looks as out of place as a tractor in a Cadillac plant." Havemann concluded, "There are so many legends about Yogi that it is very difficult to separate fact from fiction."[3] Especially when they make good copy.

In *Collier's*, Gordon Manning seemed bent on recycling every nasty joke and unflattering observation of Berra that could be found. In "Yankee Yogi: 'I'm Human, Ain't I?'" he wrote,

The hydrant-catcher of the New York Yankees, Lawrence Peter (Yogi) Berra . . . looks more like a professional wrestler than a diamond star—especially not like one who would be wearing the distinguished striped flannels of a class-conscious Yankee. With a body only an anthropologist could love, the 185-pound Berra could pass easily as a member of the Neanderthal A.C.

He stands five foot eight but looks shorter, partly because he is heavy-set and partly because he has about as little neck as a man can have and still turn his head. His arms and legs are ballooned with muscles the size of derby hats and his fingers are so stubby he frequently paints them with iodine so the pitchers can read his signs.

Frank Scott, the Yankees traveling secretary, was quoted on going to the movies with Yogi: "I sit next to him for Westerns and crime pictures, but I always move away at least one seat when it's a comedy . . . Yogi punches you on every gag line. I came home from one road trip all black and blue." There were also some flat-out apocryphal stories, including a new version of how Yogi wrecked his Pontiac. In this one, Yogi smashed into a fire hydrant, "causing a 30-foot geyser to erupt in downtown St. Louis. Yogi nonchalantly drove off and, when irate police caught up with him, offered this defense: 'That fire plug was only tricklin' when I left.' "[4]

Yogi Berra had indeed become famous. He wasn't just generating stories, he was inspiring fiction. But as the press was soon to discover, the most interesting Yogi story was just developing.

———

YOGI BERRA HAS often been used as a symbol of a more innocent age, a time when men played for the love of the game and money was small concern. Nothing could be further from the truth, as Yogi himself never stopped making clear. "I figure it's possible," he told Ed Fitzgerald in 1961, "to enjoy playing baseball more than anything else in the world and still expect to be paid what's coming to you for it. People are always saying I would play ball for nothing if I had to, and I'm not saying I would or I wouldn't, but I don't think it has anything to do with it. Sure, I love to play baseball, and once I sign my contract I forget about the money and just concentrate on the game. But I had made up my mind [before the 1950 season] that I should get whatever I was worth."[5] His reasoning was simple and correct: if the owners could afford to pay large bonuses to prospects who hadn't proven themselves beyond the Triple-A level, they could afford to give an All-Star catcher what he was worth.

The Yankees and, in particular, George Weiss did not see things that way. There was no open market for ballplayers in 1950. There was no union, and the American and National leagues, then as now, enjoyed a monopoly on big-time professional baseball. The reserve clause in each player's contract bound the player to that team for as long as that team wanted him; when they didn't, he would be traded or released. A player had to be both shrewd and mentally tough to get anything out of a team during negotiations. Berra was both.

Shortly after the New Year, a fat envelope with the New York Yankees logo arrived at 5447 Elizabeth Avenue. Berra recognized it immediately: it was an offer of $16,000, a $4,000 raise. He did a gutsy thing, something few ballplayers of that pre-agent era had the nerve to do: he sent it back to the Yankees GM with a note saying he wanted $22,000. Back in New York, Weiss was furious; he immediately fired off another contract, with another contract. Damn near it back again.

The legend persists that Yogi sent back both contracts unopened, even though he dispelled that notion in his 1961 autobiography. A sportswriter who got wind of the holdout called to ask him what the Yankees were offering. Berra told him he didn't know; he knew, of course, but like most players in a time before Marvin Miller and the Players Association, he didn't think it was appropriate to mention the sum in public. Yogi thought "I don't know" would be understood by the writer as code for "I don't think I should disclose the amount in public." The writer apparently didn't read between the lines and kept asking "You didn't even look at it?" Trying to make a joke of it, Yogi replied, "Nope."[6] More than likely, the story, when it was printed, made Weiss even angrier, as if Berra was going out of his way to insult him publicly. That the story hurt Yogi's negotiations with the Yankees is problematic at best.

As Weiss was getting madder, Yogi got more stubborn. He was sure of his position. He had, after all, been an All-Star and led the World Series champions in RBIs, despite playing in just 100 games. He knew that Charley DeWitt in the St. Louis Browns front office had told writers how much he'd love to have Berra back in St. Louis and that the lowly Browns would actually be willing to pay Yogi a higher salary than the Yankees. Yogi also knew that Tommy Henrich would soon be thirty-seven, and Joe DiMaggio was beginning the season at age thirty-five. Yogi was the only player on the Yankees roster under thirty—in fact, he hadn't turned twenty-five when the season began—who looked like a potential superstar. He was clearly the best all-around player in the league at the game's toughest position. And he knew that if he knew these things, George Weiss must know them, too. There weren't too many times before free agency when a player had an edge in bargaining, but with the 1950 season coming up, Berra had one, and he would use it. Meanwhile, if papers back East picked up photos of a smiling Yogi in a tux greeting customers at a St. Louis restaurant, well, that would give the Yankees something more to think about.

In later years, sportswriters would speculate that Carmen was the force that screwed Yogi's courage to the sticking place. In truth, Berra, to whom the memory of the Yankees' double dealing on his $500 signing bonus was still fresh, needed no impetus to hold out. Though neither the press nor the Yankee front office ever seemed to get the point, the most affable and upbeat player in the game was a hard case where his money was concerned. Perhaps if Weiss had known that when Berra was sixteen he had turned down Branch Rickey for want of $250, he'd have treated his catcher with more respect.

Which didn't mean, of course, that being married to a woman such as Carmen, who was as intelligent as she was beautiful, didn't help. Years later, discussing Yogi's battles with Weiss, she told Joe Trimble that they talked things over, "as any husband and wife would, during the winter and figure out about what we think Yogi is worth to the club. Then Yogi sets the figure, and it is his number, not mine. After he sets it, he takes a solemn oath to God that he will not take anything less. He is very superstitious about that. Once he crosses his heart and says that a thing is true or that he is going to do something a certain way, you can bet he is going to do so. He won't go back on his promise to the Lord."[7] As George Steinbrenner would discover decades later.

Berra's firmness in the negotiations, coupled, perhaps, with the lingering thought that Yogi might be serious about staying in St. Louis and going into the restaurant business, bore fruit. On the day the Yankees began their spring training camp, Weiss phoned him from St. Petersburg. His tone was diplomatic. This is foolish, Weiss told his catcher. He wasn't doing either himself or the Yankees any good in St. Louis, so why didn't he get on a plane and fly down to Florida where they could talk over their differences? They weren't so far apart that they couldn't settle things. Once again, the school dropout did a mental jujitsu and floored his boss. Okay, Yogi replied. But if I come down there and don't like the deal, who's going to pay for the ticket? Weiss seethed but held his temper. The Yankees would pay his expenses. Just hurry and come down.

Berra met with Weiss at the Soreno, the ostentatious beachfront hotel

where the Yankees housed their players during spring training—perhaps, some said, to make up for the relative shabbiness of Miller Huggins Field. Built in 1921, the Soreno was one of St. Petersburg's Boomtime hotels.*
Ballplayers who had grown up in small towns or, like Berra and Ford, in working-class neighborhoods of big towns, were supposed to be awed by the ornate chandeliers and the violinists in the lobby playing ballroom music (the average age of the guests, Ford wisecracked, "was deceased"). Or at least that's the reaction George Weiss hoped for when he scheduled salary negotiations there. That effect was lost on some, particularly Yogi, who understood that if the Yankees could afford to put up players in hotels like the Soreno, they could afford to pay him more money.

Once again, Weiss was stunned at Berra's implacability. He presented Yogi with all sorts of arguments as to why he did not deserve $22,000; Berra, like the good amateur boxer he was, slipped each jab and counter-punched. A Yankee, Weiss told him, had a great deal because he had a better chance than a player on any other team at a fat World Series check. Just look at the money Yogi made for the 1949 Series—nearly half his seasonal salary. Well, replied Yogi, that's good money, but I think I had a little something to do with earning it. He wanted to be paid as if he was a superstar, Weiss insisted, yet he did not hit .300 or even drive in 100 runs in 1949; okay, Berra countered, but he had missed more than 40 games with a bad thumb and still led the team in RBIs. And so on. Yogi didn't budge. "I thought I had a pretty good year last year," he told his GM, "but to listen to you, you'd think I was the flop of the year."[8] Then Yogi threw a lead of his own: perhaps he should talk to Weiss's bosses, Yankee owners Del Webb and Dan Topping. Weiss balked. It was a shrewd move on Berra's part. Everyone knew Yogi was Topping's favorite; in a newsreel narrated by Mel Allen after the Yankees' 1949 World Series victory, the world could see Yogi tussling the hair of the Yankees' millionaire owner. At victory parties, Berra never hesitated to walk up to Topping with a grin and ask him what he thought he was worth. Webb never hesitated to answer, and the answer was usually more than what Weiss had been offering.

Knocked back on his heels, Weiss called in the closest thing to a mediator: Casey Stengel. Stengel had been hard on Yogi during the 1949 season when he needed him back in the lineup. Now, having won his champi-

*It was also the last. Imploded to make room for a condominium complex, the footage of the Soreno's demise was shown on newscasts all over the country and used in the opening scenes of the Mel Gibson–Danny Glover 1992 action flick *Lethal Weapon 3*.

onship, Casey took Yogi's side. He had seen Berra's resolve up close and understood that his holdout wasn't a bluff, and he needed him in training camp as quickly as possible. Weiss was a tightwad with his team's money, but he was light-years from being stupid; he knew when he heard Casey out that the time had come to compromise. He offered Berra $18,000, a $6,000 raise. What he didn't know was that $18,000 was not a compromise at all but precisely the amount Yogi had determined he would settle for in the first place. "How smart was Yogi Berra?" says Phil Rizzuto. "A bunch of Yankees held out for more money that year, but Yogi was the only one who got what he wanted."

Business was business, and there were no hard feelings about the salary dispute. It was time to get on to spring training and prepare for another run at the pennant. There were no grudges. Berra never disliked Weiss, whom most of the players hated. Yogi later admitted that his GM "was sort of a cold fish" but "actually, he wasn't a bad guy to know when he wasn't working, but he was always working."[9]

———

LATER, IN RETROSPECT, it all seemed so inevitable. The Yankees from 1949 through 1953 seemed like a mere continuation of the DiMaggio-Gehrig-Dickey juggernaut that had won four straight World Series from 1936 to 1939. It wasn't that way for the Yankees who were there. "Everyone thought we had so much power," Ed Lopat reminisced. "That just wasn't so. We had the ability to win a lot of one-run games."[*][10]

In the spring of 1950, there was every reason to believe that the Boston Red Sox with Walt Dropo, Bobby Doerr, Vern Stephens, Dom DiMaggio, Billy Goodman, Mel Parnell, Ellis Kinder, and, of course, Ted Williams would take the pennant. In a preseason poll of baseball writers, the Red Sox got 116 first-place votes to the Yankees' 38. Few thought the pennant race would be between the Yankees and the Detroit Tigers, who received just 26 votes. Fewer still, if told that Joe Page was washed up as a reliever, that Joe DiMaggio would hit more than 25 points lower than his career average, or that Tommy Henrich would play in just 73 games, would have picked the Yankees.

---

[*]Lopat's memory, like that of many old-timers, was a bit off on this point. From 1949 to 1953, the Yankees finished third, second, first (tie), second, and second in home runs. Lopat would have been correct if he had said the Yankees had power *and* the ability to win one-run games.

CASEY STENGEL WASN'T the only Yankee thrilled to see Yogi report to training camp. Bill Dickey told reporters, "This year, Berra has picked up where he left off in the World Series. He hasn't forgotten the things he learned last season. In fact, he's absorbing a few new tricks of the trade. The wild pitch and the blocked ball no longer bother him. He stops everything. And we of the coaching staff, as well as Stengel, know how well he handles the pitchers. There isn't another catcher in the majors for whom I'd trade Berra."[11] The last comment was a reference to the comparisons that writers in New York area papers were now making between Berra and Roy Campanella. In 1949, Campanella had appeared in 130 games to Yogi's 116, hit 22 home runs to Berra's 20, and drove in 82 runs to Yogi's 91. Beat writers for both teams loved to argue about who was quicker out of the batter's box to field bunts and which man blocked the plate better. Over the next eight seasons, comparisons of the two would practically constitute a light industry.

The Yanks made a statement on opening day when the Red Sox thrashed Allie Reynolds at Fenway Park to build a 9–0 lead, only to see the Yankees score nine runs of their own in the eighth inning and then six more in the ninth for a 15–10 victory. The Yanks had lost some things— Charlie Keller had been dealt to Detroit, Henrich had slowed to a crawl, the outfield had lost much of its punch, and it was quickly apparent that alcohol had taken Joe Page's fastball. In other ways they had improved. The Big Three were the glue of the pitching staff, and the acquisition of previously unheralded Tom Ferrick temporarily plugged the hole at closer created by the deterioration of Joe Page. Woodling and Bauer, "The Gold Dust Twins" as sportswriter Tom Meany referred to them, platooned brilliantly in the outfield. And Berra, catching nearly every game, pulled the many-tooled pitching staff into a cohesive unit, all the time hitting a ton.

Tommy Byrne, whose eye-popping $10,000 bonus in 1940 was still his greatest claim to fame, posted eight straight victories after losing his first start and for the second consecutive season won 15 games. He also led the league in giving his manager and catcher heartburn with his control problems: both in 1950 and 1951 he was the AL leader in walks. Byrne was, in the words of teammate Hank Bauer, "a genuine smart ass, the only pitcher I ever saw smart off openly to Ted Williams." It was common knowledge in 1950 that Ted Williams and his wife were separated; Yogi, who enjoyed chatting with Ted in the batter's box, had the good taste not to bring up

Williams's marital problems. Byrne had no such compunction. According to Bauer, "He would stand on the mound asking the game's greatest hitter, 'Have you heard from your wife? Any plans to get back together, Ted?' Meanwhile Williams stood in the box, his teeth clenched, gripping the bat so hard that he threatened to snap the handle. Behind the plate, Yogi tried and failed to keep from laughing. Someone once said 'Tommy is the kind of guy that you hate when he's on the other team but love when he's on yours.' I said that once to Ted. He said, 'If that little bastard was on my team, I'd choke his f——n' neck.' "

First base turned out to be an unexpected source of strength. In Joe Collins and Johnny Mize the Yankees had both a fine fielder and a great hitter who could play first base. Mize, who had been acquired from the Giants in August 1949, was a steal. Nicknamed "The Big Cat," the Georgia-born Mize had compiled a batting average of better than .320 and had led the NL in home runs four times in eleven seasons with the Cardinals and Giants. By 1949, at age thirty-six, he was nearly forgotten, languishing on the Giants bench as Leo Durocher favored younger, faster players who could bunt and steal bases. Durocher was a smart manager, but Casey Stengel was smarter. Casey put out a feeler to Mize and found that he was unhappy riding the bench. If we had you, Casey told him, you'd be playing. Stengel urged Weiss to make a deal, and in 1950 the Yankees hit the jackpot: Mize hit 25 home runs in just 274 at-bats and drove in 72 runs with only 76 hits.

The Yankees won 26 of their first 36 games, but in June they were 15–17 and didn't look much like the defending world champs. The Detroit Tigers, managed by former Yankee star Red Rolfe and paced by future Hall of Fame third baseman George Kell (the batting champion in 1949 and a .340 hitter in 1950) and slugging first baseman Vic Wertz (who wound up the season with 123 RBIs), moved ahead of the Yankees as early as May and forced Stengel into some tough decisions. Collins, a rookie, wasn't hitting well, and Henrich was hurting, so Stengel pressured Joe DiMaggio into trying out first base. The move seemed less out of concern for solving the first base problem than for relieving the strain on DiMaggio's weary legs in the outfield. Anyway, DiMaggio hated it and refused to go back to first base for a second try; the rift between DiMaggio and Stengel deepened. Page blew one lead after another, and hitters around the league began wising up to Byrne's control problems.

But Yogi Berra and Phil Rizzuto held steady. By the time of the All-Star game on July 11, American League base runners had learned their lesson:

Berra had thrown out 16 of 29 base stealers and, in the words of Phil Rizzuto, "Yogi would have thrown out half the others if our pitchers had held the runners on base a little better." No longer worried about defensive problems and comfortable with batting in the cleanup position, Yogi flourished at the plate, hitting around .320 for most of the season. Just before the All-Star game, he hurt his knee, twisting a tendon while chasing a foul ball in Boston. He played in pain, but caught a remarkable 148 of 154 games—11 more than the great Bill Dickey had caught at his peak in 1937. Phil Rizzuto, making use of a bat owned by Johnny Mize that some wags said was bigger than Phil, was hitting at an amazing .350 clip for much of the season. Berra, Rizzuto, and the trio of Reynolds, Raschi, and Lopat held the fort; after the All-Star game, the cavalry arrived in the form of yet another smart-ass Irish southpaw.

Edward Ford was born in Manhattan in 1928 and grew up in Astoria, Queens, in a predominantly Catholic neighborhood comprised mostly of Irish, Italian, and Polish immigrants and their children—"sort of Archie Bunker country" Ford would later recall it.[12] His father ran a bar, and his mom worked at the local A&P. His neighborhood produced two national celebrities—Eddie and Anthony Benedetto, who wasn't much interested in sports but aspired to be a singer. He would make it, but only after changing his name to Tony Bennett. Ford's local school couldn't afford a team, so he tested for and was accepted by the Manhattan School of Aviation Trades, which had a student body composed of black, Hispanic, and white ethnics. The easiest way to describe it, he would later tell Phil Pepe, "is to compare it to the one in the movie *The Blackboard Jungle*. Manhattan Aviation was exactly like that."[13]

In the spring of his senior year, he went to a tryout at Yankee Stadium. At scarcely 150 pounds, he displayed little power, and being left-handed, the only infield position he could play was first base—and light-hitting first basemen weren't much in vogue in the big leagues. Luckily for him, Paul Krichell saw him whipping the ball around the infield and asked him if he'd tried pitching. Eddie told him he hadn't; Krichell showed him how to throw a curveball. In 1946, age seventeen, he played for a team in the Queens-Nassau League, and in September pitched a 1–0 victory to give his team the Journal-American sandlot championship. He was awarded the Lou Gehrig Trophy as the game's MVP; twenty-four years later, his son, also an Eddie, won the same trophy. The publicity from the game had the Red Sox and Giants bidding for him; the Yankees won with a bid nearly twice that of the Red Sox when they could have had him for virtually any offer at all. He never dreamed of being anything but a Yankee. On September 22, he signed with the Yankees, and to celebrate Krichell took him to the Stadium, where the Yankees were playing the Philadelphia A's. He was introduced to a catcher who had just been brought up from the Newark Bears. Eddie Ford and Larry Berra shook hands. The next time they shook hands nearly four years later the world wouldn't know them as Eddie and Larry.

Ford was feisty and brash—the latter to hide his shyness. At Binghamton in the Eastern League he was managed by the greatest south-paw in Yankee history, Lefty Gomez, who had so many players in camp he couldn't remember the young pitcher's name and kept referring to him as "Blondie" and "Whitey." Ford was irrepressible; the Yankees tried to pressure him out of pitching winter ball in Mexico, but the money was twice as good as he was making in the Yanks minor league system, so he defied them and went anyway. In 1949, twenty years before Joe Namath audaciously predicted his legendary Super Bowl win, Ford had the gall to call Paul Krichell—who was still peeved at him for going to Mexico—and tell him to let the Yankees know that if they brought him to the majors, he would "guarantee" them the pennant. And if they wouldn't let him pitch in a game, "I thought I might be able to pitch batting practice or go in as pinch runner or something."[14] George Weiss was reluctant to bring up a twenty year old at the tail end of a white-hot pennant race, but he was impressed by the kid's aggressiveness. Krichell told him that if he behaved himself, he'd get to go to spring training with the Yankees in 1950.

Ford wanted much more than that, and in the heat of a July pennant race, he got it. By this time, he had filled out to about 170 pounds; he had a good humming fastball to go with his killer curve, but he had a lot to learn and, luckily, Milkman Jim Turner and Junk Man Eddie Lopat took him under their wings and made him learn it. His debut was a disaster. Pitching in relief of Tommy Byrne against Boston, he got hammered. Ford was baffled: he was sure his stuff was good, and Yogi seemed to agree. But Tommy Henrich noticed that Ford was tipping his pitches, and it had also been spotted by Red Sox first base coach Earle Combs, who passed it along to his batters. The next day Turner, Lopat, and Berra went over the pitching sequence with him and found his "tells"—on a fastball from the stretch, the inside of his wrist was flat against his rib cage, and on a curve, he would grip the ball so that his wrist was against his midsection.

Whitey was a quick study, and his debut as a starter, on the 6th of July, was more promising. Yogi had him versed in the signals, and he quickly built a rhythm with his catcher and learned to trust him. He went seven innings against the Philadelphia Athletics and left with a 3–3 tie (the Yankees won 5–4). Besides his pitching, the front office saw an immediate plus to having him on the roster: the Stadium was jammed with his family, friends, and neighbors. If Ford caught on, the Yanks would have a home-town drawing card.

There were also drawbacks. Ford, the son of a saloonkeeper, was imme-diately attracted to the team's rougher elements. The player he bonded with most quickly was another rookie, Billy Martin, whom he had met in spring training. When Ford was called up and arrived at the Yankees' hotel in Boston, the Kenmore, he went to Martin's room to take him down to breakfast. In the lobby Martin had two women waiting for him and his buddy. The team's family men, particularly Allie Reynolds and Bobby Brown, looked askance at such behavior. Management tolerated Martin—Stengel thought his fiery temperament could be valuable in a pennant race—but they were truly concerned about Ford, who they thought might prove to be a major talent. They decided to try rooming Whitey with Yogi Berra—what arrangement could be better for a rookie pitcher than to bunk with his catcher? At the time, Berra was rooming alone. Ford could understand why—as roommates, "we were the original odd couple. Yogi used to like to go to bed early and wake up early. I liked to go to bed late and sleep late." Not unusual habits for left-handed pitchers, who were thought to be a little looser in their habits than their right-handed counter-parts. But if Weiss thought that Yogi's good habits would influence Whitey, he was badly mistaken. Berra usually arose around six, by which time Ford might have been asleep for only a couple of hours. Yogi liked to talk in the morning; Ford would pull the pillow over his head. When Ford came in late, he'd crawl into bed only to have Yogi switch on the light and begin a conversation about the previous day's game or a movie he had seen the night before. "The pain in the ass," said Ford, "was awake all the time."[15] It didn't seem to occur to Whitey that the reason Yogi found it easy to be awake so early was that he had already had several hours sleep by the time Ford stumbled in.

The end of the Yogi-Whitey roommate experiment came in Chicago at the Del Prado Hotel on a day Ford was scheduled to start. Berra, as usual, was up at six, dressed, and ready to go down to the restaurant for a morn-ing paper and breakfast. Did Whitey want to join him? Ford mumbled no. Just wake me before you leave for the ballpark, he told his catcher, and I'll take a cab out there. Just before noon, the phone rang. It was the Yankees

PR director, Red Patterson. Where in hell, Patterson wanted to know, was Ford? Did he forget he was pitching that day? Stengel was furious. Ford leapt out of bed, dressed, grabbed a cup of coffee, and jumped in a cab to Comiskey Park. He got there thirty minutes before game time. Setting a land-speed record for preparations, he was warming up at 12:45. The veterans glared at him. Reynolds, who Ford was terrified of, articulated their anger. Rookie, he told Whitey, don't go fooling around with our money. Ford won their respect that afternoon, blanking the White Sox as the Yankees won 2–0. But Whitey wanted to know why his catcher hadn't awakened him. "He gave me one of his typical, profound, philosophical answers. 'I forgot. ' "[16]

Stengel didn't yet trust Ford to pitch against the contenders—the Tigers, Red Sox, and Indians. At first he would only start him against the Washington Senators, Chicago White Sox, Philadelphia Athletics, and St. Louis Browns—but as Stengel put it, "We gotta play those teams, too, and a win against them counts as much as a win against anyone else."[17] The pennant race was nearly as hot as in 1949. The Red Sox had come on strong, but the Yankees held even, trailing the front-running Tigers by just a game. In September, finally, the greatest big-game pitcher in Yankee history got to start in his first big game, maybe the most important game of the regular season. The Yanks and Tigers split the first two. In the rubber game, Ford was matched against the smart thirty-five-year-old veteran, Dizzy Trout, who would finish 13–5. Prior to the first pitch, Phil Rizzuto walked to the mound to give his young teammate a pep talk. Ford told his veteran shortstop to relax: "All I gotta do is throw my glove out there, and I can beat these guys."[18] But, of course, he was nervous. The atmosphere in Briggs Stadium evoked a World Series. Ford recalled, "I was full of butterflies. Yogi came up to me just before the game, slapped me in the arm with his glove, and said 'Hey, this is excitin', ain't it? This is what you came here for, huh?' I thought, 'Hey, he's right. This *is* what I came here for. It's the kind of game I've always dreamt of.' I was no longer nervous. I was excited." He was confident, too, because Yogi, already acting like a veteran, was confident in him. Several times when behind on the count 2–0 and even 3–1 Berra called for curveballs, and Whitey threw them for strikes.

Whitey put his faith in Yogi and never shook him off. After eight nail-biting innings, the score was 1–1. Ford was scheduled to lead off the Yankees' half of the ninth. Stengel knocked everyone for a loop by letting his rookie pitcher hit. Improbably, Ford drew a walk, sparking a seven-run rally for an 8–1 victory. Ford's win put the Yankees in first place, and that's where they would finish.

On September 23, 1950, the Yankees began a two-game series with the Red Sox at Yankee Stadium which Red Smith called "the itsy-bitsy World Series." It was a chilly, gray afternoon, and it was, wrote Smith, Yogi Berra "who called attention to the weather. His comely features were unshaven, and somebody remarked about the thick shrubbery on his jaw. 'I'm wearin' it to keep warm,' Yogi explained sensibly. 'I got a little cold.' Physicists were still studying this when Ed Lopat went to work on the pitching rubber."[19] New York won in a walk, 8–0.

The clincher came the next day. Ted Williams hit a home run off Vic Raschi to give the Red Sox an early lead, but the Yankees' two MVP candidates, Berra and Rizzuto, turned the game into a rout. Yogi had four hits, including a triple, while Phil had three, one of them a home run. In the ninth inning, the Yanks heard that Cleveland had beaten the Tigers. That was it. Stengel had won his second improbable pennant. The Yanks finished just three games ahead of Detroit, four in front of Boston, and six ahead of Cleveland, all of whom were thought by many at the beginning of the season to have more talent than the Yankees. The Yankees failed to lead the league in a single key hitting or pitching statistic; the Red Sox led the AL in batting, slugging, runs scored, and OBA while the Indians had the most home runs and posted the lowest ERA. A year earlier, in a fit of youthful bravado, Ford had bragged that he could guarantee the Yankees a pennant. In 1950, a slightly more mature Ford kept his mouth shut and made the difference between the Yankees and Tigers. He won nine of ten decisions, including seven complete games.

History has been unfair to the Philadelphia Phillies Whiz Kids of 1950. The product of a smartly conceived rebuilding program, the young Phillies, paced by future Hall of Famers Richie Ashburn and Robin Roberts, won a thrilling pennant race against the powerful Brooklyn Dodgers on the last day of the season. Roberts, pitching his third game in five days, beat the Dodgers at Ebbets Field on a three-run, tenth-inning home run by Dick Sisler. This led to just the second World Series appearance in the franchise's history, the first since 1915.

The record book shows that the Yankees swept the Phillies, thus adding to the myth of Yankee dominance. On the field, the first three games were tense, one-run contests—the second decided in the tenth inning—which made the fourth game, won by the Yankees 5–2, look like a rout. Yankees pitching was decisive; the Phillies had no home runs and just 26 hits in the four games. The Yanks got all the breaks; their hotshot lefty, Whitey Ford, was still available to pitch even though he would soon report for military service. The Phils' ace southpaw, Curt Simmons, 17–6 during the regular season, wasn't granted such a privilege by the draft board.° Phillies manager Eddie Sawyer was forced to yank ace reliever Jim Konstanty, the NL's MVP for the season, into the starting rotation. Konstanty pitched brilliantly in two starts, but, except for a brief time, he was unavailable for the bullpen. Berra and DiMaggio had the only two home runs of the Series; DiMaggio's came in the tenth inning of Game Two off Robin Roberts and won the game, while Yogi's was a two-run shot off Konstanty in the sixth inning of the final game that all but buried the Phillies. Richie Ashburn remembered it vividly, "We all heard that Yogi was a free swinger, but that gave us the wrong impression about him. The scouts told us he would *swing* at anything—they never told us he might *hit* anything."[20]

Ford pitched the clincher, the first of what would become a record World Series win total for him, and Allie Reynolds got the final out. "Champagne and lobster," Berra said eleven years later, recalling the World Series that gave him his third championship ring. "It's good when you win."[21] You've got the world by the tail, a sportswriter told him during the celebration in the locker room. How great, said the writer, it must be to be young and a Yankee. What he meant, of course, was that it was great to be young and a winner. Of course, from 1949 through 1953, to be a Yankee was to be a winner.

Despite the four-game sweep and even though it was played by two East Coast teams, the Series was an enormous hit with viewers all over the country. An extraordinary average 35 million viewers per game watched on NBC, CBS, and ABC, which shared the broadcasting rights.

Yogi Berra had now played in three World Series and had three rings to show for it. That, of course, is the important statistic. But a word should be said about his individual stats. In the 1940s and 1950s, fans and most sportswriters seemed to understand better than today that postseason performance was, by and large, luck of the draw. A best-of-seven series just didn't offer enough opportunities to judge a player's true value. Yogi Berra has always had the reputation as a great clutch player and the consummate

---

°Simmons would have to wait fifteen years to get his chance to pitch against the Yankees in the World Series, and it would come in 1964 against a team managed by Yogi.

World Series performer, yet, in his first three World Series, he had a composite batting average of only .140 in 14 games with two home runs and five RBIs. This was overshadowed, as it should be, by the fact that the Yankees won all three Series. If the Yankees had lost, Berra might have been saddled early on with the label of a guy who couldn't come through in the big games.

He hadn't hit that much, but his catching had been superb. He had been unjustly blamed for the loss in Bill Bevens's near no-hitter in 1947 when actually he had struggled mightily to keep Bevens, who walked ten batters, from getting blown off the mound. In the 1949 and 1950 Series, his handling of the Yankee pitching staff was impeccable, best summed up by Vic Raschi after his two-hit shutout against the Phillies in Game One of the 1950 Series. "Yogi," Raschi told him in the clubhouse, "you called a perfect game. I didn't shake you off once. Thank you." It was just the first of many such accolades from Yogi's pitchers.

The Most Valuable Player vote of 1950 came as something of a surprise. Berra had had a sensational season, hitting .322 and once again leading the team in RBIs with 124 (two more than DiMaggio). Phil Rizzuto, though, easily led in the voting. Phil had his best season ever in the majors, hitting .324, two points higher than Yogi though with only seven home runs. His 200 hits were second in the league behind the Tigers' George Kell. Many felt Rizzuto's defensive contributions had earned him the votes; he led the AL in put-outs and fielding average—.982, a whopping 21 points higher than the league average at his position. But Yogi's defensive statistics were equally impressive: he led the league's catchers in games caught, put-outs, assists, and double plays. Much was made of Rizzuto's uncanny ability to make contact with the ball in key situations—he struck out just 39 times in 617 at-bats. However, Yogi, who batted 597 times, had accomplished something even more amazing: he struck out *just twelve times* while hitting 28 home runs, 30 doubles, and six triples.

The surprise in the MVP voting was not so much that Rizzuto won—he was a favorite with sportswriters for his hustling play and had finished second in the MVP voting the previous season when he only hit .275—but that Yogi finished *third* behind the Red Sox multiposition player, Billy Goodman. Goodman did lead the league in batting at .354, but injuries had limited him to 110 games, and though he played in hitter-friendly Fenway Park, he had only four home runs. Yogi grinned and shrugged it off; Rizzuto was now thirty-three years old and wasn't likely to get any more shots at winning the MVP.

———

JUST BEFORE THE end of the Series, Berra was asked by Ed Sullivan to appear on his television show for the hefty sum of $1,000. There was no bigger honor for a professional athlete in 1950 than to appear on Sullivan's Sunday night show, which was one of the most popular variety programs of the era. Though it seems inexplicable to a modern-day fan, Yogi, always uneasy at the thought of taking money for personal appearances, balked. He and Carmen had already planned to go back home to St. Louis, and they didn't want to miss any time with their families. Before the final game, Sullivan himself visited the Berras and made his pitch to Carmen. You'd only have to stay over another day or so, he told her. Could she possibly talk to Yogi about it? Did he say $1,000? Mrs. Berra asked. Yes, Sullivan assured her—$1,000. Don't worry about it, Mr. Sullivan, Carmen promised, Yogi will be there.

It was a problem Berra was going to have to learn to live with. The calls for appearances would soon become too many (and too lucrative) to ignore. The following year, Yogi would again be on live television, grinning to the quips of America's favorite comic, Milton Berle.

———

BERRA DID NOT win the 1950 MVP trophy, but just before Christmas he walked away with a more intriguing award: the National Association of Women Artists voted Yogi's as one of "the most stimulating faces in America." Others cited as having stimulating faces were Ava Gardner, Lauren Bacall, Arturo Toscanini, General George C. Marshall, Vice President Alben W. Barkley, and Ernest Hemingway. The voters included the leading female painters and book and magazine illustrators in the country. Their press release said, "Yogi has the most-down-to-earth face in America. It stimulates women's subconscious yearning for the Neanderthal man." As if to soften the Neanderthal reference, Ruth Yeats, the president of the association, added that most celebrities "carry faces which have no more stimulation than a bowl of oatmeal." Yogi's face, then, stimulated women, at least artistic women, more than oatmeal.

Berra was back in St. Louis spending his nights as the greeter at Ruggeri's when the results were announced. When his friends from the Hill kidded him, he blushed, partly because he didn't know what having a stimulating face actually entailed. "He phoned me up to ask me," says

Garagiola. "I told him don't worry, it means women go for you. Damn, he said to me, I hope Carmen doesn't find out about this."

———

THE CELEBRATION OVER winning the 1950 World Series had scarcely died down when the reality of world politics intruded the insular world of Yankees baseball. Four months earlier, near the end of June, the Russians had tested their first nuclear weapon. On June 25, war had broken out between North and South Korea, and on October 25, just eighteen days after Whitey Ford won the fourth and final game of the World Series, American and Chinese Communist troops clashed for the first time. On November 19, Ford was drafted into the Army and would miss perhaps the two peak years of his career. In May of 1952, Jerry Coleman, who had been an inactive Marine Corps reservist since World War II, was recalled to active duty. He returned in August of 1953, but Coleman, a Marine pilot, was never the same player and would play in only 310 games the rest of his major league career. "It's funny how a lot of us in baseball didn't want to think about Korea," recalled Hank Bauer. "Guys like me and Yogi who fought in World War II just kind of took it for granted that we wouldn't see another war in our lifetime. We never talked much about the Korean War or the Cold War when the Rosenbergs were on trial in 1951 for selling nuclear secrets to the Russians. The only thing I remember someone saying was hearing a pitcher say 'The way they're hitting home runs now. They must have sold atomic secrets to the companies that make the baseballs.' "

———

AS SPRING TRAINING of 1951 neared, the Yankees' adversaries knew all of their weaknesses: Joe DiMaggio was merely a shadow of his former self, Phil Rizzuto was thirty-four and unlikely to repeat his .324 BA of the previous season, and Whitey Ford was lost to the Army. Allie Reynolds was thirty-four, Johnny Mize was thirty-eight, and Tommy Henrich was retired. On the other hand, Yogi Berra, who would turn 26 in May, was a superstar in his prime and the player that any general manager in baseball would have liked to build his team around. Berra knew he'd never have a better opportunity to cash in on his real worth. Shortly after the holidays, Yogi got his offer from George Weiss: $22,000, just $4,000 above what he had made in 1950 and, in fact, what he had asked for that year—practically a case of déjà vu all over again. The Yankees' pitch was low and away: Berra wanted $40,000, or at least said he did, though he later admitted he would have settled for $30,000. But $40,000 was not unreasonable, and there was little doubt Yogi would have gotten it had baseball had an open market; $40,000 was, after all, the sum that Rizzuto had been paid after the 1949 season when he had hit .275 with six home runs. The contract went back to Weiss, accompanied by a respectful letter from Yogi—written with an assist from Carmen—relating in some detail why he was worth more than what Weiss was offering. His argument was sound. Yogi was tired of being told that he was young and had a long career ahead of him in which he would surely make big money. Even great players sustained injuries that brought a sudden halt to careers, and in any event, catchers tended to have short shelf lives. If the Yankees weren't willing to pay him big money after hitting .322 and driving in 124 runs, when *would* they pay him? He was also tired of having Weiss use his World Series share (a whopping $5,737.95 for 1950) as an excuse for holding his salary down; as he never ceased to remind them, he had had something to do with producing the World Series revenue, too. He got a boost from the annual All-Star team picked by the *Sporting News*: Walt Dropo of the Red Sox at first, Jackie Robinson of the Dodgers at second, George Kell of the Tigers at third, and Rizzuto at short; an outfield consisting of the Cardinals' Stan Musial, the Pirates' Ralph Kiner, and the Indians' Larry Doby; a three-man pitching staff of Vic Raschi, the Indians' Bob Lemon, and the Phillies' Jim Konstanty; and beating out Roy Campanella by nearly a three-to-one vote, Yogi Berra at catcher.

The Yankees' second offer was for $25,000; Berra assumed—correctly, as it turned out—this meant "they were willing to give me $3,000 for arguing."[23] The contract was accompanied by a polite letter from Weiss saying how much the Yankees appreciated Yogi and how much they wanted to be fair to him. Berra sent off an equally polite letter telling Weiss that he appreciated his appreciation, but he didn't consider a $3,000 raise a fair offer. As usual, phone calls from Weiss to the Hill yielded no tangible results. Then Yogi got a call from Roy Hamey, Weiss's assistant, who just happened to be flying across the country and thought he'd stop off in St. Louis for a couple of days. How about dinner? Sure, Yogi said, why not meet at Ruggeri's? Did Roy want a table by himself or did he want to have dinner with Yogi and some of his pals and gas about baseball? Hamey told Yogi he wasn't interested in dinner; he was there to talk about the contract. The steaks are good, Yogi told him. The spaghetti is better, and the lobster better still. Just tell me what you'd like, he insisted.

What Hamey wanted was for Berra to sign his contract and mail it in—

the Yankees would even pay the postage. Was he ready? Carmen was still reading the contract, said Yogi; she hadn't gotten to the fine print yet. Let's stop kidding, said Hamey. All right, let's, replied Berra. He would talk about the $40,000 but refuse to even discuss $25,000. And that was that. Why wasn't a $7,000 raise enough? Hamey wanted to know. It wasn't enough, Berra informed him, because the club had made him wait till the end of the first season to collect his $500 bonus and because of the $90 a month they made him take at Norfolk—and a few other sore spots that he had not forgotten. He was adamant: "They always told me I would get the money if I did the job. Well, I did the job, and now I want to get the money."[24] Hamey sighed and told Yogi they had reached an impasse. What the hell is an impasse? Yogi asked.

The toughest part of winter was dealing with the unending stream of invitations to speak at banquets. It was tough to turn down requests from old pals, no one on the Hill wanted to be accused of having become a *pezzanovante*—a big shot. Yogi avoided as many banquets as he could and cut back on eating at the ones he did attend. When the sun was out, Yogi played golf again with Stan Musial or went by Grassi's or one of the taverns on the Hill. Carmen spent time with her family in Salem, and sometimes the two would go to a basketball game at St. Louis University. One Sunday, the Hill paisans went to Chicago to see the Bears and Lions play. (So inexpensive were NFL tickets in 1951, they could all afford them.) And there were poker fests in the Berra basement—after Paulina went to sleep, of course. Someone told Yogi it wasn't fair to his boyhood pals to keep playing cards with them, as he was earning several times what they were. Yogi retorted that his friends told him, "How are we going to make expenses if you don't play?"[25]

———

SPRING TRAINING OPENED on March 1, and the Yankees began without their best player. Weiss was beside himself and broke one of the Yankees' unwritten rules in an effort to pressure his catcher into signing. Salary figures, though they were often leaked to writers, were almost never revealed. Weiss told reporters, "Berra has been offered $25,000, and he's asking for $40,000. In his first four years with the club, Berra has made more money than any other Yankee in history except DiMaggio. We think his demands"—baseball executives always referred to a player's asking price as a "demand"—"are too far out of line for comment. This is positively the club's last offer. When he comes down out of the clouds, we'll be happy to bargain with him."[26] Just who did Yogi Berra think he was, Weiss asked the press rhetorically, another Joe DiMaggio? What was forgotten was the rancor that surrounded DiMaggio's own holdout in 1938. When he finally appeared in a Yankee uniform, he heard boos in the stadium.°

Much to Weiss's chagrin, the tactic left Berra entirely unfazed. A few days after ripping Yogi in the press, he called him in St. Louis and talked compromise. Sure, said Berra, how about $35,000? Weiss replied, How about $28,000? Yogi knew he had him and proceeded to reel him in: How about $30,000? Deal, said Weiss. It was, of course, the sum Berra had been aiming at all along. He would later find out that he had had a secret partner in the negotiations: once again, Casey Stengel had urged Weiss to cut a deal with Yogi. That season the Yankees, in an unusual agreement, traded spring training camps with the New York Giants. Del Webb, Berra thought, wanted to flaunt his world champions in front of friends from Arizona and California, so he made a swap with Giants' owner Horace Stoneham. The Yankees came to Arizona, and the Giants went to Florida. When Berra arrived in Phoenix, a writer asked him if Weiss had gotten mad during the negotiations. He did, Yogi replied, but he had gotten pretty mad himself.

It was to be Yogi's last big contract squabble with the Yankees; from then on, in his estimation, the front office always offered him what he considered a fair figure. Once a player reached big money, he thought, the Yankees brass was smart enough to accept it and deal with him realistically. After the season, Berra saw his biggest fan, Dan Topping, at the New York Baseball Writers dinner. How much, Topping asked with a grin, did Yogi plan on taking from the Yankees for the next year? Yogi grinned, looked into the eye of one of the most powerful men in sports, and informed him that he was worth $40,000. Extending his hand, Topping informed him it was a deal.

Back in February of 1951, Berra had noticed a story in a St. Louis paper that said the Yankees' nineteen-year-old phenom from Oklahoma, Mickey Mantle, hadn't reported for spring training. When the team wired him and asked why he hadn't reported, Mantle wrote back and said he couldn't

---

°DiMaggio wanted $40,000 and, without leverage, eventually signed for the $25,000 the Yankees offered him in the first place. The Yankees owner, Colonel Jacob Ruppert, rubbed in the humiliation by telling the press, "I hope the young man has learned his lesson." If DiMaggio had learned his lesson the way Berra did, he might have gone back to San Francisco and had himself photographed greeting customers in a neighborhood restaurant.

afford a ticket and no one had sent him any money to buy one. Just like the Yankees, Yogi thought. Weiss apparently had saved a few bucks by getting rookies, even ones from poor coal-mining families in Oklahoma, to pay their own expenses; Stengel, irritated that his prize rookie wasn't in camp, pressured Weiss to send the money immediately.

When Berra finally got to camp, he found that the press's attention wasn't on DiMaggio, Rizzuto, or himself but on the deeply muscled switch-hitting kid whose speed and power had even the veterans' jaws dropping. Mantle had played shortstop in Class C ball, though not very well, and in any event, Rizzuto wasn't about to retire, so Tommy Henrich was assigned to teach Mantle the outfield just as Bill Dickey had taught Yogi how to catch. That was the Yankee way. Webb had himself been a professional baseball player. In 1917, barely seventeen years of age, he had tried out for the minor leagues team in Salt Lake City. Confused, depressed, and unable to find anyone who would give him adequate attention and instruction, he was cut from the team before, he felt, he was given a proper chance to develop his talent. This, thought some of the Yankees veterans, was the reason Webb so strongly supported the franchise's instructional programs. If a kid was good enough to merit a shot with the Yankees, Webb reasoned, he deserved the best opportunity to display his talent.

Yogi found Mantle to be "bashful, a hillbilly kid, really."[27] Mantle was indeed fortunate to be on the same team as Berra, who joked with him and made him feel they were old teammates, or the kid's rookie season might have been even bumpier than it was. Like all young players, Mickey idolized "the great DiMaggio," as he would forever be known after the publication of Ernest Hemingway's *The Old Man and the Sea*, in which he served as the inspiration for an elderly Cuban fisherman. But in 1951, DiMaggio was inspiring no one, limping through camp with a sullen demeanor that indicated that this would be his last season. "Mickey was really hurt by DiMaggio's aloofness," recalled Hank Bauer. "It was Yogi and Scooter who made the difference by helping him along. After all, they were the best players on the team in 1951."

The preseason prognosticators still hadn't wised up. After two consecutive years of underrating Stengel's Yankees, most of them still hadn't caught on to the wisdom of the platoon system and the strength of the Big Three starters. Most writers continued to favor the Red Sox. (How could a team with all that hitting not win?) In the *Sporting News* poll, the Red Sox received 149 first-place votes to the Yankees' 32. There seemed to be many practical reasons for not picking the Yankees, beginning with the bone chips in Allie Reynolds's right elbow; the surgery would cause him to miss all of spring training. Whitey Ford was still in the Army, and DiMaggio could no longer turn on a fastball. Mantle might well be the next DiMaggio, but he was, after all, just nineteen.

Mickey, it turned out, would mature faster than a normal nineteen year old. For one thing, he had Tommy Henrich to help him learn the outfield. What none of the experts had counted on in their preseason predictions was the increasing power of the Yankees' minor league system and the benefits their young players would get from the Yankees' innovative instructional camp. Weiss and his scouts invited more than three dozen promising minor leaguers to the early camp, where they received a course in fundamentals from a superb coaching staff which included Dickey, Henrich, Frank Crosetti, and Jim Turner. They also got to play with Berra, Bauer, Rizzuto, and other Yankees—at least until Commissioner Happy Chandler found out that Weiss and Stengel were trying to circumvent the rules by "inviting" veterans to report before March 1 and closed the camp a week early. Among the prospects' ranks were several players who would make contributions to future Yankee pennant winners, including Bill Skowron, Bob Cerv, Andy Carey, and, perhaps the most promising of any player besides Mantle, a fiery twenty-three-year-old infielder named Gil McDougald. McDougald played a solid third base and a more than adequate second, batted .306 with 14 home runs and 14 stolen bases, and won the Rookie of the Year award.

All spring long, Casey whined about how many "green peas" he'd have to start on opening day; he couldn't win with his old men any more, he told reporters, he had to rebuild. But on opening day the Yankees were a mix of experience and youth. Rizzuto, age thirty-four, started at short with DiMaggio, thirty-six, in center and Mize, thirty-eight, at first in the same lineup with four rookies—Mantle, nineteen, in right, former UCLA football star Jackie Jensen, twenty-four, in left, McDougald, twenty-three, at third, and most amazing of all, twenty-one-year-old Tom Morgan starting. The only superstar in his prime was Yogi Berra, age twenty-six. They whipped the Red Sox, 5–0.

———

DURING THE SPRING of 1951 some producers approached Yogi with an offer for a TV program, reading comic strips to New York area kids. Columnists had a field day when the story leaked—Berra would be reaching out to his intellectual equals, things like that. Others thought Mayor Fiorello La Guardia reading the comics over the radio during the newspaper strike of 1945 was a better analogy.

When the show fell through, it was widely assumed that Weiss and the front office had pressured Yogi out of it, that reading the funny papers on television wasn't in keeping with the Yankee image. (This was apparently the part of the Yankees image not associated with Babe Ruth and Lefty Gomez.) Whatever Weiss thought about the danger to Yankee dignity, it was Berra who had pulled the plug on the show. "They didn't have a sponsor," he told *Sport*. "You know, they want you to do it, and then they'll see if they can pick up a sponsor. If they do, okay. If they don't, you don't get paid."

At home, Yogi Berra read the comic strips for fun. If he read them on TV it would be for money.

———

AS USUAL, THE 1951 pennant race was spirited, but this time the Yankees didn't seem like the underdogs, even when they faltered. The Tigers stumbled early, and the Indians and Red Sox waited until the last two weeks of the season to collapse. By July 20, the Yankees were only a handful of percentage points ahead of the Red Sox and the surprising Chicago White Sox with their new manager, Paul Richards, and exciting new Cuban-born outfielder, Orestes "Minnie" Minoso. After a promising start, Mantle could do almost nothing but strike out; frustrated with his inability to hit outside curveballs and high fastballs, and depressed over the controversy over his having been turned down by the draft board because of osteomyelitis, he was temporarily demoted to Kansas City. By August it was clear that DiMaggio would not be making much of a contribution to the pennant run that year. Some of the slack in the Yankees hitting was taken up by the rookie MacDougald, who would finish over .300, and by the platooning outfielders Bauer and Woodling. But it was obvious that the Yankees' most valuable player was Berra, who had hit .304 and driven in 55 runs in the first half of the season. Behind the plate, he had shut down the opposition's running games, throwing out 16 of 29 runners. By the All-Star game on July 11, he was clearly the leading MVP candidate. Casey acknowledged this in mid-September by moving Yogi into the cleanup spot. But it wasn't a move that pleased Yogi, who was uneasy about replacing Joe as the team's leader, even though on the field he was clearly the most important player both on the field and at bat. Stengel had come to rely on him so much in the handling of new pitchers and his positioning of fielders that he routinely referred to him as "*Mister* Berra, which is my *assistant* manager." By 1951, writers pinched for a deadline started going to Yogi rather than Casey for the short form on team strategy.

━━━━

IN AUGUST, YOGI was proclaimed by *Sport* magazine as "a legend in his own lifetime."[28] The story, by Ed Fitzgerald, was to be the start of a beautiful friendship. It was Yogi's first cover story for *Sport*, a magazine that regularly featured the best sportswriters of the decade. If *Sport* didn't represent the golden age of sportswriting, it reflected a handsome silver age, with such writers as Fitzgerald, Red Smith, Roger Kahn, Frank Graham, and Arnold Hano, to name only a few of the regulars. In lengthy well-written profiles which told you all you wanted to know about an ath-lete in an era before fans began to feel the need to know about their heroes' private lives, Yogi Berra was *Sport's* perfect cover boy. And for the rest of the decade each new cover story would add fresh stories, quips, and anecdotes by and about the game's most quotable player—many of them true, or at least partly so.

Missing, though, from the jokey stories were the rare but virulent flashes of temper which Yogi still displayed on occasion. On August 28 in St. Louis, in front of the neighborhood crowd, he had his most serious meltdown since his blowup with Cal Hubbard in 1948. Jack Maguire Jr., his old friend from the Hill, had made the major leagues and recently been acquired by the Browns. With Vic Raschi on the mound, umpire Ed Hurley made what looked to be a routine ball four call on Maguire when Yogi went ballistic. Turning around and whipping his mask off, Berra grabbed Hurley's left arm and seemed to be on the verge of taking a swing at the ump. At any rate, that's how it looked to Hank Bauer and, appar-ently, several of Yogi's teammates. "We were stunned," said Bauer. "No one quite knew exactly what had happened or why. We were all looking at each other and saying 'Yogi wasn't going to hit him, was he?' " From the visitor's dugout, Stengel's rickety old legs suddenly had new spring. He could see the entire season going down the drain in a suspension for his catcher if he didn't get there in time. Casey collided with Yogi in an attempt to get between the umpire and Berra. Like a father bawling out a rebellious son in a Little League game, Stengel yelled at Yogi all the way to the dugout and into the locker room, where he ordered him into a cold shower.

After the game, in anticipation of Hurley's filing a nasty report to

American League president Will Harridge, Casey commanded a repentant Yogi to dress and go apologize to Hurley in person. Fortunately for manager and catcher, Hurley, a tough, good-natured Irishman, was as surprised by Berra's behavior as everybody else. Having had some of his most enjoyable afternoons chatting with Yogi before and after at-bats, Hurley not only held no grudge but was touched by Yogi's choked, mumbled apology. Hurley had to mention the incident in his report, but he downplayed it, and Berra got off with a mere $100 fine and no suspension. Was it the pressure of playing in front of the hometown crowd? Was, perhaps, the burden of carrying the team as DiMaggio faded starting to tell? Did Maguire remind him of some embarrassing play in a sandlot game some fifteen years earlier when they were kids? No explanation has ever been offered for what came within a wisp of being the biggest humiliation of Berra's career.

———

WEISS, EVER WATCHFUL for National League castoffs, picked up from the Boston Braves thirty-three-year-old Johnny Sain—immortalized by the Braves fans' chant "Spahn, Sain, and two days of rain" during the 1948 pennant race.* No one else wanted Sain, who was just 5–13. Raschi, Reynolds, and Lopat, though, all knew Sain from the minor leagues and knew that with the proper backing he could still be an asset.† In this case, the proper backing meant Berra, who would be as adept at handling Sain's

---

*By 1951, Johnny Sain's fortunes had fallen so low that many Yankee fans didn't realize he was the same Sain who, along with Warren Spahn, had been the subject of the chant by Boston Braves fans during the 1948 pennant run: "Spahn, Sain, and two days of rain!," also recited as "Spahn, Sain, and pray for rain!" Actually, the lines were a condensed version of a poem by *Boston Post* sports editor Gerald V. Hern who wrote in 1948

> First we'll use Spahn
> then we'll use Sain
> Then an off day
> followed by rain
> Back will come Spahn
> followed by Sain,
> And followed
> we hope
> by two days of rain.

†"In later years," Casey said to Harry Paxton in his 1962 memoirs, *Casey at the Bat*, "I'd often pick up old pitchers during the pennant race, like John Sain and Sal Maglie and Jim Konstanty. I'd get the old man to fool the youth of America. You have the old man go two or three innings in relief, and the young ballplayers can't hit him. He's too slick for them. He gets them off stride and makes them hit at a bad pitch." (p. 126)

assortment of curveballs and junk pitches from the right side as he was in handling Lopat's from the left. In mid-September, the Indians came to New York for two games, and once again Stengel, as he often did, had been able to manipulate his rotation, this time to match Allie Reynolds against Bob Feller. Feller was having a fabulous season and was 22–7 going into the game. Reynolds shut down Cleveland with just one run, and the Yankees scored three runs off Feller. They put it away in the fifth when Mantle, back from the Kansas City Blues, knocked a Feller fastball to the wall for a double; Berra, who loved fastballs, even Feller's 98-miles-per-hour heater, watched helplessly as Feller walked him intentionally to get to DiMaggio. DiMaggio had gone through the humiliation of being dropped to fifth in the batting order behind Yogi and took out his anger on Feller by lining a triple into left-center field. The Yankees won 5–1. In the second game, Lopat outdueled Bob Lemon and the Yankees had a one-game lead with 12 to go.

But it was a pennant race that few fans outside those of the teams involved were paying attention to. There were too many other distracting things happening in 1951.

On August 19, St. Louis Browns owner Bill Veeck captured headlines everywhere with a stunt of sending 3'7" Eddie Gaedel—who had, in the words of sports historian Bert Randolph Sugar, "a strike zone smaller than George Weiss's heart"—to bat. He walked in his only major league at-bat. The sports pages soon turned from the subject of Eddie Gaedel to the remarkable late-season surge of the New York Giants, who had opened the season by losing 11 of their first 12 games. On August 12, they were still trailing the Brooklyn Dodgers by 13½ games before beginning the charge that would result in the most famous game in National League history. Meanwhile, Yogi Berra and Allie Reynolds combined to produce the second-most famous game of 1951.

On July 12, Berra finally got to catch a no-hitter when Reynolds over-powered the Indians at Cleveland, which was especially satisfying not only because it came against Allie's former team but also because he out-dueled the hardest-throwing and best pitcher in the game, Bob Feller. With two outs in the last of the ninth, the Indians' Bobby Avila, who would hit .304 that year, stepped up to the plate. From the dugout, Casey Stengel, seeing something he didn't like in the way Avila was gripping the bat, called for Gil McDougald, the rookie third baseman, to move in for a bunt. Reynolds growled for McDougald to move back. McDougald ignored him; Reynolds kept growling. Yogi called time and sprinted to the mound. Halfway there, he heard McDougald snap at his pitcher, "Hey, Indian, what's your number?" The hell are you talking about, replied Reynolds. "If your number don't read 37"—Stengel's number—"don't tell me where to play." Reynolds was in no position to argue with the brash Irish rookie; anyway, it was nice to know that the guy playing in back of him was as tough-minded as he was.[29]

Reynolds fired two quick strikes to Avila and then, rearing back for a titanic effort, threw a fastball so hard he skipped and fell face down in front of the mound. (The pitch was high, for a ball.) Yogi, startled, ran out to see what was the matter and found his pitcher laughing. What was so funny? Just imagine, said Reynolds, what all these people must be thinking. On the next pitch he fired a high fastball by Avila to win the game. The next thing Reynolds knew, he had Yogi Berra on his back hugging him like a madman and very nearly went down a second time.

Yogi had worked hard to win that confidence. According to Sol Gittleman in his book *Reynolds, Raschi and Lopat*, "At the beginning of the 1949 season, Stengel knew that The Big Three would not allow Berra to call the pitches. They had worked out a system of signs that informed Yogi of what to expect. They were in charge, and they didn't even allow Casey to intrude."* Early in the season, Stengel, who felt he ought to be calling the pitches, yelled to his catcher to look over to the dugout for his signals. If Raschi and Lopat caught on to this, they said nothing, but it wasn't part of Reynolds's makeup to be silent about such things. "Yogi," he shouted. "If you look toward the dugout I'll cross you up! Keep your damn eyes on me!" With an angry Allie barking out one set of orders from the mound and a stern Stengel growling at him from the dugout, Yogi was nonplussed. A livid Casey went into the clubhouse and came back with a wad of dollar bills and waved them in Berra's direction, indicating that this, dammit, is what you're going to be fined if you don't listen to me! Milkman saved the day. He told Casey not to worry, that the three of them— Reynolds, Raschi, and Lopat—would work it out with Berra. That was the way it had to be "if you want him to be the catcher you hope to have for the next ten years." Stengel wisely slipped the bills in his back pocket and sat

---

*Vic and Yogi had even created a phony shake-off in order to confuse opposing hitters. Yogi would flash the fastball sign; Raschi would lean forward and glare at his catcher as if to say "The hell are you thinking?" He'd then shake his head contemptuously. Yogi, almost as if in exasperation, would flash a couple of meaningless signs, and Raschi would shake his head no to them, too. Finally, Berra would flash the original sign again—fastball.

down. All through the incident Lopat and Raschi sat in the dugout "laugh-ing into their gloves."[30]

Berra was no ideologue. Some catchers demanded control over their pitchers and what they threw. If accommodation, though, would win their trust, then, okay, that's how Yogi would do it. He never allowed any differ-ences of opinion on a little thing like calling pitches to interfere with their personal or professional relationships; to Yogi, Allie was "Chief," to Reynolds, Berra was "Dago." The rest of the world might regard those two words as ethnic insults. To Allie and Yogi, they were terms of respect and affection.

Still, Reynolds always insisted that he was the one in charge.* "You might be surprised," he told Yankee historian Dom Forker, "that he [Yogi] didn't call our pitches for us. We [Raschi, Reynolds, and Lopat] called our own pitches."[31] The others did not say this, at least not after the 1949 sea-son. For what it's worth, Yogi's infielders thought *he* was the one in com-mand. Jerry Coleman thought Berra was the one who taught the Big Three. "He had the keenest baseball mind I ever saw," he said.[32] Rizzuto was even more emphatic. "Yogi called the pitches for all of them. Not at first, but after a while. Everyone came to rely on him. Allie, Vic, Ed, Whitey, everybody. And any stories you hear about Casey calling pitches from the dugout are baloney."

Ultimately, whoever called the shots when Reynolds and Berra were the Yankee battery, were, to Reynolds's way of thinking, irrelevant. "My prob-lems with Berra," said Allie, "were minor, considering his value to the team. I might get mad as hell with him in the third inning, but with men on in the eighth, I was glad he was on our side."[33]

═══════

ON FRIDAY SEPTEMBER 28, 1951, with just five games left in the sea-son, the Red Sox came to Yankee Stadium for a doubleheader. Most of the Yankees were excited, but not nervous, needing just one victory to clinch a tie for the pennant and two to win it. The angry Red Sox were eager to play the role of spoilers, and in the first game they sent their ace, Mel Parnell,

---

*In a bizarre story told by David Halberstam in *Summer of '49*, Reynolds said he would "cross Yogi up, to hit him in the chest with a fastball if he keeps trying to call the pitches." In his book, *The October Twelve*, Phil Rizzuto said, "I played right behind Allie at short and never heard Allie say it [that he would cross Yogi up]. I talked to both Allie and Yogi about it, and they say it never happened." (p. 41) Halberstam never said where he got the story.

an 18-game winner, against Reynolds. There was a great deal going on that day to distract Allie; just before the game, his wife Earlene had collapsed. (She had been suffering from fits of dizziness, as it turned out, from an inner-ear infection.) As if Reynolds didn't have enough on his mind, when he got to Yankee Stadium there was a celebration of American Indian Day paying special homage to Allie. Reynolds bore down. In the top of the third inning, he looked over to the wives' section and saw Earlene waving to him. As usual, in her hand was the notebook where she recorded her husband's pitch count, a good thirty to forty years before that practice was fashionable. Suddenly, Reynolds felt a charge, and the Yankees could feel it, too. They hammered Parnell to build an 8–0 lead that they took into the ninth inning. But Reynolds had not merely overpowered the Red Sox, he had shut them down completely—no hits. He now needed just three outs.

In the late innings of Reynolds's first no-hitter in Cleveland, he had shocked Berra and the others in the dugout by talking about the game in blatant defiance of baseball's time-honored superstition. When New York sportswriters wrote of this the next day, Reynolds received some harsh letters from fans admonishing him for not respecting tradition. As if to appease them, this time, as the ninth inning began, Allie was silent.

A pinch hitter, Charlie Maxwell, hung tough, fouling off several pitches before grounding to second base. Dom DiMaggio worked the count full and drew a walk. The well named Johnny Pesky, a dangerous contact hitter, took a curveball for a third strike. Then, into the batter's box stepped the last hitter anyone wanted to see with two outs in the ninth inning and a no-hitter on the line. "Usually I tried to walk that damn Williams if I could," Reynolds said years later, "because I'll tell you, I couldn't pitch to him, and to me it was stupid to let the outstanding hitter get a hit and beat you. It just wasn't worth it. When I pitched to him, I usually walked him."[34] But Reynolds's pride would not allow such a thing now, and Berra would never have thought to ask it.

Yogi walked to the mound and told his pitcher, "Take it easy, now. What do you want to throw to him?" "Anything," Reynolds replied. Allie knew what he *didn't* want to throw and Yogi wouldn't call for: a fastball, at least not on the first pitch. The first pitch was a curveball, down and away. Strike one. It was dangerous to try to get away with the same pitch again, and Reynolds knew it. This was the time when he must suck it up and challenge the greatest hitter in the game. Reynolds nodded to Berra's sign and fired a high hard fastball, chest high—precisely Ted Williams's power zone. Williams's whiplash swing was a microsecond off; he sent a dizzying pop foul between home plate and the Yankee dugout. That was it. Reynolds had become the first pitcher in the American League to throw two no-hitters in one year—but not quite. In the broadcast booth, Mel Allen, respecting the time-honored tradition of the game, hadn't said a word about a no-hitter. Now he was ecstatic as Williams's pop-up rose into the sky: "Berra's underneath it! This could be it!" Yogi had thrown off his mask as Dickey had instructed and sprung toward the ball. But as he waited, a strong gust of autumn wind swept across the home plate area and made the ball float—backward. He stopped and lunged back desperately, and the ball bounced off his mitt as Yogi sprawled unheroically in the dirt.

Across the Hudson River at Mountainside Hospital in Montclair, New Jersey, Carmen Berra was listening to the game from her bed in the maternity ward; Tim, their second son, had been born on the twenty-third. Suddenly she heard Mel Allen exclaim, "Berra drops the ball!" She let loose with a scream that echoed down the hallway, "Yo-giiiii!" The nurses came running into the room. "My husband dropped the ball," she told them.

Back at Yankee Stadium, Berra was wishing he could stick his head into the turf. To make matters worse, Reynolds, who had made a play for the ball himself, stepped on his catcher's throwing hand. "You stepped on my hand!" Berra told his pitcher with a weak grin. As he walked back to the plate, Yogi was distraught; Ted Williams would now be given a second chance to ruin Allie's place in history, and baseball superstition said it was bad luck for a pitcher to give any hitter, let alone a six-time batting champion, a second chance. Reynolds felt worse for Berra than for himself. According to the *Daily News*, Allie "carefully picked the squat man up, patted him on the fanny, and threw an arm around his shoulders—like a father comforting a small, unhappy boy."

Don't worry about it, Yog, he told him. We'll get him. Back behind the plate, Berra had to endure Williams's scorn. You blew the chance, he told him. Now I'm going to bear down even more. To his amazement, Reynolds fired the same high fastball, and Williams's magnificent swing produced another high pop—almost in the same place, but this one closer to the Yankee dugout, "a far more difficult play," thought the *Daily News* beat writer.[35] Again Berra whipped off his mask and scurried to his right; Tommy Henrich yelled, "Plenty of room!," lying through his teeth. "There was about three feet of room," Henrich later confessed, "but it looked like a lot to me right then. I figured if Yogi falls in the dugout, our guys would catch him." No matter; Yogi wasn't going to let this ball get away for anything. As he grabbed it, the Yankee players poured out of the dugout hugging Berra first and then Reynolds.

There was bedlam in the clubhouse but it quickly subsided; everyone was aware that serious work remained. Allie, his mind on the pennant more than his no-hitter, sat in front of his locker and stumbled through questions. "Come back in about two hours," he said apologetically, "and I'll give you some better answers." Someone showed him *The Old Farmer's Almanac* and reminded him it was American Indian Day. "Does it say anything about Creeks?" he asked.[36]

The Yankees had clinched a tie for the pennant; they would win it in the nightcap. In the clubhouse, Del Webb smiled and extended his hand to his most valuable player. "When I die," said the Yankee owner, "I hope I get another chance just like you."[37]

With their fourth pennant in five seasons in the bag, several of the Yankees decided to take the day off and go to—a ball game. The Dodgers and Giants were about to conclude their storied pennant race with a third and final playoff game. Yankee players went to scout out their World Series opponents, who they hoped would be the Giants. (The Polo Grounds had a whopping 23,000 more seats than Ebbets Field, and in 1951 the players' shares were based on ticket sales.) Before the game, Berra and Bauer went out on the field during batting practice and kidded their counterparts. Bauer asked the Dodgers right fielder Carl Furillo for advice on playing the Polo Grounds' right-field wall. Yogi and Campy traded quips, but there was a note of sadness in Roy's banter: Campanella had a groin injury and would miss being behind the plate for the most famous home run ever hit.

In the eighth inning, with the Dodgers up 4–1, Berra and Bauer decided that it was time to get a jump on traffic and head home. While driving across the George Washington Bridge, they listened to Giants announcer Russ Hodges's near hysterical reaction to Bobby Thomson's two-out homer in the ninth: "The Giants win the pennant! The Giants win the pennant!" About half a century later, a fan watching the World Series with Yogi at his museum asked him what he thought when he heard about Thomson's home run on the radio. Yogi replied, "I guess we should have stayed."

As he would say twenty-two years later, it ain't over till it's over.

———

THE YANKEES' REACTION to the Giants' phenomenal finish was summed up by Casey Stengel, "They still got to play us for the championship of the world, which my men and I are much looking forward to, competing against them all, Mr. Durocher and his very excellent players, who'll give us a fine contest, I am sure, when we play the Series games, which no matter what Mr. Thomson has done, remains as yet, if you catch the drift. My men are ready."[38]

"All that talk about the Giants being 'the team of destiny' really rankled us," said Phil Rizzuto. "We had had a pretty tough pennant race, too, and, after all, we had won the previous two World Series." Actually, the predictors were about evenly split among those who saw the Giants as the team of destiny and those who thought their intensity had peaked against the Dodgers. "The World Series *was* kind of a little anticlimactic for us," recalls Monte Irvin. "We had done what we wanted to do all season: beat the hated Dodgers. We got emotional for that. It was hard for us to get emotional to face the Yankees, because we didn't hate them." Anyway, says Irvin, "after the playoff we would have loved to rest a couple of days before the Series."

The Yankees would have liked to have had a couple extra days rest as well, or at least a tired Allie Reynolds would have. The two teams were evenly matched: counting the playoff wins, the Giants had won 98 games to the Yankees' 98, but had more power, with 179 home runs to the Yankees' 140, while both teams' pitching staffs had led their leagues in ERA, the Giants with 3.48, the Yankees 3.56. The Giants' big three—Sal Maglie, Larry Jansen, and Jim Hearn—had gone 69–26, while the Yankees' Big Three were 59–27. Monte Irvin, the thirty-two-year-old Negro Leagues star in his third season with the Giants, hit .312 during the season and drove in 121 runs; he was, thought Yogi, "the guy we knew we'd better stop."[39] The Giants also got 32 home runs from Bobby Thomson (not counting his heroics in the playoffs), and their rookie outfielder, Willie Mays, hit 20 home runs. Mays's all-around ability had sportswriters comparing him to Mickey Mantle.

The Yanks' one definite advantage was supposed to have been their rotation, which they had time to set. Reynolds started the first game, while the Giants were forced to go with the relatively undistinguished Dave Koslo, who had started just 16 games during the season (pitching in 23 others in relief) and posting a 10–9 record. But Reynolds, though he would not admit it until later, needed a little extra rest. He had pitched in 40 games that year, the most on the staff; he hadn't thrown as many innings as either Raschi or Lopat, but had nonetheless expended a lot of extra energy in making 14 relief appearances. (He led the team with seven saves.)

In the first game, the Giants shocked the Yankees, knocking out Allie in the seventh while Koslo cruised for a 5–1 win. Irvin stroked four solid hits off the man many regarded as the AL's best starting pitcher and stole home off Reynolds—the first time that feat had ever been accomplished in the World Series. When Irvin came to bat in the ninth, Berra introduced him to the joys of Yogi-chat. "He told me 'We don't know how to pitch to you 'cause you're hittin' everything that we throw, Monte, so I guess we'll just throw it down the middle and take our chances.' " Tom Morgan did indeed throw it down the middle, and says Irvin, "I was so surprised I didn't get a good swing. I think I grounded to second base. It was the only time they got me out."

In the second game at Yankee Stadium, though, Lopat let the Giants know that the coach was turning into a pumpkin, shutting the crosstown rivals down on just two hits. The Yanks lost Mantle when he wrenched his knee stepping on a drainpipe in right field while going for a fly ball hit by Willie Mays. No one knew it at the time, but the injury probably kept Mantle from staking a claim as the greatest player since Babe Ruth.

The next day, at the Polo Grounds, Eddie Stanky kicked the ball out of Rizzuto's glove and into center field on a key play, and the Giants went on to win easily, 6–2. Afterward, Leo Durocher was ecstatic. "Listen, gentlemen," he told reporters in the Giants clubhouse. "You cannot tag Mr. Stanky with a ball held nice and easy in your glove . . . It ain't a fuckin' tea party out there. Not against my guys." Stengel, in the Yankees locker room was more philosophical. "It was a bad game by both teams," he said, "but it was particularly bad for us, because we lost. You all saw what happened at second base. They come up with a field goal"—meaning Stanky's kick—"good for five points. They beat us. I may have my men work overnight on blocking field goals."[40]

Surely, thought Giants fans, Stanky's kick signaled a turnaround in the Yankees' fortunes, but getting ahead of the Yankees and beating the Yankees were two different things. The weather broke the Yankees' way: a rainout gave them a full day to think things over, and in the clubhouse before Game Four, Stengel put it all in perspective. "You have not done well," he told his two-time World Series winners, "and the manager has not done well, but we are going to be all right if you just go out and play the way you can and I commence managing as I should be managing. We have all been lousy together. Now, let's all be goddamned good."[41] "That rain killed us," Monte Irvin would say many years later. "It took away our momentum. It gave them a chance to regroup. The Yankees always had the luck. I'm not denying that they were a fine team, but they always got a break when they needed a break most. And that gave them confidence. Those Yankee teams beat you with confidence and with Casey. The talent just flowed easily under those conditions."

This time Reynolds held steady. In the fifth inning, Berra, batting cleanup, singled and DiMaggio followed with his final World Series home run. The Yankees won 6–2. In Game Five, the Giants' hopes must have begun to die. They made three errors—which gave them nine for the Series—and never came close to touching Lopat's baffling soft tosses. McDougald hit a grand slammer, and the Yankees won 13–1. In the final game, Raschi was matched against Koslo. The Yankees led 4-1 going into the ninth, three runs coming on a sixth-inning triple by Bauer over the head of Irvin, who fought a torn muscle in his left thigh in a desperate effort to reach the ball. In the ninth inning, trailing by a run, the Giants seemed certain to tie the Series, loading the bases with one out. Unsung reliever Bob Kuzava, who had started the season with the Washington Senators, shut the Giants down, getting the third out courtesy of a diving catch by Bauer. Thus ended the season for the New York Giants and the Miracle of Coogan's Bluff. The Lord had giveth, but the Yankees had taken away.

———

LIKE AN EFFICIENTLY run motor pool, the Yankees added and discarded parts all during the season. Tommy Byrne, his fastball fading and his control worse than ever, had been dealt to the St. Louis Browns. Byrne's fellow Irishman, the affable and irrepressible Frank "Spec" Shea, finished with a 4.31 ERA and did not get to pitch in the Series.° Like Byrne, he was banished to the nether regions, posting a respectable 23–24 record for the Washington Senators over the next two seasons and closing out his career with a lifetime 56–46 record—not bad, he was quick to remind everyone with a laugh, for someone who had spent four years in Washington. Yogi missed both of them, particularly Spec, his former roommate and fellow rookie in 1947.

In November, Yogi was in New York City instructing schoolkids at a baseball academy. When he arrived back home in New Jersey, he got a call

---

°One of Shea's favorite verbal targets was Ted Williams. As Shea once related to Dom Forker, "Ted would say to Yogi, 'Who's that popping off over there? Is that Shea?' 'Yeah, that's him,' Yogi would say. 'Tell him to get out on the mound.'" (*The Men of Autumn*, p. 56)

informing him that he had been voted the American League's Most Valuable Player for 1951. He had edged out Browns right-hander Ned Garver, who had won 20 games; Reynolds, who finished with 17 wins, two of them no-hitters, and who had saved seven games coming out of the bullpen, was third. Yogi, who had played in pain from June on with a wrenched knee and who had slumped badly in September—though still finishing with a .294 BA and 27 home runs—was being sincere when he said, "I honestly thought Allie would win it."[42] He had been saying that to sportswriters from the beginning of September. But, he told the writers, he didn't intend to throw the award in a lake. Just to give New York fans something to argue about over the winter, the Dodgers' Roy Campanella, who finished the season with a .325 BA and 32 home runs, was voted the National League's MVP. The debate over who was the best catcher would continue for much of the decade.

It had been a great run under Stengel, the experts agreed: three consecutive pennants and World Series championships that the experts never thought they would win. It was a feat, Stengel reminded anyone who would listen, that the 1920s Yankees with Babe Ruth and Lou Gehrig had failed to achieve. The problem with those teams, Casey suggested, was that, despite the superstars, they had grown a bit complacent, and he had no intention of letting that happen to his teams. But now, surely, thought most observers, the Yankees' glory days were over. DiMaggio was retired, Mantle was recovering from a knee operation, and by the next season Johnny Mize would be thirty-nine, Reynolds and Rizzuto thirty-five, Lopat and Sain thirty-four, and Raschi thirty-three, and Whitey Ford would spend another year in the Army. All good things had to end. But it was time for Yogi Berra, the American League's MVP and perhaps the most famous athlete in America, and Phil Rizzuto, the AL MVP in 1950, to get back to work at their second job, selling men's suits at a Newark department store.

The kid from Dago Hill had now achieved his share of the American Dream—or at least most of it. Just to remind him of how far he still had to go, he was refused membership in a New Jersey country club where he had lunched with friends and played on the golf course. He never got a reply on his application and was later told by a friend that he wasn't accepted because of his Italian heritage. There was some consolation, though: one of the club's board members asked him for World Series tickets. Berra shrugged off the insult. "Getting into a country club," he told Tom Horton nearly four decades later, "is not as important as where you can buy a house."[43]

———

MAYBE SOME NEW Jersey snobs were reluctant to have Yogi Berra as a golfing partner, but the New York Yankees co-owners had no such qualms. The late winter newspapers were filled with pictures of Berra chipping and putting with Dan Topping. "Did you read about Yogi playing golf with Topping on our off day last week?" Stengel asked reporters in St. Petersburg. "I'm very fortunate in having these two young men. Billy [Martin] tells me how to run the ball club, and Yogi stands in good with the bosses."[44]

PART THREE

Chapter Six

Residue of Design
(1952–1953)

He played as if he enjoyed the whole damn thing.

—CLEM LABINE

IF YOU COULD send a youngster back in time to show him the primary difference between the lives of current-day ballplayers and those of fifty to sixty years ago, you could do no better than this scene: in the winter of 1952, Yogi Berra—proud owner of four World Series rings, the most famous member of the most famous team in American sports, Most Valuable Player in his league—was taking guff from a ten-year-old in a clothing store, the All-American Shop in Newark, New Jersey. Otherwise, things weren't bad. For the first time in his career, Berra would not have to worry about fighting a salary war with George Weiss: the Yankees had met his expectations.*

But he had two children, a new home in New Jersey, and plenty of relatives back on the Hill to think about. In 1952 there were no memorabilia shows for players to cash in on during the off-season; it was players like Yogi Berra who would create the memories that created memorabilia. There were, though, endorsements for every product from cigarettes to salad dressing, most of them arranged through Frank Scott, the Yankees

---

*Some other Yankee veterans weren't so fortunate. Allie Reynolds had won 17 games as a starter, come out of the bullpen seven times to save victories for others, pitched two no-hitters, and finished third in the AL MVP vote, but when he met with Weiss to discuss his contract, he was greeted with a promise that he wouldn't be docked too much for not finishing more games. Reynolds had actually completed 16 of his starts, but Weiss didn't want to credit the seven games he had saved. After much bitterness, Reynolds finally got the salary he thought he deserved.

traveling secretary, but they paid in hundreds, not the thousands it would take to put two children (and who knew how many more?) through college. And there was never any question that Yogi's kids would be going to college.

The owner of the All-American men's and boys' clothing shop in Newark was thrilled to let everyone know that his staff now included the American League's last two MVPs—Phil Rizzuto and Yogi Berra. The customers were thrilled, too, which was fortunate for Yogi, as he knew as little about men's and boys' suits as he knew about hardware back in St. Louis. Berra handled the job okay but found that it reminded him what it was like to really work for a living: "I thought it was tough catching doubleheaders in July, but that sure beats selling coats and slacks. Too many fusspots, too many know-it-alls." Like the ten-year-old boy who, when Yogi measured his sleeve length, told him to be careful not to misjudge it like he did the pop-up by Ted Williams in Allie Reynolds' second no-hitter. Berra grimly reminded him that he had caught the second one. Worried that he had intimidated the boy, Yogi volunteered to autograph both sleeves. The kid thanked him, but told him that Sherm Lollar of the White Sox was really his favorite catcher. "He wasn't," Yogi remembered, "a bad kid, though."[1]

A GLOOM SEEMED to settle over the Yankees early in 1952. DiMaggio's retirement had left a hole in the clubhouse where his locker had been. It also left a hole in the batting order. "Who's gonna hit the fence this year?" Stengel asked sportswriters rhetorically. "Who's gonna make home runs now Joe DiMaggio is gone?"[2] (Though in fact Joe had hit only 12 the previous season.) Casey, of course, knew the answer: the Yankees hoped Mickey Mantle would quickly come of age, but the only hitter in the lineup who could be relied on was Yogi Berra.

The draft to feed the Korean War still claimed Whitey Ford, and it would soon take Bobby Brown, Jerry Coleman—unfairly, many thought, in Coleman's case since, like Ted Williams, he had served as a pilot in World War II. Mantle was still gimpy from his knee operation—as was young Tom Morgan, who was 9–3 in 1951. In mid-March, Billy Martin, who Casey counted on as a team spark plug and replacement for Coleman, shattered his right ankle in two places while taping a segment on base running for Joe DiMaggio's new television show. That was disaster. The next day, Yogi Berra sprained ligaments in his right foot during an exhibition game. That was worse. Robert Creamer, later to become Casey Stengel's most popular biographer, recalled, "The sportswriters agreed that this was Casey's worst team with the Yankees."[3]

Hank Greenberg, the great slugger of the Detroit Tigers, was now the Cleveland Indians GM. "The 1952 Yankees," he confidently told reporters, "were going to be a second division team." The leader in the first division, of course, would be his Indians, led by former Negro Leagues stars Luke Easter (who had hit 27 home runs the previous year) and Larry Doby (20 home runs and 100 RBIs), slugging third baseman Al Rosen (24 and 102), and, it went without saying, all that pitching—the foursome of Bob Feller, Mike Garcia, Early Wynn, and Bob Lemon had won 79 games. The Yankees' Big Three of Reynolds, Raschi, and Lopat were age thirty-seven, thirty-three, and thirty-four, respectively, and none figured to be as good in 1952 as they had been in 1951. Just to make it official, the *Sporting News* picked the Indians to win the AL pennant. In other words, the chances for the Yankees in 1952 looked no better than in the previous three seasons. They had their American League rivals exactly where they wanted them.

———

THERE WERE SEVERAL things the Yankees did have going for them, though, in 1952. The most important of these was the blond, deeply muscled, twenty-year-old Mickey Mantle, who showed remarkable maturity in his second season, hitting .311 with 23 home runs, 75 walks, 37 doubles, and 7 triples—numbers that were almost, but not quite, good enough to make Stengel overlook the 111 strikeouts. The platoon of Hank Bauer and Gene Woodling produced 29 home runs. The master stroke of obtaining Johnny Sain helped take some of the pressure off the Big Three starters: Sain would win eleven games and save seven that season. Billy Martin overcame his ankle injury enough to play 107 games at second base, hit a respectable .267, and learned to make the double play connection with Rizzuto almost as well as Coleman. Charlie Silvera had no power but was a superb backup catcher who batted .327 in twenty games filling in for Berra. There was also the hard-nosed Gil McDougald, who did superb work at both third and second. McDougald and Berra hit it off immediately. Gil moved to New Jersey, and the Berras and McDougalds shared babysitters over the years.*

---

*One of those babysitters was a teenager named Martha Kostyra from the town of Nutley; at the 2000 Subway Series between the Yankees and Mets, the former Miss Kostyra asked Carmen Berra if she remembered her from those days. By then, she was known as Martha Stewart.

Most of all, though, the Yankees had Casey Stengel and his amazing ability to plug a hole with the right substitute or to play mix-and-match with his pitching staff—the Yankees had 15 pitchers who worked at least 17 innings that year, and, of course, Yogi Berra had to break them all in.

As summer approached, the Yankees were scraping by, just a game above .500 at 18–17, and Cleveland seemed ready to run away with the pennant by the midseason All-Star break. The Indians were the mirror opposite of the Yankees, a team with great frontline talent but virtually no depth. First baseman Luke Easter hit 31 home runs, second baseman Bobby Avila hit .300, Al Rosen was the game's best at third base with 28 home runs and a .302 BA, and outfielder Larry Doby was the AL's best slugger with 32 home runs and 111 RBIs. But that was all there was: no one else on the team had as many as eleven home runs. On paper, the Indians' best three starters looked younger and better than the Yankees'— Early Wynn, Mike Garcia, and Bob Lemon would win 67 games among them, accounting for 72 percent of Cleveland's victories. But Bob Feller went 9–13, and no one else won as many as eight games. Casey was certain that if the Yankees kept up the pressure, the cracks in Cleveland's armor would widen as the season went on.

The Yankees found themselves in fifth place at the beginning of June. Berra had been sluggish, but both Stengel and Dickey noticed that he was hitting the ball to the same spot and thought that perhaps moving him several inches back in the batter's box would give him a better perspective on pitches. Berra exploded, hitting ten home runs in twelve games. The Yankees exploded with him. By June 14, the Yankees had pulled even with the Indians. Through the end of August and into September, the two clubs were like express trains rushing for one tunnel entrance. Stengel, as always, grew testy under the pressure. On September 5, the Yankees lost a bitterly contested game to the lowly Athletics, 3–2, in Philadelphia. On the train to Washington to play the Senators, some of the players loosened up by playing twenty questions. Stengel's bark called a halt to the frivolity; Yankees, he told them, shouldn't laugh when they lose. The incident made an impression on Berra, and, a dozen years later would lead to the most memorable moment of his managerial career.

The loss to Philadelphia didn't faze the Yankees, but the pressure of the pennant race did get to Indians manager Al Lopez, who used only Wynn, Garcia, and Lemon for the rest of the season. Stengel got off a line that sounded as if it had been written by Yogi: "I always heard it couldn't be done, but sometimes it don't always work." It didn't work this time, either. On September 14, New York played Cleveland for the final time that season before 73,609 fans—the largest crowd of the season. The Indians, who trailed the Yanks by only a game and a half, had won nine straight, while the Yankees had won fourteen of their previous nineteen.

The game matched two starters who were the opposing team's nemesis. Garcia was 4–0 against New York, while Lopat had won 39 of 43 career decisions against the Indians. After two scoreless innings, a bases-loaded single by Berra broke the game open, and the Yanks went on to win 7–1. Eleven days later, Allie Reynolds, who won twenty games that year with a microscopic 2.07 ERA, beat the Red Sox to assure the Yanks of at least a tie, and the next day Lopat and Sain stopped the Philadelphia A's to give the Yankees the pennant—a mere two games ahead of the Cleveland Indians. Stengel's Yankees were now on the verge of greatness. The 1936–1939 Yankees of Joe McCarthy were the only team in baseball history to win four consecutive World Series; only the Brooklyn Dodgers stood between Casey's Yanks and that achievement.

The Dodgers had beaten out the Giants for the NL pennant, capitalizing on two bad breaks: an injured Monte Irvin missed all but 46 games, and Willie Mays's military service kept him out for all but 34 games. Brooklyn, like Cleveland, was a team with tremendous frontline talent: future Hall of Famers Jackie Robinson, Pee Wee Reese, and Duke Snider, and, of course, Roy Campanella at catcher, with near-Hall of Famer Gil Hodges at first base. The Dodgers actually outscored the Yankees by 48 runs, and their pitching staff, like the Yankees', led their league in ERA. But their rotation was thin, and to compensate manager Chuck Dressen did what Phillies manager Eddie Sawyer had done in the 1950 series, namely take his relief ace out of the bullpen and make him a starter. Joe Black, a graduate of Morgan State College in Baltimore, had been a star in the Negro Leagues; he was twenty-eight before he got his chance to pitch in the big leagues, and in this, his first season, he was sensational, winning 15 games and losing four with a 2.15 ERA. He appeared in 56 games, 54 of them in relief, and had saved 15—an extremely high total in an era before bullpen strategy became sophisticated.*

In the first game of the Series, though, at Ebbets Field, Black looked as if he had been starting games all season. The Dodgers entered the Series

*Roger Kahn, among others, still maintains that Black was the real MVP of 1952 and he lost it only because a block of white sportswriters—there were no black ones voting for the award in 1952—preferred Chicago Cubs outfielder Hank Sauer. Black, like the other great relievers of his era, Joe Page and Jim Konstanty, burnt out quickly. The following spring, Charlie Dressen pressured Black into learning new pitches to go with his fastball and curve; he hurt his arm and won only 15 games before leaving the big leagues for good after pitching in seven games for Washington in 1957.

as 8-to-5 favorites, and Black pitched as if to justify those odds, holding the Yankees to six hits en route to a complete-game victory. It was the second year in a row that Allie Reynolds lost the opening game of the World Series. They would be the only two Series defeats of his career, and Black's win over Reynolds would be his only World Series win.

Faced with the unthinkable—that they would lose two consecutive World Series games for the first time in four years—the Yankees pulled together behind Raschi. Billy Martin, who hit just three home runs all season, slammed one off Carl Erskine in the sixth inning, leading the Yanks to a 7–1 win. But in Game Three, at Yankee Stadium, the Yanks lost again in what was probably their most inept performance since Stengel had joined the club. Berra and Johnny Mize hit home runs, but the Yankees made two more errors (to give them a total of four for the Series), and that wasn't the worst of it. In the ninth inning, with Brooklyn ahead by a run, Pee Wee Reese and Jackie Robinson stirred up memories of Yogi's 1947 nightmare by pulling off a double steal. Stengel did not blame Yogi, he blamed the pitcher who was in for Lopat, Tom Gorman, for not holding the runners. More than that, Stengel blamed Gorman for crossing signals with Yogi and throwing a low fastball that broke down and off Berra's glove, allowing both Reese and Robinson to score. To add injury to insult, the pitch split Yogi's left index finger, which he kept outside the glove, when he turned his hand trying to block the ball. The Dodgers won 5–3. After the game, Berra told the sportswriters not to blame Gorman: "If you don't have your pitcher's trust, you got nothing."[4]

There was no issue of trust over the next four games. In Game Four in the Bronx, Reynolds and Black pitched on two day's rest. Reynolds overpowered the Dodger hitters, throwing a four-hit shutout to beat Joe Black, who allowed just two runs himself. Reynolds had ten strikeouts and fanned Jackie Robinson three times. The big defensive play for the Yankees was made in the sixth inning with Andy Pafko on third base and the Yankees leading 1–0. Charlie Dressen, doubling as the Dodgers' manager and third base coach, called for a suicide squeeze. Billy Martin, who had played for Dressen at Oakland in the Pacific Coast League, caught the signal: at the end of an elaborate series of gestures, Dressen put his hand to his throat. Martin passed the signal to Berra, who flashed it to Reynolds; Allie's fastball was low and away, too far out of the strike zone to be bunted. Yogi backhanded it, wheeled to his left, and nailed Pafko at the plate. The Yankees went on to win 2–0 and evened the Series.

The Dodgers rebounded the next day in the fifth game to win 6–5, with Berra taking a rare called third strike to end the game. With the Dodgers ahead three games to two and the Series retuning to Brooklyn, it looked like Stengel's team would finally go down to World Series defeat. In Game Six, Duke Snider hit a solo home run off Raschi to put the Dodgers ahead 1–0. It looked to be a coffin nail, but in the seventh inning, with his team just nine outs from Series extinction, Yogi gave the Yankees a huge lift by sending a pitch from the Dodgers' Billy Loes over the right-field wall to tie the game. The Yanks took the lead later in the inning and extended it into the eighth when Mickey Mantle blasted a high fastball from Joe Black into the right-field seats for his first World Series home run. The Yanks held on in the ninth when Allie Reynolds came out of the bullpen to spell Raschi, winning 3–2.

The final game of the 1952 Series at Ebbets Field was, incredibly, not a sellout. Maybe because of a mechanical slip, and one game away from their first World Series victory ever, Dodgers fans weren't tearing down the ticket booth to get in. In fact, it was the smallest crowd of the Series, probably, wrote the *New York Herald Tribune*'s Rudd Rennie, "because many did not think they would be able to get tickets."[5] Stengel chose Lopat, a surprise, as left-handers were usually battered at Ebbets Field. With the Yankees leading 1–0 in the fourth, Casey again went to Reynolds when the Dodgers loaded the bases with no outs. Gil Hodges, 0-for-17 in the Series at that point, seemed spectacularly overdue and nearly delivered with a hard line drive to left. Gene Woodling caught it, but it scored Duke Snider from third to tie the game. By the end of the sixth, Reynolds was exhausted and Stengel made a daring move, bringing in Raschi, who had pitched 7⅔ innings only the day before. But Raschi walked Pee Wee Reese to load the bases, and Stengel, having used up his Big Three, made another gutsy call, bringing in another southpaw, Bob Kuzava, who was 8–8 during the regular season. Stengel knew what the fans and press did not, which was that Kuzava had been effective against Snider when they faced each other in the International League. Kuzava then proceeded to induce two Hall of Famers, Snider and Jackie Robinson, to hit pop-ups; the second one would become immortal. Robinson's fly went straight up like a geyser and dropped like a rocket between first base and the pitcher's mound. Yogi yelled for first baseman Joe Collins to make the play, but Collins, having lost the ball in the late afternoon glare, froze. Dodger base runners Carl Furillo and Billy Cox had already crossed the plate as the ball screamed earthward; diving in from second base as the wind pushed the ball back toward the mound, Billy Martin snagged it inches from the turf, saving the game and the Series. In the press box, George Weiss, unaware of the problems the sun and the wind had created on the play, thought Martin had called off the others in order to hog the play for himself. "Little show off," he muttered.[6]

"Them Brooklyns," said Casey to reporters afterward, "is tough in this little park, but I knew we would win today. My men play good ball on the road."[7] It was a pitcher's Series. Berra hit .214, the same as his Brooklyn rival, Roy Campanella. Rizzuto hit .148, McDougald .200, and Martin, despite his showing off in the final game, just .217. If not for Mantle and Duke Snider, both of whom batted .345, and Yogi, who hit two home runs, there would have been no fireworks at all. Robinson was held to a mere .174, and Gil Hodges, in the most nightmarish Series of his career, was 0-for-21. Berra had something to do with that. The Yankees scouting reports suggested pitching Hodges high and tight; having seen Gil up close in the 1949 World Series and in numerous exhibition games, Yogi thought Yankee pitchers would have more success if they pitched him outside—if they got two strikes on him, then pitch him tight, but before then, keep it away. Stengel knew enough to listen to his assistant manager. Later, Stengel gave Yogi the credit for keeping Hodges hitless; Berra divided the credit between his pitchers and his manager for having the good sense to listen to him.

Unfortunately, the 1952 World Series is also remembered for things other than baseball. The Series was marred by the ugliest racial overtones anyone could remember—in fact, it was the first time that most people could remember race even being an issue. Before the first game, Dodgers pitcher Joe Black lit a match by telling a reporter, "They aren't the same Yankees I used to pay to see. There is nothing in that lineup to be scared of." It shouldn't have been an issue that Black was black, but it was. A more serious matter was something that wasn't public knowledge. Larry Doby told Jackie Robinson that Allie Reynolds liked to knock down black players, which was certainly true since Reynolds had no qualms about knocking down white players. But whether or not Reynolds singled out blacks is a question that has never been answered. At any rate, after the 1952 World Series, that's what many would believe.* Roger Kahn, for his part, thought

---

*As with so many stories about Reynolds, the basis for this one is hard to pin down. In *Summer of '49*, David Halberstam told it a little differently: "Larry Doby, the first black to play in the American League, had complained to [Don] Newcombe that the first few times Cleveland had played the Yankees, Reynolds had knocked him down almost every time he came up. Robinson too was convinced that Reynolds had a vendetta

that it was true. "I remember Reynolds talking to me impersonally—I wasn't interviewing him at the time, so I didn't use this—about how to pitch in the major leagues, and he told me he believed knock downs worked against black players. Of course, this is stereotypical thinking, which was pretty characteristic of the time. I would say in Allie's defense that I never heard him talk in a bigoted manner about any black athlete. I think his favorite fighter was Sugar Ray Robinson, of whom he was a huge fan."

In truth, though, tension had been building even before Black's remarks. On April 15, the American Labor Party, an integrated organization, had picketed outside Yankee Stadium and distributed leaflets calling the Yankees "the only lily-white team left in New York." George Weiss could try and dismiss the picketers as "agitators" and "communists," but he couldn't blind everyone to the fact that the protestors were right. The Yankees were lily white. Jackie Robinson was outspoken on the subject and saw no reason to stifle his criticism of the Yankees. He agitated all season long and even after it. In November, after the Series, he appeared on a television show called *Youth Wants to Know* and stunned the live audience with his reply to a young girl's question about why the Yankees had no black players. "I think," he said, "that the Yankees management is prejudiced." There was no evidence to the contrary, and there would be none for another three years. Robinson wasn't just trying to be provocative; he was, after all, asked the question, and it was true that the Yankees had passed up the chance to sign Willie Mays three seasons before. ("The mind

---

against blacks, and there was obvious bad blood between the Yankee pitcher and the Dodger infielder. What made it even worse, Newcombe thought, was that Reynolds *was* good. When he was at his best, the Dodgers could not touch him. 'He would stick our bats up our ass,' was Newcombe's picturesque phrase." (p. 255)

At the 1997 Montclair Booktober Fest, I asked Doby about the stories. He was puzzled. "I don't know where all of that came from," he told me. "I do remember telling the black guys on the Dodgers that Reynolds was a 'red-ass' "—not intended as a slur on Reynolds's American Indian blood but a term which might be translated as "hard-nosed"—"and that he wouldn't hesitate to pitch inside. He was tough, but I don't think he ever hit me with a pitch, and he didn't knock me down more often than some of the pitchers in the Negro Leagues. I always thought my teammate Early Wynn was the worst. I was always glad I didn't have to bat against *him*." Doby also told me that for some reason Halberstam did not interview him for *Summer of '49*. "He got the stuff he wrote about me second hand from Newk [Don Newcombe]. I don't know why he didn't call me."

When Reynolds saw Halberstam's comments in *Summer of '49*, he was livid. He told writer Tom Horton, who was working on Rizzuto's book, *The October Twelve*, that "Mr. Halberstam said . . . that I threw at hitters and at black players in particular. During 13 years of regular-season play, I hit six batters. My recollection is that they were all white. By comparison, the late Don Drysdale hit 154 batters." (p. 188)

boggles," says Kahn, "at how dominant the Yankees would have been in the 1950s and right on into at least the mid-1960s if they had both Mickey Mantle and Willie Mays in their outfield.") Robinson had been careful, however, to emphasize that he wasn't talking about the Yankee players but about their general manager, George Weiss. To be honest, said Hank Bauer, who had seen the heroism of black Marines in the South Pacific, "We didn't talk that much about it. We knew integration was coming, though we didn't know when. A lot of us just thought that it would come a little sooner." For his part, Yogi was "really not sure why we had none [black players]. I know us players couldn't care less about color, we just wanted guys who could help us win."[8]

Robinson had touched on an issue that the Yankee players could not get around. The Yankees had two black players in their minor league system and neither one was slated for promotion to the majors. They could see the quality of the black players they went up against, and they knew in their hearts that Robinson was right. Meanwhile, no one could deny that during the Series tempers had flared. In Game Four, Allie Reynolds struck out Jackie Robinson three times, after which Stengel bellowed in the locker room in a tone loud enough to be heard by sportswriters (though none would quote him in print), "Before that black son of a bitch accuses us of being prejudiced, he should learn how to hit an Indian."[9] As Yogi would later say when told that a Jew, Jack Briscoe, had been elected mayor of Dublin, "Only in America."

In November, the MVP vote was announced. Berra finished fourth. It was the fourth straight year he had finished in the top ten, the sixth straight time he had finished in the top 20 (actually, the top eighteen), the fifth straight time in the top 13, the fourth straight time in the top nine, and the third straight in the top four. Despite the late season slump, he had hit .273 with 98 RBIs, the third time an injury had prevented him from reaching the magic 100 RBI mark. In later years, Yogi would get a bit defensive when someone would imply that his numbers were good "for a catcher." Weren't they good for *anybody*? he would ask rhetorically. And, of course, they were. But Berra's numbers in this period were among the most explosive ever put up by a catcher. He hit 30 home runs in 1952, a mark which had never been reached by an American League catcher and been surpassed only in the National League by his great rival, Roy Campanella, who hit 30 home runs in 1950 and 33 in 1951. Bobby Shantz, who had won an amazing 24 games for the miserable Philadelphia Athletics, made a handsome MVP, and Allie Reynolds, who had won 20 games and saved six more, was second. Mantle, who hit .311 with 23 home runs, took third.

If ever there was a season where Yogi didn't get proper credit for being a catcher, this was it. Even with a split index finger, he led the AL in games caught for the third straight season (so much for Casey's complaints of his constant malingering) and in put-outs, assists (for the third year in a row), and double plays (for the fourth consecutive year). His fielding percentage of .992 was seven points higher than the league average. In addition to handling his regular trio of Reynolds, Raschi, and Lopat, he had helped coax eleven precious wins out of Johnny Sain's thirty-four-year-old arm and guided Bob Kuzava, Tom Gorman, Ray Scarborough, Tom Morgan, Bill Miller, Jim McDonald, Bobby Hogue, and Joe Ostrowski—none of whom ever distinguished themselves in the major leagues without Yogi behind the plate—to a combined 44 wins.

No one questioned Allie Reynolds's status as the Yankees' ace, and everyone acknowledged that Mantle was a budding superstar, but as Hank Bauer said fifty-three years later, "If you had put it to a team vote, Yogi would have been our MVP that season."

———

IN THE SPRING of 1953, Berra arrived in St. Petersburg and went to Weiss's office at the Soreno Hotel to sign his contract. He had already agreed on the terms, so Weiss had released the contract amount to the press. But as Yogi glanced at a story in a newspaper on his general manager's desk, he saw that one reporter had announced a number $500 more than what they had agreed upon. What's this all about? asked a curious Yogi. "Yogi," said Weiss, still basking in the glow of a fourth straight World Series title, "the sun's out and it's such a nice day, I just decided to give you an extra $500."[10]

———

CASEY STENGEL'S YANKEES had won four consecutive World Series, each one, unlike the 1936–1939 powerhouses of Joe McCarthy, after a bitter and brutal pennant fight. By preseason consensus, the Yankees were underdogs in their own league in all four seasons. This time the prognosticators were determined to be on the right side: all ten of the beat writers who covered the Yankees' 1953 spring training picked them to take the pennant.

They were right, but they shouldn't have been. Reynolds was thirty-six,

Lopat thirty-five, Raschi thirty-four, and Johnny Sain, who bolstered the staff when acquired late in 1951, was thirty-five. No one could be certain that any of the swarm of no-name pitchers the Yankees had shuffled in and out of games during the 1952 season would still be effective. Rizzuto was thirty-six, had batted just .254 the previous year, and didn't look to get better in 1953. Johnny Mize, the great pinch-hitter, was forty. Jerry Coleman never regained the spark he had before going to Korea, and it was clear that Billy Martin, whatever his motivational value, would never be a bona fide All-Star. Despite his age, most American League hitters would have conceded that Allie Reynolds was about as good as anyone in the league, but no one knew that early in July he'd be hurt in an accident on the team bus that would impair his effectiveness. (Berra, Woodling, trainer Gus Mauch, and several members of the team were thrown forward, but none seriously injured. Newspaper reports also indicated that several players were cut from broken glass, though whether from soda bottles or glasses that held something stronger wasn't specified.)

The Yankees were left with just three candidates in the category of superstar: Berra, Mantle, and, returning from the military just in time to save the fort, Whitey Ford. "Whitey got there just in time," Hank Bauer recalled. "Our pitching staff really needed a boost. Someone told me later that without Whitey [who was twenty-four that year] we'd have had the oldest starting rotation of any team to ever win a pennant. I don't know if that was true, but I bet we were close."

Fired by the twin incentives of a World Series bonus and their place in history, the Yankees won nine of their first eleven games and were never out of first place after May 11. At the end of May, they obliterated the other two contenders, the Indians and the White Sox, by winning 18 straight (three short of the 1935 Cubs, the twentieth-century record holders with 21). Incredibly, 14 of those wins were on the road. On June 12 they began a four-game series at Cleveland and stunned the second-best team in the league by taking four straight. In the process they beat three Hall of Famers—Early Wynn, Bob Feller, and Bob Lemon—and another very good pitcher, Mike Garcia, who had won 20 games in 1951 and 22 in 1952. Cleveland was supposed to have the best starting four in baseball, but the Yankees matched them pitch for pitch and beat them.

Branch Rickey, then the GM of the Pittsburgh Pirates, was widely quoted as saying, "Allie Reynolds, Vic Raschi, Eddie Lopat, and Whitey Ford are the best balanced rotation in the history of baseball," but he wasn't entirely correct. It was Reynolds, Raschi, Ford, Lopat, and *Sain*—

who would start 19 games that year and win 14—who made up the rotation. When Reynolds was in the bullpen between starts, the Yankees might have had the best pitching staff of all time. Stengel used Reynolds twice in the Cleveland series, in relief of Ford and Lopat in the first two games; Allie pitched five innings of scoreless relief. Although he was thirty-eight, Reynolds was so feared that even the great Ted Williams was sometimes rattled when facing him. "Gee," Berra would needle Williams, "I'm sure glad I don't have to bat against the Chief tonight." "Shut up, you stumpy little sonofabitch," Williams would growl back.[11]

The only sour note to the Yankees' fast start was Berra's sluggishness. It was suggested that the strain of leading the league in games caught for several consecutive seasons might be catching up to him—or, some whispered, he had simply begun the season in poor condition. Yogi himself was baffled. "I felt tired and pepless from some virus, and my skin was real dry. I felt itchier than a hound dog."[12] Finally, George Weiss called in a special nutritionist to check Yogi out. The culprit was soon discovered: chocolate milk. The man who would one day make a bundle from his involvement with Yoo-hoo chocolate drink was addicted to chocolate milk. "Man, could he guzzle it down," recalled Phil Rizzuto. "He'd gulp down a quart before a game and, sometimes, one right after. Maybe more. I don't know how much he drank of it at home." While Billy Martin and Mickey Mantle were risking their health with the hard stuff, Yogi Berra nearly ruined his with chocolate milk.

———

THE INJURY TO Reynolds's back from the bus accident seemed to affect his stamina more than his velocity. From Stengel's perspective that wasn't so serious, as he preferred to have Reynolds in the bullpen anyway. But age was definitely taking a toll on Raschi. For years, Berra had been teasing American League hitters by telling them, "Jeez, don't get hit by one of this Dago's fast balls. It could kill you!"[13] In early June, though, he was on the verge of losing his spot in the rotation. Berra and Jim Turner worked with Raschi to develop a new pitching plan that involved more deception. It was a measure of how Berra's stature as a field general had grown that Raschi never resisted such a makeover. For the rest of June and in July, August, and September, Vic won 10 of 13 games with four shutouts.

Whitey Ford never questioned his catcher's authority. With Whitey, brashness and humor from his batterymate were all he needed to steady his confidence. He threw whatever Berra called for, and he learned to trust in his own ability to throw for a strike in any situation. If Yogi thought Whitey needed a break, he'd call time, walk slowly to the mound, and say something like, "Okay, Slick,"—Ford was Whitey to the world but Slick to his teammates—"the main feature at the movies starts at six. It's four now, and I want to be there on time. Let's get this thing over with."[14] Years later, Ford summed up his professional relationship with his catcher, "I'd say I probably threw more of what Yogi wanted than any other pitcher. I very seldom shook him off, [even though] Yogi did everything crazy. A batter couldn't believe the combination of pitches he would call for. I'll tell you, he outguessed a lot of good hitters. He had a natural instinct. He *knew* what the batters were looking for. Yogi made you bear down."[15] By the end of the 1953 season, Lopat and Ford were the aces of the staff, with a combined 34 wins, 20 complete games, and six shutouts.

After an eighteen-game winning streak in May the Yankees lost nine in a row. Stengel, with his eye on a record fifth straight World Series victory, was edgy and looking for ways to keep the team sharp. After the ninth loss, he came out of his office and railed at his "assistant manager" about the pitch calling on the previous day. The assistant manager fired back. "If I'm doing so bad," he told him out loud in the locker room, "why don't *you* catch?" Wisely, Stengel, who knew when Yogi had been pushed far enough, walked away. Later that afternoon Yogi got three hits, and the Yankees won. Stengel came over to him at his locker, put his hand on his shoulder, and said, with a smile, "Got you mad, didn't I?"[16] It's doubtful that Yogi or any of the Yankees needed that kind of stimulus, but Stengel, like nature, abhorred a vacuum and was ever on the lookout for ways to stir his team up. For the most part, Stengel was calm during the bad stretches. "In a losing streak," Yogi remembered, "he'd be quiet and gentle. He used to say as long as we were playing our hardest, he couldn't do a thing."[17] When the team was winning, Stengel was irritable and jumpy, chewing them out for small things to keep them from becoming complacent—and the Yankees usually won.

On September 14, the Yankees clinched their fifth straight pennant with an 8–5 win over the Cleveland Indians. The big blow was Yogi's two-run homer off Cleveland's bear-like Early Wynn. They finished 8½ games ahead of the Indians, the biggest margin of any of Stengel's flag winners up to that time.

But the season had been nowhere as easy as it looked on paper. After years of playing doormat for the Yanks, several teams decided that if they couldn't beat them, they would at least beat them up. In the tenth inning of an early season game against the Browns, Gil McDougald, running from second base, decided to try for home on an infield chopper. The throw had him beat, but McDougald slammed into St. Louis catcher Clint Courtney (Yogi's roommate in the minor leagues and his backup catcher for a few days in 1951) and knocked the ball away. The Yankees led by a run when the Browns came to bat in the bottom of the tenth. Courtney informed Berra that someone on the Yankees was going to pay for his indignity. He singled to right field and continued on to second as Phil Rizzuto waited to apply the tag; Courtney slid in thigh-high, badly gashing Rizzuto's right leg. The intention to foul had been so obvious that Allie Reynolds, first baseman Joe Collins, McDougald, and, of course, Billy Martin bolted from their positions for second base before Courtney even reached Rizzuto—they had no intention of letting their diminutive shortstop take a cheap shot from anyone. Outfielder Bob Cerv was so angry he found Courtney's glasses and smashed them into slivers. Showing no consideration for Yogi's hometown ties, Browns fans took to bombarding the Yankees outfielders with empty soda bottles. When left-fielder Gene Woodling complained to the umpire, he was told to ignore the glass missiles. When one just missed him, Woodling picked it up and hurled it on the ground next to the ump, suggesting that they could ignore it together. It was nearly that bad all season long. One game with the Red Sox became so heated that Boston outfielder Jim Piersall and Billy Martin decided to settle it under the stands at Fenway.[*]

The World Series promised to be even more of a battle than anything the Yankees had faced all year. These were the same Dodgers the Yankees had beaten in a bitter seven-game Series the previous year, only better. On the whole, though, the Yankees were solid at bat, leading the AL in batting, runs, OBP, and slugging. At first glance, though, they looked anemic compared to the Dodgers, who led the majors with 955 runs—no one besides the Yankees, with 801, scored as many as 800—as well as home runs (208 to the Yankees' 139), batting, on-base percentage, and slugging. Brooklyn was paced by Roy Campanella (who led the league in RBIs), Duke Snider (who led in total bases and slugging), Carl Furillo (who won the batting

[*]Piersall, the author of *Fear Strikes Out*, had a famous history of breakdowns under stress. During one Red Sox game when Allie Reynolds brushed back one of the Red Sox sluggers, Piersall, stepping into the batter's box, informed Berra that if Reynolds threw near him, he would wrap his bat around the catcher's neck—and then get off by pleading temporary insanity. Yogi cheerfully informed him that he needn't worry: the Yankees didn't brush back .250 hitters.

title), Gil Hodges (who drove in 122 runs), and Jackie Robinson (who hit .329). For the season, the Dodgers had won 105 games, six more than the Yankees, with a phenomenal 41–9 record after the All-Star break. Yogi led the Yankees in home runs (27) and RBIs (108); Mantle, who hit 21 home runs and 92 RBIs, was the only other Yankee to surpass 20 and 90, respectively.

The Yankees went into the World Series as the betting favorite, albeit a slim one. Newspaper polls around the country indicated that the Dodgers were the fan favorites, but the oddsmakers, who put the Yankees up at 6-to-5, took two things into consideration that the fans didn't: the Yankees' big edge in pitching—they had led both leagues in ERA at 3.21, to the Dodgers' 4.11—and the fact that the Dodgers' hitter-friendly park, Ebbets Field, tended to inflate run scoring. In other words, if the Dodgers and the rest of the National League scored more runs in Ebbets Field than in other parks, the Yankees were likely to do so as well.

The 1953 season marked the fiftieth anniversary of the World Series, and as part of the pregame ceremony, Cy Young threw out the first pitch to Berra. Yogi was in awe. "It was like watching a statue come to life." He caught the ball from Young and then handed it to him. "It was humbling, like meeting Babe Ruth a few years earlier."[18]

Stengel threw everyone, including his own team, for a loop by selecting Allie Reynolds to pitch the opener against Carl Erskine, who had won 20 games in 1953 and 15 of 17 decisions since July 1. Allie had pitched three of the previous four World Series openers for the Yankees, but this year his value had largely been as a relief pitcher. It turned out not to be the smartest World Series move Casey had ever made; Reynolds blanked the Dodgers for four innings and then, as he had done more than once since his back injury, suddenly lost his velocity. Johnny Sain came in for the sixth, held the Dodgers, and the Yankees went on to win 9–5.

The next day, President Dwight Eisenhower, relaxing now that the Korean War had been over for almost three months, began his press conference with, "I received a terrific kick out of Yogi Berra's home run. That fellow really slammed it out of the park."*

Yogi's home run was his fifth in World Series play, but his real contribution came in the field. With the score tied 5–5 in the seventh inning and runners on first and second with none out, Dodgers infielder Billy Cox laid

---

*The day before, Eisenhower had remarked offhand to some reporters, "It would be nice if someone besides the Yankees won for a change."

what looked to be a perfect bunt down the third base line. Yogi, springing from behind the plate and missing a collision with Cox by a whisker, grabbed the ball and fired to third base to get Gil Hodges in a force. Relief pitcher Clem Labine, the third pitcher for the Dodgers, laid down another bunt. "I swear, it stopped in *exactly* the same spot," recalled Labine. "I can't remember if I moved out of the batter's box or not. I have a vague memory of Yogi streaking right in front of me so fast that I didn't have time to start to first. He was on that ball so quick that Carl Furillo, who was on second, never had a chance to make it to third. That really killed us. In later years I'd hear people say things like 'Well, the Yankees just did all the little things better than you guys. That's why they won.' But that wasn't true. Many times we *did* do the little things right, but they simply did them better. Billy [Cox] and I did our job perfectly, and after both plays we stood there shaking our heads and saying 'That S.O.B. Yogi.' "

Mantle, in center field, had a perfect view of Yogi in action. "One of the benefits of being a centerfielder," he wrote in his World Series memoirs, *All My Octobers*, "is having those plays in front of you. I would see the entire action unfold. I'm not sure that the fans really appreciated how nimble Berra was . . . Twice in his career I saw him grab a squeeze bunt, tag the batter before he could get out of the box, then dive to double the runner trying to score from third. There was no doubt in my mind that the two best catchers in the game were on display when the Yankees and Dodgers met in the 1950s."[19]

In Game Two, Eddie Lopat went all the way on a five-hitter, beating the Dodgers' Preacher Roe 4–2. In Brooklyn, Carl Erskine rebounded to beat Vic Raschi 3–2, and then the Dodgers, behind Billy Loes—who had predicted before the Series that the Yankees would beat his team—beat Whitey Ford, prompting pundits in all the New York papers to wonder why Stengel hadn't started Whitey in Game One at Yankee Stadium, where left-handers were so effective. With the Series tied, the Dodgers had a chance to jump ahead three games to two before returning to the Bronx. Stengel had nothing better to throw at them than Jim McDonald, a twenty-seven-year-old right-hander who was better known for playing pranks on Phil Rizzuto—a smoke bomb in Phil's car got the most laughs—than his pitching (he was just 12–11 in his two seasons with the Yankees). But the Dodgers, too, were thin in starting pitchers and could only counter with a twenty-year-old lefty named Johnny Podres. Within two years, Podres's name would become indelible in the minds of Brooklyn Dodgers fans, but in 1953, he had not yet mastered the art of pitching in the hitter's paradise of Ebbets Field. He lasted three innings. McDonald, despite pitching in constant trouble, made it to the eighth. (He was aided in large part by a great throw from Gene Woodling in left field in the bottom of the second and a great sweeping tag from Berra to nail Gil Hodges at home.) In the third inning, Mickey Mantle, who had destroyed a water cooler in the first inning after striking out for his fifth straight time in the Series, hit a grand slammer off Dodger reliever Monk Meyer. Yogi had been on first base when Mickey hit the ball and circled the bases behind Joe Collins and Hank Bauer. Red Smith later wrote that, "Berra, straddling the plate, flapped his fins like a circus seal applauding his own cornet solo. They leapt upon Mantle as he arrived, and struck him repeated blows."[20]

Billy Martin, on a tear, later hit a two-run homer for insurance, and suddenly everything was turned around: the Yankees led three games to two and the Series was headed back uptown.

Game Six seemed to sum up every World Series game the Yankees and Dodgers had ever played. Ford, who had been humiliated in Brooklyn, rebounded to shut the Dodgers down for five innings, surrendered one run in the sixth, and led 3–1 into the eighth. As he had done so often in nail biters, Stengel went to Allie Reynolds, who pitched a scoreless eighth but ran out of gas in the ninth inning, walking Duke Snider and giving up an opposite-field home run to Furillo. The game went into the top of the ninth tied 3–3. When the Yankees came up to bat, the Dodgers had their only reliable reliever, Clem Labine (a 2.78 ERA and seven saves), on the mound. He doomed himself by walking Hank Bauer; Mantle then hit a high chopper between Labine and Billy Cox at third that, with his speed, Mickey beat out cleanly. Billy Martin got to be the hero, lining Labine's third pitch to the right side of the field, bringing Bauer home with the winning run.

It was the Dodgers' seventh consecutive World Series defeat and, worse, the fifth straight to the Yankees. A disappointed Dodgers fan said, in words that would be oft-paraphrased over the next several years, "Rooting against the Yankees is like rooting against United States Steel."* Indeed, it must have seemed that way to fans who only remembered how

---

*Exactly who first said this or wrote it isn't clear. Some attribute it to a Brooklyn sportswriter of the period, though no one has ever come up with a name. Red Smith was often credited with inventing the line, but in his *New York Herald Tribune* column of October 5, 1955, he wrote that he heard it from a New York character actor named Jimmy Little at The Players Club in Manhattan. Little would work with Berra, Ford, Mantle, and other Yankees in an episode of *The Phil Silvers Show*, on which he regularly appeared.

the seasons ended. But for those who played the games, each season had been a dogfight, and each World Series, including the four-game sweep of the "Whiz Kid" Phillies in 1950, had been excruciating. This one, as most of the players later testified, had been grueling. The Dodgers lived up to their reputation as hitters, compiling a .300 BA, actually 21 points higher than the Yankees. They also made seven errors to the Yankees' one, a fact which baffled them, as they had had the best fielding team in baseball that season and had by far the fewest errors in the major leagues, 118. "Pressure?" said Clem Labine fifty-three years later. 'No, I wouldn't call it that. I'd call it wanting to win too much. The Yankees weren't more fired up than us. If anything, they were more calm. Especially that Yogi. I couldn't get over him. He played as hard as we did, but he played as if he enjoyed the whole damn thing."

He certainly should have enjoyed it. Berra hit .423, was dazzling in the field, and handled the pitchers brilliantly, though no one could deny that Billy Martin, who had batted .500 with 12 hits and 8 RBIs, was the Series MVP. Almost all of Martin's reputation as a great clutch hitter was based on this series, but in the other 22 World Series games he played in, he batted .280.

Having just accomplished what no team in baseball history had ever done, the Yankees themselves seemed slightly awed by their achievement. Stengel, who had been so rude and obnoxious during the second half of the season that he was actually boycotted by some beat writers, was relaxed and friendly in the clubhouse. "If you win," Yogi would later recall, "you have the responsibility of knowing how to act like a winner. We never went around bragging. We learned to be appreciative and humble. The Dodgers respected us, and we did the same with them."[21] Except Billy Martin, who said, "The Dodgers are the Dodgers. If they had eight Babe Ruths they couldn't beat us."

The next month the MVPs were announced. In the National League, Roy Campanella took his second trophy. The Cleveland Indians' Al Rosen had a dream season, one of the greatest ever by a third baseman, just missing the triple crown. He batted .336 but lost the batting title to Washington's Mickey Vernon on the last day of the season, and led the league in home runs with 43 and RBIs with 145. Yogi was second. He had missed hitting .300 by just four points. In the field he had, for the fourth straight season, led the league in games caught and was second in double plays.

During the Yankees' incredible five-year run, Yogi had finished ninth, third, first, fourth, and second in the MVP voting. By 1953 he was, along with Ted Williams, Stan Musial, and Jackie Robinson, one of the four most famous baseball players—meaning one of the four most famous professional athletes—in America. As Edward R. Murrow remarked when he visited the Berras' home in New Jersey for a TV interview, they seemed as a couple to embody the ideals of American sport.* Just ten years earlier, Larry Berra had left the Hill in St. Louis to play minor league ball and had to borrow money—and depend on the kindness of fans—to get enough to eat. Now, in 1953, he was wealthy, famous, and had five World Series rings. There had even been a Yogi Berra comic book, telling the story of his life from growing up on the Hill to his unprecedented success in New York. Like David Copperfield, Yogi Berra had become the hero of his own life.

"They said we couldn't win in 1949," Yogi would say later. "They said we weren't good enough in 1950. They gave us just a little chance in 1951. In 1952, all the experts said Cleveland was going to win. We won again. And we will keep winning. With the kids we got playing down at Kansas City, we not only could win in 1953, but in 1954, and again in 1955, too."[22] As it turned out, he was right about all of those years but one.

———

ALL SEASON LONG, Eddie Lopat was putting together a group of players to go on a goodwill barnstorming trip to Japan after the World Series. He kept at Berra, telling him what a good time he'd have. Yogi was not convinced. On July 14 at the All-Star game in Cincinnati, a Japanese sportswriter who was helping Lopat with his recruiting, approached Berra. Unbeknownst to Yogi, he was already a legend in Japanese baseball circles, and the writer felt Yogi would be a valuable addition to the team. Aware of Yogi's reputation as a gourmand, he told Berra about the wonderful exotic foods he would discover in Japan. Yogi was skeptical: Did they have bread in Japan? If they had bread, he said, he would definitely go. Both the sportswriter and Lopat assured Yogi they had bread in Japan.

———

IN FEBRUARY OF 1954, Vic and Sally Raschi were at their rented house near the Yankees' facilities in St. Petersburg when the phone rang. On the

---

*Murrow's *Person to Person* visited both Phil and Cora Rizzuto and Yogi and Carmen Berra. According to Phil, "CBS did not pay guests for letting them come into their homes, and it cost Yogi because they messed up a flower bed and he knows less about flowers than I do, so he had to pay someone to fix what they messed up." (*The October Twelve*, p. 77)

other end was a photographer who asked if he could be the first to take a picture of Raschi in a Cardinals uniform. He was stunned—what did the man mean? That was how Victor John Angelo Raschi found out that after eight years, a 120–50 record for the best won-lost percentage (.710) in Yankee history, a World Series ERA of 2.24, and five championship rings, he had been traded. His teammates were shocked but not surprised. He had gone 13–6 in 1953, down from 16–6 in 1952, 21–9 in 1951, and 21–8 in 1950, but no one on the Yankees thought that even at age thirty-four he was in serious decline. Moreover, no one, least of all Casey Stengel, knew how the Yankees would replace him. Phil Rizzuto took the news hard; the magic, he thought, was now gone from the New York Yankees.

Raschi had received his contract about three weeks before Christmas. The amount offered was $25,000, $15,000 less than his 1953 salary. He had expected a cut, but nothing like that. It was the maximum possible cut allowed by the rules. Raschi's pride was stung, and many thought that was precisely George Weiss's purpose. Sol Gittleman, who chronicled the careers of the Yankees Big Three, is convinced that "Weiss wanted to humiliate his players, especially his stars. He was going to take them down a notch and send a message to the rest of the Yankees." Gittleman may be right. Near the end of 1953, Weiss told a *Sporting News* reporter, "We've made at least eight of our players independently wealthy, and they were acting as if we had to get down on our hands and knees and beg them to play for us."[23] The boldness of the lie was breathtaking. It was the players, of course, who had made the Yankees into the most valuable commodity in American sports. The only Yankee who was independently wealthy was Allie Reynolds, who had made money from his oil interests back in Oklahoma and had invested wisely. Yogi Berra was doing very well, better than anyone else on the team, in the area of personal endorsements, but he was nowhere near complete financial security outside of baseball. Watching his friends and teammates who had contributed so much to the greatest Yankee dynasty get ruthlessly cut was a sobering experience. The school dropout who had sold newspapers on a St. Louis street corner determined to become a business tycoon so that his family would never have to depend on the kindness of baseball executives.

There was a long-standing rumor that one of the reasons Weiss was so tough in salary negotiations was that he was receiving a percentage of the money he saved the organization for coming in under the proposed salary budget. In *Summer of '49*, David Halberstam wrote, "Weiss firmly believed that a well-paid ballplayer was a lazy one. That gave him a philosophical justification to be penurious, but unbeknownst to the players, he had a more basic motive. The lower the sum of all the players' salaries, the greater the additional bonus he received from the owners."[24] This was vigorously denied by a Yankees accountant, Joe Cosin, who had access to all the check disbursements from 1949 until the Yankees were sold to CBS in 1964. "George Weiss's income, and he was paid handsomely for that time, was in no way connected to the budget for players' salaries."[25] Sol Gittleman, for one, remains unconvinced. "There were all kinds of ways for an executive to be reimbursed that did not have to show up on the team's checks disbursements," he says. Gittleman points out that the rumors that Weiss was getting a percentage for holding salaries down were rife at the time; a *Sports Illustrated* article just before the 1953 season titled "The Yankees' Real Boss" stated that "He [Weiss] is a shrewd, practical businessman . . . who would like [*sic*] to win the pennant but won't be too disturbed if his team loses this year." The implication was clear: whether or not George Weiss was getting a cut of the money he saved the team on salaries, his purpose going into the 1954 season, or at least many in the press thought, was more to cut costs than to win.

In truth, Weiss never denied the rumors about profiting from cutting salaries. He simply ignored them. When asked point blank by a reporter if he "received a percentage of the money that represented savings under a certain gross dollar amount that he had available for players," Weiss's eyes turned to slits, and he walked out.[26] The day was coming when the players would not have to submit to such humiliation from their bosses, and fittingly, one of the men who set the wheels in motion was Allie Reynolds, who never forgave Weiss for the way he treated Raschi.

In 1954 a new pension agreement was negotiated between the owners and the players, who were fed up with management's miserly attitudes. Ralph Kiner and Allie Reynolds, the player representatives for the National and American leagues, hired veteran labor lawyer J. Norman Lewis in 1953 to help with their upcoming negotiations. Thirteen years later, Robin Roberts, Bob Friend, and others selected Marvin Miller, formerly the chief economist for the steelworkers union, to accept the position of executive director with the Major League Baseball Players Association, thus creating a real union, not one responsive to the owners. Less than ten years later, after numerous victories for the players in pension and salary arbitration rights, Miller succeeded in overturning the dreaded Reserve Clause in the Basic Agreement which bound a player to one team for life, thus creating free agency.

For Vic Raschi, free agency came a quarter of a century late. Miller credits Allie Reynolds with being one of the forces that would come to shape the new players union. "In the early years of the Players Association," he says, "you'd hear Allie Reynolds's name mentioned by everyone as the man who raised their consciousness about what was needed. He was one of the first players to say 'We don't have to take this' and to do something about it. And he did it all in the interest of his fellow players, because he was one of the few players so well off that he wasn't dependent on the pension money." Says Yogi, "I hope all those hitters he knocked down over the years remembered him in their prayers when they got their pension checks."[27]

As the 1954 season began, many of the Yankees felt a bit uneasy. As bad as Yogi felt about Raschi, he still thought the Yankees would win more games in 1954 than they had in 1953. Rizzuto had "a gut feeling that somehow we just couldn't win it without Vic." Amazingly, they both proved to be right.

Chapter Seven

The House
That Yogi Built
(1954–1956)

When I think about the World Series, I think about Yogi.

—Charlie Silvera

By the autumn of 1954, the Korean War had been over for more than a year, Dwight D. Eisenhower had been president for nearly two years, and America, at least in appearance, was more complacent. The generation who had survived the Depression as youth and who had gone out and won World War II had now reached the status of middle class. Its values seemed rock-solid, its dreams and sentiments preserved as if in amber by the soothing sounds in the records of Doris Day, Perry Como, Patti Page, and Eddie Fisher. It was, in the words of Roger Kahn, "a simpler time. *Not* a more innocent one, but a simpler one." There were ominous rumblings as early as 1953 in the success of the Marlon Brando film, *The Wild One*, and later *The Blackboard Jungle* (1955), and in *Rebel Without a Cause* (1956) starring the deceased cult star, James Dean. The Cold War grew colder, and in 1955 Eisenhower sent $60 million to aid the French in their conflict in Vietnam, but nothing disturbed the surface of life in the United States. America was the center of the world, and New York set its pace.

"Daddy," says Meadow to her father, Tony, in an early episode of *The Sopranos*, "stop being so old-fashioned. It's 1999." "Out there," Tony replies, "it's 1999. In here, it's 1954."

"YOU DIDN'T COME to New York," says Gay Talese, "unless you planned on being lucky." During the 1950s, everyone in New York who got lucky sooner or later came to Toots Shor's place.

In 1930, a young Jewish kid in his twenties named Bernard Shor— though no one had ever called him Bernard except his mother, and even she did for only a short time—left his native South Philadelphia for Manhattan. His mother had died tragically when a car jumped the curb where she was sitting on the stoop when he was fifteen, and his despairing father committed suicide a few years later. His uncle, legend has it, had called Toots a bum, and Tootsie (the name was coined by an aunt when he was still a toddler with long curls) decided he would go to New York and prove his uncle wrong. He planned on being lucky.

Instinctively, he knew that Branch Rickey was right about luck being the residue of design. Toots had two talents: toughness and an ability to ingratiate himself with others who were tough. In the last years of Prohibition he became an "inside bouncer" at a speakeasy run by a bootlegger named Billy LaHiff and eventually came to run the place. By happy coincidence, LaHiff's was frequented by the writer Damon Runyon and many of the celebrities and lowlife characters whom Runyon ran with. The job and his association with Runyon became Shor's introduction to the New York demimonde. In the words of Frank Gifford (the first professional football player in New York to approach the status of baseball players such as Berra, Ford, and Mantle), "Toots knew all the mob guys—and he liked them. They made him Toots Shor."

In 1940, he finally opened his own place, Toots Shor—no "s" at the end, just plain Toots Shor—at 51 West 51st Street. The famous and the infamous were drawn there as if by a magnet. Shor's saloon *was* New York nightlife. A scene from the quintessential New York noir film, *Sweet Smell of Success* (1957), says it all. When predatory publicist Sidney Falco (played by Tony Curtis) wants to schmooze with a U.S. Senator and New York's most influential gossip columnist, J. J. Hunsecker (Burt Lancaster), he goes to Toots Shor's. The saloon— Toots' favorite description for his establishment—was a place where a salesman from Iowa or one from South Philly, like my father, who was born just a couple of blocks from Wharton Street, where Toots grew up,* could rub elbows with the most famous athletes in America from Joe DiMaggio to Sugar Ray Robinson and bump into Frank Sinatra on the way to the men's room, and maybe have to step over Jackie Gleason to get there.† The atmosphere was so congenial that one remarkable evening Frank Costello, the head of the New York mob, smiled across the dining room, nodded, and tipped a glass to Supreme Court Justice Earl Warren. The country's highest-ranking judge smiled at America's most powerful gangster and tipped his glass in return.

Tourists might have to wait a while in line before being granted tables vacated by newspapermen who had dropped by in the late afternoon on a "bombing run" before returning to put their late editions to bed. No one, wrote David Halberstam, "had ever been known to praise the food excessively. That did not bother the proprietor, who made fun of fancy cuisine, anything that had *sauces*. Shor would sit down at select tables with his favorites and have a drink or two, sometimes quite a few more. The only night of the year he did not drink, Shor liked to boast, was New Year's Eve. 'That's amateur night,' he would say. The draw was the crowd and the proprietor himself, who would introduce athlete to politician to Broadway or Hollywood star."[1] It was at Shor's, according to legend, that two of America's great stylists were introduced. Toots said to Yogi, "I want you to meet Ernest Hemingway, an important writer." Berra (the story goes) replied, "What paper you with, Ernie?" Sadly, Hemingway's response was not recorded.

Toots was a master at the art of the genial insult. If he insulted someone, according to Halberstam, "that person was welcome. He was particularly skillful at using the technique with some of his more serious celebrities. It allowed them to shed some of the burden of their fame and relax—while being treated as VIPs."[2] Shor was surprisingly nimble, indeed almost delicate, in knowing how far to go and when to stop. He suffered no man's insolence. No matter how famous or powerful. When Louis B. Mayer flew in from Hollywood to test his own star power in New York, he was irritated

---

*One of my father's fondest memories was of meeting former heavyweight champion Rocky Marciano and gassing with Shor about the old neighborhood, which they had left at the same age and had never seen again.

†Don DeLillo's sprawling 1997 novel *Underworld* begins with Toots Shor, Frank Sinatra, and Jackie Gleason in attendance at the Polo Grounds in 1951 when Bobby Thomson hit the ninth-inning home run off Ralph Branca to win the pennant. The fictional Gleason, having overindulged in whiskey and hot dogs, heaves just before Thomson connects with the ball, thus, like Yogi and Hank Bauer, missing the immortal moment.

about having to wait for a table. "I trust the food will be worth all the waiting," he said to Shor with a huff. Toots shot back, "It'll be better than some of your crummy pictures I stood in line to see."

All through the 1950s, movie stars, gangsters, ballplayers, journalists, Nobel Prize–winning novelists, and five men who either were or would become President of the United States breathed the cigarette smoke–filled air of Toots Shor. No one made the scene more frequently and were insulted with more affection than the players of the New York Yankees. "*Whitey, Yogi*, you bums, you guys are playing lousy but I'll feed you anyway."[3]

"Everyone was a crumb-bum," Whitey recalled. "It was always 'Whitey, you pitched like a crumb-bum today' or 'Yogi, you played like a crumb-bum.' When Toots called you a crumb-bum, you knew you were in."[4]

Toots's clientele was mostly male. Wives were by no means unwelcome, but the food was so basic and hearty that it often seemed like it was prepared for a men's club—which, for all intents and purposes, Shor's saloon was.[*] If a regular did appear with a woman, however, it was expected to be his wife; Shor was a stickler for observing the proprieties. It would be unfair to call Toots Shor's saloon a bastion of privilege. Many of the regular visitors such as Frank Sinatra, Joe DiMaggio, and Yogi Berra were, like Toots himself, the children of immigrants or, like Mickey Mantle and Frank Gifford, had come from hardscrabble, blue-collar backgrounds. They had all fought their way up the social and economic ladder and were only accorded privileges after having earned their celebrity status. But with the exception of an occasional boxing champion like Joe Louis or Sugar Ray Robinson, they all had one thing in common: they were white.

---

[*]When my father died in 1997, I was surprised to find among his papers a menu from Toots Shor's saloon dated Monday, May 18, 1953. There were three steak entrees: sirloin ($4.95), double sirloin ($9.90), and filet mignon ($4.95). Broiled lobster was $4.50, and shrimp cocktail was $1.15 while lobster cocktail was $2.50. There were five soups, but ox-tail vegetable and cream of tomato (both 50 cents) were the only ones in bold on the menu. There was nothing more exotic on the dessert list than Old Fashioned Strawberry Shortcake (80 cents), Homemade Rice Pudding (50 cents), and Petit Fours (50 cents). Among the dinner specials were Yankee Pot Roast with Onion Sauce and Potato Pancakes ($2.60), Breaded Veal Cutlet with Tomato Sauce and Buttered Noodles ($2.50), and Hamburger Steak with Tomato Sauce, Smothered Onions Rissolee Potatoes ($1.95).

There was "half broiled chicken" but no mention of it being free range, Waldorf salad but no Caesar, chocolate ice cream but no chocolate mousse.

On the back of the menu was a photograph of a smiling Toots with fourteen baseball greats, including Jimmie Foxx, Mel Ott, Mickey Cochrane, Rogers Hornsby, Pie Traynor, Cy Young, and Ty Cobb.

So, at the end of the 1954 season, were the New York Yankees. Change was coming.

———

YOGI BERRA STARTED the 1954 season on a high note. In late January, the Yankees offered him $42,000, which he accepted. They were no longer taking any chances. The reason for their generosity was prompted in part by the Brooklyn Dodgers and Yogi's great rival for unofficial title of best catcher, Roy Campanella. After being awarded the 1953 National League MVP, Campy had been given a substantial pay boost by the Dodgers which raised his salary to $35,000. After winning five consecutive World Series and six in seven years with Berra as the keystone, the Yankees could hardly pretend that they couldn't afford to pay their five-time All-Star more than the Dodgers were paying *their* star catcher.

The 1954 Yankees were almost entirely retooled from Casey Stengel's first World Series winners in 1949. Prominent among the holdovers were Allie Reynolds, who, at thirty-seven with a bad back, won 13 and lost 4, though he started only 18 games (he appeared in 18 more as a reliever, with seven saves). Ed Lopat, at thirty-six, struggled at times yet still finished 12–4, but his 3.55 ERA was more than a full run per nine innings higher than the previous year. Jerry Coleman was back, but his hand-eye coordination seemed to be gone; in 107 games he batted just .217. At thirty-seven, Phil Rizzuto was scarcely able to hit major league pitching; his batting average was .195 in 127 games with only two home runs and three stolen bases. Bobby Brown hit .217 before leaving in July to begin his medical career. Johnny Mize had retired. Vic Raschi had been traded, and Billy Martin, the spark plug who had joined the team in 1950, had been drafted. Their departure seemed to matter not at all: the 1954 Yankees won 103 games, the most of any Yankee squad since the 1942 team (which also won 103) and more than the powerhouse DiMaggio-Dickey teams from 1936 to 1938. It was the first time a Stengel team had won more than 100 games.

The 1954 Yankees had enormous strengths to more than counterbalance the players they had lost. A twenty-four-year-old fireballer named Bob Grim won 20 games and the Rookie of the Year award, and Whitey Ford, with a staff-low ERA of 2.82, led in complete games with eleven. Hank Bauer and Gene Woodling continued to play fine platoon ball in the outfield, driving in 94 runs between them. Andy Carey won the third base job, hitting .302. A powerful young football player from Purdue (where his baseball and football coach had been future Kansas City Chiefs coach, Hank Stram) turned first baseman, Bill "Moose" Skowron, appeared in 87 games and hit .340, and more than any of the rest, Mickey Mantle blossomed into a major star, driving in over 100 runs for the first time in his career and leading the league in runs scored with 129. And with Roy Campanella hobbled by injuries, Yogi Berra, while leading the Yankees in batting, home runs, and RBIs, was recognized, without argument, as the best catcher in the game. He caught for a swarm of mediocrities and retreads and coaxed fine seasons from nearly all of them: Tom Morgan (11–5), Harry Byrd (9–7), thirty-six-year-old Johnny Sain (6–6), Jim McDonald (4–1), Martin Stewart (3–0), Tommy Byrne—back for another time and this time throwing off-speed junk (3–2), and two late-season pickups, former National Leaguers Jim Konstanty, the MVP of the 1950 Philadelphia Whiz Kids, and former Dodger ace Ralph Branca, burnt out at twenty-eight but still hanging on. The last two didn't set the American League afire, but they did their bit, appearing in 14 games, pitching 31 innings, and winning two games. Five Yankees pitchers put double digits in the win column, and at bat the team led the majors in RBIs with 747.

And absolutely none of it mattered: the Yankees were never in the pennant race, though it almost seemed that way in the first week of September, when they surged within 3½ games of Cleveland. A week later, the gap widened to 6½ after the Yankees came to Municipal Stadium for the kind of doubleheader they had become accustomed to winning. This was their last shot, and they knew it. If they won both games they could at least hope for a late Yankee-type miracle. The largest crowd in the history of professional baseball—86,000-plus, including perhaps 12,000 SROs— saw Bob Lemon win the first game 4–1, and Early Wynn win the second, 3–2. The only Yankee home run in the two games was a titanic shot by Berra off Wynn. Reynolds and others mumbled within earshot of reporters that if the Yankees had had Vic Raschi, it might have made all the difference. It seems unlikely that Raschi could have made up the eight-game difference between the Indians and Yankees, particularly since Raschi had won just six games with a bad St. Louis Cardinals team. But without Raschi many Yankees didn't feel they had a shot.°

°Near the end of the season, with nothing at stake, Casey tried a strange experiment: an "All-Hitters" lineup that, among other oddities, saw Mickey Mantle return to his minor league position of shortstop for four games and even second base for one. Moose Skowron played two games at second and five at third. Yogi played one game at third where, in the words of Red Smith, he looked like "a man trying to put up a pup tent in

When it was over, the Indians won 111 games, an American League record that held until the Yankees broke it in 1998. Their pitching was, as always, outstanding: Bob Lemon, Early Wynn, and Mike Garcia combined for a 65–26 mark, and Art Houtteman and thirty-five-year-old Bob Feller accounted for 28 more. Rookies Don Mossi and Ray Narleski won nine games and saved another 20 out of the bullpen. Second baseman Bobby Avila led the league in hitting at .341, Larry Doby led the league in home runs and RBIs, and third baseman Al Rosen hit .300 and drove in 102 runs. Most regarded catcher Jim Hegan as the best defensive catcher in the game, even better than Yogi. If the Indians' 1954 season looked too good to be true, that's what it turned out to be—in the World Series they were swept by the New York Giants (who had won 14 fewer games during the regular season) in four games.

It was, as Berra acknowledged fifty-two years later to a fan at the Yogi Berra Museum, "a really strange feeling. I really didn't know anything but winning. We had won every year that I had been a regular since 1948. It felt so strange walking around New York seeing people wearing Giants caps. I thought, 'Man, they sure forget about you fast when you don't win.'" It was small consolation to Yogi that he won his second MVP award in a vote that surprised most Yankee fans and angered not a few Cleveland fans. He had had an amazing season on both sides of the ball, hitting .307, with 22 home runs and a career high 125 RBIs—just one less than the Indians' league leader, Doby. Hitting over .300 for the first time in four seasons, Yogi attributed the extra snap in his swing to his new bats, 33½ ounces, replacing his 35-ounce bats: "As you get older, the bat gets heavier and you have to go to a lighter one."[5]

To some it seemed odd that Cleveland could win the pennant so easily without having the league's MVP. (Berra finished first with 230 points, beating Doby by just 10 and Bobby Avila by 17.) Then again, as Mel Allen pointed out, the Yankees had won the pennant and World Series the season before and Yogi lost the MVP to Al Rosen of the second-place Cleveland Indians. As Hank Bauer put it, "If they had given Yogi the MVP

---

a high wind." Not surprisingly, Yogi had never played a major league game there, though he had tried the position a few times during spring training.

Stengel's experiment resembled the kind of strategy sometimes used by Strat-O-Matic players, where a strong hitter is played at a position, like second base or shortstop, that would normally be played by a relatively weak hitter. The results of Casey's experiment were inconclusive, partly because the number of games was too small a sampling and partly because the opposition's pitching was weak.

just about every year from 1950 through 1955, there wouldn't have been much argument from most of the guys around the league."

In July, he had been elected to his sixth All-Star team with the highest vote total of any player in either league. He caught the whole game as well as collecting two hits to break the National League's four-game winning streak, 11–9. Berra's pal Stan Musial came to bat in the ninth inning with two outs as the potential tying run, with Detroit's Virgil Trucks on the mound and Duke Snider at first. As Yogi signaled for the pitch, he decided to ease the tension with some light conversation: "Stan, where will we meet for dinner tonight?" Musial, in his coiled-spring batting stance, eyes glaring at Trucks, hissed, "At Cavioli's, eight o'clock." He then grounded to Mickey Vernon for the final out.

Despite the Indians' record-setting season, the feeling could not be shaken by most observers of major league baseball that even though the Indians had won 111 games, they were merely the temporary holders of the American League flag. The feeling was best expressed by Roger Kahn in the lead sentence for his recap of the 1952 World Series for the *New York Herald Tribune*: "Every year is the next year for the Yankees." [6]

———

BASEBALL HISTORIANS HAVE expended a great deal of effort on the subject of whether George Weiss and Casey Stengel were racists. Most of the Yankee players thought not; but then, all of them were white and, like most whites in the time and place, were content to look the other way. Mickey Mantle's attitude was typical: "I don't think Del Webb and Dan Topping or George Weiss were bigots. But the Yankees were winning, and Casey felt no pressure to seek out the gifted players who were available, as the Negro Leagues, once the only option for such heroic names as Satchel Paige and Josh Gibson, faded away." [7]

Most of the evidence against Stengel comes from a single, widely quoted statement made when he heard that the organization was bringing up Elston Howard to the parent club: "They finally get me a nigger, and I get the only one who can't run." Howard took Stengel's comment in stride; what offended him was the inference that he was slow. (He had run track at Vashon High School in St. Louis.) "Elston never really thought that Stengel was racist," said Arlene Howard. "Casey was just being Casey. He was 65 years old. That was how people of his era talked, Elston thought, and so he accepted it." [8] So when Stengel would refer to him as "Eight Ball," Howard would grit his teeth and pretend not to notice in the hopes that his old white manager would become more enlightened. Meanwhile, while Howard waited for Stengel's consciousness to be raised, he at least found that his manager treated him with respect and fairness. When the Yankees were on their goodwill tour of Japan after the 1955 World Series, Arlene Howard stayed in a St. Louis hospital, awaiting the birth of their first child. Elston phoned her every day, "and Casey himself paid for the phone calls. While I was in labor, I received a phone call from Elston. At Casey's insistence, it was switched to me in the delivery room. The Yankee organization was very thoughtful." With an expanded family to take care of, Howard talked to Stengel about interceding with George Weiss. When Howard received his 1956 contract in the mail, he saw that Weiss was offering him $7,000, just a thousand more than he had made as a rookie. Howard was disappointed but determined to wait the Yankees out. He didn't have to wait long. A short time later, he received another offer, $10,000. Stengel had taken Elston's part with management, just as he had done for Yogi.*

The case against George Weiss as a racist is far more substantial. Larry MacPhail, for all his faults, had seen that black talent was going to be a sig-nificant factor in the success of any major league team and began sending Yankee scouts to cover the Negro Leagues even before Jackie Robinson made his Brooklyn Dodgers debut. George Weiss, in most respects one of the smartest baseball men of all time, had no such insight. At a cocktail party, apparently after several drinks, Weiss proclaimed loudly enough for everyone to hear and remember that he would "never allow a black man to wear a Yankee uniform. Box holders from Westchester don't want that sort of crowd. They would be offended to have to sit with niggers."[9] After two years of compiling notes, Joe Press, who had seen many of the best black prospects, told head scout Paul Krichell in a letter that it was "quite hard for me to understand your complete turnabout as far as the Negro Baseball players are concerned . . . You could have had practically all of them, just for the asking."[10]

What might the Yankees have done if they had signed Willie Mays and played him alongside Mantle? In 1959, the Yankees finished 15 games in back of the pennant-winning Chicago White Sox; Mays couldn't have

---

*In her memoirs, *Elston and Me*, Arlene Howard called George Weiss "a dog when it came to negotiating contracts. Boy, could we have used an agent. But they did not exist back then. Weiss would always point to those World Series checks as if they were taken for granted as part of your income"—something Yogi and Carmen were also quick to note about Weiss.

made up that difference. In 1954, though, Mays was the NL's MVP and batting champion at .345 with 41 home runs, and his Giants swept Cleveland four straight in the World Series. If Mays had been a Yankee, there's a good chance the Yankees would have gone all the way in 1954. And could a Yankee Mays have tipped the 1955, 1957, and 1960 World Series, all of which went seven games, in the Yankees' favor? One has to think there's an excellent chance that he could have. Stated another way, for want of a few thousand dollars and an enlightened racial policy, except for 1959, *the New York Yankees might have been the World Series champions every season from 1951 through 1962.* Give Sandy Koufax and the Dodgers their sweep in 1963 and allow that Mays would have made a one-game difference in the 1964 Series against the Cardinals, and *the Yankees, with Willie Mays, might have won 12 of 14 World Series from 1951 through 1964.*

It's indeterminate as to whether or not Weiss was racist or simply reflecting the racist attitudes of much of his time and place. But what is beyond question is that he helped implement a racist policy. In the early 1950s, the Yankees, like several big league teams that were more interested in tokenism than in integration, signed several promising black players to contracts, including pitcher Ruben Gomez, who would beat the Cleveland Indians in Game Three of the 1954 World Series, and Vic Power, who would later be regarded as the best first baseman in baseball. Both found themselves stuck in the Yankees minor league system and wound up in the majors with other organizations, and Gomez actually bought back his own contract. By the spring of 1954, Elston Howard was the last black player left in the farm system, and orders were given to convert him from an outfielder to a catcher—the position at which he was least likely to become a starter with the parent club as it happened to be occupied by arguably the most valuable player in the game, Yogi Berra. Criticism in the black press became more open that the front office was doing everything possible to keep a black player from reaching the parent team. Howard was consumed with a desire to become the first black Yankee; he swallowed his pride, buckled on the shin guards, and did what he was asked.

While the Yankees were not winning the American League pennant in 1954, Elston Howard, catcher, was tearing up Toronto in the International League, batting .330 with 22 home runs and 109 RBIs. Around the same time Berra was announced as the AL's MVP, Howard was given the same honor in his league. The Orioles' Paul Richards offered Weiss $100,000 and a top prospect for Howard's contract; Weiss took a deep breath and rejected the offer. Howard had played by the Yankees' rules and won: his perform-ance made it impossible for the Yankees not to bring him up in 1955. When spring training began for that year, Paul Krichell walked over to Elston Howard to say hello. "How do you do, Mr. Krichell," said Elston. "I've heard so much about you." "I like that young man," Krichell reported to Weiss, "even though he's black, he has manners."[11]

Ellie, as Yogi and his other teammates came to call him, was, as Berra said in the foreword to Arlene Howard's *Elston and Me*, "a high-class guy, and darned good ballplayer. We had several things in common—we both came from St. Louis, were catchers, and made room for each other by moving to the outfield."[12] In truth, Ellie's and Yogi's St. Louises were so far apart that they could have lived in the city their entire lives and never met each other. Four years younger than Berra, Howard was born to Emmaline Webb, a young schoolteacher from Arkansas who had fallen in love with Travis Howard, an educator from Tennessee. Travis was, in the words of Arlene Howard, "a tall slender man who dressed smartly in con-servative suits and knew how to talk and not sound like a preacher. He was a Tuskegee University scholar; as a student, he had lived next door to George Washington Carver."[13] Travis balked at the idea of marriage to Emmaline, who was not of his social class. She went to live with her family in St. Louis, where Elston was born in 1929. She found a steady job as a dietician at a St. Louis hospital and married a steelworker. Like Yogi, Ellie grew up on "the Hill"—in this case, Compton Hill, which Arlene remem-bered as "a soot-splattered neighborhood on St. Louis's southside, its nar-row streets packed with scores of industrial sites, corner churches, and rows and rows of red-brick tenement houses. The air was filled with the pungent smell of the Portland Cement and Scullin Steel plants. The neigh-borhood bustled with sweat shops and cluttered marketplaces; the con-stant grinding noise came from the railroad yard across LaSalle Street."[14]

Though their St. Louis worlds were far apart, Larry Berra's and Ellie Howard's boyhoods were similar in many ways. Both loved to catch rabbits in vacant lots near their homes and both were enthusiastic all-around ath-letes. Both grew up as fans of the local professional teams, Yogi the Cardinals and Browns, Elston the St. Louis Stars, who featured two great players, Cool Papa Bell and Luke Easter. And both were turned down by the St. Louis Cardinals. Howard had been scouted by George Sisler Jr., son of the Hall of Fame first baseman who played twelve of his fifteen years with the Browns. "I worked him out for two days," Sisler told the head of the Cardinals farm system, Joe Monohan, "and I'll stake my job on his ability to make it."[15] Howard never heard back from the Cardinals, who didn't sign their first black player until 1954.

By 1948, Howard had athletic scholarship offers from a dozen schools (including Michigan and Illinois in the Big Ten Conference) in football, baseball, basketball, and track. He chose a different path. A friend got him a connection with the Kansas City Monarchs, who were managed by Buck O'Neil. The Monarchs were the Yankees of the Negro American League, the team Jackie Robinson had played for. Elston had no way of knowing that the team's owner, Tom Baird, who was white, had plans to phase out the Monarchs and make windfall profits by selling his best players to the major leagues—and the team that had the most money to spend was the New York Yankees. Tom Greenwade, who had discovered Mickey Mantle, found that O'Neil was more than prepared to steer his twenty-one-year-old into the Yankees way. "He was already a professional ballplayer when I had him," said O'Neil. "I wanted the Yankees to have a black ballplayer, and I thought Elston could be the first. I knew after a short time that he was the kind of player that they were looking for."[16]

In fact, Elston Howard was a much more polished player by his twenty-first birthday than Yogi Berra. "By the time we saw him," says Jerry Coleman, "he was 26 and better than a lot of guys we had on the roster, players who had been in the big leagues for several years. If he had gotten his break three or four years earlier, he would have been in the Hall of Fame." However, like Berra, Howard was lacking experience as a backstop, and like Yogi, Ellie got to work with Bill Dickey, who quickly learned him all of his experience. "Place your confidence in me," he told Howard. "You and I can't go wrong."[17] At first, Howard was understandably reluctant to trust his future to the middle-aged white man from Arkansas who was trying to teach him a position he didn't want to play.

On March 21, 1955, having decided that Elston Howard was "the Yankee type," Weiss announced that Howard had made the team. "He has big-league talent and character," he told reporters. "That's the only yardstick the Yankees ever used in fielding a team."[18] If Weiss had said talent and character were the only yardsticks he ever used in evaluating *white* players, he would have been telling the truth. Howard was given the minimum salary of $6,000. On Sunday, April 10, three days before the season opener, Casey Stengel presented his three new players—pitchers Tom Sturdivant and Johnny Kucks and left fielder and catcher Elston Howard—on *The Ed Sullivan Show*. On April 14, in the second game of the season, Howard batted for the first time in the major leagues, singling home a run against the Red Sox in an 8–4 loss. The Red Sox, Tigers, and Phillies were the only remaining all-white teams in the big leagues. The next day Howard started and had four hits in a 6–4 victory. On May 14, with two outs in the ninth, he delivered a game-winning triple against the Tigers. Upon entering the clubhouse, he found a trail of white towels from his locker to the showers, a tradition for new Yankees who had won their spurs. A row of grinning Yankees, including Mantle, Berra, Rizzuto, Joe Collins, and Hank Bauer, made up the reception line. Elston Howard, the man who would finally replace Yogi Berra as catcher and become the first black player in the American League to win the MVP award, had arrived as a Yankee.

If the policy of their front office in regard to integration was reprehensible, the attitudes of the players were admirable. "Hell," said Hank Bauer, who during a home game with the Red Sox jumped on top of the Yankees dugout to show up a fan who was shouting slurs at Howard, "do you think we weren't ready for integration? Every guy on that club knew we needed some new blood, and we all knew that Elston was going to help. The only grumbling was from some guys who felt that he should have been there a year earlier when we might have had a chance to win *six* World Series in a row." Rizzuto and Berra quickly became two of Howard's best friends on the team. "Yogi took to Elston right away," recalls Arlene Howard, "and they'd go to the movies on road trips. Rizzuto took Elston out to play golf. Hank Bauer was another good friend."[19] With the exception of an occasional heckler, there were no ugly racial incidents after Howard joined the team—though the Yankees management had, shamefully, not taken him along with them in the spring when playing exhibitions in the Deep South—and the players themselves saw that there were none when they were on the road in big league cities.

In Kansas City, Howard was nervous about spending his first night in what had been a hotel with an all-white policy; he double locked his door and jammed a chair under the door handle for extra protection. Rizzuto eased his fears by taking Elston to his favorite Italian restaurant in Kansas City and introducing Elston to the owner, a friend of his. In Chicago, several Yankees were having breakfast before an early afternoon game with the White Sox. Howard entered the room, saw his teammates, and stopped; Bauer made a space and brought in a chair for Elston to sit beside him.

On the distaff side, Arlene Howard was quickly accepted into the most elite female circle in baseball: the Yankee wives. "And let me tell you," she says, "there wasn't a sharper dresser than Carmen Berra."

ELSTON HOWARD'S IMPACT was considerable. In the equivalent of half a season—75 games in left field, 9 relieving Yogi behind the plate—he batted .290 and drove in 45 runs. Stengel found another sensational platoon combo at first base: left-handed-hitting Eddie Robinson, who had power (16 home runs) but no consistency (.208) and, best of all, the right-handed-hitting Skowron, who continued to be a sensation, hitting .319 with 12 home runs and 61 RBIs. "Moose," as he quickly came to be called, was so shy that when Yogi asked him if he wanted to be his roommate, he stuttered and then politely refused; Skowron thought his teammates would regard him as a social climber if he roomed with one of the most famous players in the game. Only persistent back problems and Yankee Stadium's ridiculous left-center field dimensions would keep Skowron from posting superstar-like numbers. And 1955 was the year that Mickey Mantle firmly established himself as the best young player in the American League, batting .306 and leading the AL in home runs (37), walks (113), and slugging average (.611). Yogi, though, would again lead the Yankees in RBIs, as he had done every year since 1949.

Over the winter, Weiss had pulled off a sensational seventeen-player deal with the Baltimore Orioles' Paul Richards. The biggest names involved were Harry Byrd, Jim McDonald, Gene Woodling, and catching prospect Gus Triandos, sent by the Yankees for, essentially, a young shortstop named Billy Hunter, who was expected to replace Rizzuto but hit 32 points lower than Scooter, and two pitchers, Bob Turley and Don Larsen. Everyone recognized the twenty-three-year-old Turley's ability: he was 14–15 with a 3.46 ERA and a league-leading 185 strikeouts for a wretched Orioles team. The Yankees would need him desperately, as Bob Grim would hurt his arm and win just seven games in 1955. The acquisition of Larsen, though, had jaws dropping in New York. "Gooneybird," as his teammates called him, was a free spirit who didn't appear at all to be cast in the Yankee mold; he had posted a horrendous 3–21 record for Baltimore in 1954, walking more batters than he struck out. Why, some players asked out loud, did the Yankees want him?

Working with a great pitching coach in Turner, a better set of infielders, and, best of all, a great catcher did wonders for Larsen. In limited use as a spot starter and occasional reliever, Larsen, despite a sore shoulder and a display of bad attitude when Stengel sent him to Denver for rehab, was everything the Yankees could hope for in 1955, winning nine of eleven with an ERA of just over three runs a game. Whitey Ford, as expected, quickly confirmed his status as the ace of the staff, winning six of his first seven decisions, three by shutout; he finished the season with 18 wins, tied with the Indians' Bob Lemon and the Red Sox's Frank Sullivan, and, despite a reputation as a pitcher who couldn't finish what he started, led the league with 18 complete games. Turley stepped right in where Grim had left off, winning 17 games and striking out 210 batters. Jim Konstanty, finding a second life in the American League, was terrific out of the bullpen, winning seven and losing two with eleven saves.

It wasn't as good a Yankee team, though, as the 1954 squad, winning seven fewer games. But 96 victories proved to be enough. The Indians hung tough, but even with first baseman Vic Wertz crippled by polio and third baseman Al Rosen plagued by back problems, they couldn't keep pace with the Yankees at the end. By September 16, with just eleven games to play, the Yanks were half a game behind Cleveland and had to play a crucial three-game series with the Red Sox in New York. Boston's starter was their only first-rate pitcher, 6'6" Frank Sullivan, an eventual 18-game winner. Stengel juggled his rotation, as he often did, to match Whitey Ford against the Boston ace. Berra slammed an early home run, but by the bottom of the ninth the Yankees were down 4–3 with Mickey Mantle out of the game with a torn thigh muscle. (Skowron had left the game earlier, breaking his big toe on a water cooler after striking out.) With one out, Hank Bauer, finally getting a chance to play full time with Woodling gone, hit a soaring drive off Ellis Kinder into the left-field seats to tie the game. Shaken, Kinder got the next batter and then decided to start off Yogi Berra with a fastball. Yogi swung as though the count was 3–0 and he had been waiting for that pitch. The ball landed in the lower right-field seats, just missing the second deck. When they reached the locker room, they heard the news that the Indians had lost to Detroit, so the Yankees were back in first place. They would stay there for the final nine days of the season. The Indians had to return more than $3 million in World Series ticket orders.

The victory over the Red Sox, sparked by Billy Martin's return from the Army and Bauer's and Berra's home runs, lit a fire under the team; the Yankees went on to finish three games ahead of the Indians and five ahead of the White Sox. "I never have been on a yacht in my whole life," wrote Jimmy Cannon in Newsday the day after Yogi's ninth-inning home run. "But I imagine rooting for the Yankees is like owning a yacht."[20]

IF CANNON WAS right, rooting for the Brooklyn Dodgers at World Series time must have seemed like owning a submarine. After the first two games, Dodgers fans must have felt as if their team was doing a crash dive with the hatches still open. Before the first game, just before the national anthem a sellout crowd at Yankee Stadium bowed their heads in silence, praying for President Eisenhower, who had suffered a heart attack four days earlier. It was the only moment of silence for the next three hours as Yankee fans rocked the Bronx in anticipation of winning back the World Series flag they all felt was rightfully theirs. Ford wasn't sharp in the early going, allowing a solo home run by Carl Furillo and a triple by Jackie Robinson; in the third, a towering home run by Duke Snider off a hanging curveball traveled into the third deck of the right field stands. Fortunately for the Yankees, Newcombe, who had led the National League with twenty wins, wasn't sharp either. In the second inning, Elston Howard came up for his first World Series at-bat and hit a two-run homer—the first home run in World Series history by a black hitter against a black pitcher. Ford settled down, and the Yankees took a 6–3 lead into the eighth. The Dodgers pushed a runner to third and got a run on a sacrifice fly. Then came one of the most talked about plays in World Series history.

With his team down by two runs and Frank Kellert at bat, Jackie Robinson, inching off third base, shrewdly anticipated that Ford and Berra would not be expecting an attempt to steal home. He was right about Ford, wrong about Berra. Yogi, whose reflexes were as fast as Jackie's, reacted the moment Robinson shifted his weight and broke for home even before Ford released the ball. Snagging Ford's pitch right over the front edge of the plate, Berra simply allowed Robinson to slide into the tag. The umpire, Bill Summers, flashed the safe signal, and Yogi, as if on a pogo stick, jumped up and down, screaming his lungs out in protest. To this day Berra insists Robinson was out. Robinson always insisted that he was safe.

Who was right? The play, replayed frame-by-frame, clearly shows that when Robinson is seven or eight feet from the plate, Berra, who had sprung into position, is waiting for the ball. When Jackie's right foot is perhaps three to four feet from the plate, the ball is already in Yogi's glove, which is about a foot off the ground. Robinson slides right into the tag; it's close, but Jackie is out.

Well, at least that's the way I call it after watching the play several times in slow motion, though in truth I'm still not absolutely certain—and never will be. What can be said for certain is that anyone watching a replay of the steal has a better view than umpire Bill Summers did, who was standing at least five feet behind home plate *directly in back of Berra.* Unless Summers was wearing X-ray specs, there is simply no way he could have seen whether Robinson's right foot made it to home plate before touching Yogi's glove. Jackie, no doubt, took this into consideration when deciding to take his chance.

Considered from yet another perspective, though, history must come down on the side of Jackie Robinson. In January of 1955, the Baseball Rules Committee had approved a new rule establishing a "catcher's box behind the plate." The expressed purpose of the rule was to limit a catcher's lateral movement; he could not cross the white lines until the ball left the pitcher's hand. The apparent intent was to stimulate the running game, which by the mid-1950s had become almost stagnant. The idea was that keeping the catcher in the box for an extra fraction of a second would make the pitch-out slightly less effective and, as it were, level the playing field between catcher and base runner. That it also limited a catcher's forward movement toward the plate wasn't noticed at the time.

Berra and Campanella, the best catchers in the game, spoke out against the rule, Yogi telling the *New York Daily News'* Joe Trimble that it was a "blow at the profession of catching . . . I want the umpires to explain to me how we can call for a pitchout and still stay in that narrow box without the ball flying past you. I suppose it can be done, if we move when the pitcher lets go of the ball, but I still want them to tell us what we can and cannot do. After all, you have to call for a pitchout once in a while."[21] The rule book in use for the 1955 season clearly states, "Each runner, other than the batter, may without liability of being put out advance one base when, while he's attempting to steal a base, the batter is interfered with by the catcher."

As the first frame in the sequence (see first photo section) clearly shows, Berra is already into the batter's box standing directly over home plate before the ball has arrived. Had Frank Kellert decided to swing, he would have been unable to get to the ball without swinging through Yogi. So, according to the rules, Robinson would have been awarded home because of Berra's interference. For purists, of course, that doesn't end the argument; after all, Summers did not notice the interference, and neither, for that matter, did Kellert. It is still argued by some, with a logic that would cause a Jesuit to despair, that an interference call made or missed by the home plate umpire is just part of the game. Summers missed the call in this instance, but even if he had made it, it wouldn't have been a *steal* of home for Robinson but a base awarded on interference.

———

FOR THE LAST five years, my daughter Maggie and I have attended the World Series broadcasts at the Yogi Berra Museum and Learning Center. Each year, during the between-innings Q&A sessions, I've asked Yogi if he's changed his opinion on whether or not Jackie Robinson was out in the 1955 World Series, much to the delight of Yogi and the audience. Here are the questions along with Berra's responses.

2003

BARRA: Mr. Berra, I was just wondering if I could ask you if you've changed your mind over the years about one of the most controversial World Series plays you were ever involved in. In 1955, with Whitey Ford on the mound, Jackie Robinson stole home. It's hard to tell from the film, but it certainly looks as if he could have slid right into your tag. Have you watched the tape recently, and if so, has your mind changed about the call?

BERRA: Jackie was out in 1955, he was out when I saw the replay twenty years ago, and he's still out!

2004

BARRA: Mr. Berra, I was wondering if you had somehow changed your opinion about Jackie Robinson's stealing home in the 1955 series . . . ?

BERRA: Naw, he's still out.

2005

BARRA: Mr. Berra, tomorrow is the fiftieth anniversary of one of the most famous plays in World Series history, and I was wondering if your opinion has changed over the years? Jackie Robinson on third . . .

BERRA: Still out!

2006

BARRA: Mr. Berra, I was wondering if there was any possibility that you had changed your mind about Jackie Robinson in 1955 . . .

BERRA: Out!

2007

BARRA: Mr. Berra, I've asked you this question every year for the last four years, but I just wanted to see if you still feel the same way. 1955 World Series . . .

BERRA: (raising his hand and giving an umpire's call) OUT!

———

WHATEVER SHOULD HAVE been, when the dust had cleared from Robinson's slide and Berra had cooled from hopping mad to simply mad, the Yankees were ahead by only one run, 6–5. Bob Grim pitched the ninth and saved the win for the Yanks. Afterward, in the clubhouse, Yogi was still steaming. "What a lousy, showboat play. They're two runs behind. Anyway, I had him out. The damn umpire blew the call." Like an old ladies' sewing circle, the writers took Berra's words and went next door to the Dodgers' locker room and relayed them to Robinson. "Lousy?" said an indignant Robinson. "Whitey Ford was winding up. With me on third? Any time they give me a run that way, I take it. And Berra *didn't* have me. He made a lazy tag. He stayed *behind* the plate. By the time he put the ball on me, my foot was across the plate."[22]

In the second game, Tommy Byrne, enjoying the second act of his career, stopped the Dodgers on five hits for a 4–2 win and put the Yankees up two games to none in the Series.

This, though, was a different Dodgers team than the Yankees had faced in 1947, 1949, 1952, and even 1953. Yanks pitchers had led the American League with a 3.32 ERA, but this time they faced a Dodgers staff that had led *their* league at 3.68, half of it compiled in perhaps the best hitters park in the big leagues, Ebbets Field. As it turned out, the two pitching staffs were just about evenly matched, and this time the Yankees starters didn't have a big edge in experience; Ford and Byrne were the only Yankees who had ever thrown a pitch in October. Stengel had other things to worry about: Mantle, the best hitter on either team, was in terrible pain. As it turned out, he would play in just three of the Series' seven games, batting .200.

Down two games to nothing and looking at their fifth humiliation at the hands of the Yankees in nine years, the Dodgers, back in Brooklyn, sent out the twenty-two-year-old left-hander Johnny Podres, who pitched a complete game while the Dodgers shelled Bob Turley and three other Yankees pitchers for eight runs. The next day, the Dodgers outscored the

Yankees 8–5 to even the Series. And then, with both Mantle and Bauer hurting on the bench, the Yanks watched as rookie Roger Craig, with relief help from Clem Labine, gave the Dodgers an edge, three games to two. The big hit was an unimpressive 300-foot home run down the right-field line by the Dodgers' left fielder, a Cuban named Edmundo "Sandy" Amoros. Even some Dodger fans didn't know Amoros's name; before the 1955 World Series was over, they would never forget it. Despite home runs by Bob Cerv and Berra off Craig, Labine stopped the Yankees over the last two innings for a 5–3 win. The next day, in the Bronx, Whitey Ford was nearly unhittable, going all the way and allowing the Dodgers just a single run while the Yankees scored five in the first for an easy win.

The Series was tied, and the Yankees simply did not lose the seventh game of a World Series, particularly to a Dodger team that had never won one.

In the deciding game, Johnny Podres and Tommy Byrne traded goose eggs for three innings. In the fourth and then again in the sixth inning, the Dodgers scored solo runs. Yankee fans remained cheerily optimistic. Hadn't games like this always gone their way? Their patience was rewarded, or so it seemed, in the sixth inning when Billy Martin led off with a walk and Gil McDougald followed with a single. The next batter, of course, was Yogi Berra. Wasn't this the way it was supposed to be? Did Yogi ever fail in these situations? "There was no one I would rather see batting in those situations than Yogi," Mickey Mantle would later say, "unless it was me."[23]

Yogi didn't fail now. All day long, Podres had been frustrating the Yankees, whose scouts had told them the Dodger lefty was essentially a curveball pitcher. But on this day, in key situations Podres was throwing fastballs, and good ones. He threw one to Yogi, who got around on it late but with good wood. Everyone knew Yogi was a pull hitter, and although this shot went to the opposite field, Dodger fans knew in their hearts that it would somehow end up bad for them. At the crack of the bat, it looked like it would end up a home run over the fence and into the short left-field corner, but as it reached the halfway point, it began to slice to left and seemed likely to drop in for a double. The fans, thought Roger Kahn, "quickly did the math in their heads: if it dropped in front of and ricocheted off the fence, it would probably tie the game. If, on the other hand, it dropped and bounced over the fence, it would be a ground rule double and only one run would score. I believe in that instance a couple of million Dodger fans said a lightning-fast prayer that it would be the latter, for if the Yankees were able to tie the game in their own home park, there was surely no way that the Dodgers could win."

For once, and only once, in the history of the Brooklyn Dodgers their fans were granted more than they prayed for. For once, and only once, the wind blew their way. A stiff breeze, moving from left to right, kept the ball in the air just long enough for Sandy Amoros, seemingly out of nowhere, to run the ball down. Skidding to a halt so he would not break his neck on the wall, Amoros stretched out the glove on his right hand and snared the ball in the webbing. He then stopped, wheeled around, and fired to his cutoff man, Pee Wee Reese, on exactly the kind of fundamental play the Dodgers had failed to make so often against the Yankees. Reese fired to Gil Hodges at first, perhaps a foot ahead of a desperate McDougald, for a double play.

Yankee fans were stunned. On radio, millions heard Mel Allen announce, "And Amoros makes the catch! How *about* that?" Allen's signature phrase had so many times signified something positive for the Yankees that most fans never dreamed of hearing it in this context. "We just couldn't believe it," recalls Jerry Coleman. "In the dugout, we just shook our heads. There's no way he should have made that catch. There was no way he should have been playing Yogi so close to the outfield fence. It was a great play, but at the same time it was also a colossal fluke." To compound the element of flukiness, Amoros had only gone into the lineup a short time before, substituting for Junior Gilliam, who was right-handed.

The catch may have been a fluke, but Podres's pitching wasn't. In the ninth inning, Skowron smacked a shot right back up the middle, but Podres saved a hit by spearing the ball and tossing it underhanded to Hodges. Cerv hit a mile-high fly to Amoros in left. Elston Howard hit a hard hopper to Reese at shortstop. Pee Wee fired to Hodges, and, for Yankee fans, hell commenced to freeze over.

In the Dodgers clubhouse, Sandy Amoros explained how he had made his game-saving catch. "I kept my eyes on the ball . . . never looked anywhere else. It stayed up just long enough to fall into my glove . . . I never hit the fence, but I was only this far from it," he said, holding out two hands about twenty inches apart.[24]

Of all the Yankees, Billy Martin took it the hardest, crying and smashing his locker door with his fist—some said you could still see the dents when Yankees Stadium was renovated in 1975—and couldn't get control of himself for almost an hour. Hank Bauer was the most philosophical. Noting that the Yankees had come within inches of victory, he said with a shrug,

"Maybe it's a good omen, now we can start over again."[25] This was the first Stengel team ever to lose a World Series—only Phil Rizzuto among the players and Bill Dickey and Frank Crosetti among the coaches had ever been on a losing World Series team (in 1942 against the Cardinals).

Yogi Berra spotted Jackie Robinson, mad with joy and shaking hands with everyone in sight near the entrance to the Yankee clubhouse. He walked over to him, grinned, and extended his hand, "Hey, Jack, what's new?"

Berra had hit .417, with 10 hits in 24 at-bats, and though he had driven in just two runs had scored five. His performance was no consolation for the absence of a World Series ring, or, for that matter, a World Series check—or rather, a *winner's* share World Series check.

The next day, Dana Mozley wrote in the *Daily News*, "Perhaps because of a breeze that grew in the Bronx, a world's championship flag can now be raised in Brooklyn for the first time. Certainly the one play that broke the Yankees' back was Sandy Amoros's great sixth-inning catch and resultant double play. He said an incoming wind held the ball just long enough for him to catch it."[26]

Berra never got over the sting of Robinson's steal of home. His humiliation in the 1947 World Series, even though the Yankees won, was still fresh in his mind; he had expected Robinson to try something daring, and he had been ready for it. As he saw it, the umpire's bad call had stolen his triumph. But he quickly regretted his heated remarks to the press after the first game, and when the Series was over wasted no time in making amends. After talking to reporters, he put a smile on his face, walked into the Dodgers clubhouse, and shook hands with Robinson and Campanella. The gesture was much appreciated by his Dodger opponents. Next year, they would get a chance to reciprocate.

Over the years, Yogi apologized several times for his "lousy showboat play" remark. In his book of World Series memoirs, he said, "I learned later he [Robinson] did it because he wanted to rouse his team; he thought they were playing like losers. So it was a good play, even though he was really out."[27]

———

GEORGE WEISS DIDN'T allow his players to brood for long. On October 18, the Yankees, having assembled in San Francisco, embarked on a goodwill tour of the Far East that would last almost till Thanksgiving. The State Department, Pepsi-Cola, and the New York Yankees pooled their efforts to bring America's favorite pastime to Hawaii, the Philippines, Guam, and Japan. Everywhere the crowds were enthusiastic, and in Japan there was near hysteria. There seemed to be no awareness among the Japanese that the Yankees had lost the World Series; the exhibitions regularly drew over 60,000 people, and hundreds of thousands lined the streets of Japan's major cities to see their motorcades pass. The Japanese gaped in awe at Mickey Mantle's tremendous home runs and at Bob Turley's 95-miles-per-hour fastballs; every utterance from the mouths of Casey Stengel and Yogi Berra was greeted by the Japanese with the dignity accorded scripture. The errors in translation which must have made their way into Japanese papers that fall are inconceivable.

Sometimes, the baseball the Yankees played didn't translate. The combination of no curfew and pregame cocktail parties sometimes left the Yankees playing sloppier than in spring training. In a game with the Tokyo Giants, Whitey Ford gave a pickoff signal that his middle infielders, Billy Martin and Gil McDougald, did not catch—or perhaps Ford neglected to give it. In any event, Ford wheeled and fired toward second, and the ball sailed into center field, where it knocked a Japanese umpire nearly unconscious while the puzzled base runner trotted home. It was perhaps not coincidental that the night before Ford, Martin, and McDougald had been investigating Tokyo nightlife.

Weiss, perhaps mistakenly assuming that their presence would cause the players to behave with more dignity, allowed the players' wives along on the trip. One afternoon Stengel, Mantle, Ford, and Martin slipped away from theirs and went to a geisha house for a massage. Hank Bauer declined. "I don't even think they asked Yogi," he remembered. "There was no way he was going to leave Carmen to go to a geisha house."

Two years later, during spring training, Yogi shook hands with a Japanese reporter whom he had met on the 1955 trip. The reporter handed him a story he had written about Yogi for a Tokyo newspaper. "It looks real nice," Berra replied, "but I can't read Japanese."[28]

———

IN THE EARLY part of the decade, a hot topic among New York baseball fans was "Who is the better shortstop, Phil Rizzuto or Pee Wee Reese?" With the emergence of Mickey Mantle and Willie Mays as superstars, the Mays-Mantle-Snider debate heated up (though Mantle would make his biggest statements with his 1956 and 1957 seasons). But from 1949 through 1955, no baseball topic in New York was argued more fervently than Yogi Berra versus Roy Campanella. The two men didn't simply dominate their league's All-Star votes, they dominated the Most Valuable Player voting.

On December 4, the American League MVP was announced. Yogi Berra won his third award, with Tigers rookie and batting champion Al Kaline second. Yogi's batting average had fallen to .272, but he had 27 home runs and once again led the Yankees in RBIs with 108. Behind the plate, he led AL catchers in games caught for the sixth straight year and for the fifth time in put-outs. The next day, the National League selection was announced: Roy Campanella, who had batted .318 with 32 home runs and 107 RBIs, won *his* third MVP. At the Baseball Writers Dinner in New York a couple of weeks later, a grinning Campy spotted Yogi walking into the room. "Hey, there," he called out. "How's the best catcher in this big ball-room out in old for me?" Yogi smiled and took the joke. After all, Boyo team had won the World Series. *This* year, anyway.

FROM 1950 THROUGH 1955, Yogi Berra had the highest combined vote for Most Valuable Player in baseball. But 1956 would be Berra's last great year as a player. In the spring, it would be clear that Mickey Mantle, who was on his way to a triple crown and one of the landmark seasons in baseball history, was the dominant force of the Yankees (and the league). On May 12, Yogi would turn thirty-one; he would lead AL catchers in games caught, although the total, 135, was his lowest in seven years. But the high points of the 1956 season would be momentous, the most memorable of Berra's career.

The year got off to a promising start when George Weiss made Yogi, at $50,000, the highest paid catcher ever. As usual, Weiss gave it to him grudgingly. Berra told him that since he had been the MVP the previous year, he should be paid what an MVP was worth. Weiss told him that the award wasn't official, yet—some papers were saying there were players more valuable than Yogi. Berra told him that *he* only read the papers that said *he* was the most valuable. Weiss also warned Yogi that he needed to get his batting average back up to around .300. No problem, Yogi told him. If he wasn't worked so hard in August doubleheaders he'd hit .320.

While many of his contemporaries spent their money with no thought beyond the next road trip, Yogi Berra, who had never graduated from high school, transformed himself into a businessman. A close friend, Ugo Antonucci, became his business manager and advised him on what proved to be a brilliant venture. It would take nearly three years for the project to come to fruition, but the Rizzuto-Berra Lanes finally opened on State Highway No. 1 on the approach to the Lincoln Tunnel in Clifton, New Jersey.

One afternoon on a golf course he met two brothers named Olivieri whose father had invented Yoo-hoo chocolate-flavored drink more than three decades earlier.* In February of 1956, Yogi became vice president of Yoo-hoo Chocolate Products. Who could possibly be a more convincing spokesman for a chocolate drink aimed at children than the man who, just a couple years before, had gotten sick from drinking too much chocolate milk? Acting on shrewd advice, he did not take a salary but stock in the company.

By the winter of 1956, Yogi was the most ubiquitous pitchman in sports. Frank Scott quit his job as the Yankees' traveling secretary in the early 1950s to concentrate on finding endorsement jobs for players. According to Carmen Berra in an interview with the Hall of Fame: "One day Frank was at the house and not wearing a watch. Yogi had plenty, as compensation for appearing in advertisements. I brought out a bunch and had Frank pick one. He realized Yogi was not getting paid, immediately quit his job with the Yankees, and became a marketing agent for Yogi and some of the other players, like Mickey Mantle and Whitey Ford. Frank was probably the first '10%-agent.' He made sure the players were compensated as they should have been."

"It was great," Yogi remembered. "I had nothing to do in the winter, so I did all these non-baseball things. The money was good, and the commercials were always a lot of fun."[29]

For the next few years, there were two seasons for Yogi Berra, the baseball season and the endorsement season. In 1960, he hooked up with a rising young advertising executive named George Lois in what would be Berra's most famous TV spot till the coming of the Aflac duck. Lois, working on an account for the Quaker Oats Company's Puss 'n Boots cat food, wanted Yogi for a new style of commercial he was developing. The Quaker Oats people were skeptical; American women, they had learned from their research, bought the vast majority of cat food, and they weren't sure that

---

*There has always been some confusion as to whether or not there should be a hyphen in Yoo-hoo. The earliest ads for the drink show a hyphen, but for some reason in the 1950s the logo was hyphenless. This might be because of Yogi's famous reply to the woman who asked him if the drink was hyphenated. "No, ma'am," he said, "it isn't even carbonated."

Berra was well enough known among American women. Lois quickly proved otherwise, conducting a survey that showed that more than 180 of 200 average American women knew very well who Yogi Berra was. Yogi got the commercial. Lois's idea was not to use Berra directly as a pitch man but to exploit Yogi's appeal by making him a character in the commercial, in which he voiced his amazement at a cat who was jumping on a trampoline. Viewers quickly noticed what a nice relationship Yogi developed with the talking cat; he certainly should have, as the cat's voice was that of Whitey Ford. The commercial won several awards.

The Puss'n Boots commercial was a meeting of two great minds. George Lois went on to become as accomplished in advertising as Yogi Berra was in baseball. Among Lois's most spectacular successes were his famed covers for *Esquire* in the 1960s, the "I Want My MTV!" commercials in the early 1980s, and his "In Your Face" campaign for ESPN. Like Yogi, Lois was a Hall of Famer, inducted into both the Art Directors and the Copywriters Hall of Fame.

Berra took a lot of ribbing from his teammates and other ballplayers for the commercial. He had a standard comeback for all of them: "Who do you know that got paid pretty good for talking to a cat?"

────

HIS RESPECT FOR Yogi aside, Mickey Mantle was mildly irked that he had not received more votes for the 1955 MVP award. After all, he would tell some sportswriters, his batting numbers were clearly superior to Yogi's. Yes, some of them replied, but you don't have to squat behind the plate in 140 games and make the right decision on hundreds of pitches.

How tough could that be, Mantle wondered, particularly with Whitey Ford pitching? Before a game against the Red Sox at Fenway, Mantle began needling Berra, telling him it wasn't so tough to call a game. Okay, then, Yogi told him, go ahead—you call the game. They agreed on a signal: when Mantle, in center field, stood straight up, he wanted a fastball. If he bent over with his hands on his knees, that meant a curve. There was no real risk since, if Berra didn't approve of Mickey's call, he'd change it. Whitey, who knew of the arrangement, had final approval in any event. Mantle must have done a pretty good job; by the seventh inning the Yankees led 2–0. But he found the task mentally exhausting. When they reached the dugout to begin the eighth, Mantle walked over to Yogi, slapped him on the shoulder, and said, "Okay, I got you this far. Take it the rest of the way."[30]

THE YANKEES' ANNUAL Old-Timers Day was on August 25. Phil Rizzuto was summoned to Casey Stengel's office, where he found both his manager and his general manager, George Weiss, waiting for him. He was told, in effect, that the Yankees would need another player, probably an outfielder, for the World Series. "I was surprised and a little bit flattered that they asked for my opinion," Rizzuto recalled. "It was almost like they were considering me as a future manager." But no matter which player he suggested might be dropped, he found an objection from Weiss. After several minutes, it dawned on him: he was the one to be released. He was startled to realize he was crying; he left Stengel's office before any of his teammates or coaches could see him, accompanied only by Snuffy Stirnweiss, who was there to play in the Old-Timers game.

His teammates were shocked but not surprised. Phil was thirty-eight and, with a month to go in the 1956 season, he had played in only 31 games, hitting .231. What hurt Rizzuto and irked the other Yankees, particularly Billy Martin, was that he was released for a National Leaguer back for his second stint with the Yanks, who was even older than Rizzuto: Enos Slaughter. Rizzuto never completely forgave either Weiss or Stengel and seldom missed an opportunity to take a swipe at Stengel's managerial reputation in public—but then, Phil had never made any secret of the fact that, like Joe DiMaggio, he regarded himself as a Joe McCarthy man.

Rizzuto didn't brood for long. Over the winter he was invited to join Mel Allen and Red Barber in the Yankees' broadcast booth. But in the late summer of 1956, to his best friend Yogi Berra "it just seemed real strange without him in the clubhouse especially going into a World Series. It felt almost illegal."[31]

The pennant secured, Stengel turned a steely eye toward the World Series, knowing that his bosses would not tolerate a third straight failure to win the championship, especially by a sixty-five-year-old manager. Over the last few games Yogi was freed from his tools of ignorance and given some rest in the outfield. "It was a breeze out there," he thought, "easy on the knees. Aside from the mosquitoes and being a little bored, I didn't mind."[32] He had had a terrific season, driving in 105 runs and tying his own AL record for home runs by a catcher with 30; no one was going to take the MVP award away from Mantle that year, but Berra had the satisfaction of finishing second in the voting. It irked his professional pride, though, that his batting average went two points under .300 for the year.

There were, however, mitigating circumstances. Back in St. Louis, Paulina, who suffered from diabetes, was not doing well. Just prior to the start of the Series, she had gone into the hospital, where the doctors told the family they must amputate her leg to save her life. Yogi called Pietro and told him he wanted to be there; his father assured him that his mother wanted him to play well and wanted to see him on television. And so he played.

———

MICKEY MANTLE'S FAVORITE Yogi Berra story actually happened. Mantle had just completed his incredible triple crown season and was a sure bet for the MVP award, "but there wasn't much danger that I would get a fat head because I had teammates like Yogi to keep me square." Before the Yanks met the Dodgers in the World Series that fall for the fourth time in six years, Berra was interviewed for a radio show.

> The broadcaster said, "We're going to do free association. I'm going to throw out a few names and you just say the first thing that pops into your mind."
> "Okay," said Yogi.
> When they went on the air, the announcers said, "I'm here tonight with Yogi Berra and we're going to play free association. I'm going to mention a name, and Yogi's going to say the first thing that comes into his mind. Okay, Yogi?"
> "Okay."
> "All, right, here we go then. Mickey Mantle."
> "What about him?" said Yogi.[33]

———

IN 1955, THE Brooklyn Dodgers had been a little better than the Yankees. In 1956, the Yankees were the better team. The Dodgers, who had beaten out the surprising Milwaukee Braves by one game in the National League, were starting to show their age. Roy Campanella, in and out of the lineup with injuries, hit just .219 and 20 home runs in 121 games and often played in pain. Pee Wee Reese at age thirty-seven hit only .257, and Jackie Robinson, also thirty-seven, missed 37 games and hit just .275 with 10 home runs. No one could deny that there were also strengths. Duke Snider led the league in home runs, 43, and walks, 99, and Gil Hodges hit 32 home runs. The Dodgers' biggest assets, though, were Don Newcombe, who at age thirty had reached his peak, winning 27 games against just 7 losses, good enough to earn him the NL's MVP award, and former Giants star Salvatore Anthony Maglie, who was 13–5 with an ERA of just 2.87. Maglie had been nicknamed "The Barber" by the *New York Daily News'* Jim McCulley for his willingness to graze the whiskers on a batter's chin if Maglie thought he was standing too close to the plate. Newcombe and Maglie were really the Dodgers' only starting aces, but in the bullpen, Clem Labine had won 10 games and saved 19 more.

But this year the Yankees could match and even trump anything the Dodgers could throw at them. In addition to Mantle and Berra, Skowron, though limited by injuries, hit .308 with 23 home runs, and McDougald, performing brilliantly at shortstop, second base, and sometimes third, hit .311 with 13 home runs. Hank Bauer hit just .241, but with 26 home runs. The Yankees' 190 home runs broke the American League record of 182 set by their 1936 predecessors. Ford finished 19–8, leading the league in won-lost percentage, and was, the Yankees argued, as good or better than Newcombe, finishing with the same number of complete games as Newk (18) and posting a lower ERA (2.47 to 3.08). Stengel spread his starts among several pitchers; if Casey had gone with a normal four-man rotation, Whitey could have won as many as 25 games. Johnny Kucks, Tom Sturdivant, and Don Larsen, though their names didn't generate the same heat as Ford's, won 45 games while losing just 22. Tommy Byrne, Bob Grim, and Tom Morgan accounted for 22 saves—Morgan in particular won Stengel's praise for coming out of the bullpen and "throwing ground balls," induced by a hard sinker that often resulted in double plays.

Berra got off to his best start ever, hitting 12 home runs from the season opener to mid-May. When he faded, Mantle picked up the pace and revived the national excitement for a hitter who could surpass Babe Ruth's record 60 home runs in a season. (He would fall eight short.) It was the easiest pennant race enjoyed by a Stengel team up to that time, and the Yankees were itching to get another crack at the Dodgers.

After the first two games, the itch turned to shellshock. Ford, who always had trouble in the bandbox of Ebbets Field, was knocked out in the fourth inning of Game One as Maglie went all the way for Brooklyn for a 6–3 win. In the second game, Larsen, who had been an excellent starter (11–5 in 20 starts during the regular season, especially after switching to a new, no-windup delivery), couldn't locate the plate and walked four batters in just 1⅔ innings, leading a parade of six other Yankee pitchers as the

Dodgers won again, 13–8. The only consolation for the Yankees was that the dreaded Newcombe was equally ineffective, surrendering a grand slammer to Yogi in the second inning. At any rate, the Yankees left Ebbets Field to the Dodgers' fans chants of "The Yankees are dead! The Yankees are dead!" They were an empire teetering on the edge. It had now been nearly three years since their last World Series triumph, and they had now lost six of their last nine Series games to their bitterest rivals.

Then, as so often happened when the Yankees seemed to be on the verge of extinction, God—or at least the weather—intervened. A rainstorm delayed Game Three for a day, giving Stengel a chance to bring back his ace. Whitey Ford had had just three days rest, but he had gone only four innings in his first outing against the Dodgers—and this time he would be pitching in Yankee Stadium, with its spacious left and center fields where Ebbets Field home runs went to die. Ford went all the way to shut down the Dodgers and put the Yankees back in the Series with a 5–3 win. The next day, Tom Sturdivant pitched another complete game as the Yankees evened things up 6–2, the big hit coming in the sixth inning with New York trailing 2–1—Enos Slaughter, as if to justify Weiss's release of Rizzuto, hit a long three-run homer to provide the winning margin.

The problem for Stengel was whom to give the next start to. Ford was out of the question, Bob Turley had been plagued with arm trouble all season, Don Larsen had been wild in Game One, and Johnny Kucks and Tom Sturdivant had been hit hard in relief. Who, then, to start Game Five? When Don Larsen had arrived, in front of his locker he found a ball in his shoe, placed there, in accordance with Yankee tradition, by Frank Crosetti.° And that is how Don Larsen found out that he would be starting the most famous game in baseball history.

Hank Bauer, just arriving at the clubhouse, saw Crosetti and asked him who would be starting that afternoon. Larsen, Crosetti told him. "Oh, God," said Bauer, shaking his head.[34]

°In an interview for Don Larsen's book, *The Perfect Yankee*, Crosetti, a year before his death, explained, "The baseball-in-the-shoe ritual originated when I was forced to take care of the bags of baseballs in the first place. Nobody else would do it because it was a pain in the ass. Bill Dickey didn't want to, and of course [Jim] Turner wouldn't, so I was left to take care of the damn baseballs. It was then that I started to put the warm-up ball in the shoe before each game." (p. 33)

Larsen had his own theory as to why the Yankees put Crosetti in charge of the balls. "He had quite a reputation for one simple thing: he was as tight with the baseballs as he was with his nickels and dimes." (p. 33)

THE AFTERNOON OF October 8 was clear and bright, about sixty
degrees at game time—perfect weather, everyone agreed, for baseball. On
radio, Mel Allen informed his audience that a slight wind was blowing out
to left field.

Larsen was matched with Sal Maglie, the victor in Game One, who was
pitching for the first time ever in Yankee Stadium. In *New York City
Baseball,* Harvey Frommer described Maglie in his prime as "sallow with
sunken cheeks, black hair, black eyebrows . . . He looked like an under-
taker coming in to pitch."[35] By 1956 Maglie was thirty-nine, and the
description pretty much held. He was one of the favorite characters of the
New York baseball world; the writers all referred to him as a "money"
pitcher, and the 1956 World Series was his third.

In contrast, Larsen had pitched in two Series games, including four
innings in a start against the Dodgers in 1955, and had been dreadful. His
composite World Series record at that point read 5⅔ innings, six hits, five
earned runs, six walks, and two strikeouts, and the only reason it wasn't
worse was that a Yankee error had absolved him of official blame for the
four batters he walked in Game Two who had all scored. "Frankly," says
Roger Kahn, "a lot of people looked at the two of them and thought 'This
is a mismatch. Why is Casey giving Larsen the ball in a do-or-die situation?' " Despite his baffling control problems in that game, Larsen was
confident: Yogi, he knew, had a book on the Dodgers hitters. Here's how
some of it read:

- Pee Wee Reese: "Tough to pitch to. He had a good eye, and he could
  wait for his pitch. He didn't have a lot of power, but for a little guy he
  could hurt you . . . a great hit-and-run man . . . We mixed the pitches
  up on him, tried to move the ball around."

- Duke Snider: "Always been an impatient hitter . . . He takes that real
  big swing and fishes for bad balls a lot . . . Duke will get the ball out
  on you without pulling it. We would pitch him in tight and try to make
  him take a cramped swing at the ball."

- Jackie Robinson: "Strictly a big-ball hitter, and we tried to keep the
  ball down on him and change up on him. He held his arms very high
  when he stood up there, it was hard for him to get down for a low
  one."

- Gil Hodges: "We tried to keep the ball away from him all the time, because he was a dead-pull hitter and could kill you if you let him have his pitch inside."

- Roy Campanella: "The same type of hitter [as Hodges], and we tried to crowd him as much as we could, then we would pitch him far away and make him reach. He liked to tomahawk the ball and he loved to see the pitch come in up around his eyes. But we didn't give him many like that."

- Carl Furillo: "A high-ball hitter who hits to all fields . . . We used to pitch him in tight and make him pull it."

- Junior Gilliam: "A switch-hitter and a slap-hitter, not much power. He can guide the ball better when it's away from him, and we liked to give him nothing at all out there."[36]

Gilliam, the Dodgers' first batter, was a classic leadoff man; he had hit .300 during the season with 95 walks and 21 stolen bases. He seldom struck out, but Larsen, his fastball and slider crackling, got him on a called strike three. Berra liked the way Larsen's slider was working and called it again with Pee Wee Reese at bat, Reese also took the third strike. With Duke Snider, true to his book, Yogi called for an inside fastball; Snider popped it up to Hank Bauer in right field. Larsen, pitching without a windup, was in a groove. But so was Maglie. In his half of the first, he lived up to his nickname, "The Barber," throwing a pitch which narrowly missed Hank Bauer's head. Bauer glowered and then popped up to Reese. Maglie, like Larsen, ended up with a one-two-three inning. In the Dodgers' second, Robinson hit a shot toward Andy Carey at third base which caromed off Carey's glove to that of Gil McDougald, who scooped it up and, as he would later tell reporters, "threw that ball so hard I could feel the muscles pull right down to my toes."[37] Carey later acknowledged that they'd never have gotten the Jackie Robinson of a few years earlier.

Larsen got out of the second unscathed and so did Maglie; the pattern continued on into the third. In the fourth inning, Duke Snider, the hitter Larsen and the Yankees most feared, was up again. For once and only once, Larsen slipped up; behind on the count 2–0, he delivered the Duke a fastball down the middle—"like it was a beautiful present on Christmas Day." Snider smashed it down the right-field line and began his home run trot. But umpire Ed Runge, in his first World Series, correctly ruled the ball foul. Up in the broadcast booth Mel Allen sighed, "Mighty close!" Two pitches later Larsen threw what he thought was his sharpest slider of the day, and the Duke went down with his bat on his shoulder. In the Yankees' half of the fourth, Maglie made *his* first mistake, a curveball that hung in Mantle's power zone; Mickey deposited the mistake a few feet to the left of the foul pole that Snider had missed. In the booth, Mel Allen recited his famous, "It's going . . . going . . . GONE! How 'bout that!" The Yankees led 1–0. Then, Berra hit a pitch into center field that looked like a sure double or even a triple, but Snider ran it down.

Robinson hit a soft fly for the first out in the fifth inning. Larsen then threw a hard slider to Hodges, who caught up with it and hit it deep to left-center field, the ball riding the wind Mel Allen had mentioned in the first inning. In center, Mickey Mantle began his pursuit with a quick backpedal, then turned and ran furiously on a hard angle toward the left-center field wall. In Ebbets Field, it would have been a home run, but this was Yankee Stadium, and as the ball began its descent, everyone realized it would not reach the fence. But, thought Hank Bauer in left field, "Damn, that ball is maybe a triple or even an inside the park home run." It would have been, too, but Mantle, in full stride, extended his glove and, backhanded, speared it. Radio listeners heard Mel Allen call out, "Ball hit to left field, Mantle digging hard. Still going . . . *How about that catch?!*" Mickey would later describe the play: "I just put my head down and took off as fast as I could. I caught up with the ball as it was dropping, more than four hundred feet from home plate. I had to reach across my body to make the catch. And luckily the ball just dropped into my glove . . . It was the best catch I ever made. Some people might question that, but there's certainly no question that it was the most important catch I ever made."[38]

Mantle's catch put an electric charge into the crowd that would remain for the rest of the game. The next batter, Sandy Amoros, the Dodgers' hero in the previous year's Series, made his bid for 1956 MVP honors by sending Larsen's fastball into the right-field seats. Umpire Ed Runge had his second close call in as many innings; he quickly waved the ball foul, to the relief of the Yankees and millions of their fans—but by no more, he told reporters after the game, than by the space between his thumb and index finger. Had the home plate umpire Babe Pinelli called it, it would certainly have been a home run. Two pitches later, Larsen threw Amoros a hard breaking slider on the inside corner, the kind of pitch a hitter might lay off if he didn't have two strikes. The ball dribbled into Billy Martin's glove at second base, who flicked it to Joe Collins at first. Larsen had now recorded fifteen consecutive outs. For want of perhaps a foot—five or six inches on Hodges's drive to Mantle and Amoros's drive into right field—he was ahead 1–0 instead of behind 2–1.

By now, of course, Larsen and the entire baseball world were aware that he was pitching a perfect game, and in the Yankees dugout they were honoring the sacred tradition of not jinxing the pitcher by talking about it. For his part, Larsen was, as he would say more than half a century later at the Yogi Berra Museum, "excited, relaxed, and focused. I followed Yogi's orders exactly. He knew what I was capable of doing, and all the weaknesses of the Dodger hitters. All I had to do was throw the pitch he told me where he told me." For instance, in the second inning, pitching to Sandy Amoros, he threw three consecutive sliders, the third one missing low to even the count at 2–2. "I figured Yogi might go elsewhere," he recalled, "but either he was gaining faith in my slider or had figured worth one together, because he signaled for a fourth consecutive slider. Amoros connected and a pop fly danced to the right of second base toward right-fielder Hank Bauer."[39] The ball was hit so softly that Bauer might not have been able to make the play, but Billy Martin, backpedaling furiously, grabbed it and stumbled to the ground, immediately holding up the ball for the umpires to see.

———

UNTIL THE SIXTH inning, Mantle's home run was the only score. Andy Carey led off for the Yankees with a hard single. The next batter was Larsen, a superb hitter who collected 13 home runs over his major league career and had hit a grand slammer off the Red Sox during the 1956 season; Stengel had even used him as a pinch-hitter against Boston, and he responded with a home run. Many thought when he first came up that his best position would be first base or outfield. In this situation, everyone in the ballpark knew he would be bunting. He couldn't handle Maglie's first two pitches, though, and with an 0–2 count it was assumed that he would be swinging away. At least that's what the Dodgers figured as Jackie Robinson, at third base, moved back a few steps. Stengel tripped them up, calling for a bunt, which Larsen delivered right out in front of the plate that moved Carey to second. Bauer then hit a sharp single between Robinson and Reese, and the Yankees were up 2–0. Maglie escaped further damage, but just barely, when Mantle smashed a grounder right at Gil Hodges, who stepped on first and threw to third to nab a sliding Bauer. In later years, Larsen would ask himself what might have happened had

Mickey's ball gone through for a hit and the Yankees had been able to build a bigger lead. "I might have relaxed a bit," he said at the Yogi Berra Museum in 2007. "I might have relaxed too much."

In the Dodgers' seventh, with Pee Wee Reese up with an 0–1 count, Berra called for a fastball. Larsen thought he erred in putting it out over the plate, but Reese, evidently surprised to see such a fat pitch, hit a harmless fly to Mantle in center. Now Duke Snider was up again; if he got past the Duke, Larsen felt, the eighth and ninth innings might be, despite the tension, a little easier—at least he wouldn't have to face Snider. "Again," he recalled, "Yogi Berra's sage wisdom surfaced. After throwing a slider for Ball One too far outside, I threw an outside and low fastball and got Snider to lift a fly to Enos Slaughter in left."[40]

As the game went into the seventh inning, the radio announcers were having a terrible time trying to convey to their listeners the historical import of what was taking place without actually using the words "perfect game." For the Dodgers, Vin Scully told his audience, "Mr. Larsen has been brilliant, retiring 18 men in a row." Mel Allen told Yankee fans, "No Dodgers on base yet. Larsen's gottem' all. *How 'bout that?*" Everyone— Yankees, Dodgers, fans, even umpires and officials—was on the edge of their seats. No ump wanted the burden of calling a close play; if he was wrong, his judgment would be forever questioned. The official scorer, Lyall Smith, was hoping that there would be no close call requiring a decision on a hit or error. If he called it wrong, or at least what Yankee fans perceived to be wrong, he might never make it out of the Bronx.

In the Yankee bullpen, Tom Morgan, his bladder full, was afraid to run to the restroom for fear he'd miss something. In the Yankee dugout, there was a stony silence; on returning to their seats at the end of the inning, everyone took care to sit in the same spot and keep their caps on in exactly the same way. Mantle, his heart pounding, flopped down in the seat that had been occupied by reserve shortstop Billy Hunter; Hunter stared at Mickey, the best player in the game and one of his idols, and politely asked him to move. Wordlessly, Mantle shifted back to his original spot on the bench.

Larsen thought something was needed to break the tension, not add to it. After retiring the Dodgers in the seventh, he sat down and said to Mantle, "Look at that scoreboard! Wouldn't it be something . . . Two more innings to go." Mantle was horrified and decided there would be less of a possibility for a jinx if he moved to the other side of the dugout. 'It was like a big, black shadow surrounded me and kept me apart from everyone else. To be honest, the silence was awful, unlike the usual dugout buzz where everyone is kiddin' around. It was like I was the uninvited guest. No one wanted anything to do with me."[41]

The Yankees put two runners on base in the seventh with two out and again got a sharply hit ground ball, this time by Andy Carey, but it went straight to Pee Wee Reese, who threw to Junior Gilliam at second for the force out. Larsen walked to the mound with everyone in the baseball world knowing that he needed six outs for baseball immortality. On the Dodgers' radio network, Vin Scully informed his listeners, "All eyes are on Don Larsen as he goes to work in the eighth inning." Another radio announcer, Bob Wolff, would later recall, "With every pitch, there would be the roar of the crowd. Then the roar would subside just like the waves going out. Then they waited for the next pitch."[42]

Just before Jackie Robinson stepped into the batter's box, his manager, Walt Alston, whispered to him suggesting he do something to disturb his mound rhythm. Larsen stepped on the mound and "tried to remember back to what Yogi had told me about Jackie. 'Keep the ball on the inside part of the plate and jam him as much as possible.' "[43] He threw a hard-moving fastball which Robinson took for a strike. Before Larsen could throw anther pitch, Robinson called for time, walked to the on-deck circle, and began chatting with Gil Hodges. He then took a couple of casual practice swings as 60,000 Yankee fans booed the obvious delaying tactic. But the booing only succeeded in giving Larsen a comforting feeling; he'd been booed enough to know what it felt like and was now invigorated by the support of the crowd. Jackie fouled off the next pitch, a slider, and had an 0–2 count. Yogi called for another slider, and Larsen threw; Robinson, with two strikes, could take no chances and bounced a ground ball back to the mound. One out. Then came Hodges. Berra called for a fastball, which Hodges, apparently expecting a breaking pitch, took for a strike. "Nice pitch," Yogi said as he threw the ball back. The simple words of praise from his catcher gave Larsen a jolt of confidence. "It was a funny thing," Larsen recalled years later, "but I could look down there and see Yogi—I don't want to say smiling—but looking as if he was enjoying himself. He was *playing ball*. I thought, 'If he's having a great time, I'm gonna have one, too.' " He threw what he thought was a mediocre fastball at Hodges, who topped it on a line toward Carey at third base. Hodges swung so hard that he produced what players call a "frozen rope," a ball hit just hard enough to be a line drive but the trajectory of which the eye can follow. Carey was actually startled, catching the ball low off the ground and then unnecessarily throwing the ball to first baseman Joe Collins.

Larsen would not know this until later, but on retiring Hodges he had set a major league record for the most consecutive batters retired in World Series play. The previous record of 22 was shared by the Yankees' Herb Pennock against Pittsburgh in 1927 (Pennock would wind up with a complete-game three-hitter, allowing one run) and the Tigers' Schoolboy Rowe in 1934 against the Cardinals (Rowe would allow runs in the second and third and then retire 22 consecutive batters into the eleventh inning before winning in the twelfth, 3–2). Nor would it have meant anything to him if he had known; on this day he had a much bigger fish to fry.

Eighth inning, two down. With one strike against Sandy Amoros, Berra called for a curve, one of the few he called that afternoon and, Larsen thought, "one of several excellent calls he made that day." It was not, Larsen agreed, a bad time to mix things up. Amoros, surprised by the pitch, hit a soft fly to Mantle in center field. "Imagine," Vin Scully said into his microphone, "when the [Dodgers] ninth inning comes, the nation will stand still."

Sal Maglie struck out the side in the bottom of the eighth. One of his victims was Larsen. "I'm sure I tried to hit the ball," he said, "but I can't remember anything about that time at the plate."[44]

WHEN HE LEFT the dugout to take the field for the ninth, Larsen's legs felt like they were made of rubber. One of his infielders patted him on the back; if they gave him any verbal encouragement he did not hear them for the roar of the crowd. At 2:57 p.m., Vin Scully told those listening all over the world (Dodger games aired overseas on the Armed Forces Radio Network), "Let's all take a deep breath as we go to the most dramatic ninth inning in the history of baseball."[45] Incredibly, as he stood on the mound at Yankee Stadium to throw his first pitch, Don Larsen *did not know that he was pitching a perfect game.* He knew he had a no-hitter, but as no one had ever thrown a perfect game in the World Series—indeed, there had only been three perfect games in the twentieth century before Larsen, the last one in 1922 from an obscure White Sox pitcher named Charlie Robertson—he had never even heard the term "perfect game." Behind him, Billy Martin said to his fellow infielders, "Nothing gets through." His teammates, coaches, and manager were all shouting instructions to him: "I had more managers helping me than I knew what to do with." The only manager he needed was the one behind the plate.

In the broadcast booth, veteran Dodgers publicist Irving Rudd jumped on a table and yelled to his Dodgers: "Get a fucking hit!" Luckily for Rudd and the Dodgers, there was so much crowd noise in the background no one heard his remark on the air. In center field, Mantle would recall, "the crowd was on its feet, and I was so nervous I could feel my knees shaking. I played in more than 2,400 games in the major leagues, but I never was as nervous as I was in the ninth inning of this game, afraid I would do something to mess up Larsen's perfect game."[46]

Carl Furillo—perhaps the smartest Dodger hitter, Berra and Larsen thought—led off. Larsen was concentrating so hard on Berra's face that "if Yogi would have positioned the mitt ten feet outside the plate or over the batter's head, I would have tried to throw the ball there. I intended to follow Yogi's instructions all the way."[47] Berra flashed the signal for a slider and Furillo looked at it for strike one. Yogi wanted another, Larsen threw it, Furillo fouled it off. Strike two. Yogi wanted the slider again—this time it was a bit outside. Then, a fastball; Furillo fouled it off. Then he fouled off another slider. In a tight situation, Berra always believed, make the batter hit your best pitch; he called for another slider. Furillo didn't quite get around on it and hit a harmless fly to Bauer in right field. Though it didn't seem possible, the crowd grew louder.

Then came Roy Campanella. Campy rubbed dirt on his hands, turned and smiled at his pal and rival behind the plate, said something, and both men chuckled. "There they were poking fun," thought Larsen, "and I was dying out there." Campy fouled off a fastball for strike one. Then Yogi called for a slider. Larsen wasn't sure how much gas he still had in him, "but Yogi was the boss." Larsen thought it was ball one, but Campanella, guarding the strike zone, swung and tapped it to Martin at second. Martin flipped to Collins. One more to go.

Maglie was due up, and Alston sent up left-hander Dale Mitchell. Mitchell had played in only 19 games for the Dodgers that year, but was a fine pinch-hitter. In center field, Mantle was thinking, "Please don't hit it to me." He couldn't decide whether to move back to play a drive that might be hit over his head, or move closer in case Mitchell hit a sinking line drive. He decided to stay exactly where he was. For the first time all day, Berra and Larsen were a bit nonplussed—Mitchell was the only Dodgers hitter they hadn't given pregame attention to. "Yankee Stadium," said Vin Scully, "is shivering in its concrete foundations right now."

Yogi called for a fastball. It was low and outside by perhaps an inch. The crowd let loose a torrent of boos, but Larsen thought umpire Babe Pinelli's call was correct. Then, a slider; Larsen threw it hard, more of a fastball than a breaking pitch, and it caught the outside corner. One and one. Berra stood up to throw the ball back to Larsen, pounding his own glove with enthusiasm. "Seconds later," Larsen wrote in his account of the game, "the robust, barrel-chested catcher I'd come to love resumed his squatting position. He carefully flashed me the sign for another slider." Low, Larsen thought as he released the ball, but Mitchell swung and missed. One ball, two strikes. Berra suggested a fastball, and Larsen threw it as hard as he could. Pinelli began to raise his right hand for strike three, but Mitchell fouled it off. The combined oohs from the crowd created a "whoosh" sound that someone thought sounded like a small tornado.

Before the next pitch, the crowd went eerily silent. Pinelli placed a new baseball in Yogi's hand. Larsen, as if to savor the moment, stepped off the rubber to the right of the mound. He wiped his brow with his forearm sleeve, put his cap back on, and bent down for a resin bag. Then he stepped back on the mound. Coming up was Larsen's ninety-seventh pitch, and most of them had been sliders, a fact that Berra knew had been relayed to Mitchell by the Dodger hitters.

So Yogi called for a fastball.* The ball hit Berra's mitt with an audible "splat!" sound; Mitchell glanced toward Pinelli to see the call. It was irrelevant. As endless replays over the following decades would show, Mitchell's bat had crossed the plate before he pulled it back.

Larsen later said that he did not fully realize what had happened until Yogi leapt full force into his arms.

In the pandemonium of the locker room, Yankee club officials swarmed around Larsen while reporters fired him question after question. A reporter from *The New York Times* shouted one at Stengel. "Casey," he said, "was that the best game you ever saw Larsen pitch?" "So far," the manager replied.[48]

A few of them thought to walk over to the locker of the man who had called every pitch of the game. They found Berra sitting on his stool in his undershirt, a green-bottle Coca-Cola in his right hand. "So," he said with a grin, "What's new?"

---

*Why Yogi deviated from his usual practice of calling for a pitcher's best pitch in a tough situation was explained in the Q&A session of the replay of the perfect game at Yogi's museum in 2006: "I thought maybe we had one pitch to play with since we were ahead in the count, one and two. If Don had missed with the fastball, I'd have told him to come back on the next pitch with the slider."

———

OVER THE NEXT half century, Larsen would so much come to associate Yogi with the perfect game that when he talked about it, he began to sound like Yogi. "Sometimes a week might go by," Larsen told the Yes Network in 2005, "when I don't think about that game, but I don't remember when it happened last."

Neither before nor since has any pitcher in a World Series come close to equaling Larsen's achievement. Bill Bevens had come within one out of pitching a World Series no-hitter in 1947, but he had walked ten batters. It's worth noting, though, that the catcher for the only two games in Series history where a pitcher went into the ninth inning without allowing a hit were caught by Yogi Berra. Not only did Yogi call Larsen's game, he managed it up better than anyone else! It's never happened in World Series history, and it hasn't happened since."

———

ON MAY 17, 1998, Yankees left-hander David Wells, or "Boomer," as he was affectionately known by his teammates and friends, pitched a perfect game against the Minnesota Twins. Afterward, as the party raged in the Yankees clubhouse, Billy Crystal put his hand on Wells's shoulder and asked him to sign his ticket stub. "I got here late," said Crystal. "What happened?"

Wells took call after congratulatory call from well-wishers all over the country, including Mayor Rudy Guiliani. The call that drew the broadest grin from Wells, though, was from a former Yankee who had graduated from the same high school, Point Loma in San Diego, thirty-four years before Wells. "Two guys from the same high school doing this?" Wells gushed to Don Larsen. "What are the odds? Who would ever believe it?" A reporter later phoned Larsen and asked him what he and Wells had talked about. "I told David we have to have a few drinks this summer and raise a little hell," Larsen replied.

———

BERRA WAS ON a flight from Pittsburgh to Newark when Wells was pitching his masterpiece and didn't find out about it until he arrived home. Carmen asked him why he hadn't heard about the game. "They didn't have a radio on the plane," Yogi told her.

═══

"ODD AS IT may seem," Tommy Byrne said years later, "I think Don's perfect game may actually have hurt us a little bit. It was such an emotional thing with everyone jumping and yelling and congratulating Don that it seemed like we had just won the World Series. And some of us may have forgotten that we hadn't won anything yet." Clem Labine, who would pitch against Bob Turley the next day in Brooklyn, agreed. "I'm not going to say that their hitters were distracted," recalled Labine, "especially because it was about the best game I ever pitched. But considering that a win for them would have wrapped up the Series, they did seem a little off." The sixth game of the 1956 World Series was also one of the best Bob Turley ever pitched; he scattered four hits over nine innings and allowed just one unearned run on a fly ball misplayed by Enos Slaughter. (Billy Martin would later berate Stengel for starting "that National Leaguer," but Slaughter, after all, hit .350 with four RBIs in the Series to Martin's .296 and three.) But Labine scattered seven hits in a complete-game victory.

The loss was a jolt to the Yankees. In Gil McDougald's words, "It was now clear to us what was on the line in that seventh game. It has been three years since we had won a championship, and we were on the verge of losing our second straight World Series to our biggest rivals, right there in New York. If we'd lost that game—and I hate to say this—but the memory of Don's perfect game would have stuck in some of our throats, I'm sure. At least, it would have in mine."

So inevitable do many of the Stengel-era Yankee victories seem in retrospect that it's difficult now to remember how desperate the team's situation was on the afternoon of October 10, 1956. Not only were they facing the Dodgers in their home park, they were facing Don Newcombe, the winningest pitcher of 1956. The Yanks had bombed him in his one start in the 1955 Series and hit him hard again in Game Two of this one. Surely it was time for his luck to change. He was, after all, matched up with a twenty-two-year-old, Johnny Kucks, who had won 18 and lost only 9 during the regular season. But Kucks's ERA was an uninspiring 3.85, which looked like a number that would inflate at Ebbets Field. His World Series experience up to that point didn't inspire confidence: in 1955 and in two brief appearances in 1956, he had pitched a total of five innings and given up seven hits. And Kucks hadn't won a start since September 3.

Stengel had lost sleep the night before deciding who to start in what he would later reveal he regarded as the most important game of his career. He made his decisions based on the advice of his assistant manger, Berra.

Whitey Ford was, of course, the Yankees' best pitcher. Even great left-handers, though, got hit hard at Ebbets, as Ford had in Game One; the short outfield of the Dodgers' park was where Yankee Stadium outs became home runs. Kucks, reasoned Berra, was superior to the other Yankee pitchers in one specific area: he could, as Stengel liked to say, throw ground balls. Effective sinkerballs played to the strength of the Yankees' outstanding infielders. Still, Stengel was taking no chances; when Kucks took the mound for the Dodgers' half of the first inning, he saw Whitey Ford and Tom Sturdivant warming up in the bullpen.

Shortly before Game Six, Yogi had called Paulina, who was still in a hospital in St. Louis, and promised his mother he'd hit a home run for her. He failed. In the first inning of Game Seven he would redeem himself.

In the first inning Newcombe faced Berra with a runner on base. Towering over Yogi by more than a full foot, the Dodger right-hander fired a high fastball; Yogi stepped into the pitch with his familiar whiplash swing, and the ball rocketed high over Ebbets' right-field wall. "My heart just soared," remembers McDougald. "Suddenly I just knew that we were going to win." At that moment, the world seemed right again. It was one of the most important home runs in Yankee history, but as he was rounding third base, Yogi Berra wasn't thinking about that. His first thought was, "That's for you, Mom." ("It was a day late," he would later muse, "but I was sure she didn't mind.")[49]

His second thought was for his beaten opponent, Don Newcombe, who stood on the mound in shock to a chorus of boos. In the third inning, Paulina got a bonus when Yogi slammed another two-run shot out of the park and onto Bedford Avenue. As he rounded third, he called out the only thing he could think of to try to soften the blow: "It was a good pitch, Newk." ("I don't think," he would recall forty-seven years later, "that it made him feel any better, though.")[50] Tommy Byrne, thinking back on the game half a century later, thought Berra's second home run "took the starch right out of them. They were tough guys—Jackie, Pee Wee, Gil, Campy and the rest. But you could see the let down in their faces when Yogi hit that second ball off Newk. They knew it just wasn't going to be their day."

Berra's two home runs fueled the Yankees' fire; Newcombe was relieved in the fourth inning after Elston Howard, who had missed the first six games with strep throat, hit a solo homer. In the seventh, Moose Skowron hit a grand slammer off Roger Craig, as if to rub it in to the Dodgers that their one-year reign as champions was over. The Yanks went on to score nine runs. Johnny Kucks shut out the Dodgers with just three hits. In the clubhouse after the final game in the 1956 Series, a gracious Jackie Robinson returned the noble gesture Berra had made the previous year. Putting his arm around a champagne-soaked Yogi, he told reporters, "This guy is a great competitor. He's one of the greatest clutch hitters who ever lived."

Dodger fans left the park muttering, as they always had, "Wait till next year." But no one knew that there would be no next year. In 1957, they would finish third, and before the 1958 season the team was moved to Los Angeles. The Dodgers would never play a World Series in Brooklyn again.

———

YOGI BERRA AND Don Newcombe would live forever in the minds of baseball fans as the classic examples of clutch performer and choke artist, respectively. It was widely believed that the sting of the World Series loss caused a rapid decline in Newcombe's performance; he was just 11–12 the following season, though with a respectable ERA of 3.48. But after that, he disintegrated quickly; the primary culprit was alcoholism. "In 1956 I was the best pitcher in baseball," he later said. "Four years later, I was out of the major leagues. It must have been the drinking. When you're young, you can handle it. But the older you get, the more it bothers you."[51]

Newcombe's heartbreak in the World Series certainly didn't help his drinking problem, but were the reps hung on Yogi and Newk really fair? Roger Kahn addressed the question in a story for the November 1957 issue of *Sport* magazine: "Why Yogi Wins and Newk Loses: A Study in World Series Psychology."

Dozens of honest reporters have written, and thousands of sincere fans believe, that the big leagues are divided into two groups. There is the Honorable Order of Heroes, men who thrive on the seventh game of a World Series and become unhappy if they do not come to bat in the ninth inning with two out and the tying run at second base. So far as can be learned, Yogi Berra is generally accepted as president. Then there is the American Federation of Cowards. Here you find second-basemen who can't make a double play later than the fifth inning, sluggers who can't hit home runs after Labor Day, and pitchers who can't win games in the World Series. The head man of this outfit is Don Newcombe, or so the story runs . . .

Newcombe has pitched in five World Series games for the Brooklyn Dodgers. He was knocked out in four and beaten in the fifth. Last fall, after winning 27 games during the regular season, he started two Series games. He passed the third inning in neither and finished the Series with his earned-run average a snappy 21.21.

Berra, a splendid hitter, will bat .280 in an ordinary season. In the New York Yankees last three World Series Berra has hit .429, .417 and .360. He apologized for dropping below .400 last October by setting a record for runs batted in.

Berra also hit three home runs, all when Newcombe was pitching. Followers of the choke theory cheerfully rubbed their hands together even before the third homer left the bat. Here, they thought, was a perfect case to support their point, a classic meeting of extremes, as when a cowardly Trojan met Achilles, or when Abbott and Costello met Frankenstein. Newcombe said "Ulp." Berra did not, and so inevitably the Yankees had to win. The Yankees won.[52]

Berra's explanation to Kahn as to how and why he had such great World Series wasn't very illuminating: " 'I was hitting good,' Berra says now. 'The thing just happened. Why does it happen? Who knows!' I don't feel different in a Series. I don't bat different. I don't do nothing different. It just happened.' " Newcombe told Kahn pretty much the same thing. "Before the game, my wife kissed me, like she always does. She said, 'Good luck at the ball park' like she always does. In the game, I don't know, I guess I tried too hard, but there have been games I tried like hell and I pitched good."°

Frank Crosetti didn't think Newcombe had choked. "Hell, no," he told

---

°Berra's postseason performance before the 1956 World Series makes an interesting comparison to that of Alex Rodriguez, universally reviled by Yankee fans and the New York press for his failures to "hit in the clutch"—the postseason. Though Yogi was the linchpin of the Yankees' seven World Series teams from 1947 through 1955, it might be argued that his reputation as a great World Series performer didn't begin until 1956. Here's a look at five great Yankees sluggers and their postseason numbers—World Series games for DiMaggio, Berra, and Mantle, and playoffs and World Series for Jackson and Rodriguez—after a similar number of games. DiMaggio's numbers reflect his performance through the 1949 Series, Berra's through the 1955 Series, and Mantle's through 1958. Jackson's are just prior to his famous 1977 World Series in which he hit five home runs to win immortality as "Mr. October."

	Games	AB	Homeruns	RBI	BA
Joe DiMaggio	41	153	6	23	.270
Yogi Berra	40	146	6	14	.260
Mickey Mantle	38	135	11	20	.259
Reggie Jackson	37	134	5	16	.253
Alex Rodriguez	39	147	7	17	.279

You'd probably win some money at your local neighborhood tavern by betting someone that after a similar number of postseason at-bats, Alex Rodriguez hit more home runs than DiMaggio, Berra, or Jackson. It's worth noting that the pitching on Rodriguez's Yankees teams was vastly inferior to that of the other players in the chart, so A-Rod's hits and RBIs had substantially less impact on the outcome of the games than those of the others.

Kahn. "It wasn't Newk's fault that Berra hit him. I thought he had good stuff when I watched him warm up before the last game. When the game started, I thought we'd never get a foul off him. The Yankees were just good, but the writers wouldn't give credit so they said Newcombe choked. (Expletive) And then all over the country people read it, and they fall for it. They believe it about Newcombe. What a crime; it's a damn shame."

Yogi's pal and rival, Roy Campanella, thought that it wasn't a case of Berra rising to the occasion: "Yogi don't play favorites. He gets a lot of hits. He hits homers off the rest of them. He makes no exceptions. He don't pick out who he's gonna hit homers against, you know," Campy told Kahn with a grin. "This game ain't that simple."

So what happened, Kahn wanted to know, to turn Yogi from Series flop in 1950 to chronic Series hero a few years later? "Nothing," Berra replied. "Nothing happened. It's one of them things. It's different from the season. The Series is so short. You play as good as you can. You can have a bad Series or a good one. You can't figure it."

What about Newcombe? Kahn wanted to know. "He's a good pitcher," said Yogi. "He was throwing good in the Series. He just got hit."[53]

———

IMMEDIATELY AFTER THE game, Berra rushed to the airport and home to St. Louis to see his parents. To his relief, Paulina was recovering and in good spirits after the surgery. He had scarcely returned home when he got a call from George Weiss. His offer for the 1957 season was $55,000; Yogi and Carmen had already decided on a fair number and accepted on the spot. It was a big day for Weiss; he had already gotten Whitey Ford to agree to $35,000 and decided to make the most of it by signing them both at a press party in New York. Berra raised eyebrows when he arrived driving a new Cadillac that the papers reported as being "golden brown" but which Berra recalled as a "beige-and-pink job." Whitey, who had driven there in a less impressive automobile kidded him: "I came further than you did and used half the gas." "Listen, son," Yogi tossed back, "You're right. Don't have nothin' to do with these Caddies. Us stars can afford this kind of thing, but you better save your money."[54] None of the reporters present recorded Ford's reply. It was the most expensive car he had ever bought, but after eleven full seasons with the Yankees, Yogi figured he was by-God entitled. He would need all of the salary and the $8,700-odd dollars of the World Series check. Dale, his third son, was born at Valley Hospital in Ridgewood, New Jersey, on December 14.

Also in December, the Yankees traded Charlie Silvera to the Cubs, where he played in 26 games before retiring. Silvera had been Yogi's backup for nine seasons but now, with the emergence of Elston Howard, he was no longer needed. He was a capable receiver and had batted .282 in just 482 at-bats, less than the equivalent of one full season.

Silvera never regretted playing for the Yankees: "How could I? Where else could I have gotten six World Series rings?" He knew his place early on: "I figured what the heck, it's not so bad backing up a Hall of Famer and getting a World Series check every year. My wife Rose got so used to that money that when I came home after the 1954 season [when the Yankees lost the pennant to Cleveland] she said, 'Hey, where's my World Series check?' " Silvera refers to his house near San Francisco as "The House That Yogi Built."

"To this day when I think about the World Series I think about Yogi

Chapter Eight

The Silver Age
(1957–1960)

I never play a game without my man in the lineup.

—CASEY STENGEL

FOR MOST AMERICANS of the postwar generation the phrase "the Eisenhower years" would evoke an image of middle-class prosperity backed by economic and military power. This image was false. The world, as always, was a seething cauldron of potential firestorms, from the Middle East to Southeast Asia to the ghettoes of U.S. cities. And during what would be recalled as a time of complacency, every American woke up every morning under the threat of nuclear annihilation.

Against such a backdrop, baseball scarcely counted as anything but trivial, but that is not how most Americans felt. In the mid-1950s, baseball was the country's unchallenged national pastime, and by the end of 1956, the baseball universe was once again stable. The New York Yankees were again the champions, for the sixteenth time in three decades.

When the Yankees went to spring training in 1957, they probably had more talent than any team since Stengel had arrived in New York nine years earlier. Still, like all good managers, Casey hedged on his team's pennant chances. After all, he told the beat writers, Mickey Mantle was the best player in baseball but he might get hurt, "and suppose something happens to Yogi Berra?"

Something was indeed happening to Yogi Berra: he was getting older. He would appear in 134 games during the 1957 season, 119 of them behind the plate—his lowest numbers of the decade. There were so many good players around him, though, that hardly anyone noticed. Hank Bauer, playing regularly in 1956, had batted only .241 but had hit 26 home runs; Bill Skowron, getting into 118 games at first base, hit .308 with 23 home runs; and Elston Howard played well both in left field and behind the plate. Gil McDougald was coming off a superb season. And, of course, Mickey Mantle *was* the best player in baseball. The pitching staff, featuring Whitey Ford, Don Larsen, Tom Sturdivant, Bob Turley, Bob Grim, and Johnny Kucks, was versatile and deep. Added to the roster were several new names that Yankee fans would come to know, including an outfielder-shortstop named Tony Kubek and a flashy-fielding second baseman named Bobby Richardson, both twenty-one years old. And if that wasn't enough, the Yanks acquired two useful pitchers and a dazzling glove man from a Kansas City Athletics organization that some were beginning to call the Yankees' Major League Farm Team.[*] The third baseman's name was Cletis (Clete) Boyer, who would go on to become one of the greatest-fielding third basemen of all time, while the pitchers were Art Ditmar and Bobby Shantz. Ditmar had been a dismal 12–22 for the Athletics in 1956 as a starter but as a spot-starter and reliever for the Yankees in 1957 would win eight games and save six more. Shantz had beaten out, respectively, Allie Reynolds, Mickey Mantle, and Yogi Berra for the AL 1952 MVP award when he won 24 games for an otherwise undistinguished Philadelphia Athletics team. The latest National League retread to get a second life in pinstripes, Shantz in 1957 started 21 games, came out of the bullpen nine times, won eleven, saved five, and had the lowest ERA, 2.45, on the team.

It was almost unfair. Mantle was once again fabulous; he hit fewer homers, 34, only because pitchers were so terrified of him that they walked him 146 times. His .365 batting average was the highest of his career, and for good measure he led the team with 16 stolen bases, the only Yankee with more than seven. Added to Sturdivant, Turley, Grim, and Larsen (who were a combined 51–24) the Yankees were so good that they

[*] Kansas City owner Arnold Johnson, a Chicago millionaire, was a close friend of both Dan Topping and George Weiss—in fact, it was Weiss who had suggested Johnson buy the Athletics from Connie Mack when the team was still based in Philadelphia. (Topping then relocated his minor league franchise, the Kansas City Blues, to Denver.) After the Athletics moved to Kansas City in 1955, the Yankees began a string of trades that sent over-the-hill big leaguers to the Athletics in exchange for fresh talent which fueled the Yankees pennant drives. Though several of the league's owners and general managers complained vociferously, no action was taken by either the president of the American League or the commissioner of baseball. Such was the Yankees' power within the structure of major league baseball. The Indians GM, former major league slugger Hank Greenberg, was widely quoted as saying, "It sure must be great to have your own farm team right there in your own league."

Greenberg was not exaggerating. The roster of the 1957 Kansas City Athletics consisted almost entirely of players who had been or would be affiliated with the New York Yankees.

survived Ford's two-month bout with tendonitis, a condition that depressed Ford so much that he actually thought of quitting baseball.

They could also afford a slow start from Berra. Some players regard a good spring performance as a bad omen, Yogi more than most. "I don't like to waste hits in spring training exhibition games," he told a reporter when he hit .458 in the 1955 preseason. In 1957, though, he hit poorly in spring training and his woes continued for the first three months of the season. Adding injury to insult, in a night game against the Indians on June 5, Larry Raines hit a flukish foul ball that shattered the protective metal bar of Berra's mask. The jagged edge slashed Yogi's nose as Roman Polanski's switchblade cut Jack Nicholson's proboscis in *Chinatown*. After several stitches, Berra was back in the lineup but batting only .228—but reminded everyone, in a line that would reverberate fifteen years later, "The season ain't over yet, y'know."

Enos Slaughter suggested special glasses to help Yogi's vision while at bat. Berra's trouble, according to the *Daily News*, was " 'Tired eyes.' He was told to wear the specs while reading and watching TV in order to rest his optics for baseball. But when his average stayed down around .230, he started to use the glasses in batting practice and then in games. Now he's a confirmed believer."[1] The glasses, noted the *Daily News*, were tinted yellow. His hitting picked up, but toward the end of August he discarded them and went on an 11-for-20 tear. Casey wasn't satisfied, "Maybe if he had worn them, he would have been twenty for twenty."[2] Perhaps, and maybe too Berra would have snapped his slump earlier had Stengel given his veteran catcher a bit more rest. Thinking back on the season many years later, Yogi said, "I'd never gotten that many injuries before. I was thirty-two, and people were wondering if my reflexes were slowing. All those foul-tip injuries were annoying."[3] The following January Yogi gave up the glasses altogether because, the *Daily News* reported, Carmen didn't think he needed them.

Batting fifth behind Mantle and Skowron, Yogi continued to hit well, finishing with 24 home runs and 82 RBIs, easily the best numbers of any catcher in the league. His .251 batting average, though, was the lowest of his career. The Yankees, never really pressed, left the surprising Chicago White Sox behind, taking the pennant by eight games.

———

ACCORDING TO MICKEY Mantle, it was he and Whitey Ford who came up with the idea "of inviting the fellows, Yogi, Hank Bauer, Gil

McDougald, Johnny Kucks, and their wives, to celebrate Billy's twenty-ninth birthday on the night of May 15 (a day early)"[4]—the sixteenth was supposed to be an open date, so an early morning rise was not expected, but after the birthday plans were made, a rainout makeup game was scheduled for that night. "We had dinner at Danny's Hideaway and then someone said we had time to catch Sammy Davis Jr. at the Copa. We hailed some cabs and hustled over."[5] (Actually, they hustled over from the Waldorf Astoria, where they had gone after Danny's to hear Johnny Ray, the histrionic pop singer whose single "Just Walkin' In The Rain" the year before had put him back on the hit parade.)

The Copacabana, where, it was said, "every night was New Year's Eve," opened in 1940 at 10 East 60th Street. It was frequented by news-papermen, show business celebrities, athletes, Wall Street moguls, and mobsters—pretty much the ~~same clientele any night that or took that's The Copa, though, was no saloon, it was a~~ nightclub which featured, according to Walter Winchell, "the best girl show in town," with its famous line of chorus girls known as "ponies" (for some unknown reason, the club's owners preferred dancers between 5'0" and 5'4"). The decor was art deco by way of ersatz Brazilian; the main room featured palm trees illumi-nated with blue and pink lights.*

From the beginning, the Copa was no stranger to intrigue and scandal. Though nightclub impresarios Monty Proser and Jules Podell were on the lease, everyone knew that the real boss was the most powerful man in organized crime, Frank Costello, who had assumed titular head of the national syndicate when his friend Lucky Luciano was deported to Sicily. Podell had maintained a public policy of segregation, bringing bad public-ity to the Copa in 1944 by keeping Harry Belafonte from performing there; Costello, who had oddly progressive attitudes for a mobster, finally gave the order to allow black entertainers as well as customers, and Belafonte became one of the club's leading headliners. Anyone who was anyone in show business—Frank Sinatra, Rosemary Clooney, and Dean Martin and Jerry Lewis—appeared there frequently (Martin and Lewis's final performance as a duo was there in 1956).

Exactly what happened on May 16, 1957, has never really been explained. The Yankee players, to a man, always insisted that some intoxi-

---

*In the mid-1970s the Copa became a discotheque, but the classic Copa look has been re-created in numerous films, including *Goodfellas, Raging Bull, Tootsie, Carlito's Way,* and *Beyond the Sea,* the film biography of Bobby Darren, who often played there.

cated members of a bowling club were peppering Davis with racial slurs. All the Yankees, particularly Hank Bauer, who was Elston Howard's room-mate, began to object. No punches were thrown by Yankees—or so the players said—and Bauer maintained this until his death in 2007. But shortly after 1:00 a.m. a scuffle broke out near the men's room involving perhaps half a dozen guys, and Bauer was at least nearby. Edwin Jones, a delicatessen owner who lived in upper Manhattan, was punched by some-one and wound up in Roosevelt Hospital with a broken nose and jaw and bruises on his arm and shoulder. Some later claimed that his injuries were exaggerated, but that's the way they were described by the hospital, and subsequently, the police reports. The police were summoned, and Yogi and Carmen, thinking quickly, left for New Jersey. So did Mantle, Martin, and Kucks (Ford later said he didn't get out in time and was stuck with the tab). Bauer, who stayed, was booked; Edwin Jones preferred charges.

Stengel found out just before dawn when Joe Trimble of the *Daily News* called his home to fill him in and to get a comment. His brain fogged with sleep, Casey told Trimble he'd call him back, pulled on his bathrobe and staggered to his front door to get the morning papers. After scanning the stories, he called Trimble to inform him that Ford and Berra would be out of the lineup that day. In the May 17 afternoon edition of the *Daily News*, in a story by Arthur North and David Quirk, Stengel was quoted as saying, "I won't pitch Ford because the whole world knows he was out until two in the morning. He knew days in advance that he was supposed to pitch this game. He has no right to be out after hours. If I pitched him and he was hit hard, people would wonder what I was doing . . . Berra has been around long enough to know better. The way he's been hitting, he could use a rest instead of being out late.° Anyway, with a lefthander pitching against us, I think he can stand a night off."[6]

Casey was playing to the press—certainly it was no great loss to have Yogi sit out a game and put in the gifted Elston Howard to face a left-handed pitcher. For the game, Bauer was demoted to eighth in the batting order, but Mantle stayed at the number three spot. "I'm not mad enough," said Casey, "to take a chance on losing a ballgame and possibly the pennant."[7]

°Stengel should have been the last person to criticize Yogi. In an oft-told story that in fact Casey was fond of repeating himself, his New York Giants boss and mentor, John McGraw, had hired a private detective to shadow Stengel and his drinking buddy, Irish Musel. When Casey found out, he supposedly confronted McGraw and said, with no little indignation, that he didn't deserve that kind of treatment: "I got a right to have a whole detective to myself."

Stengel's statement was pure press release fiction. Ford had only been told shortly before that he was to pitch on that day because the game had been rescheduled. In any event, Casey knew that on the road, Ford had often returned to his hotel after one in the morning and still pitched well enough to compile baseball's best won-lost percentage. He also knew that his assistant manager and his wife seldom went nightclubbing and usually only on special occasions, such as Martin's birthday. Mantle and Martin were the team's most notorious night owls—or so said the reports Weiss and Stengel received from private detectives on their players' after-hours activities—and neither was called down in Casey's comments to the *Daily News*. Why, then, was Yogi mentioned at all? Apparently to let the world know that the Yankees were serious about at least making it seem that they were not taking the incident lightly.

The Yankees' statement to the press added little to what the papers had already reported. "The Yankees have made a preliminary examination of the facts surrounding Billy Martin's birthday party, which was attended by certain players—all with their wives with the exception of Martin, who is a bachelor—and are convinced that neither Bauer nor any other Yankees player struck anyone last night." Hank Bauer, they announced, "has engaged counsel of his own and the legal aspects of this matter are in the hands of said counsel."

Only later, when witnesses gave testimony, did a clearer picture begin to emerge. Allegedly, someone at the bowling team's table called Davis a "jungle bunny"; Mantle said he recalled hearing "Little Black Sambo." Davis, telling his band to stop playing, leaned toward the man and said into his mike, "I want to thank you very much for that remark. I'll remember it." Bauer then told the man he regarded as the chief instigator to "shut the hell up." "Make me shut up," or some similar response followed. At that point, someone in the bowlers' group recognized the men sitting at the table next to them and the Yankees became the targets of heckling. It was then that the ever pugnacious Billy Martin entered the fray, telling Jones, reportedly the loudest of the bowlers, that he'd be happy to go somewhere else to discuss the matter. The drunk got up and Martin left the table. When Martin stood up, Bauer asked him where he was going; Martin replied, "I'm just going to talk to him." Mantle, tossing his napkin on the table, told his wife Merlyn, "I'd better see that Billy doesn't get into trouble." When Bauer began to rise from his chair, his wife Charlene whispered to him that this was none of his business. Bauer left the table anyway, and several people from surrounding tables rushed in to keep the incident from escalating. Jones's brother talked to Martin, and both testi-fied later that they did their best to restore order. Meanwhile, in the men's room, patrons said they saw Berra and Ford restraining Bauer.

At about this point, Jones was on the men's room floor, out cold and bleeding from his nose and mouth. The front page of the *Daily News* read "Bauer in Brawl in Copa." "The next day," Bauer quipped half a century later, "I got bigger headlines than for any home run I ever hit." Bauer swore, "I never hit anybody. The Copa had two pretty good bouncers, and one of them pulled Jones away from me. Jones looked as if he was going to take a swing, and the bouncer, who I later heard was a former light-heavyweight, laid him out."

Whatever happened at the Copa might have been forgotten if not for its aftermath. George Weiss summoned the participants to the Yankees' Fifth Avenue office. Weiss's feelings were clear to everyone present. "He thought Billy had thrown the first punch," recalled Bauer, "and he wanted someone to say it. It was that simple." No one would. Frustrated, Weiss took Berra aside and asked him to relate the sequence of events—at least Yogi, he thought, would be honest about it. Berra, miffed that he had even been called to the meeting since he had done nothing but act as a peace-maker, composed one of his best Yogiisms on the spot. "Nobody done nuthin' to nobody." There was no rebuttal to Yogi's word.

Berra's statement aside, somebody most certainly *did* do *something* to *somebody*: somebody beat the stuffing out of Edwin Jones. Did Yogi not see it? It's entirely possible that he didn't. But he knew Jones had been hit. So, if Yogi was telling the truth, what he must have meant when he said "nobody done nuthin' to nobody" was that none of the *Yankees* punched Jones. Since everyone who has ever known Yogi Berra has taken him at his word, so must we: nobody—no Yankee at least—done nuthin' to nobody.

Still, Weiss—and, as it turned out, Dan Topping—had their own agenda. Topping fined Mantle, Berra, Bauer, Ford, and Martin an exorbi-tant $1,000 apiece; Kucks, who made only a fraction of what the older stars pulled in and who most certainly did nuthin' to nobody, was fined a stiff $500. The Yankee players, and not just the ones who had been at the Copa, were furious. "Gil McDougald was so mad," Tommy Byrne recalled, "that I really thought he was going to say or do something crazy." "What angered everybody," said Bauer, "is that the fines were announced before we even got our day in court."

A short time later, the participants met at the Criminal Court building to testify before a Manhattan grand jury. Only three were questioned—

Kucks, who seemed as bewildered then as he must have felt around 1:00 a.m. on May 16, along with Martin and Berra. The district attorney took less than an hour to determine that the case should be thrown out for insufficient evidence. The DA's decision also pulled the rug out from under Jones, who subsequently dropped his case against Bauer. But Weiss did not drop his case against Martin. On June 15, just hours before the trade deadline, Stengel tracked down Billy in the Yankees bullpen and told him to report to his office. Martin, who must have known what was coming, was quietly told by his manager that he had been traded to the Kansas City A's, whom the Yankees were playing that day.° Martin burst into tears, as did Mantle and Ford when they heard. Martin, who should have known better, childishly blamed Casey. "I needed Stengel only one time in my life," Martin told Peter Golenbock, "and he let me down."[8] It was years before the two reconciled; in his 1960 autobiography, Stengel didn't mention the trade.

Martin's attitude, of course, was unrealistic and immature. There was no way he could not have known that both Weiss and Topping wanted him gone; those who knew Weiss say that he regarded Martin as a bad influence, particularly on Mantle, though why exactly Mickey needed Billy with him to stay out past two a.m. isn't clear. Ford and Mantle were often out late together as well; but then, Ford, unlike Martin, wasn't an average ballplayer—he was the best left-handed pitcher in the American League. Phil Rizzuto summed up the "bad influence" charges on Martin this way: "He roomed with me in 1950, and I won the Most Valuable Player award. He roomed with Yogi for a year, and Yogi was MVP. Then he roomed with Mickey, and Mickey won the MVP *both* years. If that's a bad influence, then the Yankees should have spread it around, had Billy room with a different guy every year."

Bad influence or not, Martin had hastened his own departure with a ridiculous attack on the Chicago White Sox's Larry Doby on June 13. In the second game of a doubleheader, Art Ditmar decked Doby (who, along with Minnie Minoso, had been traded to the White Sox from Cleveland). The knockdown was supposedly in retaliation for an incident in the first game in which the Yankees' Al Cicotte had thrown at Minoso. Minnie had responded by flinging his bat toward Cicotte's ankles. It wasn't clear that

---

°Martin was traded, along with Ralph Terry, for Harry "Suitcase" Simpson, so named for having often been "the player to be named later," and Ryne Duren. Duren arguably gave the Yankees more value than Martin ever did, posting an ERA of 2.02 in 44 games in 1958 and 1.88 in 41 games the next season before his drinking caught up with him.

Cicotte's pitch had been intentional—Minoso was always among the league leaders in hit-by-pitches—but Doby didn't cut the Yankees any slack. Dusting himself off, Doby told Ditmar that if he ever threw a pitch that close again, he'd stick a knife in his back.° Ditmar suggested Doby have sexual relations with himself. The two came together, and Doby threw a punch, missing but knocking off Ditmar's cap. The benches, of course, emptied, and Bill Skowron wrestled Doby to the ground. When a semblance of order was restored, a still seething Martin asked Ditmar what Doby had said to him, and Ditmar mentioned the knife comment. Martin went ballistic and attacked Doby. Shocked Yankees and Indians pulled Doby and Martin apart. "I got to be honest," said Tommy Byrne, "I loved Billy, but this was something different than the usual brawl. Even the guys who had been fighting just a few minutes before were kind of stunned. Billy really lost his nut." Two days after the attack on Doby, Martin was out of pinstripes.

Berra and the rest of the Copa Yankees remained incensed about the fines until the end of the season. When they received their World Series check, though, they each found the amount of the fine had been added back. It was understood that they were to remain silent on this, as the Yankees' front office had to keep face with the public. It took Yogi a while to understand that in the interest of team unity, all players who were at the Copa, guilty or no, had to be publicly chastised. The lesson would mean more to him seven years later when, as a manager, he was forced to dispense his own discipline.

After the season, journalist Irv Goodman interviewed Carmen and Yogi at home. Carmen, he wrote,

blames herself for Yogi's involvement in the Copacabana incident. He was deep in his slump at the time, hitting about .176 and feeling miserable. Some of the Yankees had planned to take Billy Martin to the Copa to celebrate his birthday. Yogi didn't want to go, but Carmen felt it would do him some good to shake his deep moodiness, and she talked him into it. Then Hank Bauer had the argument with the delicatessen man, and the story ran for weeks . . . Carmen felt terrible she had pushed her husband into such a noisy and embarrassing scandal. What made it so much

°If that sounds like an overreaction, it should be remembered that Doby, the first black player in the American League, had endured much of the same brutal treatment as Jackie Robinson had in the National League. Minoso, too, was black—according to some historians the first black Latin player in the big leagues.

more galling for her—although Yogi never reminded her of this—was that she knew he didn't enjoy going nightclubbing, and that, if left alone, would have been 20 miles from the Copa, sound asleep, when the mess broke.

Whatever distrust Berra had for the press in general had become aggravated as a result of the incident . . . They insisted on alluding to the scandal on every turn with lines like "If the Yankees (or Berra) had as much punch in the field as they had in the Copa that night . . ."[9]

As if winning seven World Series in the previous ten seasons, including the previous year, wasn't an indication of sufficient "punch."

———

WHAT THE YANKEES would miss in the 1957 World Series was a Hank Lumpkin. The night before the first game of the 1957 World Series, Berra, Ford, Mantle, McDougald, and Turgul were seen in an episode of the hugely popular sitcom, *The Phil Silvers Show*, about the enterprising Sergeant Bilko, played by Silvers, and his get-rich-quick schemes. The plot to "Hillbilly Whiz" (which had been filmed a few weeks earlier in New York on an off-day) involved a hotshot left-handed young pitcher from Tennessee, Private First Class Hank Lumpkin, whom Bilko—a full two decades before sports agents appeared on the scene—tries to get under contract so he can sell him to the Yankees for the astonishing sum of $125,000. Hank, played by a rising young comic actor named Dick Van Dyke, is reluctant to play for the Yankees because they're, well, Yankees. To make the deal, Bilko must convince Hank that the Yankees players are all good old Southern boys, so the Yankees—which presumably meant George Weiss—send several players to Bilko's base dressed as the vaudeville version of Kentucky colonels, replete with broad-brimmed hats, long coats, and nineteenth-century bow ties. Each is introduced as "Colonel," as in Colonel Yogi Berra, who has a dreadful Southern accent. Yogi's closing line as he says goodbye to Lumpkin is, "Arrivederci, ya'll."

———

THE REAL-LIFE HANK Lumpkin who got away from the Yankees was Selva Lewis Burdette Jr. of Nitro, West Virginia, a raw-boned 6'2" country boy who pitched in two games for the Yankees in 1950, at age twenty-three, before being dealt to the Boston Braves in the Johnny Sain deal. Lew Burdette never forgot what he regarded as a grievous insult, and he was determined to make the New Yorkers pay.

The Braves, who had moved to Milwaukee from Boston at the end of the 1952 season, had electrified not only Wisconsin but all the Midwest throughout the summer of 1957. They had won the National League pennant, eight games ahead of the Cardinals and eleven ahead of the Dodgers. Their two best players were twenty-three-year-old Hank Aaron, the league's MVP who had hit .322 and had led both leagues in home runs with 44, and third baseman Eddie Matthews, who had hit 32 home runs. But the story of the 1957 World Series would not be hitting (though Aaron topped them all at .393 with three home runs).

Mantle summed up the 1957 World Series this way: "The way Lew dominated us proved two points that I believe in. One is that, unlike the regular season, pitching isn't 75% of the World Series but 90%. The other is that the so-called book on hitters means very little in such a short competition. Yogi told our pitchers, 'Don't fool around, give me your best pitch.' Every pitcher has to rely on what has been most effective in a jam, and the hitter knows what that pitch is. So it boils down to that very basic duel. And this time the Braves pitching was the best."[10] Or at least it was when Burdette was pitching. In point of fact, the Yankees' pitching was better than the Braves', with a 3.00 ERA over the course of the season to Milwaukee's 3.47. Before the Series, Lew Burdette didn't even appear to be the Braves' second-best starter: Warren Spahn, who in his thirteenth season was still commanding, led the NL in wins with 21, and Bob Buhl had finished 18–7 with an ERA of 2.74 to Burdette's 17–9 and 3.71. But fortunately for the Braves, Burdette was focused, and his turn in the rotation came up in time for him to get three Series starts.*

The first game, in New York, matched the American and National leagues' candidates for best left-hander of the decade, Whitey Ford and Warren Spahn. Ford scattered six hits and went all the way for a 3–1 victory. In the second game, Burdette, aided by two Yankee errors, pitched a complete game and beat Bobby Shantz 4–2. Game Three, the first World Series game ever in Milwaukee, was played before a crowd whose acrimony shocked the Yankees, who generally found Midwestern fans to be a little nicer than those in Brooklyn. Braves fans might actually have been that if not for some comments from Casey Stengel that were picked up by the local papers. When several whooping Braves fans attempted to board

---

*Also, the Yankees believed, Burdette got mysteriously better when he applied certain substances to the ball. According to Hank Bauer, "Some of his pitches were so damned moist you didn't know whether to bring a bat or an umbrella to the plate." Of course, no Yankee complained too loudly, as Whitey Ford had a similar reputation.

the Yankees bus, Stengel called their behavior "bush league." His remarks were an indication of annoyance at some unruly fans rather than an insult to Milwaukee; Stengel had, after all, managed there for a year in 1944 and had always expressed fondness for the city. But the press and fans chose not to take it that way. For three consecutive days, Braves fanatics waited along the road that the Yankees team bus took to County Stadium flashing signs and banners; the most polite of them read "The Yankees Are Bush."

Tony Kubek, the twenty-one-year-old rookie shortstop who had been born and raised in Milwaukee, silenced the hometown fans in the first inning by slamming a Bob Buhl pitch into the right-field seats. The New Yorkers went on to introduce the Braves to Yankee power, winning 12–3 behind Don Larsen, who replaced a wild and ineffective-looking Bob Turley in the second inning. Larsen stayed in to pitch the last seven innings and got the win. (After getting Hank Aaron to fly out in the second, Larsen sat down six consecutive batters, which, counting his perfect game against the Dodgers the previous year, gave him an other-worldly total of 34 straight retired in World Series play.) Kubek, who had just three home runs all season, later hit his second of the game. "It was probably the greatest day I ever had in baseball," he recalled. "After the game Casey came up to me in the locker room, put his hand on my shoulder, and said 'Go home and thank your parents for me.' " In fact, Kubek's parents weren't particularly happy that night; their yard was strewn with garbage, and someone left a sign which read "Get out of town, you bush traitor!"[11]

———

SOMETIME DURING THE 1957 World Series—neither man remembers exactly when—Yogi Berra and Hank Aaron had a brief but famous conversation. Berra, the Braves had been warned, was a notorious talker, expert at distracting enemy hitters. For his part, Yogi insisted that that was never, or at least seldom, true. "I talk to the hitters all the time," he said in his 1961 autobiography, "but I don't very often [sic] do it to distract them or upset them. I just like to talk, that's all. 'How's the kids?' I ask them, or 'Playing any golf lately?' Just something to get a conversation started." Some hitters didn't take the overtures in the spirit they were intended and complained to umpires. Larry Doby, who would later be a close friend, would ask umpires to tell Yogi to shut up; Doby's teammate, Vic Wertz, didn't so much mind the conversation as Yogi's needling him for never tipping his cap to the crowd—Wertz was sensitive about his baldness. Yogi thought Minnie Minoso was a fun guy to talk to and teased him by tossing pebbles on him when Minnie dug in at home plate. When batters complained, Yogi told them, "If you don't talk to me now, I'll never speak to you again."[12] If a guy was particularly nasty and hurt Yogi's feelings, he would sometimes throw dirt on their shoes, but for the most part the distractions were verbal, on the order of "Be careful, it's hard to see the ball out there tonight. That's a bad background."

In the 1957 Series, despite the hostility between the Yankees and Braves, Yogi went out of his way to learn his experience to the twenty-three-year-old Henry Aaron, who, after all, had hit only .322 that season. "Hank," Yogi reminded the NL's batting champ of 1956 in a tone of avuncular concern, "you need to hold the bat so you can read the label. You're gonna break that bat. You've got to be able to read the label."

"Didn't come up here to read," Aaron calmly replied.

Over the years, Berra often repeated the story until it became part of baseball lore. Many took it as a sign that Yogi's needling tactics couldn't penetrate Aaron's mental armor. "I didn't take it that way," Aaron told me in a 1992 interview. "I always enjoyed coming to bat when Yogi was catching. He helped me relax, and I hit better. I had no problem talking to him. I just wasn't very interested in talking about the label on my bat. I just wished he had talked to me about movies, or fishing, or something else."[13]

━━━

THE BRAVES TIED the Series in Game Four as Spahn survived a rough outing, giving up eleven hits but winning 7–5. It was one of the most bizarre games ever played in the World Series. One strike away from victory in the ninth inning, Spahn gave up a three-run homer to Elston Howard which tied the game. In the tenth, with the Yankees leading 5–4, Vernal "Nippy" Jones, a journeyman pinch-hitting for Spahn, led off by taking a pitch off his right foot. Or so he claimed; umpire Augie Donatelli didn't believe him. Tommy Byrne, who threw the pitch, claimed to the end of his life that Jones was fibbing: "It wasn't even that close. It hit the ground first, then spun up and clipped off the top of his shoe. He knew it didn't hit him, but he also knew that it was close enough to argue it. Augie's [Donatelli] first call was the right one." But the ball, which had hit the wall behind home plate, rolled slowly back to exactly where Jones and Donatelli were arguing. Jones, seeing a black spot on the ball, picked it up and shouted, "See? It's the polish from my shoe!"—but, then, the ball could have picked up the spot by hitting the ground first and then Jones's shoe, as Byrne said. Donatelli gave in; Jones went to first and was replaced by a pinch-runner, Felix Mantilla. No one in the Yankees dugout was sure quite what had happened; Stengel, for once, seemed nonplussed and scarcely put up an argument. He finally had the presence of mind to relieve Byrne with Bob Grim so he could pitch to the right-handed Red Schoendienst, who promptly bunted Mantilla to second base. Then the roof fell in. Shortstop Johnny Logan doubled to tie the game at 5–5, and Eddie Matthews hit a long home run into the right-field bleachers to win it 7–5. Things like that were not supposed to happen to the Yankees, and Yogi Berra would have to wait twelve years to even the score in games involving shoe polish.

Game Five may have been the most important of the Series. Ford and Burdette exchanged zeroes until Joe Adcock singled home Eddie Matthews for a 1–0 lead that held up the rest of the game. In the fourth inning McDougald ripped a long fly over the left-field wall, but Wes Covington jumped high and pulled it down; if the ball had traveled another six inches, it would have been the Whitey Ford instead of the Lew Burdette World Series. Back at Yankee Stadium, the Yankees evened things up again, winning Game Six 3–2 when Berra pulled a Buhl fastball into the lower right-field seats. It was Yogi's fifty-third World Series game, a record, surpassing Phil Rizzuto's total by one.

The final game was a shock. Spahn was ill and Burdette was chosen to start on only two days rest. Everything appeared to be in the Yankees' favor, including the fact that Mantle was in the lineup after having injured his right shoulder on a pickoff attempt in Game Three. He was still in pain by Game Seven and would later say the injury bothered him for the rest of his career.

Things started going badly for the Yankees in the third inning, when Kubek, the hero of Game Three, muffed a throw on what looked like an automatic double play. The Yankees committed two more errors and, despite nine hits off Burdette, could not find a way to push a run across the plate. The 5–0 loss, the Yankees' poorest performance under Stengel in a key Series game, left a bad taste in everyone's mouth. Yogi had hit well, .320, and Ford pitched brilliantly, with a 1.15 ERA in two starts. But Burdette's ERA was 0.67. If he had not given up two runs in his first start, he would have equaled Christy Mathewson's incredible achievement in the 1905 Series of pitching three shutouts.

Not only were the Yankees forced to watch the hysterical Milwaukee fans shower their heroes with confetti on television, they had to endure remarks from Burdette which were given much ink in the New York papers. "We'd like to play them again next year," Lew told sportswriters in the Braves locker room after the victory. "I'm sure we're going to win the pennant, but I'm not sure about them." Warren Spahn added another verbal knockdown: "The Yankees couldn't finish fifth in the National League." Those comments would not be forgotten the following October.

IN MANY WAYS, the loss to the Milwaukee Braves in 1957 had stung worse than the loss to the Dodgers in 1955, in large part because they had lost three games to a pitcher whom they respected but knew in their hearts was no better than numerous pitchers they beat regularly in the American League. Another reason was the unexpectedly poor quality of their play: in Games Two and Five, they had made five errors, and in the Series final against Burdette they had left eleven runners on base. Once again, to the Yankees and their fans, the world seemed off its axis.

On October 4, when the Yankees were traveling to Milwaukee for the third game of the Series, the Russians had launched Sputnik, and the nation was stunned to find out that America no longer led the world in aerospace technology. We had lost the first step in the race for space. The Cold War, it now appeared, would get worse before it got better. And in the insular world of baseball, the Yankees found that the rumors they had been hearing for so long were true: on October 9, with the Series tied, a spokesman for the Brooklyn Dodgers had read to the press an announcement that "the directors of the Brooklyn baseball club have met today and unanimously agreed that the necessary steps be taken to draft the Los Angeles territory."[14] To everyone's disbelief, the Dodgers would be leaving New York for the West Coast, and the Giants would soon follow. "New York," wrote Dick Young, "is left without a National League club for the first time in 67 years."[15]

Berra, like his teammates, was stunned by the news. "No one ever truly believed they'd leave the city," he reflected more than forty years later. "Whoever leaves New York City to get rich? I was friendly with some of the Dodgers players, guys like Campy, Pee Wee Reese, and Gil Hodges and can tell you they didn't want to leave. Brooklyn was the Dodgers. It was their home."[16] The rivalry between the Yankees and the other New York teams even in exhibition games brought out an intensity that the Yankees were hard pressed to match when playing anyone else—the Milwaukee Braves, for instance. They would have to do something about that.

SPORTS ILLUSTRATED'S 1958 preseason baseball issue contained a scouting report on Berra that accurately summed up his reputation late in his career. "Game's most famous home plate conversationalist, the stocky veteran is once again most feared clutch hitter on roster. Vicious pull hitter who can murder anything in strike zone . . . Has tremendous Series record, runs well, a fine receiver with quick arm."[17]

The season began for Yogi with a pill that was almost as hard to swallow as the World Series loss: he took a pay cut of $5,000. (For a reason that has never been explained, the papers reported the amount as $2,500, and the real figure was not revealed until Yogi wrote his memoirs.) At the press conference at the team's Fifth Avenue offices, Yogi seemed uneasy. His official statement was "I deserve the cut." Then he added, "I'll get it back." The feeling, according to at least one reporter, was that "the Yankees made an unnecessary and foolish error in insisting that Berra take a cut, of whatever size . . . It had been his first bad year after ten good ones—and it hadn't been that bad—and the thought must have occurred to him that the Yankees, as a token, could have allowed him to sign for the same money as the year before. But they didn't."[18]

After the terms of the contract were made public, Stengel told Yankee beat writers, "Now, about Berra, he is 3–2 [years old]. True, he hit 24 home runs and drove in 82 runs, but he wasn't the old Yogi. It is possible that from now on he will need more help than I have been giving him. We will be ready to do that in 1958 with Elston Howard possibly confining himself to catching . . . No don't misunderstand me, I ain't retiring Yogi, not just yet, not for some years."[19] As it turned out, Yogi would outlast Casey by three years.

PRIOR TO THE 1958 season, statistician Allan Roth accurately summarized Yogi's career for *Sport* magazine's May edition. Under "Highlights," Roth noted that "Berra was selected MVP in A.L. in 1951, 1954, and 1955 . . . was named catcher on the major-league All-Star team in 1950, 1952, 1954, 1956, 1957 . . . named to A.L. All-Star squad in last ten seasons, played in the last nine All-Star games, started the last eight . . . holds the major-league record for home runs by a catcher—262 . . . holds the A.L. record for home runs in a season by a catcher—30 in 1952, 1956 . . . has hit 20 or more home runs for nine consecutive seasons . . . has struck out only

252 times in 6,087 times up, once for every 24.15 times up, one of the best strike out records in the majors."

Then "World Series Highlights": "holds Series records for most games played (54), most games caught (52), most Series for a catcher (9), most RBIs in one Series (10 in 1956) . . . Hit the first pinch home run in Series history (Oct, 2, 1947) . . . is one of the six players to hit a Series grand slam HR (Oct. 5, 1956) . . . needs three Series hits to tie Frank Frisch (58) and four total bases to tie Babe Ruth (96) for all-time Series lead . . . ranks second, tied with Lou Gehrig and Duke Snider, in Series home runs with 10 behind Ruth (15) . . . has led Series hitters twice, in 1955 (.417), 1956 (.360)."

And, finally, under "Defensive Highlights": "has led A.L. Catchers in games caught 8 times (the last 8 years) for a major-league record . . . has led in double plays 6 times, sharing major-league record with Josh "Gabby" Hartnett . . . has led in putouts, total chances for 4 consecutive years and 7 times in the past 8 seasons." If Roth waited one more year, he could have added that Berra had played 148 consecutive games at catcher without an error, another major league record.

———

"YOGI IS A bit more subdued this year," wrote Jimmy Powers in the *New York Daily News* in 1958. "He isn't the comic-book TV detective serial and gangster movie type he has been painted. 'Some of those wise cracks they credited to me I never heard of before,' he says. 'I still don't understand 'em when I read 'em.' Yogi has turned into an efficient, well-dressed, well-spoken businessman. Off-season he is doing effective work for a soft drink concern. He has several retail businesses going for him, and he regularly has to turn down offers to come into still more . . . 'I'm concentrating on baseball. I owe everything to the game. I was tickled to death to play for $90 a month in my first job.' "[20]

Yogi had turned into more than a businessman; by the summer of 1958 he had morphed into an animated TV bear. Hanna-Barbera Studios, creators of Huckleberry Hound, caricatured Berra's verbal gymnastics and piped them through a voice which resembled Art Carney's Ed Norton character on *The Honeymooners*. The resulting character, Yogi Bear, was an instant hit and by 1961 had his own TV show.

Berra was not pleased. The new Yogi pulled his image back to the cartoon caricature he had spent ten years getting away from. For a while, he thought of suing Hanna-Barbera for using his name without permission, but his lawyers told him that, after all, his real name was not Yogi. For scores of American League batters, though, Yogi Bear was a minor godsend: players who had been driven to distraction by Yogi's chatter could now shout, "Hey there, it's Yogi Bear!" every time he took the field.

———

AFTER YOGI HAD caught ten consecutive seasons of over 100 games, Irv Goodman wrote in the May 1958 issue of *Sport* magazine,

> Yogi had become something of a griper about his bumps and bruises, and Stengel will warn him off with a jibe, and the scene will be reported in the press as a very funny piece of business. It runs something like this:
>
> BERRA, on the dugout steps, "I ain't feeling so good."
> STENGEL, looking at his lineup card: "Neither am I. Must be this New York climate."
> BERRA, putting on his shin guards: "The legs are stiff."
> STENGEL: "Yeah. Who's pitchin' for them?"
> BERRA: "I think it's in the muscle."
> STENGEL: "It'll work out. See you after the game. I gotta go change my lineup."

For the first time in a national magazine, Berra was portrayed not only as an entertainer but as a serious person, one who, after twelve full seasons in the major leagues, was getting a little, well, tired: "Yogi doesn't do it with as much enthusiasm as he used to . . . It isn't easy, somehow, to think of Berra as getting old. I'm not sure why this is, but try it. Musial is getting old, Williams, despite his .388 average last year, you know is old. But Berra, you figure, will always be around. Yogi knows better."

Yogi still wanted to play, wrote Goodman, but his level of enthusiasm had "lowered." Goodman cited a minor incident that occurred before the last game of the 1957 Series against the Braves which would have been unlikely even five years earlier. Berra, after taking his batting practice cuts, reneged on the Yankee practice of running the bases. " 'Run around,' [Frank] Crosetti said. 'You kidding?' Yogi gasped. 'This is the last game.' 'What of it? Run.' 'You run!' said Yogi as he walked back to the dugout."

"The Other Yogi Berra" was the last *Sport* cover story on Yogi and the most in-depth profile on Berra ever written, capturing the aging but still amiable Yogi as he made the transition from superstar to fading icon. By

1958, Yogi, said Goodman, had developed a second image that ran counter to the public one of "a simple clown who could read comic books relentlessly, hit a ball with a bat enthusiastically, and was destined forever to remain an innocent child of the streets." The second image was of Berra "'the assistant manager' [who] not only knew more than he let on in public but knew as much about the game of baseball as anyone around. This is the picture that prevails today, although there is still a distinct residue of the earlier, shabbier image in the funny lines that get recited around Yankee Stadium, Toots Shor's, and other way-stations for baseball's camp followers." This other Yogi "is not blind to the facts of life, he ponders where it will all lead, he has pride and moods and a defensiveness that could never be found in a mound of pliable clay . . . this man Berra can be cold and aloof to visitors and he can be distrustful of writers, and yet utterly ingenuous with friends away from the game who want a favor of him."

Goodman revealed the private life of a celebrity athlete—and Yogi Berra was, by then, as well known as any professional athlete in America—at a time when superstar athletes still had private lives, lives that weren't radically different from those of most of their fans.

The three Berra boys, Yogis all, came tumbling into the room. They had just finished lunch. Larry, eight, had been inducted into the Cub Scouts a week before, and Yogi had to go down there with him. Timmy, six, is called "The Bouncer" by the family. He likes to rough-house with his father; his father likes it, too. Dale, one-year-old last December, is the best-fed member of the family.

Yogi picked up the conversation himself while holding Dale. "I go to some affairs in the neighborhood, Communion, breakfasts, Holy Name meetings. I go to places for the local Little League. You get so many calls from people, you could go every night if you wanted to." . . .

. . . "I don't like to go much [to the city] except to the shows," Yogi said. "I like to go to some clubs, [Toots] Shor's, the Harwyn Club, and a few others. We saw *My Fair Lady* and *That Square Root of Wonderful*. It closed down, but I thought it was pretty good. I've been trying to get tickets to *The Music Man*, but no luck yet. We go into the city for dinner about once a week. I like to eat home better. I get enough of that restaurant food on the road."

Most notably, Goodman reported that Yogi "has no very close friends on the Yankees now that Phil Rizzuto has moved over to the radio and televi-

sion booth. Today, Berra associates socially with the New Jersey contingent
of the Yanks—Gil McDougald, Jerry Coleman, Bill Skowron, and some
others. But it is to Rizzuto, currently his business partner and a fellow who
always knew his way around a dollar, that credit generally goes for Berra's
surprising financial acumen. Through Phil's advice and teaching, Yogi surrounded himself with people who knew about finances—a good lawyer, an
accountant, able business advisors—and has become strikingly solvent."
Many major leaguers, Goodman pointed out, came from similar working-
class backgrounds. "The only difference worth pointing out here is that
Berra has not forgotten what it was like then. Some others, drunk by the
flush of success, do forget."

After a couple of hours of discussion, Yogi had to leave to run some
errands. Goodman continued to interview Carmen who spoke up cand
donly. "Yogi is a jovial fellow, really. He is happy with his life. But he's
temperamental. Not like Maria Callas, but pretty moody. One day he can
feel like talking to you, and not the next. I know about that. I've heard people mention it often enough. That's the way he is. It's embarrassing. Here
he was talking to you like a brother, and I bet he doesn't know your name.'
We bet, and I tested Yogi on it later. He didn't know my name."

In some ways, Goodman found Mrs. Berra more forthcoming about her
husband than Yogi himself. "When he's finished playing," Carmen said,
"Yogi would like to coach. But never manage, although I think he'd be
good at it. Don't you?"[21] She was wrong about her husband never managing, but correct that he would be good at it.

———

THE YANKEES STORMED through the American League with such
ease that by the summer some writers were calling them Stengel's best
team, better in fact than any Joe McCarthy team and maybe even better
than the 1927 Yankees. As if to irritate his players, Casey went out of his
way to discourage such notions. After the bitter loss in the 1957 World
Series, he didn't want anyone getting complacent, but that's what happened. By the first week in August, the Yanks had built a 17-game lead
over the Chicago White Sox and then, unaccountably, went into a swoon.
On August 8, Ford threw his seventh shutout of the season, a six-hitter
against the Red Sox, his fourteenth victory. It would be his last win of the
season. Two days later, Stengel, probably managing a bit more than was
needed, called his ace left-hander in to relieve. Stengel had always pulled
Ford out of the rotation to hold him for first-division opponents and fre-

quently used him as a reliever, but with such an enormous lead there seemed to be little point in overworking his best pitcher. In any event, Ford hurt his elbow warming up and pitched the rest of the season in pain. He led major league starters with an outstanding 2.01 ERA, but he might have made history if Stengel hadn't called on him during that game. Along with Gil McDougald's and Bill Skowron's back problems and Hank Bauer's decline at age thirty-seven, the Yankees suddenly began to look ordinary. Yogi might have offered the best explanation to Mel Allen in a TV interview when the Yankees announcer asked him why the team had gone flat. "We coasted," Yogi admitted.

Berra caught just 88 games, by far his lowest number since becoming a regular, and played 21 more in the outfield despite getting hit in the face by a fungo fly from Milkman Turner while taking outfield practice on August 6. It was far from normal for a thirty-three-year-old catcher to find a second career as a sub outfielder, but Yogi did okay and hit better than he had the year before, finishing at .266 with 22 home runs and 90 RBIs. Elston Howard, who hit .314, was easing into the role of first-string catcher, putting in 69 games behind the plate. Despite the surge by Mickey (who would finish at .304 and lead the league with 42 home runs) and Yogi, the Yankees won only 25 of their last 53 games, causing some to doubt if they were really poised to wreak revenge on the Braves, who finished eight games ahead of the surprising Pirates.

After clinching the pennant with a doubleheader win against Kansas City on September 14, the Yankees, feeling flat despite the wins, had a tame victory party and then hopped a train to Detroit. A few players weren't satisfied and wanted more party. Ryne Duren, whose drinking was an increasing problem for his teammates, picked a fight with first base coach Ralph Houk. By the time they reached Detroit, a fuming George Weiss, determined to prevent a repeat of Copa-like publicity, hired private detectives to follow the usual suspects. Inevitably, Weiss's gumshoes were found out, inspiring even more of the headlines he didn't want. Mantle and Ford, suspecting they were being tailed,* bribed a cab driver to pull away at breakneck speed; trying to catch up, the detectives nearly killed a female pedestrian. Mickey and Whitey took the cab around the block and got out in front of their hotel, laughing and waving at the shamuses as they

---

*In his memoir, *Slick*, Ford recalled that their detective "was no Mike Hammer. He wore white rabbit-skin shoes and you could spot him a mile away. Some detective!" (p. 145)

walked in. Other detectives were inexplicably assigned to Tony Kubek, Bobby Richardson, and, of all people, Johnny Kucks. "We couldn't believe it," said Kubek. "We went to the local YMCA to play ping pong. We thought 'Why do these guys care that we're playing ping-pong? We decided to play a joke. We went to a movie theater and bought some popcorn. They went to the box office and bought tickets. Then we walked out of the theater. I always wondered if they stayed to see the show."

The next year, said Kubek, "when I got my contract from the front office, I thought about asking them to also give me what they were paying the private eyes."

The Yankees, nerves frayed by Stengel's constant haranguing and his extra practices, were tired and distracted by the time the World Series started on October 1. The two teams were, on paper, evenly matched: both had won 92 games, both had led their leagues in hitting (the Yankees at .268, the Braves at .266) and ERA (the Yanks at 3.22, the Braves at 3.21). Both had power—the Yankees hit 164 home runs, the Braves 167. But the Braves, still smoking from their victory the previous fall, were recklessly confident and not shy about letting that fact be known to reporters. The Yankees flew to Milwaukee—the first time they had ever traveled to the Series by plane—and, instead of going to a downtown hotel, went to Brown's Lake Resort, about a half hour drive from County Stadium. Weiss's reasoning was sound; Braves fans were so boisterous that the verbal assaults going in and out of a Milwaukee hotel would have been distracting. Still, not all the players enjoyed their suburban surroundings. "A fine place," said Yogi, "if you liked checkers and billiards."[22]

The Braves, on fire, won the first two games in Milwaukee, 4–3 when Spahn outdueled Ford, and then 13–5 when the Braves bombed Bob Turley and four other Yankees pitchers. Lew Burdette got the victory—though, ominously, after tiring late in the game. Nonetheless, the Yankees again found themselves at the crossroads of baseball history. They had now lost six of nine games to Milwaukee in two World Series, and losing a second Series to the Braves was something that neither their reputations nor Casey Stengel's job would survive.

Game Three, at least, would be played in the Bronx. But the pregame ceremony featured a grim reminder to both the Yankees and the Braves about how ephemeral a ballplayer's career could be. Roy Campanella, whom the Yankees had faced in five World Series against the Dodgers, had been paralyzed in an automobile accident earlier in the year. Since there was no longer an Ebbets Field in which to honor him, Campanella was brought before the crowd at Yankee Stadium, who gave him a roaring standing ovation. Yogi called it a moment he would never forget. As he left the field to go back in the dugout just before the game, "I turned and waved to Campy. I felt a strange chill seeing him helpless and unfortunate. It was still heartening to see him."

———

AS SO OFTEN happened with Stengel's Yankees, when a great performance was needed from a non-star, they got it. The ball for the crucial third game was handed to Don Larsen, who had pitched well during an injury-plagued season and was 9–6 with a 3.08 ERA. Luckily for Don, instead of Spahn or Burdette he was matched against another journeyman, Bob Rush, who had posted a 10–6 mark. After seven shutout innings, he got relief help from Ryne Duren, and the Yankees were down just two games to one. Any elation, though, from that game quickly vanished when Warren Spahn dominated the Yankees the next day. Ford, still pitching with a sore arm, was sharp, but his fielders, notably Kubek (who let a ground ball go through his legs to give the Braves a run in the sixth), betrayed him. Spahn gave up just two hits in a 3–0 victory. Over two World Series the Yankees had lost seven of eleven games to the Braves and were now behind three games to one, a deficit no American League team had ever overcome in October. Johnny Logan told reporters that the last two games at County Stadium would be unnecessary; the Braves would take the Series in New York.

A brash, abrasive young radio reporter named Howard Cosell cornered Stengel in the clubhouse and asked him if he thought the Yankees had choked. "If there's any choking," Casey shot back, "it'll be you when I shove this microphone down your throat." Cosell started to reply to Stengel and then thought better of it. He told his listeners, "Well, there you have it."

A couple of years later, Berra would reflect that he had never seen a Yankee team as steamed up as this one was when they arrived at the Stadium for the fifth game. Bob Turley recalled that "the mood changed quickly when Mickey Mantle walked into the clubhouse with one of those trick arrow things sticking through his head. You know, like Steve Martin used in his routines. We were all pretty grim, but Mickey was smiling. He said, 'Now I know how Custer felt'—we were playing the Braves, remember? That cracked us all up. After that, we all felt looser."

In Game Five, Turley showed the Braves—particularly Spahn,

Burdette, and Johnny Logan, who was popping off to any reporter who would listen about how satisfying it was to bury New York two seasons in a row—that they should have kept their mouths shut. Turley, another of those pitchers who, in the words of Berra, "really didn't learn how to pitch until he was a Yankee,"[23] had been terrific in 1958—in fact, he had been voted the Cy Young award after leading the AL in wins with 21 and complete games with 19. Turley, nicknamed "Bullet Bob" for his fastball, overpowered the Braves on five hits and the Yanks won 7–0.

Game Six, one of the all-time Yankee classics, once again pitted Spahn against the still-hurting Ford. Hank Bauer, the Yankees' hitting star with four home runs in the Series, gave them an early lead with a solo shot, but Whitey, pitching with a bad elbow on two days rest, had to be relieved by Art Ditmar in the second inning when the Braves moved ahead 2–1. This was the Braves' best chance — playing in Milwaukee, up three games to two, leading after two innings, with their ace, Spahn, on top of his form, and a damaged Whitey Ford out of the game. But Ditmar did his job, getting the Braves' shortstop Johnny Logan to fly to Elston Howard, and then Howard did his, delivering a perfect throw to Berra to nail Andy Pafko at the plate and prevent further damage. Spahn stopped the Yankees until the sixth inning, when Mantle singled, went to third on an error, and scored when Yogi, reaching out of the strike zone to get one of Spahn's curves, lifted a sacrifice fly to center field, tying the game, 2–2.

The student of the modern game of baseball would immediately note one major difference between baseball in our time and the late 1950s: the absence of relief aces. In most key games back then, ace pitchers were expected to finish what they started. And so, Warren Spahn, who had pitched 28 innings so far in the World Series, was still on the mound in the tenth when McDougald came to bat. Gil ripped a mediocre Spahn fastball over the left-field fence; Howard then singled, Berra sent him to third with a single, and Skowron greeted reliever Don McMahon with another single to give the Yankees a 4–2 lead. The Braves scored a run in their half of the tenth, and then, with Hank Aaron on third and Joe Adcock on first with two outs, and with victory almost within their grasp, Stengel called on Turley, the hero of Game Five, to pitch to Frank Torre, who promptly lined a ball to the edge of the outfield grass. McDougald leapt and caught it, and the Series was tied.

The next day, the Yankees drove from Brown's Lake to County Stadium for the seventh game of the 1958 World Series escorted by police cars with sirens blaring. Both Stengel and Braves manager Fred Haney chose pitchers of destiny for the seventh and deciding game: Burdette, last year's hero, for the Braves and Larsen for the Yankees. Berra, though, was so wound up that he thought the question of starting pitchers was irrelevant. "I don't think it mattered who pitched for who," he said. "We were going to win this one and that was all there was to it."[24]

In a rare display of bravado, Yogi began telling the Milwaukee team just that, starting with batting practice and then throughout the game. In the third inning with the Yankees up 2–1, the Braves got two singles and Stengel, taking no chances, once again called on Bob Turley. Bullet Bob got the Yanks out of a bases-loaded situation. In the sixth, though, Braves catcher Del Crandall, a one-time Yankee farmhand, hit a long home run into the left-field seats. Now it was 2–2. In the eighth inning, Burdette was still on the mound. He got McDougald to fly out, then struck out Mantle for the second out. Then Berra came to bat.

Neither Yogi Berra nor Elston Howard had a good World Series in 1958, both batting just .222 and driving in only two runs apiece. But during the season, it was clear that Howard's star was on the rise while Yogi's was waning. In the eighth inning of the seventh game of the World Series, though, they both put their mark on the Yankees victory: Yogi slammed a hard double off the right-center-field wall and Elston drove a single to center to score him and put the Yankees ahead. It must have seemed to Braves fans as if the wrath of history had now fallen on their team: Andy Carey singled off Eddie Matthews's glove at third base, and Moose Skowron hit perhaps his biggest home run as a Yankee, a three-run shot delivered into the left-field bleachers in almost total silence—except for the screaming coming from the Yankee dugout. Bullet Bob mopped up in the ninth.

For the second time in four years, the Yankees had avenged a World Series loss in their opponents' home park, this time accomplishing what had been thought impossible by coming back from a three-games-to-one deficit. (Actually, the 1925 Pittsburgh Pirates had come back from a three-to-one deficit to defeat the Washington Senators, but there was a prevailing attitude among New York sportswriters that if the Yankees hadn't done something then it really hadn't been done.) That they had beaten Spahn and Burdette in back-to-back games made it all the sweeter. "I wanted to win it so bad," Gil McDougald told Yankees executive Bob Fishel, "I would have played this one for nothing. I mean it."

No World Series victory during the Stengel years elicited such a euphoric reaction as this one. All the way back to New York, the players and coaches sang, popped champagne corks, and mocked the Braves who had mocked them. Whitey Ford, who had been dubbed by Elston Howard "The Chairman of the Board,"* took over the celebration, proclaiming Yogi "Wing Commander Berra." (Though all he was in charge of, said Yogi, "was putting away a couple of martinis and a filet mignon.")[25] His bad arm no longer an issue, Ford collected the corks and burned them, using the charred tops to make designs on the players' faces. The players howled when it was Casey's turn. "There sat Casey," Hank Bauer recalled decades later, "his eyes closed while Whitey made dollar signs on his cheeks. We stood around watching and laughed out butts off." After the plane touched down at the airport, Stengel, charcoal dollar signs on his cheeks, spoke to the crowd of reporters, "I guess we *could* play in the National League after all."

———

New York's victory over Milwaukee in the 1958 World Series was Casey's last with the Yankees—and with it, the Yogi Berra era of the Yankees came to an end. There would be four more pennants and two more World Series rings, but Yogi would no longer be a decisive factor. In the dozen seasons from 1947 through 1958 he was one of the most valuable players the Yankees or any other team had ever seen.

That one never even hears the phrase "the Yogi Berra era" is one of the puzzles of baseball history. Babe Ruth had his era; Ruth played with the Yankees for fifteen years, from 1920 through 1934, in which time the Yankees won seven pennants and four World Series. Lou Gehrig, too, had an era, though it was shorter than Ruth's (1925 to 1938), over which time the Yankees won seven pennants and six World Series. There was a Joe DiMaggio era, 1936 to 1942 and 1946 to 1951, which saw the Yankees win ten pennants and nine World Series. And there certainly was a Mickey Mantle era from 1951 through, let's say, 1964, when Mickey played on his last pennant-winning team. In those fourteen seasons, the Yankees won twelve pennants and seven World Series. In the Yogi Berra era—which is what 1947 to 1958† most certainly is—the Yankees won ten pennants and eight World Series, including five consecutive World Series victories from

---

*Howard, a jazz and big band aficionado, liked to listen to WNEW while driving to and from Yankee Stadium. WNEW's most popular disc jockey was William B. Williams, a Frank Sinatra devotee who dubbed his favorite singer "The Chairman of the Board." Elston thought Whitey, the Yankees' best big-game pitcher, deserved the title.

†Of course, 1949–1958—or 1949 to 1960, if you will—should also be called the Casey Stengel era. For what it's worth, though, let us remember that Casey never won a pennant or World Series without Yogi, but Yogi did win a championship without Casey, in 1947.

1949 to 1953, something not achieved by Ruth, Gehrig, DiMaggio, or Mantle.

Of course, no player, no matter how great, can create an era on his own. Yogi's era overlaps DiMaggio's and then Mantle's. From 1925 to 1934, Gehrig and Ruth shared ten full seasons. (Strange in retrospect that the combination of two of the greatest hitters in the game's history didn't produce more than four World Series titles.) Gehrig overlaps DiMaggio for three full seasons, 1936 to 1938. Nobody makes an era on their own. No Yankees era, though, was longer and better than Yogi Berra's.

The biggest knock against Berra as a hitter—one, in fact, made frequently by Stengel—is that he wasn't selective enough at the plate and didn't draw enough walks. Yet, from 1950 to 1956 Berra was among the top ten in on-base percentage five times and in the top eight (or better) in total bases every season. From 1948 to 1956 he was in the top ten in slugging average every year, finishing as high as third in 1953, fourth in 1956, and fifth in 1949. No major league catcher before Berra—not Bill Dickey or Mickey Cochrane or Gabby Hartnett—had been so productive a hitter in his time as Yogi was in his.

By the end of the 1958 season only two players, Yogi Berra and Hank Bauer, were left from Stengel's first World Series winner in 1949. Berra was the only regular player during all of those ten years. The Yankees of Yogi's era won six pennants and four World Series *after* DiMaggio's retirement, and Yogi already had three World Series rings *before* Mantle's rookie season. Does Yogi deserve to have an era named for him? Consider this: in the twelve seasons from 1947 to 1958, Berra led his team in RBIs for *seven consecutive seasons*, 1949 to 1955. In two other seasons, 1956 and 1958, he was second in RBIs, and in two others, 1948 and 1957, he was third. That's what he did on offense; behind the plate, he caught more than 100 games for nine consecutive seasons (and led the league in games caught for *eight consecutive seasons*, from 1950 to 1957). In seven of those seasons, he led the league's catchers in put-outs (he would lead the AL again in this category in 1959); in three of them, in assists; and in six of them, in double plays. Intangibles? He caught old pitchers, new pitchers, fastball pitchers, junk-ballers, righties, lefties, proud veterans, cocky rookies, castoffs stopping off in New York for one more lucky break, and flash-in-the-pans who were never quite as good anywhere else when Yogi wasn't behind the plate. And when his era was over, when Mickey Mantle and then Mantle and Roger Maris led the charge, Yogi was still a fine ballplayer.

After the 1958 World Series, Stengel gave an interview from his home in

Glendale, California, that was widely circulated in the national press. Next to DiMaggio, he said, Yogi was the greatest player he had ever managed. Casey, of course, hadn't seen DiMaggio at his peak, and the two men did not get along. But it was understood that no one who had managed the Yankees while Joe DiMaggio was playing could possibly say anything but that DiMaggio was the greatest player he had ever seen. The suggestion was that Yogi was really the greatest player he had ever managed—he just wasn't free to say so. Yogi was touched when he read the interview.

───

NEAR THE END of 1958, Yogi, Carmen, Larry, Tim, and Dale boarded a plane for Christmas in St. Louis. There was already a feeling that this could be their last Christmas together. Paulina was only sixty-four but had endured much in the previous two years, first with the amputation of her leg and then oncoming blindness. In his memoirs, Yogi recalled numerous details of the holiday: "Early Sunday morning I took the kids to mass at St. Ambrose's, where I met a lot of people I know, and then, after mass, I walked up the hill to Grassi's. John Prachelli, who was behind the bar, saw me come in and said, 'Oops, we got a live one,' and I bought a drink for everybody and John gave me a bottle of wine to take home to Mom and Pop. When we got back home, the women were cooking enough food for an army, and pretty soon my brothers were there, and we were mixing martinis and manhattans and eating slices of cold meat and cheese . . . After dinner, all the kids from St. Ambrose's choir came to the front door and stood in the living room, twenty of them, and sang Christmas carols for Mom because she hadn't been able to get out to go to church. 'I wish I could see them,' Mom said, and she cried a little . . . It's hard to realize that we can't all be together any more. But we're all getting older and things change."[26]

───

IN THE SPRING of 1959, Toots Shor announced that after twenty years he had sold his lease for $1,500,000 and was closing his famous saloon at 51 West 51st Street. (The Zeckendorf Hotel would go up in its place.) On June 23, Toots threw his "final black-tie dinner party" for nearly 300 sportswriters, athletes, and pals who, according to *The New York Times* "have gotten some sense of belonging" when Mr. Shor called out their name, insulted them, and pounded them on the back."[27] Yogi, Whitey, Mickey, and the other Yankees who might have attended were playing ball in Kansas City. Shor told them that he was planning a new restaurant around the corner on West 52nd Street, but to the old crowd, the new Toot Shor's would never be quite the same.

Early in May, after the Yankees had completed a series in Detroit and were preparing to leave for Kansas City, Berra called Stengel and asked him for permission to fly back to St. Louis to see his mother. Sure, Casey told him, for once showing some warmth and a sense of appreciation for what Berra had meant to the Yankees for so long, you go on, and get back to us later. Paulina had been hospitalized for several days; Yogi had called before and after each game to check on her. Her doctor from St. John's Hospital in St. Louis called him before 6:00 a.m. and told him that he should come home as fast as he could. He arrived at St. John's Hospital before noon. His father, brothers, and sisters were all there. Paulina had slipped into a coma. Leaning over her bed, he whispered in her ear, "It's me Mom, Lawdy." Paulina moved a bit but did not speak; a short time later a priest performed the Catholic sacrament of last rites. A few hours later, she died. Yogi's sister, Josie, told him that the doctors were surprised that Paulina hadn't died hours before he got there; she had, thought her daughter, waited for Lawdy. "I hope she heard me and knew I was there. I loved her very much. I took the rosary that she was holding in her hands, and I kept it with me all the time."[28]

Thirty years later in Los Angeles, Berra was taping a session of *Yogi at the Movies*. During a break, the talk turned to parents, and someone asked Yogi about his. Yogi took out his wallet and showed them photos of Pietro and Paulina. One of the tech people began to tear up. "How many 63-year-old men do you know," he asked rhetorically, "who still carry pictures of his mother and father around with him?"[29]

———

BERRA'S AND RIZZUTO'S bowling alley opened in the summer of 1958 and was immediately popular; by winter, it was booked weeks in advance. Yogi and Phil made it a family business: Rizzuto's brother Al worked there, and Yogi asked his older brother John to quit Ruggerio's, come east, and run the cocktail lounge. "You know," Yogi told *Sport* magazine, "we can seat 54 people in the bar, and John wants to figure out how much liquor we can stock. I don't know. It's something we're going to have to find out, what they drink around here. I figure there are the bowlers and the whatchacallthem, the stiff-shirts. Uh, no, the white collar people. The bowlers will go for beer, but them, I don't know."[30]

Berra was proud of his business acumen—if the ninth-grade dropout didn't have a head for business, he had a head for knowing those who had a head for business. "We aren't fronting for anybody," he told Ed Fitzgerald. "We really own it ourselves. We put our own money into it and borrowed the rest on our own names . . . unless the country runs into another Depression or something, it should take care of both of our families for the rest of our lives . . . It's our insurance policy for the future."[31]

In the *Daily News*, Dick Young called it a "snazzy no-post palace, complete with automatic pinsetters and two bars . . . located in a busy shopping center off a highway near Clifton, New Jersey, and it is there that Yogi spends his time now."

> "Those pinsetters cost $7700 apiece," says Yogi proudly, "and each alley costs $3500." Even the huge bar is shaped like Yankee Stadium. "We call it the Stadium Lounge," beams Yogi.
>
> Near the broad entrance a glass-encased trophy case on the wall bears numerous Rizzuto and Berra trophies—the three MVP plaques won by Yogi, and the one Rizzuto received.
>
> Yogi pointed out the bronzed beat-up catcher's glove on the lower shelf. "That's the one I caught two no-hit games with. You know, Reynolds."[32]

Several months later, the building was broken into. The morons who committed the robbery stole money and overlooked the most valuable items in the place, namely the MVP plaques and bronze glove. When asked years later why he thought the burglars had missed a chance to walk off with some pieces of baseball immortality, Rizzuto shrugged, "I always wondered that. Those guys were really stupid. They must have been Red Sox fans."

————

YOGI PLAYED WELL in 1959, catching 116 games (28 more than the previous season) and hitting .284 (eighteen points higher than in 1958), with 19 home runs and 69 RBIs. His most notable regular season game came when he made an error. On May 10, in the second game of a double-header against the Senators, he threw wide of second base and was charged with an error, thus reminding sportswriters that he had set a record for catchers by playing in his previous 148 consecutive games without an error—969 flawless chances—a streak going all the way back to 1957. His season's highlight probably came on August 3 in the second All-

Star game° when he hit a home run off Don Drysdale.† He made a contribution to the American League in the first All-Star game, too. In a pregame
meeting, the other AL All-Star pitchers and catchers were discussing possible ways to pitch to Stan Musial. Yogi cut them off: "You guys are trying to
figure out in fifteen minutes what nobody could in fifteen years."[33]

Elston Howard played well, too, splitting his time between catching, the
outfield, and first base, batting .273 with 18 home runs and 73 RBIs, but
most of the rest of the Yankees had off seasons. Mantle, playing most of the
season in pain, had his worst year, .285 with just 31 home runs. Gil
McDougald hit only .251 with four home runs, and Bill Skowron, hobbled
by injuries, played in only 74 games. The young middle infielders, Bobby
Richardson and Tony Kubek, fielded well but batted with little power.
Whitey Ford won 16 games, and Don Larsen, his talent eroded by extreme
nightlife, was 6–7. The Yankees never really got on track and finished a dismal third, 15 games in back of the Chicago White Sox (who, according to
Stengel, "were not a good hitting team, so they made their living running
bases")[34] and ten behind the Indians. The low point of the season came
from July 9 to 13 when the Yankees were swept in a five-game series by the
Red Sox at Fenway Park.‡ Losing five straight to the Red Sox was like an
open sore. And to rub salt in the wound, a month later the Yankees lost
three straight to Boston at Yankee Stadium.

"This bad season," Casey said, "was an emergency to our owners. They
thought the manager was slipping. They thought the coaches were slipping. They thought the players were slipping. But maybe those people in
the front office didn't have such a good year themselves."[35] Yogi stated it
more simply: the Yankees failed to win the pennant because "it was just
one of those years. Nobody did nothing."[36]

For reasons not yet known, Topping and Webb, after winning the World
Series, decided to cut corners in 1959 by doing away with Stengel's off-
season instructional school and created resentment among the veterans
and young players alike by taking a hard line on salaries. Rumors of Casey's
demise as Yankee manager, which had surfaced near the end of the previ-

°From 1959 to 1962, there were two All-Star games, one each in an AL and a NL park;
the proceeds went to the players pension fund.

†Oddly enough, this would be the last home run by a Yankee in an All-Star game until
forty-one years later when Derek Jeter hit one in the 2001 game.

‡It had been twenty years since anything like that had happened to the Yankees. In July
1939, the Yanks had inexplicably lost five straight games to Boston at Yankee
Stadium—but since they had won 106 games that season, finished 17 ahead of Boston,
and swept the Reds in four straight in the World Series, no one remembered.

ous season, now was revived; also revived were the rumors that Berra would be traded to the Cardinals for Stan Musial. (Musial, age thirty-eight in 1959, hit just .255 with 14 homers, five fewer than Yogi.) Other rumors suggested that Berra would be moving over to first base, but Yogi, who remembered the miserable time DiMaggio had had playing first near the end of his career, didn't like the idea. Stengel chided him: "You know why he don't want to play first base?" Casey said aloud in the clubhouse one day. "He's afraid of the dirty look Skowron will give him if he picks up a first baseman's mitt."[37] But as Showron's back got worse, a Berra switch to first seemed more likely, especially with Howard ready to step in behind the plate. At least it seemed like a possibility to everyone except Yogi. When coach Johnny Neun suggested that Berra get himself a first base-man's mitt, Yogi told him that if the Yankees wanted him to have a first baseman's mitt, they could buy it for him. "I ain't gonna buy the whole, he said, for a glove I ain't going to use."[38] Once day Larry Jr. came to the ball-park with him and saw a catcher's mitt and outfielder's glove in his daddy's locker. Why, his son wanted to know, didn't Yogi also get a first baseman's mitt? Yogi told his son to mind his own business or he'd stop bringing him to the games.

THE SECOND YOGI Berra Day was September 18, 1959 at Yankee Stadium. Only five other Yankees—Babe Ruth, Lou Gehrig, Joe DiMaggio, Phil Rizzuto, and Charlie Keller—had been given their own day. Casey, of course, was the keynote speaker, reiterating for the Yankee Stadium crowd his statement to a West Coast newspaper the year before that "outside of DiMaggio, the man behind the plate, Berra, is the greatest player that I ever had to manage." He then added, in enigmatic Stengel-ese, "Which is a great thing to enhance my career." There were dozens of gifts, from gold cuff links and a vacuum cleaner to a year's supply of coffee and new hats for Carmen; there was a beautiful watch from Joe DiMaggio (who was co-chairman of the event, along with Mel Allen). Ted Williams, who had enjoyed so many fine conversations with Yogi in the batter's box, presented him with fishing equipment. Berra turned over cash gifts of hundreds of dollars to Columbia University for a scholarship fund rather than sending it to a St. Louis college "because New York was my home now."* Though bored to distraction by school when he was a youngster,

---

*Though in fact he was living in Montclair, New Jersey, in a large Tudor mansion which Carmen called her dream house.

Yogi had developed a keen interest in education as he grew older; he became a regular contributor to numerous scholarship funds and made clear to interviewers (just in case his sons happened to be reading the papers) that he had no intention of letting Larry, Tim, and Dale follow his own academic path.

It was Yogi's second "appreciation day" in the major leagues, the first in St. Louis in 1947. At the microphone, Yogi, introduced by Mel Allen, who called for and got a standing ovation, teared up and said how much he appreciated the good wishes and the gifts. "Everything up until now has been fine," he said. "I was enjoying myself and hope you are, too. On behalf of myself and family, I want to thank you, not for the gifts, but for showing up."[39] This time, he didn't thank the fans for making the day necessary.

Pietro came from St. Louis to see his son honored. Looking at the mountain of gifts—fifty-eight in all, according to the *Daily News*—he turned to Yogi's brother John and said, "Everything's for him. What's for me?" After the game (a 3–1 win over the Red Sox on a great pitching performance by Whitey Ford), George Weiss invited Pietro and the rest of the family up to Topping's private lounge. When he shook hands with the Yankees GM, Pietro asked, "You the man who gives my boy all that money?" Yogi hustled his dad out of the room "before he talked me into a cut."[40]

One of the best presents given to Berra was an assortment of baseball equipment intended for the Baseball for Italy Club.* Yogi (or Lorenzo Pietro Berra, according to his passport), Carmen, and Yogi's business manager, Ugo Antonucci, flew to Italy to deliver the equipment to the organization and do some sightseeing, which included a trip to St. Peter's in Rome and, later, a performance of *Tosca* at La Scala.† The highlight of the

---

*The organization's commissioner was Prince Borghese, the infamous Black Prince, an unrepentant Mussolini supporter and neo-Fascist organizer up to the time of his death in Spain in 1974, who led a failed coup attempt on the Italian government in 1970. In his 1961 memoirs, Berra recalls meeting him but showed no awareness of the Black Prince's political past. American baseball has had some bad commissioners, but no one whose record is on a par with Borghese's.

†Two famous stories out of the Berra's Italian vacation were, first, that Yogi, on meeting Pope John XXIII, said "Hello, Pope." The second is that after seeing *Tosca*, he was asked what he thought of La Scala and replied, "It was great, even the music." Neither of these stories were mentioned at the time; they appear to be of later development and are probably fictional. The Pope John story appears to be a variation of Jim Thorpe's response to King Gustav of Sweden at the 1912 Olympics: "Hello, King."

Surprisingly, no one ever quoted Yogi's own line from his 1961 memoirs, "They really know how to build beautiful buildings in Rome." (Berra and Fitzgerald, *Yogi*, p. 214)

trip was a drive from Milan to the village from which the Berras and Garagiolas hailed, Malvaglio. Yogi met family he had never seen, including five aunts, an uncle, and assorted nephews, nieces, and cousins. He also discovered that he could speak Italian after all. During the war, he had not been able to fathom the Roman tongue, but in Malvaglio he discovered the same dialect he had heard around the house back on the Hill in St. Louis. "I was right at home. It was just the same as talking to Mom and Pop."[41] On a visit to the local cemetery, he saw the headstones of numerous Berras, including one which startled him: relatives had put up a headstone for Paulina, of which he and the family back in St. Louis had been unaware.*

SOMETIME IN 1959, movie star and Yankee fan Angie Dickinson invited two of her favorite players, Whitey Ford and Yogi Berra, to dinner. "They thought I was at least a little bit nifty," Ms. Dickinson recalled. "They said they did, anyway. They did, that is, until Marilyn Monroe sat down at a table about fourteen feet away. Then both of them became unraveled."[42] Whitey, she says, was ga-ga, and Yogi couldn't eat. He kept muttering *"Madonne"*—apparently forgetting for the moment that Monroe was the ex-wife of his good friend Joe DiMaggio.

BY THE START of the new decade, Yogi Berra was the only remaining player from Casey Stengel's first championship club in 1949. Before the 1960 season, Hank Bauer and Don Larsen were traded to, of course, Kansas City, in a seven-player deal which gave the Yankees a somewhat unremarkable left-handed-hitting outfielder, Roger Maris, who had hit .273 with 16 home runs in a park, Weiss and Stengel noted, not suited to his power. (In 1958, Maris had hit 28 home runs in a season split between Cleveland and Kansas City.)

At age thirty-five, Yogi was far from old but found himself the Yankees' elder statesman. He began the year by signing again for $58,000—not a bad salary, all things considered, since the Yankees had a second-string

---

*Many an Italian-American found, on a visit to the old country, that their parents were better remembered by relatives in Italy than in the United States. In Frederick Reiken's 2000 novel *The Lost Legends of New Jersey*, a character who had tamed a wild wolf in her native village met her husband on a journey to America. She moved to New Jersey, scraped by during the Depression, married, "had five children, and had lived to be almost ninety. She was a legend still in Italy, but in New Jersey all that was forgotten."

catcher just as good as he was. Yogi thought so, too. "I'm plenty satisfied," he told the press. "I never thought I'd be making this much money." His plan, at this point, was "to catch for five more years or so, on a diminishing basis, then to become a Yankee coach 'for the rest of my life, if they'd have me.' "[43]

The years and the constant travel had changed and sobered him—"the worst part about baseball is the road trips, and the worst part about road trips is being away from the family."[44] If all the games were home games, he'd play forever; it was the traveling, he felt, that got harder as he got older. Never a night owl, he saw little of his teammates on the road except at the ballpark. His evenings were often lonely; if a hotel was comfortable and had a good restaurant, he often didn't go out. Paperback novels had replaced the comic books; he mentioned James Jones's *From Here to Eternity* and Robert Ruark's *Something of Value* as favorites to a reporter. He had always loved to play cards on the road, but there was less of that as the Yankees traveled more and more by plane. Also, now that he was the senior member of the team, he didn't enjoy taking money from younger players who weren't making much more than minimum wage.

One thing he did not mind, though, was giving up his job as starting catcher. Left field was far easier to play—no squatting, no taking foul tips off your shins, no base runners crashing into you. At this point in their respective careers, he knew, Elston Howard had become a better catcher—Yogi had worked overtime to help make that true. "Elston," thought Arlene Howard, "always appreciated the way Yogi and Bill Dickey had worked with him to develop his catching skills. Elton said being a Yankee catcher was like being in a special fraternity."[45] (In later years, Howard would help learn Thurman Munson all his experience.) In 1960, for the first time, Howard, despite nagging injury, caught more games than Berra, 91 to 83.

It was neither Berra nor Howard, though, who powered the 1960 Yankees. Mantle led the league in home runs with 40. Roger Maris, the latest gift from Kansas City, hit 39 home runs, led the league with 112 RBIs, and won the MVP award. Bill Skowron was superb, rebounding from his dismal 1959 season, hitting .309 with 26 homers. On May 20, the Yankees had been in dead last in the American League, 8½ games behind the Indians, and their dismal performances suggested that 1960 would be a reprise of 1959. A May 21 *New York Post* headline read "The Day the Yankees Hit the Bottom." Disgruntled beat writers were suggesting that this season *would* be worse than the previous year. When writers would ask

Yogi, though, if the Yankees still had a chance, he would tell them, "This season ain't over yet." It wasn't quite as catchy as "It ain't over till it's over," but it was just as prophetic.

On May 26 Weiss pulled off another terrific deal with, of course, the Athletics, trading the fading pitcher Johnny Kucks, along with light-hitting infielder Jerry Lumpe, for outfielder Hector Lopez and pitcher Ralph Terry, whom Weiss had sent to Kansas City in the Billy Martin trade. It was, as angry American League officials called it, a steal. Kucks won just four games for the Athletics and lost ten while Lumpe hit .272. Terry won ten games for the Yankees and Lopez batted .284 with nine home runs. In June, the Yankees suddenly came alive, winning 14 of 15 games, including a four-game sweep of the defending champion White Sox. They finished with a spectacular flourish, winning their last 15 games and clinching the pennant on September 25 when Ralph Terry beat the Red Sox 4–3, finishing eight games ahead of the Orioles. Their opponent was a surprise to nearly everyone, the Pittsburgh Pirates, who hadn't won a pennant since 1927, the year the Ruth-Gehrig Murderers' Row swept them in four straight.

The 1960 World Series is one of the most written about ever, and much of what's been written is wrong. The overwhelming majority of writers thought the Series a mismatch as the Yankees had the best record, 97–57, and hit the most home runs, 193, in the major leagues—and, after all, they were the Yankees. But the Pirates had won only two fewer games, though they had 70 fewer home runs, and had led the league in RBIs with 689, just ten fewer than the Yankees. The Yankees pitching was supposed to be their weak spot, largely because they appeared to have no ace. (Whitey Ford was just 12–9 after missing the first six weeks of the season but pitched well over the last two months.) In fact, the Yankees staff finished first in the AL in ERA with 3.52—tied with the Orioles and just .03 higher than the Pirates, who led the NL. The Pirates had no reason to fear the Yankees. The previous season they had only won 78 games, but the Yankees had only won 79.

Stengel would be forever criticized by fans, the press, and by Whitey himself for not allowing Ford to pitch until the third game of the World Series, when the two teams played in the Bronx. In truth, Casey's most trusted coaches—Ed Lopat (who had returned to his old team as a pitching coach when Jim Turner was made the scapegoat for the dismal 1959 season), Frank Crosetti, and Ralph Houk—thought it was a sound strategy. In hindsight, of course, the starter should have been Ford, who was about to embark on the greatest World Series streak of any pitcher ever, but in October of 1960 Whitey Ford did not have the reputation as a great World Series pitcher he would have after the 1960 and 1961 World Series, in which he pitched 32 consecutive scoreless innings to break Babe Ruth's record of 29⅔ consecutive scoreless innings. As good as Ford had been in the Series up to 1960, he was just 5–4, though with a superb 2.81 ERA. What is not remembered now is that prior to the first game against Pittsburgh in 1960, Ford had not won a World Series game in more than three years, in fact since he had beaten Warren Spahn 3–1 in the first game of the 1957 Series. The normally astute Rob Neyer, in his *Book of Baseball Blunders*, flat-out states that "Casey should have started Whitey three times."[46] But in October 1960 there was no reason why the uncharismatic Art Ditmar shouldn't have been set up for three starts. He had gone 15–9 to Ford's 12–9, and their ERAs were almost identical, Ditmar 3.06 and Ford 3.08.*

Ditmar looked like a good match for the Pirates' Vernon Law, the aptly named Mormon deacon who led the National League in wins with 20. Maris staked Ditmar to a 1–0 lead in the first inning with a home run, but the Pirates knocked Ditmar out of the box in their half with three runs. A big play was a throw from Berra to try and nail Pittsburgh center fielder (and future Yankee manager) Bill Virdon at second base. The ball flew untouched into center field—shortstop Tony Kubek and second baseman Bobby Richardson weren't clear as to who was supposed to cover. Shortly after, with Roberto Clemente up, Berra again tried to nail a runner at second, Bob Skinner, and the ball sailed over Richardson's head. This one was Yogi's fault; Kubek, backing up the play, kept Skinner from going to third, but Clemente bounced a single to the rock-hard infield to score him. Jim Coates relieved Ditmar for the next four innings, and Bill Mazeroski hit a two-run homer off him to give the Pirates a 5–2 lead in the fifth. Yogi very nearly atoned for the throw in the fourth inning, slamming a high drive between right and center, but Virdon and Clemente, both running at full speed, converged on the ball with Virdon making a leaping catch that drew a standing ovation from the Forbes Field crowd. Elston Howard, pinch-hitting in the ninth inning (he had sprained a ligament in his right ring finger in the last game of the season), hit a two-run homer off the Pirates relief ace, Elroy Face. But it wasn't enough, and the Pirates won 6–4.

---

*For the record, Ditmar had been at least as effective as Ford the previous season, posting a 2.90 ERA in 38 games to Ford's 3.04 in 35.

The second game, won by the Yankees 16–3, might have given them too much confidence. Turley, who had not pitched well all season, nearly went the distance, giving up just one run before being relieved in the ninth by Bobby Shantz. The Yankees pounded starter Bob Friend and five other Pirate pitchers (including their former Dodger foe Clem Labine) for 19 hits, two of them titanic home run shots by Mantle. Stengel, enjoying the show, walked up and down the dugout clapping his hands, telling his boys to "Pour it on! Don't let up on 'em!" They didn't. They poured it on again in the next game, this time at Yankee Stadium, with 16 hits and 10 runs, four of them on a stupefying grand slammer by Bobby Richardson, who had hit only one home run all season. The battery of Ford and Berra, clicking on all cylinders, shut out the Pirates on four hits. The 26 runs in the previous two games went to their heads; the Yankees seemed to forget that baseball games can be decided by a single run as Vern Law, with help over the last three innings from Face, beat Ralph Terry 3–2 to even the Series. The next day, though, the Yankees were really shocked when Ditmar, making his second bad start of the Series, was outpitched by Harvey Haddix 5–2. Now the Yankees, having lost two straight at home, were down three games to two and facing elimination as they headed back to Pittsburgh. Ford, who had been plagued with arm trouble all year except down the pennant stretch, pitched another gem, his second shutout of the Series, as the Yankees shelled six Pirate pitchers for 12 runs in Game Six.* The Yankee batters beat the Pirate pitchers so badly that Yankee fans scarcely noticed when Elston Howard took a pitch on the little finger of his left hand and had to leave the game. Howard was batting .462 with 4 RBIs, but he would not be available for the crucial seventh game.

The seventh game of the 1960 World Series might be the most famous baseball game ever played after Don Larsen's masterpiece in 1956, and so it's fitting that Yogi Berra was a major player in both. Unlike the Larsen game, this one was a wild, poorly pitched affair in which nine pitchers gave up 24 hits and 19 runs. The Yankees seemed a bit overmatched with a rested Vern Law ready to go for Pittsburgh. And because of his decision not to start Ford in Game One, Stengel's options for Game Seven were limited. Bob Turley was no longer the blazing fastball pitcher of 1958, but he had pitched well in Game Two and was rested. Twenty-year-old Bill

---

*Amazingly, though he had pitched well in several World Series losing efforts, this was Whitey Ford's first Series win outside Yankee Stadium. He later said he believed that if he had lost it, the Yankees would have traded him after the 1960 season.

Stafford had impressed everyone with his poise down the stretch for the pennant, and Casey told him the night before that he would start the seventh game. Then Casey changed his mind and gave the ball to Turley. At the end of the second inning, both Turley and Stafford had been knocked out as the Pirates took a 4–0 lead. In the fifth, Skowron hit a solo home run off Law. In the dugout Yogi could be heard telling his teammates, "If we can get Law out and Face in, we'll win"—he was that confident that he could hit the Pirates ace reliever. In the sixth, he got his chance.

Before the Series, Pirates manager Danny Murtaugh had told reporters that Berra was the Yankees' most dangerous hitter, more to be feared in tight situations than either Mantle or Maris. With Richardson and Kubek on base, Mantle singled to make it 4–2. Yogi came to the plate. His advice to pitchers in the World Series had always been "go with your best pitch." Applying that straegy, Face threw Yogi his best pitch, a forkball; Yogi's wrists snapped at the moment of impact and the ball soared into Forbes Field's right upper deck. It was as if the Yogi of 1955 was back. Like a kid hitting a home run to win a Little League game, he rounded first and leapt around the bag with an enthusiasm he hadn't shown in years. It was the biggest home run of his career—or should have been. The problem was that it was only the sixth inning and the Yankees led by a single run, 5–4. In the eighth inning, things looked even better as the Yankees added two more runs for a 7–4 lead. Then, all the things that weren't supposed to happen to the Yankees in the World Series began to happen.

Stengel's late-innings strategy when Yogi was in the outfield was to protect a lead by putting Kubek in at left and moving Joe DeMaestri to short, not because DeMaestri was a better shortstop than Kubek but because Kubek was a better left fielder than Yogi. But with Berra playing in left field and scheduled to hit in the ninth, Kubek stayed at short. Gino Cimoli, pinch-hitting for Face, led off the bottom of the eighth with a single. Then Bobby Shantz, who had been pitching since relieving Stafford in the third inning, did exactly what Stengel wanted him to do: namely, coax a double play ball, this one from Bill Virdon. It seemed tailor-made for a twin-killing. The play that should have decided the World Series became a nightmare for Yankee fans and decades later still causes veterans to wince. On its third hop, the ball did not skip harmlessly into Kubek's glove but instead hit something—some said a pebble, but Kubek, recalling it in 2007, thought it was a clot of dirt that had been dislodged by a base runner—and shot over the shortstop's glove, striking him flush in the Adam's apple.

In one of the most dramatic scenes in World Series history, millions of television viewers gasped as Kubek lay on the ground, clutching his throat and struggling to breathe. Virdon reached first and Cimoli slid into second. Richardson called time and the Yankees swarmed around their stricken shortstop. "Give him room! Give him room!" Stengel shouted. Kubek recalled, "I wanted to stay in the game, but Gus Mauch, our trainer, said 'No dice.'" Joe DeMaestri came in to play short. As they carried Kubek off the field, he had a piece of advice for Casey. The Pirates were in a bunting situation, and Bobby Shantz was perhaps the best fielding pitcher in the majors. Shantz, Kubek told Stengel, should stay in the game.

Good advice, but the Pirates didn't bunt. Dick Groat, the league's batting champion and future MVP, slapped a grounder by Clete Boyer at third, and the Pirates were down by two, 7–5. The next batter, Bob Hannon did bunt, moving Virdon and Groat to third and second. Rocky Nelson flied out without getting the run home, and the Yankees were still up by two with two outs and the tying runs on base. Coates should have gotten the third when Roberto Clemente chopped a grounder to Skowron at first, but when he turned to flip the ball to Coates there was no one there. No adequate reason has ever been offered for Coates's failure to cover, but the play was nearly as important as the double play ball that hit Kubek in the throat.

Casey elected to have Coates pitch to Hal Smith, who was recorded as the Pirates' "defensive" catcher; Smokey Burgess was the hitter but Smith could hit, too. Coates did, carefully—but not quite carefully enough. On a full count he threw a fastball, and Smith hit it over the left-field fence. Coates, in frustration, threw his glove high in the air, but not higher than the fans at Forbes Field were jumping. Ralph Terry came in and got Don Hoak to fly out.

Pittsburgh, now leading 9–7, needed just three more outs to win their first World Series in thirty-five years, their first since what seemed like the stone age of 1925. Bob Friend had been a reliable starter for the Pirates all season long, but in this, his third Series appearance, he was once again ineffective. In the ninth, Richardson and Dale Long opened with singles, and Harvey Haddix, in for Friend, forced Maris to pop up. Mantle, with the game on the line, cracked a single to score Richardson and make the score 9–8. Gil McDougald became the potential tying score when he pinch-ran for Long at third base.

The crowd held its breath as Yogi Berra, the man Danny Murtaugh said the Pirates least wanted to see in this situation, came to the plate—it was exactly the scene Pirates fans had been dreading. Berra got nearly all of Haddix's pitch, smashing a hard one-hopper down the right-field line. "When I saw it," said Turley, "I figured that's the game. McDougald scores to tie it, and Mantle with his speed might make it, even with Clemente's arm in right field." But first baseman Rocky Nelson snagged the ball on one hop and stepped on first base to retire Yogi. Mantle, lunging desperately under Nelson's glove, dived back to first, while McDougald scored from third. In two critical situations in the sixth and ninth, Yogi had hit a three-run homer to give the Yankees the lead and a near extra-base hit that at least tied the game. Skowron then grounded to Groat to force Mantle at second, ending the rally.

With the game tied at nine and Ralph Terry on the mound, Bill Mazeroski led off Pittsburgh's half of the ninth. "Mazeroski beat out a bunt in the second inning, popped to short and grounded to short into a double play," Mel Allen told NBC viewers. "Ralph Terry on the mound. Sudden death now, last of the ninth, 9 to 9." Terry's first pitch, a slider, tailed high for ball one. Johnny Blanchard, the Yankees' third-string catcher, cautioned him to get his pitches down. The next pitch was lower, belt high. Mazeroski swung and connected. "There's a drive into deep left field," Allen shouted to millions watching on TV. "Look out now! That ball is going, going, *gone!*" Berra, in left field, drifted back toward the high, ivy-covered wall. He then began to retreat, back, away from the wall; he thought the ball might ricochet off the top for a play at second base. He took one glance up and decided to keep on going, tucking his glove under his arm and trotting to the Yankee clubhouse as berserk Pirates fans swarmed out onto the field.

The Yankees did not take the loss well. They had outhit the Pirates by a whopping 82 points and had outscored them 55–27. They had won Games Two, Three, and Six by a total of 38 runs and had hit ten home runs to Pittsburgh's four. They should have known from past experience that this alone was not enough to guarantee World Series superiority; in fact, all it really indicated was Pittsburgh's weakness in left-handed pitching, which the Yankees pounded unmercifully. In the three Yankee routs, Pirates manager Danny Murtaugh quickly decided to concede the game and not waste his best pitchers, which is why the Yankees' run totals had little meaning. The Pirates won Games Four and Seven by one run, Game One by two runs, and Game Five by five runs; they had pitching when they needed it. Moreover, the Yankees committed eight errors to Pittsburgh's four. The ground ball that nearly killed Tony Kubek was not an error, but it might be called fate, or luck—and we all recall what Branch Rickey said about luck. Aside from Ford—who was masterful, striking out eight and walking just two in pitching two complete game shutouts—the Yankees could scarcely find a pitcher who distinguished himself. Ditmar, who had led the team in wins and starter's ERA during the season, was dreadful, recording only five outs in his two starts, losing both games, and finishing with an ERA of 21 runs per nine innings. (He would, of course, be gone before the 1961 season began.)

To a man, the Yankees were stunned at the defeat. Mantle, now a ten-year veteran, wept inconsolably in the clubhouse; he was so distraught he was saying out loud that he thought the Yankees were going to trade him. Berra said things he should not have: "We were the better team. That dirty, lousy infield beat us. What an excuse for a major league ballpark. We didn't lose this one, it was taken away from us." Yogi apparently forgot that the Pirates had beaten them in Games Four and Five at Yankee Stadium and that in the latter the Yankees had made two errors in their own infield.

STENGEL KNEW HE was gone. He staggered around the clubhouse like a ghost. Still trying to manage the Yankees, he put his hand on Ralph Terry's shoulder and asked him what had happened on the last pitch. Terry told him he had tried to keep the ball low. Well, Casey told him, as long as you tried to keep the ball low, I'll sleep at night.

Aside from outscoring the Pirates by 28 runs, a big reason the players took the loss so hard was because they all knew it was the end of an era. The rumors had been rife for some time that Casey would be out as manager even if the Yankees won the Series; the realization that this was Casey's last game was harder to take because they lost. Few of them actually liked Stengel, and all of them at one time or another had chafed under his relentless nagging and prodding, but no one could deny that Casey knew baseball. In twelve seasons, he had won ten pennants and seven World Series. Yes, the front office had given him the best horses to race, but surely that was God's way of evening up for all those years with inferior clubs where he practically had to pull the horses himself. Despite all Casey's questionable decisions—should Ford have been the stasrter for Game One? should Casey have gone with Stafford instead of Turley in Game Seven?—the team knew they were the ones who had lost the World Series. Or, as Yogi later said upon reflection, "We made too many wrong mistakes."

The biggest question was whether or not Ford should have started Game One so he could have been available for three World Series starts. When Casey told him that he wanted to "save" him to pitch the first game at Yankee Stadium, Whitey was "really ticked off. It was the only time I ever got mad at Casey . . . The way I was pitching, I know I could have beaten the Pirates three times, and we would have been world champs again."[48] Whitey was so upset that on the plane ride back to New York he refused to talk to his manager. But who knew that Ford was going to pitch two shutouts, especially one on the road, which he had never done in World Series play before? Still, it was hard to understand Stengel's logic. If he wanted Ford to start Game Three only because it was the first game at Yankee Stadium, why wouldn't Game Four have done just as well? If he slotted Ford for the fourth game in New York, he could have used him in the first game at Pittsburgh as well as the seventh, if there was one.

Bob Turley, who was eventually given the seventh game start, says, "I never blamed Casey for starting Art instead of Whitey in that first game. I thought the problem was that he didn't have Ryne Duren in to pitch the ninth inning." Turley pinpointed the Yankees real problem: Duren had pitched well enough—two games, four innings, one run—but Casey had lost confidence in him during the season when he ran up an ERA of 4.96; in contrast, he had been nearly unhittable in 1959 with a 1.87 ERA. "I should have been in that game," Duren said years later. "Everyone else was. In 1972, I was sitting with Casey at an Old Timer's Day game in Los Angeles, and he congratulated me on conquering my addiction and praised me for working so well with problem kids. He said, 'You know the biggest mistake I made in the 1960 World Series? I brought that right-hander in the eighth inning.' He meant Jim Coates . . . 'I should have brought you in instead.' "[49]

Casey went with Coates. His other option, screwball pitching Luis Arroyo, had been terrific during the regular season, winning five games and saving seven, but Casey soured on him when he had given up two hits in a key situation in Game Five, which the Yankees lost 5–2. No one knew that the following season Arroyo would be the best reliever in baseball. Turley adds, "It's not second-guessing to say that Arroyo should have been in there to pitch to Hal Smith. We all thought he was a fine reliever. Even though he was a leftie, with that screwball he was very effective against right-handers. He was a much better choice than Coates, and we all knew it at the time. Casey was a great manager, but it was evident by the choices he made during the Series that he was losing it."

In retrospect, the best solution to the Yankees bullpen problems seems obvious in light of the way the game has changed over the last few decades. At the annual World Series broadcast at the Yogi Berra Museum and Learning Center in 2006, Berra was asked by a fan why Stengel didn't take Whitey Ford out of Game Six when the Yankees were up 8–0 after six innings, or even when the Yankees were leading 10–0 after batting in the seventh. That way Ford might have been available for an emergency situation should it arise in Game Seven. After all, the fan said, the Arizona Diamondbacks had used a similar strategy against the Yankees in 2001 when Randy Johnson, with Arizona leading 15–2 in the seventh, was relieved so he could rest and possibly pitch in relief if needed in Game Seven. The decision to rest Johnson probably saved the Series for the Diamondbacks: he got four crucial outs in the eighth and ninth innings of Game Seven, and the Diamondbacks took the Series.

"Who knows?" Yogi replied. "We didn't think like that. That wasn't the way the game was played then." No one wants to second guess Bill Mazeroski out of his moment of baseball immortality, but it's worth noting that the potential double play ball that struck Kubek in the throat hurt the Yankees in more ways than one. If Kubek had not been out of the game, he would have been in left field in the ninth inning with DeMaestri at short and Yogi Berra behind the plate. And, with all due respect to Blanchard, how many Yankees fans wouldn't have taken their chances with Yogi Berra behind the plate?

———

THE MORNING AFTER the Yankees returned to New York, Webb phoned Stengel and said he wanted to see him at his suite in the Waldorf-Astoria. When Casey arrived, he found Dan Topping there, too, and was pretty sure what was coming. "There wasn't any big conversation," he noted two years later in his memoirs. "Nobody said 'You did a good job this year. Look at the attendance we had at home and on the road. The team hasn't gotten away from you, except in the eighth and ninth innings of the last World Series game.' And there was also no contract on the table." When you don't see the contract, he said, "you know the ball"—the wrecking ball?—"is there." According to Stengel, the Yankee owners wanted to announce that day that Casey was leaving, but he insisted that it be done in a press conference. Topping presented him with a check for $160,000. He made it sound, Casey thought, "like it was some special gift from the owners. Actually, this was the money that had been set aside for me over the twelve years as my share in the Yankees profit-sharing pension plan. All full-time Yankee employees are in on this except for the ballplayers, who naturally have their own pension program."[50] It was, Stengel shrewdly noted, the success of the teams Casey had managed that made the plan possible and produced the profits that were shared by the owners themselves. The exact share accumulated by Stengel in his twelve seasons was $158,747.25. His "gift" amounted to $1,252.75—or a little over a hundred dollars a season.*

On October 18, five days after the Series was over, the press conference was held at Le Salon Bleu at the Savoy Hotel. It would prove to be one of the more awkward and unflattering moments in Yankee history. Dan Topping announced that Stengel would not be returning as manager because of his "advanced age." That an ashen-faced Casey was standing alongside Topping made the news seem even more mean-spirited. After reading an obviously prepared speech meant to appease the press and fans, Stengel seemed angry. Associated Press baseball editor Joe Reichler asked Casey flat out, were you fired? "You're goddamned right," Casey spit back. "I was fired." Then came a whole litany of things Casey had been saving up all season to complain about: they took away his instructional league, they fired his pitching coach, he was told who to play at shortstop, and several more items he had been waiting to get off his chest. This never happened, he told the assembled writers, when George Weiss was the boss. (That Weiss wasn't in charge would soon be public knowledge.) The nation's newspapers took Stengel's side despite Del Webb's protestations that the Yankees needed to keep Ralph Houk, who had been promoted from coach to manager, in the organization. Had they not made their move then, Webb insisted, they'd have lost Houk to another team. True or not, Webb's argument failed to sway the press and public.

Dan Topping didn't know what else to say so he responded, "Twelve years ago we were ridiculed when we hired Casey Stengel. Today when Casey is leaving, we are ridiculed again." Many weren't sure as to precisely what point Topping was aiming at, but they had to at least acknowledge that his statement was correct. For his part, Casey simply added, "I'll never make the mistake of being seventy again."[51]

Two weeks later, on November 2, at a press conference which, like

---

*Of course, neither Stengel nor anyone else in the Yankees organization acknowledged that one of the reasons the profits were so high for executives was that they had kept salaries—at least relative to the Yankees' revenue flow—so low.

Stengel's was held at the Savoy Hotel, writers were treated to an astonishing sight: George Weiss burst into tears. He was announcing his "retirement," though as Casey dryly noted, "The age program also caught up to Mr. Weiss, who is several years younger than I am."[52] At a private party afterward, Weiss apologized to several writers for never getting close enough for them to really know him; his job had just been too time consuming. According to Leonard Koppett, "Some of us looked at each other sideways: *he* regretted that we had never gotten to know *him*." All of them knew of the cold-blooded manner in which Allie Reynolds, Vic Raschi, Phil Rizzuto, and others had been treated. Weiss was red-eyed, but none of the newspapermen at his party were.

Some of Casey's players—Phil Rizzuto, for instance—also failed to shed tears at the news that the Stengel era was over. Phil never stopped suggesting that Stengel was overrated, that with the talent the Yankees had, they would have won just as many games without him. Rizzuto's best friend and Stengel's assistant manager did not agree. "Old Casey really knew how to handle a ball club," said Yogi a year later, "and never better than when you're in trouble. Now that he has left the Yankees, people will begin to realize how much he meant to us."[53]

Chapter Nine

Manage Who?
(1961–1964)

You can observe a lot by watching.

—YOGI BERRA

YOGI ONCE OBSERVED that 1961 "wasn't the fifties anymore. It was like that famous Bob Dylan song about the times changing. President Kennedy was like a symbol of the young taking over for the old. The country seemed a little more charged up."[1]

The post-Stengel Yankees seemed less like a well-run family business and more like the corporation that would soon own them. Stengel had helped give the Yankees a folksy and personal public face; the new manager, Ralph Houk, had the personality, as former Yankees pitcher Jim Bouton says, "of a regional sales manager."

Ralph Houk had been the Yankees bullpen catcher, more or less taking Charlie Silvera's place after 1956. A former Marine, he was a tough disciplinarian, but much more open and emotional with the players than Casey—he wasn't shy about giving someone a slap on the back and saying "good play" and "good game," something Stengel almost never did. He was more of a players' manager than Stengel, though cold and corporate when dealing with the press, often with a cigar clenched between his teeth. The Yankee owners and the new GM, Roy Hamey, understood that some of Stengel's criticisms of the two seasons that failed to produce a championship were on the mark, and the Yankee preseason instructional school was resumed—no sense in not taking advantage of Yogi Berra's experience.

But the players quickly learned that baseball under Houk was going to be radically different. The first change was that they would no longer be a platoon team; Houk was a set-lineup kind of guy, and he had the frontline talent to make a set lineup work. (Except in left field, where he could find no suitable single player, so Berra alternated with the right-handed-hitting Hector Lopez.) Elston Howard, it was understood, would be the number one catcher. Clete Boyer, who wasn't much of a hitter but was as great as Baltimore's Brooks Robinson, was given the third base job.

There was another big change: Houk went with a four-man, not a five-man rotation. The biggest beneficiary was Ford, who had been just 28–19 in the previous two seasons but was once again recognized as one of the best starting pitchers in baseball. Not that he hadn't been that under Stengel, it was just harder to notice how good Ford was because he had fewer starts and therefore fewer wins. (Many of those wins, though, were against first-division teams—Stengel would often set up the rotation so that Ford would have to pitch more games against the Yankees' tougher opponents.) Whitey had won 133 games and lost 50 for a superb won-lost percentage of .693, though in none of those seasons did Ford win as many as 20 games; in four years after Stengel, from 1961 to 1964, he *averaged* over 20 wins per season for an almost inhuman won-lost percentage of .769. Under Stengel, Ford only once had more than 30 starts, in 1955, when he began 33 games; after Stengel, Ford *averaged* slightly more than 37 starts a year.° But after Stengel, he wasn't expected to finish as many. In 1961, for instance, the Yankees had the best relief pitcher in the game, screwballing Luis Arroyo, who won 15 games and saved 29 more. Arroyo finished so many of Ford's games that Yankee fans joked, "Ford and Arroyo are pitching tonight."† The new arrangement was fine with Whitey. "I never liked waiting four days before it was my turn to pitch," he said. "I found it boring. I enjoyed pitching. I didn't like watching."²

Like Ford, Elston Howard flourished under Houk, coming into his own as the best catcher in baseball. In 1961 he challenged for the batting title for most of the year, finishing at .348, 26 points higher than Yogi's highest average (and also 34 points higher than Howard's second-highest average).

°ESPN's Rob Neyer suggested to me in an email that while the extra starts gave Ford more opportunities for wins, they may also have shortened his career. Perhaps, but under Stengel's system it would have taken Ford at least five seasons to win as many games as he won in four seasons with Houk. On the other hand, Neyer points out that under Stengel's system Ford might have had another three or four effective seasons.

†At the Cy Young Award Dinner, Ford announced that he couldn't finish his speech; Arroyo came in from the wings to close it out.

In 1963, he hit 28 home runs and became the American League's first black MVP. But he was thirty-four years old that season and had only one more good season, 1964, before his performance fell off sharply. On another team, Howard probably would have been a Hall of Fame catcher, particularly for a team whose home park didn't have a cavernous left-center-field area which swallowed up most of his long flies. Yankee Stadium, with its short, friendly right-field porch, was suited for left-handed pull hitters like Berra, but the right-handed Howard hit just 53 home runs in all his seasons in the Bronx compared to 113 home runs in other AL ballparks.

Was Ellie as great, or at least potentially as great, a catcher as Yogi? It's a good question, one which Yankee players who knew them both argued over the years. Bobby Shantz, who worked for many seasons with both of them, thought "Elston was a pitcher's best friend. He got more strikes for his pitcher than any other catcher I saw. When the ball hit his glove, it didn't move, his glove stayed right there. Most catchers give a little. The umpires can tell the difference between great ones and not-so-greats. They give them the call." Whitey Ford wouldn't choose between the two: "They were both great catchers with different styles. You would throw the ball to Elston and hear a big crack when he caught it. I would tell Yogi 'Get closer like Elston,' but Yogi was afraid of getting hit. I would get so mad at Yogi. Elston had a better arm, but Yogi was quicker getting out from behind the plate. Both called great games; I hardly ever shook them off."[3]

Ryne Duren, the fireballing reliever, told one interviewer that "Howard was the best catcher" he ever threw to, and "Yogi was the worst." Howard blocked everything in the dirt, he explained, and his glove didn't move. Yogi's glove would always move, Duren insisted. He was a poor target, and he didn't have Howard's arm. "One day I said to Howard, 'Ellie, you're so much better than Yogi. Suppose you catch me. Let's go tell the Old Man.'" After making his case to Stengel, Casey, according to Duren, said, "I know all that. But who's going to tell Mr. Berra?" Duren said he went to Yogi and explained his reasons. " 'I don't give a damn,' Yogi said. 'Make the switch. I don't like to catch you, either.' How about that! Who ran that club any-way? You had to get his permission to make the switch."[4] But that, of course, is how the situation should have been handled. Most teams didn't have the luxury of two first-rate catchers; in the rare situations where two men could do the job, pitchers would often make a deal to work with their favorite. In any event, Duren's statements are difficult to reconcile with the facts. When his primary catcher was Berra in 1958 and 1959, Duren's

ERA was 2.01 and 1.87, respectively; in 1960 and 1961, when he was mostly caught by Howard, his ERA was 4.96 and 5.40.

Jim Bouton suggests that choosing between Berra and Howard "isn't an entirely fair question. By the time most guys got a chance to work with them both, Yogi was a little past his peak after a decade of catching 120 games a year. He was older than Ellie and more banged up. I didn't work with Yogi much. He was 37 when I arrived [1962], and I thought he was pretty damned good then. Ellie was better, of course, but he was four years younger, and that's a lot for a catcher. Was Howard as good at 37 as Yogi? I don't know. I'd have to say that they were both great, and anyone who worked with either one of them was privileged."

Don Larsen says,

I worked mostly with Yogi, of course, and Elston was just becoming a great catcher in the late fifties. I think even then, though, Yogi got out of the box quicker. I mean, people thought he really slowed down around 1959, and I suppose he did. But when he had to move, he could get out of the box even quicker than Elston. I would say there were two differences. Elston made the hard plays look easy, and Yogi made the hard plays look hard. But, really, they could both make the same plays, so what did it matter?

There's one more thing, though. The most important thing for a catcher is his pitch calling. Howard was good when I worked with him, and I heard he got even better after I left the Yankees. But Yogi was the greatest pitch caller I ever saw.

For what it's worth, in his 2002 book *Win Shares*, Bill James did a career study of fielders at all positions using a brilliant system too complex to go into here. (The reader who wants more information is urged to seek out the book, which contains the most detailed study to date of fielders.) Berra, for his career, gets an "A" defensively, as do Roy Campanella, Mickey Cochrane, and Bill Dickey. Howard is graded an A–, as is Johnny Bench.

―――――

ON A WEST COAST road trip to play the Los Angeles Angels in June of 1961, Hollywood finally beckoned. Maris, Mantle, and Berra were hired to play themselves in the Cary Grant–Doris Day romantic comedy *That Touch of Mink*. Seated in the dugout at Wrigley Field, the Angels' home park in LA, Doris Day hotly disputes an umpire's call, and the ump, in a blatant violation of major league baseball rules, comes over to confront her. Mantle is swiftly ejected for disagreeing with the ump; so is Maris. Berra then agrees with the ump's call, to which the ump responds, "I don't like sarcasm, Berra. You're out of the game."

"It wasn't one of the great scenes in Hollywood," Yogi said. "Let's put it that way. But it was fun."[5] The scene, of course, was pure fiction, and not merely because Cary Grant and Doris Day are sitting in the Yankees dugout. No umpire who ever lived accused Yogi Berra of sarcasm.

Two years later, in 1963, Yogi did a solo. The producers of the hugely popular daytime soap opera *General Hospital* were Yankee and Yogi fans and asked him if he'd like to do a guest appearance. Yogi said sure. The pay was ridiculous—around $150—but all his kids and the rest of his family back in St. Louis and everywhere else would get to see him acting. It would be easy, the producers told him, you won't have any lines. But when he got there, they gave him something to read; he did it well and wound up with a speaking part. It was perhaps the most unlikely casting television has ever seen: Yogi Berra played a brain surgeon.

———

THE YANKEES WERE hoping for a rematch with the Pittsburgh Pirates in 1961, as they had with the Brooklyn Dodgers in 1956 and the Milwaukee Braves in 1958, but in those days, the Lord gaveth, and the Yankees tooketh away. The Pirates were never in the NL pennant race in 1961, finishing sixth, 18 games behind the Cincinnati Reds, while the Yankees fielded one of the greatest powerhouses in franchise history, winning 109 games and hitting an all-time record 240 home runs. One of Yogi's fears was being a hanger-on, a veteran who stayed around just to collect a paycheck without making a substantial contribution to the team. He didn't have to worry about that; in 1961 he played in 119 games (87 in left field) and batted .271 with 22 home runs (5 of which came after the sixth inning, and all 5 in close games). No one accused him of being a Gold Glover in left, but at age thirty-six and after nearly 1,700 games behind the plate, he did surprisingly well as an outfielder, finishing with a .988 fielding percentage, eleven points higher than the league norm. The stars of the team, of course, were Mickey Mantle and Roger Maris, whose twin assault on Babe Ruth's season record of 60 home runs helped distract Americans from an escalating Cold War, hitting 114 home runs between them. They also distracted the press from the fact that Howard, who hit .348, would have been MVP in a normal season. The Yankees were so good that they overwhelmed the Reds in the World Series in five games almost without Mantle, who was kept out of all but two games with injuries. Yogi hit a home run in Game Two, his last ever in a World Series.

For the 1961 Yankees, Yogi was a combination of mascot, good luck charm, and a walking piece of team history—one still capable of hitting a ball into the right-field seats in the late innings of a close game. It was a great way to play out a career. Yogi's presence in the clubhouse reduced tension—particularly for Maris, whose hair was falling out from the pressure. And Yogi wasn't the only Berra who helped relieve pressure in the Yankee clubhouse. In one game during his 1961 home run chase, Mantle struck out three times and dropped a fly ball in a Yankee loss. Little Timmy Berra, ten years old, walked up to Mantle's locker and told him that he stunk. Mantle, who had been famous for assaulting watercoolers after striking out in his early days, stared down at him and burst out laughing.

―――――

ON NOVEMBER 7, Pietro passed away at St. Mary's Hospital in St. Louis. He was seventy-six and died almost half a century after arriving at Ellis Island. Because his death occurred during baseball's off-season, few in the press noted the passing of Yogi's father, which was fine with Yogi. "Pleasing your parents," Yogi once said, "is a good way to grow up." Larry had displeased his father when he told him he wanted to quit school and play "a bum's game," but that had long been forgotten. Pietro never got to see his son play in a World Series game in person, but he saw him play dozens of times on TV. "My dad never told me," he related years later, "but I think he was happier to see me on TV in his home with some of his friends than watching in person in New York."[6]

―――――

THE BIG NEWS for New York baseball fans who didn't care about the Yankees was that there would be a new National League team in New York in the 1962 season. Just prior to the first game of the 1961 World Series, it was announced that Casey Stengel would be the first manager of the New York Mets. Yogi bumped into Casey before the first game against Cincinnati. How long, Yogi asked, did he think he'd be managing his new team? Stengel wasn't sure. Stick around, Yogi told him, and maybe I'll come over and help you out. Casey told him he couldn't wait that long, that Yogi would probably be with the Yankees till retirement.

The joshing, of course, was all in good spirits, but Yogi had begun to think more seriously of managing, seriously enough to consider taking a minor league job. The 1962 season had been his worst as a player in the major leagues (a .224 batting average with just 10 home runs). For the first time in thirteen years, he wasn't voted on the All-Star team—though Houk very sensibly added him to the squad for the second All-Star game at Wrigley Field in Chicago. What would an All-Star game be without Yogi Berra?

Yogi uncharacteristically spent most of the year on the bench, trying for a change to watch the games through a manager's eyes and noting how Ralph Houk handled the Yankees' mix of veterans and young players. The Yankees again won the World Series, beating the Willie Mays–Orlando Cepeda–Juan Marichal Giants in seven exciting games, but it was the least satisfying ring of Yogi's career. ("I was kind of an afterthought," he felt.)[7] For Yogi, there was little drama in the season except for the final game of the Series in San Francisco. The night before the game, Berra, Mantle, Ford, Clete Boyer, and Ralph Terry were playing poker in Mantle's hotel room. Yogi was reputed to be the best poker player on the team, but Terry beat him. Terry was ecstatic; if he beat Yogi, he told everyone, it had to be an omen. The next day, with two outs in the ninth, the Yankees leading 1–0, Matty Alou on third, and Willie Mays, the potential winning run, at second, Terry got a chance to make amends for allowing Mazeroski's home run two years earlier. Willie McCovey hit a hard liner to Bobby Richardson at second, and the Yankees had won their second World Series in a row, Yogi's tenth. Yogi may have lost a poker game, but Berra's Luck had struck again.

In January of 1963, before spring training, the Yankees offered Yogi a new deal, a job as a player-coach. He had to take a pay cut, down to $45,000, but that was more than just about any part-time player and certainly more than any coach was making.

———

THE NASHVILLE BANNER'S Fred Russell liked to tell this story. Yogi made an appearance at a sports banquet in Houston in the winter of 1963. As he was leaving, some locals approached him with a program they asked him to autograph. At the same time, an old baseball pal called out to him from across the room. "Wait a minute," he told his friend, "I've got to sign this first. These people came all the way from Texas."

———

"THE YANKEES," Billy Martin once noted, "were more interested in Yogi's movie reviews than what they saw in the papers. I mean Mickey,

Whitey, and Bobby Brown and even Joe D. would ask Yogi what to see. If Yogi says it's a good movie, it's a good movie."[8]

Berra, more than most ballplayers, maintained friendships with writers. Roger Kahn, regarded by his colleagues as the most intellectual of sports journalists, often sought out Berra's companionship for films. After a day game with the Minnesota Twins in 1963, he invited Yogi to go with him to see Federico Fellini's two-hour-and-twenty-minute phantasmagorical semiautobiographical 8½. "When we came out," said Kahn, "my head was spinning. It was like a multi-ringed circus of the mind. I was dazzled and a little shaken, and I wasn't sure exactly how I felt. We walked about half a block, and I finally said to Yogi, 'Well, Yog, what did you think?' Berra shrugged and gave a two-word review: 'Too long.' " In her 1965 collection of reviews, Pauline Kael wrote, "It's a deluxe glorification of creative crisis, visually interesting (the dark and light contrasts are extraordinary magical). But in some essential way, conventional-minded." When I read Kael's review to Kahn he laughed and said, "They're on the same page, aren't they?"

A few years later, the *New York Daily News'* Vic Ziegel invited Yogi to go with him to see the Audrey Hepburn–Albert Finney sophisticated romantic comedy, *Two for the Road*, about a couple working out the problems in their tumultuous marriage through a series of long car trips. "What did you think, Yogi?" Ziegel asked after the movie. "I don't know," Berra responded. "They got in the car, they got out of the car. They got in the car, they got out of the car."

———

THE 1963 SEASON was something of a comeback for Berra. He appeared in just 35 games, nearly all behind the plate, but batted .293, his highest average in seven years, and hit eight home runs in just 147 at-bats. Though the Yankees won the AL pennant by 10½ games over the White Sox, they lost four straight to Sandy Koufax and the Dodgers in the World Series, including 1–0 and 2–1 defeats in the last two games in which Jim Bouton and Whitey Ford had allowed just six hits between them. Yogi made only one appearance, as a pinch-hitter; a hard line drive to right field was his last at-bat as a Yankee.

Aside from the Yankees' loss, Yogi felt no sadness. He had spent the entire season with his mind on a new goal. In the spring of 1963, Ralph Houk asked Yogi to join him, Roy Hamey, Del Webb, and Dan Topping for a cruise on Topping's yacht. Once at sea, Hamey told Yogi that he would be retiring at the end of the season and that Ralph Houk would replace him as GM. How, Hamey wanted to know, would he like to manage?

A startled Yogi asked, "Manage who?"

———

MANY THOUGHT THAT the Dodgers victory in the 1963 World Series was a fluke, or at least that the sweep was a fluke. There was probably something to that—the Yankees had, after all, won 104 games that season to the Dodgers' 99. Even if the Yankees had won, though, there would have been an undeniable sense that, even more than in 1960, a time had passed. In 1963, though he would play in four games two years later with the Mets, Yogi Berra ended his career as a professional ballplayer, a career that had begun twenty years before with a modest bonus from the Yankees.

Outside of Yogi Berra's world, John F. Kennedy, the first son of Catholic immigrants to become president, had brought new vigor to the White House—and shortly after the World Series his assassination sent shock waves throughout the country and the world. The civil rights movement and the war in Vietnam, which would break into full force in 1965, were beginning to bring the country to a boiling point. Culturally, Bob Dylan had released his first album the year before; approximately four months after the 1963 World Series was played, the Beatles appeared on *The Ed Sullivan Show*, and Berra's sons were singing songs around their Montclair home that would have been incomprehensible to Yogi and Carmen just a few years earlier. Cassius Clay, the new heavyweight champion, would, within a short time, become Muhammad Ali and symbolize the zeitgeist of his time as no athlete of Yogi's generation possibly could.

A new kind of blatant celebrity worship began to reveal itself in American culture, and the time was soon coming when ballplayers and fans no longer seemed to be part of the same society. Looking back on the 1950s many years later, Mickey Mantle would reflect on a time when "We would wait on the corner of Fifty-ninth Street and Sixth Avenue for the team bus to pick us up for the trip to Brooklyn, during the World Series. By then a lot of people knew my face, and Billy's. But we just stood there and waited and people walked around us, maybe with a glance here and there. I think back to that image of Billy and me standing on the corner of Sixth Avenue, talking, swinging aboard the bus, and nobody troubling us. You couldn't do that today, not in New York, not anywhere."[9]

LATE IN 1963, Casey Stengel visited New York trying to recapture some of the old spirit. He went by Toots Shor's new place on West 52nd. Birdie Tebbetts, who had just become manager of the Cleveland Indians and was in town for a series, walked in, hoping to find someone to make baseball conversation with. "Casey," he recalls, "was sitting in what they called the quiet corner where guys like managers and people like that were seated." Stengel motioned for Tebbetts to come on over.

> Soon Toots came by to insult us for a while, and Casey looked up at Toots and said, "Let me tell you about this feller." And he started describing a play when I was catching for the Red Sox against the Yankees. "And our feller led off with a double and gets over to third and the tall guy hit a lineout to the feller out there with the arm, and he throws bee-line to this here one who just stands there not noticing the ball is going to hit him on the head so the guy coming in from third thinks he don't have to slide, but he does have to slide because this here feller has been faking not caring until the last second when he grabs the ball and tags my guy out with his bush play in front of the whole goddamn world. Smart feller here."
>
> Toots wandered off to insult somebody else . . . Finally I couldn't hold it in any longer and said, "Casey how do you do it?" He looked at me as if he didn't understand. So I said it again. "How do you do it?" And he wrinkled up that ugly face until he figured out what I was asking and said— and the story has been printed, but it hasn't been printed the way it happened—he said, "Birdie, I never play a game without my man in the lineup." Then he waited and took a sip of his bourbon. In the pause, I'm thinking "He's talking about DiMaggio, he's talking about Mantle, he's talking about this guy, and that guy, and suddenly I realize he's talking about Yogi Berra."[10]

IN OCTOBER 1963 when the news was announced that Yogi Berra would be managing the Yankees, much of the nation's sporting press was incredulous. That was because they had not been paying attention. Contrary to Carmen Berra's remarks to *Sport* in 1958, Yogi had been contemplating managing for some time, and rumors were everywhere. On the back cover of Berra's 1961 memoirs, Orioles manager Paul Richards, generally thought by his peers to be the smartest baseball man then in the game, was quoted as saying, "He'd make a fine manager, and why not? He's deadly serious even though he gives the impression of kidding around behind the plate. He's smart . . . Why can't a fellow like him manage?" No reason at all, thought the front offices of the Boston Red Sox, Washington Senators, and Baltimore Orioles, who all put out feelers in Yogi's direction,° and in the September 13, 1963, issue of the *Newark Evening News*, Hy Goldberg predicted correctly that within the next few weeks the Yankees would announce that Ralph Houk would be the new GM and Yogi Berra the new field manager.† Critics of the Yankees' decision maintained that Yogi had no managing experience, which was absurd: he had been watching Houk operate for nearly two seasons, the second as a player-coach, and, more than that, for twelve seasons he had been, as Casey was always happy to remind everyone, the Yankees' "assistant manager." Stengel had learned Yogi all his experience. Better on-the-job training was not to be had.

Berra's problem wasn't lack of experience, it was getting his friends to think of him as a manager instead of a pal. The year before, when Carmen took the Berra boys to visit family in St. Louis, Yogi had thrown a pool party and invited Mantle, Maris, Ford, Bobby Richardson, Tony Kubek, and some of the younger Yankees. A few of them stayed over; it was, Yogi said, "like we were just a bunch of brothers, and they even helped me out with some yard work, too."[11] How do you make your brothers keep curfew?

———

DAN TOPPING WANTED to keep the agreement with Yogi a secret for a whole year, and, amazingly, considering that the Yankees' managerial job was the most visible in baseball, he succeeded.‡ "The way he likes to talk," Carmen Berra told Joe Trimble, "I thought sure he'd say something to let

---

°Berra was flattered by the offers but told reporters that he didn't want to manage a second-division club because "you only have the job for two years, then you get fired."

†Thus helping to sell a ton of newspapers in Old Bridge, New Jersey, for a paper boy named Allen Barra, who ended up winning a Hartland baseball statue of Yogi Berra, which is on my office bookshelf as I write this.

‡Exactly why Yankee management wanted to keep it a secret has never been satisfactorily explained, though it was thought to have something to do with Hamey's difficulty in selling his East Side co-op apartment. Apparently, it was thought that the knowledge that he would be stepping down as GM and presumably leaving New York would bring the price down.

it out. I'm surprised he could keep a thing like that to himself for a whole year."[12] That Yogi did keep it to himself is one way in which he convinced Yankee management that he was serious about the job. On October 22 at the Sheraton Plaza Hotel, where the Yankees held their press conferences, Hamey's retirement and Houk's promotion were announced, but the big story was that Yogi would be managing the Yankees for the 1964 season. Asked about his salary, Berra bluntly replied that he would be taking a cut; Topping, recalled Leonard Koppett, grabbed the microphone and did a spin, saying, " 'Yogi is signing for the same amount that Casey Stengel and Ralph Houk did in their first years as manager.' Which was true, but Casey had signed for $35,000 in 1949! Fourteen years later, they were paying Yogi the same money and making it sound like he should be happy to get it. They were promoting him and giving him a pay cut at the same time."

The contract was for one year. Why, one of the reporters wanted to know, hadn't Yogi asked for a two-year deal? "I want to see if I can manage," he replied. "At the end of the year, if my managing hasn't turned out good, nobody will have to tell me that I've had it. I'll know if I've been good or not."[13]

Though many couldn't get past Berra's early clown image, baseball vets, almost to a man, were on his side. Joe Garagiola, almost as well known as Yogi through his NBC baseball broadcasts, told a national audience, "I see no change now that he's a manager. Yogi was always a leader when we kids . . . He knows how to boss." White Sox manager Al Lopez said, "He has baseball in his blood. He'll manage and do it superbly."[14] Casey Stengel stood up large for Yogi: "He's been studying for many years, calling the pitches and learning the hitters . . . He's familiar with the tactics of the team and the skills of the players. And he's got the same ownership, which is important. He's got no problem like going to a strange league."[15] Stengel hit the ball on the nose: Yogi knew the skills and limitations of the players on the Yankees organization and had been taking mental notes on most of them for at least two years. There was no sense in wasting that knowledge in the minor leagues. If Yogi was going to get his shot, now was the time.

Bill Dickey also gave a vote of confidence as well as a note of caution. "Yogi knows baseball, and he knows himself. The problem he'll face is one of discipline. He'll be managing men who were his teammates for many years. It's a different life. Just how he will handle that, no one can say. It's a very complicated question. But that will be the key to his success, handling that problem."[16]

Many in the press were not so sure, and at the Sheraton Plaza conference kept peppering him with questions about where so-and-so would play and how so-and-so would pitch. "If you ask me a question I don't know," he told them, "I'm not going to answer." He also told them that though he had never managed a professional team, he had picked up a lot in sixteen seasons with the Yankees and that he had been "watching and learning" and that "you can observe a lot by watching."

When he got home later that day, Larry Jr. couldn't believe the news: "*You* the Yankee manager?"

————

THERE WERE A lot of questions about the 1964 Yankees that Yogi did not know the answers to, especially those regarding Mantle's ongoing injury problem (he had played in just 65 games the previous season), Whitey Ford's age (he would be thirty-five that year), Tony Kubek's back (which kept him out of 19 games in 1963 and lowered his batting average to .257), and the lack of reliable relief pitchers. Bill Skowron, the great slugging first baseman, had been dealt to the Dodgers after the 1962 season (and come back to haunt the Yankees in the 1963 World Series), and no one knew whether Joe Pepitone, the irreverent twenty-three-year-old first baseman who had surprised everyone by hitting 27 home runs the year before, would continue to perform at a Skowron-like level. And, in what was potentially the most serious problem of all, Elston Howard was thirty-five, an advanced age for a catcher, and there was no young Elston Howard–type on the horizon, despite Johnny Blanchard's presence, to step in for the second game of doubleheaders.

Though it was not obvious at first, there was in fact little depth at all, surprising since the Yankees had been such powerhouses just a few years before. Jerry Coleman, seven years retired in 1964 and by then a broadcaster, had been thinking that for some time when he visited the Yankees in spring training. Before going to the broadcasting booth, Coleman had worked briefly in the Yankees' player personnel department and had been dismayed to discover, on a trip to a farm team in Nebraska, that there wasn't a single solid, big league prospect on the roster. The team had been cutting back on almost every level. Preseason prognosticators, noting that, despite the World Series loss, the Yankees had won 104 games in 1963 without Mantle in most of them, picked the Yankees to run away with the 1964 pennant. Coleman was not so sure. " 'You know,' he said to his broadcasting partner Red Barber at dinner, 'I don't think the Yankees are going to win it this year.' Barber nodded his head in agreement."[17]

In truth, the front office felt that Berra himself was a question. Though no one said it quite this way, it was felt by the owners that one of Yogi's primary competitors was Casey Stengel, who, by 1963, was manager of a Mets team that drew over a million fans. The Yankees topped that, selling more than 1.3 million tickets, but the Yankees had won 104 games while the Mets had won 51—what would happen, the Yankee brass asked themselves, when the Mets moved, amid the fanfare of a World's Fair on the premises, into their new ballpark, Shea Stadium, in 1964?* Dan Topping thought that Berra's popularity with the press would take some ink away from the daily clubhouse show that Stengel was putting on over at the Polo Grounds. But Topping's support was thin. Del Webb didn't want Yogi at all, but gave in when Houk told him Yogi was "the type of guy I can keep my arm around."[18] Webb was not reassured; Berra flew to California to talk to him in person. Webb told Yogi that he had some misgivings. He thought a manager should have minor league experience, something which made little sense in Berra's case, and that it might be a bad idea for someone to play on a team one year and manage it the next, which did make sense. In any case, Webb told Yogi that he was in his corner and the job was his.

Recalling the 1964 season nearly thirty years later, David Halberstam would conclude, "The truth was that the Yankees had made a serious miscalculation if they hired Berra because he was good with the media. Rather the media was good with him—inventing a cuddly, wise, witty figure who did not, in fact, exist."[19]

Some of the things that Berra did say to writers before the season, though, didn't get much play but, in retrospect, had an eerie prescience: "If we win, they'll say that Mickey Mouse could have managed the club to the pennant. If we lose, they'll say that it's my fault. Maybe I'll quit even if we win."[20]

———

THE 1964 SEASON started bad and got worse. The Yankees lost their first three games, all in extra innings, after a spring in which the team barely hit .200. Jim Bouton, the brash, young right-hander who had won 21 games in 1963 and who looked to be the ace of the Yankees' future, was erratic after missing part of spring training following a nasty contract spat

---

*Their fears were justified: the Mets drew over 1.7 million in their first year in Shea while winning just 53 games; the Yankees won 99 and pulled in a little more than 1.3 million. It was the third straight year Yankee attendance declined after the 1.7 million plus of 1961, fueled by the Mantle-Maris home run race.

with Ralph Houk. Both Mantle and Maris pulled up lame in the first couple of weeks, then Tom Tresh, the switch-hitting young slugger who had hit 45 home runs in his first two seasons, pulled a hamstring. So, early in the season, Berra was faced with the loss of his entire starting outfield. Johnny Blanchard, who had been the third-string catcher on the 1961 championship team, was pressed into service as an outfielder. The parallels between the injuries of the 1964 team and Casey Stengel's 1949 team were striking, but there was one distinct difference: in 1949, the Yankees had sufficient bench strength to overcome misfortune. In 1964, they did not. They were able to win the pennant mostly because Elston Howard avoided injury and Mantle, who was hurting all season, played through his.

The starting pitching, though, looked good through the first month. Ford looked like his old self, Bouton came around (he would lead the team in wins with 18, one more than Ford), and a twenty-three-year-old southpaw named Al Downing, the Yankees' first African-American pitcher, was striking out an average of nearly one batter per inning. Then, this too looked as if it might fall apart. Bouton suffered a muscle pull in his right arm, and the high-kicking Downing strained a back muscle. Berra's relief pitchers began grousing about overwork, particularly being made to warm up in games they never got to pitch in. Players began to knock on Houk's door to complain about their manager; the general manager, said one Yankee historian, "listened patiently—too patiently."[21] From the other side of Houk's door, the relief corps could be heard complaining the loudest.

———

ON JUNE 16, Berra took a night off from the Yankee pressure cooker and did a guest appearance on CBS's popular panel show, *What's My Line?* Even with the panelists blindfolded and with Yogi using a high-pitched voice, it wasn't too hard to figure out that the mystery guest was Yogi Berra. They figured it out so quick, in fact, that host John Daly was stuck with a couple of minutes to fill. Carmen was brought out from backstage and introduced as "Yogi's lovely bride."

CBS and Daly were bombarded with indignant calls and letters over the next few days. Appalled viewers, when they saw Carmen, thought Yogi had left his wife and the mother of his three sons for a younger woman.

———

THE YANKEES WENT to Chicago to play the first-place White Sox on August 17 in what looked like a crucial four-game series; they lost all four to give them a 5–10 record over the previous 15 games, and it looked like, if not the end, at least the beginning of the end of the season. The team then left Comiskey Park for the ride to O'Hare Airport, and by the time they reached Boston for a series with the Red Sox, news of what happened on the bus trip dominated the nation's sports pages. The Harmonica Incident, as it was called, became such a part of Yankees lore that even stories about where the harmonica came from became legion. According to Joe Trimble, Tony Kubek and twenty-five-year-old utility infielder Phil Linz had bought themselves harmonicas and a third for Bobby Richardson so they could practice hymns from the *Billy Graham Hymn Book*.[22] Tom Tresh and Phil Linz tell the story with a little less Billy Graham. In an interview with Yankee historian Richard Lally, Tresh, an amateur musician who played guitar and harmonica, had his new harmonica appropriated by Kubek, and before the Yankees left Chicago, Tresh took him to Marshall Field's department store to buy one of his own. On their way out of the store, they bumped into Linz coming in. They told him about their harmonicas, and Linz wanted in. He hadn't gone there thinking about music: "Jim Bouton and I loved hanging out in department stores because, well, it was a great place to pick up girls. You talked to them, let them know you were a ballplayer, then saw where it went."[23] If Linz had bumped into a girl he liked before he saw Tresh and Kubek, Yankee history might have been radically different.

Bouton recalls what happened on the bus:

It was hot, we were tied up in Sunday traffic, we'd blown a doubleheader, we'd lost four or five in a row, we were struggling for a pennant and tempers were short. Linz was sitting beside me, stewing because he hadn't played, and all of a sudden he whipped out a harmonica he'd bought that morning and started playing "Mary Had A Little Lamb." The reason he played "Mary Had A Little Lamb" was that it was the only song he knew how to play. He really played very respectfully and quietly, and if "Mary Had A Little Lamb" can sound like a dirge, it did.

Yogi, who was sitting in the front of the bus, stood up and said "Knock it off."

Legend has it that Linz wasn't sure what Berra said, so he turned to Mickey Mantle and asked, "What did he say?"

"He said play it louder," Mantle explained.

Linz didn't believe that. On the other hand, he didn't stop. In a minute, Yogi was in the back of the bus, breathing heavily and demanding that Linz shove that thing up his ass. "You do it," Linz said, flipping the harmonica at him. Yogi swatted at it with his hand and it hit Pepitone in the knee. He was up doing his act, called '*Oooohh*, you hurt my little knee." Pretty soon everybody was laughing, even if you're not supposed to laugh after losing, especially a doubleheader. And that was really all of it, except that I should point out that in the middle of it all [Frank] Crosetti stood up and in his squeaky voice screamed that this was the worst thing he'd ever seen in his entire career with the Yankees.[24]

Mantle's version was a little different. After losing the doubleheader,

the bus ride from Comiskey Park to O'Hare Airport was a quiet one. Linz, who was in the back of the bus, pulled out a harmonica he was learning to play and softly tooted "Mary Had A Little Lamb." Berra turned around and shouted toward the back, "Shove that thing up your ass!"

Linz didn't hear him, so he asked me what the manager had said. I told him, "He said, if you're going to play that thing, play it faster."

Which Phil did. Now Berra stormed to the back of the bus and knocked the harmonica out of his hand. The instrument hit Joe Pepitone on the knee, and Pepi let out a yelp in mock pain. Soon everybody but Yogi was laughing.

After Berra returned to his seat, I retrieved the harmonica and said to Whitey, who was sitting across the aisle, "It looks like I'm going to be managing this club pretty soon. You can be my third-base coach. And here's what we'll do. One toot, that's a bunt. Two toots, that's a hit and run."[25]

Linz's story is a little different than Bouton's. The harmonica "was one of those Marine Band–type harmonicas with a song sheet I was playing by the numbers. Mary Had A Little Lamb. Very basic. Yogi was hot. He yelled 'Shove that thing up your ass.' I didn't hear what he said. I asked Mickey, who was seated across the aisle from me 'What did he say?' 'Play it louder,' Mick said. Everything happened so quickly. But I played it again and I played it louder." If Linz didn't believe Mantle that Yogi said to play it louder, one wonders why he played it louder. Linz admitted to being "resentful." "They [the White Sox] had pitched lefties, and I was a right-handed hitter who had a ten-game hitting streak going, and I always played well against the White Sox. But Yogi had put Boyer at third and benched me." So it must be assumed that Linz was in a bad mood, and that he played the harmonica louder just to irritate his manager. Then, "Yogi charged me. I stood up on the seat and threw the harmonica at him. He threw it back at me. It hit Joe Pepitone, who was seated nearby. He started rolling on the floor, like he was half dead. That didn't make things any better. 'What are you yelling at me for?' I yelled at Yogi. 'I give one hundred per cent.' After about five minutes I finally sat down."[26]

The reason Yogi was yelling—though no one seems to have understood it at the time and indeed seemed not to understand it decades later—was that the Yankees were playing terribly and he felt his job was on the line. There were several different levels of Yankee sensibility clashing in this one incident: Berra and Crosetti, the old-schoolers, who had joined the team before Stengel, when a DiMaggio-type dignity was the appropriate attitude following losses; the Stengel-era veterans, Mantle and Ford, who had always chafed at Casey's attempts at discipline; and the young, irreverent, post-Stengel players—Bouton, Linz, and Pepitone—to whom the solemnity of the old Alch Vankoog, particularly after a loss, was a source of amusement. Pepitone was simply being Pepitone, but Linz was being a brat. He provoked his manager and undermined his authority in front of the team, not over what might have been a legitimate point—that Yogi hadn't started him that day against the White Sox—but over something as ridiculous as a children's nursery song.

The real culprits, though, were not Linz and Pepitone but Mantle and Ford, who should have known better and shown some maturity and leadership in supporting their friend and manager. Berra had thought enough of his batterymate to ask him to be the Yankees pitching coach; Ford did not act like a coach on the occasion of the harmonica incident. According to Whitey, when Mantle said, "He said to play it a little louder," he was playing "the agitator." Yogi lost his temper when he heard Linz playing the harmonica the *second* time: "He got out of his seat, came back, and said, 'Stick that harmonica up your ass.' " The one thing that all accounts agree on is what Yogi said, but Bouton and Ford placing it after Linz played the harmonica a second time makes more sense. Ford also adds what Linz did not, that Yogi "was yelling at Linz about not caring if we won or lost."[27] It's doubtful that Linz actually felt that way, but from Yogi's perspective he wasn't acting as if he did.*

It never seems to have occurred to Ford, or Mantle, that they might have defused the entire incident by putting a hand on someone's shoulder

---

*Whitey claims to have picked the harmonica up off the floor and kept it: "I still have that harmonica."

and asking them to cool it. Mantle seemed to feel that by egging Linz on, he had actually helped clear the air. "I'm not trying to brag," he recounted to Mickey Herskowitz, "but in a way, unintentionally, I may have turned the team around for Yogi . . . It may have been a coincidence, but from then on the players seemed to have more respect for Berra. They had seen his temper and believed he had drawn a line. We played some of our best ball the rest of the season." He also added, "Yogi had named Ford as pitching coach, and we were the team's senior citizens, but what the heck, we still broke a few curfews."[28] What the heck.

Mantle helped create the legend that the Yankees did a sharp turnaround after the harmonica incident, so it must have been a good thing. But in fact, the Yankees lost their next two games and three of their next six. They then won three out of four against the Red Sox at Yankee Stadium before losing two of three to the lowly Angels in Los Angeles. So the Yankee malaise continued for some time after Mary had a little lamb. Not until early September did the team seem to come together. "The most interesting thing about 'the harmonica incident,' " says Jim Bouton, "is the way the press portrayed it. Stuff like that happens in just about every season, and when it does, players have pretty much forgotten about it by the next day. That was really the way it was with most of us on the bus. We had a few laughs about it, and that was that. But then we got to Boston, and every newspaper story we saw said that Yogi was losing control of the team. But he didn't lose control of the team, and we weren't falling apart like everyone said. We just went through a bad stretch. Then we won something like 18 out of 23 games,* and the same writers who used the harmonica incident as an example of our falling apart then started saying that it was some kind of catalyst. Man, every time I hear that, I laugh. Pennants aren't won by things like that except in sportswriters' fantasies."

The late-season surge was stimulated by a twenty-two-year-old starter, Mel Stottlemyre, who won nine of twelve decisions, and the newly acquired hard-throwing right-hander, Pedro Ramos, who saved eight games down the stretch. (The Cuban-born Ramos had grown up idolizing Yogi, partly because he thought Berra was a Spanish name.) He was so thrilled to play for Yogi and the Yankees that he voluntarily gave up his trademark five-gallon Stetson hat so he would blend in with the rest of the team. "Yogi don't tell me not to wear my hat," he told reporters, "but I

---

*Actually, they won 23 of 29 from August 29 against the Red Sox through September 30 against Detroit.

want to be nice. I don't want to break no rules." He did not, however, give up his embroidered boots, black cowboy pants, and black cowboy shirt with shining mother-of-pearl buttons.[29]

Another reason for the Yankees' turnaround was Mickey Mantle, who ended up hitting .303 with 35 home runs and 111 RBIs in a down year for hitters. "I wanted to be healthy for him," Mantle later said about Yogi. "I wanted to have a good year for him."[30] It would be Mickey's last great season.

Yet one more factor anchored all these: Berra's patience and his belief that the Yankees would come back even when times were worst. Presaging his 1973 slogan, he repeatedly told them, "The world ain't come to an end yet." Though Hal Reniff and other relievers would later criticize his methods, the Yankee bullpen was remarkably strong all season. (Peter Golenbock noted that over the summer, when the relievers were bitching the loudest, they didn't notice the bullpen had a 20–7 record with 15 saves.)

Still, "the harmonica incident" was exactly the kind of publicity that Topping and Webb did not want as they were preparing to officially announce the big sale of the team to CBS—a deal which was finalized about the time the Yankees arrived in Boston after the White Sox series.* Yogi had absorbed the lesson of the Copa fallout seven years earlier: if you involve the team in negative publicity, you must be fined, whether or not you've done anything wrong. According to Linz, after they left Chicago for Boston, he immediately apologized to Yogi; they shook hands, hugged, and all was forgotten. But Berra told him, " 'Phil, with all the writers there, I have to fine you. How much do you think it should be?' 'You're the manager,' Linz replied." Yogi suggested $250, and Linz said okay; he knew he had been wrong to show up his manager.

"We were friends after that," Linz says. "The most ironic thing about all this is that Yogi and I always got along before and after the harmonica thing."[31] Actually, that was the second-most ironic thing. The first was that the Hohner Harmonica Company paid Linz $5,000 to endorse their product. When the Yankees started winning again, the whole thing was looked back on with a chuckle; Joe Pepitone told Linz he should have carried a piano on the bus, he'd have gotten a bigger endorsement. When Berra and

---

*The news of the deal had leaked as early as August 8, when American League president Joe Cronin had wired the offices of the other nine AL clubs asking if they would approve of the sale. (Seven approvals were needed to clear the deal.)

Linz were together on the Mets in 1967, they posed for comic publicity pictures: Linz pretended to toot on his harmonica as a grinning Yogi stood by with his fingers in his ears.

———

ON OCTOBER 3, the next to the last day of the season, the Yankees clinched the American League pennant with an 8–3 win over the Indians at Yankee Stadium, finishing one game ahead of the White Sox and two ahead of the Orioles. The headline on *The New York Times* sports page the following day was concise and accurate: "Berra Vindicated as Tactician, after Bumpy Road to the Pennant." The *Daily News* described the scene: "In the Yankee clubhouse, Yogi was the center of the celebration in the champagne-splattered dressing room. Berra was bathed in the bubbly, most of it poured over his balding pate by Phil Linz, the harmonica rascal who inadvertently helped turn the tide in August."[32] Macy's, beating Gimbel's to the punch, ran an ad in New York and northern New Jersey papers with a picture of an eight ball with the bold caption, "You made it. We always knew you would. Because you can't keep Yogi Berra on a team like the Yanks behind the 8 ball. Congratulations to the New York Yankees and a sigh of relief for Macy's and all of New York." As it turned out, Macy's sigh of relief was premature.

To Berra's delight, the St. Louis Cardinals had edged out the Cincinnati Reds and the late-swooning Philadelphia Phillies for the National League pennant, and at least two of the Series games would be played at Busch Stadium.

Some World Series are great when you watch them, and some look great in the rearview mirror of history. The 1964 World Series looked terrific at the time and has only gotten better, watched on DVD with commentary by the great Harry Caray. The Yankees were the favorites and deserved to be. They were the better team that year, winning 99 games to the Cardinals' 93, out-homering St. Louis during the regular season 162 to 109, and with a better team ERA of 3.15 to the Cardinals' 3.43. The Series went the full seven games: each team won a game by one run and each won a game by five. The Yanks hit more homers, 10 to 5, and four more RBIs, 33 to 29. But little things—the Yankees had racked up nine errors to the Cardinals' four—plus an avalanche of bad luck made the difference.

The Cardinals had two Hall of Famers, Bob Gibson and Lou Brock, with several near-Famers, including outfielder Curt Flood and third baseman Ken Boyer, the National League's MVP that year. The Yankees also had two HOFers in the lineup, Mickey Mantle and Whitey Ford, and in Roger Maris a two-time MVP winner. Some Series have boasted more Hall of Famers, but none has ever featured so many players who have had such an enduring impact on the game both on and off the field. The most controversial would prove to be the Yankees' Jim Bouton, who would win two games in the Series, and in 1970, with his arm damaged and his fastball gone, would change the sports world forever with his candid and acerbic revelations about the game in *Ball Four.*[*]

St. Louis's lineup was dotted with rebels, most notably Curt Flood, whose 1970 lawsuit against Major League Baseball very nearly succeeded in removing the infamous "reserve clause," which bound a player to one team for life. (Flood's suit led to arbitration in disputes between players and owners, and in 1976 an arbitrator declared all players free agents after their contracts had expired.) There were other rebels on players on their roster, and like Flood, they were black. The seemingly invincible Bob Gibson, the Series MVP, had two victories, including the seventh and final game, and first baseman Bill White, later to become the first black American League president, were both unyielding in their views on integration and equal treatment for black ballplayers. (Both were instrumental in pressuring the Cardinals front office out of its segregationist hotel policy when the team was on the road.)

In time, two more Cardinal players from the 1964 team would make an impression, both of them catchers. Starting catcher Tim McCarver would become, by the mid-1980s, the most astute and quoted of baseball announcers, one of the first commentators attuned to racial and political issues that affected baseball. (Tony Kubek, the Yankees shortstop through much of the season but injured and unable to play in the Series, was, for a while, regarded as McCarver's equal as an announcer and analyst.) McCarver's backup, Bob Uecker, would go on to become a staple of late-night talk shows with his humorous and generally self-denigrating stories, as well as a fine character actor in films such as *Major League.*

The 1964 Yankees and Cardinals were a microcosm of the changes that were transforming professional sports. Bouton and Flood, most notably, exemplified the new breed of articulate professional athletes who were skeptical of authority and unafraid to challenge the traditions—both written and unwritten—of America's national pastime. In truth, it seems in ret-

---

[*]By some estimates, *Ball Four,* which has never been out of print in nearly forty years, is the best-selling sports book of all time.

rospect that nearly every member of the two teams had something to say:
Bouton, Berra, Mantle, Ford, Kubek, Pepitone, Flood, McCarver, Gibson,
and Uecker are credited with twenty-two books among them, which makes
them the writingest teams ever to play in the World Series.

The first two games in St. Louis were of course a homecoming for Yogi.
He was bombarded with requests for tickets by old friends and neighbors;
those who couldn't get to the ballpark crowded around radios and televi-
sions in neighborhood taverns and restaurants such as Ruggeri's. As
Garagiola would recall, "During the second game in St. Louis, I remember
looking down at the dugout and it really hit me: Yogi was managing the
Yankees in the World Series and I was broadcasting it for NBC. That we
could be the same two kids who spent so many nights sitting underneath
the lamppost barely seemed possible."[33]

The fairy-tale atmosphere ended abruptly with Game One, in which
Ford, matched against Ray Sadecki, struggled through an erratic five
innings. With the Yankees leading 4–2 in the sixth, Ford was pulled after
getting just one out. Whitey was suffering from a circulatory ailment and
suddenly did not have the strength to grip the ball. Al Downing, not used
to appearing in relief roles, gave up four runs, and the Cardinals took the
first game 9–5. The second game went more the way the Yankees *thought*
the Series should go, with twenty-two-year-old Washington native
Stottlemyre scattering seven hits and the Yankees getting good wood on
Bob Gibson en route to an 8–3 victory. At Yankee Stadium in Game Three,
Jim Bouton pitched a complete-game gem. His opponent was Curt
Simmons, the former Phillies Whiz Kid who didn't get a chance to pitch
against the Yankees in the 1950 Series. It took Simmons fifteen years, but
he finally got his shot and pitched well, before losing in the ninth inning
when Mantle blasted a knuckleball from reliever Barney Schultz into the
upper deck. It now looked as if things would go Yogi's way.

Even without Ford, New York could match St. Louis with three solid
starters, and the Yankees, as they had in the first game, hit Sadecki in
Game Four with authority, scoring three runs in the first while Downing
threw shutout ball through five innings. In the sixth, though, came an
absolutely mystifying moment. Bobby Richardson, regarded by many as
the best defensive infielder in the league, muffed a sure double play when
he couldn't get the ball out of the webbing of his glove; his toss to Phil Linz
was late and wide, loading the bases for Ken Boyer. Boyer jumped on a
Downing fastball and deposited it in the left-field seats. The Cardinals won
4–3 and tied the Series at two games each. In Game Five, Stottlemyre and

Gibson once again stifled the hitters, but St. Louis scored two runs in the fifth after Bobby Richardson, amazingly, committed another miscue on a sure double play ball hit by Curt Flood. (Slow motion replay reveals a bad hop, but nothing that Richardson shouldn't have handled cleanly.) The Yankees scored two in the ninth off a tiring Gibson to tie the game, but in the top of the tenth McCarver walloped a three-run homer off Yogi's favorite reliever, Pete Mikkelsen. An exhausted Gibson held the Yankees in the last of the tenth, and the Cardinals were up three games to two with the Series headed back to St. Louis.

Three times in Yogi's playing career the Yankees had been down 3–2 in a World Series with the final games to be played in their opponent's home park. In 1952 and 1957 they had come back to win; in 1960 they had suffered the most heart-rending defeat of Yogi's career. As he had during the troubled moments of the 1964 pennant race, Berra played calm; the Yankees already knew Busch Stadium and didn't need an extra day of practice. He would keep them home for an extra day of rest, he told beat writers. Though the decision would be second-guessed by the press, Berra's plan was a good one. A cocky Jim Bouton routed the Cardinals and the star-crossed Curt Simmons in Game Six, with Mantle, Maris, and Pepitone all hitting home runs in an 8–3 decision.

It was left to the seventh game and two tired pitchers, Bob Gibson and Mel Stottlemyre, to decide the World Series. The Cardinals started Gibson, though he had pitched ten innings in Game Five three days earlier, because they had no one else; the Yankees went with a rookie because Whitey Ford's arm problem had taken him out of the Series. The two right-handers matched goose eggs for three innings, but in the fourth the Yankees once again suffered defensive lapses, misplaying yet a third double play opportunity and allowing a run on a double steal (actually a failed hit-and-run). The Cardinals scored three more in the fifth to go ahead 6–0, and it looked like the Series was over until Mantle, bearing down, finally caught up with Gibson's fastball and slammed a three-run, opposite-field home run that cut the Cardinals' lead in half. It was a record eighteenth World Series home run—the record he broke was his own—and, sadly, it would be his last. As Mantle rounded the bases, some Cardinal fans picked up a piece of news on their transistor radios: Nikita Khrushchev had given his resignation as premier of the Soviet Union, and Leonid Brezhnev had assumed leadership as general secretary of the Communist Party of the Soviet Union. The fans murmured, but at the moment, more were concerned with whether or not Mantle's home run meant that Gibson was fading. He was. The Cardinals scored one more in the seventh, and the Yankees rallied for two runs in the ninth on solo home runs by Clete Boyer and Phil Linz. Cardinals manager Johnny Keane had no one in his bullpen worth taking a chance on, so Gibson, heroically, finished his own game. The Cardinals won 7–5 and took the Series, best of seven.

Disappointed as Yogi and the Yankees were, no one compared this Series to the 1960 loss to the Pirates. The Yankees' luck had been horrible, beginning with the front office's failure to acquire Pedro Ramos before the September 1 deadline, which made him ineligible for the World Series. Worse, the Yankees' fielding was horrendous throughout the Series, more so even than their nine errors indicated. They made bad throws, missed three sure double plays, and the pitchers had been slow to cover bases. Mantle looked terrible in the field even when he wasn't making errors. On one embarrassing play, he couldn't get to a simple pop-up. In Game Three, with the game tied, he stumbled going after a line drive by Curt Flood; if the ball had gotten past him into the vast Yankee Stadium center field, the speedy Flood would easily have rounded the bases.

The worst piece of luck, though, was Ford's arm trouble in Game One, which resulted not only in a loss but also forced Stottlemyre to go with just two days' rest in the final game. Jim Bouton recalls knowing of Ford's arm problems *before* the Series began. If true, and if Ford's condition had been diagnosed in time, Berra could have reset his rotation to give Bouton, who was outstanding in two starts, a third try—Bob Gibson was the Series MVP with an ERA of 3.00 in three starts, but Bouton had a 1.56 ERA in two games. Or perhaps Stottlemyre, who was effective in his first two starts, could have gotten more rest before the seventh game. At the least, Al Downing would probably not have been rushed into service to relieve in Game One. Many believed that Stengel and the Yankees had lost the 1960 World Series because Casey had not started Whitey Ford in Game One; it now seemed very much as if the Yankees had lost the 1964 World Series *because* Yogi had started Whitey Ford.

On the flight back to New York, Yogi immediately started calculating the odds for next season. He had held the team together despite early-season injuries that recalled 1949, and if not for a couple of missed double plays they would have won it all. Should he ask for a two-year extension on his contract? On the plane, he dropped the question to Betsy Richardson, Bobby's wife. "Why not?" she replied. "If it hadn't been for Bobby, you'd have won the World Series."[34] (It should be mentioned that he set a World Series record with 13 hits and led both teams in batting at .406.) The consensus about Berra's performance was expressed by David Halberstam: "Baseball men compared what he had done in New York to what Gene Mauch"—Yogi's old American Legion foe and regarded by many as the smartest manager in the National League—"had done in Philadelphia and concluded that Berra's lighter touch and willingness to let the players find their own way was the superior job—particularly for a team that had suffered so many injuries."[35] Mauch had blown a sizable lead in September by pressing his players too hard and pitching his aces with two days' rest; Berra had held his team together in a torrid pennant race in large part by refusing to press the panic button.

ON OCTOBER 18, approximately seventy-two hours after the final game of the 1964 World Series, Yogi Berra was playing golf in Ridgewood, New Jersey, with old teammates Joe Collins and Eddie Lopat when he was summoned to the clubhouse phone and asked to meet with management at the team's office in the Bronx. About two hours later, Jerry Coleman was going into Yankee Stadium when he literally bumped into his old teammate, who was on the way out. "Hey, Yog," Coleman beamed, "did they give you one or two years?" "They fired me," Berra answered.

Coleman, Berra, and the rest of the baseball world were stunned; no one had any idea of the duplicitous goings-on in the Yankee front office. There had been rumors, but no one had taken them seriously. All season long, Ralph Houk had been keeping tabs on the situation in St. Louis, where General Manager Bing Devine was at odds with Cardinals owner Gussie Busch. Cardinals Manager Johnny Keane was a close friend of Devine's, so everyone assumed that Houk also knew that at the end of the season Keane would be gone, with Leo Durocher, one of Yogi's boyhood idols with the Gashouse Gang Cardinals, a likely replacement. (Devine was fired in August with the Cardinals in third place.) Or at least that was the scenario Houk envisioned. At almost exactly the same time Yogi was fired, a bizarre situation occurred in St. Louis where, at a press conference, Busch prepared to announce that Keane would be rewarded for his World Series victory with a new contract. Keane was late to his own press conference. When he arrived, he handed the puzzled Busch a letter. It was a formal resignation, which a startled Busch then read to the assembled reporters. After the announcement, someone asked Keane what he would be doing next. "I'm going to do some fishing," he replied.[36] In truth, Keane had already reeled in his fish: it was in the Bronx.

Houk had already offered Keane the job. There was nothing new in a manager, even a successful manager, being fired; no one knew that better than Yogi, who had seen Casey Stengel dismissed supposedly because of old age after winning seven World Series. But the audacity of Houk's and the Yankees' machinations drew double takes from even the cynical veterans of the game, and they haven't lost their power to shock when recalled decades later. According to Joe Trimble, as early as August 12, Houk had been in touch with San Francisco Giants manager Alvin Dark* about managing the Yankees.[37] Had any hard evidence ever surfaced that Houk asked Dark about taking the job, he could have been in deep trouble with AL president Joe Cronin for tampering with another team's employee. Then, in September, Houk sent Mayo Smith from the front office to ask Keane if he would be interested in Berra's job. Keane told Smith yes, which means that he was lying the day after the World Series when he told Busch he wasn't sure he'd be returning to the Cardinals. (Busch set up the press conference assuming that a two-year contract and a hefty raise would settle Keane's mind.) Of course, considering that Keane had managed the entire World Series knowing that if he lost, he probably would not be rehired, he might have been justified. In essence, both managers' jobs depended on the outcome of the Series—the difference was that Keane knew what *his* situation was and Berra did not.

If management was counting on everyone making a good show at the press conference to announce Berra's dismissal as a manager, it didn't happen. Yogi was offered a position as "special field consultant" at, it was rumored, $40,000. No one had the slightest idea what the title meant or what Yogi would be doing; it was created, according to Houk, "because we didn't want to lose Yogi."[38] But Berra had no intention of taking the money

---

*Dark had been a popular player in New York as a three-time All-Star with the Giants and the shortstop on the 1951 pennant winner and the 1954 World Series champion team. Houk had managed against him in 1962 when the Giants took the Yankees to the seventh game before losing. Many, including the *Daily News'* Joe Trimble, believe that Dark would have been the Yankees manager if not for an interview he did in July 1964 with Stan Isaacs of *Newsday* in which he was quoted as saying that the Giants had many Negro and Spanish-speaking players and that "they are just not able to perform up to the level of the white player when it comes to mental alertness." But Dark, who had previously won praise from black leaders for making Willie Mays the team's first black captain, always claimed that he had been misquoted, and in later years, many of his players supported him.

Rumors after Berra was fired indicated that Dark would indeed have been offered the Yankees' job had CBS not been worried about having a Yankee manager surrounded by racial controversy. Given the chance to manage again by the Oakland A's owner, Charlie Finley, Dark earned a World Series ring with the A's in 1974.

and sitting around for the 1965 season pretending to look important. "At least," he told *The New York Times*, "I'll be spending the year at home. Where else can you get a job like this? I don't have to sign in or punch a clock, and the pay is good."[39] Houk told the press that Berra had been let go because he couldn't communicate with his players. It was assumed that this was a reference to the harmonica incident, and Houk was happy with letting it stand at that. After all, every reporter there had written about it and knew about Yogi losing his temper.

The harmonica incident, though, had occurred on August 20, and if Joe Trimble was correct, Houk had contacted Al Dark about replacing Berra on August 12, which means he had already made up his mind. Which means by definition that Topping and Webb had also made up their minds.

At the press conference, Houk was asked by Leonard Koppett who was going to replace Yogi. Houk responded that twelve three men were under consideration. He was asked if Johnny Keane was one of the men being considered. "He's not available, is he?" Houk asked, looking more disingenuous than a California blonde. The reporters in the crowd glanced at each other and shook their heads; a couple of them snickered. Someone shouted out that Keane had resigned from the Cardinals a couple of hours earlier. Houk said that he hadn't known that; in that case he would add Johnny Keane to the list. Stan Isaacs was one of the new breed of inquisitive sportswriters known collectively by the old-timers as "the Chipmunks." In his column the next day, Isaacs wrote that he had created an award for "the number-one charlatan, mountebank, quack, fop, fraud and ass of the sporting panorama."[40] The first winner of the award, he announced, was Ralph Houk.

It would have been interesting to see how they would have handled the situation if the Yankees had won the World Series. In 1960, after all, Casey Stengel was seventy years old and likely to have been fired even if the Yankees had won. But what would the front office have done if Bouton or Ford had been available for Game Seven in 1964 and the Yankees had won it? It's a fascinating question, but ultimately an academic one: in the end, the owners and the GM wanted Berra gone.

Why, exactly? That question has never really been answered, but as Harold Rosenthal wrote in the *New York Herald Tribune*, "Not the players, maybe, but somebody gave Yogi a push."[41]

Webb's misgivings about Yogi's abilities as a manager were known before they offered him the job, but it's doubtful that Yogi would have been fired without Ralph Houk's approval. And all the evidence indicates that Houk decided he wanted a new manager. There *is* something to the charge of Yogi not having the support of the players—or at least all of them. Some rumors had it that Tony Kubek and Bobby Richardson both told Houk they would not play the next season if Berra was the manager. (Precisely what they would have done, short of asking to be traded, isn't known.) Phil Linz, for one, insisted that Kubek and Richardson both went to Houk to complain that Yogi was letting Linz take too much playing time away from Kubek. But twenty-six years later, talking to a Yankee historian, Richardson said, "It was a tough spot for Yogi. One day he was our friend. The next day he was our boss. But I thought Yogi did a great job. He showed a lot of growth in the position. He handled the pitching staff really well, and he led a stretch drive that nipped the White Sox and Al Lopez at the wire." Perhaps, too, Richardson was one of the players who complained about Yogi early in the season and changed his mind at the end.° In any event, Richardson's final verdict was that firing Berra "was the biggest mistake the Yankees ever made."[42]

Bud Daley, who appeared in just 13 games for the Yankees, thought Berra had mishandled him and several other Yankee pitchers. "Yogi was such a good catcher that I thought he'd know pitchers better. He didn't." Hal Reniff, who pitched 41 games in relief with a respectable ERA of 3.13, agreed with Daley, at least to a point: "Yogi shafted me all year long. It was very disappointing." But, he added, "When you're trailing two teams [Baltimore and Chicago] by that much at that stage, you shouldn't win it. I have to give Yogi credit. He did some juggling at the end."[43]

Al Downing enjoyed pitching for Yogi. "He was a pleasure to play for . . . He never said much, but when he did it made sense." What stuck in Downing's mind was "he knew exactly what was going on, and it was your job to give him that strike out or ground ball. You didn't always do it, of course, and if you didn't, he would come out to get the ball and say 'Nice try, kid' or something. You would bust your butt for him."

The real question, says Jim Bouton, is "Why the hell did Ralph Houk leave his door open for people who wanted to complain about Yogi? What kind of GM encourages complaints about his own manager? Houk was a bad GM. He made bad baseball decisions and then he undermined Yogi. It was Yogi who wanted to bring Mel Stottlemyre up and give him a shot,

---

°Perhaps, too, Richardson felt bad about his missed double play opportunities in the World Series. "If I had made one play," he told Dom Forker in *Sweet Seasons*, "we would have won the World Series. Would they have released Yogi then?" (p. 8)

it was Houk who resisted the idea." Clete Boyer had even stronger words on the subject of Houk:

> That stuff he said about Yogi having communication problems with the players was bull shit, and everyone knew it. Who did Yogi have trouble communicating with? Not with me. Not with Ellie Howard, who hit over .300 that year. Not with Mickey or Whitey, who played their hearts out for him. Did Mantle and Ford stay out late a few nights when Yogi was manager? Hell, yes, and they did it when Casey was manager, and you know what? They even did it when Houk was manager.
>
> I'm going to tell you something that should have been said a long time ago, and I mean no disrespect to any of the guys I played with. We weren't the best team in the league in 1964. We got to the World Series and damn near won it because, in the end, Yogi had faith in us and we had faith in him. And you know what else? He did the same thing with the New York Mets in 1973, and no one's going to tell me that they were the best team in the National League that season. Now don't tell me that it's just a coincidence that he did that twice.
>
> The truth was that Houk was jealous of Yogi. Houk had been nothing but a scrub, a backup, for years, and he resented the fact that Yogi was a much greater player and much more popular. And, in my opinion, just as good a manager.

Whether or not Houk was resentful of Berra, their relationship had changed drastically when Yogi was made manager under him. In an interview with *The New York Times* twenty years after Yogi was fired, Carmen Berra said, "I remember it as being a totally frustrating year. We had always been such great friends with Ralph and Betty Houk, but once Yogi became the manager and Ralph the general manager, Ralph no longer was Yogi's friend. Yogi was suddenly working under someone who wasn't available and wasn't communicating with him. He was kind of left out there, hanging alone."[44]

Billy Martin, who loved Yogi, said later, "He was the greatest coach in the world. He knows so much. But he couldn't be a good manager because he wasn't mean enough."[45] Bouton calls Martin's remark "crap. How many pennants did Billy win being so mean? Two? That's what Yogi won by not being mean. Forget that talk of 'not mean enough' or 'lost control of his players.' Yogi was a fine manager."

Let's let Del Webb have the last word. Webb and Berra shared the same physician. A few months before Webb's death in 1974, he asked the doctor if he had seen Yogi lately; he replied that Yogi was in the office every now and then. Webb asked a favor of him: the next time the doctor saw Yogi, would he please "tell Yogi I made an error."[46]

———

DEL WEBB OR Dan Topping or perhaps Ralph Houk made another error. There had been numerous complaints from one of the Yankees' sponsors, Ballantine Beer, that Mel Allen's on-air commentary was often too long and rambling. What they meant, of course, was that Ballantine Beer sales were flagging because the Yankees were losing both attendance and television ratings to the Mets. Even when Allen didn't ramble, he had a tendency toward verbosity which did not lend itself to the new, hipper audience the Yankees were seeking. ("Mel is an articulate man," Jimmy Cannon famously said, "his hellos are longer than the Gettysburg address.") According to Allen's best biographer, Stephen Borelli, Houk regarded Allen "as a friend of all the players." Allen maintained "an amiable working relationship with Houk. When Houk managed the club, Mel would sit on the bench next to him before games and inform out-of-town writers about Yankee happenings. 'I thought he was one of the most secure people in the world,' Houk says." Things began to change when Houk became Topping's right-hand man. Jack Lang, who covered the Yankees for the *Long Island Press* from 1958 through Houk's first season as manager in 1961, thought "Houk was a very forceful figure. When Stengel was gone after 1960, Mel became the biggest name around the Yankees, and Houk didn't like that."[47] According to the *New York Post*'s Maury Allen (no relation to Mel) in 1964, on a road trip to Minnesota, Houk reacted with disgust to a beer-fueled Mel Allen press gathering with some writers. "I knew," Maury Allen would later relate, "that Mel was in trouble. That one incident put him [Houk] over the top. He had to go out of the press room because Mel dominated the scene, and that was really the essence of his [Allen's] leaving the Yankees, why the Yankees decided they didn't want him.[48]

On September 21, sixteen days before the start of the World Series, Topping called Allen and asked him to meet at his Fifth Avenue office. Topping lit cigarette after cigarette while beating around the bush. "He was the most nervous guy I ever saw," Allen said later. Finally, he got to the point: the Yankees weren't going to renew his contract. Topping offered nothing more specific by way of an explanation except that his decision wasn't based on Allen's performance. Later Allen would tell Jack Mann, "Dan never gave me any reasons. He said it had nothing to do with me or my work. He said, 'You know me.' . . . I guess nobody told Yogi anything either."[49]

The next day at Cleveland, Allen told his listeners, "At the end of the year we like to express our appreciation to many people." He began thanking Webb, Topping, and Houk and numerous other people in the Yankees organization, from executives to stadium administrators. Then, the Indians' Luis Tiant interrupted Allen by hitting his first major league home run. Mel Allen told his television audience in his by-now familiar cadence, "There's a drive to deep left field. That ball is going . . . going . . . gone!" No one knew that Allen, who had broadcast more than three thousand games and made his trademark home run call more than five thousand times, had just done it for the last time. When Red Barber took over the fourth inning it was the end of Mel Allen's twenty-five-year career broadcasting games for the New York Yankees.

Over the winter of 1963–1964, Allen had written a book on his years as a broadcaster, *You Can't Beat the Hours*. "Ralph Houk," he had written before his dismissal, "isn't the kind of man you would ever likely disregard or even take lightly."[50] Of all the broadcasters in all the cities in the league, the one the Yankees signed to replace Allen was Joe Garagiola, who joined the Yankees at precisely the time his boyhood pal was moving across town to Queens.

THE 1965 YANKEES, with Johnny Keane managing, tumbled precipitously to sixth place with a 77–85 record, their worst record since finishing 69–85 in 1925. If some thought Berra had lost control of the players through lack of discipline, it was quickly obvious that Keane had lost control of his players through trying to impose too much discipline. In one game, he had the take sign flashed to Mantle, whose jaw almost dropped. "We couldn't f——ing believe it," Clete Boyer said. "Here was Mickey Mantle, the greatest slugger of his generation, and this guy comes in and tries to tell him when he should swing." In the third week of the season, with the Yankees three games below .500, Keane called a meeting and, according to Phil Linz, "started bawling the hell out of us for not hustling. We all thought 'What is it with this guy?' "[51] "He was the wrong guy for the wrong team in the wrong town at the wrong time," says Bouton.

In 1966, the Yankees would finish dead last. Just twenty games into the season, with the Yankees 4–16, Keane was fired. He moved back to Texas and later accepted a scouting job with the Angels. In January of 1967, in Houston, Texas, he died at age fifty-five of a heart attack, one accelerated, many felt, by the stress of the 1965 season.

Houk replaced Keane, but the Yankees still finished 26½ games behind the league-leading Orioles. Apparently, what Houk wanted to do all along was manage: he stayed on nine more seasons, but the Yankees were challengers only once, in 1970, when they finished second in the American League's Eastern Division. (Both leagues had split into two divisions after expansion.) Some of his former players, such as Tony Kubek, would remember him fondly. Others, like Ralph Terry, would not. "He's a bullshitter, and a smoke-blower," Terry told Peter Golenbock, "and he's lied to a lot of players and come up short." After the Yankees were sold to CBS, "Houk sews up a three-year contract, and he's smoking cigars, and the Yankee attendance went to zero. And after he hired Johnny Keane, and Keane couldn't have been worse, then Houk comes back to manage like the Messiah."[52]

By the end of 1964, for the first time since he had signed his first professional contract in November 1942, Yogi Berra was not a Yankee. No one could have possibly predicted that Berra, and not Ralph Houk, would manage another team to the World Series.

———

IN NOVEMBER OF 1964, the Columbia Broadcasting System purchased 80 percent of the Yankee franchise for the astonishing sum of $11,200,000. No one knows precisely how the deal originated (though William S. Paley, president of CBS, and Dan Topping were old country club pals). Topping and Webb each retained a 10 percent share; Webb sold his share in 1965, just before the franchise began its nosedive, and Topping divested his in 1966, presumably for less money than Webb got.

An unnamed writer in the August 21, 1964, issue of *Time* magazine had written, "Topping and Webb had already taken tremendous profits since purchasing the club with Larry MacPhail in 1945 for $2.8 million. Two years later they bought out MacPhail for $2 million, got that back and more when they sold Yankee Stadium and the land under it for $6.5 million in 1953. All the rest was gravy." So why did they sell the team to CBS? "The gravy was getting thinner. Last year's attendance (1,308,920) was the lowest since World War II and may be heading lower this year." Yogi Berra, said the story, "grinned at the news."

It's doubtful that Berra was grinning at the sad fate that had befallen his friends and former teammates. Elston Howard, often playing hurt in 1965, caught just 95 games and batted .233. Roger Maris missed nearly three-quarters of the season and hit only eight home runs. Mantle, playing in pain, hit only .266 with 19 home runs. Whitey Ford thought that "what really happened to us wasn't that we got old but that we got injured all at once, which made us seem older than we were." But then, old teams tend to lose players to injury more often than young ones.

Mel Stottlemyre, twenty-three, blossomed into a full-fledged star, winning 20 games; Whitey Ford, gritting his teeth and trying to work his way back from the previous season's arm trouble, won 16 games. He would pitch for two more seasons and win only four more games. When he called it quits after the 1967 season, twenty years after the Yankees signed him as an untrien, he had won 236 games against 106 losses with a career E.R.A. of 2.75. Those were impressive stats, but they don't begin to tell his whole story. His career ERA was .89 runs per nine innings lower than the league average over that period. His career won-lost percentage of .690 was the highest of any twentieth-century pitcher, yet neither his win total nor his won-lost percentage indicates how tough many of those victories were. It was conceded by everyone that he was the best left-handed pitcher in the American League in the 1950s and second only to Warren Spahn among southpaws in both leagues. Probably he ranked only behind Phillies right-handers Robin Roberts and Spahn as the best pitcher of the decade. Casey Stengel summed him up: "If you had one game to win, and your life depended on it, you'd want him to pitch it."

It was hoped in 1965 that Ford, at thirty-six, would help to anchor the rotation for a few more seasons while Bouton, Stottlemyre, and Downing gave the Yankees the kind of starting pitching that the Big Three had given them in Stengel's first five seasons. It was not to be. The irreverent Bouton, winner of 38 games in the two previous seasons, hurt his arm and lost his fastball forever, and won only 4 games. At the end of 1968, he was sold to the Seattle Pilots in the Pacific Coast League and rejoined the American League the next year when the Pilots became an expansion team. Mel Stottlemyre would be an effective pitcher for ten more seasons, winning 20 or more games three times from 1965 through 1969 despite scanty support. In 1974, after pitching in just 16 games, he tore his rotator cuff and was through. Downing, the young left-hander of whom so much was expected, was effective through the 1967 season, when something snapped in his left elbow. In 1969 the Yankees traded him to Oakland, and in 1971, with the Dodgers, he made a comeback and won 20 games. Unfortunately, he is better remembered for serving up Hank Aaron's 715th home run than for the World Series games he should have won for the Yankees.

Several Yankee regulars were also plagued with bad luck. Tony Kubek never recovered from his back problems; a specialist warned him that one hard collision might result in paralysis, and he retired after the 1965 season. The case of Tom Tresh was even sadder. Cursed with the label of "the next Mickey Mantle" when he came up in 1962, he was in double digits in home runs every season and four times had 20 or more, including a high of 27 in 1966, the year of the Yankees collapse. He was also a Gold Glove–caliber outfielder. In 1967 Tresh hurt his knee in an exhibition game and underwent surgery, but never really recovered; he was traded to Detroit in 1969 then retired.

There were no young hotshots to replace the injured or fading regulars. The old farm system had dried up due to neglect and budget cuts; in fact, it had been drying up for years. The last significant product of the Newark Bears was Berra back in 1946, and the last blue-chipper to come out of the Kansas City minor league franchise was Bill Skowron in 1953. In truth, without the trade pipeline from the major league Kansas City A's, the Yankee dynasty post-1953 might not have been possible. Another blow to Yankee supremacy was the new draft rule, first implemented in 1965, which kept the Yankees from stockpiling talent as they once had. (Teams were limited to signing one prospect per round.)

For all that, the Yankees might have held on to some of their productive veterans, or at least got something more for them when they traded them away. Clete Boyer, for instance, was dealt to the Atlanta Braves after the 1966 season where, in addition to being the best defensive third baseman in the National League, he hit 26 home runs. The oft-injured Roger Maris went to St. Louis in 1967 where, as a platoon player, he helped the Cardinals win the pennant and World Series. Hal Reniff, a useful relief pitcher with an ERA of 3.21 and nine saves in 1966, was cast off to the Mets the next season and then left the game.

The saddest waste of talent, many felt, was the career of Joe Pepitone. In 1964, he hit 28 home runs, drove in 100 runs, and made his second consecutive All-Star team. By 1966, as the Yankees were fading, Pepitone seemed to be peaking, hitting a career high 31 home runs and winning a Gold Glove. After that, nightlife, gambling, and a general inattention to the game eroded his skills. He would occasionally miss games by claiming he was being pursued by vengeful bookies; Houk put up with him for a while because he could not replace his power, but by 1970 the Yankees gave up and sent him to Houston. Within five years he was playing for the Yakult Atoms in Japan. His reputation was so bad that the Japanese press coined a new Americanism: a "Pepitone" meant a goof-off.

The biggest reason, though, for the decline of the Yankees could be traced back to George Weiss himself. Everyone's minor league system was shrinking in the 1950s, but many teams compensated by expanding their scouting to develop black and Latin talent. In 1965, the year after Yogi Berra left, the Yankees were scarcely more integrated than they were during his playing days; the only nonwhite starter on the team, thirty-six-year-old Elston Howard, had been their first black player eleven years earlier.

———

THE PHRASE "Berra's Luck" was not yet known in 1964, but no more spectacular example of it can be found in Yogi Berra's life. Though no one could possibly have known in the wake of the heartbreak and humiliation of the Yankees firing him, Del Webb and Ralph Houk had done him an enormous favor.

On August 9, 1959, Yogi hit his 300th career home run, and Elston Howard won the game with a home run in the eleventh inning. (Charles Hoff, *New York Daily News*)

The catcher who pitched. Berra may have been the most sought-after athlete for endorsement in the 1950s. No one was asked to endorse a wider range of products than Yogi. Here, Kraft Salad Dressing—Italian, of course! (Courtesy of Kraft Foods)

"For me it's got everything... sure makes swell salads!"
says Yogi Berra

star catcher of the New York Yankees, and three-time winner of the American League's Most Valuable Player Award (1955, 1954 and 1951)

Yogi Berra really goes for Kraft's new Italian Dressing

KRAFT Italian dressing

8 FLUID OUNCES

Cat-alysts. Yogi and visionary ad man George Lois changed the face of advertising by putting Berra in a cat food commercial with a talking cat. The cat's voice was supplied by Whitey Ford. When asked if he recognized the voice, Yogi said no. Lois told Yogi it was the Chairman of the Board, to which Yogi replied, "What company?"
(Courtesy of George Lois)

Reunion of the Stags at Yankee Stadium, circa 1960. Joe Garagiola is center front.
(Courtesy of the Yogi Berra Museum and Learning Center)

That touch of Yogi. It's hard to tell Cary Grant from Yogi Berra—Yogi is the one in pinstripes. Here, Cary explains the finer points of strategy to Yogi between takes on the Grant–Doris Day comedy *That Touch of Mink*. Precisely what Cary Grant and Doris Day were doing in the Yankees dugout was never explained.
(Republic Pictures; photographer unknown)

The Berras and family pet in 1964, the year Yogi managed the Yankees. The boys from left to right: Larry, Dale, and Timmy.
(*Life* magazine)

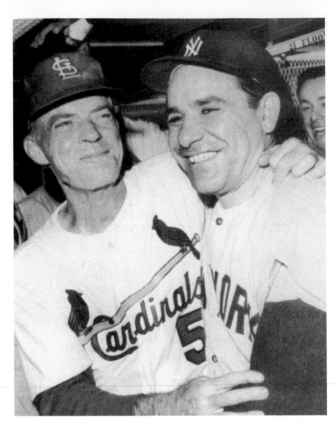

All smiles. Yogi Berra, the biggest winner in baseball history, proves he can be a good loser, congratulating St. Louis manager Johnny Keane after the Cardinals beat the Yankees four games to three in the 1964 World Series. Yogi had no inkling that he had already been fired by the Yankees management and that the front office would choose Keane to replace him.
(Courtesy of the St. Louis Mercantile Library / University of Missouri)

Yogi Berra was one of the few ballplayers of the 1950s who deserved to be on the cover of the Boy Scouts' magazine.
(Courtesy of the Boy Scouts of America)

"There are no second acts in American lives," wrote F. Scott Fitzgerald. But Fitzgerald never saw Casey Stengel and his assistant manager in New York Mets uniforms. April 12, 1965.
(Courtesy of the *New York Daily News*)

I've heard that song before. Years later, in 1967, Yogi and Phil Linz, newly acquired by the New York Mets, reprise "The Harmonica Incident."
(Courtesy of the *New York Daily News*)

Two immortals, Yogi and Willie Mays, celebrate the Mets' division title, 1973. The friction between Berra and Mays was scarcely reported by the New York press.
(Frank Hurley, *New York Daily News*)

"Ya Gotta Believe!" Manager Berra chats with two of his aces, righty Tom Seaver and southpaw Jon Matlack, before the start of the 1973 National League playoffs against Cincinnati's Big Red Machine. Seaver wasn't always as well disposed toward his manager as he was on this day. (Courtesy of the *Houston Post*)

Together again. Whitey Ford, his wife Joan, Yogi, and Mickey Mantle. In 1974 both Ford and Mantle were elected to the Hall of Fame, two years after Yogi was inducted. Whitey's number was retired at a ceremony at Shea Stadium. (Courtesy of the *New York Daily News*)

Pride of the Yankees. Roger Maris, Berra, and Mickey Mantle—representing eight MVP awards among them—meet to celebrate Maris's Pride of The Yankees Award, circa 1978. (Courtesy of the *New York Daily News*)

In the footsteps of Columbus. Yogi as grand marshal in New York's annual Columbus Day Parade, 1978. "I'm glad my father came over." (Courtesy of the Yogi Berra Museum and Learning Center)

Half a century of Yankee catching greats: Bill Dickey (who first caught over 100 games in 1929), Yogi Berra, Elston Howard, and Thurman Munson, who died the year this photo was taken, 1979. (Courtesy of Lou Requina)

Two Hall of Famers, Yogi Berra and Nolan Ryan, pose with the former captain of the Yale baseball team, August 1988. (Courtesy of the *Houston Post*)

Two thumbs up. While coaching the Houston Astros in the late 1980s, Yogi hosted his own movie review show. Always a movie fan, Yogi's favorites include Greer Garson, the Marx Brothers, and Steve McQueen.
(Alphonse Normandia, artist; courtesy of Marty Appel)

Yogi poses with the author's childhood friend Joe Casamento (on left), then vice president of Human Resources at Twin County Grocers, Inc., in Edison, New Jersey, 1994. Berra was promoting Yoo-hoo chocolate-flavored drink, which Casamento drank as a Little Leaguer in Old Bridge, New Jersey.
(Personal collection of Joe Casamente)

Former Montclair neighbors Bruce Willis and Yogi Berra are awarded honorary degrees from Montclair State University in 1996.
(Courtesy of the *Newark Star-Ledger*)

Another great honor: throwing out the first pitch at the dedication of the Yogi Berra Stadium adjacent to the Yogi Berra Museum and Learning Center on the campus of Montclair State University, New Jersey, May 1998. When the Yogi Berra Museum was built, Yogi remarked, "This is a great honor, you usually have to be dead to get your own museum." (Robert Rosamillo, *New York Daily News*)

Berra and the Barras, Allen and Maggie, at the Booktober Fest, Montclair, New Jersey, 1998. (Photograph by Jonelle Barra)

All's well that ends well. Yankees owner George Steinbrenner reconciles with his former manager, January 7, 1999, at the Yogi Berra Museum. They had not spoken in the fourteen years since Berra was fired. "You're late," Yogi chided George, as Steinbrenner pulled up in front of the museum.

(Courtesy of Arthur Krasinsky)

Greatest living Yankee, greatest current Yankee. Yogi and Derek Jeter at the season opener in Japan, March 27, 2004. (Reuters)

Yogi links arms with Dan Keiser, Tony Pasqua, and Bill Chemerka of the Yankee tribute band, Yankee Blue, at a celebration of the fiftieth anniversary of Don Larsen's perfect game. (Linda Pasqua)

More than any other baseball great of his era, Berra has remained in the public eye. (Photograph by Eddie Adams, *Parade* magazine)

Myth American. Ben Gazarra as Yogi Berra in the play *Nobody Don't Like Yogi* by Tom Lysaght, written to celebrate Yogi's return to the Yankees after his much-publicized falling out with owner George Steinbrenner. "I've reworked this myth in terms of a mythical American. What took Odysseus twenty years and the Jews forty, took Yogi Berra fourteen years—to get 'home.' " Performed at the Syracuse Stage in 2003. Yogi was too shy to come and see the play about him. (Photograph by Gary Mornay; courtesy of the Syracuse Stage)

Yogi and Carmen served as grand marshals at the Montclair, New Jersey, Fourth of July Parade, 2005.
(Photograph by Margaret Barra)

Barra snaps Berra. Margaret Barra photographs Yogi greeting an unidentified fan at Watch the World Series with Yogi Night, an annual event at the Yogi Berra Museum and Learning Center. October 24, 2006.
(Photograph by Margaret Barra)

Better than perfect. Fifty-one years after the only perfect game in World Series history, Yogi Berra and Don Larsen relive the moment at a replay of the game at the Yogi Berra Museum and Learning Center.
(Courtesy of the *Newark Star-Ledger*)

Yogi Berra by David Levinthal. This photo of the Danbury Mint statue is part of a series, *Baseball,* in which the New York–based artist used "soft focus to blur the distinction between still life and action shot." This one is a particular favorite of Levinthal's: "I think this image captures both the grace and competitiveness of Yogi."
(Courtesy of David Levinthal)

LAWRENCE PETER BERRA
"YOGI"
NEW YORK, A.L. 1946-1963
NEW YORK, N.L. 1965
PLAYED ON MORE PENNANT-WINNERS (14) AND
WORLD CHAMPIONS (10) THAN ANY PLAYER IN
HISTORY. HAD 358 HOME RUNS AND LIFETIME
.285 BATTING AVERAGE. SET MANY RECORDS
FOR CATCHERS, INCLUDING 148 CONSECUTIVE
GAMES WITHOUT AN ERROR. VOTED A.L. MOST
VALUABLE PLAYER 1951-54-55. MANAGED
YANKEES TO PENNANT IN 1964.

Yogi's plaque in Cooperstown. A Mets fan might object to the omission of the 1973 pennant to which Yogi managed them.
(Courtesy of the National Baseball Hall of Fame)

And thanks for making this book necessary.
(Courtesy of Bill Gallo and the *New York Daily News*)

It's over. September 21, 2008. Yogi stands at home plate in Yankee Stadium for the last time.
(Robert Deutsch, *USA Today*)

PART FOUR

Chapter Ten

It Ain't Over
(1965–1975)

We were overwhelming underdogs.

—YOGI BERRA

"YOGI BERRA A MET? What could be more wonderful?" Joe Trimble wrote less than two weeks after the Yankees fired Berra. "The deposed Yankee manager yesterday received a definite offer from the Mets and will let them know in about 10 days if he will accept the offer—and a reunion with his old boss, Casey Stengel."

"I talked with Yogi on the phone," Mets president George Weiss said.* "He is going to Pinehurst [North Carolina] on a golfing vacation and will think things over." Weiss was up front about his reasons for contacting Yogi: "I would like to have a man like Berra, for his baseball knowledge and [sic] popularity."[1] The extent of the Yankees' public relations disaster soon became evident when former Dodgers and Giants fans, by the tens of thousands, voted to hire Yogi via petitions and bedsheet banners at Shea Stadium. No sooner had Berra hit the golf course at Pinehurst for some R&R than the rumors began to fly. Everyone from Gil Hodges in Washington to Al Lopez in Chicago were said to be seeking his services as a coach. The most likely story was that Red Schoendienst, who had assumed the Cardinals job when Keane left, wanted Yogi in St. Louis.

*Weiss was the Mets team president because his Yankee contract, though he had been released, had not expired. The contract, which ran until 1965, guaranteed him $35,000 a year, but specified that he could not take a job as another team's general manager. Front offices in this period wouldn't give ballplayers multiyear contracts but had no qualms about giving them to baseball executives.

When asked if he had made a commitment to anyone, Berra smiled, driver in hand, and repeated some variation of "I ain't signed nothin' yet." The signing would take place on November 17, 1964, with scores of newsmen from the tristate area clogging the clubhouse at Shea. Berra signed for two years at $40,000 a year,* though it wasn't made clear whether Yogi was joining the team as a coach or player-coach. One thing *was* clear up front: Berra was not being groomed to succeed Stengel, though Casey could not possibly be managing much longer. Yogi merely smiled and said that he hoped to learn much more from Stengel and that he would be available if "a chance to manage comes along."[2]

That afternoon Ralph Houk, preparing the Yankees' new spring camp in Fort Lauderdale (they had just made the move from St. Petersburg) received a wire from the New York Mets: "As per agreement, have signed two-year contract with Mets as coach. Regards and best wishes—Yogi Berra." Houk and Topping wired back: "The Yankees wish Yogi Berra continued success in his new position with the Mets. Yogi has been one of the truly great Yankees and, while we were hoping he would continue with our organization, we can understand his desire to remain in uniform. We are proud to have had Yogi as a Yankee since 1946, and we all join in wishing the Berras the best of luck in the years ahead." The telegram sounded as if Yogi had been a part of Topping's and Houk's tradition, whereas Berra had been with the Yankee organization three years before Topping and had joined the team as a player before Houk.

Though Berra had said at the press conference that he would be available to manage if the chance came along, that it would, oddly, not come for nine seasons has never been sufficiently explained. One possible reason is that the Mets already had managerial candidates in Eddie Stanky and Wes Westrum, who Stengel liked and had already chosen as his successor. It was also likely that everyone knew the Mets, playing like a minor league team totally out of its depth, were awful and were likely to stay awful for quite some time and there wasn't anything Casey or Yogi or any other manager was going to be able to do about it. The first-year Mets in 1962 were an abominable 40–120; the next season Stengel was able to coax 11 more wins out of his collection of castoffs, has-beens, and never-weres. In 1964, while the Yankees were the winningest team in the major leagues, the Mets were still mired in the National League cellar, though Stengel squeezed another two victories out of his club. The Mets could do no bet-

*Though a writer for the *Daily News* reported at the time it was $35,000.

ter until they acquired some genuine talent. In fact, the highlight of their first three seasons was a March 22, 1962, spring training game with the Yankees. Richie Ashburn, the two-time batting champ of the Philadelphia Phillies now playing out his career with the Mets, pinch-hit a single to win the game 4–3. Mets fans happily deluding themselves about what the near future held, jammed into New York bars for victory parties. Toots Shor, phoning Stengel in Florida from his new location on West 52nd, told Casey, "It's like New Year's Eve in this joint."[3]

THERE WOULD BE no more New Year's Eve–like celebrations by Mets fans for years. The 1965 team was actually a game worse than the previous season's. Ron Swoboda, a twenty-one-year-old outfielder of part-Chinese ancestry, led the team in home runs with 19, and Charlie Smith, the third baseman, led in RBIs with only 62—a total Yogi had equaled or exceeded thirteen straight seasons. Lefty Al Jackson and right-hander Jack Fisher paced the Mets with 8 wins each, though, unfortunately, they lost 44 games between them. Shortly after Berra joined the team, Warren Spahn, age forty-four, was signed as a player-coach. He won 363 games in his career, but only 4 were as a Met (he lost 12).

On April 27, the Mets activated Yogi, giving them two future Hall of Fame player-coaches. Yogi was asked what it was like to be a teammate of someone he had played against in two bitterly contested World Series. Did he like Spahn? "I like him better now than I did when I was playing against him," Berra replied.[4] Yogi, though, didn't want to play again. On May 25, after all, he would be forty, and it had been two years since he was an active player. On May 1, against Cincinnati, he pinch-hit and grounded out to first.

Back at Shea three days later against the Phillies, there was a brief flashback to the golden years; Berra caught Al Jackson and got two singles in three trips, scoring the winning run in a 2–1 game. Jackson, a diminutive (his baseball cards listed his weight at around 160 pounds) African-American southpaw from Texas, had the distinction of being Yogi Berra's last major league batterymate. He was dubbed "Little Al" by Mets announcer Bob Murphy. Jackson recalled the game more than twenty years later: "Yogi was famous. I knew all about his Series records, but to tell the truth it didn't mean much. But at the end of the first inning, it was clear to me that he was remarkable . . . Yogi was an asset, a huge asset, to me. He didn't know the National League hitters, but he knew hitters. I went along with him. You had to. You had to listen to him. You looked in for the sign like he had some magic. He did." In the sixth inning, Yogi singled, moved to second, and then scored to put the Mets ahead 2–1, a lead they would, for once, hold on to. When he got back to the dugout, said Jackson, "he looked tired. After he sat down for just moments, he got up and went over to talk to Casey. I was sure he wanted out. I didn't have the nerve to go down and say anything when they were talking. I can't think of anybody on that team walking up when Yogi Berra and Casey Stengel were talking business." Jackson was right: Berra wanted out of the game. When Yogi stepped out of the dugout, Jackson went over to Stengel and told him that he would "just as soon not have to establish rapport with a new catcher this late in the game." He wanted to finish with Berra. Casey stared at him, then talked to Yogi. "Yogi looked at me," said Jackson. Berra was tired and not happy to have to go back into the game, but after all, there are worse things in the world than having a pitcher who wants you.

After the game, Jackson was a guest on Ralph Kiner's radio show, and Kiner told him that Yogi had announced his intention to retire as a player. "We have never talked about that game," Jackson later said.[5] But Berra liked Jackson's account of his final game so much that he later included it in the book of memoirs he wrote with Tom Horton.

Five days later, Berra struck out three times, all on fastballs, to the Milwaukee Braves' Tony Cloninger (who, it should be noted, won 24 games that year with 211 strikeouts). Failing to get a hit was one thing, but striking out was another. Though he never shook the reputation as a wild swinger, Berra was always proud of his ability to make contact. One of George Will's favorite Yogi stories involves a rare whiff: "Once, after striking out swinging at three bad pitches, Yogi Berra had the brass to ask indignantly, 'How can a pitcher that wild stay in the league?' " The answer to Yogi's question, Will wrote, is "such pitchers stay in the major leagues because there are a lot of hitters who, like Berra, do not discipline themselves to swing only at what is in or near the strike zone, and who, unlike Berra, do not have the talent to compensate for their indiscipline."[6]

In 7,555 at-bats in the big leagues, Yogi had struck out a ridiculously low total of just 414 times. (In contrast, Ted Williams, by consensus the greatest hitter of his era, batted 7,706 times and struck out 709 times. Stan Musial, probably the second-greatest hitter, batted 10,972 times with 696 strikeouts. Worse, Yogi had been fanned on fastballs—he just couldn't get the bat around fast enough anymore. And so, on May 9, 1965, in front of a lukewarm crowd of Mets' fans, most of whom had never seen Berra play,

Yogi made his famous sweeping swing with the lasso-like follow-through for the last time. He had gone 2-for-9 over the stretch. Yogi's time as a player was up, and he knew it. A week later, Berra and Stengel had a heart-to-heart, and Yogi, insisting that he no longer felt comfortable as a player, asked to be removed from the active roster.[*]

The day before, at West Point in upstate New York, where the Mets were playing an exhibition game, Stengel slipped and fell outside the locker room and fractured his wrist. He was seventy-four, and looked and felt older. For two months, writers and fans speculated about whether Stengel was physically capable of managing the team. The issue was settled on July 24, the night before the Mets' Old-Timers game. (The participants, of course, were mostly older Dodgers and Giants; Stengel, a writer quipped, was the only Met old enough to qualify.) There was a party at Toots Shor's, and one of two things happened, according to which county you believe. Either Casey slipped in the men's room—which certainly wouldn't have been the first time something like that happened—or he fell getting out of a friend's car. Either way, he fractured his hip and his career was over. Five days later, the Mets made it official. "I got this limp," he told reporters from his hospital bed. "If I can't walk out there to take the pitcher out, I can't manage."[7] On September 2, he hobbled into a pregame ceremony at Shea Stadium where his number 37 was retired. Thus officially ended a career in professional baseball that lasted fifty-five years.

Once again, Yogi was lucky: Wes Westrum got the managerial job. The Mets played worse under Westrum than they had under Casey, losing an unbelievable 48 of their last 67 games. There was only one memorable moment over the last three months of the 1965 season. On August 26, an impish-looking left-hander named Tug McGraw, not quite twenty-one years old, beat Sandy Koufax, 5–2. It was the first time the Mets had ever defeated the best pitcher in the game.

With Westrum managing, they inched up to ninth place in 1966 with a team record 66 wins,[†] but it was a false dawn. In 1967 they were back in last place, and Westrum was fired with eleven games to go. Poor Westrum

[*]In a 1967 game against the Dodgers, the Mets lost their starting catcher, Jerry Grote, to an injury and their backup catcher, John Sullivan, when he was thrown out of the game for arguing pitches. Berra, a grin on his face, said to umpire Ed Sudol, "Let me catch the last two innings." "No chance," said Sudol.

[†]One of those wins, by the way, was credited to Yogi. On April 29, against Pittsburgh, Westrum came down with the flu, and Berra managed the game. It was his first in the National League. Arthur Daley of The New York Times suggested that Yogi's success hastened Westrum's recovery." (April 1, 1966)

must have known he had no chance. About two months before he was fired, he was sitting with Berra at the Hilton Hotel bar in Los Angeles when a fan walked up to Yogi and asked for an autograph. Yogi obliged and handed him back his book. "Is the guy next to you," the fan asked, nodding in Westrum's direction, "anybody?"

A sacrificial lamb, Salty Parker, one of Westrum's coaches, finished out the season. The New York press was puzzled that Berra had not been elevated to the top spot by Mets chairman of the board Donald Grant and Bing Devine, who had become general manager upon George Weiss's retirement. Devine in particular made a show of praising Yogi publicly; at the Parker press conference, he told him, "The Board of Directors loves you and wants you to stay with the Mets as long as your health permits."[8]

The press also seemed puzzled that Berra had to make a public play for the job. In *The New York Times*, Robert Lipsyte wouldn't let the issue go. "At 42," he wrote, "Berra is often pleasant, patient, and concerned with ways to make money for his family. He had enough pride at the end of the 1964 season to leave the Yankee organization rather than being demoted from manager."[9] The implication was that Yogi didn't have enough pride to quit now after being passed over because he had become "too concerned with ways to make money for his family"—as if anyone connected with major league baseball (including sportswriters) wouldn't have similar priorities. In reality, there was no puzzle at all. Though Berra wanted to manage again, he was smart enough to avoid campaigning for a job where there was as yet so little opportunity for success. Other teams had openly expressed their interest in Yogi, but he wanted to stay in New York. "I'm very satisfied," he told Lipsyte. "If I left, y'know, it would have cost me money to move to another city."[10] For their part, Grant and Devine understood that having hired Berra was in part a public relations jab at the Yankees; it would look bad if they made him manager only to fire him if the team continued to lose. There could be someone out there who was just as qualified as Yogi and who might be a safer choice.

There were some glimmers of hope in 1967. Ed Kranepool and Cleon Jones were developing into major league hitters, and a twenty-three-year-old shortstop named Bud Harrelson played as if he wanted to make the position his own. Jerry Grote, though he could not hit at age twenty-four like Yogi probably could have at forty-two, was at least a dependable backstop—Yogi had learned him some of his experience. Best of all, a young fireballer from California named Tom Seaver won 16 games and seemed destined to become the first genuine star in the franchise's history. And in

1968, a man who could make something of such players, Gil Hodges, was named their manager.

———

IF A POLL HAD been taken in 1968 among players, managers, and front office people, Gil Hodges would probably have been named as the most respected man in baseball. A near Hall of Fame first baseman, he was smart, authoritative, and the natural leader that many managers pretend to be. Hodges had paid his dues managing the expansion Washington Senators for five years. (The old Senators had moved to Minnesota and become the Twins.) In his first season, 1963, taking over for Mickey Vernon after 40 games, Hodges won just 42 of 121 games. The next year, though, saw a sharp improvement, 62–100, as did the third, 70–92. By 1967, the Senators amazed the American League by winning 76 games. Hodges knew this was about as far as he could go in Washington. When the Mets opportunity came along, he jumped at a chance to get back to New York in front of all those Brooklyn Dodger fans who still remembered him so fondly. Hodges cleaned house with the Mets coaching staff, retaining only Berra—he knew, liked, and respected Yogi, who, after all, had been in the NL for three seasons and knew its players. Hodges valued Berra's storehouse of knowledge, including the kind of savvy which had helped make Hodges 0-for-21 in the 1952 Series against the Yankees. Three men came over with Hodges: pitching coach Rube Walker, third base coach Eddie Yost, and bullpen coach Joe Pignatano—all men who, like Hodges, had played for or against New York teams and lived in Brooklyn. It was the first time a Mets manager had been allowed to choose his own coaches, and it was a signal that Hodges meant business.

Hodges did not treasure the Mets' image as loveable losers, and instituted the toughest spring camp any of the Mets regulars had ever seen. The front office stopped going with grizzled veterans such as Warren Spahn and Ken Boyer, and started sending some young talent Hodges's way, including a twenty-five-year-old outfielder from Alabama, Tommie Agee, who came over to the Mets in a multiplayer deal, and a twenty-one-year-old flamethrower from Texas named Nolan Ryan who, Berra was happy to tell reporters, threw harder than Allie Reynolds, Vic Raschi, or even Sandy Koufax.

Under Hodges, the Mets began to show some swagger, and Berra was there to apply some polish. When Swoboda altered his batting stance in the mode of his idol, Frank Robinson, Yogi gave him some immortal advice: "If you can't imitate him, don't copy him."[*] The players loved everything about Yogi except, thought outfielder Art Shamsky, his batting practice: Yogi threw much too slow. Shamsky took his complaint to Berra, who told him, "Go complain to a coach."[11]

The 1968 Mets won 73 games, twelve more than the previous year, and finished out of last place, a game ahead of Houston. Jerry Koosman, a twenty-five-year-old left-hander who hadn't won a game the year before, was 19–12 with an ERA of 2.08, Tom Seaver won 16 games for the second straight season with an ERA of 2.20, and Nolan Ryan averaged a strikeout for each of his 134 innings. Cleon Jones hit .297, and behind the plate, Grote still showed no power but hit .282. All the Mets needed, their fans thought, was a little pop at the plate and . . . who knew?

The only bad note came on the final road trip of the year against the Braves in Atlanta. Just before a night game, Hodges tossed some batting practice, but after a while, stopped and walked into the clubhouse, telling Rube Walker that he wasn't feeling well and was going to lie down for a while. The trainer Gus Mauch, yet another former Stengel Yankee now working for the Mets, called for a doctor, who sent Hodges to a nearby hospital; he had suffered a heart attack. It turned out to be a "mild" heart attack, exacerbated by Gil's habit of smoking at least three packs of cigarettes a day. He would be back for the next season.

The year of Woodstock, 1969, was also the year Neil Armstrong walked on the moon. It was the year President Richard Nixon began the program of "Vietnamization," in which the war was supposed to be gradually turned over to the Vietnamese; it was also the year that Nixon escalated the war by bombing Cambodia and Laos. In sports, it was the year that began with Joe Namath and the New York Jets scoring the biggest upset in Super Bowl history with the young American Football League's first victory over the old National League's Baltimore Colts. Baseball and the traditional values it represented seemed to many to be on the wane. Professional football had far surpassed baseball as a TV attraction, and even with the expansion of the major leagues to twenty-four teams, average attendance was down from ten years earlier—in 1969 average attendance was 1,134,600 compared to 1,196,500 in 1959 (for that matter, the average 1959 attendance

---

[*]There are reports that Casey Stengel had actually said this to Berra in a conversation some time around 1960, years before Yogi said it to Swoboda. But Tommy Byrne swore that he remembered Berra saying this sometime during spring training in 1957 to a young left-hander who was trying to imitate Byrne's pickoff move. It's possible that, like so many great minds, Berra and Stengel recycled each other's words of wisdom.

per team was down from 1949). A line from a 1973 movie, *Bang the Drum Slowly*, seemed to express what many in the era were feeling: "Baseball is a dying game." No one in 1969 could know how much new stadiums, free agency, and cable television would revitalize the game. In 1969, baseball did, in the parlance of the times, seem a little less . . . relevant.

Perversely, then, 1969, professional baseball's centennial year, was the year that the New York Mets—100-to-1 long shots to go all the way, according to Las Vegas—picked to stage the most amazing run in the team's, and perhaps all of baseball's, history. And, of course, Yogi Berra was in the middle of it.

The season began with a thud with the Mets losing to the expansion Montreal Expos. It wasn't until early in July that the possibility they were a first-division club began to suggest itself. On July 9, Seaver beat the Cubs 4–0 and came within just two outs of a perfect game. The Mets were now out of three from the division-leading Cubs, after which Chicago manager Leo Durocher, when asked if what the team reporters had just seen were the "real Cubs," replied, no, those were the real Mets. On July 16, at Wrigley Field, the Mets won 9–5 and found themselves, to their own amazement, just 3½ games out of first place. By early August, the possibility of the Mets challenging for the pennant seemed like a dream. The Mets fell 9½ games back, but then Tommie Agee (who proved to be the hitter with the "pop" the Mets were searching for, finishing with 26 home runs), Cleon Jones, and others began to surge. On September 10, the Mets took two from the Cubs at Shea Stadium and, for the first time in their existence, were in first place. They finished with 100 wins—a total that seemed unbelievable at the beginning of the season—and went on to beat the Western Division Champion Atlanta Braves in three straight games. This left only the Baltimore Orioles standing between the Mets and the World Championship.

Berra, back in the World Series five years after being fired from the Yankees, was ecstatic. "I've played, managed, and now will coach in a World Series. I've done it all."[12]

There are supposed to be no upsets in baseball; too many variables, the experts say, for one team to dominate another. But the 1969 World Series comes about as close to an upset as baseball has ever seen. The Mets were good; the Orioles were far better, winning 109 games, hitting 175 home runs to the Mets' 109, scoring 779 runs to the Mets' 632, and even stealing more bases, 82 to New York's 66. The Orioles' slugging average was 63 points higher than the Mets', and their on-base average was 36 points higher. Their fielding average was better, .984 to .980, and they made just

101 errors to the Mets' 122. The Mets' strong suit was their pitching, but the Orioles' team ERA of 2.83 was lower than the Mets' 2.99. New York did have a superstar pitcher, Tom Seaver, who was at his blazing peak, winning 25 and losing just 7 with an ERA of 2.21. But the Orioles had great starters, too, in left-handers Mike Cuellar and Dave McNally, who won 43 games between them, and they had a superstar right-hander of their own, Jim Palmer, who won 18 games and had a won-lost percentage better than Seaver's. The Mets had a great manager, but the Orioles had future Hall of Famer Earl Weaver. In short, there wasn't a single aspect of the game in which the Mets seemed to be superior or even equal to the Orioles.

So, the Orioles won the first game, Cuellar outdueling Seaver 4–1 at Baltimore, which was supposed to happen. The Mets won the next four, and the Series, by a total of 14 runs to 5. Frank Robinson, who had batted .308 with 32 home runs during the season, and Boog Powell, .304 with 37 home runs and 121 RBIs, had a combined zero home runs and one RBI for the Series.

The fifth and final game was the most memorable, and not just because it decided the Series. Trailing 3–0 in the sixth with Cuellar coasting over Koosman, Cleon Jones pulled away from a curveball in the dirt and immediately began yelling that the ball had hit him in the foot. The home plate umpire, Lou DiMuro, ordered Jones back into the batter's box. Berra, in the first base coach's box, howled and came running in toward home plate, pointing at Jones's foot. Since the pitch looked very much as if it *could* have hit Jones, one wonders in retrospect why DiMuro was so quick to dismiss the possibility that the ball might have caromed off his shoe. A possible explanation is that the Orioles appeared to have been shafted on two previous calls, starting with a tenth-inning call in the previous game. With the game tied, the Mets' J. C. Martin attempted to bunt Rod Gaspar from second to third base. The Orioles pitcher, Pete Richert, fielded the ball and threw to first, clipping Martin on the wrist. The ball dribbled toward second base, Gaspar kept right on going around third to home, and Martin, in the words of sportswriter George Vecsey, started " jumping up and down like a sheep in an animated cartoon, and Gaspar landed on home plate and was greeted by a dozen teammates."[13] Leonard Koppett, then writing for *The New York Times*, studied photographs of the play which proved that Martin's feet were both in the baseline, and noted that Rule 6.05(K) specifically states that a runner must stay outside the baseline when a pitcher or catcher is throwing to first base to avoid exactly the kind of play that happened with Richert and Martin.

The next day, Koppett's story appeared, claiming that home plate umpire Shag Crawford had blown the call, that Martin should have been called out for interference, and the game continued from that point. When confronted with the photographic evidence, Commissioner Bowie Kuhn shook his head and told reporters, "I'll have to pursue it." There was, of course, nothing to pursue since Crawford's decision was a judgment call and could not be reversed.

The next controversial call to go against the Orioles occurred in the top of the sixth of Game Five when Frank Robinson was obviously hit by a Koosman pitch and DiMuro simply missed it. Robinson and his manager, Earl Weaver, argued to no avail, but DiMuro must have been told by his colleagues between innings that the pitch certainly looked as if it had hit Robinson.

So, after two important calls had gone against DiMuro, DiMuro may have been hesitant to make a quick call in favor of the Mets. At any rate, Hodges, in his usual style, did not react immediately to the pitch to Jones, but as George Vecsey later wrote in *Joy in Mudville*, came out of the dugout

> plodding toward home plate carrying a baseball in his hand. The ball had skittered into the Met dugout after hitting—or not hitting—Jones on the foot. Now Hodges was carrying a ball.
>
> The manager could have quickly antagonized the umpire with the wrong word or the wrong motion. But Hodges was impassive as he reached home plate. Then, he extended his giant paw, still wrapped around the baseball. "Lou," Hodges said slowly. "The ball hit him."
>
> DiMuro looked up at Hodges. DiMuro was willing to be reasonable. After all, Hodges was being so polite about it, the least DiMuro could do was inspect the ball. And when Hodges plunked the ball into DiMuro's hand, sure enough, there was a smudge of shoe polish. . . .
>
> DiMuro was alone, terribly alone, the hero in history, faced with a momentous decision. The last sound he had heard was the solemn voice of Gil Hodges. The words may still have been ringing in his ears.
>
> "Lou, the ball hit him . . ."[14]

The first words Lou DiMuro heard after Jones's claim were from two of the great bastions of honesty in baseball, Yogi Berra and Gil Hodges. Against them Earl Weaver, perhaps the greatest baiter of umpires the game had ever seen, was powerless.

Jones was awarded first base. Then, with a count of two balls and two strikes, Donn Clendenon hit one over the left-field wall to make it 3–2. In the next inning, Al Weis, who had hit .215 with two home runs during the season, tied the game with his first and last home run ever in Shea Stadium. In the eighth, the Mets got doubles from Jones and Swoboda, and the Orioles came apart, committing two errors that allowed two unearned runs. That completed the scoring.

Mets fans, though, are still convinced that it was the shoe polish play that decided the game, and, incredibly, it was the *second* shoe polish incident in Yogi Berra's career. "I've been in two shoe polish games," he said during a break in the 2005 World Series telecast at the Yogi Berra Museum. "Both times the ball hit a guy named Jones. I won one of those games, and I lost one."*

New York was delirious. No local sporting event—not any World Series won by the Yankees nor the Jets' 1969 Super Bowl victory—had ignited anything like the street celebrations after the Mets' victory.† It wasn't Yogi Berra's show, it was Gil Hodges's, but Yogi was a supporting player. Almost as an afterthought, Leonard Koppett wrote, "No Yankee triumph had ever been sweeter. He was aware he might never have another chance at another one. But neither Yogi nor anyone could imagine at that moment [when he was fired] that five years later he'd be standing in the first-base coaching box at Shea Stadium, a part of the Mets and of a triumph incomparably greater, because of the odds, than any the Yankees had ever won. And I can't help remembering that the Yankees haven't won anything since."[15]

Years later, in Houston, reminiscing with Nolan Ryan about the 1969 World Series, Yogi summed it all up: "We were overwhelming underdogs."

The Mets' World Series victory, while not a fluke, was certainly fluke-*ish*, and the next season the magic was gone, as if 1969 was only a mirage. The next year the Orioles again overpowered the American League, win-

---

*The shoe polish game is an important plot point in the 2000 movie *Frequency*. The story is both absurd and ingenious: a rare atmospheric phenomenon allows a Queens firefighter, played by Dennis Quaid, to communicate with his son (James Caviezel) thirty years in the future via shortwave radio. At first, Quaid's character is justifiably skeptical that he is actually talking to his son in the future. The son convinces his father by describing the shoe polish play before it happens. Since no one could have possibly predicted anything so bizarre, the father believes his son and takes action which saves his wife's life.

†Though Roger Kahn claims it did not exceed the public euphoria across the river in 1955 when the Dodgers finally won the World Series.

ning 108 games, sweeping the Twins in the playoffs, and crushing the Cincinnati Reds four games to one in the Series. The Mets didn't slip back into the second tier, though they were third among the six teams in their division and were never serious contenders.

————

SHORTLY IN OR around 1970, Joe DiMaggio, who was appearing at a memorabilia show in Chicago, hooked up with Yogi for breakfast when the Mets were in town to play the Cubs. Berra glanced at the menu and said, "I only have eggs in Cincinnati." "I didn't ask him why," said DiMaggio, mulling over the remark some years later, "but you can bet he had a good reason."[16]

————

IN 1971 THE New York Mets finished with the identical 83–79 record as the previous year. The Mets still had the pitching, but without a superstar hitter in the batting order, they were stuck in a cycle of near mediocrity. On April 5, 1972, just before the season began, the Mets finally swung a deal to get that hitter, but he arrived too late to help Gil Hodges.

Just three days earlier, on the afternoon of April 2, Gil Hodges and some of his coaches—Rube Walker, Eddie Yost, and Joe Pignatano—were in West Palm Beach and took a day off from spring training for a round of golf. Walking back to their hotel, Hodges collapsed. He was rushed to the nearby Good Samaritan Hospital, where the attending physician pronounced "complete heart arrest." Gil had never given up smoking, contrary to the wishes of his doctor and his wife. When he had boarded the plane for Florida, his wife Joan told him, "Watch the cigarettes." Those were the last words he heard from her.

The Mets, like all the baseball world, went into collective shock, no one more than Berra. Many years later, Yogi would raise eyebrows when he wrote in his memoirs, "If I had to name the best manager I ever saw, I guess I would have to say Gil Hodges."[17]

Most of the players and press had flown home after the players had voted to strike.* Among the writers, only Red Foley of the *New York Daily News* remained behind. At the Mets headquarters at the Ramada Inn,

————

*The first work stoppage in the game's history, a strike by the players, was the result of a unanimous vote to hold out for increased contributions to their pension and medical funds. It wiped out the remainder of the spring exhibition games and postponed the beginning of the season.

Foley heard from the hotel manager that Hodges had been rushed to the hospital; he and Jerry Koosman, who had been hanging around the hotel, jumped in a cab for Good Samaritan and found out the worst. Within a few minutes, Foley phoned Donald Grant and Bob Scheffing and asked if they had given thought to who the new manager would be. The executives acted as if Foley was being insensitive at a time of tragedy, but in fact the season would begin as soon as the strike was over, and the Mets would have to be ready. Despite their denial to Foley, Grant and Scheffing had, of course, already made their decision.

Hodges's funeral in New York seemed like a Who's Who of major league baseball over the previous twenty years—former Dodgers, Giants, and Yankees all mourning together. "Gil's coaches," wrote Red Smith, "sat near the front . . . perhaps all of them shared Yogi's knowledge that he had been selected to move into Gil's office."[18] Berra later said he came to terms with Grant and Scheffing "in less than an hour. I didn't feel right about asking for a two-year contract. Gil's death was hard on me, and I just wanted to help out."[19]

The players had been whipped into shape by Hodges, and Berra maintained his system. The big addition to the team was Rusty Staub, who the Mets had obtained from Montreal for three prospects just three days after Hodges's death. Staub had hit .311 and driven in 97 runs for the Montreal Expos the year before. That and the acquisition of a hotshot twenty-two-year-old left-hander named Jon Matlack (who would win 15 games) should have made New York the division leader. But Agee and Jones had terrible years (.227 and .245, respectively); Grote, missing most of the season with an injury, hit just .210; and Staub, of whom so much was expected, played in only 66 games (though he hit well, .293 with nine home runs). Seaver was brilliant, winning 21 games, but Koosman had his worst season as a Met, winning just 11 games in 23 decisions. With the strike settled, the season began late, April 15, with Seaver shutting out the Pirates 4–0.

After the game, Berra was sitting in his office with his feet on his desk when the phone rang. Yogi picked up the phone and beamed. "Hi 'ya, Casey," he said. "It was easy, just like you said." Stengel had watched the nationally televised game back in Glendale, California, and had called to give Yogi a notebook-full of advice, then repeated it. Afterward, a grinning Yogi told reporters, "He still doesn't let you get in a word."[20]

By the beginning of June, the Mets were leading the Eastern Division by five games—then they lost Staub, third baseman Jim Fregosi, second baseman Ken Boswell, Jones, and Agee, all to injuries. June and July were dismal, with the Mets winning just 23 of 53 games. In September, they recovered and finished strong, but there was no catching the Pirates, who won the East by 13½ games. The Mets, 83–73, finished third in the strike-shortened season. But some fair-minded writers pointed out that Yogi's won-lost percentage of .532 was twenty points better than Hodges's in both the 1970 and 1971 seasons.

The year 1972 was grueling in just about every way possible. Yogi's election to the Hall of Fame was about the only break from the pressure. Almost a month after Hodges's death, John Berra, who had continued to manage the bowling alley and moved to Nutley to be close to Yogi's family in Montclair, died of cancer. There had been great comfort in having his brother so close by, working for the family business, and now he was gone.

A week after John's death, the Mets dominated the sports pages, not for an achievement on the field but by signing a forty-one-year-old outfielder. Willie Mays was the most popular ballplayer in New York baseball history, more popular than Yogi, Mickey Mantle (whom Yankee fans, at times, booed loudly for striking out too much), Joe DiMaggio (who had alienated fans for a while when he held out for more money during the war), Lou Gehrig (who was sometimes booed for not being Babe Ruth), or Babe Ruth (who was booed several times early in his career with the Yankees for boorish behavior on and off the field). For New York fans, Willie Mays was pure love, though he had spent a little more than five full seasons in New York before the Giants went to San Francisco after 1957.

In 1971, when the Giants won the National League Western Division, Mays, the greatest player in the NL and perhaps all of baseball over the previous twenty years, was still a useful player, hitting .271 with 18 home runs and 23 stolen bases. By 1972, though, his skills were badly eroded, and he was able to play in just 69 games with the Mets, batting .267 with eight home runs, 19 RBIs, and just one stolen base. Though Mays had become, some said, an insufferable prima donna by the end of his career, the New York press's affection for him was unlimited. He was a huge pain in the ass, though, to Berra. Indeed, he had been a pain in the ass to his manager in San Francisco, Charlie Fox, who told the *San Francisco Chronicle*'s Glenn Dickey, "They should have traded him five years ago. I'm supposed to be the manager, but I f——ing had to come to him every day and say 'Willie, can you play today?' " In a 1971 column, Dickey wrote,

Mays is certainly the best and most exciting ballplayer of his generation, but he sheds his greatness like a cloak when he leaves the playing field, the Willie Mays myth not to the contrary. You know the myth, created in New York: Mays, the "Say-Hey" Kid, a happy-go-lucky fellow with a kind word for everyone.

Try that on an autograph seeking kid who has been brushed off, a sportswriter who has been cursed, a manager who has tried to exercise authority, a black who has tried to get Mays to speak out against racial inequalities as Hank Aaron, Bill White and Bob Gibson do.

Mays has always had an idolatrous press, but that has not made him cooperative. He talks only to the sycophants and those he thinks can help him. Questions from the others are met with obscenities or silence . . . Giant managers are hardly more fortunate. They know they must give Mays preferential treatment or Willie will become fatigued or beset by one of his mysterious ailments.[21]

Dickey's words, controversial enough in the Bay Area, were completely ignored in New York. Two years later, reflecting on Berra's tribulations with Mays in his book, *The Jock Empire,* Dickey wrote, "As a Met, Mays's behavior toward manager Yogi Berra was the same as that towards the Giant managers. He left the club in spring training without consulting Berra. He was fined upon his return; half of the fine, said one writer, was for leaving, the other half for returning. During the regular season, he was on the disabled list early. When he came off—ironically against the Giants in San Francisco—he spent one game up in the Giants broadcasting booth . . . instead of on the bench with his teammates. The next week, Berra put his name on the lineup card without consulting Willie. Mays not only didn't play, he went home—again without permission."[22]

Tug McGraw would later recall that Mays and Berra "had a tough time as far as the lineup went, and a lot of times Willie didn't want to come to the ballpark at all."[23] By the final month of the season, with the Mets playing well but out of the pennant race, Mays was openly criticizing Yogi for playing him too much—a strange complaint, as Mays batted just 195 times during the season.

Berra soon had another problem that he didn't need. In a game against the Cardinals during the summer slump, Cleon Jones made a lackadaisical play on a pop fly; Yogi benched him for three days, and Jones sulked.

UP IN THE Bronx, Ralph Houk's Yankees were having even a worse time than the Mets. They would finish with four fewer victories, 79 to the

Mets' 83. On July 22 at the Yankees' Old-Timers Day, the team retired the number 8, worn by both Bill Dickey and Yogi Berra. Larry Jr. represented his dad, and Yogi, in a recorded message, thanked Yankee Stadium fans and regretted that he couldn't be there; he was on the West Coast with "my Mets." At the word Mets, the fans began a loud booing. Dickey, chuckling, pointed out to everyone, "Those boos, you know, are for the Mets, not for Yogi."

On August 7, Yogi was given leave to go to Cooperstown to be inducted into the Hall of Fame with Sandy Koufax and Early Wynn. He would have made it sooner had he not had those nine at-bats with the Mets in 1965, as a player must be retired for five full seasons before being eligible for the Hall. In fact, he had missed induction the year before by 28 votes but showed not the slightest bitterness, pointing out that "even Joe DiMaggio didn't make it his first year. But whenever you make it, it's a great thrill." Since Yogi was not insulted by the 1971 snub, we should not be either. Still, a fan is entitled a simple question: Yogi Berra had ten World Series rings, eighteen All-Star selections, three Most Valuable Player awards, pages of World Series records, and the most home runs and RBIs ever at his position. He had caught three no-hitters, one a perfect game in a World Series. How could any baseball writer—anywhere, anytime—have thought Yogi Berra didn't deserve to be in the Hall of Fame?*

———

GEORGE WEISS DIED at the age of seventy-eight on August 13, 1972, at his home in Connecticut. Yogi would later say, "I liked him a lot. Hazel and George Weiss were good friends of ours."[24] There is no known public record of anyone else saying they liked George Weiss.

In the space of four months, Yogi had lost a close friend, a brother, and his former boss, but trying as the 1972 season was, there was reason to hope that 1973 would be much better.

———

*In 1971, Yogi got 242 votes, followed by Early Wynn with 240. The next five were Ralph Kiner (212), Gil Hodges (180), Enos Slaughter (165), Johnny Mize (157), and Pee Wee Reese (127). In 1971, it seemed like just a matter of time till Hodges would get in. All the other five eventually did. In fact, Red Schoendienst (123 votes in 1971), George Kell (105), Phil Rizzuto (92), Bob Lemon (90), Duke Snider (89), Bobby Doerr (78), Nellie Fox (39), and Richie Ashburn (10) have all made it since, but not Gil Hodges, despite the pleas of hundreds of thousands of fans. Such are the vagaries of Hall of Fame voting.

AT HOME, YOGI'S life was storybook. Larry Jr., catching for his high school team in Montclair, was beginning to look like he would be attracting major league scouts. Tim was also a superb baseball player but thought football was more exciting; he starred as a runner and pass catcher at both Montclair High and Seton Hall Prep, and at the University of Massachusetts. In 1974 he was drafted by the Baltimore Colts.* Many thought Dale was the most promising athlete of all and looked to have a future in big league ball.

"I tried," Carmen told the New York press, "to get the boys to take piano lessons to broaden their horizons, but they became athletes despite me."[25]

Around that time, Frank Sinatra was on tour and Larry Berra wanted tickets. He found that all the nearby shows were sold out. "Don't worry," his father told him. "I'll see what I can do." "Who are you going to call?" Larry asked. "I'll call Frank," Yogi said. Larry's jaw dropped. I've been your son all these years, he told his dad, "and I didn't even know you *knew* Frank Sinatra!"[26]

AT THE END of the 1972 season, Yogi Berra was forty-seven, and many of his friends wondered why he wanted to continue managing under such difficult conditions. "1972 was such a strain on him," Phil Rizzuto recalled, "and no one really thought the Mets were going anywhere. I'll tell you, though, Yogi really wanted that World Series ring as a manager."

"Here's a guy," says Joe Garagiola, "who had every reason to stay home in 1973, just enjoy his life, everything he'd built up. Why go back into that New York madhouse again? You've really got to hand it to him, Yogi was always tougher and grittier in his own way, than anyone ever gave him credit for." Berra did go back in 1973, and he produced his masterpiece as a manager.

WILLIE MAYS SHOWED up at spring training—a day late—wearing tape around both knees. He was eager to play, he told attendant writers, "If

---

*In fact, Tim Berra was selected by Colts GM Ernie Accorsi, who, before retiring from the New York Giants in January 2007, was the architect of the team's phenomenal Super Bowl run by drafting, among others, quarterback Eli Manning.

I can do it my way." Berra, wisely, did not take the bait but didn't back down. "I appreciate that Willie isn't 18 years old—he's 42," he told *The New York Times'* Joseph Durso, "but you can't have two sets of rules. I'll have to talk to him tomorrow to see what he can do." Mays chose to communicate with Berra through the press: "I'll explain to Yogi what I'd like to do, and if he doesn't like it, we'll have to go somewhere else."[27] It was obvious that they weren't on the best of terms, but neither player nor manager wanted to start the season with any controversies; both men understood this could well be their last shot in New York.

The Mets' 1973 season started well. They went 12–8 during April, but May saw a dismal 9–14, and by the end of June, the Mets were seven games under .500, 32–39. Maddeningly, the injury bug returned. Essential players Rusty Staub, Jon Matlack, and Jerry Grote missed significant time and, playing hurt when they returned to the lineup, were subpar. At the end of June, Berra walked on the field to relieve a pitcher and heard something he had scarcely heard in twenty-seven seasons in the major leagues: boos. They were scattered, but they could be heard for the simple reason that the fans who weren't booing were silent. Grant issued an ominous vote of confidence: "We have no intention of firing Berra unless [*sic*] the public demands it."[28] That Yogi kept his job was probably because the public *did* demand it; in mid-July, the *New York Post* ran a poll asking readers to vote on who was responsible for the Mets' debacle and who should be fired. More than four thousand responded by mail: Scheffing, the GM, won, with Grant finishing second. Only about six hundred of the four thousand thought Yogi should go. Grant, apparently, was for firing Berra, and would have done it if Scheffing had taken the heat. But Scheffing would have none of it; he had no intention of being remembered as the Mets' Ralph Houk. "If you want to fire Yogi," Scheffing told his boss, "you do it."[29]

By August 15, the Mets were 7½ games from the top of the Eastern Division, and Berra's demise seemed imminent. Everyone, it seemed, had quit on the team except Yogi. "There's lots of time yet," he told a cynical press. "We can still do it . . . all we have to do is put a few good games together."[30]

Words can't win pennants, but they can light sparks. Sometime in late summer, Yogi said, "You're never out of it until you're out of it. It's not over until it's over," or some variation thereof. Later, Yogi would say he was actually quoting Clint Courtney, the much traded catcher from the 1950s—or at least that Courtney had said something like that. Whatever Yogi said, it wound up as "It ain't over till it's over." It was often thought but never so well expressed, and his players seemed to take heart. Around the same time, Tug McGraw first said, "Ya gotta believe!"* The Mets may not have had much hitting, but they had some great slogans.†

One thing Berra believed in was Tug McGraw, and in turn Tug came to believe in Yogi. "Yogi Berra never took a course in child psychology . . . but I remember one thing he did that wasn't too dumb. He got a hold of a clipping that said the Mets were horse shit, and that we were just going through the motions, and he came around to each player and held it up and said, 'See, you're going through the motions.' You might think Yogi just wanted to get us riled up. But I think it went deeper than that." What Yogi was trying to tell his players, McGraw thought, "was that he didn't feel that way."[31]

It wasn't until August 22 that McGraw picked up his first win of the year, but things only got worse. They lost three of the next four, and on August 27, staring at the final month of the season, the Mets were twelve games under .500. And then, suddenly, dramatically, and inexplicably, they turned around. They capped the month of August by sweeping the Padres at Shea; Rusty Staub won the second game with a dramatic grand slammer. In the clubhouse, Koosman shouted, "It's beginning to feel like 1969!"[32] What it was really like, though, was 1964, when Berra's cool calmness and simple faith in his players provided the bedrock for a comeback. With 23 games to go and trailing the division-leading Cardinals by 5½, Berra made a decision: he would go with a four-man rotation down the stretch—Seaver, Matlack, Koosman, and George Stone, who would finish the season with a 12–3 record. By September 10, the Mets had climbed into fourth place, only three games back of St. Louis. By September 17, the fading Cardinals had slipped to third place, and the Mets were 2½ games behind the first-place Pirates—with a huge string of games on the schedule for September 17 through 21, the first two at Three Rivers Stadium

---

*A legend grew up that McGraw said "Ya gotta believe!" to mock a clubhouse speech by Grant. Tug denied this to Maury Allen: "Grant came into the clubhouse for this meeting. He started telling us the front office was behind us, they thought we could still win and we could if we only believed we could. As he was leaving, I was all fired up. I screamed, 'Ya gotta believe!' He thought I was making fun of him; I wasn't. I was just overtaken by the emotion of the moment. Kranepool said to me, 'You better get your ass upstairs and explain it to Grant, or you're gone.' I went up in uniform and told him I was just excited. He seemed to understand." (Allen, *After the Miracle*, p. 40)

†Oddly, "It ain't over till it's over" didn't become common currency outside the Mets' clubhouse until around the time Yogi left the Mets in 1975, though Joe Pignatano, among others, swear that Yogi did say it, or something very close to it, in the dark days of 1973. Some Mets historians think that it took so long to catch on because McGraw's "Ya gotta believe!" was easier to put on signs and tee shirts.

and the last three at Shea. They needed to win three of the five just to cut a single game out of Pittsburgh's lead. When the Pirates wiped them out 10–3 in the first game, the race seemed over.

What happened in the next four games of the Pittsburgh series was more amazing than anything that happened in 1969. In the second game, they went into the ninth inning trailing by three runs, rallied for five, and then watched McGraw record the final out with the winning runs on base. Back home at Shea, McGraw again finished out the game as the Mets won 7–3. The fourth game was a microcosm of the Mets' season: going into New York's half of the eighth, the Pirates were leading 2–1; the Mets tied the score, the Pirates took a one-run lead in their half of the ninth, the Mets tied it in the bottom of the inning, and, in the thirteenth inning the Pirates' Dave Augustine hit a two-run homer to give the Pirates the victory—but wait! Augustine's shot hadn't cleared the top of the fence but bounced back into the glove of an astonished Cleon Jones, who, not lollygagging on this play, whirled and threw to third baseman Wayne Garrett, who in turn fired to catcher Ron Hodges, who tagged the runner, Richie Zisk, out at the plate. The Mets won 4–3 on a Ron Hodges single in the bottom of the thirteenth inning. Now the odds were in the Mets' favor, and Tom Seaver finished the series by scattering five hits in a 10–2 victory. With seven games to play, New York had pulled even at .500 and were in first place in the East.

Three weeks before, McGraw had predicted that the Mets would be the first team ever to be in last place in August and go on to win the division. The Mets won five of their last seven to finish a game ahead of St. Louis. Tug McGraw saved two of those games and helped fulfill his own prediction.

———

IF THE 1969 World Series against the Orioles had looked beforehand like a mismatch, the 1973 National League Championship Series redefined the term. The 1969 Orioles had won nine more games than the 1969 Mets; the 1973 Reds, the Big Red Machine, had won *seventeen* more games than the Mets. Cincinnati had hit 137 home runs to the Mets' 85 and scored 741 runs to the Mets' 608, and the Reds had stolen 148 bases to the Mets' 27. New York had a slim edge in team ERA, 3.26 to 3.40, though Shea Stadium was a much better pitcher's park than Riverfront Stadium. The Reds were heavy favorites, and when a Johnny Bench homer off Tom Seaver in the ninth inning won Game One for Cincinnatti, 2–1, it once again looked like the end of the Mets' season. In the second game, though, Matlack, who had pitched well all year nursed a 1–0 lead into the ninth, watched his teammates blow the game open with four runs, and wound up with a two-hit shutout. Game Three is the one every Mets fan remembers though, oddly enough, for a play that had little to do with the outcome.

With the Mets up 9–2 in the fifth inning, Pete Rose slid hard and wide into Bud Harrelson at second, trying to break up a double play. Rose was just playing good, hard-nosed baseball, but when Harrelson came up pushing and Rose pushed back, the best baseball fight anyone had seen in years broke out. The dugouts and bullpens emptied, and within seconds nearly sixty players and coaches were fighting or wrestling. The Shea Stadium crowd was hysterical, and it soon became apparent that though play had resumed, order had not been restored. Rose, in left field, was bombarded by garbage. He later swore that fans were throwing uneaten chili dogs at him. "Imagine that," he said a few years later, recalling the incident on *The Tonight Show* for Johnny Carson. "They were *buyin'* them just to throw at me." But when an empty whiskey bottle landed just a few feet from him, Rose trotted off the field and into the dugout. Reds manager Sparky Anderson then called the rest of his team off the field.

Luckily for the Mets, their manager had a cooler head than they did. If the game had been suspended, the Mets might have had to forfeit a crucial victory. After a request from league president Chub Feeney, Yogi and Willie Mays, for once in agreement, came out on the field and begged the fans to calm down and let the field be cleaned up. Meanwhile, Rusty Staub, Tom Seaver, and Cleon Jones walked around the foul territory near the fences, exhorting the fans to stop throwing garbage. When the game was finally finished, the Mets found themselves just one win from one of the most improbable pennant victories ever. But in Game Four, Pete Rose galled the crowd in the twelfth inning, winning the game with a solo home run. That left the deciding game right where the Mets wanted it, in the hands of Tom Seaver. Even without Staub, who had bruised his right shoulder while making a great catch in the eleventh inning the day before, New York scored two runs in the first on a single by Ed Kranepool and then broke the game open with four runs in the fifth. They coasted to a 7–2 win and took the NL pennant. Yogi Berra had become just the second manager—Stengel's predecessor, Joe McCarthy, was the first—to win pennants in both leagues.

By the ninth inning, with McGraw on the mound, chaos had erupted at

Shea; the mob, Jack Lang later wrote, "was uncontrollable. The wife of the Reds doctor was almost trampled in the crush. Fearing for the safety of the Cincinnati people, the umpires halted the game and allowed the wives and officials to leave the stands through the visitors' dugout."[33] The barbaric display tarnished what should have been one of the most joyous moments in both Berra's and the Mets' history. In the clubhouse following the game, Yogi seemed more embarrassed than happy.

After the exhausting pennant race and playoff, the Mets could have been forgiven had they regarded the 1973 World Series as an afterthought. They were, after all, facing a team in the defending champion Oakland A's who had scored 758 runs, more even than the Reds, and, led by future Hall of Famers Catfish Hunter and Rollie Fingers, had the best pitching in baseball. Reggie Jackson led Oakland with 117 RBIs, 39 more than the Mets' RBI leader, Rusty Staub.

Playing at Oakland–Alameda County Coliseum, the A's took Game One 2–1 with Ken Holtzman outdueling Jon Matlack. In the second game—to the surprise of the A's and probably the Mets, too—New York scored ten runs to win 10–7, the big hit coming on a twelfth-inning single by Willie Mays, the last big hit of his career. Game Three, at Shea Stadium, was a heartbreaker. The Mets scored two runs in the first inning off Catfish Hunter, but the A's tied it up in the eighth, and in the eleventh, when Jerry Grote, one of the most dependable defensive catchers in the game, dropped a third strike and let Angel Mangual go to first base, Ted Kubiak went to second and then scored the winning run on a single by Bert Campaneris. But dominating pitching performances by Matlack and Koosman gave the Mets the next two games, 6–1 and 2–0. Suddenly, a team with baseball's shallowest talent pool was on the verge of overcoming the team that was, by consensus, the best in baseball.

Yogi chose this time to make one of the most hotly debated decisions ever by a Mets manager. As he had with the rookie Mel Stottlemyre in Game Seven of the 1964 World Series, Berra asked Tom Seaver to pitch on short rest—or rather, he asked him if he thought he could. Seaver looked Yogi and pitching coach Rube Walker in the eye and told them yes. In Game Six, at Oakland, Seaver was touched for solo runs in the first and third innings, both on doubles by Reggie Jackson, but pitched well into the eighth. The Mets, though, never laid a glove on Catfish Hunter, and the A's won 3–1, tying up the Series.

The 1973 New York Mets were just one game from immortality as the David who slew two Goliaths of baseball that year—Cincinnati's Big Red

Machine and the World Champion Oakland A's, both loaded with Hall of Famers. The wonder is that Berra's Mets came so close. The dream came to an abrupt halt early in the seventh and final game of the 1973 World Series. After three terrific postseason efforts with only three runs in just over 23 innings, in the fourth inning Matlack gave up home runs to both Campaneris and Jackson, and the A's won 5–2. But from August 27 till October 21 the Mets were on a tear their fans would never forget.

"Now I'm finally going to relax," Yogi told *The New York Times'* Joe Durso. "I'm finally going to get to see Timmy play football this Saturday."[34] He could not know it at the time, but the 1973 World Series was the high point of Berra's post-playing career. There were great moments ahead, but he would witness them as a supporting player. A World Series ring as a manager would be the only honor in baseball Yogi Berra would be denied.

———

BERRA WAS REWARDED for his great work in 1973 with a two-year contract, but 1974 saw a sad follow-up to a legendary season. Once again, the Mets were plagued with injuries, and Berra's relationship with Seaver, never warm in the first place, began to sour completely. The Mets system was producing practically no first-rate talent and seemed unable to acquire any through trade. Their 71–91 mark was the worst since 1967. The front office, it seemed, was content to bask in the glow of a completely unexpected pennant run the year before and enjoy the boost in ticket sales without investing in the team's future. "Even though the other teams made moves to strengthen themselves," wrote Lang and Simon in their history of the team, "the Mets did not make a single off-season deal. That subsequently appeared to have been a mistake."[35]

The 1975 season got off to a terrible start when Cleon Jones, who had had off-season knee surgery, was left behind in Florida to get into shape while the team left to start the season. A short time later, Jones was arrested by St. Petersburg police for indecent exposure after being discovered nude in a van with a twenty-one-year-old woman who was not his wife. The woman was not a concern of the police, but the drugs in the van were. The Mets fined Jones and ordered him to make a public apology at a press conference with his wife standing beside him. The press was not impressed, and came down harder on Grant for staging the conference than on Jones for his behavior. Jones lasted less than two months into the season. Once again, he stopped hustling and Berra pulled him out of the starting lineup. On July 18 Yogi ordered him off the bench and into left field as a late-inning defensive replacement. Jones refused in full view of the rest of the team; Yogi then ordered him back into the clubhouse. Joe McDonald, who had replaced Scheffing as GM, and Grant knew about Jones's rudeness to his manager, but for four days after the incident, they refused to suspend Jones. According to a Mets historian, "Yogi was adamant. He insisted Jones be suspended and ordered to apologize for his insubordination in front of the entire team. It was a test of Berra's strength as a manager at a time when some players were laughing behind his back at his lack of discipline. On this issue Berra was firm, and he was right. Unfortunately, he did not get the support he deserved."[36]

In the gutsiest decision of his career, Yogi told Grant that he would not back down when Jones did not apologize: the Mets could have Cleon Jones on the team or Yogi Berra managing it, but not both. Grant called Berra's coaches to get them to pressure him. Yogi knew how precarious his situation was and, in essence, understood that he was simply giving Grant, who did not appreciate getting an ultimatum from an employee, an excuse to fire him if the team didn't win. Finally, Mets management had no choice: on July 26, they announced that Jones had been released.

Yogi never understood why he couldn't communicate with Jones. "Some people thought it was racial," he said years later in his memoirs. "It was not . . . I don't mind going into what happened, but I really don't know. I think it probably is that way on most teams and in business, too. Things get started."[*37]

The Mets lost five of their next six games. Against the Pirates, Berra took Seaver out after six innings; Seaver thought he should have been allowed to stay and let reporters know it. On August 5, after losing to the lowly Expos, Yogi was asked to come to Grant's office. He knew why and took the news calmly. First base coach Roy McMillan, a one-time slick-fielding shortstop for Cincinnati, was named as Berra's successor. Grant told the press, "We are trying to salvage something from the season." Actually, the Mets were three games over .500 when Yogi was fired, and something might have been made of the season if Grant had exhibited the same patience that he had shown at the same time the year before when the

---

*Donn Clendenon, one of four black players on the 1969 Miracle Mets, insisted that there was no racial tension on that team. "I would get to the clubhouse early and kid around with the guys. The coaches were important on that team, Yogi, Eddie Yost, Rube Walker, Joe Pignatano . . . One of the reasons there were no racial problems is because they wouldn't allow it." (Allen, *After the Miracle*, p. 63)

Mets were several games *under* .500. Under McMillan, the team lost 27 of the remaining 53 games and went nowhere.

A week after Yogi was fired, Joe Durso summed up the episode neatly in *The New York Times*:

> Make no mistake about it, Yogi Berra was not dismissed as manager of the New York Mets because the team skidded into a five-game losing streak. That would be like saying Richard M. Nixon resigned as president a year ago because our balance of payments was a little low that month. Yogi was gunned down after a series of reverses that were not altogether his fault. The Mets lost nearly one million in home attendance over the last four years. The Yankees crowded their way into Shea Stadium with Catfish Hunter and other new talent [this was when Yankee Stadium was being renovated] and then they signed Billy Martin as their manager. The Mets meanwhile found that their winter of trading wasn't producing a summer of winning, and several of their elite players developed a habit of sniping at Berra through the front office.
>
> So the gun was already pointed at Yogi's head when the chairman of the board of directors, M. Donald Grant, pulled the trigger. And the stage was set for the execution when Yogi stood up to his boss on the tricky issue of Cleon Jones . . . It leaves them with the difficulty of explaining why they dismissed a national folk hero in the middle of a three-year contract that was bestowed after he had won an improbable pennant in the final four weeks of 1973. And that explanation so far has been shrouded . . .

Everybody, said Durso, was overlooking the fact that they were dismissing a sound baseball man who had played in fourteen World Series and fifteen All-Star games, had managed both the Yankees and Mets to pennants, and who had "helped pay the bills with an image probably matched only by Stengel in our time."[38]

Durso concluded, "Gene Mauch, the manager of the Montreal Expos, watched the Mets play out their strange little drama last week and said: 'It's a shame a man like Yogi Berra is fired because of recalcitrant ballplayers.' And bosses with short memories."[39]

Berra's four seasons with the New York Mets were one long continual struggle, but no one really should have expected anything else. The sad truth is that the 1969 and 1973 seasons notwithstanding, the Mets from the late 1960s through the 1970s made little commitment to winning, as exhibited by their failure to make even a single important deal after winning the pennant under Yogi. Berra's four-year record was slightly under .500, 292–296; Hodges's four years had been better, 339–309, but that includes the 1969 season, which, in retrospect, was an aberration. In Hodges's other three seasons, the Mets won 239 and lost 247. In the four years after Berra, under Joe Frazier and then Joe Torre, the Mets drifted back to the losing ways they had known before Hodges, winning 279, losing 339, and finishing last in the NL East three times.

With the exception of Tom Seaver and Cleon Jones, Yogi's players loved him. Shortstop Bud Harrelson—always referred to by Yogi as "Shorty" though he "never understood why . . . I was at least two inches taller than him"—appreciated Berra's virtues: "He never complicated anything, and that is why some of the players didn't understand him . . . I know this he was fair and he knew the game as well as anyone. I don't think he was the best manager I ever played for. Gil Hodges was. I'm not saying Gil knew more about baseball because he didn't. Nobody knows more baseball than Yogi, but sometimes he thought that everyone wanted to win as much as he did. They didn't."[40] Jerry Coleman said something very similar. The only mistake Yogi made as a manager, thought Coleman, was that "he thought the players wanted to win as much as he did."

Berra seemed curiously placid about the abrupt ending of his tenure with the Mets. "Don't worry about me," he told the writers, "I'll be around."[41]

———

ON SEPTEMBER 29, Casey Stengel died in Glendale, California, only fifteen days after discovering he had cancer of the lymph glands. He was eighty-five. He had outlasted the men who hired and fired him, Del Webb and Dan Topping, by a year. The next day in the *Los Angeles Times*, Jim Murray wrote,

> Well, God is getting an earful today. I hope he understands the infield fly rule, the hit and run, how to pitch to Hornsby with men on, when it would do you some good to bunt and what happened in the 1913 World Series. He will get an illustrated lecture on the hook slide, the best place to play Babe Ruth, when to order the infield in and how to steal on left-handers.
>
> At the end of all this, the narrator will doff his cap and a sparrow will fly out. They finally slipped and called a third strike past Casey Stengel.

He can't argue the call. The game is over. Dusk is settling on the bleachers, the lights are turned on in the press box . . .[42]

In November, there was a memorial service at St. Patrick's Cathedral, attended by scores of Casey's old players, friends, and fans. Yogi and Toots Shor were both there with tears in their eyes. So many of the old crowd from Shor's saloon showed up that Bert Randolph Sugar quipped, "Except for the absence of cigarette smoke and booze, the inside of the cathedral looked like a typical night at Toots's." Toots would outlive Casey by less than two years, passing in 1977.

Though they are joined at the hip in baseball lore, the relationship between the Yankees' greatest manager and his assistant manager was always more complex than most observers realized. In his 1962 memoirs, Casey picked his all-time All-Star team. Surprisingly, Yogi was not Stengel's number one pick at catcher. "There have been some tremendous catchers in the American League," he wrote. "You've got Mickey Cochrane, you've got Bill Dickey and Yogi Berra. They're possibly the best catchers that have ever been in baseball—better than any in the National League."[43] That was the order Casey picked them in—Cochrane, Dickey, and Berra.

What is odd is that Stengel wasn't in the American League when Cochrane and Dickey were playing and could rarely have seen them up close. He saw Yogi Berra every day of the twelve seasons he managed the Yankees, praised him to high sky, and called him his assistant manager. Yet, in his final analysis, he ranked Yogi behind two catchers he knew almost entirely by reputation only (though, of course, he had known Dickey in his years as a coach for the Yankees).*

Several years later, Berra seemed to return the compliment, telling Tom Horton, "If I had to name the best manager I ever saw, I would have to say Gil Hodges. Stengel was good, but probably not as good as he thought. He had a great team. The catcher was really outstanding."[44]

"I liked and respected Casey," Yogi said, but he knew him too well to get sentimental about him. Casey was tough, he recalled: "Billy Martin was his pet, and Casey sent him away when it suited him." He likened playing for

---

*It's odd, too, that Stengel went out of his way to remark that the three were "better" than any he had seen in the National League. Casey had seen Roy Campanella, both in exhibition games and in the World Series, and knew that he was just about on a par with Yogi. It's hard to see how Stengel could not have known that Campy was, at the very least, also on a par with Cochrane and Dickey.

Casey to working in a factory: "If you felt good when you went to work and saw your foreman, that would be a fringe benefit. I worked in a factory next to my brother, Tony, and that was a fringe benefit, too, but Casey was not like a brother, not like a father. Casey was not like anybody."

Once, Yogi and Carmen went to see *Auntie Mame*. "Angela Lansbury played the part. She was terrific—better, I think, than she is in *Murder She Wrote*. Maybe not better, but she sang in *Auntie Mame*. It was a great show. We took some friends, and one of them said on the way home, 'Gee, wouldn't it be great to have an aunt like that?' After seeing the show, you had to say yes. Casey was an Uncle Mame for most of the Yankees."

Yogi, though, never claimed to understand Casey. "Casey always used to say 'You can look it up.' But he never said where."

But, "I miss him. Billy Martin told me he loved the old man, I didn't But I miss him."[45]

Chapter Eleven

Déjà vu All Over Again
(1976–1985)

Yogi was the Yankees. Yogi *is* the Yankees.

—Ron Guidry

"I DID NOT steal the crown," says Rod Steiger's Napoleon in the 1970 film, *Waterloo*, "I found it lying in the gutter and picked it up." Something similar might be said of George Steinbrenner.

Later, particularly in the 1980s, when the high-salaried Yankees always fell a player short in the pennant races, those who didn't like Steinbrenner—and there weren't many of the other kind to be found—would accuse him of being a carpetbagger, of having bought the Yankees to acquire instant status in New York—as though millions of others beforehand hadn't discovered that if they could make it there, they could make it anywhere. In truth, Steinbrenner and a syndicate of limited partners had purchased the Yankees from CBS for an amount reported as high as $10 million and as low as $8.7 million. CBS, which had understood less about running a major league baseball franchise than baseball owners knew about the potential of TV, had led the Yankees into a spiral of decline; by 1973, they ended up selling the team for less than they had bought it for in 1964.

Steinbrenner, in the words of Yankee historians Bill Madden and Moss Klein, "was a man of action and vision, and in the course of three seasons he rebuilt the Yankees into pennant winners."[1] Volatile and exacting, Steinbrenner understood better than any of his fellow owners that free agency was here to stay—and that it would change the game. Marvin Miller, head of the Players Association and the man who brought free agency to baseball, summed him up well in his 1991 autobiography, *A Whole Different Ball Game,*° "Throughout the 1978 season, the owners and [Commissioner] Bowie Kuhn continued to pop off about the need to put me and the players back 'in our place.' George Steinbrenner was a prominent part of the chorus, though I felt that George's comments were made largely to persuade the other owners that the man who was leading the way in signing free agents was still in their club."[2] While talking publicly about the need to limit the free-agency rights of players, Steinbrenner was, "at the same time . . . busy signing Catfish Hunter, Don Gullett, Reggie Jackson, Luis Tiant, Goose Gossage, and Tommy John to lucrative contracts."[3] The staggering influx of new money from television and the electric charge brought to the game by free agency created what *Sports Illustrated* proclaimed on its August 11, 1975, cover as "The Baseball Boom." And thin was the atmosphere in which Yogi Berra came back to the Yankees in 1976.

———

CARMEN WANTED YOGI to take a year off from baseball, but Billy Martin and George Steinbrenner did not. Both men knew that Berra's baseball knowledge was an invaluable asset,† and both, too, were anxious to make associations between the 1976 team and the Golden Era—or, put more crudely, hiring Yogi gave George instant credibility. It wasn't hard for Billy to persuade Yogi to come back to the Yankees; his duties would not be overly taxing—help Martin plan strategies, handle substitutions, and so on—and, after all, there was no reason to harbor bad feelings over what had happened in 1964. Webb and Topping were dead, and Houk had left the team after the 1973 season. Yogi had outlasted them. Besides Billy, there were other old friends around; Elston Howard was also on the Yankees coaching staff, and, in one of the good deeds that George Steinbrenner seldom got credit for, Mel Allen had been asked to come back, first as a guest announcer at special events like Old-Timers Day and then, later, to do some play-by-play on cable with the regular announcers, including Phil Rizzuto. It wasn't like old times, but it wasn't bad.

"Yogi is coming back," Yankees president Gabe Paul announced at a

---

°Partly written, in the interest of full disclosure, by the author of this book.

†Such things are said about almost every former player who becomes a coach, but in Berra's case, it was true. George Will's *Men at Work* quotes him as saying, "If a pitcher's uniform fits too good, the base runner can see his buttocks tighten just before a pickoff attempt." (p. 198)

press conference. "Yogi who?" asked a wiseacre in the crowd. "I didn't," said Paul with a smile, "think we needed a second name."[4]

Berra quickly found out that it wasn't going to be dull. He discovered in the spring that part of his job consisted of being a buffer between his old friend Billy Martin and their new boss. After a loss to the Mets in an exhibition game, an angry Steinbrenner accosted Martin. "I want to talk to you. You told me you were going to take the bus!" Billy told him that he and his coaches rode together in a car so they could share their thoughts without the players overhearing. "I don't care," George shouted. "Get Yogi in here. I want to straighten this out." When Yogi was a manager, George wanted to know, didn't he ride on the bus with the players? Apparently Steinbrenner wanted to at least emulate the procedures followed by the old Yankees. No, Yogi told him. "You didn't ride on the bus?" Steinbrenner said. "No, I liked to ride in the car with my coaches so we could talk, just like Billy does."[5] For the time being, at least, The Boss was silent.

The 1976 season, as if plucked out of history, seemed like one out of the golden years. Paced by slick fielding, power-hitting third baseman Graig Nettles, and a pugnacious catcher named Thurman Munson, the Yankees won 97 games and, in the playoffs, beat the Kansas City Royals on a dramatic ninth-inning home run by Chris Chambliss. The season ended, though, on a very un–golden age note when the Cincinnati Reds of Johnny Bench, Joe Morgan, Tony Perez, Pete Rose, and George Foster swept the Yankees in the World Series. A team Yogi had played on, the 1963 Yankees, had been swept, but those four games had been decided by just eight runs and they had lost twice to the game's greatest pitcher, Sandy Koufax. The Reds, with a lineup stocked with Hall of Fame candidates, had no ace pitchers but still held the Yankees to just eight runs while scoring 22 themselves. Steinbrenner was not satisfied with the season, and when the Yankees took the field in 1977, Reggie Jackson, already wearing three World Series rings from the Oakland A's, was in the lineup. And for good measure, Steinbrenner also bought Don Gullett, the stylish left-hander who had beaten them in the first game of the 1976 World Series.

The 1977–1978 Yankees were the franchise's first back-to-back World Series winners since the 1961–1962 edition. Their story has been told so often in books, documentaries, and, most recently, in the 2007 miniseries, *The Bronx Is Burning*, that Yankee fans born after 1978 can recite the great moments from those years—Reggie's three home runs in Game Six of the 1977 Series, Bucky Dent's home run in the one-game playoff that gave the Yankees the Eastern Division title in 1978—and most fans probably feel they actually lived through them. Yogi's biggest contribution came in 1977: he saved Billy Martin's life. The Yankees weren't, as has sometimes been reported, in desperate straits at the time of the most famous dugout clash in team history—in fact, they were nine games over .500, though playing erratically. Jackson and Martin were often said to be like oil and water, but in practice they were more like oil and fire—an old-style manager and a new-style mercenary superstar who couldn't, in the words of Leonard Koppett, "pass the salt shaker across the table to one another without finding something to argue about."

In a June 18 game against the Red Sox, a team one might have expected Jackson to go all out against, Jim Rice hit a soft, opposite-field bloop into right field. Reggie, in no particular hurry, fielded the ball and flipped it back in while Rice, hustling around first base, took second. Martin called Jackson off the field and sent in a replacement. This was really nothing more than Stengel and Berra had done in many similar situations, Yogi most notably with Cleon Jones. Jackson, though, was a new species: a superstar who would openly confront the team's authority figures. This surprised Berra, who liked Reggie, and positively appalled Martin, who did not. Just two decades earlier it would have been unthinkable for Mickey Mantle to have taken out his frustrations on Casey Stengel instead of an unfortunate watercooler, and Mantle was Martin's ideal of a superstar.

What Martin *did* do that Stengel and Berra would *never* have done was confront his humiliated superstar on national TV. Jackson, doing a slow burn, came to the dugout, stood on the steps, and stared at Martin. A simple stare right back at Jackson would have been sufficient. Instead, Martin screamed, "You show me up, and I'll show you up!" Reggie threw up his hands disingenuously. "What did I do?" he pleaded. "How could you do this to me on national television?"[6]

It was right about this time that, according to Martin, Jackson touched things off by saying, "Don't you dare ever show me up again, you mother f——er!"[7] This does not ring true. Other Yankees do not recall Jackson using this kind of language to Martin, and in any case, Jackson's reaction in such situations was to act like an injured innocent. Martin made the first move; Elston Howard, playing the thankless role of peacemaker, tried to stop him but underestimated Martin's fury, and Billy pushed him aside. But, as Martin later recalled, "I couldn't get past Yogi. Yogi has those iron hands, and he grabbed me by the crotch and pulled me back. I swear, if Yogi hadn't stopped me, I would have beat the hell out of him. It's a good thing that Yogi grabbed me . . . Reggie's big, but I wasn't afraid of him. He was lucky Yogi was there."[8] Jackson certainly was lucky that Berra was there, or Reggie might have been arrested for battery. Jackson had nearly twenty years and forty pounds of muscle on Martin. Trying to brush off the clash a couple of days later, Martin showed reporters his bruises and quipped, "That damned Yogi—picking on a 160 pound guy!"[9]

———

ELSTON HOWARD DIED of a heart attack at age fifty-one on December 14, 1980, after a history of heart trouble. Red Smith wrote of the loss, "The Yankees' organization lost more class on the weekend than George Steinbrenner could buy in 10 years."[10] Both Smith and the *Los Angeles Times'* Jim Murray had long been roasting Steinbrenner in print for not giving Howard a chance to manage the team, a move which, Murray thought, "would restore Yankee class."[11] Privately many writers were glad that he never got the job, considering how humiliating it would have been if Howard had gotten off to a poor start and Steinbrenner fired him. Steinbrenner, to his credit, knew the destructive capabilities of his own temper and impatience and admitted to Arlene Howard that that was his reason for not giving Elston the manager's job. In 1973, Mrs. Howard was returning to New York from spring training when she saw George at the Fort Lauderdale airport. She was flying coach, and Steinbrenner whipped out his credit card and had her moved to the seat next to his in first class. They talked all the way back to New York, and before they landed there was one thing Arlene had to ask her husband's boss, "Did he know how badly Elston Howard wanted to manage?" "Yes," Steinbrenner told her, "but Elston is too good to be a manager. Managers are hired to be fired. He deserves better than that."[12]

Elston didn't buy Steinbrenner's explanation, but was pleased when, in February of 1980, Steinbrenner offered him a front office job, which he accepted. "I don't have a title yet," he told reporters, "but George convinced me to give up coaching to take this job because he said anybody could be a coach, but not anybody could get to be an assistant to the owner of the most important team in baseball. I guess this move makes me the Jackie Robinson of the Yankee front office."[13]

In the fall of 1979, about a year before he died, Howard had been in the hospital recovering from a heart attack. He was bombarded with flowers, fruit, get-well cards, and even calls from unlikely sources—Reggie Jackson, with whom he had not always gotten along—Howard represented an era when a player was proud to be a Yankee, and Jackson felt the

Yankees should be proud to have *him*—and Thurman Munson, who seldom got along with anyone. "But no one," Arlene Howard remembered, "called more than Yogi Berra." "Many people don't realize how close Yogi and I are," Elston told *The New York Times*. "Yogi is one of the nicest guys in the world."[14]

———

FROM 1978 THROUGH 1983, George Steinbrenner fired managers faster, literally, than Topps could print their baseball cards. During that time, says Moss Klein, Yogi was "an island of calm in a sea of turbulence." In 1983, with Martin back managing the team for the third time, the Yankees finished 91–71, not bad considering the available talent he had, but it was good for only third place in the AL East behind Baltimore and Detroit. This time there was no confusion. Martin was simply fired.

At a boy scout dinner in West Orange, New Jersey, Berra was asked if he had been offered the job as Yankees manager. Doing his best Robert DeNiro impression, Yogi replied, "A little bit."[15] "A little bit" meant that Steinbrenner had asked, and Yogi had told him he would think about it. By December 16, the Yankees made it official: Yogi would get one more shot at managing. Why, he was subsequently asked by the *Daily News'* Bill Madden at the press conference, would he consider taking the job after having seen firsthand how erratic Steinbrenner's behavior was? Yogi was direct. "My age had something to do with it. I've achieved just about everything a man can achieve . . . But I've never won a championship [as a manager]." He had been offered the job by Steinbrenner a couple of times in the previous five seasons. So, Madden said, why had he not accepted them? "In the past," Yogi explained, "George talked to me about the job. I really didn't know the players then, but I think I know these guys real well, and I think they can win." What about Steinbrenner's penchant for butting in? "I don't care what he does. That don't bother me. I don't get mad." Why did he agree to a two-year contract, someone wanted to know? Because, he said, I want to retire after that. "I just hope George takes care of me, too."[16]

What Berra meant was that Steinbrenner at least had a reputation for honoring his contractual agreements. He fired managers like rock stars fire agents, but he always paid them off. Yogi would soon find out that Steinbrenner kept his contracts, but he did not always keep his promises.

Probably the reason why Yogi came back to manage a third time, knowing full well the perils of working for Steinbrenner, was best expressed almost twenty years later in a CNN interview: "If I had to do it over again,

I would do it over again."[17] He was making a general statement about life, of course, but his words can also be applied to specific circumstances in his life. If he thought a goal was worth pursuing, he'd take a chance. If he failed, he'd have no regrets, and if the opportunity arose to try again, he'd try again. Simply put, in 1984 he had a chance to do it over again, and he did it over again.

———

ON APRIL 2, 1984, *Sports Illustrated*'s cover featured a man facing a baseball field. He had a broad back and short legs and was wearing pin-stripes with the number 8—was any ballplayer ever so identifiable from the back as Yogi Berra?

"Yogi's Back!" proclaimed the headline, and the story was by the only writer who could have written it, Roy Blount Jr. Blount's was the first exten-sive visit to the Berra household since Irv Goodman's for *Sport* magazine twenty-six years earlier, and Blount's task, or rather tasks, were monumen-tal. The first was to reconcile Yogi with yogis: "Berra," he wrote, "hasn't fol-lowed the traditional regimen of a person who gives his life over to yoga. He has never attempted to assume the Lotus, the Plow, the Fish, or the touching-the-top-of-your-head-with-the-soles-of-your-feet position. In his playing days, it's true, he so mastered the Bat Swing and The Crouch that he's now in the Baseball Hall of Fame. And this spring, in the Yankees new flexibility program, he stretched, bent, and folded himself pretty well for a man of 58. But when he's asked whether he knows the body toning postures of yoga, he says, 'Nahhh. A couple of people wrote me, "What exercises do you give?" thinking I was a, you know . . . Ahhhh, I don't do no exercises.' "

In tracking down the origins of Berraisms, Blount tried to invent one and found it was far more difficult than he anticipated. After four weeks, he came up with: " 'Probably what a pitcher misses the most when he doesn't get one is a good target. Unless it never gets there.' Nope, it's too busy. A real Berraism is more mysterious, yet simple. Stengel once asked Berra what he would do if he found a million dollars. Yogi said, 'If the guy was real poor, I'd give it back to him.' "

To come up with a genuine Berraism, Blount concluded,

you have to start with some real Berraistic raw material, which, in itself, may *not* ring true. Take the famous utterance "It ain't over 'til it's over," which is so distinctively descriptive of a baseball game—a football or bas-ketball game is often over with five minutes to go—and which we would like to think is even more true of life.

Research through old sports-page clippings indicates that what Berra probably said was, "In reference to the 1973 pennant race, 'We're not out till we're out.' " That quickly became "You're not out of it till you're out of it," which somehow evolved into "The game's never over till it's over," which was eventually streamlined into "It ain't over 'til it's over."

But I wouldn't call that wholly manufactured product. Berra sprouted its seed. And he did so at a time when the expression "The game is never over till the last man is out" had become hackneyed, even if its meaning still held true. One thing Berra doesn't deal in is clichés. He doesn't remember them.

AS THE 1984 spring camp opened, with Yogi telling his boys to "pair up in threes," he knew the players were behind him. Second baseman Willie Randolph, who would someday manage the Mets, said, "Yogi has helped us all over the years. I want to give something back to the man. It makes a difference when you can say I'm going to go out and give something for that man." He added, "And Yogi can be tough when he wants to. Everybody says 'good old Yogi,' but just try that nonchalant stuff, and he'll put you in your place." Perhaps the biggest vote for Yogi came from a player he had never really been close to. Tom Seaver, who had just left the Mets for the Chicago White Sox, was generous in describing Yogi's best qualities: "He doesn't over-manage. He puts the players in the field who he thinks are the best players. He also doesn't come apart under pressure . . . You don't see him get upset unless it's with a player who gives something less than his best effort."[18]

The problem with the 1984 Yankees, though, wasn't lack of effort. Billy Martin's 1983 team had won 91 games, and Yogi's would win 87—like Martin's squad, was good for third place in the division. The sharp decline of Ron Guidry left the Yankees without a left-handed ace; he went 21–9 for Martin with an ERA of 3.42, but just 10–11 and 4.51 for Yogi. Phil Niekro, at age forty-five, was sensational, finishing 16–8, but no one besides Guidry and Niekro won more than ten games. First baseman Don Mattingly had everyone remembering Stan Musial, winning the batting title at .343, driving in 110 runs, and winning a Gold Glove.° Dave Winfield lost the batting crown to Mattingly by just three points, driving in 100 runs. Randolph played a fine second base and hit .287, and DH Don

°When asked by reporters if Mattingly had exceeded his expectations, Berra replied, "I'd say he's done more than that."

Baylor hit 27 home runs. Still, the Yankees' power base was underwhelming: the team hit only 130 home runs.

Berra began his tenure with an unpopular decision. Taking a page from Casey's book, Yogi wanted to platoon Graig Nettles, one of the stars of the 1977–1978 teams in his prime, at third base. Nettles howled. A potent power hitter and a fine fielder, he was thirty-nine years old in 1984 and had been in sharp decline for the last two seasons. Much to the chagrin of the fans and the other Yankee players, the front office dealt him to the San Diego Padres, and Nettles at least got to play in the World Series against Detroit.* Though it was unpopular, Yogi's decision was sound: Nettles hit only .228 for San Diego and ended up playing in about as many games, 124, as he would have had he stayed in New York.

A more important Berra decision involved moving left-hander Dave Righetti from the starting rotation to the bullpen because, as Yogi had said while managing the Mets, "If you ain't got a bullpen, you ain't got nothin'." This decision, too, was resisted, but soon it was clear that Yogi was right again. Righetti, twenty-five in 1984, had been a promising starter the previous two seasons, and his no-hitter against the Red Sox on the Fourth of July in 1983 was the season's highlight. But he had won just 25 of 43 decisions in the previous two years, and after becoming a reliever he posted an outstanding 2.34 ERA and saved 31 games. In 1984, he would save 29. Righetti was the Yankees' biggest surprise in a season of disappointments, the biggest of whom was Steve Kemp, who had been a terrific hitter with the Tigers in 1979 and 1980, driving in more than 100 runs both seasons, and then batting in 98 for the White Sox in 1982. But Kemp had been plagued with injuries since coming to the Yankees; he played in just 94 games for Yogi in 1984, with only 41 RBIs.

In truth, it really didn't matter what the Yankees did that season as the Detroit Tigers picked 1984 to have the franchise's greatest year. The Tigers ended every other American League team's season early by winning 10 of their first 11 games and 35 of their first 40. By the All-Star break, everyone had conceded the East to the Tigers and assumed they would win the playoffs and probably the World Series, which is exactly what happened. The Yankees under Yogi followed their usual pattern: things started slowly, and by the end of June, they were eight games under .500. Then, like Yogi's pre-

---

*In fairness, Nettles cited more reasons for discontent than Yogi's platoon plan. He was fond of telling writers that he was tired of "Steinbrenner's big mouth." (*Sports Illustrated*, April 2, 1984)

vious teams, things began to gel. For the rest of the season, they were twenty games above .500 with a record of 54–34 for a won-lost percentage of .614.

———

IN THE WINTER of 1985, the New York Yankees acquired Dale Berra from the Pittsburgh Pirates. It was understood from the start that there was no possibility of nepotism: "If he don't hit, he don't play," Yogi repeatedly reminded the press, and in spring training, the Yankees' chances looked good.

Eleven years earlier Tim Berra had made it to the NFL and played one full season with the Baltimore Colts as a kick returner despite the enormous handicap of being only 5'11" and weighing about 185 pounds—not a lot of meat for a football player, but in the words of his general manager, Ernie Accorsi, "all of it choice." Many thought Larry Jr. would be better than his father. At 6'1", taller than his dad and built more in the mode of a classic athlete, he attracted attention while catching for the Montclair State University baseball team and went from there to the Mets' minor league system. There he suffered the serious injury—in Larry's case, a damaged knee that required surgery—that his father had been able to avoid in more than 2,100 big league games, and his professional career was over.

Dale, though, made it to the major leagues. In 1977 at age twenty-one, he was signed by the Pirates as a shortstop and a third baseman. He had his problems; from 1982 through 1984 he made 30 errors each season, earning him the nickname "Boo Boo"—a name which was, in his case, particularly irritating as it was also the name of Yogi Bear's cartoon sidekick. But in those same seasons, Dale's range was impressive, and he started to show some pop, hitting 10 home runs and 25 doubles in both 1982 and 1983.

The winter of 1985 was a good time for the Berra family: big family dinners, rounds of Trivial Pursuit, home movies, and endless sports arguments. There was reason for hope as the season approached. Surely, American Leaguers were saying to each other, the Tigers can't be as good this year as last. And they were right: in 1985 Detroit got off to a dismal start, floundered, and finished fifteen games off the pace. Surely, too, the way the Yankees had played from July 1984 on indicated that they had a good chance of dethroning the Tigers and taking the Eastern Division flag in 1985. The problem was that, although the Yankee manager was blessed with patience, Yankee management was not.

Like all of Yogi's teams, the 1985 Yankees crawled out of the gate. On April 25, they beat the Red Sox 5–1 at Yankee Stadium to salvage just one game of three. They were 6–7, hardly cause for desperation, but already the rumors were flying. Berra, leaning back in his office chair with his feet on the desk, responded to the rumors by telling the assembled writers, "All I know is that I'm still here." Don Baylor, the team's DH and one of the team's unofficial leaders, made it clear that the Yankees were pressing, telling reporters, "No question, the guys are playing uptight. They're trying to do more than they're capable of, and it's all for the manager. It would be different if there was a manager here who nobody respected or gave a damn about. Losing is hurting us, but nobody . . . is hurting more than Yogi, and we realize that."[19]

The next three games were excruciating. The Yanks lost three straight games to the White Sox at Comiskey Park by scores of 4–2, 5–4, and 4–3; in two of the losses, they blew late-inning leads, and in the other they went down with the winning run on base.

On April 28, with the Yankees 6–10, Steinbrenner made the announcement: he had reneged on his promise that Yogi would get the whole season. The players were shocked and angry, but not surprised. Don Mattingly sat outside his locker and wept. Baylor picked up a trash can and threw it across the locker room. Yogi's immediate reaction was to walk around the clubhouse shaking hands and saying goodbye to players and attendants.

The team bus, headed for O'Hare Airport and a flight to Texas, was silent. Berra was seated at the front. The bus stopped at the passenger gate to let Yogi out; he was headed back to New York. He picked up his carry-on bag and turned to say something to his players, but his throat caught and no one could make it out. As he walked away, the bus erupted in cheering and clapping. When the players on the second team bus saw Yogi walking into the terminal, they also stood and cheered. As the buses pulled away, everyone had a clear view of Yogi, alone and looking older than his sixty years, walking through the door. It was a sight none of them would ever forget.

Sixteen years later, writing with Dave Kaplan, Berra would say,

I've always been a devout Catholic . . . I've always believed in brotherhood, redemption, and forgiveness. But my firing by George Steinbrenner as Yankee manager in 1985 was more than hurtful and disappointing. It struck deeper than that.

The hurt wasn't so much that I was fired. Or that it was only sixteen games into the season. Or that George had promised that I'd be the manager all season, no matter what. Heck, nobody knows better than me that managers are hired to be fired. What bothered me most was the disrespect; to me, that was unforgivable.[20]

After thirty years as a player, coach, and manager, Berra felt he had a right to be told face-to-face that he was fired. Steinbrenner "triggered an anger in me I didn't know I had."[21] He would not, he vowed, return to Yankee Stadium so long as George was in charge.

No satisfactory explanation has ever been offered for Steinbrenner's overreaction, but later, in retrospect, Yogi thought he might have discovered the real reason he was fired. Sometime in the 1984 season—the exact time was never specified—there had been a meeting in Steinbrenner's office. (Berra thought that under Steinbrenner, the Yankees held too many such meetings.) The topic of discussion was the twenty-four players on the roster, and the point of contention, as Yogi recalled it, was that "the twenty-four guys I wanted to be on the team were not the same guys who the owner wanted to be on the team. It was not just one guy like Willie Mays when he came to the Mets in 1973,* it was four or five guys who the owner wanted and the coaches and I didn't." At some point in the meeting, Berra got exasperated and said, "If you want that team, can I say that it is *your* team if we lose?" after which Steinbrenner, according to Berra, questioned Yogi's knowledge of baseball. "I have been called some awful things," Yogi said later, "but I have never been told I didn't know baseball, or who can play baseball." He later admitted that "I called the owner some bad things and threw a pack of cigarettes at him"—managing under Steinbrenner had driven Yogi back to smoking. "One of the coaches said I threw the pack down on his desk, and it bounced up and hit him. I don't know. I know I threw them, and I know I was hot." Yogi recalls Steinbrenner saying either "nobody ever talks to me that way" or "nobody can ever talk to me that way." After the meeting, several coaches told him, "Atta boy, Yogi! Stand up to the bastard!" But Berra would later wonder "if the thrown pack of cigarettes came back my way the next year."[22]

Don Mattingly, one of the players on the bus who applauded Yogi as he walked away would tell Tom Horton four years later, "I can't tell you how happy it makes me that he [Yogi] won't come back . . . All I can say is it is a deep profound joy that Yogi won't sell out. The man has character. He has

---

*Thus an admission many years after the fact that Berra did not want Mays on the Mets roster.

pride. It is an honor to say I played for Yogi Berra."[23] Dave Winfield, who had his own much-publicized differences with Steinbrenner, said, "George thought he could push Yogi around. He couldn't, and he fired him. He thought Yogi would crawl back. Then the next time he gave him the job that he would dance the George Jig . . . It makes him crazy that Yogi won't play his game." Steinbrenner, Winfield thought, was going nuts asking himself "How come this funny little man everyone used to make fun of won't do what I want?"[24]

Ron Guidry agreed with the many who thought that Steinbrenner had made a major miscalculation: "What George didn't understand was that Yogi was different from all the guys he had hired and fired. Yogi was the Yankees. Yogi *is* the Yankees."

DALE BERRA'S PROBLEM was revealed in 1985 when he, along with several former Pittsburgh Pirates, including Lee Mazzilli and Dave Parker, and stars from other major league teams, including Keith Hernandez and Tim Raines, were subpoenaed to testify before a grand jury investigating the use of cocaine in major league baseball. In the twenty-first century, baseball owners were soft on the issue of drug use, but the drugs they tried to ignore were thought to *enhance* the performance of their most valuable property, the players; in the 1980s, the issue was recreational drugs, which devalue the property, so there was no hedging on taking appropriate action. One of seven players granted immunity in exchange for his testimony, Dale Berra was suspended for a full season and allowed to play in 1986 only after donating 10 percent of his salary to drug-related charities and performing one hundred hours of drug-related community service. Dale could never get his career back on track. He played 46 games for the Yankees in 1986 and 19 for the Houston Astros the following season, then called it quits. He had picked a good family to be born in; with help from the rest of the Berras, he recovered from his habit and resumed a productive life.

BILLY MARTIN, YET again, replaced Yogi, and the Yankees finished 97–64—good enough to win in most years, but this season two games in back of the Toronto Blue Jays. Yankee fans were left wondering what might have happened if Yogi had been given a chance to work one of his second-half pennant rushes. The next season, Martin was gone again, replaced by Lou Pinella, who lasted through the 1987 season and was then replaced in 1988 by . . . Billy Martin, who, in turn was again replaced by Pinella before the mid-season mark.

Oddly, it wasn't a sportswriter who gave the best assessment of Yogi as a manager, but Marvin Miller, the first executive director of the players union, in his 1991 autobiography. Comparing Berra with Gene Mauch, who was regarded by many as the smartest of baseball managers from the 1960s to the 1980s, Miller wrote, "Some writers and even some players think Mauch had ability. Perhaps. But the fact that he talked so much about the 'art' of managing probably explained why reporters often wrote about his baseball acumen and blamed losses on his players, not on his tendency to overmanage. Conversely, Yogi Berra—the king of the malapropism— managed seven seasons, had a winning percentage of .522 (to Mauch's .483), produced pennant winners in both leagues. And came within two games of winning two World Series. Yet, he was never considered in Mauch's league as a manager."[25]

It ain't over till it's over, but when it's over, it's over. Though he was approached about managing by Astros owner John McMullen, Yogi never again managed in the big leagues. So at least one dream in a dream life went unfulfilled.

Chapter Twelve

Eternal Yankee
(1986–)

"But it is a game, not life. Although if you play it
for money, you can learn a lot about life."

—YOGI BERRA

IN THE MID-1980s, when the New Jersey Devils hockey team was trailing late in games at the Continental Arena in the Meadowlands, fans were heard to shout in unison, "It ain't over!" Often, Yogi Berra, from his box seat, would respond with a smile and a wave or a thumbs up. The Devils were owned by John J. McMullen, a former naval officer with a degree in naval architecture from MIT and a PhD in mechanical engineering from the Swiss Institute of Technology. McMullen, a neighbor of the Berras in Montclair, made his fortune in various maritime industries and bought the Colorado Rockies hockey team in 1982. He relocated the team to New Jersey and renamed them the Devils. The Berras were given passes to the Devils home games.

McMullen had also been the owner of the Houston Astros since 1979. It came as little surprise when, on November 5, 1985, the Astros announced that Yogi Berra would be returning to Major League Baseball as a coach. And so an unlikely pair of New Jerseyites took up residence in Houston during the baseball season in an apartment near Houston's prestigious shopping mall, The Galleria—at the time, so said the Houston Chamber of Commerce, the largest hotel/retail facility in the world. Berra was an immediate favorite with the fans and press. "They'd never seen anything like him in Houston," said Mickey Herskowitz, longtime Houston sportswriter. "Texans had had football idols for half a century, everyone from

Bear Bryant to Darrell Royal to Tom Landry, but they never had a baseball icon." The Berras loved Texas—the food, the margaritas, the collegiate-like enthusiasm of the fans. Yogi even liked the Astrodome, which was disliked by many Astros fans because its dimensions and air currents killed potential home runs and cut down on run production. Yogi didn't care about that. "What's the difference?" he asked local reporters, "if you win 3–2 or 6–5, as long as you win?" And there was something else: "The good thing about it is that you know you're going to play every day, even if the weather's lousy."[1]

Neil Hohlfeld, who covered the Astros for years for the *Houston Chronicle*, remembered that "being on the road with Yogi was like traveling with the Pope. Everyone knew Yogi." On one occasion in Montreal, Hohlfeld picked up a Yogiism. Berra, he found, was somewhat befuddled by the twenty-four-hour military clock at Jarry Park. "Yogi," said Hohlfeld, "you were in the Navy, you should understand how that works." "Yeah, but those clocks were for the *Navy*."

Houston fans embraced Yogi, and in turn he brought them a huge dollop of Berra's Luck. Under manager Hal Lanier, the Astros, paced by first baseman Glenn Davis and outfielder Jose Cruz but mostly by pitchers Mike Scott, Jim DeShaies, and Nolan Ryan, won the National League West and played—quel irony!—the New York Mets for the pennant. The Mets had a super team with a starting rotation of Dwight Gooden, Ron Darling, Bob Ojeda, and Sid Fernandez who led the NL in team ERA at 3.11, and a lineup full of All-Stars, including catcher Gary Carter, first baseman Keith Hernandez, and slugging outfielder Darryl Strawberry. The Mets also led the league in batting, on-base average, slugging, and runs scored. In many ways, it looked like a rematch of the 1969 World Series, with the Mets this time playing the part of the Baltimore Orioles and the Astros as the overwhelming underdogs.

Scott beat Gooden 1–0 in the first game. In the second game, Ojeda beat Ryan 5–1 at the Astrodome; it was the only easy game of the Series. The Mets squeezed out a 6–5 win in Game Three to take a two-games-to-one lead. Scott came back to pitch another complete-game victory, 3–1, in the fourth game, and the Mets won Game Five, 2–1, on a twelfth-inning single by Gary Carter.

Game Six, the most exciting in the pressure-packed series, was one of baseball's all-time classics. With the Mets up three games to two and the seemingly unhittable Scott poised to go the next day, the Astros took a 3–0 lead into the ninth inning, the Mets scored three times to tie it, and both teams scored a run in the fourteenth. Finally, in the sixteenth inning, the Mets again scored three runs to blow the game open—or so it looked until Houston scored two in the bottom of the sixteenth and went down with the tying and winning runs on base. Many—including Tim McCarver, who called the game on TV—thought the 1986 National League Championship Series was the best since the playoffs were instituted in 1969. Houston out-hit New York .218 to .189, but lost three games played over a total of 34 innings by just three runs.

The Mets went on to beat the Boston Red Sox in the World Series, becoming the first New York team since the Brooklyn Dodgers thirty-one years before to win the championship without having Yogi Berra on the roster—but to do it they had to win a grueling series against a team which Yogi coached.

Berra liked the young Houston players, though he found them a bit more sophisticated than the ones he had known on the 1950s and 1960s Yankees and Mets. "Some of my Astros teammates heard about what they called the 'self thing' [i.e., Berra's lack of ego] and called me an id, or said that I had no id. Stuff like that, worse stuff than I had ever heard on the Yankees. A lot of the Astros went to college and know about ids and libidos and even quantum physics . . . All this bush league head shrinking I was getting bothered me a little. Not a lot, but a little."[2]

Before he left the Astros in 1989, Yogi helped to make one more lasting impression on the team's history. Houston had a promising catcher named Craig Biggio with whom Berra spent significant time. "Yogi told him 'See the ball, hit the ball,' " says Matt Galante, an old friend and then a fellow coach with the Astros. "You could see Craig getting more confident all the time from working with Yogi." But Berra thought Biggio, who stole 109 bases in his first five seasons with the team, was too fast to waste that speed crouching behind the plate. He helped persuade Biggio to become a second baseman, where he would play 1,978 games and make seven All-Star teams; Yogi's legacy with the Astros lasted through 2007, when Craig Biggio, regarded as a sureshot Hall of Famer, announced his retirement.

═══

IN 2002, WHILE working on a chapter for a book of baseball essays, *Brushbacks and Knockdowns*, I wrote to Leonard Koppett to ask him for an evaluation of Yogi's career as a manager. "Don't you think it's appropriate that Yogi finished his career as a coach?" he asked me.

A lot of the New York writers I know felt that it was something of a come-down for him to spend his last years in Houston, wearing a black-orange rainbow uniform, teaching fundamentals, and telling stories to kids just out of Triple-A and college. Most of the old guys thought it would have been nicer if he could have gone out as a manager.

I don't agree, though. There was something about coaching, about learning these young guys all his experience, that seems so much more in character for Yogi than managing. I always thought there was something about managing that was alien to Yogi's character. I'm not saying he wasn't a good manager; he was a very good manager, not as good as Casey and probably not as good as Gil Hodges, but as good or better than Billy [Martin], who was a great manager only in his own mind. What I mean is that there was something very good about Yogi that was suppressed when he was managing.

There was a playfulness and spontaneity to Yogi that never showed up when he was managing, which is why a lot of writers who saw him for the first time when he was a manager thought the whole Yogi legend thing was bull shit. They had been told about this nice guy who was really fun to talk to and was always good for a couple of quotes, and then they saw this real serious guy and they said "This ain't the guy I heard so much about." A manager, after all, is a company man. His primary responsibility is to the company, not the players, no matter how much he likes the players and wants to help them. A coach works for the company, too, but he doesn't have the same relationship with the players. One aspect of a coach's job is to develop relationships with players and help them along. A manager who doesn't sit a guy who's not performing because he likes the guy isn't being responsible to his boss. Coaching isn't like that. A manager's job is to win, but a coach's job is to help a guy be the best player he can be.

Yogi could never entirely give himself over to being a company guy. On some fundamental level, he was temperamentally unsuited to be a man-ager because managing means being 100% loyal to the boss even if the boss was an asshole like Steinbrenner.

People always talk about a guy being "good in the clubhouse" but they never say exactly what that means. When I was in the Yankee clubhouse before important games, I could tell one primary difference between the Yankees and their opponents. It wasn't professionalism—the Yankees were professional, of course, but all ballplayers were professional. What was different about the Yankees is that in all situations, even when they were down, they were always eager to get out on that field and play. And it seemed to me that a lot of that started with Yogi. He always reflected that truth that says you play a game much better if you enjoy it. Outside the ball park, he was business, but on the field, in the clubhouse, you could always sense more than just business, you could feel his joy at being a ballplayer.

I think that coaching was the ideal way for Yogi to end his baseball career.

———

WHILE BERRA WAS coaching for the Astros, his friend and coauthor Tom Horton arranged a breakfast with Yogi and Milton Friedman in San Francisco. The *Houston Post* ran a headline on the sports page, "Odd Couple's Breakfast," but the two men got along splendidly despite the fact that Yogi admitted "he is not a baseball fan, and I am not as much a money fan as most people think I am." Berra thought America's most famous economist to be the opposite of Casey Stengel: "When he [Stengel] finished talking, people scratched their heads . . . when he [Friedman] finished talking, everything is clearer."

Inevitably, the discussion turned to money. Friedman asked Berra what jobs he had before baseball, and Yogi told him about working in the shoe factory back in St. Louis for $60 a week. In return, "I got a speech on Adam Smith. He was a Scottish economist who did some of the same sorts of labor-savings things in a pin factory that we did in a shoe factory."[3] Yogi told Friedman he gave his mother his entire paycheck and that she gave him back $2. Of course you did that, Friedman told him, you were a good son. Yet another topic of discussion was Little League baseball. Berra had made some criticisms of Little League ball in *USA Today*—too much competition and organization, he felt, and not enough actual *play*. Friedman agreed with Yogi, adding, "A lot of our life is too organized."

Finally, they talked about literature. Berra told him the story about meeting Ernest Hemingway at Toots Shor's and asking him what paper he worked for. Friedman laughed heartily and told Yogi that he thought Hemingway's two best books were *The Sun Also Rises* and *The Fisherman and the Sea*. "He meant *The Old Man and the Sea*," Yogi said later. "Do you suppose anyone called him on it? No. Suppose I had said the same thing?"

Berra's concern was "Who was going to spring for breakfast? I knew it would go for $50 plus tip." Who did pay is not recorded, but according to

Yogi, "He said that if I had been in his class, I would have gotten a good grade."[4] Shortly before his death in 2006, Friedman said, "I don't remember telling Yogi that, but it's probably true. I think he had a good grasp of basic economic principles, apparently much better than some of the better educated people in the Yankees front office that he used to negotiate salaries with. One thing he said that I have always remembered is 'A nickel isn't worth a dime any more.' He was right."

———

RETIREMENT FROM BASEBALL gave Berra more time to indulge his second passion, movies. Shortly before he retired, an article in *The Washington Post* announced, "Yogi Berra isn't catching pitchers anymore, just movies . . . Once a month, the Houston Astros' coach leaves the ball park and trades his baseball cap for the hat of a movie critic." Yogi at the Metros' marketing agent Tom Villante, a former Yankees bat boy who knew Berra from his first game as a Yankee in 1946, recalled that Yogi had always been his teammates' resident film critic: "The players would ask Yogi, 'Hey, Yog, what movie did you see?' and he would give the most interesting reviews, probably better than the movie itself. This got to be a daily thing, and I remember thinking that I was going to do something with it someday."[5]

Some of Yogi's lines sounded a bit scripted, such as "I *love* movies, if I like them." But some were genuinely Yogi. Of *Good Morning, Vietnam*, he said, "I've always been a fan of Roger Williams." Sean Connery was "Sean Conrad." The star of *Fatal Attraction* was "Glenn Cove" (actually a Long Island suburb close to Shea Stadium). Of the movie itself, he was scared "only by the scary parts." *Three Men and a Baby* "proves that three men can be just as good as one woman." Neil Simon's *Biloxi Blues* "reminded me of being in the Army—even though I was in the Navy." He could not guess the ending to *Masquerade*, "but towards the end I could." Yogi enjoyed *Moonstruck*, which costarred the Berras' neighbor in Montclair "Olympia Du-cactus, or what's her last name? She did a good job." He predicted that Dukakis and Cher would both win "the Golden Glove award."*

---

*Berra was a student of all film genres but one. A veteran sportswriter who asked not to be named recalled an old story: "A bunch of writers thought it would be fun to take Yogi out to see a skin flick. He kept saying, 'I dunno,' and said he wanted to go see *Airport*. They insisted, 'C'mon, Yogi, let's go see the dirty movie. Come on with us.' 'I dunno,' Yogi said, 'Who's in it?' "

===

THE YEARS PASSED, but Yogi did not waver in his decision to stay away from Yankee Stadium. On August 22, 1988, he and Bill Dickey were given plaques on the wall of Yankee Stadium's Monument Park; Dickey was there, Berra was not. The Astros were playing the Cubs in Chicago that day, and McMullen certainly would have excused Yogi to attend his own ceremony, but Berra did not ask. Tougher for him to miss was Phil and Cora Rizzuto's fiftieth wedding anniversary celebration at Yankee Stadium on June 23, 1993. Rizzuto expressed his regret at Yogi's absence in his memoirs: "I had hoped Yogi would come to the affair at the Stadium, but he didn't. I respect him for his convictions. He won't go back to Yankee Stadium as long as George owns the team. End of subject."[6]

By the early 1990s, Yogi Berra, one of the four or five most famous living ballplayers, had emerged as one of the game's most marketable names. LTD Enterprises—the initials stand for the Berra boys, Larry, Tim, and Dale (with Tim's wife Betsy as the fourth partner)—was formed as a logical response to the carload of mail being delivered to Yogi's house every week requesting autographs, appearances, and other favors. "I couldn't sell widgets," Dale Berra told *The New York Times*, "but I can sell Yogi Berra."[7] Berra trailed only Joe DiMaggio and Mickey Mantle in popularity among memorabiliaists. By the end of the decade, he would be number one.

The 1990s marked a time of increasing popularity for Yogi. It seemed as if everyone wanted Yogi, and sometimes Carmen, to endorse their product. Filming one commercial together, Carmen had only one line: "And a free cup of coffee!" "It took her twenty-one takes!" Yogi recalled. Carmen had laughed when he slipped up during his movie reviews. "Now she knows what it's like."[8]

By the twenty-first century, nearly four decades after his last major league at-bat, Yogi Berra's face was more recognizable to TV viewers than that of the cartoon bear that had annoyed him so much in the late 1950s. In 2002, "Berra At The Barber," created by the Kaplan Thaler advertising agency for Aflac Insurance, made its debut on ESPN's *Sunday Night Baseball*. It proved to be one of the most popular commercials of the decade and is still running.*

---

*Bart Starr Jr., son and business partner of the great Green Bay Packers quarterback, told me about coming up to New Jersey for the Yogi Berra Museum Celebrity Golf Classic. Delighted to meet one of his all-time sports heroes, Bart Jr. remarked to Yogi that he liked his Aflac commercial. How, Bart asked, did Aflac choose Yogi for the

The Aflac commercial capitalized on one of Yogi's most appealing traits, his blissful unawareness of his own celebrity. Ira Berkow relates a story about Yogi at a spring training game where, while he busily signed autographs, a lady yelled at him, "Yogi, have you got a minute?" "For what?" he responded.[9] Another story about Yogi may or may not have happened, but it sounds very much to me as if it could have, so I'll relate it here: a woman from St. Louis—and that's the way the story was told to me, and it's this bit of verisimilitude that leads me to believe that it's probably true—visited the Yogi Berra Museum and Learning Center and, suddenly, was thrilled to actually find Yogi there in person. "Mr. Berra," she gushed, "could you make up a Yogiism for me?" "Ahh, ma'am," Yogi said with a blush, "if I could do that, I'd be famous." Indeed.

———

IN RETIREMENT, YOGI played touch football with his grandchildren, golfed with presidents,* and received honorary degrees. Dale Berra had graduated from Montclair State University in 1977, and in May 1996 a second Berra earned a degree from MSU, an honorary one. Yogi's fellow honoree was Bruce Willis, a former neighbor in Montclair when he had been going to college. Berra described Willis as "a perfect neighbor—he never said a word." Yogi saved some of his all-time best lines for this address: "I don't know yet whether people should call me Dr. Yogi or Dr. Lawrence." He was going to call Bobby Brown and "tell him I'm a doctor now, too." Of his contributions to *Bartlett's Familiar Quotations*, he said, "I wish I could say them when I wanted to because I would have made a fortune by now."[10]

He also found time to update his memoirs. His rambling and hugely entertaining volume of memoirs, *Yogi: It Ain't Over*, written with Tom Horton, was published in 1989 and quickly became a bestseller. Doing publicity for the book, Yogi met old friend Arlene Francis ("Are you in show business?") at Sardi's in Manhattan for a radio interview. After Berra

———

spot? "I don't know," replied Yogi. "My agent just said 'Do you want to do a commercial with the Amtrak duck?' "

*In his book, *Slick*, Whitey Ford relates a story involving Yogi and President Gerald Ford: "They happened to be playing golf one day in the same foursome, and Yogi mentioned to the President that he owned this racquetball club in New Jersey. 'Do you play racquetball, Mr. President?' Yogi asked. 'Yes, I have on occasion,' the President said. With that, Yogi pulled a card out of his pocket and handed it to the President. 'Here, Mr. President,' said Yog. 'Just in case you're ever in New Jersey and you want to play racquetball.' The card said the bearer was entitled to play racquetball at Yogi's club, free of charge. On the other side of the card was stamped: 'Good Tuesdays only.' "

stumbled through a couple of questions, Francis leaned over to him during a commercial break and asked, "Yogi, have you read this?" "No," he replied, "Why should I? I was there."[11]

As the years went by, though, there were fewer of those who had been there with him. Roger Maris was one of the first of his old teammates to go, dying of cancer in a Houston hospital in December 1985. He was fifty-one. Yogi was in Houston shortly before Maris died and went to the hospital, but Roger was too ill to have visitors. Maris's biographer, Maury Allen, related that Yogi left the hospital in tears. The Big Three—Vic Raschi, Ed Lopat, and Allie Reynolds—died within a span of six years, in 1988, 1992, and 1994, respectively. With each of their funerals, Berra told a journalist, "I felt like a piece of me died."[12]

Like Maris, Billy Martin came to a far-too-early end. After his 68-game stretch in 1988, Billy Martin never managed again, though he continued to work for Steinbrenner as a special consultant. On Christmas Day in 1989, he was killed in Binghamton, New York, when either his friend William Reedy or Billy himself drove Martin's pickup truck off the road. Both men had been drinking heavily. Martin was sixty-one. All that was certain was that Martin died as he had lived, without a seat belt. He was buried in Hawthorne, New York, perhaps sixty yards from Babe Ruth. Berra and numerous Yankee teammates made the trip for the funeral. The words written on Billy's tombstone had been spoken by him some years before: "I may not have been the greatest Yankee to put on the uniform, but I was the proudest."

Bill Dickey died in November 1993, in Little Rock, Arkansas, at the age of eight-six. "He was a great man," said Yogi. "A gentleman and a Yankee. That's a lot to say for anyone."[13]

Mickey Mantle, who thought he would die before he was forty as so many men in his family had, outlived Maris and Martin. He died in a Dallas hospital, sixty-three years old, on August 13, 1995, after liver cancer spread through his body. He had undergone a transplant earlier in the year, as his own liver was ravaged by years of chronic drinking, resulting in cirrhosis and hepatitis C. In his time, Mantle had squandered more money than Berra had made playing baseball and never acted sufficiently to provide for himself or his family when he was still making the big money. By the end, he had destroyed his once magnificent body through alcohol, pills, and a reckless personal life. Worse, he had been a terrible influence on his own family; his long-suffering wife Merlyn and all four of his sons were treated for alcoholism. His third son, Billy (named for Billy Martin), had, like many of the Mantle clan, Hodgkin's disease, which led to an addiction to prescription painkillers. Both Mantle and Berra had sons who developed drug problems, but Billy Mantle did not have the strong family support to help him through his crisis. Only thirty-six, Billy died of heart trouble caused by substance abuse just five months before his father passed. (In 2000, the oldest son, Mickey Jr., died at age forty-seven of liver cancer, and Danny later successfully fought prostate cancer.) In an interview shortly before he died, Mantle confessed that what he most regretted was that he had been "a bad father."

Mickey loved Yogi, who had tried to make him feel comfortable from his first day on the Yankees, unlike Joe DiMaggio, who didn't speak a word to the nineteen-year-old rookie. "As my friend," Mantle said years later, "Yogi worried about me. About why I didn't pay more attention to the game and how easy I was with my money. I threw money around pretty good as a reaction to growing up without any. Yogi's family was almost as poor as mine, but he had the other reaction. He tossed half dollars around like they were manhole covers."[14]

Berra's friendships with his teammates were widely known, but few knew how close Yogi was to Don Drysdale. Many in the media were surprised when Yogi attended the memorial service following Drysdale's sudden death from a heart attack on July 3, 1993, but in fact the 6'5" movie-star good-looking Californian and the stumpy Italian guy from the Hill in St. Louis had been close since the winter of 1957. Drysdale, fresh off his rookie season, checked into a Florida hotel for a charity golf tournament and found out he had a famous roommate. "When I got to the room," he later told Tom Horton, "his stuff was all there, his name on the bag and all. I made some phone calls and said, 'Guess who my roommate is?'"[15]

"We shared a room once during a golf tournament in Florida," Yogi recalled, "and he let me use his car. It was a brand-new Ford station wagon, 1957, I think, and I lost the keys." Drysdale's version was a little different; he remembered Yogi as having locked the keys in the car. Yogi took Drysdale's death hard. "I never lost my respect for him. He hit a lot of batters. One more reason to like playing in the American League."*[16]

Every year, it seemed, there came a call from someone putting together a benefit for an old ballplayer in need of help. None were refused. On June 20, 1992, Yogi appeared in a parade for Sandy Amoros Day in

*Yogi enjoyed chiding Don about the home run he hit off him to win the August 3, 1959, All-Star game.

Brooklyn, an event organized to help pay for his growing medical expenses; Sandy, a refugee from Castro's Cuba, suffered from circulation problems which resulted in the amputation of a leg. Yogi appeared at the event for the man who had stolen his 1955 World Series ring. Dodgers fans cheered him as if Branch Rickey had had the good sense to sign him for the Dodgers back in 1941. Sandy was too ill to be there and died a week later of pneumonia.

The hardest loss of all was Phil Rizzuto, who never missed a Yankees Old-Timers game until June 24, 2006. His health had been failing for some time, and in September he was moved from his home in Hillside, New Jersey, to a rehabilitation facility in West Orange. According to attendants, Yogi would come by at least once a week to play bingo with his oldest and best friend. Phil died in his sleep on August 13, 2007, after a bout with pneumonia. The year before he died, Rizzuto had decided to sell some of his personal mementos to raise money for his favorite charity, St. Joseph's School for the Blind; his 1950 MVP plaque alone went for $175,000.

Rizzuto's election to the Hall of Fame in 1994 was tainted, some said, by the fact that Yogi, Pee Wee Reese, and other friends of Rizzuto were on the Veterans Committee that finally voted him into the Hall. (It was Berra who called to inform him of the vote: "We got you in.") But Ted Williams, among others, thought the honor had come some thirty years late. Just before the final vote, Williams made an emotional speech on Rizzuto's behalf. After the announcement, a reporter asked Berra, "What would you say to those who claim Rizzuto would not have been a Hall of Fame candidate if he hadn't been on all of those Yankee World Series teams?" Yogi shot back, "If he hadn't been on the team, we wouldn't have been in all those World Series."[17]

———

THE SIGN AT the entrance proclaims "The House That Yogi's Friends Built." The Yogi Berra Museum and Learning Center on the Montclair State University campus opened in December 1998, with Whitey Ford, Ralph Branca, Larry Doby, and Ted Williams, in a wheelchair, among those in attendance. Adjoining the facility is a picture-perfect minor league ballpark, Yogi Berra Stadium, home to both the Montclair State Red Hawks and the New Jersey Jackals, currently in the Canadian-American Association of Professional Baseball (the Can-Am League). When construction for the museum and the ballpark began in the spring of 1997, George Steinbrenner had been frantically pulling strings to get the Yankees a new stadium west of the Hudson; when Yogi Berra Stadium was completed the next year, some wits observed, it was Yogi, not George, who had a ballpark in New Jersey.

Berra wasn't sure what to say when he was presented with the idea of having a museum named after him. "Every museum I ever went to as a kid," he told me in an interview for an article for *The New York Times* in 2003, "was named after somebody who was dead." Rose Cali, an MSU board member who founded the museum and learning center, admits, "Yogi was a little uncomfortable at the idea of having a place named after him. 'Some times I feel ashamed,' I heard him once say, 'I feel humble.' When I explained to him that what we wanted to do was build a learning and resource center and use his name to attract people, especially kids, he was convinced."

The interiors were designed by Frank Gehry, who worked with the Baseball Hall of Fame in Cooperstown for more than nine years. Permanent exhibits feature Yogi's ten World Series rings, replica Hall of Fame plaques, and the mitt (now bronzed) he used to catch Don Larsen's perfect game in the 1956 World Series. Exhibits over the years have included "Pride Against Prejudice," a tribute to the Negro Leagues in the Larry Doby Gallery, and "The History of Women in Baseball," which earned Yogi a letter from one Mariah Levinson. "Dear Yogi Berra, I just wanted to know if you could maybe teach girls how to be a great legend and star just like you. The ages that you could work with are girls 7–14." Thousands of school children a year attend workshops, sports camps, and clinics; one of the museum's first speakers was Roberto Clemente Jr., who spoke on the history of Latinos in baseball.

Hundreds of photos, some of them enlarged to cover entire walls, tell Yogi's own story—pictures of Berra with his dad, Joe DiMaggio, Mickey Mantle, Casey Stengel, current Yankees such as Derek Jeter, and half a dozen American presidents. "I've got pictures of me here," Yogi observed to one journalist, "that I've never seen before."

One exhibit, housed in a long glass display case, reflects Yogi's place in American pop culture, with such artifacts as Yogi figures, cereal boxes, ads, comic books, and panels from various cartoons, including, inevitably, Yogi Bear. There is also a state-of-the-art theater designed to look like the bleachers at Yankee Stadium. Symposiums have included such subjects as "Baseball and Race," "Women's Sports and Gender Equity," and, during Math and Science Month, "Exploiting Baseball's Connection to Physics and Kinetics." And in April 1999, it was announced that the New York

Yankees' 1998 World Championship Trophy was being sent to the museum by George Steinbrenner.

As early as 1993, Steinbrenner had been seeking a path toward reconciliation with Yogi. He had been widely quoted as saying, "I will try the best I can this year to reach out to Yogi. This is something that really bothers my family. Everybody loves Yogi."[18] To which Dick Schaap, commenting on ESPN, said, "When I read that Yogi won't go back to Yankee Stadium as long as George is there, I think to myself how different the two men are. Yogi doesn't need George, but George seems to need Yogi."[19]

The thaw between Berra and Steinbrenner had been coming for some time. The catalyst was Joe DiMaggio, who was in Memorial Regional Hospital in Hollywood, Florida, with a lingering case of pneumonia. According to a report in the *New York Daily News*, during a visit from Steinbrenner, Joe urged George to make amends with Yogi.* From there, events moved quickly. Two months after Steinbrenner saw DiMaggio, Yankees broadcaster Suzyn Waldman went to The Boss and asked him if he would be willing to visit Berra at the museum in Montclair. Waldman also suggested that an apology would be appropriate.

"My immediate instinct," Yogi said, "was to say no. It seemed like just another scheme to break me down and make me return to Yankee Stadium. I was upset about it until my son Dale spoke to me."[20] Dale Berra had inherited some of the wisdom of his father; this was not easy for a man like George Steinbrenner to do, he told his dad, and if Yogi turned him down, George would be humiliated. Yogi should do the honorable thing and agree to meet him. The kicker came when Dale told him that Yogi's grandchildren had never been to Yankee Stadium. Imagine what it would be like to take his grandchildren there! Yogi had but one stipulation, that Carmen be there with him. So the mountain finally came to Mohammad.

When Steinbrenner's car pulled up in front of the museum on January 5, 1999, Yogi told his former boss, "You're ten minutes late." One report, uncorroborated, is that Steinbrenner replied, "Yogi, I'm fourteen years late." One wants to believe that George actually said that.† Yogi later described his and Carmen's meeting with George as "a heartfelt talk for fifteen minutes." Later, Steinbrenner said in front of reporters, "I know I

---

*DiMaggio's lawyer denied the report, but according to the *Daily News*, Steinbrenner spokesman Howard Rubinstein confirmed that George and Joe had at least talked.

†Steinbrenner may not have said this at the time, but he did say it to me in a phone interview in February 2007. After all, not even Yogi said all of his best lines on the spot.

made a mistake by not letting you go personally. It's the worst mistake I ever made in baseball."[21] A careful reading of Steinbrenner's apology reveals that he regretted not the firing of Yogi but not firing him "personally," but George was swallowing a lot of crow that day, so Yogi pretended not to notice. "If I could get Yogi to come back," Steinbrenner told the press, "I'd bring him back on a rickshaw across the George Washington Bridge." (However, George did not offer to pull the rickshaw himself.) He promised another Yogi Berra Day at Yankee Stadium—"He's got to forgive me and come back," George told Carmen.[22]

In his own way, Steinbrenner took his guardianship of the Yankee dynasty seriously. "We almost lost Joe," he told Yogi. "We don't want to lose you." His concern was well founded; DiMaggio died of lung cancer on March 3, a little more than two months after Steinbrenner and Yogi's meeting.

"It's over," Yogi announced. He had accepted George's apology. "Things have been terrific with me and George since," Yogi said two years later, "though I think it's nice I don't work for him any more."[23]

On July 18, 1999, approximately fourteen years, two months, and three weeks since he had been to Yankee Stadium, Yogi Berra made a triumphant return, grandchildren in tow, to watch the Yankees defeat the Montreal Expos in an interleague game, 6–0. Don Larsen and the Yankees starting pitcher, David Cone, had a superb sense of occasion: Larsen threw out the first ball to Yogi, and Cone celebrated Yogi Berra Day by pitching a perfect game. The glove he used in that game can be seen in a permanent exhibit at the Yogi Berra Museum.

———

SO PERVASIVE WAS Yogi's fame and his estrangement from the Yankees that by the mid-1990s a play about this period was in the offing. Thomas Lysaght had begun work on the first draft of his play, *Nobody Don't Love Yogi*, a few years before Yogi and George came to terms. After the reconciliation, Lysaght finished it.

The premise is simply Yogi's return to Yankee Stadium after a fourteen-year self-imposed exile. "The concept of coming home," wrote Lysaght in the play's introduction, "has been the controlling metaphor in myths and movies since Homer's Odysseus left Troy and Moses' Jews crossed the desert—long before Dorothy got back to Kansas. We all have to leave home in order to find our true home. What took Odysseus twenty years and the Exodus Jews forty took Yogi Berra fourteen years—to get 'home' to Yankee Stadium, to 'arrive,' as T.S. Eliot wrote, where we started and know that place for the first time."

Lysaght reworked the "quest" myth in terms of a mythic American. The play is a monologue delivered by Yogi in the Yankee clubhouse and manager's office on Yogi Berra Day, before and after David Cone's perfect game. Lysaght uses Yogi as a prism for looking back through Yankee history. At one point lights rise on the uniforms of the Yankee greats in their lockers—Ruth's number 3, Gehrig's 4, DiMaggio's 5, Mantle's 7, Casey's 37—and you can feel Berra's awe at being there, and, even more, being included as one of them. Yogi is halfway between being a fan, like us, and one of the immortals, and at the close of the play the lights fade and a spotlight catches the number 8 on the back of Yogi's jersey, hanging on the wall with the others.

In May 2003, the one-man show starring Ben Gazzara premiered at the Bay Street Theater in Sag Harbor, New York. On October 30, the production at the Lamb's Theater in Manhattan opened to excellent reviews. "At 73," Bruce Weber wrote in *The New York Times*, "Mr. Gazzara actually looks a little like Mr. Berra, who is 78. Wearing a jacket and tie and wire-rimmed glasses, he effects quite well Mr. Berra's gruff vocal tones, and he plays the role with great aplomb, gently embodying the soft-spoken legend that Mr. Lysaght has chosen to outline here."[24]

Yogi and Carmen were given an advance copy of the play, and the author and lead actor met with the family at the museum in Montclair to seek Yogi's endorsement. Over vodka and cranberry juice, Berra and Gazzara exchanged stories about growing up Italian. Gazzara recalled, "Yogi brought out photographs—of him jumping all over Don Larsen after the perfect game, of Jackie Robinson stealing home on a slide that Yogi still believes was an out—and I thought to myself, 'Ah, we got him.' "[25] But there was a problem. Carmen felt she could not sit and watch Dale's problems rehashed, however briefly, on the stage. And, says Lysaght, there was something else: "Dale told me, 'My dad just doesn't want to revisit George.' " Lysaght says he totally understood, and that "Yogi did autograph my script." In the end, though, Lysaght thought there was another factor involved. "I think," he says, "that Yogi was too humble to watch himself on stage."

———

WHY, I ASKED Lysaght, with all the great heroes in Yankee history—Ruth, Gehrig, DiMaggio, Stengel, Mantle, etc.—did he pick Yogi for his subject? Because, he replied, Yogi represented the best of all of them. He was the essence of the team of immortals over the decades. "He was—he *is*—the eternal Yankee."

In W. P. Kinsella's 1982 novel, *Shoeless Joe*, a fictionalized J. D. Salinger says, "The one constant through all the years has been baseball. America has been erased like a blackboard, only to be rebuilt and then erased again. But baseball has marked time while America has rolled by like a procession of steamrollers. It is the same game that Moonlight Graham played in 1905. It is a living part of history . . . It continually reminds us of what once was, like an Indian-head penny in a handful of new coins."

Baseball's most *constant* constant over the last sixty-some years has been Yogi Berra. Like baseball itself, Yogi has never really been in fashion. Like baseball, he is too popular to be fashionable at all, and his life and achievements transcend fashion pointing to something indelibly good in the American character.

Yogi is more than a living part of our history; he does more than remind us of what once was; he is a symbol of the best of what is and can still be, of what baseball, the way he played it and lived it, has to tell us. "But it is a game," he once observed, "not life. Although if you play it for money, you can learn a lot about life."[26] That's Yogi: learning us all his experience. That's Yogi: pragmatic, realistic, and playful. That, at its best, is America.

EXTRA INNINGS

Appendices

Appendix A

Was Yogi the Greatest?
Yogi Berra, Johnny Bench,
Roy Campanella, Mickey Cochrane,
and Bill Dickey Compared

WHO WAS THE greatest catcher of all time?

In the first half of the twentieth century, most greatest-catcher debates had Mickey Cochrane and Bill Dickey in the first two spots with the Cubs' great backstop, Gabby Hartnett, finishing third. From there to the end of the century, six more candidates were thrown into the mix: Berra, Roy Campanella, Johnny Bench, Carlton Fisk, Gary Carter (one of the most underrated catchers ever), and Josh Gibson, who many feel would have been the greatest of all had he been given his fair shot at the big leagues.

I would add yet two more names who, as I wrote this, were still active: Mike Piazza and Ivan Rodriguez. Piazza just retired, and Pudge plays under a constant cloud created by the steroids scandals. Piazza may be the best-hitting catcher in baseball history, but by no standard of evaluation I've ever seen has he been regarded as more than a mediocre defensive catcher. I think if we were considering the greatest at just about any other position, defense wouldn't weigh so heavily, but catcher being the only regular position where a player is on the line for every pitch makes defense far more important in determining overall value. In any event, though, I'm going to simplify this debate. I'm going to eliminate Piazza and Pudge, if only because they are contemporary and their careers have not yet been properly evaluated. For now, let's stick with the twentieth century.

Josh Gibson might well have been the best ever had he been given the chance; then again, Roy Campanella, had he come up a couple of years earlier and not suffered quite so many serious injuries, might also be in first place. My suspicion is that against the same competition and under the same circumstances, Campy would have proved to be better than Gibson, if only because Campanella was a great defensive catcher and none of Josh Gibson's contemporaries thought he was. While I haven't read anyone who says Gibson was a *bad* one, I don't know anyone who thought he was particularly good, so I'm going to eliminate Josh Gibson from the debate because, simply put, I just don't have any relevant statistics to work with.

Of course, those who do lots of stats aren't always in agreement. For instance, in 1984, two years after Johnny Bench's retirement, John Thorn and Pete Palmer published their groundbreaking book, *The Hidden Game of Baseball*. Using their complex linear-weights method that normalizes statistics from different eras, they concluded that the most productive hitting catchers of all time were, in order: Johnny Bench, Gene Tenace, Mickey Cochrane, Bill Dickey, Gabby Hartnett, and Yogi Berra (actually, Joe Torre was ranked higher than all of them, but of course he played many more games at other positions). I won't dwell on this because any explanation of their methods would be shallow and incomplete; I direct the reader to either the original 1984 edition or the 1985 paperback, which is revised and updated.

To further complicate the issue, Palmer and Thorn contributed much to *Total Baseball: The Encyclopedia of Major League Baseball*, which, in the 2001 edition, ranks "The Top 100 Players of All-Time" by Palmer and Thorn's TPR, or Total Player Rating, which is defined as "the sum of a player's Adjusted Batting Runs, Fielding Runs, and Base Stealing Runs minus his positional adjustment, all divided by the Runs Per Win factor for that year." (Again, the reader is advised to go directly to the source for details.) By TPR, the best catchers of all time were Gabby Hartnett, Yogi Berra, Mike Piazza, and Bill Dickey—at least they were the best catchers in the 100 top players. Johnny Bench, Mickey Cochrane, Roy Campanella, Carlton Fisk, and others didn't make the cut.

In the 2000 book *Baseball Dynasties: The Greatest Teams of All Time*, by Rob Neyer and Eddie Epstein, Epstein contributes a section titled "The Greatest Catcher," which turns into an essay of the relative merits of Johnny Bench, Yogi Berra, Roy Campanella, and Mickey Cochrane—Dickey does not make Epstein's cut. "Much of the evaluation of a catcher," he writes, "revolves around things that are difficult to measure, such as calling a game or blocking pitches. Ideally, one would like to compare, for example, the ERA of their pitching staff with and without them behind the plate. But we don't have that data for these guys . . . Bench caught 125-plus games in ten different seasons. Berra did it seven times and led the league in games caught in eight consecutive seasons (1950–57). Campanella didn't catch quite as many games per year, but did lead the league four times in games caught. Like Campanella, Cochrane had a relatively short career but he did lead the league in games caught in five of his eleven seasons as a regular." Epstein then proceeds to discuss the vagaries of fielding statistics but concedes the obvious, which is that though the Gold Glove has only been awarded since 1957, with Bench winning ten, the others would certainly have won their share, too, had there been such an award during their time.

As for hitting, "this is something we can measure with some degree of accuracy. All of these catchers were productive hitters. Bench, Berra, and Cochrane were better than the overall league average in runs created per 27 outs (RC/27) every year that they were regular catchers. Nagging injuries kept Campanella from doing this, but he finished in the top five in his league in RC/27 four times, more than any of the other players in this group. *In terms of where they ranked among catchers in their league while they played, Berra and Cochrane dominate* [emphasis mine]. They led their league's catchers in RC/27 ten times. Campanella led six times, and, somewhat surprisingly, Bench led 'only' four times."

Epstein calculates the RC/27 of his four top candidates relative to their league and multiplies the result by each man's number of plate appearances. (He ignores Bench's and Berra's appearances at other positions, which is okay by me as I doubt it would make much of a difference in the outcome.) Here are his results:

Player	Plate Appearances	Player RC/27	League RC/27	Relative RC/27	Net RC/27
Bench	8,669	5.47	4.07	1.34	11,651
Berra	8,361	6.14	4.45	1.38	11,536
Campanella	4,816	6.17	4.48	1.38	6,633
Cochrane	6,206	7.60	5.08	1.50	9,825

(To fully explain Epstein's chart, he uses Bench as an example: he had 8,669 career plate appearances and a career RC/27 rate of 5.47 while the league average during the time he played was 4.07. Dividing 5.47 by 4.07 gives the result of 1.34—by the standard of runs created, Bench was 34 percent more productive than the average league player. Epstein then multiplies 1.34 by 8,669 to get 11,651, which he calls Net RC/27.)

Epstein takes the comparison a bit further. What would the rankings look like if only the seasons in which they caught at least 100 games—which would presumably mean their peak seasons—were used? The answer is below:

Player	Plate Appearances	Player RC/27	League RC/27	Relative RC/27	Net RC/27
Bench (13)°	7,607	5.69	4.07	1.40	10,620
Berra (10)	5,782	6.46	4.48	1.44	8,334
Campanella (9)	4,531	6.23	4.48	1.39	6,298
Cochrane (11)	5,902	7.59	5.06	1.50	8,854

°The number in parentheses next to each player's name indicates the number of seasons he caught at least 100 games.

Cochrane comes off a little better than the other three in Relative Runs Created when evaluating both career and seasons of 100-plus games. He played, of course, in an era in which runs were more plentiful than the other three did, but essentially all four, at their respective peaks, hit at pretty much the same level of effectiveness. For what it's worth, both Cochrane and Bench had a slight edge on Berra and Campanella, as they became regular catchers earlier in their careers. Bench had his first 100-plus-games caught season at age twenty, Cochrane at twenty-two. Yogi didn't get to catch over 100 games until he was twenty-four, and Campy, alas, not until he was twenty-seven.

Yet another evaluation of the great catchers has been done by Bill James—actually, several evaluations, including his *Bill James Historical Baseball Abstract* (1988). James originated the Runs Created formula, though his evaluations in the *Historical Abstract* are based on more than just that single statistic. In 1988, these were his lists for the top catchers:

Peak Value	Career Value
1. Roy Campanella	1. Yogi Berra
2. Mickey Cochrane	2. Johnny Bench
3. Johnny Bench	3. Mickey Cochrane
4. Yogi Berra	4. Gary Carter
5. Gary Carter	5. Carlton Fisk
6. Gabby Hartnett	6. Gabby Hartnett
7. Thurman Munson	7. Bill Dickey
8. Carlton Fisk	8. Ernie Lombardi
9. Bill Dickey	9. Roy Campanella
10. Bill Freehan	10. Ted Simmons

James also lists the catcher's offensive winning percentage, defined by him as "a mathematical answer to this question: If every player on a team hit the same way this player hits, and the team allowed an average of runs to score, what would the team's winning percentage be?" Here's James's top ten catchers ranked by career value with their offensive winning percentages:

Catcher	Offensive Winning Percentage
1. Mickey Cochrane	.683
2. Gabby Hartnett	.654
3. Yogi Berra	.643
4. Gary Carter	.638
5. Bill Dickey	.626
6. Johnny Bench	.621
7. Ernie Lombardi	.610
8. Roy Campanella	.602
9. Ted Simmons	.584
10. Carlton Fisk	.568

In an even more advanced version of the *Historical Abstract*, his 2001 edition, James did yet another more sophisticated set of player rankings and listed his top ten catchers this way:

1. Yogi Berra
2. Johnny Bench
3. Roy Campanella
4. Mickey Cochrane
5. Mike Piazza
6. Carlton Fisk
7. Bill Dickey
8. Gary Carter
9. Gabby Hartnett
10. Ted Simmons

In 2002 James's *Win Shares* was published, which is perhaps the most sophisticated method yet devised for rating players. James explained that Win Shares are "in essence, Wins Created . . . Win Shares takes the concept of Runs Created and moves it one step further, from runs to wins. This makes it different in essentially two ways: first, it removes illusions of context, putting a hitter from Yankee Stadium on equal footing with a hitter from Colorado, and putting a hitter from 1968 on equal footing with a hitter from 2000. Second, the Win Shares system attempts to state the contributions of pitchers and of fielders in the same form as those of hitters." Suffice it for our purposes to say that a detailed explanation of James's method would take up more space than is reasonable here, and the reader is urged to search out his book for the specifics.

Here are the candidates for greatest catcher ever, ranked by Win Shares (the top eleven, actually, as Ted Simmons and Joe Torre are tied). According to James, a Win Share is worth about one-third of a win.

Catcher	Win Shares
1. Yogi Berra	375
2. Carlton Fisk	368
3. Johnny Bench	356
4. Gary Carter	337
5. Gabby Hartnett	325
6. Ted Simmons	315
7. Joe Torre	315
8. Bill Dickey	314
9. Mickey Cochrane	275
10. Bill Freehan	267
11. Mike Piazza	255

Because these numbers are for entire careers, Roy Campanella, who played nine full seasons and 83 games of another, didn't make this list.

I am throwing in all of these evaluations to provide as wide a range of opinion as possible. Here is one more:

In order to pay me back for scores of checks picked up whenever we get together, I asked several members of the *Baseball Prospectus* team, plus ESPN's Rob Neyer, SI.com's Alex Belth, *Baseball Prospectus*' Steven Goldman, and my *Wall Street Journal* colleague Allen St. John, to give me their top ten catcher list of all time. I gave just one ground rule: to leave Josh Gibson off the list for the reasons already specified. For the record, everybody said they would include Gibson among their top five or six, but since they are all statistics people, I wanted their opinions on catchers whose numbers could be calculated. Their top ten in order:

1. Johnny Bench (tie)
   Yogi Berra
3. Mickey Cochrane
4. Gary Carter
5. Carlton Fisk
6. Bill Dickey
7. Roy Campanella
8. Gabby Hartnett
9. Ivan Rodriguez
10. Mike Piazza

(Joe Torre, it should be noted, finished eleventh, and Buck Ewing, who caught from 1880 to 1897, was twelfth, the only catcher before Cochrane and Dickey to be ranked.)

I asked all my voters if they had weighted their choices more toward career than peak value. All confirmed that they did and said if they had been choosing on the basis of peak value, Campanella would have rated higher.

———

NO MATTER HOW you toss it, I think, it comes down to Yogi Berra and Johnny Bench for best all-around catcher over the course of their careers in the second half of the twentieth century, and Yogi versus Campy for best catcher at his peak in that same period.

I think it's also clear that the three best catchers in the first half of the twentieth century were Mickey Cochrane, Bill Dickey, and Gabby Hartnett. Most analysts I've talked to favor Cochrane; most of the old-time sportswriters preferred Dickey. The 1960 book *Big-Time Baseball*, edited by Ben Olan of the Associated Press, has a chapter on "The All-Star Team of All-Time," in which "164 top flight sportswriters of the country's leading newspapers as well as 76 nationally-known public figures" picked the top nine players in the game's history up to that time. Bill Dickey beat out Cochrane, Hartnett, Berra, and Campanella as the team's catcher. If nothing else, that settles the issue as to what most leading sportswriters thought in 1960.

A second poll in the same book, "The All-Star Team of the Past Decade"—meaning 1950 to 1959—was taken among 190 of the country's leading sportswriters and editors from 137 cities and 41 states (as well as the

District of Columbia). Each voter indicated a first, second, and third choice at each position; a first-place vote earned a player three points, a second-place vote two points, a third-place vote one point. Yogi received 506 points to 412 for Campanella. Del Crandall finished third with 90 points.

So, we can conclude that (a) judged by their contemporaries, Yogi was considered a little better than Campy, and (b) most analysts agree with that opinion today. Near the end of Yogi's career, most of the experts regarded Dickey as not only better than Berra but the best the game has ever seen. Today, most would favor Berra.

Mickey Cochrane and Bill Dickey compete with each other for the title of best catcher in the first half of the century, and in the second half, virtually all experts who don't go with Berra choose Johnny Bench. Berra and Bench are easier to compare to each other than either is to Dickey or Cochrane, who, in comparison, played a radically different game.

Berra and Bench actually square off quite nicely. Here are their career numbers at the plate (and my thanks to both men for having the decency to play almost the same number of games).

	G	AB	HR	RBI	R	BB	SO	GDP	BA	OBA	SA°
Berra	2,120	7,555	358	1,430	1,174	704	414	146	.285	.348	.482
Bench	2,158	7,658	389	1,376	1,091	891	1,278	201	.267	.342	.476

°Slugging average

As Eddie Epstein noted, both men played other positions: Yogi put in 260 games as an outfielder, while Bench played 111 in the outfield, 195 at third, and another 145 at first. It seemed picky not to include all their batting numbers here.

If there is an edge for Bench over Berra in hitting, it isn't apparent from these raw statistics. There is, of course, far more to the debate than these basic stats, but anyone making a case for Bench would have to argue past these figures. Yogi played in 38 fewer games and hit 31 fewer home runs than Bench, but he also drove in 54 more runs and scored 83 more. Bench walked 187 more times, which is significant, and Berra struck out 864 fewer times, which may or may not be significant. It certainly sounds better to say someone struck out 864 fewer times, but what that means in terms of actual runs is difficult to pin down. Since major leaguers in the second half of the last century caught about 97 percent of the balls hit to them, it might mean that the extra balls put in play by Berra produced a handful more runs than Bench's batted balls. But though Yogi made contact more often than Bench, he *didn't*, as you might have expected, ground into more double plays. In fact, Bench hit into 55 more double plays.

But look at the categories Yogi leads Bench in: batting average, by 18 points; on-base average by 6; and slugging average, also by 6. Figured by SLOB, or slugging average times on base average, Yogi produced 16.7 runs per 100 at-bats to Bench's 16.3. Not much of a gap there, and it certainly fits into the category of possible margin for error.

What about their relative worth as defensive catchers? Fielding statistics, of course, are never as definite as batting stats, and it is easier to make sense of Berra's and Bench's batting numbers than their fielding numbers. This is particularly true regarding stolen bases, since runners simply didn't attempt many steals in the 1950s and went wild when Bench was catching in the late 1960s and early 1970s.

Bill James's meticulously researched Win Shares method gives Berra an A as a defensive catcher for his career and Bench an A–. (Roy Campanella, Bill Dickey, and Mickey Cochrane all got A's, too.)

The defensive statistics seem to me to be slightly on Yogi's side. (The numbers in parentheses indicate how many times they led the league.)

	Games	Put-outs	Assists	Double Plays	Fielding Average (FA)	League FA
Berra	1,697	8,738 (8)	798 (5)	175 (6)	.989 (2)	.987
Bench	1,742	9,249 (2)	850 (1)	127 (1)	.990 (1)	.987

For what it's worth, Roy Campanella led National League catchers *six* times in put-outs in only nine seasons, four times more than Bench; once in assists, the same as Bench; and twice in double plays, one more than Bench, even though one of the seasons he accomplished this was his first, when he played in just 78 games.

In comparison, Cochrane led the American League catchers in put-outs six times in twelve seasons, and led twice in assists and twice in double plays. Dickey, in thirteen seasons of catching 100-plus games, led his league in put-outs six times and led three times in assists and just once in double plays. Whatever the value of leading the league in fielding stats, the edge goes to Yogi.

Of course, the reason sportswriters in the 1950s and 1960s regarded Cochrane and Dickey as better hitters than Berra and Campanella was because they had higher career batting averages, and sportswriters' faith in batting average in those dark ages of baseball analysis was unshakable. But even without using statistics which level the playing field, it's possible to compare one important fact about hitters in any era: how they compared against hitters in their own time.

Total Baseball ranks the top five hitters in every year since 1871 in runs, hits, doubles, triples, home runs, total bases, runs batted in, runs produced (runs plus RBIs), bases on balls, batting average, on-base average, slugging percentage, and their own complex evaluation system, Total Player Rating (TPR). Catchers aren't expected to lead their leagues in key hitting categories; the defensive job is just too demanding on legs and backs. But Berra and Bench show up an amazing number of times in the top five spots, not just for catchers, but for anybody. Let's do a year-by-year search, starting with Yogi:

1949	Fifth in slugging percentage
1950	Fifth in runs, fourth in hits, third in total bases, third in RBIs, second in runs scored, **second in TPR**
1951	Fourth in total bases, **fifth in TPR**
1952	Fourth in runs, third in HRs, fifth in RBIs, **fourth in TPR**
1953	Fourth in HRs, fifth in total bases, fifth in RBIs, third in slugging, **third in TPR**
1954	Fourth in total bases, second in RBIs, third in runs produced, fifth in batting average, fifth in slugging, **fifth in TPR**
1955	Third in RBIs
1956	Third in HRs, third in RBIs, fourth in runs produced, fifth in slugging average, **third in TPR**

These are Yogi's eight best seasons, and I think that, relative to his era, it's the most impressive batting display ever put on by a catcher. Johnny Bench's is almost as impressive:

1970	First in HRs, second in total bases, first in RBIs, second in runs produced, **second in TPR**
1972	Third in total bases, first in RBIs, fifth in runs produced, third in walks, third in slugging, **third in TPR**
1973	Fourth in RBIs
1974	Third in runs, third in doubles, second in HRs, fourth in total bases, first in RBIs, first in runs produced, fourth in slugging

| 1975 | Fourth in doubles, fourth in homers, second in RBIs, fifth in runs produced, fourth in slugging, **third in TPR** |
| 1977 | Fifth in slugging |

It's easy to see why some people regard Bench as the greater catcher, or at least the greater hitter. At his best, Bench was better than Yogi, finishing relatively higher than Berra in the power categories—HRs, RBIs, and slugging average—in several seasons. But note Yogi's consistency. He shows up in something in every year for eight straight seasons, while in 1971 and 1976 Bench fails to place anywhere in the top five in anything.

Whether you come down on the side of Berra or Bench as the better hitter, you must concede that, at least from the point of TPR, both Berra and Bench leave Cochrane and Dickey in the dust.

Cochrane had a pretty good run from 1930 to 1935. In 1930, he was fifth in batting and fifth in TPR; in 1931 he was fourth in batting and fifth in TPR; in 1932 he was fifth in walks, fifth in on-base average, and fourth in TPR; in 1933 he was second in walks, first in on-base average, fourth in slugging, and fifth in TPR. In 1934 he was fourth in on-base average, and in 1935 he was fifth in on-base average. Dickey's best seasons were from 1936 to 1939, when he finished, fifth, fourth, fifth, and fifth in TPR, respectively. But the only hitting categories he ever placed in were batting average (third) and slugging average (fifth) in 1936 and RBIs (fourth) in 1937.

I think it's safe to say that in their own time Yogi Berra and Johnny Bench were better hitters than Mickey Cochrane and Bill Dickey were in theirs. I think it's also safe to say that Berra and Bench were the two most valuable catchers of the century. Their hitting and fielding numbers are too close to declare either one a clear winner, so let's call the statistical comparison a draw and move on to the question of "team skills," loosely defined here as "leadership," as in the handling of pitchers.

How many truly great pitchers did Yogi Berra work with? I think Whitey Ford obviously qualifies as great from just about any perspective, but what other Yankee pitchers could justifiably be called great, from the late 1940s when Berra assumed the regular catching duties till the end of the next decade?

Allie Reynolds is close. But despite some flashes of greatness with the Indians, Reynolds didn't become a consistently effective pitcher until he came to the Yankees. In addition to better fielding and, of course, working with the Yankees' new pitching coach, Jim Turner, one of the likely reasons

Reynolds brought his game together was his ability to work well with Berra, who caught 51 games in 1947, 71 in 1948, and 109 in 1949. There is no clear evidence that Yogi made a star out of Reynolds or Eddie Lopat or Vic Raschi or Tommy Byrne, the Yankees' four starting aces of the post–World War II period, or any of the Yankees' other pitchers, but look at how they all improved as Berra eased into regular duties:

Year	Reynolds Team	W-L	Lopat Team	W-L	Raschi Team	W-L	Byrne Team	W-L	Berra Games Caught
1946	Cle	11–15	CWS	13–13	NYY	2–0	NYY	0–1	6
1947	NYY	19–8	CWS	16–13	NYY	7–2	NYY	0–0	51
1948	NYY	16–7	NYY	17–11	NYY	19–8	NYY	8–5	71
1949	NYY	17–6	NYY	15–10	NYY	21–10	NYY	15–7	109
1950	NYY	16–12	NYY	18–8	NYY	21–8	NYY	15–9	148
1951	NYY	17–8	NYY	21–9	NYY	21–10	2 Teams°	6–11	141

°NYY and StL-AL.

    This isn't scientific, but when you see the records of these four good-to-very-good-but-not-great pitchers alongside Yogi's increasing total of games caught, it's hard to escape the conclusion that they matured together. Tommy Byrne's case stands out even more than the others. In 1951 the Yankees traded Byrne to the Browns after arm trouble limited him to just nine ineffective appearances and a 2–1 record. He was just 4–10 for the rest of the season with St. Louis. In 1953 he bounced from the White Sox to the Senators, going 2–5 with an ERA of 6.16. At the tail end of 1954, the Yankees reacquired him and he went 3–2 with an ERA of 2.70 in five starts. In 1955 he had his best season, starting 22 games and going 16–5 with an ERA of 3.15.

    Yes, he had some arm trouble, and the Yankees were a much better team. But a huge portion of that better team, both at bat and behind the plate, was Yogi Berra. Byrne had some effectiveness in both 1956 and 1957 with the Yankees, mostly as a relief pitcher, but when you add it all up, Tommy Byrne not only pitched ineffectively when he was outside the Bronx, *he had all his best seasons when Yogi Berra was his catcher.*

    And so did most of the Yankees' other pitchers in the 1950s. From 1954 to 1959, the last season Berra served as the Yankees' workhorse catcher before giving way to Elston Howard, the Yankees won four more pennants and two more World Series, and in one of the two years they didn't win the pennant, 1954, they won 103 games. Their pitching pretty much consisted of Whitey Ford, youngsters having one or two great seasons, a couple of aging veterans, and a long list of career mediocrities who had a couple of good seasons with the Yankees and then faded into obscurity. Even Yankee fans can't remember most of their names. Season by season, the most important ones were:

1954

The staff included Ed Lopat and Allie Reynolds, hanging on in 1954 (Reynolds's last season, Lopat's next to last); Johnny Sain (playing out a productive three-year stretch with the Yanks; the next season, after a few appearances, he would be dealt to Kansas City); Bob Grim; Tom Morgan; Harry Byrd; and Jim McDonald. Let's look carefully at the last four:

• Bob Grim was 20–6 for the Yankees in his rookie season of 1954; for the next three seasons, he was plagued by arm trouble but was effective when he could pitch, winning 25 games and losing 14, and by 1957 making the transition into a reliever (he led the AL in saves with 39 that year). For the rest of his career, with four other teams, he was a combined 16–20.

• Tom Morgan was a combination starter-reliever for the Yankees from 1950 to 1956, when he was dealt to—you guessed it—Kansas City. For his five seasons in New York, he was 38–22, with his best season coming in 1954 when he started 17 games and went 11–5. He lasted in the big leagues for six more seasons, winning 29 and losing 25.

• Harry Byrd was with the Yankees just one season, going 9–7 in 21 starts and posting the best ERA of his career, 2.99. For the rest of his six seasons in the bigs he was 37–47 with an ERA of over four runs per game.

• Jim McDonald was with the Yankees for three of his nine major league seasons, 1952 to 1954, when, as a reliever and spot starter, he was a combined 16–12 with an ERA under four runs for all three seasons. For the rest of his career he was 8–15, and his overall ERA was 4.27.

There you go. Four more guys who, for whatever reason, pitched very well when Yogi Berra was behind the plate and very lousy when anyone else caught them. Let's move on to 1955.

1955

The Yankees rebounded from their second-place finish in 1954 to beat out the Indians by three games for the American League pennant. After Whitey Ford (18–7), the staff was paced by

- "Bullet Bob" Turley, who had compiled a three-year record of 16 wins and 22 losses with the Cardinals and Orioles, but was to go 76–44 from 1955 to 1960 with the Yankees before arm trouble reduced him to spot starting and middle-innings relief. In 1945, with the Orioles, he was 14–15 with an ERA of 3.46; in his first year with the Yankees and Yogi he was 17–13 with an ERA of 3.16.

- Don Larsen's perfect game in the 1956 World Series is always regarded as a colossal fluke—which, of course, it was. But for four seasons, 1955–1958, Larsen was a pretty good pitcher as both a starter and a reliever. After enduring two horrible seasons with the St. Louis Browns and then with their incarnation in Baltimore, he won 10 games and lost 33 with an ERA of over 4.20. In 1955, Larsen started 13 games for the Yankees, went 9–2, and saved two others, posting an ERA of 3.06. Overall, in his four good seasons in pinstripes, Larsen went 39–17 and his ERA never exceeded 3.74. In 1959, he dipped to 6–7, and the next year the Yankees dealt him to—need you ask?—Kansas City, where he was 1–10 with a 5.38 ERA.

- Johnny Kucks was a rookie in 1955 and started in 13 games, relieved in 16, and had an 8–7 record and a respectable 3.41 ERA. His best year was 1956, when Yogi and the Yankees coaxed an 18–9 record out of him. Overall, in four seasons and part of a fifth with the Yankees, he was 42–35 with six saves. In 1959 the Yankees traded him to—have I already mentioned this?—Kansas City, where, for the next two years, he was 12–21 with an ERA of over four runs per game.

- Jim Konstanty—yes, the Jim Konstanty who won the MVP award for the Phillies in 1950. After going 16–7 for the Phils at the beginning of the decade, Konstanty was 23–24 over the next three seasons with an overall ERA in that span of over four runs per game. In 1954, when he was thirty-seven, the Phillies traded him to the Yankees, where he made nine relief appearances, saving two, and recorded an ERA of 0.98. In 1955 he was again sensational for the Yankees, winning seven and losing two in 45 relief appearances. He saved 11 games and posted the best seasonal ERA of his career, 2.32. The next season the Yankees dealt him to the Cardinals (the Athletics' phone must have been busy), where he closed out his career.

1956

This time the Yankees not only won the pennant but the World Series as well. Ford, of course, was the ace that year at 19–6. The staff was fleshed out by Kucks (18–9), Larsen (11–5), Turley (8–4), Byrne (7–3), Grim (6–1), and the new addition of Tom Sturdivant (16–8).

Sturdivant pitched in 33 games as a rookie with the Yankees in 1955 with an excellent ERA of 3.16. The next season he started 17 games and relieved in 15, winning 16 and saving five with an ERA of 3.30. In 1957 he had his best year pitching exclusively as a starter, leading the AL in won-lost percentage (16–6, or .727), with his career-best ERA, 2.54. That was about it for Tom. After a disappointing 1958 season, 3–6, and a slow start in 1959, the Yankees dumped him on—am I starting to sound like a broken record here?—Kansas City, where he went 2–6. He pitched indifferently for six seasons after leaving the Yankees, never approaching the 32–14 record he had in 1956 and 1957.

1957

The Yankees won the pennant but lost the World Series to the Braves. The most significant addition to the staff was Bobby Shantz, who had won the MVP in 1952 for the lowly Philadelphia A's when he went 24–7, but he had spent the next four seasons struggling with arm trouble and had a won-lost record of 13–26. The Yankees squeezed four more good seasons out of him—two (1957–1958) as a spot starter and reliever and two (1959–1960) almost exclusively as a reliever. In 1957 he was brilliant, starting 21 games, going 11–5, saving five, and leading the league with a 2.45 ERA. Over the next three seasons he was 19–13 with 14 saves, recording ERAs of 3.36, 2.38, and 2.79. In 1961 the Yankees traded him to Pittsburgh, and he spent his last four seasons bouncing around the National League.

1958

The Yanks again won it all. The pitching staff was paced by "Bullet Bob" Turley (21–7), who had his best season and walked off with the Cy Young award. Whitey Ford, at 14–7, was the only other pitcher to win more than *nine* games. Perhaps more than any other of the Yankees' pennant-winning seasons with Berra as the regular catcher, the Yankees staff was an incredible pastiche of one-shot wonders and also-rans. Let's go down the list:

- Duke Maas had a record of 19–32 with the Tigers and Athletics before the Yankees acquired him early in the 1958 season. He promptly went 7–3 for them with an ERA of 3.82. Maas wasn't much of a pitcher, but he lasted with the Yanks for two more full seasons and part of a third before retiring in early 1961. From 1959–1960, incredibly, he managed to win 19 and lost only 9.

- Ryne Duren, of course, is one of the great weird stories of the 1950s and 1960s. A terrifying fastball pitcher, he suffered from bad eyesight. In a brief (one game) appearance with the Orioles in 1954 and 42 innings with—is there an echo in here?—Kansas City in 1957, Duren had an ERA of 5.3 runs per nine innings. In 1958, after coming to New York, he did an immediate about-face with a 6–4 won-lost record, a league-leading 20 saves, and a spectacular 2.20 ERA. In 1959, despite a 3–5 won-lost record, he was even more effective, with an ERA of 1.88. After a bad spring and slow start in 1961, the Yankees let him go to the expansion Angels, where he went on to lose 12 of 18 games and collected only two saves, with a horrendous ERA of 5.18. He hung around for four more seasons, having some success in 1963 with the Phillies (6–2, ERA 3.30), but he won only one more major league game after that.

- Art Ditmar was one of the most amazing Yankee success stories of the 1950s. From 1954 through 1956, he struggled with the (natch!) Athletics—winning 25, losing 38, and watching his career ERA climb precariously toward five runs per nine innings. In 1957 he came to the Bronx, went 8–3 with six saves, and saw his ERA drop to 2.35. In 1958, the Yankees' last championship season under Casey Stengel, he was a useful pitcher, going 9–8 in 13 starts and saving four games with an acceptable 3.42 ERA. From 1959 through the first month of 1961, Ditmar was 30–21 before leaving New York for—stop me if you've heard this one—Kansas City, where over the next two seasons he was 0–7 with an ERA of nearly six runs per game.

Have I left anyone out? Oh, yeah, I almost forgot. There was Zach Monroe. I don't know anything about Zach except that his first season in baseball was 1958 and that he started six games for the Yankees and went 4–2 with a very good ERA of 3.26. The following season he pitched in three innings and was out of baseball forever. (The upside is that he never got traded to Kansas City.)

There are, of course, all kinds of reasons why all these pitchers had their best years with the Yankees: better hitting (though that doesn't explain the improved ERAs), better fielding, better coaching, and Casey Stengel's shrewd application of their mostly modest talents. But there is one connection common to all of them that is more direct: Yogi Berra. Yogi worked with just one undeniably great pitcher in his career, Whitey Ford, and in 1951 and 1952 when Ford was in the service Yogi was at his peak, winning the MVP in 1951.

Throughout the late 1940s and most of the 1950s, the Yankees had the best pitching in baseball, even though they seldom had the best pitchers. All of them, no matter what their talent or background or fate, shared two things—World Series money and a catcher. Not Mickey Cochrane or Bill Dickey or Johnny Bench ever displayed anything like Yogi's talent for handling a pitching staff. They might have, if they had been faced with the same circumstances and the same talent to work with. But they didn't have the chance; Yogi did, and he won—seasonal games, pennants, World Series rings—more than any other catcher. In fact, he won more than any other baseball player of the century.

If Yogi Berra's record as handler of Yankee pitching staffs isn't a clear indication of an extraordinary talent for leadership, then we may as well dispense with the word altogether.

Appendix B

Yogi Berra and the Great Minds:
A Comparative Study

Hardly anybody would quarrel . . . that Winston Churchill
has been replaced by Yogi Berra as the
favorite source of quotations.

—*The New Yorker*, July 1991

1. Never, never, never give up.
   — WINSTON CHURCHILL

   It ain't over till it's over.
   — YOGI BERRA

2. This is the best of all possible worlds.
   — VOLTAIRE

   Even if the world were perfect, it wouldn't be.
   — YOGI BERRA

3. One thing you cannot copy, and that is the soul of another person
   or the spirit of another person.
   — SIKH GURU YOGI BHAJAN

   If you can't imitate him, don't copy him.
   — YOGI BERRA

4. It is human to err; and the only final and deadly error, among all
   our errors, is denying that we have ever erred.
   — G. K. CHESTERTON

We made too many wrong mistakes.
—YOGI BERRA

5.   Two roads diverged in a wood, and I—
     I took the one less traveled by.
                    —ROBERT FROST, "The Road Not Taken"

When you come to the fork in the road, take it.
—YOGI BERRA

6.   The moments of the past do not remain still; they retain in our
     memory the motion which drew them towards the future,
     towards a future which has itself become the past, and draw us
     on in their train.
                    MARCEL PROUST

It's déjà vu all over again.°
—YOGI BERRA

7.   Concentration is the narrowing of the field of attention, the fixing
     of the mental eye upon a chosen object.
                    —ERNEST WOOD on yoga

You only got one guy to concentrate on, he throws the ball.
—YOGI BERRA on catching

8.   Act the part and you will become the part.
                    —WILLIAM JAMES

He learned me all his experience.
—YOGI BERRA

9.   The distinction between past, present, and future is only a
     stubbornly persistent illusion.
                    —ALBERT EINSTEIN

We may be lost but we're making good time.
—YOGI BERRA

°Actually there's some confusion about this quote. In fact, Yogi himself is confused. In
his 1989 book, *Yogi: It Ain't Over*, he denies having said it. In *The Yogi Book—I Really
Didn't Say Everything I Said!*, published in 1998, he says he remembers saying it after
watching Mickey Mantle and Roger Maris hit back-to-back home runs. Perhaps he did
say some things that he never said.

10. If none observe me, I have to observe myself all the closer.
         — FRANZ KAFKA

     You can observe a lot just by watching.
         — YOGI BERRA

11. It is impossible for anything to signify nothing.
         — G. K. CHESTERTON

     No one did nothin' to nobody.
         — YOGI BERRA

12. In war, the moral is to the physical as three to one.
         — NAPOLEON BONAPARTE

     Half this game is 90 percent mental.
         — YOGI BERRA

13. The time is now and now is the time.
         — SIKH GURU YOGI BHAJAN

     You mean right now?
         — YOGI BERRA (when asked what time it was)

14. By prevailing over all obstacles and distractions, one may
     unfailingly arrive at his chosen goal or destination.
         — CHRISTOPHER COLUMBUS

     You got to be very careful if you don't know where you're going
     because you might not get there.
         — YOGI BERRA

15. Every day is a journey, and the journey itself is home.
         — MATSUO BASHŌ

     Yeah, but we're making good time.
         — YOGI BERRA (when told that he was lost)

16. By dispelling that ignorance of the true self he has realized the
     Changeless Total Universal self as his own true form, and through
     this realization ignorance has been destroyed.
         — THE VEDANTASARA (Fifteenth-century Hindu text)

I'd be pretty dumb if I started being something I'm not.
— YOGI BERRA

17. A conversation is a dialogue, not a monologue. That's why there are so few good conversations: due to scarcity, two intelligent talkers seldom meet.
— TRUMAN CAPOTE

It was hard to have a conversation with anyone, there were so many people talking.
— YOGI BERRA

18. Thinking should be done beforehand and afterwards, never while actually taking a photograph.
HENRI CARTIER DILLISSION

You can't think and hit at the same time.
— YOGI BERRA

19. If one advances confidently in the direction of his dreams, and endeavors to live the life which he has imagined, he will meet with a success unexpected in common hours.
— HENRY DAVID THOREAU

Go out live your life like every day is opening day.
— YOGI BERRA to the Class of 2007, St. Louis University

Of course, as Yogi Berra had occasion to remind us, he didn't actually say everything he said. But whether he actually said something or not, he usually said it one way or another. Whether or not Yogi said all the things included here exactly as they are written isn't the point; as Shakespearean scholar Michael Macrone points out in *Brush Up Your Shakespeare!*, Shakespeare didn't say everything that Shakespeare said either—or at least he didn't say it first. Or perhaps, as with Yogi, he always said it best.

Appendix C

Casey Interviews Yogi

IN 1960, CASEY STENGEL interviewed Yogi Berra for the Armed Forces Radio Network. The transcript offers a rare look at two great American stylists.

CASEY: I'd have to say, Mr. Berra, that you was one of the three outstanding catchers in the American League—there was Bill Dickey and Mickey Cochrane—and in the National League there was Hartnett and Campanella. So that's pretty good company for you. Now, you've talked to so many umpires, and you've conversed with them, the umpires are your friends, and so on and so forth, and I know they haven't fined you so much in the last few years. How do you account for that?

YOGI: Well, you know, a lot of people think I'm always arguing with the umpires when I turn around, but actually I'm not. I'm just talking conversation to them.*

CASEY: That's what they told me for years. They never missed one from the heart. But they use their eyes. You know, they call them with their eyes. But from the heart they never missed one. Do you think your hitting has

---

*Many umpires appreciated this, some tolerated it, some hated it. Once, Tom Gorman, when asked by Yogi how his family was doing, shouted, "Shut up! My family died last night!"

held up, Yogi? In the fourteen years you have been playing for the Yankees, do you think you can use your bat or can you swing as quickly or do you have the same wrist action that you used to have when you first started in baseball? Do you think you've overcome the fact that you don't chase as many bad balls as you used to when you were first in baseball? I thought you were getting over it. But this is one thing that you did this year. You almost hit a one-hopper.* Some day you may hit a home run on a pitch like that.

YOGI: I had a bad year last year, and maybe the reason was I tried to hit too many good pitches.

CASEY: I think you're right. There's nobody playing where they go. They can't be playing for a ball over your head or one that's pitched on the ground. Now, let's get into something else. You used to be a millionaire, Yogi, and I know you got a lot of friends out there among the men in the services, and there's one thing I would like to ask in their behalf. You used to wear a white glove when you were catching, and I wondered why you would wear a white glove like you had just come from a wedding and you forgot to take off the white gloves. Why is it that you used a white glove when you was a catcher?

(*End of available transcript.*)

————

THERE IS NO simple answer as to what Stengel was talking about. He might have been referring to a glove Yogi slipped over his catching hand to cushion the impact of fastballs, or he might have been referring to gloves he wore to prevent cuts on his hands from getting infected. Those gloves resulted in one of his most widely quoted Yogiisms: "The only reason I need these gloves is 'cause of my hands." In *The Yogi Book* (1998), Berra explained that "Carm, Tim, and I were in the back yard gardening. I began complaining about getting scratches and mud all over my hands. Carmen really let me have it. She finally threw me a pair of gloves . . ."

Whatever Casey might have been talking about, he was probably making a joke about how effete his catcher looked wearing a white glove.

*Casey did not mean that Yogi hit a ball that one-hopped, but rather that he swung at, and hit, a ball that hit the ground before reaching home plate. There are many stories of Berra having done this, though none have been verified; in any case, a ball that hit the dirt before reaching home plate would be considered a dead ball, and the resulting hit nullified—that is, if the umpire actually saw it hit the dirt.

Appendix D

Distant Replay:
Watching the 1956 Perfect Game
with Yogi and Don Larsen*

"IT WAS PERFECT the first time," says Yogi Berra of Don Larsen's perfect game in the 1956 World Series, "and it was even better tonight." A packed house in the theater of the Yogi Berra Museum and Learning Center on the campus of Montclair State University was in full agreement. Roberta Ziemba, who was in her early teens when she saw the game at Yankee Stadium on Oct. 8, 1956, thinks, "It was better than perfect. It was more fun this time around."

In the fifth game of the '56 fall classic, Mr. Larsen faced 27 Brooklyn Dodgers and retired them all, including future Hall of Famers Jackie Robinson, Pee Wee Reese, and Roy Campanella. The feat was unprecedented in the previous 52 World Series, and it hasn't been duplicated in the 49 that have followed—or, in the immortal words of Mr. Larsen's catcher, "It's never happened in World Series history, and hasn't happened since." Last Friday, 80 guests paid $300 each to watch the game, with proceeds benefiting the museum and charities designated by Messrs. Berra and Larsen. It was the first time either man had seen a replay of more than brief highlights of the game.

In fact, it was the first time that anyone in attendance had seen a replay of more than short clips of any baseball game played before 1965—except Doak Ewing. Mr. Ewing, a sports film collector, says that there may be only 10 complete or near-complete baseball games (the recording of the

*Reprinted with permission of *The Wall Street Journal*.

Larsen perfect game is missing only the first inning) prior to that season still in existence, all World Series games. "There are newsreels of high-lights from thousands of games," says Mr. Ewing, "but nobody thought to keep entire games. Games were looked on as entertainment; nobody knew that we'd regard them as history."

Mr. Ewing bought this piece of history at a flea market; it had been put up for sale by the son of the man who kinescoped it for the Armed Forces more than half a century ago. "The games were recorded in order to be shown to servicemen and then destroyed," Mr. Ewing notes. "We have this one by luck and accident."

Those lucky enough to watch the eight innings of the game looked through a window back to a vanished world. "The first thing you notice," says Berra museum director Dave Kaplan, "is how much faster the game moved then than now. I mean how quickly they got the game going again after each side was out. There was only one commercial after each team's at-bat. Today, you've got three or four."

There was just one sponsor for the perfect game, Gillette safety razors. Some of the commercials were done by the game's TV announcers, the Yankees' Mel Allen and the Dodgers' Vin Scully.

Audience member Don MacNair, who admitted to faking illness to stay home from school and watch the game on television, noticed something else: "All you saw on the screen was the game. I didn't realize how clut-tered up modern telecasts are until I saw this one. There was no box score in the corner, no ticker tape running across the bottom with scores of other games, no logo for the network or Major League Baseball, and no com-mercials for other shows flashing on the screen between batters. It was so enjoyable just to sit and watch the ballgame." Jim Pascuiti felt the same way about the commentary: "Mel Allen and Vin Scully were so good. Everything they said was to the point, and when there wasn't anything to say, they kept quiet." Or, as Yogi added, "If they didn't have anything to say, they didn't say it."

Everyone was quick to notice one thing when the first batter was retired—no instant replay. "Everyone had better pay attention," Mr. Ewing quipped to the crowd, "because you're only going to see everything once." Once was enough for Mr. Larsen, who got chuckles from the audi-ence when he remarked, "Yup, that's pretty much the way I remembered it happening." As the game progressed, Mr. Larsen recalls, none of his teammates would talk to him. "They were superstitious. I wasn't. I wanted to talk about it. I sat down next to Mickey Mantle"—who helped preserve the perfect game with a great running catch off a drive off the bat of Gil Hodges—"and he was shocked. He got up and moved away from me."

Mr. Larsen wasn't superstitious, but the announcers were. Bob Wolff, who called the game on radio, told the museum crowd: "I never actually said 'He has a perfect game going.' I kept talking around it, saying things like 'Well, all the base runners tonight have been Yankees.' "

Mr. Berra thought that his pulse raced just as fast watching the replay as it did 51 years ago: "I kept worrying before each pitch as if I was playing the game tonight: 'Is this the right call? Am I set up in the right location? I don't want to ruin this by calling for the wrong pitch!' But watching the game again, I guess I did OK." Larsen concurs: "People forget that half the credit should go to Yogi. It was his perfect game as much as mine. He called every pitch of the game, and I had total confidence in him. I never shook him off once. Why spoil a good thing?"

For some, the evening was an opportunity not just to relive a great memory but to pass it on to the next generation. Dr. Paul Lioy, who saw the game with his father, watched the replay with his son, Jason, who flew in from Pittsburgh. Dr. Lioy remembers: "My father actually suggested leaving around the sixth inning so we could beat the traffic. Can you imagine?" Dr. Lioy's father took him out of school early that day so they could go to the game. "I sure hope my grammar-school principal doesn't read this."

In honor of the occasion, Dr. Lioy paraphrased a "Yogi-ism" on the spot: "It was like 'Back to the Future' all over again."

Acknowledgments

If you don't write a good book about Mr. Yogi Peter Berra,
I will have you killed!

—TED WILLIAMS to a prospective Yogi biographer

I DON'T KNOW when or where Ted Williams said that, but I'm positive he did. I've worked with Ted's quote taped to my wall every day while working on this book. I sincerely hope this book lives up to Ted's demand, because if it doesn't, I will lose sleep at night thinking about a reconstructed Ted Williams rising up from his frozen DNA and knocking on my door late some night, custom-made, whip-handled Louisville Slugger in hand.

Writing this book was so logical for me that I don't remember when I decided to do it, or why it took me so long to get around to it. Probably from my father, Alfred Barra, who used to laugh every time someone asked him, "Are you related to Yogi?"

Yogi Berra was never my idol in the same sense as Mays or Mantle; Yogi was more like family. (I don't think we're related, by the way; my father's family was Neapolitan and Yogi's ancestors were from farther north—"practically Germans," as Carmen Berra once put it—but it's possible that some Irishman at Ellis Island changed a vowel.) All I remember for sure is that when I mentioned the idea of writing a book about Yogi to Bob Weil, who edited my biography of Bear Bryant, *The Last Coach*, he jumped on it like Yogi fielding a bunt.

Most authors, I've noticed, tend to thank their publishers and agent last, but if Bob, Bill Rusin, Tom Mayer, and Lucas Wittmann at W. W. Norton, and Jay Mandel of the William Morris Agency, weren't so enthusiastic about this book from its inception, you wouldn't be reading this now.

I get a catch in my throat every time I walk into the wonderful Yogi

Berra Museum and Learning Center in Little Falls, New Jersey, and I want to thank everyone connected with it, particularly Dave Kaplan, who has gone into extra innings answering my questions. Marty Appel gets a tip of the cap for both his image permissions and for sharing his extensive knowledge of Yogi's life and career. My deep appreciation to Jeff Idelson and Tim Wiles of the National Baseball Hall of Fame in Cooperstown, who never went home before answering my emails. Roy Blount Jr. and Rob Neyer did yeoman work in researching what Yogi said, what he didn't say, and how he did and didn't say it, whether he said it or not. Jim Baker supplied research material and DVDs of *Mystery Science Theater 3000* that considerably boosted morale during my low periods. Both Rob and Jim came out of the bullpen to read through this manuscript. Rob, you're still wrong about Bench, but I thank you for arguing his case.

I thank the following people in the order I spoke to them.

Roger Kahn provided a wonderful background into New York baseball in the 1940s, 1950s, and 1960s and added much priceless insight in both his books and in personal interviews. Professor Gary Mormino's *Immigrants on the Hill: Italian-Americans in St. Louis, 1882–1982* opened a door for me into the wondrous world of the Hill and made it come even more alive in our interviews. Joe Garagiola—of course—was a treasure trove of information on all things Yogi, but especially on their childhood in the Hill. A special thanks to the Ossana women, Diana and her mother, Marian. Diana, who won the Academy Award for her *Brokeback Mountain* screenplay while this book was being written, took time off from her breakneck schedule to connect me with her mom, who had my mouth watering with stories of the great Italian restaurants and bakeries of the Hill.

My thanks to Joe Montefusco and the Newark Bears front office for taking the time to send clips, information, and images, and South Orange's own Joe Murphy for lending me the scorecard for Yogi's first Bears games and for his recollections of Yogi's early years with the Yankees. Dr. Bobby Brown did a great job of setting the record straight on that season at Newark and what it was like to be Yogi's roommate. Frank Shea Jr., son of the late Spec Shea, was generous with anecdotes about his father's friendship with Yogi from 1947 to 1951.

Arlene Howard, Elston's widow, deserves special thanks not only for the generous use of text from her book on her late husband, but for the time she gave me talking about her husband's trials and tribulations, his friendship with Yogi, and her own friendship with Carmen Berra.

Lynn Faupel, Ballantine Beer's advertising manager in the 1950s, recalled stories so vividly I felt I had actually seen a "Ballantine Blast." The man who coined that phrase, the late Mel Allen, granted me several interviews over the years with wonderful stories about both Bear Bryant and Yogi Berra, all of which, in *The Last Coach* and now in this book, I've tried to put to good use. Thanks to Mel's brother, Larry, back in Alabama, who had valuable information not only about his brother but also about Yogi during his early years with the Yankees.

Thanks to Mel's biographer, Steven Borelli, who shared his knowledge of Mel Allen and the Yankees of his time. This is probably the best place, too, to thank the late Red Barber, who, when I was working on Marvin Miller's autobiography, *A Whole Different Ballgame*, was candid about the Yankees and Dodgers in the early 1950s, particularly on the racial attitudes of the Yankees front office. And now that I mentioned him, thanks to Marvin Miller who in his capacity as executive director of the Players Association, saw a different side of Yogi than most people. Before I get out of this paragraph, I want to thank another broadcaster, Bob Wolff, who shared his memories of the Larsen perfect game as well as other stories of the Yankees and Yogi.

Tony Kubek, Bob Turley, Jerry Lumpe, Ryne Duren, Monte Irvin, Don Larsen, Gil McDougald, Charlie Silvera, and Hank Aaron contributed wonderful stories about playing with and competing against Yogi. Particular thanks to Jim Bouton, who, as always, wasn't afraid to go against the grain then or now.

Thanks to Richard Snow, managing editor of *American Heritage* magazine, for helping bring the New York of the 1950s alive for me. Thanks to Bert Randolph Sugar for information, pictures, anecdotes, phone numbers, and, mostly, for continuing to be Bert Sugar.

Thanks to Kristi Jacobsen, granddaughter of the late Toots Shor, for her marvelous photographs and for making me feel as if I had been to her grandfather's saloon and rubbed elbows with Yogi, Jackie Gleason, Frank Sinatra, Joe DiMaggio, and Ernest Hemingway.

Thanks to Robert Creamer and Steven Goldman for bringing Casey Stengel back to life for me.

Richard Lally and Dom Forker, both of whom have written oral histories of the Yankees, were generous in sharing their books and their opinions. Thanks to Peter Golenbock for graciously allowing me to quote from his *Dynasty*, his history of the New York Yankees from 1949 to 1964.

Tom Lysaght and Ben Gazzara were delightful in evoking their memories of bringing Yogi to life on stage for Lysaght's play, *Nobody Don't Love Yogi*.

Ray Robinson, Vic Ziegel, Steve Jacobson, Jerry Eisenberg, and Moss Klein shared a lifetime of great memories on the subject of Yogi in New York; any of them could have written a great book on Yogi, and I am eternally grateful that they chose not to. Mickey Herskowitz, Neil Hohlfeld, Larry Dierker, and Yogi's longtime friend Matt Galante had a wealth of information on Yogi's years in Houston.

A very special thanks to George Steinbrenner for relating the events leading up to the reconciliation between Yogi and George. God knows I've been rough on Mr. Steinbrenner over the years, and he has responded to me only with kindness. This is the second book of my books to which he has contributed. And there's probably no better spot to thank the late Curt Gowdy, the only man besides George Steinbrenner who had a close relationship with both Bear Bryant and Yogi Berra.

It never occurred to me when I started this book that I would be engaging in conversation with the late Dr. Milton Friedman, and I wish he could have lived to see this book in print. The same is true for David Halberstam, who was enthusiastic in sharing his memories and research of the 1949 and 1964 seasons.

Jane Levy was writing her Mickey Mantle biography at the same time I was writing about Yogi. It was delightful to share contacts, quotes, and sources.

Thanks to Bob Costas and George Will for loving Yogi as much as I do.

Thanks to Ron Shelton, writer and director of *Bull Durham, Tin Cup,* and others, for relieving the tension during the writing of this book with stimulating email debates on such subjects as the relative merits of Whitey Ford and Warren Spahn.

And thanks to the late Dick Schaap, George Plimpton, and W. C. Heinz for their encouragement over the years.

Sadly, many great players passed away while I was working on this book, and I regret that I have to thank them posthumously. In the order I spoke to them, Hank Bauer, Phil Rizzuto, Larry Doby, Billy Johnson, Clem Labine, Tommy Henrich, Clete Boyer, Tommy Byrne, Tom Tresh, and Johnny Podres.

The idol of my boyhood, the late Richie Ashburn, took time to reminisce about Yogi and the 1950 World Series when I interviewed him for a story I wrote on Dick Allen for *Philadelphia* magazine in 1995.

Charlie Einstein was a great writer and a great friend to me for many years. When I moved back to New Jersey in 1992, I noticed that Newark's

Star-Ledger had a Charles Einstein covering the Atlantic City beat. I asked around to find out if that could possibly be the same Charlie Einstein who wrote about New York baseball so lovingly in the 1950s and was the author of one of the greatest baseball books ever, *Willie's Time*. (My father, a life-long Willie Mays fan, bought two copies.) Sadly, no one at the *Star-Ledger* knew who Charlie was or was aware of his great writing. I'll relate the story briefly here: when the Giants moved to San Francisco in 1958, Charlie went with them and wrote for many years for the *San Francisco Chronicle*. A few years after Mays retired, Charlie's wife passed away, and he moved back to the East Coast—or near the East Coast, at any rate, in a little town near the Jersey Pine Barrens called—swear to God—Mays Landing. Outside of editing the *Fireside Book of Baseball*, Charlie seemed to me to be out of touch with most of his old cronies. He had little to do with baseball over the last two decades of his life, but he always found time to write me witty and needling notes commenting on stories I wrote for *The Village Voice*, *The New York Times*, and *The Wall Street Journal*. (How in the name of God he saw *The Village Voice* down in the Pine Barrens I'll never know.)

For those of you who may have heard of Charlie but never met him, he was the half-brother of comic and filmmaker Albert Brooks, which means, yes, Albert Brooks's birth name is Albert Einstein. Over the years Charlie passed on a wealth of great stories about Willie, Mickey, Yogi, and other players in their New York primes, for which I'll always be deeply grateful.

This book could not have been written and illustrated in the form you see it now had it not been for the generosity of Wayne Parrish and the Sport Media Group (Wayne is now the executive director of Canada Basketball), who graciously gave me carte blanche access to all of *Sport* magazine's stories, photographs, and covers. A few years ago, writing for Salon.com, I stated that the real golden age of American sportswriting was the work (both articles and photography) featured in *Sport* from the late 1940s through the mid-1960s. I hope this book reflects that belief. A nod to my two boyhood pals—Allan Nordstrom, who, though a die-hard Brooklyn Dodgers fan, is the only person I've ever known who could perfectly imitate Yogi's swing; and Joe Casamento, who gave me the Topps Yogi card that appears in the front of this book.

My thanks to the late Allie Reynolds, whose inspirational words stayed with me: "Yogi is worth a book, maybe two."

And, finally, thanks to you, Ted Williams. Wherever you are, please let me know what you think.

Notes

Introduction: Inventing Yogi Berra

1. Berra and Fitzgerald, *Yogi*, p. 61.
2. Ibid.
3. Ibid.
4. Ibid., p. 64.
5. Rickey and Riger, *The American Diamond*, p. 159.
6. Manning, *Collier's*, p. 68.
7. Mantle and Herskowitz, *All My Octobers*, p. 103.
8. Ibid.
9. Berra and Fitzgerald, *Yogi*, p. 11.
10. *Daily News* Legends Series, *Yogi Berra*, introduction by Bill Madden.
11. Mann, *The Decline and Fall of the New York Yankees*, p. 195.

Chapter One: King of the Hill (1925–1942)

1. Manning, *Collier's*, p. 68.
2. Berra and Fitzgerald, *Yogi*, p. 33.
3. Gambino, *Blood of My Blood*, p. 91.
4. Berra and Fitzgerald, *Yogi*, p. 34.
5. Garagiola, *It's Anybody's Ballgame*, pp. 111–112.
6. *Yogi Berra: Déjà vu All Over Again*, tape prepared by the Yogi Berra Museum and Learning Center, 1999.
7. Garagiola, *Baseball Is a Funny Game*, p. 5.
8. Berra and Fitzgerald, *Yogi*, p. 36.

9. Ibid.

10. Garagiola, *Baseball Is a Funny Game*, p. 3.

11. Berra and Fitzgerald, *Yogi*, pp. 44–45.

12. Ibid.

13. Ibid.

14. Ibid., p. 49.

15. Ibid., p. 37.

16. *Yogi Berra: Déjà vu All Over Again*.

17. Berra and Fitzgerald, *Yogi*, p. 41.

18. *Yogi Berra: Déjà vu All Over Again*.

19. Berra and Fitzgerald, *Yogi*, p. 45.

20. Ibid., p. 47.

21. Gambino, *Blood of My Blood*, pp. 80–81.

22. Berra and Fitzgerald, *Yogi*, p. 38.

23. *Yogi Berra: Déjà vu All Over Again*.

24. Berra and Fitzgerald, *Yogi*, p. 39.

25. Garagiola, *It's Anybody's Ballgame*, p. 182.

26. Berra and Horton, *Yogi: It Ain't Over*, pp. 51–52.

27. Garagiola, *It's Anybody's Ballgame*, p. 182.

28. Quoted by William James in *The Varieties of Religious Experience: A Study in Human Nature*, p. 437.

29. Berra and Fitzgerald, *Yogi*, p. 55.

30. Ibid., p. 51.

31. Ibid., p. 53.

32. Ibid., p. 54.

33. Ibid., p. 55.

34. Gambino, *Blood of My Blood*, pp. 136–137.

35. Garagiola, *Baseball Is a Funny Game*, p. 115

36. Berra and Fitzgerald, *Yogi*, p. 55.

37. Berra and Horton, *Yogi: It Ain't Over*, p. 155.

38. From the files of the Yogi Berra Museum and Learning Center.

39. Berra and Fitzgerald, *Yogi*, pp. 62–63.

Chapter Two: Larry Berra, They Call Him Yogi . . . (1943–1946)

1. Berra and Fitzgerald, *Yogi*, p. 65.

2. Gambino, *Blood of My Blood*, p. 288.

3. Allen Barra, *The Village Voice*, April 29, 1984.

4. Goodman, *Sport*, May 1958.

5. Berra and Horton, *Yogi: It Ain't Over*, p. 157.

6. Madden, *Pride of October*, p. 65.

7. Havemann, *Life*, July 11, 1949, p. 71.

8. Ibid., p. 141.

9. Montclair Booktober Fest, October 1998.

10. Berra and Horton, *Yogi: It Ain't Over*, p. 142.

11. Trimble, *Yogi Berra*, p. 42.

12. Berra and Fitzgerald, *Yogi*, p. 68.

13. Berra and Horton, *Yogi: It Ain't Over*, p. 144.

14. Berra and Fitzgerald, *Yogi*, p. 70.

15. Ibid

16. Ibid. p. 71

17. Berra and Fitzgerald, *Yogi*, p. 72.

18. Ibid.

19. Berra and Horton, *Yogi: It Ain't Over*, p. 144.

20. Berra and Fitzgerald, *Yogi*, p. 72.

21. Madden, *Pride of October*, p. 68.

22. Ibid., p 74.

23. Berra and Horton, *Yogi: It Ain't Over*, p. 146.

24. Ibid.

25. Trimble, *Yogi Berra*, p. 49.

26. Ibid.

27. Berra and Fitzgerald, *Yogi*, p. 75.

28. Ibid, p. 76.

29. Trimble, *Yogi Berra*, p. 51.

30. Berra and Horton, *Yogi: It Ain't Over*, p. 147.

31. Berra and Fitzgerald, *Yogi*, p. 80.

32. Joe Trimble, *New York Daily News*, April 13, 1954.

33. Ibid.

34. Trimble, *Yogi Berra*, p. 56.

35. Meany, *The Magnificent Yankees*, p. 101.

36. Ibid., p. 102.

37. Trimble, *Yogi Berra*, p. 57.

38. Berra and Fitzgerald, *Yogi*, p. 83.

39. Ibid.

40. Ibid.

41. Ibid., p. 84.

42. Ibid.

43. Havemann, *Life*, July 11, 1949, p. 72.

44. Trimble, *Yogi Berra*, p. 60.

45. Montclair Booktober Fest.

46. Berra and Fitzgerald, *Yogi*, p. 89.

47. *Déjà vu All Over Again*, video biography, 1999.

48. Berra and Horton, *Yogi: It Ain't Over*, p. 129.

49. Berra and Kaplan, *Ten Rings*, p. 15.

50. Berra and Horton, *Yogi: It Ain't Over*, p. 129.

51. *Déjà vu All Over Again*, video biography, 1999.

52. Jim McCulley, *New York Daily News*, September 23, 1946.

53. Ford and Pepe, *Slick*, p. 39.

54. Berra and Kaplan, *Ten Rings*, p. 21.

55. *Déjà vu All Over Again*, video biography, 1999.

Chapter Three: A Silly Hitter (1947)

1. Berra and Fitzgerald, *Yogi*, p. 94.

2. Ibid., p. 93.

3. Ibid., p. 94.

4. Berra and Kaplan, *Ten Rings*, p. 18.

5. Rizzuto and Horton, *The October Twelve*, p. 64.

6. Ibid.

7. Ibid., p. 58.

8. Ford and Pepe, *Slick*, p. 53.

9. Forker, *The Men of Autumn*, p. 58.

10. Ibid., p. 56.

11. Ibid., p. 58.

12. *The Miami Herald*, 1947.

13. Trimble, *Yogi Berra*, p. 66.

14. Berra and Fitzgerald, *Yogi*, pp.95–96.

15. Berra and Kaplan, *Ten Rings*, p. 19.

16. Arthur Daley, *The New York Times*, April 12, 1947.

17. Larry Doby, Montclair Booktober Fest.

18. Berra and Horton, *Yogi: It Ain't Over*, p. 20.

19. Trimble, *Yogi Berra*, p. 103.

20. Havemann, *Life*, July 11, 1949.

21. Schoor, *The Story of Yogi Berra*, p. 69.

22. Kahn, *The Era*, pp. 81–82.

23. Berra and Kaplan, *Ten Rings*, p. 27.

24. Berra and Fitzgerald, *Yogi*, p. 103.

25. Kahn, *The Era*, p. 82.

26. Berra and Fitzgerald, *Yogi*, p. 105.

27. Kahn, *The Era*, p. 88.

28. Berra and Kaplan, *Ten Rings*, p. 31.

29. Golenbock, *Dynasty*, p. 90.

30. Trimble, *Yogi Berra*, p. 73.

31. *New York Herald Tribune*, August 5, 1947.

32. Roswell, *The Yogi Berra Story*, p. 54.

33. Berra and Fitzgerald, *Yogi*, p. 100.

34. Milton Gross, *New York Post*, May 26, 1948.

35. Kahn, *The Era*, p. 80.

36. Montclair Booktober Fest, October 21, 1999.

37. Heinz, *Once They Heard the Cheers*, p. 230.

38. *New York Post*, October 2, 1947.

39. Heinz, *Once They Heard the Cheers*, p. 233.

40. Berra and Kaplan, *Ten Rings*, p. 35.

41. Kahn, *The Era*, p. 121.

42. Berra and Kaplan, *Ten Rings*, p. 34.

43. Red Barber, 1947, *When All Hell Broke Loose in Baseball* (Garden City, N.Y.: Doubleday, 1982), p. 127.

44. Berra and Fitzgerald, *Yogi*, p. 94.

Chapter Four: A Rather Strange Fellow of Very Remarkable Abilities (1948–1949)

1. Schoor, *The Story of Yogi Berra*, p. 58.

2. *Sports Illustrated*, April 2, 1984, p. 97.

3. Ibid., p. 97.

4. *Déjà vu All Over Again*, video biography, 1999.

5. Trimble, *Yogi Berra*, p. 92.

6. Ibid., p. 93.

7. Ibid., p. 3.

8. Letters courtesy of the Yogi Berra Museum and Learning Center.

9. Berra and Fitzgerald, *Yogi*, p. 118.

10. Ibid., p. 119.

11. Ibid.

12. Ibid.

13. Ibid.

14. Trimble, *Yogi Berra*, p. 108.

15. Ibid., p. 113.

16. Rizzuto and Horton, *The October Twelve*, p. 56.

17. Stengel and Paxton, *Casey at the Bat*, p. 12.

18. John Drebinger, *The New York Times*, February 4, 1949.

19. Kahn, *The Era*, p. 113.

20. Woolf, *The Moment, and Other Essays*, p. 50.

21. Durso, *Casey*, p. 110.

22. Ibid., p. 76.

23. Stengel and Paxton, *Casey at the Bat*, p. 172.

24. Berra and Kaplan, *Ten Rings*, p. 51.

25. Stengel, *Casey at the Bat*, p. 172.

26. Ibid., p. 175.

27. Ibid., p. 176.

28. Ibid., p. 177.

29. Berra and Kaplan, *Ten Rings*, p. 48.

30. Berra and Fitzgerald, *Yogi*, p. 124.

31. Stengel and Paxton, *Casey at the Bat*, p. 189.

32. Ibid., p. 188.

33. Campanella, *It's Good to Be Alive*, p. 30.

34. Ibid, p. 41.

35. Durso, *Casey*, p. 115.

36. Stengel and Paxton, *Casey at the Bat*, p. 179.

37. *Sporting News*, February 15, 1949.

38. Berra and Horton, *Yogi: It Ain't Over*, pp. 95–96.

39. Trimble, *Yogi Berra*, p. 122.

40. Berra and Fitzgerald, *Yogi*, p. 125.

41. Berra, *Yogi Berra's Baseball Guidebook*.

42. Ibid.

43. Ibid.

44. Berra and Kaplan, *Ten Rings*, p. 51.

45. Meany, *The Magnificent Yankees*, p. 125.

46. Madden, *Pride of October*, p. 70.

47. Havemann, *Life*, July 11, 1949, p. 77.

48. Total Baseball, *Baseball: The Biographical Encyclopedia*, p. 948.

49. Forker, *The Men of Autumn*, p. 2.

50. Rizzuto and Horton, *The October Twelve*, p. 23.

51. Ibid., p. 48.

52. Durso, *Casey*, p. 118.

53. Gittleman, *Reynolds, Raschi and Lopat*, p. 50.

54. Rizzuto and Horton, *The October Twelve*, p. 57.

55. Lally, *Bombers*, p. 46.

56. Berra and Kaplan, *Ten Rings*, p. 25.

57. Berra and Fitzgerald, *Yogi*, p. 136.

58. Ibid., p. 137.

59. Ibid., p. 139.

60. *Sporting News*, August 17, 1949.

61. Ibid.

62. Berra and Kaplan, *Ten Rings*, p. 27.

63. Trimble, *Yogi Berra*, p. 133.

64. Red Smith, *New York Herald Tribune*, August 30, 1949.

65. Halberstam, *Summer of '49*, p. 238.

66. Trimble, *Yogi Berra*, p. 132.

67. Golenbock, *Dynasty*, p. 41.

68. Linn, *Hitter*, p. 239.

69. Al Abrams, *Pittsburgh Post-Gazette*, October 10, 1949.

70. Shirley Povich, *The Washington Post*, October 9, 1949.

71. *Sporting News*, June 8, 1949, p. 23.

72. *Sporting News*, November 2, 1949.

Chapter Five: *Mister* Berra . . . My *Assistant* Manager (1950–1951)

1. Halberstam, *The Fifties*, p. x.

2. Roswell, *The Yogi Berra Story*, p. 98.

3. Havemann, *Life*, July 11, 1949, pp. 71–77.

4. Manning, *Collier's*, August 13, 1949, pp. 67–69.

5. Berra and Fitzgerald, *Yogi*, p. 154.

6. Ibid.

7. Trimble, *Yogi Berra*, p. 140.

8. Berra and Fitzgerald, *Yogi*, p. 155.

9. Berra and Kaplan, *Ten Rings*, p. 47.

10. Forker, *The Men of Autumn*, p. 31.

11. *New York Daily News*, February 27, 1950.

12. Ford and Pepe, *Slick*, p. 24.

13. Ibid., p. 31.

14. Ibid., p. 49.

15. Ibid., pp. 63–64.

16. Ibid., p. 65.

17. *New York Daily News*, August 5, 1950.

18. Golenbock, *Dynasty*, p. 42.

19. Smith, *Red Smith on Baseball*, p. 99.

20. Barra, *Philadelphia*, August 1995.

21. Berra and Fitzgerald, *Yogi*, p. 165.

22. Gittleman, *Reynolds, Raschi and Lopat*, p. 87.

23. Berra and Fitzgerald, *Yogi*, p. 168.

24. Ibid., p. 170.

25. Ibid., p. 171.

26. *Sporting News*, March 3, 1951.

27. Berra and Kaplan, *Ten Rings*, p. 87.

28. Fitzgerald, *Sport*, August 1952.

29. Gittleman, *Reynolds, Raschi and Lopat*, p. 101.

30. Ibid., p. 7.

31. Forker, *The Men of Autumn*, p. 8.

32. Berra and Horton, *Yogi: It Ain't Over*, p. 2.

33. Ibid., p. 70.

34. Golenbock, *Dynasty*, p. 67.

35. *New York Daily News*, September 29, 1951.

36. Smith, *Red Smith on Baseball*, p. 123.

37. Berra and Kaplan, *Ten Rings*, p. 97.

38. Kahn, *The Era*, p. 287.

39. Ibid., p. 99.

40. Ibid., p. 291.

41. Durso, *Casey*, p. 162.

42. *New York Daily News*, November 9, 1951.

43. Berra and Horton, *Yogi: It Ain't Over*, p. 140.

44. *New York Daily News*, February 26, 1952.

Chapter Six: Residue of Design (1952–1953)

1. Berra and Kaplan, *Ten Rings*, pp. 104–105.

2. *Sporting News*, March 1, 1952.

3. Creamer, *Stengel*, p. 251.

4. Berra and Kaplan, *Ten Rings*, p. 117.

5. *New York Herald Tribune*, October 8, 1952.

6. Golenbock, *Dynasty*, p. 96.

7. *New York Herald Tribune*, October 8, 1952.

8. Golenbock, *Dynasty*, p. 95.

9. Ibid., p. 00.

10. Berra and Fitzgerald, *Yogi*, p. 176.

11. Trimble, *Yogi Berra*, p. 123.

12. Berra and Kaplan, *Ten Rings*, p. 132.

13. Gittleman, *Reynolds, Raschi and Lopat*, p. 163.

14. Berra and Kaplan, *Ten Rings*, p. 125.

15. Golenbock, *Dynasty*, p. 111.

16. Gittleman, *Reynolds, Raschi and Lopat*, p. 130.

17. Berra and Kaplan, *Ten Rings*, p. 129.

18. Ibid., p. 133.

19. Mantle and Herskowitz, *All My Octobers*, p. 32.

20. Smith, *Red Smith on Baseball*, p. 167.

21. Berra and Kaplan, *Ten Rings*, p. 136.

22. Golenbock, *Dynasty*, p. 92.

23. *Sporting News*, December 28, 1953.

24. Halberstam, *Summer of '49*, p. 43.

25. Rizzuto and Horton, *The October Twelve*, p. 76.

26. Gittleman, *Reynolds, Raschi and Lopat*, p. 183.

27. Berra and Kaplan, *Ten Rings*, p. 154.

Chapter Seven: The House That Yogi Built (1954–1956)

1. Halberstam, *Summer of '49*, p. 123.

2. Ibid.

3. Ibid., p. 124.

4. From the documentary *Toots Shor, Bigger Than Life* (2006), directed by Kristi Jacobson.

5. Trimble, *Yogi Berra*, p. 166.

6. Roger Kahn, *New York Herald Tribune*, October 8, 1952.

7. Mantle and Herskowitz, *All My Octobers*, p. 24.

8. Howard and Wimbish, *Elston and Me*, p. 37.

9. Golenbock, *Dynasty*, p. 139.

10. Ibid.

11. Howard and Wimbish, *Elston and Me*, p. 22.

12. Ibid., p. ix.

13. Ibid., p. 11.

14. Ibid., p. 10.

15. *St. Louis Globe-Democrat*, March 15, 1980.

16. Howard and Wimbish, *Elston and Me*, p. 32.

17. Ibid., p. 33.

18. *New York Daily News*, March 22, 1955.

19. Howard and Wimbish, *Elston and Me*, p. 42.

20. Jimmy Cannon, *Newsday*, September 17, 1955.

21. Trimble, *Yogi Berra*, p. 167.

22. Kahn, *The Era*, p. 324.

23. Mantle and Herskowitz, *All My Octobers*, p. 55.

24. Dana Mozley, *New York Daily News*, October 5, 1995.

25. Ibid.

26. Ibid.

27. Berra and Kaplan, *Ten Rings*, p. 141.

28. Trimble, *Yogi Berra*, p. 137.

29. Idelson, Jeff, National Baseball Hall of Fame, *Hall of Fame News*, February 15, 2007.

30. Berra and Kaplan, *Ten Rings*, p. 147.

31. Ibid., p. 148.

32. Ibid.

33. Mantle and Herskowitz, *All My Octobers*, p. 62.

34. YES Network, *Perfect Game*, October 5, 2005.

35. Frommer, *New York City Baseball*, p. 264.

36. Berra and Fitzgerald, *Yogi*, p. 194.

37. *New York Herald Tribune*, October 9, 1956.

38. Mantle and Pepe, *My Favorite Summer*, p. 156.

39. Larsen and Shaw, *The Perfect Yankee*, p. 47.

40. Ibid., p. 152.

41. Ibid.

42. YES Network, *Perfect Game*, October 5, 2005.

43. Larsen and Shaw, *The Perfect Yankee*, p. 160.

44. Ibid., p. 158.

45. Borelli, *How About That!*, p. 148.

46. Mantle and Pepe, *My Favorite Summer*, p. 260.

47. Larsen and Shaw, *The Perfect Yankee*, p. 175.

48. Kahn, *The Era*, p. 332.

49. Berra and Kaplan, *Ten Rings*, p. 153.

50. Ibid., p. 154.

51. Total Baseball, *Baseball: The Biographical Encyclopedia*, p. 820.

52. Kahn, *Sport*, November 1957.

53. Ibid.

54. Berra and Fitzgerald, *Yogi*, p. 198.

Chapter Eight: The Silver Age (1957–1960)

1. *New York Daily News*, August 18, 1957.

2. Golenbock, *Dynasty*, p. 204.

3. Berra and Kaplan, *Ten Rings*, p. 164.

4. Mantle and Herskowitz, *All My Octobers*, p. 76.

5. Ibid.

6. Arthur North and David Quirk, *New York Daily News*, May 17, 1957.

7. Ibid.

8. Golenbock, *Dynasty*, p. 202.

9. Goodman, *Sport*, May 1958.

10. Mantle and Herskowitz, *All My Octobers*, p. 87.

11. *The Milwaukee Journal-Sentinel*, October 6, 1957.

12. Berra and Fitzgerald, *Yogi*, p. 204.

13. Allen Barra, *New York Observer*, February 13, 1992.

14. Kahn, *The Era*, p. 337.

15. Dick Young, *New York Daily News*, October 12, 1957.

16. Berra and Kaplan, *Ten Rings*, p. 160.

17. *Sports Illustrated*, March 7, 1958.

18. Goodman, *Sport*, May 1958.

19. *Sporting News*, February 12, 1958.

20. Jimmy Powers, *New York Daily News*, February 14, 1958.

21. Goodman, *Sport*, May 1958.

22. Berra and Kaplan, *Ten Rings*, p. 170.

23. Ibid., p. 168.

24. Berra and Fitzgerald, *Yogi*, p. 203.

25. Ibid., p. 205.

26. Ibid., p. 233.

27. *The New York Times*, June 24, 1959.

28. Berra and Fitzgerald, *Yogi*, p. 210.

29. Berra and Horton, *Yogi: It Ain't Over*, p. 154.

30. *Sport*, May 1958.

31. Berra and Fitzgerald, *Yogi*, p. 227.

32. Dick Young, *New York Daily News*, June 10, 1958.

33. Trimble, *Yogi Berra*, p. 195.

34. Stengel and Paxton, *Casey at the Bat*, p. 211.

35. Ibid., p. 212.

36. *New York Daily News*, January 29, 1960.

37. Stengel and Paxton, *Casey at the* Bat, p. 214.

38. Ibid., p. 212.

39. *New York Daily News*, September 20, 1959.

40. Berra and Fitzgerald, *Yogi*, p. 212.

41. Ibid., p. 215.

42. Berra and Horton, *Yogi: It Ain't Over*, p. 87.

43. *New York Daily News*, January 29, 1960.

44. Berra and Fitzgerald, *Yogi*, p. 219.

45. Howard and Wimbish, *Elston and Me*, p. 88.

46. Neyer, *Roy Neyer's Big Book of Baseball Blunders*, p. 101.

47. Trimble, *Yogi Berra*, p. 196.

48. Ford and Pepe, *Slick*, p. 150.

49. Forker, *Sweet Seasons*, p. 55.

50. Stengel and Paxton, *Casey at the Bat*, p. 221.

51. Golenbock, *Dynasty*, p. 208.

52. Ibid., p. 221

53. Berra and Fitzgerald, *Yogi*, p. 205.

Chapter Nine: Manage Who? (1961–1964)

1. Berra and Kaplan, *Ten Rings*, p. 176.
2. Ford and Pepe, *Slick*, p. 157.
3. Howard and Wimbish, *Elston and Me*, p. 89.
4. Forker, *Sweet Seasons*, p. 183.
5. Berra and Kaplan, *Ten Rings*, p. 188.
6. Berra and Horton, *Yogi: It Aint't Over*, p. 156.
7. Ibid., p. 200.
8. Ibid., p. 177.
9. Mantle and Herskowitz, *All My Octobers*, p. 79.
10. Tebbetts and Morrison, *Birdie*, p. 135.
11. Berra and Kaplan, *Ten Rings*, p. 199.
12. Trimble, *Yogi Berra*, p. 204.
13. *New York Daily News*, October 23, 1963.
14. *Sporting News*, November 3, 1963.
15. Ibid.
16. Ibid.
17. Halberstam, *October 1964*, p. 8.
18. Golenbock, *Dynasty*, p. 351.
19. Halberstam, *October 1964*, p. 15.
20. Schoor, *The Story of Yogi Berra*, p. 165.
21. Ibid., p. 353.
22. Trimble, *Yogi Berra*, p. 218.
23. Lally, *Bombers*, p. 174.
24. Bouton, *Ball Four*, p. 69.
25. Mantle and Herskowitz, *All My Octobers*, p. 83.
26. Forker, *Sweet Seasons*, p. 107.
27. Ford and Pepe, *Slick*, p. 212.
28. Mantle and Herskowitz, *All My Octobers*, p. 183.
29. Mann, *The Decline and Fall of the New York Yankees*, p. 87.
30. Mantle and Herskowitz, *All My Octobers*, p. 175.
31. Lally, *Bombers*, p. 175.
32. Joe Trimble, *New York Daily News*, October 4, 1964.
33. Garagiola, *It's Anybody's Ballgame*, p. 117.
34. Halberstam, *October 1964*, p. 351.
35. Ibid.

36. *St. Louis Post-Dispatch*, October 19, 1964.

37. Trimble, *Yogi Berra*, p. 217.

38. Mann, *The Decline and Fall of the New York Yankees*, p. 201.

39. *The New York Times*, February 17, 1964.

40. Stan Isaacs, *Newsday*, October 19, 1964.

41. Harold Rosenthal, *New York Herald Tribune*, October 19, 1964.

42. Forker, *Sweet Seasons*, p. 8.

43. Ibid., p. 136.

44. *The New York Times*, February 13, 1984.

45. Forker, *Sweet Seasons*, p. 178.

46. Ibid., p. 179.

47. Borelli, *How About That!*, p. 200.

48. Ibid.

49. Mann, *The Decline and Fall of the New York Yankees*, p. 208.

50. Allen and Fitzgerald, *You Can't Beat the Hours*, p. 194.

51. Lally, *Bombers*, p. 182.

52. Golenbock, *Dynasty*, p. 320.

Chapter Ten: It Ain't Over (1965–1975)

1. *New York Daily News*, October 30, 1964.

2. *New York Daily News*, November 18, 1964.

3. Lang and Simon, *The New York Mets*, p. 23.

4. Trimble, *Yogi Berra*, p. 215.

5. Berra and Horton, *Yogi: It Ain't Over*, p. 164.

6. George F. Will, *Men at Work: The Craft of Baseball* (New York: Macmillan, 1990), p. 191.

7. Lang and Simon, *The New York Mets*, p. 53.

8. *The New York Times*, September 22, 1967.

9. Robert Lipsyte, *The New York Times*, October 19, 1967.

10. Ibid.

11. Shamsky and Zeman, *The Magnificent Seasons*, p. 213.

12. Ibid., p. 217.

13. Vecsey, *Joy in Mudville*, p. 237.

14. Ibid.

15. Leonard Koppett, *The New York Times*, December 28, 1969.

16. Forker, *The Men of Autumn*, p. 150.

17. Berra and Horton, *Yogi: It Ain't Over*, p. 184.

18. Smith, *Strawberries in the Wintertime*, p. 265.

19. Berra and Horton, *Yogi: It Ain't Over*, p. 185.

20. *The New York Times*, April 16, 1972.

21. *San Francisco Chronicle*, May 8, 1971.

22. Dickey, *The Jock Empire*, p. 32.

23. Golenbock, *Amazin'*, p. 308.

24. Berra and Horton, *Yogi: It Ain't Over*, p. 83.

25. *The New York Times*, January 28, 1973.

26. *New Jersey Monthly*, July 2006.

27. Joseph Durso, *The New York Times*, March 2, 1973.

28. Schoor, *The Story of Yogi Berra*, p. 192.

29. Lang and Simon, *The New York Mets*, p. 128.

30. Ibid.

31. McGraw and Durso, *Screwball*, p. 295.

32. Schoor, *The Story of Yogi Berra*, p. 193.

33. Lang and Simon, *The New York Mets*, p. 136.

34. Joseph Durso, *The New York Times*, October 24, 1973.

35. Lang and Simon, *The New York Mets*, p. 141.

36. Ibid., p. 146.

37. Berra and Horton, *Yogi: It Ain't Over*, p. 188.

38. Joseph Durso, *The New York Times*, August 12, 1975.

39. Ibid.

40. Berra and Horton, *Yogi: It Ain't Over*, p. 186.

41. *The New York Times*, August 8, 1975.

42. Jim Murray, *Los Angeles Times*, September 30, 1975.

43. Stengel and Paxton, *Casey at the Bat*, p. 245.

44. Berra and Horton, *Yogi: It Ain't Over*, p. 184.

45. Ibid., pp. 26–27.

Chapter Eleven: Déjà vu All Over Again (1976–1985)

1. Madden and Klein, *Damned Yankees*, p. 1.

2. Miller, *A Whole Different Ball Game*, p. 281.

3. Ibid., p. 282.

4. *The New York Times*, December 5, 1975.

5. Martin and Golenbock, *Number 1*, p. 286.

6. Allen, *All Roads Lead to October*, p. 176.

7. Martin and Golenbock, *Number 1*, p. 288.

8. Ibid., p. 291.

9. *The New York Times*, June 21, 1977.

10. Red Smith, *The New York Times*, December 15, 1980.

11. Jim Murray, *Los Angeles Times*, December 15, 1980.

12. Howard and Wimbish, *Elston and Me*, p. 185.

13. *New York Post*, February 14, 1980.

14. Howard and Wimbish, *Elston and Me*, p. 192.

15. *The New York Times*, December 5, 1983.

16. *New York Daily News*, December 17, 1983.

17. CNN, September 4, 2003.

18. *The New York Times*, February 13, 1984.

19. *New York Daily News*, April 26, 1985.

20. Berra and Kaplan, *When You Come to a Fork in the Road, Take It!*, p. 173.

21. Ibid.

22. Berra and Horton, *Yogi: It Ain't Over*, pp. 206–207.

23. Ibid., p. 199.

24. Ibid., p. 201.

25. Miller, *A Whole Different Ball Game*, p. 79.

Chapter Twelve: Eternal Yankee (1986–)

1. *Houston Post*, May 12, 1987.

2. Berra and Horton, *Yogi: It Ain't Over*, p. 22.

3. Ibid., p. 210.

4. Ibid., pp. 209–216.

5. Ruth Rendon, *The Washington Post*, July 19, 1998.

6. Rizzuto and Horton, *The October Twelve*, p. 97.

7. *The New York Times*, April 30, 1999.

8. Berra and Horton, *Yogi: It Ain't Over*, p. 14.

9. *The New York Times*, March 21, 1986.

10. *The New York Times*, May 17, 1996.

11. *USA Today*, March 28, 1989.

12. *Newark Star-Ledger*, May 25, 2005.

13. *Newark Star-Ledger*, November 13, 1993.

14. Mantle and Herskowitz, *All My Octobers*, p. 176.

15. Berra and Horton, *Yogi: It Ain't Over*, p. 224.

16. Rizzuto and Horton, *The October Twelve*, p. 190.

17. *Newark Star-Ledger*, February 26, 1994.

18. *Newark Star-Ledger*, February 12, 1993.

19. ESPN, October 17, 1998.

20. Berra and Kaplan, *When You Come to a Fork in the Road, Take It!*, p. 174.

21. *The New York Times*, January 6, 1999.

22. Ibid.

23. Berra and Kaplan, *When You Come to a Fork in the Road, Take It!* p. 175.

24. *The New York Times*, October 31, 2003.

25. *Downtown Express*, November 2003.

26. Berra and Horton, *Yogi: It Ain't Over*, p. 124.

Bibliography

Books

Allen, Maury. *After the Miracle: The 1969 Mets Twenty Years Later*. Franklin Watts, New York, 1989.

Allen, Maury. *All Roads Lead to October: Boss Steinbrenner's 25-Year Reign over the New York Yankees*. St. Martin's Press, New York, 2000.

Allen, Maury. *Roger Maris: A Man for All Seasons*. Donald I. Fine, New York, 1986.

Allen, Mel, and Ed Fitzgerald. *You Can't Beat the Hours: A Long, Loving Look at Big League Baseball, Including Some Yankees I Have Known*. Harper & Row, New York, 1964.

Anderson, Dave, Murray Chass, Robert Creamer, and Harold Rosenthal. *The Yankees: The Four Fabulous Eras of Baseball's Most Famous Team*. Random House, New York, 1980.

Berra, Yogi. *Yogi Berra's Baseball Guidebook: Basic Plays and Playing Techniques for Boys*. McGraw-Hill, New York, 1966.

Berra, Yogi. *The Yogi Book: I Really Didn't Say Everything I Said!* Workman Publishing, New York, 1998.

Berra, Yogi, with Dave Kaplan. *Ten Rings: My Championship Seasons*. William Morrow, New York, 2003.

Berra, Yogi, with Dave Kaplan. *When You Come to a Fork in the Road, Take It!* Hyperion, New York, 2001.

Berra, Yogi, with Ed Fitzgerald. *Yogi: The Autobiography of a Professional Baseball Player*. Doubleday, Garden City, NY, 1961.

Berra, Yogi, with Tom Horton. *Yogi: It Ain't Over*. Harper Torch, New York, 1997.

Borelli, Stephen. *How About That! The Life of Mel Allen*. Sports Publishing, Champaign, Ill., 2005.

Bouton, Jim. *Ball Four: The Final Pitch*. Bulldog Publishing, North Egremont, Mass., 2000.

Bouton, Jim, and Neil Offen. *I Managed Good, but Boy Did They Play Bad*. Dell, New York, 1973.

Buckley, James Jr. *Perfect: The Inside Story of Baseball's Sixteen Perfect Games*. Triumph Books, Chicago, 2002.

Campanella, Roy. *It's Good to Be Alive*. Little, Brown, Boston, 1959.

Cannon, Jack, and Tom Cannon, eds. *Nobody Asked Me But . . . : The World of Jimmy Cannon*. Holt, Rinehart, and Winston, New York, 1978.

Creamer, Robert W. *Stengel: His Life and Times*. Simon and Schuster, New York, 1984.

Daily News Legends Series. *Yogi Berra: An American Original*. Sports Publishing, Champaign, Ill., 1998.

Dickey, Glenn. *The Jock Empire: Its Rise and Deserved Fall*. Chilton Book Company, Radnor, Pa., 1974.

Durocher, Leo, and Ed Linn. *Nice Guys Finish Last*. Simon and Schuster, New York, 1976.

Durso, Joseph. *Casey: The Life and Legend of Charles Dillon Stengel*. Prentice-Hall, Englewood Cliffs, N.J., 1967.

Durso, Joseph. *Yankee Stadium: Fifty Years of Drama*. Houghton Mifflin, Boston, 1972.

Einstein, Charles, ed. *The Baseball Reader: Favorites from the Fireside Books of Baseball*. McGraw-Hill, New York, 1980.

Falkner, David. *The Last Yankee: The Turbulent Life of Billy Martin*. Simon and Schuster, New York, 1992.

Ford, Whitey, with Phil Pepe. *Few and Chosen: Defining Yankee Greatness across the Eras*. Triumph Books, Chicago, 2001.

Ford, Whitey, with Phil Pepe. *Slick: My Life In and Around Baseball*. William Morrow, 1987.

Forker, Dom. *The Men of Autumn: An Oral History of the 1949–53 World Champion New York Yankees*. Taylor Publishing, Dallas, 1989.

Forker, Dom. *Sweet Seasons: Recollections of the 1955–64 New York Yankees*. Taylor Publishing, Dallas, 1990.

Frommer, Harvey. *New York City Baseball: The Last Golden Age, 1947–1957*. University of Wisconsin Press, Madison, 2004.

Gambino, Richard. *Blood of My Blood: The Dilemma of the Italian-Americans*. Doubleday, Garden City, N.Y., 1974.

Garagiola, Joe. *Baseball Is a Funny Game*. Bantam Books, New York, 1962.

Garagiola, Joe. *It's Anybody's Ballgame*. Contemporary Books, Chicago, 1988.

Gittleman, Sol. *Reynolds, Raschi and Lopat: New York's Big Three and the Great Yankee Dynsasty of 1949–1953*. McFarland & Company, Jefferson, N.C., 2007.

Goldman, Steven. *Forging Genius: The Making of Casey Stengel*. Potomac Books, Washington, D.C., 2005.

Golenbock, Peter. *Amazin': The Miraculous History of New York's Most Beloved Baseball Team*. St. Martin's Press, New York, 2002.

Golenbock, Peter. *Bums: An Oral History of the Brooklyn Dodgers*. Putnam, N.Y., 1984.

Golenbock, Peter. *Dynasty: The New York Yankees, 1949–1964*. Prentice-Hall, Englewood Cliffs, N.J., 1975.

Graham, Frank. *The Brooklyn Dodgers: An Informal History*. G. P. Putnam's Sons, New York, 1945.

Graham, Frank. *McGraw of the Giants: An Informal Biography*. G. P. Putnam's Sons, New York, 1944.

Graham, Frank. *The New York Giants: An Informal History*. G. P. Putnam's Sons, New York, 1952.

Graham, Frank. *The New York Yankees: An Informal History*, G. P. Putnam's Sons, New York, 1947.

Graham, Frank Jr. *Casey Stengel: His Half-Century in Baseball*. John Day, New York, 1958.

Halberstam, David. *The Fifties*. Villard Books, New York, 1993.

Halberstam, David. *October 1964*. Villard Books, New York, 1994.

Halberstam, David. *Summer of '49*. William Morrow, New York, 1989.

Heinz, W. C., *Once They Heard the Cheers*. Doubleday, Garden City, N.Y., 1979.

Henrich, Tommy, and Bill Gilbert. *Five o'Clock Lightning: Ruth, Gehrig, DiMaggio, Mantle, and the Glory Years of the NY Yankees*. Carol Publishing Group, New York, 1992.

Howard, Arlene, with Ralph Wimbish. *Elston and Me: The Story of the First Black Yankee*. University of Missouri Press, Columbia, 2001.

James, Bill. *The Baseball Book 1991*. Villard Books, New York, 1991.

James, Bill. *The Bill James Historical Baseball Abstract*. Villard Books, New York, 1988.

Kahn, Roger. *The Era: 1947–1957, When the Yankees, the Giants, and the Dodgers Ruled the World*. Ticknor & Fields, New York, 1993.

Koppett, Leonard. *All About Baseball*. Quadrangle/New York Times Book Company, New York, 1974.

Lally, Richard. *Bombers: An Oral History of the New York Yankees*. Crown Publishers, New York, 2002.

Lang, Jack, and Peter Simon. *The New York Mets: Twenty-Five Years of Baseball Magic*. Henry Holt, New York, 1987.

Lardner, Ring. *Ring Around the Bases: The Complete Baseball Stories of Ring Lardner*. Charles Scribner's Sons, New York, 1992.

Larsen, Don, with Mark Shaw. *The Perfect Yankee: The Incredible Story of the Greatest Miracle in Baseball History*. Sagamore Publishing, Champaign, Ill., 1996.

Linn, Ed. *The Great Rivalry: The Yankees and the Red Sox, 1901–1990*. Ticknor & Fields, New York, 1991.

Linn, Ed. *Hitter: The Life and Turmoils of Ted Williams*. Harcourt Brace, New York, 1993.

Madden Bill. *Pride of October: What It Was to Be Young and a Yankee*. Warner Books, New York, 2004.

Madden, Bill, and Moss Klein. *Damned Yankees: A No-Holds Barred Account of Life with "Boss" Steinbrenner*. Warner Books, New York, 1990.

Mann, Jack. *The Decline and Fall of the New York Yankees*. Simon and Schuster, New York, 1967.

Mantle, Mickey, *The Education of a Baseball Player*. Simon and Schuster, New York, 1967.

Mantle, Mickey. *The Quality of Courage*. Doubleday, Garden City, N.Y., 1964.

Mantle, Mickey, with Herb Gluck. *The Mick*. Doubleday, Garden City, N.Y., 1985.

Mantle, Mickey, with Mickey Herskowitz. *All My Octobers: My Memories of Twelve World Series when the Yankees Ruled Baseball*. HarperCollins, New York, 1994.

Mantle, Mickey, and Phil Pepe. *My Favorite Summer, 1956*. Doubleday, New York, 1991.

Martin, Billy, and Peter Golenbock, *Number 1*. Delacorte Press, New York, 1980.

Masterson, Dave, and Timm Boyle. *Baseball's Best: The MVPs*. Contemporary Books, Chicago, 1985.

McGraw, John. *My Thirty Years in Baseball*. Boni and Liveright, New York, 1923.

McGraw, Tug, and Joseph Durso. *Screwball*. Houghton Mifflin, Boston, 1974.

McMillan, Ken. *Tales from the Yankee Dugout*. Sports Publishing, Champaign, Ill., 2001.

Meany, Tom. *The Artful Dodgers*. A. S. Barnes, New York, 1954.

Meany, Tom. *The Magnificent Yankees*. Grosset & Dunlap, New York, 1957.

Miller, Marvin, *A Whole Different Ball Game: The Inside Story of the Baseball Revolution*. Ivan R. Dee, Chicago, 2004.

Mormino, Gary R. *Immigrants on the Hill: Italian-Americans in St. Louis, 1882–1982*. University of Missouri Press, Columbia, 2002.

Musmanno, Michael A. *The Story of the Italians in America*. Doubleday, Garden City, N.Y., 1965.

Neft, David, Richard Cohen, and Michael Neft. *The Sports Encyclopedia: Baseball 2005*. St. Martin's Griffin, New York, 2005.

Neyer, Rob. *Rob Neyer's Big Book of Baseball Blunders*. Fireside/Simon and Schuster, New York, 2006.

Neyer, Rob, and Eddie Epstein. *Baseball Dynasties: The Greatest Teams of All Time*. Norton, New York, 2000.

Okrent, Daniel, and Harris Lewine, eds. *The Ultimate Baseball Book*. Houghton Mifflin, Boston, 1979.

Olan, Ben, ed. *Big-Time Baseball*. Hart Publishing, New York, 1960.

Polner, Murray. *Branch Rickey: A Biography*. Signet Classics, New York, 1983.

Powers, Jimmy. *Baseball Personalities: The Most Colorful Figures of All Times*. Rudolph Field, New York, 1949.

Rice, Grantland. *The Tumult and the Shouting: My Life in Sport*. A. S. Barnes, New York, 1954.

Richards, Paul. *Modern Baseball Strategy*. Prentice-Hall, New York, 1955.

Rickey, Branch and John J. Monteleone, ed. *Branch Rickey's Little Blue Book: Wit and Strategy from Baseball's Last Wise Man*. Macmillan, New York, 1995.

Rickey, Branch, with Robert Riger. *The American Diamond: A Documentary of the Game of Baseball*. Simon and Schuster, New York, 1965.

Rizzuto, Phil, with Tom Horton. *The October Twelve: Five Years of Yankee Glory—1949–1953*. Forge, New York, 1994.

Robinson, Ray. *Baseball's Most Colorful Managers*, G. P. Putnam, New York, 1969.

Robinson, Ray, and Christopher Jennison. *Pennants & Pinstripes: The New York Yankees, 1903–2002*, Viking Studio/Penguin, New York, 2002.

Roswell, Gene. *The Yogi Berra Story*. Julian Messner, New York, 1958.

Ryan, Cornelius. *The Longest Day: The Classic Epic of D-Day*. Simon and Schuster, New York, 1994.

Schoor, Gene. *The Story of Yogi Berra*, Doubleday, Garden City, N.Y., 1976.

Shamsky, Art, with Barry Zeman. *The Magnificent Seasons*. Thomas Dunne Books, New York, 2004.

Smith, Curt. *The Voice: Mel Allen's Untold Story*. Lyons Press, Guilford, Conn., 2007.

Smith, Red. *Red Smith on Baseball: The Game's Greatest Writer on the Game's Greatest Years*. Ivan R. Dee, Chicago, 2000.

Smith, Red. *Strawberries in the Wintertime: The Sporting World of Red Smith*. New York, Quadrangle/New York Times Book Company, 1974.

Smith, Red, and Dave Anderson, ed. *The Red Smith Reader*. Random House, New York, 1982.

Stark, Jayson. *The Stark Truth: The Most Overrated and Underrated Players in Baseball History*. Triumph Books, Chicago, 2007.

Stats All-Time Major League Handbook, 2nd ed., Stats Publishing, Morton Grove, Ill., 2000.

Stengel, Casey, with Harry T. Paxton. *Casey at the Bat: The Story of My Life in Baseball*. Random House, New York, 1962.

Stout, Glenn ed. *Top of the Heap: A Yankees Collection*. Houghton Mifflin, Boston, 2003.

Sugar, Bert Randolph. *Rain Delays*. St. Martin's Press, New York, 1990.

Tebbetts, Birdie, with James Morrison. *Birdie: Confessions of a Baseball Nomad*. Triumph Books, Chicago, 2002.

Thorn, John, ed. *The National Pastime*. Warner Books, New York, 1987.

Thorn, John, and Pete Palmer. *The Hidden Game of Baseball: A Revolutionary Approach to Baseball and Its Statistics*. Dolphin Books/Doubleday, Garden City, N.Y., 1985.

Thorn, John, Pete Palmer, and Michael Gershman. *Total Baseball,* 7th ed. Total Sports Publishing, New York, 2001.

Total Baseball editors. *Baseball: The Biographical Encyclopedia*. Total Sports Publishing, New York, 2000.

Trimble, Joe. *Yogi Berra*. Tempo Books/Grosset & Dunlap, New York, 1965.

Vecsey, George. *Joy in Mudville*. McCall Publishing Company, New York, 1970.

Veeck, Bill, with Ed Linn. *The Hustler's Handbook*. Putnam, New York, 1965.

Ward, Geoffrey C., and Ken Burns. *Baseball: An Illustrated History*. Alfred A. Knopf, New York, 1994.

Woolf, Virginia. *The Moment, and Other Essays*. Harcourt, Brace, New York, 1948.

Williams, Ted. *My Turn at Bat: The Story of My Life*. Simon and Schuster, New York, 1969.

Yardley, Jonathan. *Ring: A Biography of Ring Lardner*. Random House, New York, 1977.

Magazines

Barra, Allen, "An Embarrassment of Richies," *Philadelphia,* August 1995.

Blount, Roy Jr., "Yogi," *Sports Illustrated,* April 2, 1984.

Brady, James, "Catch Yogi: In Step with Yogi Berra," *Parade,* July 11, 1999.

Daley, Arthur, "Yogi," *Boys' Life*, April 1963.

Fitzgerald, Ed, "The Fabulous Yogi Berra," *Sport,* August 1951.

Fitzgerald, Ed, "The Pitcher They Called a Quitter," *Sport,* August 1952.

Fonseca, Lew, "Most Valuable Player . . . the Catcher," *Popular Mechanics*, June 1956.

Goodman, Irv, "The Other Yogi Berra," *Sport,* May 1958.

Graham, Frank, "The MVP of the Yankees," *Sport,* October 1955.

Hann, Christopher, "It Ain't Over," *New Jersey Monthly,* July 2006.

Havemann, Ernest, "Why Pitchers Get Nervous," *Life,* July 11, 1949.

Kahn, Roger, "Why Yogi Wins and Newk Loses: A Study in World Series Psychology," *Sport,* November 1957.

Leggett, William, "Trouble Sprouts for the Yankees," *Sports Illustrated,* March 2, 1964.

Manning, Gordon, "Yankee Yogi: 'I'm Human, Ain't I?,'" *Collier's*, August 13, 1949.

Newman, Marv (photographer), "Yogi Berra Then and Now," *Sport*, June 1955.

"The Roughest Plays in Baseball," *Quick*, August 4, 1952.

Television Broadcasts

Centerstage: Yogi Berra. Michael Kay, host. YES Network, May 7, 2006.

Yogi Berra, Déjà vu All Over Again. Bob Costas, host. New River Media, 1999.

Index

About the Author

Allen Barra is a sports columnist for *The Wall Street Journal* and a contributing editor to *American Heritage* magazine, as well as a regular contributor to *The Village Voice*, the *Los Angeles Times*, *The Washington Post Book World*, *The New York Times*, and *Salon*.

He is the author of the national bestsellers *Inventing Wyatt Earp: His Life and Many Legends*, *The Last Coach: A Life of Paul "Bear" Bryant*, and *Clearing the Bases: The Greatest Baseball Debates of the Last Century*, a 2003 *Sports Illustrated* Book of the Year, recently republished by Bison Books of the University of Nebraska Press. He is also the coauthor of *A Whole Different Ball Game: The Story of Baseball's New Deal*, the autobiography of Marvin Miller. He lives in South Orange, N.J., with his wife and daughter.